Y0-GUA-283

RETHINKING PLATO

VALUE INQUIRY BOOK SERIES

VIBS

Volume 251

Robert Ginsberg
Founding Editor

Leonidas Donskis
Executive Editor

Associate Editors

G. John M. Abbarno
George Allan
Gerhold K. Becker
Raymond Angelo Belliotti
Kenneth A. Bryson
C. Stephen Byrum
Robert A. Delfino
Rem B. Edwards
Malcolm D. Evans
Roland Faber
Andrew Fitz-Gibbon
Francesc Forn i Argimon
Daniel B. Gallagher
William C. Gay
Dane R. Gordon
J. Everet Green
Heta Aleksandra Gylling
Matti Häyry
Brian G. Henning
Steven V. Hicks
Richard T. Hull
Michael Krausz
Olli Loukola
Mark Letteri
Vincent L. Luizzi
Hugh P. McDonald
Adrianne McEvoy
J.D. Mininger
Peter A. Redpath
Arleen L. F. Salles
John R. Shook
Eddy Souffrant
Tuija Takala
Emil Višňovský
Anne Waters
James R. Watson
John R. Welch
Thomas Woods

a volume in
Philosophy, Literature, and Politics
PLP
Edited by Leonidas Donskis and J.D. Mininger

RETHINKING PLATO

A Cartesian Quest for the Real Plato

Necip Fikri Alican

Rodopi

Amsterdam - New York, NY 2012

OHIO UNIVERSITY LIBRARY ATHENS OHIO
WITHDRAWN

Cover photo: www.dreamstime.com

Cover Design: Studio Pollmann

The paper on which this book is printed meets the requirements of "ISO 9706:1994, Information and documentation - Paper for documents - Requirements for permanence".

ISBN: 978-90-420-3537-9
E-Book ISBN: 978-94-012-0812-3
© Editions Rodopi B.V., Amsterdam - New York, NY 2012
Printed in the Netherlands

To my wife

Banu Beste Başol Alican

CONTENTS

LIST OF TABLES

Part One

Part Two

FOREWORD

Throwing a bright light of understanding at the real Plato, at the man who hides in the shadow of Socrates and behind dramatic dialogues while asserting his own presence so forcefully as to occupy philosophers from the fourth century before Christ to the present, this work is one of the most comprehensive, systematic, thorough, erudite, and lucid contributions to come out in the past two decades in the field of Plato scholarship. It is comprehensive in its formulation and treatment of the questions, concepts, and views that constitute the field of Plato scholarship and are essential to an adequate understanding of Plato's thought; systematic in its analysis and evaluation of these questions, concepts, and views; thorough in its method of establishing the validity of its claims; lucid and erudite in its scholarly skills; and penetrating yet versatile in its reading of Plato's dialogues.

First, what does it take to delimit the territory that contains Plato's real thought in contrast to that of Socrates and his interlocutors in the dialogues? This question is a request for a methodology by which we can secure the most appropriate means of identifying Plato's thought. In answering it, we should, to begin, proceed from a trustworthy portrayal of the historical Plato, the Plato who lived in Athens from 427 to 347 BC, studied with Socrates, established the Academy, wrote at least twenty-eight philosophical dialogues, tried to educate princes in the art of government, who, in short, was a paradigmatic philosopher and teacher of philosophy. An adequate knowledge of Plato's life, verifiable by the most reliable method of historical investigation, is a necessary condition for paving the way to an adequate understanding of his thought, mainly because there is an intimate relationship between real life and the accomplishments of a human being: One's thought originates, after all, from the bosom of one's life, from the sort of experiences one undergoes. *Rethinking Plato* provides this kind of knowledge. In putting it together, Alican consults, as the text clearly shows, critically, analytically, and evaluatively, the most authoritative sources exploring the life of Plato from antiquity to the present. The outcome is an informative and historically realistic picture of Plato; and this picture is not only consistent with the Plato we glean from the autobiographical remarks we read in the dialogues and the letters, and with the accounts of those who knew him personally, but it also illuminates, and, in fact, increases, our appreciation of Plato's character, ideas, and method of philosophizing. And he lends further clarity, substance, and credence to this picture by an equal delineation of the character and life of Socrates. By showing who Socrates the man, the teacher, and the philosopher was, Alican *ipso facto* makes more visible the line that distinguishes the teacher from the student.

Second, he renders this line still more visible by spotlighting and articulating the central questions, concepts, and views that distinguish the philosophical mind and accomplishments of Plato. But just what are these issues? This is the crux of the problem that underlies our quest for the real Plato, because he hides behind a tapestry of literary and philosophical devices that create a distance between him and his readers: images, metaphors, speakers, stories, direct confessions, and dramatic frameworks. Add to this, the fact that he did not leave behind a coherently constructed system of ideas but a large number of dialogues seemingly dealing with specific philosophical questions or problems. Confronted with this kind of legacy, how can we penetrate the tapestry of devices and the complex of dramatic presentations in our quest for what the real Plato said? Could it be that the fact that Plato chose to remain distant from his readers is itself an aspect of his philosophical method and aim? For example, the question whether Plato did or did not espouse a philosophical system, and related questions busying scholars for centuries, would automatically be solved if we could determine, to a reasonable degree, what he really said. But answers to such questions are not easily forthcoming, at least not without an adequate methodology. Plato scholars have been developing and refining ways of removing, or making transparent, the literary veils that spread over his thought. Alican's own investigative adventure goes through the contributions of these scholars, qua scholars, both evaluating and utilizing the methodological tools they have employed in identifying the fundamental questions, concepts, and views that are peculiarly Platonic. This is no mean task! With the eye of a metaphysician, the soul of an epistemologist, the heart of a social thinker, and a mind that embraces the dialogues as a philosopher and as an aesthetician, Alican lifts the Platonic veil and exposes the flesh and skeleton of what we have as the Platonic corpus. His synoptic, critical, and probing eyes reach out for both the written and unwritten doctrines, for the ideas that are crucial to a reasonable construction of Plato's thought as well as to an understanding of what they mean. In itself, this achievement is an invaluable service to Plato scholarship, not only in identifying a foundation intrinsically important for philosophical inquiry, but especially in determining the kind of ideas that may, or may not, spring from it or be consistent with it. The point which merits special emphasis here is that a significant step toward understanding what Plato said is uncovering, or reconstructing, the logical and conceptual coherence, or unity, of his thought, for no idea can be attributed to or excluded from Plato's thought if the result does not cohere with his fundamental philosophical intuition and the conceptual structure that arises from it. By exploring the logical thread that runs through the written and unwritten doctrines, and by accentuating the real Socrates in the last four chapters, Alican moves us closer to the real Plato.

Third, it is not enough to map the territory of Plato's thought; the scholar should also offer a systematic, critical, and interpretive analysis of the questions, concepts, and views that make up the structure and soil of this territory, for without this kind of analysis the territory would remain vague, dubious, and unintelligible. Implied in this condition of scholarship is the need to take into serious consideration all the texts—past, modern, and contemporary—necessary to an adequate reading of the dialogues. This condition raises the question of authentication: the extent to which the dialogues themselves and the works of the historians and commentators that deal with their genuineness or meaning represent the real Plato. It also raises the question of inclusiveness, or comprehensiveness: Successful research requires two types of analysis, external and internal. The first relates to what others have said about the authenticity and meaning of the dialogues. The second, once the question of authenticity is settled, relates to what Plato really said and how others have understood the texts. Let me at once state that *Rethinking Plato* is a spectacle of respected scholars. Whether in weaving Plato's life or in examining the formal and historical aspects of the dialogues, Alican organizes symposia to which he invites major scholars who have something to say about the authenticity and meaning of Plato's ideas. He plays two different roles at these symposia. Stepping into his first role, he creates a dialogue between the participants, and, with a skillful touch, he draws the reader into the ensuing discussion. This is a lively way of disclosing the insights implicit in their arguments and points of view. Switching to his second role, he acts as a philosopher: On the basis of what transpires in the proceedings, he contributes his own understanding of what Plato said or what was said in reference to his life, thought, or work, be it by historians or by analysts. He, in other words, performs the function of the critic, the synthesizer, and the creator. But how do we determine the reliability, or authority, of the scholars? The demand implicit in this question is exactly what makes *Rethinking Plato* distinctive in its approach and contribution to Plato scholarship. The general criteria in meeting this demand are logical coherence, critical analysis, and sound interpretation, the sort that reveals Plato's meaning and philosophical aim. Alican provides a most elaborate and systematic methodology for evaluating the logical, critical, interpretive, and historical aspects of Plato's dialogues. His coverage of the rich repository of scholarship preceding him reaches deep and far enough, not just in exposition but also in evaluation, to enrich his own work. Yet the mark of a serious scholar is loyalty to truth rather than to tradition. The two need not be in conflict, but when they are, it is best not to be caught on the side opposite the truth. No agenda—philosophical, ideological, or religious—is indispensible for the scholar, and none expendable without critical consideration. Implicit in this ideal is objectivity in the search, evaluation, and determination of knowledge. No one who reads *Rethinking Plato* can miss this feature in Alican's scholarly achievement.

Fourth, and a corollary to the preceding point, is thoroughness in establishing the validity of both Platonic and non-Platonic claims—theories, views, assumptions, and judgments. It is a generally accepted principle among philosophers that logical reasoning, formal and empirical, is the instrument we employ in ascertaining the truth or reasonableness of any claim about any aspect of reality. This is the light which reveals the validity of such claims. But when we focus our attention on research in the field of Plato scholarship, we discover that the quest for the real Plato is an elusive one, quite different from quests for truth in mathematics, physics, biology, social science, or theology. This is because, advanced twenty-four hundred years ago, Plato's thought is enmeshed in an excessively complicated web of vague and often uncertain historical facts—dubious and sometimes fragmentary historical texts, interpretations, theories, and methodologies—and a bewildering compendium of literature on the subject. How can one find one's way into this web, into this compendium? A Plato scholar has to be both a philosophical analyst and a historical investigator. His or her quest for the truth is twofold: ascertaining the validity of external commentary and working out what Plato meant in all that he said. A significant contribution of *Rethinking Plato*, which no Plato scholar can overlook, is the method Alican adopts, first, in delimiting the historical and philosophical fields that are relevant to our quest for the real Plato, which clearly shows an erudite scholarly mind that possesses a synoptic vision of Plato scholarship, and, second, in the keenness of his analytical mind, in his ability to dissect the ideas and theories under consideration with amazing logical acuity and profundity of intuitive comprehension. I would not be exaggerating to say that he is a philosophical anatomist who, following Descartes, penetrates deep into the logical relations, assumptions, and implications of the different views of scholars, and then, on the basis of what this penetration yields, makes a judgment, a generalization, or hypothesis. For how can one be an anatomist if he or she is not a taxonomist? Indeed, *Rethinking Plato* is a mosaic of logical relations and reasoning. The point of this kind of design, which is a vivid example of intellectual beauty, is simply to expose the relations in terms of which we can see what is said by Plato and by the philosophers who lived during his time and the succeeding epochs. There is a running interplay between the two types of analysis required, the external kind dealing with the strand of works, both historical and philosophical, about Plato, and the internal kind dealing with Plato's works. The one is not possible without the other. But how can we proceed with either one of them without a measure of certainty of the validity of both? Here, we cannot afford to run into a vicious circle. To avoid this trap, Alican follows a strategy enabling him to keep his philosophical eye on the two domains of investigation, so that analysis in one of the domains is intertwined, sometimes by implication, with the other. Beginning with Plato's life, onward to his main philosophical ideas, then to his works from a structural perspective, and finally to an in-depth analysis of four major dialogues, always coordinating results in historical and critical discussion with direct reference to the Platonic texts, is an illustration of what Plato would call dialectical thinking. And what better use for dialectical thinking than in dissecting the very field of Plato scholarship it inspires? The pillars of this kind of thinking are logical analysis and philosophical intuition, or comprehension. Analysis without intuition, always abstract, can be accurate, even flawless, while leaving the reader without concrete understanding; intuition without analysis is informative, but it leaves the reader without objective, valid knowledge. Both of these extremes are avoided in *Rethinking Plato*.

Fifth, a condition, and, we can say, a basic feature, of scholarship is lucidity —the ability to communicate an idea, an emotion, a feeling, or an experience of some kind clearly, transparently, distinctly, and, where applicable, expressively. Lucidity is a necessary condition of human communication in general, as the very process of communication would be obstructed without it. But it plays a pivotal role in scholarship because one of the aims of scholarship is the discovery and communication of a truth that has been buried under the dust of time, typically distorted by personal, philosophical, ideological, or religious bias, and requiring the clarification or interpretation of mystical, oracular, intrusive, or difficult ideas, views, and feelings. What is the point of writing a book or an essay, or even a letter, or of creating a work of art, if it cannot be understood or appreciated by the ordinary and educated public, or if it is not understood or appreciated adequately? Is it an accident that the most lucid writers and artists, for example, Plato, Augustine, Descartes, Phidias, Michelangelo, and Van Gogh, have always commanded the attention of the ordinary and educated public? Is it an accident that a literary genius such as Tolstoy has argued that clarity and sincerity are necessary conditions of good art? And can we separate these two conditions from each other? A lucid work, be it scientific, philosophical, or artistic, reflects a lucid mind, a mind that thinks clearly and expresses its ideas or feelings articulately. The scholar's task is to illuminate what is hidden behind a dramatic, linguistic, artistic, religious, or cultural veil; it is also to make the vague linguistic or artistic forms clearer, and to make the difficult ideas easier to grasp; it is, moreover, to liberate certain ideas, forms, and images from their accidental or intrusive associations. Lucidity is a virtue of human communication, and *Rethinking Plato* is an example of this virtue; and it is such an example, not merely in the way Alican structures his work; in the way he organizes the historical texts and facts and draws clear charts and tables that enable the reader to grasp the myriad relations between them, thus making them relevant to logical analysis; in the way he examines the chosen dialogues critically and insightfully; but also in the way he constructs his sentences, paragraphs, and chapters. The outcome of his effort is a lucid work of scholarship.

When scholarly skills and philosophical understanding intersect, that is, when rational analysis intersects with intellectual depth, when reasoning intersects with passion, when clarity intersects with expressiveness, when logical form intersects with creative insight, and when the truth of the particular intersects with a synoptic vision of the whole, we are likely to have a worthwhile philosophical adventure. *Rethinking Plato* is such an adventure.

Michael H. Mitias
Emeritus Professor of Philosophy
Millsaps College

ACKNOWLEDGMENTS

This book is a product of isolation more than collaboration. It was not inspired by students or teachers or colleagues. It is not the organized accrual of lecture notes. Nor was it occasioned or stimulated by a particular symposium, conference, or colloquium. It is the result of a spontaneous impulse in the process of reading and reflecting.

Still, debts accumulate. And notable intellectual debt is hardly ever unique to a particular project. It is timeless.

If one is lucky, gratitude starts with the family. I have been lucky. Both my father and my mother have been caring, attentive, and supportive parents. But their influence goes beyond that. My father, Fikri Alican, a physician, scientist, and scholar, one of the global pioneers of organ transplantation, impressed upon me from an early age that knowledge, specifically, its pursuit, acquisition, and dissemination, opens up a magical world, not to be valued merely for the professional success it may bring, nor even solely for the personal growth it promises, but always also as an end in itself. My mother, Halide Ihlamur Alican, a champion of the underdog, partly in reflection of her vocational dedication to nursing, was responsible for my moral education, teaching me basically the same ethical principles as the past masters, falling short, if anywhere, perhaps in the area of rational justification, which she still finds superfluous, because, after all, "what's right is right."

But education rises to its full potential outside the family. The earliest and most compelling force in my intellectual development was Feridun Baydar. To him, I owe a fair amount of proficiency in mathematics, which has withered away over the years, and an analytic mindset, which has not. In an educational system rewarding memorization, he taught me not just to answer the questions, but, more urgently, to question the answers. He even insisted on questioning the questions. He fully immersed me in the Socratic method years before I found out the name for it. He was my teacher and my hero, and I miss him dearly.

As with most professional philosophers, my first institutional encounter with philosophy was in college. Michael H. Mitias and Robert E. Bergmark were responsible for my initiation into philosophy as a formal discipline, guiding me through an undergraduate major in the field. They helped shape my ability to recognize and analyze philosophical problems, while introducing me to the philosophical classics with a childlike enthusiasm that has remained an enduring source of attraction. First teacher, then mentor, and always friend, Mitias was singularly influential in my decision to pursue graduate studies in philosophy. And this through inspiration rather than instruction. He mesmerized me as a freshman in a liberal arts curriculum, he stood by my side as the best man at my wedding, and he honors me still with encouraging words in the foreword to this book.

I was likewise fortunate to have two grand sources of inspiration in graduate school. Roger F. Gibson, Jr., showed me that philosophy could be just as enchanting at the graduate level as it is at the undergraduate level, and that the transition need not replace the charm with rigor, as there is room enough for both. At a critical juncture, when I was starting to feel pressure to write like a magician, conjuring up words to suit my purposes, or at least embracing the gobbledygook already in place, he endorsed my faith in the alternative of simplicity, with a superlative flair for clarity, cogency, and coherence. His classes were a pure joy as are his numerous publications. My other role model, Carl P. Wellman, was, and still is, one of the leading ethicists in the country, and, in fact, in the world. In the department, however, he was also revered as a rather demanding pedagogue, one to be avoided for the sake of a respectable academic transcript. This challenge, together with admiration for his steady output of extremely well-received publications, convinced me that I had better take anything he was willing to teach. I feel all the richer for that decision. Not only was he a major part of my graduate studies, but he was the single greatest contributor to my previous book.

Regarding the present work, I am indebted to several philosophers for their generosity with their time and effort in helping me develop, evaluate, or finalize specific points of interest. My gratitude to them includes moral admiration as well, because they each came to my aid on a cold call, with no prior personal relationship. Eric Brown was kind enough to share his views on Plato's argument for the immortality of the soul in the tenth book of the *Republic*. Debra Nails provided guidance regarding competing positions on the chronology of Plato's works. Holger Thesleff graciously accommodated my persistent questioning of his thoughts on the matter of chronology. I consider the book the better for their input, but any shortcomings are, of course, my own.

I am obliged to Charles Allen Scarboro for reading the entire manuscript, primarily with a view to weeding out the typographical errors and other infelicities that tend to creep in during the process of converting reasoning into reporting, but also, as it turns out, with an appetite for substantive disagreement. A sociologist by trade, Scarboro assures me that he had read the *Republic* ten times by the time he finished his doctoral program. So far, Plato is ahead: I could only get Scarboro to read my book once. But just the once has saved me much embarrassment. Any mistakes that actually made it into print most likely originate with material introduced after his editorial intervention.

Above all, I am indebted to my wife, Banu Beste Başol Alican, for her loving support and encouragement. This is not the obligatory tribute authors pay their spouses for letting them get the work done, to wit, for leaving them alone. Quite the contrary, I am grateful to my lovely wife for not leaving me alone, for forcing me to make time for life, and for making that life, our life together, the happiest that one could wish for. Combining the splendor of a Greek goddess, the intellect of an empirical scientist, and the passion of a Renaissance artist, her sheer presence has been the highlight of my own. She is, more than anything, Diotima reincarnate, showing me here on earth a love fit for the gods in heaven.

NOTE ON DOCUMENTATION

Serviceable renditions of the works of Plato, no matter the language, contain marginal references to the pagination of a standard volume known as the Stephanus edition (1578), named after its compiler and publisher, Henri Estienne, or, Henricus Stephanus in the Latinized version. These references, bearing the notation of an alphanumeric string, usually placed alongside the outside margin, indicate not only the page in the Stephanus edition but also the quintile on that page. Starting the sequence, the numerals stand for the page number, while the accompanying letters ("a" through "e") denote a particular section equivalent to a fifth of the corresponding page, so marked in the original edition. For example, "*Apology* 38b" designates the part of the text where Socrates is sentenced to death. Such standardization of references facilitates dialogue between interested parties as they engage one another in queries, comments, and debates.

This is how references to Plato work in this book as well. A systematic exposition of the scheme follows in chapter three (§ 3.6). Still, a point worth noting here at the outset, even at the risk of redundancy, is the existence of a secondary practice within the main convention: Stating the name of the work is not necessary in a Stephanus citation where the context is an essay or chapter dedicated entirely to that work. In such cases, giving the Stephanus pagination is sufficient documentation, provided that all other references in the same chapter come with the title of the relevant work. To illustrate, chapter five of this book is on the *Apology*, and references in that chapter to the *Apology* omit the title of the dialogue, while references in the same chapter to any other work of Plato provide the appropriate title. Thus, the sentencing of Socrates would there be simply "38b," while elsewhere always requiring the title before the page number.

All translations of Plato are from the Hackett edition (1997) of the complete works. This centralization should make it convenient for readers to consult the sources. However, in order to avoid repetition, the identity of the publisher is not announced each time a direct quotation is occasioned. Instead, citation details for each quote are limited to the Stephanus pagination and the name of the translator.

Other references, specifically, the modern ones, employ the author-date system, producing examples such as Brown (1997, pp. 211–238), Nails (2002, pp. 243–250), and Thesleff (2009, pp. 397–410). The first number indicates the year of publication, the second number, or range, gives the pagination relevant to the passage in question.

Classical sources, of course, constitute an exception because the publication year is seldom available. Here, academic practice requires combining the name of the author with that of the work. Page numbers are usually supplemented, and sometimes supplanted, by book, chapter, section, and even paragraph numbers, which are uniform locators, unaffected by physical variations introduced by changes in typesetting or page layout. Some of these layers partitioning the whole have traditionally been represented by Roman numerals, but that custom is no longer as inviolable as it used to be. The developing trend, even among classicists, favors a full set of Arabic numerals. The following entries, for instance, would be fairly representative of current practice: Aristotle (*Metaphysics* 987a32); Cicero (*Academicae Quaestiones* 1.12.46); Quintilian (*Institutio Oratoria* 2.17.4).

On the less trendy side, proper classical citation follows a rigid routine of abbreviation, not taken up here. The correct form for the entries just listed is rather less familiar than indicated above: Aristotle (*Metaph.* 987a32); Cicero (*Acad.* 1.12.46); Quintilian (*Inst.* 2.17.4). Actually, the names of the authors also require abbreviation. Depending on whether the author is explicitly mentioned in the sentence in question, the parenthetical reference may absorb the name of the author: (Arist. *Metaph.* 987a32); (Cic. *Acad.* 1.12.46); (Quint. *Inst.* 2.17.4). By the same token, the Platonic example regarding the sentencing of Socrates should actually be "(Pl. *Ap.* 38b)," or "(*Ap.* 38b)" where the context is exclusively or primarily about Plato, and simply "(38b)" if it is about the *Apology*. Sometimes, only one work by the author will have survived, or only one will have been produced in the first place, in which case the title of the work is customarily omitted, though not so here in this book.

The practice of abbreviating, and even partly omitting, citation information in classical scholarship obviously saves space and standardizes references. Yet a little indulgence in terms of space promises substantial returns in terms of accessibility without sacrificing standardization. The aim of this book is to attract people to the study of Plato, not to impress those already attracted. Full documentation seems far more consistent with this aim than does proper abbreviation. Anyone lacking a training in classics, whether a college freshman, a doctoral candidate, or a full professor, will surely be inconvenienced by references that cannot be followed up without the aid of a classics dictionary. This book does not require one.

Another standard that is violated, though not consistently but as needed, is the tendency to use the last name alone after first mention with a full name. The last name usually suffices in citations, even on first mention. But the full name can be more appropriate where the intention is to talk about the author, however briefly, rather than merely to cite a passage. Although reserving the full name for first mention is a popular rule, slavish obedience to rules sometimes interferes with readability, and even intelligibility, or at least clarity.

Moreover, violating the rule of first mention cannot be such a crime, given that some transgressions are expected and encouraged, not just tolerated. Kant hardly requires a full introduction as if there could be, especially in a philosophy book, the slightest risk of confusion with some other Kant. The same may be said of Locke, Berkeley, Hume, Descartes, Spinoza, and Leibniz. And the list can be extended indefinitely. Besides, the rule itself admits of various interpretations, where the first mention can be absolute, that is, anchored to the entire book so that the full name is never repeated, or it can be periodically restarted, say, by indexation to each chapter, or even to each section.

However that may be, the rule is violated here, though not persistently. The tendency here is to use last names alone, whether on first mention or on every mention, in citations geared toward documentation of the source rather than discussion of the author. Other than that, most references actually follow the rule of first mention, but anyone mentioned or discussed gets the full treatment wherever a reminder seems necessary, regardless of how many times the name has come up.

The bibliographic appendix at the end is also rather unconventional. Following the customary documentation of works cited, it encourages and facilitates further study by opening up multiple gateways to scholarship. Organized in convenient categories, it is a kind of manual for rethinking Plato beyond the intellectual adventure shared in this book. As a bibliography, it is both longer and more detailed than what might be expected of a book of this length. This is partly by design and partly by accident. The length, as in any other publication, was eventually determined by necessity, naturally growing beyond the first draft. The level of detail, on the other hand, was planned from the beginning, on the conviction that a guide or companion to such a major philosopher ought to acquaint readers as closely as possible with the relevant literature. Not all of it will have been cited in the main body of the text, but the reader should not be cut off from valuable sources just because the author cannot make room for all of them.

INTRODUCTION

Plato is an elusive writer. He does not address his audience directly. Instead, he hides behind the anonymity of the dialogue form, never positioning himself as a character with a speaking part, and, with the rarest of exceptions (*Apology* 34a, 38b; *Phaedo* 59b), never even mentioning his own name. Most of his dialogues are named after a character in the corresponding dialogue. Thus, we have Plato's *Phaedo*, Plato's *Phaedrus*, Plato's *Philebus*, and the like. But how do we get at Plato's *Plato*, so to speak?

Or, setting aside the metaphorical finesse, how do we get at Plato without the italics, whether in reference to the character that might, in a perfect world, have taken center stage to make life easier for us, or in deference to the writer silencing that character and keeping him out of sight? How do we interpret, or reconstruct, the Plato, mute as a character and invisible as a writer, communicating with us through a myriad of other characters, collectively engaged in philosophical drama? How, in other words, do we enter the mind of the man who issued a universal invitation to philosophy but refused to attend his own party?

The target may well be beyond our reach. To cover all bases, we might go through the entire corpus, comparing each dialogue with every other, in an effort to stitch together an overarching philosophical outlook. Even then, we will often be told, we cannot be sure we have penetrated into the thought of Plato himself. All the same, the attempt is worthwhile as an end in itself.

Where, then, should the study of Plato start? With what work? Time was when the answer pointed unequivocally to the *Alcibiades*, the standard introduction in antiquity to Plato. Then, for centuries, the center of attraction was the *Timaeus*, the only Platonic text available in Latin through much of the Middle Ages. Nowadays, critical focus seems to favor the *Republic*, widely hailed as the pinnacle of achievement in ancient philosophy. But surely the most enchanting and inspiring experience of all awaits in the *Symposium*, just the place to fall in love with Plato, for the art if not also for the thought. Then again, perhaps the *Parmenides* would be a good place to begin, laying out, as it does, the most nagging questions in Plato studies. We could probably commence equally well with the *Meno*, or the *Gorgias*, or the *Protagoras*. Just about anywhere would be a good starting point, especially if the intention is to go far.

The aim of *Rethinking Plato* is to make that start. This is a quest for the real Plato. Yet it is not a mission of estrangement, envisaged to abandon the received wisdom, or to cast aside the prevailing platform of Platonism. The impetus for the project is not a collective failure, real or imagined, in previous efforts to uncover the real Plato, who might, instead, be exposed for the first time here. On the contrary, the quest reflects and celebrates the accretion of academic appraisal in the area. The goal is to expand that body rather than rejecting it, or, what is worse, ignoring it. And the mode of inquiry is constructive rather than destructive or dismissive.

On the other hand, little progress can be expected where the approach caters primarily to philosophical preservationism, treating Plato studies as revolving around a core of sacrosanct scholarship. Regrettably, this tendency has been so strong that the canonical corpus now comes with select secondary literature, perhaps not appended *per se* to the dialogues themselves, but imposed through interpretive paradigms, becoming especially inhibitory from the twentieth century onward. Staying within the confines of certain reconstructive traditions has been nearly as important as avoiding contradiction with the original text. Establishmentarianism of this sort is not peculiar to the study of Plato, but it is common to it.

This book, then, is an initiative to make a fresh start. It is a proposal and a map for rethinking Plato. The goal is not to replace old paradigms with a new one but to demonstrate that we do not need any particular paradigm for the study of Plato. We may undoubtedly need help, especially at the outset, but this must not be in the form of predefined patterns of understanding that suffocate the intellect instead of stimulating it, or that condition the imagination instead of cultivating it. All we really need is a critical outlook and an open mind, thereby combining an artless and unscripted analysis of problems with a willingness to consider all alternatives as if they were our own.

As the subtitle suggests, this is a Cartesian project. It is at once rational, reflective, and foundational. What makes it quintessentially Cartesian is that it looks for Plato independently of the prevailing patterns already tracing his whereabouts. Another distinctive mark is its meditative progression, not merely sampling, or even devouring, the canonical corpus, but getting to know Plato on a personal level, treating him like a human being instead of like an ancient library. However, for all its Cartesian aspirations, the book does not remain firmly outside the established web of belief, as evidenced by its tendency to make heavy use of secondary literature, perhaps not so much in turning to it for confirmation, but certainly in deferring to it for information.

Even so, if it appears strange that a Cartesian quest should be attuned to mainstream standards, it need only be remembered that Descartes himself was anxious to reaffirm many of the judgments he suspended. Moreover, he was not operating from a standpoint of disagreement, but from one of dissatisfaction. He was bothered by the uncertainty, not by the actual dogma. Otherwise, he was just as attuned to the web of belief confronting him as we are to ours. But not everyone has a reputation for erudition rivaling that of Descartes, who could skip a survey of the relevant literature without being accused of either ignorance or insolence. The rest of us would do well to confront the scholarly output pertinent to our project, even if we really are conducting a Cartesian experiment. The objective here is not to tear down the web but to illustrate what can be done without it, which calls for a demonstrable, and preferably demonstrated, understanding of what is and can be done with it.

What this requires, more than anything, is a relationship with Plato. While that cannot be built on what third parties have to say, it also does not require an academic vacuum. As in any relationship, mutual acquaintances might initiate or facilitate the process, but the strength of the end result is commensurate with the personal engagement. Mere acquaintance is obviously not the richest relationship imaginable. And habituation and inculcation are no substitute for understanding. Plato scholars may, most assuredly without shame or folly, and often with much benefit, subscribe to one school of thought or another. But this should follow personal deliberation and reflection rather than shaping it. Their considered opinions should be the inspiration for that subscription, not the other way around.

Indeed, a quest for the real Plato would end up as a simulation, far short of a relationship, if left to enlightenment through commentary alone. Yet it would also be unlikely to reach fruition if conducted through a solitary reading of dialogue after dialogue. Fortunately, these are not mutually exclusive alternatives. Nor are they jointly sufficient means to the desired end. Understanding the man fully, or even adequately, requires understanding the circumstances of his life, the nuances and depths of his thought, and the details of his work, not merely on the level of individual dialogues, but also in regard to the whole of the corpus, that is, its structural intricacies. Only then will an examination of this or that dialogue be adequately informed. Any attempt to understand a particular dialogue, as it is essentially an episode in a developing relationship with Plato, will flourish with the holism of the effort.

A caveat is in order here: Despite the recommendation not to approach Plato from any particular perspective before approaching him through the dictates of reason alone, the attempt to find the real Plato might itself be construed as a subscription to a predefined pattern of thinking about Plato. This is because of a schism between those who claim that Plato's dialogues impart doctrine and those who claim that they do not, the first view being labeled "dogmatism," and, the second, "skepticism," or "nondogmatism." Thus, the proposal to rethink Plato and to forge a relationship with him may seem to be taking sides on this issue from the beginning, presumably, the side of the dogmatist. And this may appear to be at odds with the claim that we do not need to approach Plato from a predefined angle in order to understand him.

However, the recommendation here is not to ignore the skeptical position and instead to pretend that each and every dialogue is a direct gateway to the mind of Plato, who delivers dogma after dogma throughout the corpus. The suggestion, rather, is that we should be interested in this difference, not to mention other significant methodological issues, only as a problem dividing scholars and not as a solution demanding adoption. If the mere attempt to understand Plato counts as taking sides, simply because it implies that there is something, as opposed to nothing, to be understood, then, skepticism be damned, *Rethinking Plato* is a veritable manifesto of dogmatism.

In actuality, though, the quest here for the real Plato is not an attempt to settle methodological questions but a discovery mission making use of all the available evidence. Bringing together the essential components of a proper exegesis, an integrated platform for rethinking Plato constitutes the first part of the book. This interpretive substructure devotes a chapter each to the life, thought, and works of Plato. The natural complement to this is a demonstration of where this might lead in the analysis of individual dialogues. This is the theme of the second part.

The second part of the book proceeds with a selection of four dialogues, each in its own chapter: *Euthyphro*, *Apology*, *Crito*, and *Phaedo*. Each of these chapters is a critical commentary on the dialogue to which it is dedicated. How they stand out from existing conceptions is not necessarily in a revolutionary deviation from what may be expected but in a rogue exploration of where we can end up, independently of what is expected, in pursuing a personal relationship with Plato. The book itself is nothing if not the exposition of a developing relationship with Plato, a kind of friendship.

Why these dialogues instead of others? And if the aim and approach are purely demonstrative, why not just one of these dialogues? First, with respect to the demonstration in question, this is not a specific method to be applied or formula to be instantiated. Rather the reverse, the intention is to get away from methods and formulas. This kind of demonstration calls for more than one example. In fact, rather than an example, it calls for an experience. Second, with respect to the particular selection, these happen to be the very dialogues, almost always taken as a unit, constituting a student's first, and often only, experience with Plato. That alone makes the selection appropriate. But it also creates a special responsibility: an obligation to extract the Plato from the Socrates.

In a way, this is the opposite of the more fashionable endeavor of extracting the Socrates from the Plato. Socratic studies are at the height of their popularity, and Plato is the place to turn to for any project in that area. As for mining the Platonic corpus for pure Plato, this will never be an exact science. Presumably, throwing out everything staked out by the Socratic scholars should do the trick, leaving behind the Platonic core, and thus saving a lot of time. But there are specialists in this area as well, indicating that sifting through philosophical leftovers is not the way to go, and suggesting that their Socratic counterparts have no better claim to methodological precision. At any rate, the aim here is not to make a science out of either, but to urge sensitivity to a tendency among students exposed to these four dialogues to idolize Socrates without understanding Plato.

Idolizing Socrates, of course, is no crime, at least not of the hemlock variety. No one better can be nominated for a firm grounding in morality, and historians of philosophy would be hard pressed to come up with a more able debater. What would be a shame, however, is to let students walk away with this impression as the full extent of their intellectual return on investment in a course, or module, on Plato. Yet this is not far from what goes on in introductory philosophy courses covering Plato in any detail.

Hardly anyone graduates from college without having been exposed to Plato in some manner or degree. The exposure usually comes from the cluster of dialogues built around the story of the trial and execution of Socrates, the four dialogues taken up in this book. While this constitutes the standard collegiate introduction to Plato, it quickly turns into, and typically ends up as, an immersion course in Socrates. Granted, students understand that Plato is the author, and, Socrates, the protagonist, but the fact that Socrates is also a real person, and a singularly admirable one at that, immediately inspires hero worship. Plato can no more compete with his protagonist than Matthew, Mark, Luke, and John can with theirs. As a result, the typical orientation process scheduled for Plato often turns out to be mostly about Socrates.

The present work fortifies the Platonic side of the equation, treating the disciple as more than a narrator of the life and death of the master. An alternative would have been to let Plato shine for himself by focusing the second part of the book on a few of the works in the late period. But going there would probably be more fruitful in a later stage of rethinking Plato. Moreover, showing that Plato shines just as brightly in the presence of Socrates is a greater service, thus validating the selection of the four dialogues constituting the academic module familiar from introductory courses. In this spirit, the second part of the book can be taken as a Platonic guide or companion to standard compilations of the Socratic saga.

That said, even in its auxiliary function in that capacity, it is not a substitute for reading the dialogues themselves, and it is not a study guide for the next midterm. Nor is it an instructor's manual. Plato is so much fun that hardly anyone should be tempted to seek an alternative to reading the original, at least in translation. He is also often so easy to follow as to require no instruction or assistance. Understanding Plato does not depend on a special teacher or pedagogical approach. Nor does the effort call for spoon-feeding or sugar-coating the details. In fact, Plato can be so deceptively simple that the student, or any other reader, often needs to be shown the difficulty rather than being helped out of it. Hence, the approach here does not necessarily simplify the material. It does not even shrink from complicating what may appear to be simple. It does, however, aim to bring out all that is pertinent to the message in each work discussed and to the treatment of each topic considered.

The only obvious barrier to direct access is that Plato wrote almost exclusively in dialogue form. This is not to say that his philosophy cannot be discerned from his work but that guidance toward that end would be useful. The most common trap in drawing out the philosophy from the literature is to treat this merely as a matter of separating the logic from the drama. Indeed, a Platonic dialogue can be stripped of everything extraneous to the logic, and studied exclusively through the arguments it contains. That, too, would be doing philosophy, but it would no longer be the philosophy of Plato. Reading Plato purely for the logic would be like reading Shakespeare purely for the grammar, or, possibly worse, like studying physics purely for the math.

What is required is a balanced approach, taking stock of the logic, the drama, and the historical circumstances, all at once. This is particularly important in a typical Socratic dialogue such as the *Euthyphro*, which ends in apparent failure and frustration, and perhaps even more so in the opposite case presented by a dialogue such as the *Phaedo*, which ends in boundless and undisguised satisfaction, not to mention an infectious optimism and enthusiasm, all resting rather precariously on a series of arguments that are not very convincing. In between, what are we to make of the *Apology*, where we find the master of debate failing to win his most important argument, the one for his life, and what of the *Crito*, where we encounter an uncompromising advocate of authoritarianism? For a major philosopher, Plato can come across as embracing one too many an argument that seems questionable, to say the least, plus a position or two looking surprisingly untenable, or even unpalatable.

Yet appearances can be deceiving, especially in a Platonic dialogue. Students midway through their first course in logic revel in picking out errors in the reasoning of published writers, especially of philosophers, showing off their newly acquired skills in recognizing such faults and in identifying them as one fallacy or another. In contrast, the object in reading Plato is to determine how apparent mistakes, if any, might contribute to the overall aim or message of the dialogue, not how they might have been avoided in the first place. Plato, after all, while predating the birth of formal logic in Aristotle, is not known for outlandishly stupid arguments. Where any are found, it is better to look for an explanation than for a pat on the back.

The intermediation needed, then, is somewhat more expository than argumentative. This being so, the aim of the second part of the book is to explain each work, not to defend or attack it, and even less to wrestle with another commentator who defends or attacks it. The analytical and exegetical execution is not entirely devoid of opinion, but opinions are, as much as possible, identified as such, instead of disguised as fact. The corresponding chapters, whether in expressing opinions, advancing arguments, or reporting facts, are not interdependent. Appreciating one does not require perusing another. Inspecting just one and ignoring all the rest, hence, treating the book as a companion or a reference guide to be consulted as needed should not present any problems, though that is not the primary intention.

The primary intention, as intimated earlier, betrays a more holistic concept, a scholarly exercise in rethinking Plato. The most accurate characterization of this project is, at the risk of being cryptic, the public exposition of a personal relationship with Plato, a friendship, really. How can we become friends with a dead philosopher? The same way we do with a living one: by collaborating in pursuit of the truth. In the spirit of a legendary appraisal ascribed to his greatest student, Aristotle: Plato is a friend, and is dear to us, but the truth is dearer. This anecdotal juxtaposition of friendship and truth is quoted differently by different sources, but a strict quotation is out of the question, especially if Plato is to be identified by name. The closest we come to this in the Aristotelian corpus is a general assessment in the *Nicomachean Ethics* (1096a11–16), where the reference to Plato is only implicit albeit obvious. If we prefer to name Plato, the best we can do is to paraphrase Aristotle, not to quote him. Curiously, the aphorism has come down to us in some rigid formulations, the most popular of which seems to be this: "Plato is dear to me, but dearer still is truth." No matter what the best reconstruction may be, the spirit in which the original expression was uttered has been a guiding force here, where the aim is not to defend Plato but to show what it takes to become his friend. Hence, the aim, or rather obligation, of that friendship, has been to lay out the truth about Plato, not to glorify his thought, which, everyone knows, even when it strays from the consensus, and perhaps especially then, is glorious enough as it is. This was so for Aristotle, and it is so now.

The truth is for everyone, but a scholarly monograph usually is not. We are all laypersons about one thing or another, indeed, about well nigh everything, and we all tend to approach the expert with the same dreaded cliché: "Explain it to me as you would to a two-year old!" The age reference may vary, but the nature of the request does not. We want the explanation to be short and simple yet definitive and comprehensive. And we demonstrate the same patience with books as we do with the professors we accost at cocktail parties. No doubt, there is a perceived need for that sort of information, and perhaps, therefore, for a simple book on Plato that can be read on an exercise bike while watching television. This is not that book.

This is, however, a book for any serious student of Plato. And that category includes college professors no less than the people they teach. If students find the material a bit challenging, so much the better, for they will find it all the more useful. If Plato scholars find the material rather familiar, mission accomplished, for there is nothing new under the sun, nor inside the cave. No new book on Plato can surprise the experts; not anymore, at least not in a good way. And it is not the aim of this book to do so in any way.

Explanations, illustrations, and elaborations may often exceed the requirements of Plato scholars. But this is inevitable. Plato scholars hardly need Plato explained. And this book is not meant to educate them. Quite the opposite, it purports, with sincere appreciation and open gratitude, to be the reflection of an education by them.

What places them in the center of the target audience is the nature of Platonic scholarship as dialectic, just the way Plato himself intended. Expertise, even at the highest level, is not a terminal achievement. It is not a static state but a dynamic process. Plato scholars are not frozen in academic stasis, instead, flourishing in interaction, often with disagreement but always in dialogue. This, then, is a new voice in that dialogue.

Part One

GENERAL ORIENTATION

One

LIFE OF PLATO

Lives are shaped by basic events. This being so, they can be understood through simple principles. This is not to trivialize psychology but to draw on its fundamental clarity. For example, people tend to pursue or praise what they deem desirable, while avoiding or rejecting what they find disagreeable. Plato is a child of leisure. He is also a child of war. As a child of leisure, he advocates social stratification through a conception of collective justice grounded in the preservation of class distinctions in a perfect world where individuals are content with their lot without rocking the boat. As a child of war and chaos, he finds real goodness and beauty only beyond the realm of experience, thus relegating our interaction with the world around us to illusion, or, at best, to an imperfect reflection of reality.

This assessment begs for elaboration, especially in regard to details omitted in encapsulating Plato's conception of justice, but it is useful even as it is, as a heuristic tool bringing together biographical details on a provisional basis, that is, as a prelude to critical consideration, and does not merit dismissal merely for being laconic. Nothing can detract from the importance of Plato's having been born into the electrifying juxtaposition of privilege and strife. Either perspective on his formative years constitutes an adequate explanation of the strong emphasis on unity and order in his philosophy. Together they are compelling. His elitism, no doubt at least partly and probably largely a reflection of the Greek culture of the time, must have come all the more easily with roots firmly grounded among the elite. His low opinion of the visible, indicative of dissatisfaction with what one has seen, is particularly consistent with a protracted state of war. His drive toward unity and order speaks to both themes at once, namely, both to his aristocratic birth and to his wartime upbringing, embracing harmony of some sort as insurance for the hierarchical social order perpetuating his social position at home, and as an antidote for the war and disorder, and the constant threat of such, attracting menacing complications from abroad. He was born with a silver spoon, yet he knew the right end of a steel blade. Both are powerful forces in the formation of character.

On the other hand, this does not mean that Plato's contribution to philosophy can be reduced to a deterministic stimulus-response mechanism producing automated reactions to circumstantial developments. If this were the case, every rich kid growing up in the midst of war would have left a comparable mark in the history of philosophy. Given the turbulent history of Europe, we should have then been in a far more advanced state of intellectual achievement, which might, in turn, have precluded such a turbulent history for Europe, which, however, on the original reasoning, would have held back the intellectual progress supposedly setting the process in motion. In short, psychological profiling, whether an art or a science, is not infallible. As it is, we are grappling with the same problems troubling Plato, which suggests that not many more like him have been around, thus implying that circumstances alone cannot account for genius, his or anyone else's.

Nevertheless, ideas are not born in a vacuum. And, at least with the more important ones, it pays to examine where they were born. Biographical studies, even expository overviews such as this, are useful not so much for the facts they provide as for the connections they draw between those facts, presumably, enriching them with a plausible and insightful analysis. In Plato's case, no interpretive framework can afford to ignore the comforts of his prominent family, making aristocracy more palatable than might otherwise be expected, nor the inspirational burden of the state of war consuming his childhood and early adulthood, making a transcendent reality more appealing than might be the case under most any other scenario.

1.1. Sources

Little else is certain about Plato, though not entirely for a lack of information. Any insight we seem to have today is twice removed from reality, as Plato himself might say, through temporal gaps in two directions, the first extending back roughly three centuries from the earliest extant and datable biography to the subject, and the second extending forward more than two millennia from that first known record to the modern reader. This is not to say that absolutely nothing of note survives from the time of Plato, but indeed no full biography does. While we may count the Platonic corpus and the Aristotelian corpus among data relevant to the life of Plato, these do not add up to a coherent biography. Each makes unique and important contributions, but neither comes close to a full story.

Autobiographical entries in the received manuscripts are limited to family background in a few dialogues and to personal history in some letters. The dialogues in question (e.g., *Charmides*, *Protagoras*, *Republic*) are widely agreed to be authentic, but the information there is neither momentous nor hardly ever about Plato himself, instead consisting mostly of minutiae on relatives. The letters, in contrast, are not widely agreed to be authentic, drawing mixed assessments, depending both on the letter and on the reviewer, but the information therein is enlightening, despite covering a disappointingly short span of time in the philosopher's life.

The only two exceptions to the otherwise universal confinement of Plato's truly autobiographical remarks to letters, hence, not counting the family details he reveals through the dialogues, are his explicit confirmations that he was present at the trial (*Apology* 34a, 38b) and absent at the execution (*Phaedo* 59b) of Socrates. This is not much to go on, and going any further, namely, into the realm of letters, requires not just reference but argument as well, and, in the absence of argument, remains on the level of assumption.

On the face of it, a fair summary might seem to be that the dialogues are more reliable while the letters are more revealing. But this would be a hasty conclusion. The letters are indeed more revealing, an uncontested fact, but they are not necessarily less reliable. The questionable authenticity of the letters, or, from a less judgmental perspective, their questioned authenticity, is not a decisive factor against trusting their contents. The transmission of accurate information about a subject might well be accomplished by persons besides the subject, perhaps not just as well, but probably reasonably well. Granted, Plato's authorship of the canonical letters is in dispute, typically on the level of the individual letters rather than *en masse*, yet, either way, the question is not whether they are inaccurate but whether they are forged.

At any rate, what we get by way of an epistolary autobiography is predominantly about Plato's experiences in Syracuse and in connection with Syracuse, thereby excluding much else that would have been of interest. And what survives from the period in all, counting the entirety of the first-hand information we have, including everything remaining from whatever Aristotle saw fit to share, is a bricolage, falling short of a cohesive or comprehensive report, though not thereby short of an informative or entertaining one.

For anything more, we have to move forward hundreds of years. We know of biographies composed immediately or shortly after Plato's death, but they are all lost, and appear, on evidence from third parties, to have been meant to eulogize the man rather than to document his life. More than a dozen generations pass by before the first surviving accounts that constitute standalone stories come along.

The temporal distance does not automatically undermine the reliability of the information supplied. After all, neither the ancient nor the medieval biographers we have on record complain of inadequate source material. On the contrary, many invoke sources no longer available to us. Those who do not do this expressly no doubt do it silently. There is no good reason why one or two, or even more, of the biographies composed by Plato's contemporaries would not have been available to the biographers of late antiquity, and possibly even to those of the Middle Ages, hence, at least indirectly, to just about everyone informing us today. Even if the earliest known biographers did not themselves have access to eyewitness accounts, they might have had access to sources that did. We have neither. And it would be extravagant of us to dismiss what little we do have.

The real problem is not the hundreds of years that are invisible to us today but the biographical tendencies that are alien to us today. Plato's contemporaries were not the only ones to idealize his life. Glorification colors later biographies as well. Much of what we have is a lionized Plato.

Most embellishments are obvious, and can be weeded out. For example, we need not be confused about whether Plato really was a demigod just because tradition has him sired by a god. But fabulosity was not the only deviation from reality. Systematic intervention in the truth, not to embellish the facts but to reconfigure them in the standard biographical template of the day, leaves us with greater obstacles. For example, it was highly desirable that one important event coincide with another. An enviable life became all the more enviable, or at least more memorable, upon synchronization with another, whether birth with birth, death with death, or birth with death. And hardly anyone worth remembering seems to have led a chronologically uneven life, the most illustrious characters of antiquity going down in history as having spent their time on earth in symmetrical intervals adding up to a nice round number.

The Alexandrian biographical tradition is notorious in this regard, with Apollodorus of Athens (born c. 180 BC) leading the way. The *Chronicle* of Apollodorus, a lost work with historical influence that is still evident today, is famous for imposing a standard chronological framework on lives that are not otherwise set in stone: The height of one's career (*akmê* or ἀκμή) comes at forty, and, death, at eighty, except, of course, in the case of documentary evidence to the contrary.

A turning point in our understanding of the practice is German scholarship in the early twentieth century. Mosshammer (1976, pp. 291–306) offers a highly accessible overview invoking the authority of Jacoby (1902) and Diels (1903). Unless an untimely death is in question, an eighty-year lifespan is divided into two halves, and each half again into two halves, so that a life proceeds in intervals of twenty years, neatly compartmentalizing all the relevant milestones. Any storyline that happens to break the pattern is ignored altogether, or, if essential, reformulated for a better fit. Thus, an entire life, so long as it is not decidedly and famously out of proportion with the standard paradigm, is always a candidate for perpetuating the predetermined chronology.

Plato's life is no exception. He seems to have had his most important encounters right on schedule, meeting Socrates when he was twenty, Dion, when he was forty, Aristotle, when he was sixty, and, the maker of all things, when he was eighty. Not all the dates are certain, but this is more or less what we get through the uncritical tradition. Some of this is a matter of record, or is at least corroborated by mutually independent sources, thus constituting a happy coincidence in favor of Alexandrian chronicling, but the entire chain seems just too convenient. And several other coincidences, including Plato's founding of the Academy at his *akmê*, as he turns forty, further enhance the convenience.

On the whole, given any corruption to be expected over time, together with the timeless penchant for mythologizing, and an evidently influential practice of chronological recalibration, we can never be sure how close we are to the truth. We cannot even assume that the truth, unadulterated even if incomplete, was ever a matter of record. Yet this is no reason to ignore what is available to us. What is available consists of the following:

- Anonymous: *Life of Plato*. Not merely anonymous but still rather obscure. Available in Westermann's *Biographoi* (1845, pp. 388–396). Also appended to the Cobet edition (1850) of the *Lives* of Diogenes Laërtius. Thought to inform certain biographical details in St. Augustine of Hippo (*De Civitate Dei* 8.11; *De Doctrina Christiana* 2.28.43) and in Photius (*Bibliotheca* 249, a codex actually on the life of Pythagoras).

- Apuleius (Lucius Apuleius Platonicus [=Lucius Apuleius Madaurensis]) (c. 125–180): *De Platone et Eius Dogmate* (*On Plato and His Doctrine*). A biographical sketch (1.1–4) serves as the opening of an overview of Plato's philosophy, with an exclusive focus on his physics (natural philosophy), ethics (moral philosophy), and logic (interpretation), examined separately in three books.

- Diogenes Laërtius (c. 200–500): The third book of the *Lives and Opinions of Eminent Philosophers* (3.1–109). A widely consulted ancient biographical reference on Greek philosophers, this compendium is cherished for its use of a great many sources no longer in existence, though it is often condemned for its uncritical compilation of information, typically brought together with greater regard for completeness than for cohesiveness.

- Olympiodorus the Younger of Alexandria (c. 495–570): Introductory sections of both (1) the *Commentary on the First Alcibiades of Plato*, the biographical opening of which is often excerpted as a *Life of Plato* (*Olympiodori Vita Platonis*) in various older collections of the Platonic corpus, and (2) the *Anonymous Prolegomena to Platonic Philosophy*, the latter traditionally albeit erroneously attributed to Olympiodorus.

- Philodemus of Gadara (c. 110–35 BC): *Academicorum Philosophorum Index Herculanensis*. Fragmentary remains (Papyrus Herculanensis 164, 1021) from the eighteenth century rediscovery of Herculaneum. Traditionally attributed to the Epicurean philosopher Philodemus, this is a history of Academic philosophy beginning with the birth of Plato and ending with the death of Antiochus of Ascalon, thus tracing developments through the end of the New Academy and all the way up to the inception of Middle Platonism.

- Suidas (10th century): The entry on Plato in the *Suda* (*Souda*). Traditionally attributed to a certain Suidas, now widely recognized as the name of the work rather than the compiler, this is a Byzantine lexicon of the tenth century. Its biographical accounts, including that of Plato, are taken from the *Onomatologos ē Pinax tōn en Paideia Onomastōn*, a lost work on eminent writers by Hesychius Illustrius of Miletus (6th century).

Further details on these are available in the bibliographic appendix at the end of the book. They are invariably, or nearly so, recognized in all specialist surveys, for example, in the work of Boas (1948, pp. 439–457) and Swift Riginos (1976, especially pp. 1–8), both dedicated to the difference between fact and fiction in the biography of Plato. The only murky item on the list seems to be the first one, the anonymous *Life of Plato*. Boas (1948, p. 439) includes it in his own list, while Swift Riginos (1976, p. 1) excludes it from hers. Other than that, they both acknowledge the same sources, the ones listed above.

These sources, together with various references in the Platonic and Aristotelian corpuses, constitute the core material we have on the life of Plato. Anything else in circulation is either derivative or otherwise too brief or trivial, or possibly both, to count as a biography in itself.

Not everyone will be satisfied with the ancient accounts themselves. Fortunately, a plethora of commentary and reconstruction is available. With a few exceptions, the seminal work in English is concentrated in the hundred years between the mid-nineteenth and mid-twentieth centuries. Notable entries in this period include the following:

- Burnet: *Greek Philosophy* (1914, pp. 205–233)
- Field: *Plato and His Contemporaries* (1930, pp. 1–48)
- Grote: *A History of Greece*
  (1846–1856, volume 8, chapters 67–68; volume 11, chapters 83–84)
- Grote: *Plato, and the Other Companions of Sokrates*
  (1865, volume 1, chapter 3 [=1885, volume 1, chapter 5])
- Guthrie: *Plato: The Man and His Dialogues: Earlier Period*
  (=*A History of Greek Philosophy*: Volume 4) (1975, pp. 1–38)
- Ritchie: *Plato* (1902, pp. 1–18)
- Taylor: *Plato* (1908, pp. 1–20)
- Taylor: *Plato: The Man and His Work* (1960 [originally 1926], pp. 1–9)
- Tennemann: "Life of Plato" (1839, pp. 311–367)
- Woodbridge: *The Son of Apollo* (1929, pp. 1–31)
- Zeller: *Plato and the Older Academy* (1876, pp. 1–44)

The paginal references in this list are restricted to portions dedicated primarily or entirely to the life of Plato, as opposed to his thought or works, excepting Grote's *History*, where the philosopher's presence is incidental to the greater context. Tennemann and Zeller, in translation, are included among the otherwise anglophone scholars listed, in order to avoid the crime of fully ignoring German scholarship, arguably the most important institutional voice in the nineteenth century, and still commanding attention today.

The list can be expanded, both within the temporal scope stated and beyond it, but it is already a sufficiently representative list of excellence in biographical achievement. Subsequent efforts tend to draw on these reconstructions rather than on the core material from antiquity. Hardly any original work is being done in the area, which is understandable since there is only so much to do with the same basic information.

A prominent exception is the work of Debra Nails, who has been challenging the prevailing view in terms of both dates and events. She is one of the few contemporary scholars reconsidering the evidence with a view to refining the received chronology, purging centuries of invention and intervention, and thereby pursuing an accurate account as opposed to a merely agreeable one. Her willingness to let momentous events fall where they may, instead of forcing them into predetermined temporal slots, throws several events off by a few years and gives Plato a shorter life, pushing his birth forward by four years. Anyone interested in a sober account of this sort may find it in her prosopography (Nails, 2002, pp. 243–250, all the more enlightening when read together with other relevant entries, e.g., Socrates in pp. 263–269 and Dion in pp. 129–132), and those preferring a less discursive and less rigorous rendition should appreciate her fluid narrative in "The Life of Plato of Athens" (Nails, 2006a, pp. 1–12), her contribution to a recent generalist companion to Plato.

What follows here, with all due respect to Nails, is the traditional view of Plato's life.

1.2. Birth and Family

The tendency of drama to trump detail in the ancient biographical tradition leaves us with a wider consensus on Plato's having been fathered by Apollo than on where and when he was born (Apuleius: *De Platone* 1.1; Diogenes: *Lives* 3.2; Olympiodorus: *Commentary on the First Alcibiades* 2.21–24; Suidas: *Suda* pi 1707 Adler). In the same vein, we find greater medieval enthusiasm for perpetuating, say, Cicero's (106–43 BC) report of bees having settled on Plato's lips as an infant, thus accounting for the sweetness of his prose, than for establishing anything of significance regarding his childhood and early adulthood (*De Divinatione* 1.36.78, 2.31.66). That story seems to take on a life of its own later, as details are filled in, for example, by Olympiodorus (*Anonymous Prolegomena* 2.16–22; *Commentary on the First Alcibiades* 2.24–29), who adds that the event took place during a family trip to Mount Hymettus for a sacrifice to the relevant deities, namely, Pan, the Nymphs, and Apollo, a clever reminder of the Apollonian nature of Plato. A further nuance is that while bees land on the lips of the infant in the version by Cicero, they actually fill his mouth with honey in the version by Olympiodorus. This, however, is at most a matter of emphasis, as the intention in either case is to compare the subject's words to drops of honey. Yet quite apart from the question of whether the story is true, that is, whether bees ever had anything to do with Plato, and apart still from the question of whether this would be significant if true, in other words, whether it would make a difference what, if anything, transpired between a swarm of bees and the philosopher, the basic scenario is not even unique to Plato. It represents a standard reference to literary distinction, possibly first employed in accounting for the poetic skills of Pindar (c. 518–438 BC).

Leaving aside anecdotal and mythological boilerplate of this sort, the range of scholarly debate regarding Plato's vital statistics can be narrowed down, albeit not without nagging outliers, to bring the possibilities into close spatial and temporal proximity. Although he is now enough of a celebrity to get away with using nothing more than his first name, he was known in his own time as Plato of Collytus, Son of Ariston, the prevailing equivalent of what we would consider his full legal name.

He was born either in Athens or in Aegina, an island situated approximately twenty-five kilometers south of Athens in the Saronic Gulf between Attica and the Peloponnesus. Athens is the default assumption, but Aegina has its advocates as well (Diogenes: *Lives* 3.3, citing Favorinus of Arelate: *Miscellaneous History*; Olympiodorus: *Anonymous Prolegomena* 2.8–10; Suidas: *Suda* pi 1707 Adler).

The consensus on timing, notwithstanding reputable dissent, is that he was born in 428 BC or 427 BC, and lived to be eighty or eighty-one years of age, dying in 348 BC or 347 BC. His mother Perictione (or possibly Potone) bore him in wedlock with Ariston, and presumably as a result of coitus with her husband, with the only competing alternative represented by reports of divine intervention by Apollo (Diogenes: *Lives* 3.2). Yet his heavenly genealogy is not grounded entirely in the seed of Apollo, as Plato is said to descend ultimately from Poseidon on both sides of his earthly family (Diogenes: *Lives* 3.1).

Regarding the time and circumstances of his birth and death, we are not without guidance from the ancients. If there should be any problem at all, it is not the absence of information but an abundance of incompatible reports, all offered with comparable confidence. According to Diogenes, Plato was born on the seventh day of the month of Thargelion in the first year of the 88th Olympiad (*Lives* 3.2, invoking the chronology of Apollodorus of Athens: *Chronicle* fr. 37), and he died at eighty-one, in the first year of the 108th Olympiad (*Lives* 3.2, on the authority of Hermippus of Smyrna), coinciding with the thirteenth year of the reign of Philip of Macedon (*Lives* 3.40, citing Favorinus: *Memorabilia*: Book 3).

Happily, the seventh of Thargelion is also the birthday of Apollo, representing a permanent reminder of the link between the heavenly father and the divine son. It also happens to be the day after the birthday of Socrates, conveniently symbolizing the succession between master and pupil. The basic data is confirmed by various fragmentary sources and repeated in full biographies besides Diogenes: Apuleius (*De Platone* 1.1); Olympiodorus (*Anonymous Prolegomena* 1.41–46, 2.12–16, 6.1–7); Suidas (*Suda* pi 1707 Adler).

The information is specific enough, and, the confirmation, or repetition, promising. Yet recasting this Attic record in terms of the Gregorian calendar is not as straightforward as converting, say, gallons into liters. There are certain difficulties. Mercifully, they would throw us off only by a matter of days, giving us at least a rough idea.

The problem, however, is not so much with the day or month as it is with the year. The years given by Diogenes tend to draw criticism for falling short of the lifespan given by him in the same breath. Going by the Olympiadic timeline provided, Plato was born in 427 BC and died in 347 BC, but this does not let him quite reach eighty-one as reported in the same sentence. The years of birth and death given would make him eighty, if he died on or after his birthday, and seventy-nine if he died earlier, not eighty-one as stated. But what is actually stated is not a categorical declaration that he was fully eighty-one years old when he died, having spent no less than one plus eighty complete years on this earth. Translators expose the ambiguity, Yonge (1853) letting the philosopher finish eighty-one years, while Hicks (1925) kills him off in his eighty-first year. The Hicks translation would be consistent with death on the eightieth birthday, or anytime after that and before the eighty-first birthday.

Indeed, another tradition has Plato dying on his own birthday, though on his eighty-first rather than eightieth (Olympiodorus: *Anonymous Prolegomena* 6.1–7). This may seem to break with the chronological prescription of Apollodorus, but what is important is to reach eighty, going beyond being far less problematic than falling short. Acknowledging the man's death to coincide with his own birthday is a grand compliment. Although making Plato eighty-one instead of eighty upon death stretches his life beyond the Alexandrian template, eighty-one is an even better number, as it is three to the fourth power, which is the same as three-squared squared, or, in other words, the square of the square of the number three, a mystical product, not to mention its correlation with the number of Muses, totaling nine in all, the square root of eighty-one.

Nevertheless, additional information by Diogenes (*Lives* 3.6, appealing to Hermodorus), specifically, that Plato was twenty-eight when Socrates was executed (399 BC), points again to 427 BC as the year of birth. Strictly speaking, the text is not clear whether Plato was exactly twenty-eight when Socrates died: It affirms only that he could not possibly have been any older, as the explicit testimony is that he was twenty-eight when he left for Megara after Socrates died, which need not have been immediately after Socrates died. But the common reading is that this all refers to the same year, thus reinforcing the traditional timeline.

Zeller (1876, p. 2, n. 2), for one, interprets the birthday reported in Diogenes as 21 May 427 BC. Boas (1948, pp. 439–457) prefers 22 May 427 BC. A specific date of death is not recorded, but if we go by its legendary synchronization with the philosopher's birthday, the calculation is easy enough.

As stated earlier, the greater difficulty is with the years, not the days. One way to clean up the chronology might seem to be to stick with just one tradition, say, Diogenes, ignoring anything that contradicts it. But Diogenes can contradict his own account quite effectively with no outside help, a testament to his predilection for exhaustive coverage at the expense of coherent reporting, placing a greater value on transmitting all the information available than on making sure that everything mentioned is jointly consistent. To be fair, in this case, he does not profess to be relaying a uniform record, instead acknowledging chronological inconsistencies and openly passing on conflicting reports as competing alternatives available to him. The leading example is the alternative that Plato died at the age of eighty-four (Diogenes: *Lives* 3.3, citing Neanthes of Cyzicus). Introducing this possibility immediately after the Alexandrian opening, that is, the Apollonian chronology, Diogenes adds straightaway that Plato was born the year Pericles died, during the archonship of Ameinias. Knowing when Pericles died, we can work out the alternative timeline, despite the apparent confusion regarding the corresponding archonship (Zeller, 1876, pp. 2–3, n. 2). The alternative thereby intimated seems to be that Plato was born in 429 BC and died in 345 BC. If this ever had any currency as an alternative, it no longer does. But the point is that the record was never without an alternative, and still is not.

Tennemann (1839, pp. 311–315) and Zeller (1876, pp. 2–3, n. 2) still afford the richest insight into the intricacies of the "lifetime math" involved, perhaps not in terms of a compelling solution, but certainly by way of an enlightened and enlightening discussion. As for a definitive answer, the most cogently argued solution may easily be the one sketched by Nails (2002, pp. 243–247), who places Plato's birth in 424/423 BC and his death in 348/347 BC. Although she strays from the traditional chronology, Nails might just as well be read as explaining it, as her defiance is so erudite, confident, and transparent as to constitute a dispassionate and comprehensive overview of all relevant details.

In the midst of all the uncertainty surrounding Plato's life, one thing that is not in dispute is an established family with good connections and a strong presence in the social and political scene. Both his parents claimed an impressive lineage, even without counting kinship with the gods. Perictione's brother Charmides and their kinsman Critias (either their paternal uncle or that uncle's son) were prominent statesmen, their final position being membership in the Thirty Tyrants (*de jure*: September 404 BC – May 403 BC; *de facto*: April 404 BC – September 403 BC), the oligarchy briefly supplanting democracy in Athens at the conclusion of the Peloponnesian War (431–404 BC). Charmides was a regular member of the oligarchy, and Critias was one of its two leaders. Both are immortalized in Plato's dialogues: Charmides is the main interlocutor in a dialogue named after himself, while Critias is present as a character in that dialogue as well as in the *Protagoras*. Critias appears, in addition, to be the eponymous protagonist of a dialogue named after himself, not to mention a speaking part in the *Timaeus*, but the identity of the character in both cases is in dispute, dating back to a suggestion by Burnet (1914, p. 338) that these roles are better attributed to the oligarch's paternal grandfather of the same name. Both Charmides and Critias were killed in the revolt restoring democracy and limiting its interruption to eight months, or just under a year-and-a-half counting the political vacuum immediately preceding and following the recognized reign of the Thirty.

This is not all there is to Plato's patrician existence. Perictione is four generations away from the brother of Solon, while Ariston traces his ancestry back to the last of the legendary kings of Athens, Codrus, who, in turn, happens to be the son of Melanthus, the king of Messenia. If Plato is not the son of gods and fabled heroes, he can, we are assured, boast comparably good stock on earth.

Plato had three full siblings: two brothers, Glaucon and Adeimantus, who appear as interlocutors in the *Republic* and characters in the *Parmenides* (with Glaucon also present in a minor capacity in the *Symposium*), and a sister, Potone, whose son Speusippus took over the reins of Platonism after his death. Despite some disagreement regarding the order of the children, Plato's brothers are thought to be older, primarily on the evidence of a passage in the *Republic* (368a) making them warriors in a battle taking place in 424 BC in Megara when Plato was a child, though Xenophon makes Glaucon out to be younger than Plato by implication, specifically, by presenting him as a familial source of embarrassment for Plato and his uncle Charmides (*Memorabilia* 3.6.1–2). Biographical commentators variously state his sister to be older or younger than he, none, however, as a matter of record.

Plato also had a stepbrother, Demos (or Demus), and a half-brother, Antiphon (appearing as a character in the *Parmenides*), through Perictione's marriage to Pyrilampes, following the death of Ariston and in accordance with Greek legal and social sanctions against a solitary existence for women. Even Plato's stepfather was a prominent citizen, being an ambassador to the Persian court and an associate of Pericles, and, in general, enjoying enviable social circumstances. Pyrilampes was not only *from* a distinguished family, but he *was* family, being the brother of Perictione's mother.

1.3. Youth

We do not know much about Plato's childhood, but we do know that it took place in the thick of war. To be precise, the first quarter of a century of his existence coincides with widespread turmoil. Born in the third or fourth year of the Peloponnesian War, which might be considered a world war, or perhaps an extensive civil war, depending on one's view of warring city-states populated by a single race, he was twenty-three or twenty-four years old at the end, presumably having been in active military service in the last five years (409–404 BC).

About the possibility of combat duty, all we have to go by is the reports of Diogenes Laërtius (*Lives* 3.8) and Aelian ([=Claudius Aelianus, 175–235] *Varia Historia* 7.14) that Plato took part in expeditions to Tanagra, Corinth, and Delium. While the information is specific enough, its exclusion from other biographical sources is a bit suspicious. Another difficulty is chronological fit: The campaigns are not listed in the correct order (Tanagra, Delium, Corinth), despite a pretension to reporting the actual sequence of events (Diogenes: *Lives* 3.8). Moreover, in relation to the proper historical order, as Grote (1865, pp. 117–118, n. 1) warns, Plato was too young during the first two battles, and presumably abroad during the third. Grote assures us that even if Plato were, perchance, in Athens, and able to participate in the Battle of Corinth (394 BC), this was definitely not followed by an expedition to Delium, where, incidentally, Plato supposedly won the prize of valor (Diogenes: *Lives* 3.8), a curious coincidence given that Socrates reportedly distinguished himself with his own bravery in the very same battle (Diogenes: *Lives* 2.22–23). Although Grote is careful to acknowledge the possibility that minor incursions into the Boeotian frontier, including both Tanagra and Delium, may have taken place during Plato's military years without any record of such being transmitted through the ages, this is a testament to Grote's academic integrity rather than to Plato's service record. The admission is certainly nothing to build a military biography on. Nor are the original reports of Diogenes and Aelian. In summary, Plato could not possibly have been involved in two of the three campaigns traditionally mentioned in connection with his military experience, and he is not altogether likely to have actually been there for the remaining one. (See further: Ritchie, 1902, pp. 4, 10; Tennemann, 1839, p. 320, n. 2; Zeller, 1876, p. 6, n. 6.)

Plato may not have been a warrior, but he was certainly a child of war. With or without evidence, he is likely even to have been personally engaged in combat on more than one occasion. But this should by no means be interpreted as an indication that he was deprived of educational, professional, intellectual, or even leisurely opportunities or activities that might have been available otherwise. His family connections were so strong, and his political prospects so bright, that he had a standing reservation for distinction as a statesmen in the aftermath of the war, both as a member of the Thirty Tyrants seizing power in 404 BC and as a representative of the democracy established in the very next year. The actual course of his life, developing as it did outside the political arena, is often attributed to his enchantment with Socrates and to his growing interest in philosophy, two factors that go hand in hand, with the latter, no doubt, unavoidable, as a consequence of the former.

Given Plato's privileged place in the social structure of Athens, a good education is a biographical certainty, even without the corroboration of formal scholastic records. Unfortunately, the most familiar report available on his life at the schooling stage pertains to how he got his name: According to a wide variety of ancient sources, Plato was originally named Aristocles, after his paternal grandfather, switching to Plato sometime during adolescence (Apuleius: *De Platone* 1.1; Diogenes: *Lives* 3.4; Olympiodorus: *Anonymous Prolegomena* 1.14–18; *Commentary on the First Alcibiades* 2.36–43; Suidas: *Suda* pi 1707 Adler). Indeed, one of the epigrams on his tomb reverts to the name "Aristocles," though the rest use "Plato" (Diogenes: *Lives* 3.43).

The most colorful backstory here is that the name "Plato," which translates literally as "broad," was given to the young Aristocles by his gymnastics teacher, the wrestler Ariston of Argos, who was supposedly impressed by his pupil's robust figure. Diogenes cites Alexander Polyhistor's *Successions of Philosophers* as his source for this story, though he goes on to add two competing accounts, one by Neanthes of Cyzicus, attributing the nickname to the size of Plato's forehead, and one by an anonymous source, presenting it as a reference to the breadth of his speech (*Lives* 3.4). Swift Riginos (1976, pp. 35–38) notes that each of the three scenarios finds ample corroboration in the standard biographical tradition, with several sources repeating all three stories, and most recounting at least one. As is true of most any anecdote concerning Plato, Swift Riginos (1976) is the place to go for exhaustive documentary evidence regarding the case. As for critical commentary, Notopoulos (1939, pp. 135–145) takes a sweeping position against the authenticity of the alleged name change, rejecting the story on any rendition, while Sedley (2003, pp. 21–23) may profitably be consulted for an endorsement of the possibility.

Whatever his real name was, Plato was evidently multitalented. While he excelled in letters, which is not difficult to believe with the benefit of hindsight, he was also a champion wrestler (Apuleius: *De Platone* 1.2; Diogenes: *Lives* 3.4; Olympiodorus: *Anonymous Prolegomena* 1.26–28). Ancient sources acquaint us with a few of his teachers in his primary education: Ariston the Argive, the aforementioned gymnastics instructor; Dionysius the Grammarian, who taught him reading and writing; Draco of Athens and Metellus of Acragas (Agrigentum), who were responsible for his education in music. Not all biographers name all four, many, including Diogenes (*Lives* 3.4), leaving out the two music instructors. But all four are cited frequently enough, in isolation or all together, to constitute a common denominator. (See further: Dacier, 1701, p. 32; Tennemann, 1839, pp. 315–316; Zeller, 1876, p. 6, n. 6.)

Details of his education surviving transmission over millennia present Plato as having studied painting and having composed poetry, initially dithyrambic and later lyric, in addition to some work in tragedy. Whether true or not, this constitutes a fitting backdrop for his legendary meeting with Socrates, whereupon Plato is said, depending on the source, to have destroyed all his poems, or to have burned a tragedy that he was about to enter into a competition, or, in general, to have made some such gesture renouncing all literary production that is not philosophical.

Tennemann (1839, pp. 316, 323) reports two separate incidents on which Plato is said to have burned his poetry, once in disappointment and once in contentment: According to the first tradition, Plato initially tried his hand at heroic verse, burning his work upon the realization that it did not rival that of Homer, and according to the second, he burned all his poems and renounced poetry altogether, simply out of enchantment with philosophy and in awe of Socrates. Actually, these need not be taken as competing accounts, as they do not contradict each other. The gesture ostensibly motivated by a newfound passion for philosophy, whether or not it is the only such episode of pyrotechnical literary criticism by the aspiring philosopher, is unlikely to represent Plato's first encounter with Socrates, who already had an established relationship with Plato's family, but the story is just as effective as a representation of Plato's initiation into the Socratic circle.

Another legend regarding the meeting of the two giants is a dream by Socrates on the night immediately preceding the sublime occasion. In the dream, Socrates sees a cygnet undergoing fledging, interpreted on the next day as Plato's introduction to and prospective training by the master (Apuleius: *De Platone* 1.1; Diogenes: *Lives* 3.5; Olympiodorus: *Anonymous Prolegomena* 1.22–29; *Commentary on the First Alcibiades* 2.83–86; Suidas: *Suda* pi 1707 Adler). As typical as this might be of the storytelling conventions of yore, broadly defined as a time when the bare facts were just not good enough for a presentation, this particular metaphor has never been more fitting than here.

1.4. Serendipity

While the precise location and date of his birth are not certain, Plato was indubitably born in the right place at the right time for philosophy. The world was ripe for a breakthrough in scientific thought. Two centuries of intellectual awakening had already ended the solitary reign of mythology as the only possible source of knowledge, or at least as the only authoritative one, but the sciences were still in their infancy and barely distinct or distinguishable from philosophy, which was itself in need of direction, inspiration, and consolidation. The seeds of the Western intellectual tradition had been sown generations ago with the bold inquiry of Thales into the nature of the universe, but the response in progress required both weeding and cultivation. A paradigm shift in civilization was in the making but lacked momentum.

Such were the conditions that produced, or welcomed, arguably the greatest philosopher in history, and quite certainly the greatest three in succession. As a student of Socrates and teacher of Aristotle, Plato had the good fortune of being the pupil of one of the keenest minds in history, and the mentor of another. Each held a privileged position of influence in this ancient triumvirate of philosophy, with the benefits accruing naturally from age to youth, but even more so to humanity in general.

Socrates (469–399 BC) and Aristotle (384–322 BC) never met, but something of the master's spirit must have been transferred to the pupil through Plato (428/427–348/347 BC), whose life overlapped with Socrates for at least twenty-eight years and with Aristotle for at least thirty-five years.

Platonic Overlap with Master and Pupil

	Birth	**Death**	**Lifespan**	**Intersection**
Socrates	469 BC	399 BC	70 years	28-29 years
Plato	428/427 BC	348/347 BC	79-81 years	—
Aristotle	384 BC	322 BC	62 years	35-36 years

Notes:
1. Plato's birthday (May) comes before the date of the execution of Socrates (June or July).
2. Plato's date of death (May or June) comes before Aristotle's birthday (between July and October).

Sources: Eduard Zeller: (*Plato and the Older Academy*: 1876, pp. 2–3, n. 2) on Plato's date of birth and death. Debra Nails: (*The People of Plato*: 2002, pp. 323, 363) on Socrates's date of death, as given by the dramatic date of the *Phaedo*. Anton-Hermann Chroust (*Aristotle* 1: 1973, p. 95) on Aristotle's date of birth.

The resultant synergy produced a quantum leap in philosophy, laying out the course of Western thought through the Enlightenment.

This momentous intersection of genius in Athens proved to be the greatest boost to intellectual development the world has ever known in the history of ideas. The felicitous union reinvigorating the dawn of reason, likewise originating in the Greek world, is difficult to imagine in terms of contemporary relationships between teacher and student. In addition to temporal and cultural differences in general, and their effects on the teacher-student relationship in particular, two decisive differences in this case are that Socrates was not a teacher in the sense common for any period and that Aristotle was not driven by awe of Plato, on the contrary, finding plenty to criticize and even to reject with some urgency. Nevertheless, the elements obviously fit together well. Something about the combination, and even the sequence, must have been right, as the sparks set off by Socrates continue to carry through with growing vibrancy.

1.5. Travels

Sadly, the philosophical impetus for Plato came not merely from the life of Socrates, but just as much from the death of Socrates. The execution of Socrates in 399 BC, ironically, by the democratic regime reinstated four years earlier to replace an oppressive oligarchy, reinforced Plato's choice of a philosophical life over a political one, making him a lifetime critic of democracy. It also marked the beginning of his philosophical output, and ushered in an extensive phase of travel, the first and longest of three such periods in his life.

Plato's Travels

Dates	**Travel Locations**
399–387 BC	Megara, Cyrene, Italy, Egypt, Syracuse
368–367 BC	Syracuse
361 BC	Syracuse

Note: Evidence and testimony for the first travel period are consistent with a greater number of destinations, as well as a smaller number, not to mention an entirely different order.

Sources: Diogenes Laërtius: *Lives* (3.6, 3.18–23). Wilhelm Gottlieb Tennemann: "Life of Plato" (1839): pp. 331–339, 339–342, 346–351, 352–357. Eduard Zeller: *Plato and the Older Academy* (1876): pp. 14–24, 32–35.

As far as confirmation goes, all this is little better than legend. Hardly any agreement exists in the academic community, primarily because hardly any exists between the ancient sources. The history and possibility of debate is not limited to specific dates, places, and events along the way. Scholars tend to disagree even on whether Plato really went to all of these places, or to any of them, with particular suspicion regarding three separate trips to a place (Syracuse) proven miserable on the first visit, hardly befitting the top student of the wisest man in the world. Yet there it is, with ample documentation, be it testimony or hearsay. Sifting through the evidence is more appropriate than rejecting it out of hand.

Plato's first travel period appears to have kept him away from Athens for a dozen consecutive years following the execution of Socrates. In fact, the initial stimulus must have been more an aversion to Athens than an attraction to anywhere else. He thus fled Athens, driven out presumably by a combination of fear and disillusionment, as was the case with many other disciples of Socrates.

Diogenes Laërtius (*Lives* 3.6) gives a concise account of this first period abroad, sometimes with details not to be found elsewhere, and, thereby, arousing suspicion: Plato's first stop was Megara, the hometown of a fellow philosopher in the Socratic circle, Euclides (or Euclid), an important thinker in his own right, not to be confused with the famous Greek mathematician of the same name flourishing later in Alexandria. Next, he traveled to Cyrene, to study with Theodorus, a distinguished mathematician, later mentioned or featured in several dialogues, including speaking parts in the *Theaetetus*, *Sophist*, and *Statesman*. From there, he went to Italy to study with the Pythagoreans, Philolaus and Eurytus, the former the master of the latter and mentioned in the *Phaedo* (61d–e). The disciples of Philolaus include Simmias and Cebes, the primary interlocutors in the *Phaedo*, and Echecrates, the spokesperson for the anonymous audience at the outermost layer of narration in the same dialogue. A scholarly expedition to Egypt, in the company of Euripides, is supposed to have followed his studies with the Pythagoreans, but this is inconsistent at least with the fact that Euripides of Phlya (c. 480–406 BC) died before Socrates. Nor is the alleged Egyptian adventure well-documented in any other respect, being manifested in, or possibly being inspired by, nothing more than scattered textual references to Egyptian science or culture in a few dialogues, with the knowledge displayed therein neither requiring nor demonstrating any personal acquaintance with the land.

According to tradition, the final destination of notable stay in the first travel period was Syracuse. Diogenes does not append this to his account of the first travel period (*Lives* 3.6), preferring instead to relate it later as part of a saga combining all three visits to Syracuse (*Lives* 3.18–23). The itinerary reported by Diogenes, be it in regard to the visits to Syracuse or everything preceding that, is a familiar one. It tends to be perpetuated in modern accounts, as in the one in progress here. This is partly because Diogenes continues to be a popular source, despite his recognized faults, and partly because no alternative is guaranteed to take us nearer the truth. Sources contradicting Diogenes do not necessarily have a greater claim to accuracy, just a competing one. Hence, since Diogenes remains widely available, his account is widely circulated, usually uncritically.

Readers requiring a critical account have two options: One is to compare Diogenes with other ancient sources, the other is to consult modern sources readily offering such a comparison. Not too many commentators seem to have the patience anymore for a grassroots survey, that is, for starting from scratch, directly and severally inspecting the ancient sources, instead of adopting a consolidation paradigm from among derivative sources that have already sifted through the evidence and extracted a uniform storyline that best fits the data. As a result, modern readers are typically left, not entirely inappropriately, either with a single story and single source, or with a narration of the travels in the manner of a legendary story, drawing on and blending all the sources without documenting any. Fortunately, any current shortcomings in the critical approach are more than offset by ambitious initiatives carried out in the nineteenth century with the meticulous attention to detail so characteristic of the period. Two sources that stand out in this regard are Tennemann's "Life of Plato" (1839, pp. 331–339, on the travels between the death of Socrates and the establishment of the Academy; pp. 339–342, 346–351, 352–357, on the three visits to Syracuse) and Zeller's *Plato and the Older Academy* (1876, pp. 14–24, on the early travels; pp. 32–35, on Syracuse).

Returning to the end of the first travel period, tradition has it that a visit to Syracuse precedes resettlement in Athens. Actually, we do not know whether Plato stayed away from Athens for the entirety of the first travel period, or broke up the process into relatively shorter trips, each starting and ending in Athens, which he never abandoned permanently. Be that as it may, the final destination is Syracuse, a port situated on the eastern coast of Sicily, home to one of the most powerful city-states in the region at that time.

The original reason for Plato's trip there is not clear. Being a guest at the royal court, he was likely there on invitation. Such invitations were customary diversions for royalty in general, not to mention being particularly characteristic of the host in this case, Dionysius I (432–367 BC; reign: 405–367 BC), the tyrant of Syracuse. The known circumstances of his visit also lend credence to the hypothesis that Plato might have been there on a tutorial assignment. This is based on the evidence of a lasting friendship he formed with a young man named Dion, who enjoyed a presence in the Syracusan court through marriage, both his own and that of his sister. Dion was the brother-in-law and the son-in-law of Dionysius I: Dion's sister (Aristomache) was already (from 398 BC) married to the tyrant upon Plato's first visit, and Dion later married their widowed daughter (Arete), his own niece. Dion was twenty years old, and Plato forty, when the two developed a close relationship with obvious undertones of hero worship if not actually a formal bond as would exist between a teacher and student.

Either way, whether invited for the amusement of Dionysius I or for the education of Dion, Plato would have had to have made a name for himself, one good enough to attract the attention of prominent foreigners. This means that he might have started writing, publishing, and distributing his works prior to leaving Athens, and that he must have done so at least prior to arriving in Syracuse. It is difficult to imagine a scholar without an established reputation securing an invitation from a foreign government. Given that Plato had not yet founded the Academy, any reputation of his would most likely be attached to his writings, especially if copied in adequate quantities and circulated with sufficient coverage and penetration. Given the tradition denying that Plato wrote anything while Socrates was still alive, he must have had a quick and successful start afterwards. No doubt, his presence in Syracuse might have been facilitated, or even mediated, by influential people he either knew in Athens or met through his travels, particularly in Italy and Sicily, but this still does not dispense with the requirement for good credentials.

No matter the reasons for and circumstances of his visit, the philosopher's time in Syracuse (388–387 BC) ended in conflict with the royal host, as he angered Dionysius I, allegedly to the point of having Plato sold into slavery (Diogenes: *Lives* 3.18–21; Suidas: *Suda* pi 1707 Adler). Reports of such extreme mistreatment pose an interpretive challenge, but the Syracusan adventure in general, minus the slavery episode, is confirmed at the source, particularly in the *Seventh Letter*, which, together with the *Third* and the *Eighth*, is among those of Plato's letters engendering the greatest expert confidence regarding authenticity. As for the putative sale into slavery, nothing in the Platonic corpus, whether dialogic or epistolary, confirms the reports in the patchwork biographical tradition represented by Diogenes and Suidas. Yet the basic story of Plato's presence in Syracuse, plus the sale into slavery, is corroborated from the perspective of one of its other heroes, the young admirer, as Plutarch (c. 46–120) relates in his *Life of Dion* (especially 4.3–5.7).

Plutarch, however, can hardly be considered an additional source, given his clear opportunity, and ostensibly also his actual tendency, to draw on the letters of Plato. Plutarch, no doubt, made use of what he perceived to be reputable sources, and it is entirely conceivable that the *Seventh Letter* was chief among them. Burnet (1914, p. 205, n. 1), for one, suspects that Plutarch gets most of his information about Plato from Plato, specifically, from the epistolary tradition attached to the Platonic corpus, and he spurns the tendency to quote Plutarch just to avoid invoking the letters, a common means of circumventing the questions of legitimacy immediately associated with one but often overlooked in the other. That said, with respect to the anecdotal adventures of Plato as a slave, there can be no question whether Plutarch confirms Plato or merely repeats him, because the story is nowhere to be found in Plato, so defined to include the letters.

In the final analysis, Plutarch's testimony does not settle this particular issue. Just as the part of Plutarch that agrees with the letters looks to be a repetition of Plato rather than a confirmation of him, the part that goes beyond the letters to add the slavery episode might well be a repetition of rumors rather than a confirmation of facts. Or Plutarch may be right. We do not know. Either Plato did not wish to mention the slavery episode, say, because it is humiliating, or outside sources are entirely speculative, say, because it makes a better story.

Whatever the truth of the matter, legend has it that Plato's ransom was secured by Anniceris the Cyrenaic, who reportedly refused to be reimbursed for the expense, turning down offers both by Dion and by Plato's Athenian friends, instead graciously designating the favor a privilege (Diogenes: *Lives* 3.20). In an alternate version of the story, Anniceris, again refusing reimbursement by Dion, uses the money to buy Plato the land required for setting up a school (Diogenes: *Lives* 3.20).

Disappointment in Syracuse is a common thread running through Plato's travels. He returned to Syracuse twenty years later (368–367 BC) under circumstances resembling his first visit. This time, he was invited, on the initiative of his pupil, Dion, to tutor the original tyrant's son, Dionysius II (397–343 BC; reign: 367–357 BC and 346–344 BC), who had taken the reins upon the death of his father. Often discussed as an attempt, or at least an opportunity, to raise a philosopher-king, the engagement ended in disaster. Both Plato and Dion fell out of favor with the new tyrant within the space of a few months. Dion was sent into exile on allegations of seditious and subversive activities in preparation for a *coup d'état*, while Plato found himself effectively albeit not formally under house arrest. Plato eventually managed to talk his way out of confinement, heading for Athens, where he was reunited with Dion.

Despite comparable disappointment by all parties, the tumultuous experiment was repeated six years later in 361 BC. Dionysius II was eager to win Plato over, if not as a genuine friend, then as a celebrated companion, a symbol of prestige to adorn his court. Having agreed to let Plato go the first time (second visit for Plato) only on the condition that the philosopher would return under more favorable circumstances, basically in reference to the establishment of amicable relations between Dion and Dionysius II, the tyrant was ready to have Plato back, but without Dion. Twice turning down a summons to this effect, Plato complied with the third call. This was when Dionysius II sent for Plato with a message promising to expedite the resolution of the ongoing conflict between Dion and himself, should the philosopher agree to a visit, declaring further that the dispute would otherwise remain unresolved.

The mode of delivery was even more impressive than the message itself, as the tyrant sent a trireme, the predominant warship of antiquity, boasting three rows of oars on either side, with Plato's Pythagorean friends on board, not only bearing the letter, but also anxious personally to convince him to return to Syracuse. Chief among them was Archedemus of Syracuse, a disciple of Archytas of Tarentum, who, in turn, was a Pythagorean philosopher, specifically, a disciple of Philolaus. Archytas had befriended Plato during his earlier visits, and the Tarentian circle, represented on the ship by Archedemus, sought Plato's help regarding their relations with Dionysius II.

As indicated in the *Seventh Letter* (388e–399a), Plato suspected that Dionysius II was motivated more by expectations of a public show of good relations with the philosopher than by the prospect of learning philosophy, yet he accepted the tyrant's invitation, apparently against his own better judgment, in order to spare his friends what looked to be excessive consequences attached to refusal.

This attempt likewise ended in failure and misery, as Plato managed to secure his freedom only upon the intervention of his Tarentian friends, who sent over a vessel and convinced the tyrant to let him go. The outcome for Dion was worse: He was eventually assassinated (354 BC) by one of his own associates, Callippus of Athens (Callippus of Syracuse), shortly after invading, or, depending on the perspective, liberating (357 BC), Syracuse, and overthrowing Dionysius II.

These are the known milestones of Plato's life. Allowing for a margin of error commensurate with the uncertainty regarding his birthdate, Plato must have been roughly twenty years old when he became a student of Socrates, twenty-eight when he embarked on his first travel period, and forty when he returned to Athens. His travels have an obvious significance, but their importance is inflated by the sheer availability of records pertaining to this part of his life, making equally significant matters pale in comparison simply for a lack of information. The most salient aspect of his experience abroad is his exposure to Pythagoreanism, which accounts for his greatest intellectual debt after the central grounding in Socratic methods and topics. He is thought to have started writing philosophy shortly after the death of Socrates, quitting only upon his own death, though the temporal restriction is rather controversial because commentators still do not agree on what to make of biographical and anecdotal indications of dialogues composed while Socrates was alive (e.g., Diogenes: *Lives* 3.35).

Other notable influences include Heraclitus of Ephesus and Parmenides of Elea. Plato's first systematic introduction to both seems to have taken place during the brief interval following the death of Socrates and preceding his departure for Megara. Diogenes (*Lives* 3.6) reports him as having studied

Heracliteanism with Cratylus of Athens, who has a dialogue named after him, and Parmenidianism with Hermogenes of Alopece, who lends his name to a character in the same dialogue, with both experiences evidently coming before his international travels. Here, too, we cannot be sure of the facts, particularly in regard to the reported timeline: Aristotle (*Metaphysics* 987a32 ff.) makes Plato out to be familiar with Cratylus and Heracliteanism from an early age, which cannot reasonably be placed after the death of Socrates, as would be required by the reckoning of Diogenes (*Lives* 3.6). Moreover, the report regarding Hermogenes is not entirely convincing, especially in regard to his intellectually unimpressive presence in the *Cratylus*, not to mention the absence of external testimony corroborating the connection drawn by Diogenes.

Yet there can be no doubting the overall richness of the documented manifold of doctrine serving as a source of education and inspiration for Plato. This makes it all the more striking that the philosophical output outshines the input.

1.6. The Academy

Plato's influence is generally held in even greater esteem than the influences upon him. Apart from his works, the most important outlet for and manifestation of this influence is the Academy, the school he founded on the outskirts of Athens in 387 BC or thereabouts. Widely considered the prototype of the modern university, the Academy survived for more than nine centuries, eventually being abolished in 529 through a blanket decision banning all pagan schools in accordance with the imperial edict of Justinian I (482/483–565; reign: 527–565). The establishment of the school is traced back to the period of serenity following Plato's return from his first trip to Syracuse. Tradition has it that he was forty years old and at the height of his intellectual powers, and the truth cannot be far from this. He founded the school next to a public park just outside the city walls, about six stadia (roughly one kilometer) to the northwest of the Dipylon Gate (also known as the Thriasian Gate or the Kerameikos Gate). The homesite, a garden adjacent to the park but not contiguous with it, was possibly purchased with the contribution of Dion, and through the generosity of Anniceris (Diogenes: *Lives* 3.20). The public grounds next door were home to a sacred olive grove serving as a sanctuary dedicated to Athena, the goddess of wisdom and the divine protector of the city. The school takes its name from the locality, which was called "Akademia" (or Hecademy) in honor of the legendary hero Akademos (or Hecademus), whose exploits had already become a thing of lore by classical times (Diogenes: *Lives* 3.7–8).

Talk about the Academy is not always clear. Part of the problem is that both the public park and Plato's school have a legitimate claim to the name "Academy," as do several other things besides (Wycherley, 1962, p. 2). Thus, the reference is rarely unmistakable without a deliberate effort to make it so. But a more basic ambiguity awaits in the concept of school itself, which might equally well denote the intended institution or the buildings and grounds used by that institution. This becomes all the more significant in classical Athens, where teaching was not a stationary activity. Neither the teachers nor, for a while, the schools stayed put. Itinerant teachers of virtue, that is, human excellence (*aretē* or ἀρετή), the infamous Sophists dominated the secondary education scene in the fifth century, especially intensely for several generations in the second half of that century spilling over into the next. Stationary schools started cropping up in the fourth century, but even this transformation still left the student body with a perambulating teacher, epitomized by the legendary style of Aristotle, giving us the term "peripatetic," from the Greek *peripatētikos* (περιπατητικός), putatively in reference to his walking around while lecturing. Between the Sophists and Aristotle, we have no reason to picture Plato frozen behind a lectern, reading from his notes, until the bell frees his students just in time for them to dash off in separate directions, through the hallways, and across the quadrangle, each joining many others to form a new class taught by another instructor in another room. Even if anything remotely resembling this took place, we are not in a position to confirm it. We simply do not know enough about the physical layout of the school, nor about the organization of its pedagogical processes.

Historical documents, anecdotal references, and incidental insight, say, through depictions in the literature of the day, do not light up our world. They give us some idea, but nothing so firm as a blueprint. Nor have we had the best of luck in excavations, each one furthering the cause, but the entire network and succession still falling short of piecing together the entire puzzle. We know that the public park and the private property were separate, but this does not indicate that Plato kept to himself, carrying out the business of the school entirely on his own property. And whether he did or not, we are not sure where one ended and the other began. The existing infrastructure of the public site included a gymnasium, yet another referent of the name "Academy." This seems to have been the most conspicuous element of the local topography. Plato's own place was not a vacant lot either, but, here too, we do not know the precise nature and extent of the development involved. He definitely had living quarters for himself, plus guest accommodations, and possibly a classroom or two, though whether all this was housed in a single building or divided between several smaller ones remains undecided. Given that people can conceivably, and possibly even comfortably, eat, sleep, and study in the same room, so long as they are all doing the same thing at the same time, the question just may remain undecided, especially if reasoning is to be the only recourse, with no further empirical evidence forthcoming.

Tennemann (1839, p. 342, n. 4; p. 343, n. 1) notes that the private property traditionally associated with the school might actually be Plato's second piece of real estate in the area, the first being a garden he inherited from his father. Although Tennemann cites the testimony of Apuleius, Plutarch, and Diogenes, this is not to confirm precisely the same fact three times over but to create that one fact from different bits of testimony, with the overall appeal remaining far from a certainty. Ignoring this and focusing instead on the other property, the one purchased (or donated, not, at any rate, inherited, howsoever acquired) just after his first Syracusan adventure, should not divert us from anything vital in the life of Plato.

1.6.1. Topographical Clues

Any modern discussion of Plato's Academy runs the risk of anachronistic reconstruction, becoming all the more tempting in the dearth of hard evidence. Notwithstanding the nostalgic analogy, it was not a university as we might imagine today, neither physically nor administratively. Even if it had been precisely that, or something frightfully close, it would not have been the absolute forerunner, marking a genesis in higher education. Academic activity, so to speak, even in the very same park, predates Plato. People had started gathering in the area with a pedagogical agenda a generation or so before Plato founded a school there (Dillon, 2003, p. 2). His was not the first school either. At least Isocrates had beaten him to it, if only by a few years, starting in 390 with the establishment of a "permanent school" in Athens for instruction in rhetoric (Nails, 2006a, p. 7; see also: 2002, p. 179).

Plato's intellectual input, and, to some extent, his entrepreneurial input, cannot be overestimated, but his structural contribution does not extend far beyond the purchasing of a place for himself adjacent to the public park already used for philosophical activity. The park came readily equipped with the aforementioned gymnasium, which is where much of the philosophical discussions took place, both before Plato and in his time. Plato had his own garden, including at least one house, where he would get together on a regular basis with his associates and students, whether for philosophical pursuits or for semiformal meals. It is not clear how academic affairs, particularly the actual interplay of teaching and learning, were divided between the public park and the private property, but anecdotal evidence suggests that Plato's presence was not limited to his suburban home. Evidently, classes were held out in the open, even if they also took place indoors. An especially telling anecdote in this regard is to be found in Aelian (flourishing in the third century), while a comparable scenario in fiction dates back to fragments preserved from the comedy of Epicrates of Ambracia (fourth century BC). Dillon (2003, pp. 3–9), for one, directly quotes and fully recounts both stories, discussing their significance for the organization of classes.

Aelian (*Varia Historia* 3.19) tells the story of a public encounter between Plato in his old age and Aristotle in his prime, engaged in a battle of the wits. Unaccompanied by his usual entourage, with Speusippus ill and Xenocrates abroad, the elderly Plato has trouble fending off the elenctic assault of his presumably sharpest student. Harassed and humiliated, the master retires from the *peripatos* (περίπατος) to his own *kēpos* (κῆπος), that is, from the public grounds to his own property, avoiding the subtleties involved in a direct translation, which is not necessary to follow the move indicated. Given that the anecdote has Plato retreating to his own place, whether indoors or outdoors, only upon an unpleasant experience in the park, the implication is that lively discussions indeed took place out in public, whether or not classes were also held in private. As the story goes, Xenocrates, upon his return three months later, finds Plato still in seclusion, and promptly coordinates his return to the commons. Even if the anecdote is a total fabrication, there is no reason to reject the topographical orientation provided. What is important here is the logistics of the relocation back and forth, which clearly demonstrates that pedagogical activity was not confined to a certain building or fixed location (Dillon, 2003, pp. 3–5).

The same conclusion is supported by Epicrates (fr. 11 Kock = fr. 10 Kassel-Austin), who depicts students of the Academy, under full pedagogical supervision, huddled around a pumpkin in an attempt to determine its taxonomical classification. The supervisors named include Plato, Speusippus, and Menedemus (the Academic narrowly losing an election for the headship of the school to Xenocrates upon the death of Speusippus), thus completing the portrait of a class resembling something between a seminar and a laboratory session. The discussion is disrupted at one point by an outside critic, but Plato gently urges the class to move on. We are privy to the entire scene through a dialogue between two characters, one reporting it to the other as an eyewitness. The point is not merely that this takes place outdoors as opposed to indoors, but that it takes place out in the open where passers-by can observe, in fact, so closely as to be able to intervene if they so desire (Dillon, 2003, pp. 7–9).

Clearly, classes were not confined to the classroom. Put differently, the classroom was not necessarily a room in a building. Yet regarding the structural details of the site of the Academy, public and private, armchair archeology in the fashion of extrapolation from ancient commentary can take us only so far, representing no substitute for hands-on expertise, which can fruitfully be sought, for example, in the work of Travlos (1971, pp. 42–51) and Wycherley (1978, pp. 219–226).

Nevertheless, the two anecdotal passages invoked are significant in another respect as well, that is, in addition to what they reveal about where and how classes were held, or, more accurately, because of what they reveal in this regard. They confirm, not only that education was not restricted to a fixed location, be it outdoors or indoors, public or private, but also, on that account, that it was not, at least in the Academy of Plato, a cloak-and-dagger enterprise for the secret indoctrination of jealously guarded ideologies shared through immersion in cultic rituals. It really was education, what was going on. And it was education in the sense of intellectual enlightenment, not some sort of sectarian tutelage. To be sure, moral edification was also sought, but the teaching, moral or otherwise, was grounded in reason rather than religion. At the very least, we can be certain that the Academy was not a place of clandestine instruction or activity, not even one concealed behind a public facade.

In opposition, much has been made of the legend that Plato erected a shrine to the Muses, somewhere on the Academy grounds, as we find out incidentally in the *Life of Speusippus* by Diogenes (*Lives* 4.1). While the precise location of this shrine is not known, it was probably built on his own property, as Plato would have had no greater authority over what is to be done on or to public property than would any other private citizen. Either way, the heart of the story is the shrine, not its specific location. The dedication is sometimes interpreted as having a religious significance, standing as a testament to the cultic nature of the school. Yet it is futile to seek a religious or spiritual motivation, or even one that may be profound in any way, in such a typical act as this would have been in the time and place of Plato's Academy. At a time when gods were legion, and, honoring them, in vogue, the common grounds of the Academy were already graced with shrines aplenty, including one to Hecademus himself and another to Athena, the patron goddess of the city (see further: Judeich, 1931, pp. 388, 413; Wycherley, 1962, p. 2). No doubt, Plato's shrine to the Muses represents yet another reminder of the philosopher's Apollonian nature, as the Muses, divine though they may be, are themselves the handmaidens of Apollo, the god of music, among other things. But the erection of the shrine, rather to be expected under the circumstances, than to be questioned or explained, might simply have served, as Dillon (2003, p. 3) so astutely points out, no further aim than to mark the boundaries of Plato's stomping grounds. The fact that the Muses were the tutelary deities of education makes it all the more fitting that the shrine of the Academy should be in their honor. Aristotle had one as well in his Lyceum.

1.6.2. Institutional Character

The grand catalyst in the depiction of the Academy as some sort of religious order is a speculative scenario, highly influential in its time, that the school had to be founded as such by law. Around the same time as the heyday of this scenario, coinciding with the better part of the twentieth century, various strands of esotericism in the interpretation of Plato were championing the paradigm of a secret teaching, quite apart from discussions of the legal status of the Academy. Although the esoteric movement itself had no religious undertones, its emphasis on secrecy went well with parallel efforts to make the school out to be a sectarian organization of sorts. The esoteric platform is covered in greater detail in the next chapter (§ 2.2, § 2.3, § 2.4), but the prime catalyst just mentioned came in the form of a hypothesis introducing religious affiliation as a legal requirement of incorporation as a secondary school. This was the contribution of Wilamowitz (1881, pp. 263–291), whose assessment quickly gained a following, remaining the dominant view for nearly a century, until challenged successfully by Lynch (1972, pp. 63–67, 112–134).

Specifically, Wilamowitz put forth the thesis that registration as a *thiasos* (θίασος), essentially a cult association, was a necessary condition of incorporation as an institution of higher learning, anything beyond the education required and regulated by the state. As this sweeping stipulation covers the Academy, Plato's school was made a religious confraternity on a par with Pythagorean brotherhoods.

This was not entirely the result of this solitary piece of new insight into the history of higher education. The scenario worked well with and drew strength from existing clues, such as the shrine to the Muses, the common meals by members, and Plato's admiration of Pythagoreanism, though the philosophy rather than the lifestyle, and certain tenets of the philosophy rather than the organic system. In short, it turned out to be just the formula needed to subsume the scattered evidence under a definitive interpretation.

Perhaps the most nagging loose ends tied up in this way were the longevity of the institution and the survival of everything ever written by its founder. Giving the organization a religious dimension helps explain its longevity because piety holds greater currency than scholarship in a relationship of precedence established early on in the history of civilization and solidified through the ages. This much is confirmed, or would be on this reasoning, by the abolishment of the school only upon the erosion of its religious basis by the rise of Christianity.

This is a tidy explanation. Something along the same lines is applicable to the preservation of the entirety of Plato's works. It may be asked, of course, why, if all secondary schools of the period were required to be organized as cults, none fared so well. This is not immediately important. Perhaps Plato really set up and operated a cult while the others dispassionately observed the legal requirement. Perhaps Plato was simply more successful. What matters at this point is that the explanation works. And that explanation, made possible by the interpretive framework of Wilamowitz, is that the spiritual order, owing to its sectarian roots and bonds, thrived for centuries on end, falling victim only to the increasing intensity of efforts to safeguard and manage the growth of what was well on its way to becoming the most powerful institution in history, the Roman Catholic Church.

The credibility of the position grew with that of its advocates, as preeminent scholars adopted it as part of the standard history of the Academy. The cultic nature of the school became an essential fact to be communicated as background information in any introduction to Plato. For example, we encounter the following description in Burnet: "Like all societies of the kind, it was organized as a religious guild. It had its chapel, dedicated to the Muses, and its sacrifices at stated times. The members lived for the most part a common life" (1914, pp. 213–214).

Likewise, Guthrie reports in the third volume of his monumental survey of the history of Greek philosophy that "both Plato's Academy and Aristotle's Lyceum were legally registered as *thiasoi*" (1969, p. 374). While this is an unequivocal declaration, the tone changes in the fourth volume, the first of two tomes dedicated entirely to Plato, where Guthrie intimates less than full confidence in the same fact: "To form a society owning its own land and premises, as Plato did, it appears to have been a legal requirement that it be registered as a *thiasos*, that is, a cult-association dedicated to the service of some divinity, who would be the nominal owner of the property" (1975, p. 20; author's footnote reference marker omitted; n. 2 on the same page acknowledges Wilamowitz as a source, as well as endorsing his views, though not without qualification). To be precise, the hesitation is not in regard to the same fact but to the legal and regulatory scenario that would account for that fact, namely, the registration of the schools of Plato and Aristotle as *thiasoi*. Otherwise, there is no evidence of hesitation, anywhere in Guthrie, on the question of whether the schools were in fact registered as such, but he does seem unsure about a blanket requirement forcing the issue.

Promulgated by prominent figures, the cultic coloring remained the reigning view in the late nineteenth century and through much of the twentieth century. Yet the model fell out of favor just as rapidly and decisively as it attracted a consensus. The downfall was sparked by the challenge of Lynch (1972, pp. 54–67, 112–134), who not only rejected the thesis that incorporation as a *thiasos* was a legal requirement, but specifically reevaluated the known circumstances of the Academy and the Lyceum, with primary emphasis on Aristotle. His conclusion is that secondary education in Athens during the period in question was neither provided, nor regulated, nor in any way sponsored or subsidized by the state (Lynch, 1972, p. 66). It was, he contends, an altogether unregulated enterprise, with corporate establishment simply a matter of will and skill, as an example of which he cites the *Lysis* (203a–204b), opening, as it does, with Socrates accosted by admirers as he passes by a newly established palaestra where Miccus the Sophist has recently set up shop, evidently already with a student body eager to hear the sage of Athens as a guest speaker (Lynch, 1972, p. 65).

Lynch is not the only challenger of Wilamowitz. He is the first successful one. Many in turn have adopted his stance, whether to build on it or to recommend it as is. Tarán (1981, p. 9–11), for example, duplicates the opposition to Wilamowitz, acknowledging the contribution of Lynch, but not so much as an inspiration as a matter of fact. He has a specific point of agreement with Lynch and disagreement with Wilamowitz: "Nor is the widely accepted notion that the Academy was organized as a *thiasos* of the Muses a likely hypothesis" (Tarán, 1981, p. 9; author's footnote reference marker omitted; see n. 35 for further elaboration and for references). Tarán (1981, p. 9, n. 35) takes issue especially with anachronistically assuming what may be true of the legal status of the institution at the time of later administrators, specifically, those after Speusippus, to be true at the time of Plato as well, though, for good measure, he repudiates the assumption of religious affiliation in either case, early or late. His argument is not restricted to the Academy, as he explicitly extends it to other schools, thereby making it a general feature of the legal and regulatory framework rather than a circumstantial characteristic of a particular institution.

Examples may be multiplied indefinitely. Wallach, to cite another, agrees categorically: "The Academy was not a sophisticated religious cult (*thiasos*)" (2001, p. 65). The support of Dillon (2003) might be a good place to stop in this direction, as it represents a peak in the uprising against the cultic characterization of the Academy. Drawing on the work of Lynch (1972, pp. 108–127), Dillon (2003, pp. 3–8) rejects the religious association, with specific objections to proponents ranging from Wilamowitz to Guthrie. He blames Wilamowitz (1881, pp. 263–291), and, indirectly, Foucart (1873), as the inspiration of the former, for perpetuating what he characterizes as nothing more than an "assumption that the Academy must have been a *thiasos* dedicated to the Muses" (Dillon, 2003, p. 6, n. 12). Dillon himself denies this decisively, claiming in no uncertain terms that "nowhere in the ancient sources is either the Academy or the Peripatos referred to as a *thiasos*, but always as a *skholē* or *diatribē*" (2003, p. 6, n. 12). While this is his considered opinion on the matter, he recognizes room for disagreement in the prevailing state of scholarship, as he reports rather less decisively that "it is now fairly generally agreed that it [the Academy] was not any sort of formal legal entity, such as a *thiasos*, that we can identify" (Dillon, 2003, p. 15). Despite his own strong convictions, he admits that the matter is far from clear, in fact, less clear now than it used to be.

This is a telling admission and a fair assessment. Arguably the least controversial overview of the ongoing debate would be that allegiances have shifted from one extreme to the other, with the truth possibly lying somewhere in between. Encouraging enlightened reconciliation, White (2000, pp. 151–175, especially p. 167) objects to the readiness to characterize the Academy as a *thiasos*, but warns at the same time against going too far in the opposite direction, that is, too far toward a secular interpretation, and cautions, in general, against polarizing the matter instead of settling it. The point, of course, is not to strike a deal or to adopt the average, but to investigate the rational grounds underlying the current equilibrium. Presumably, the debate up until now has likewise rested on nothing less than investigations of rational grounds, so that recommending more of the same might seem somewhat trite. But nothing would ever be accomplished if rational inquiries did not produce ever new results on top of results.

Giving it more thought never hurt a problem. The controversy is grounded almost entirely in the inadequacy of evidence. The clues available are consistent both with the thesis of Wilamowitz and with the call championed by Lynch for rejecting it. Both sides present a convincing case, but each may be pushed further.

The question to ask Wilamowitz at this point is not whether registration as a *thiasos* was really required for incorporation as a secondary school. That, he has already answered, rightly or wrongly. We might ask instead why anyone complying with this requirement should be interpreted as doing anything more than following standard procedure, and why a group of people coming together in this way should be perceived as more of a cult than a school, or even at all as a cult if also as a school. Surely, the debate is not about whether the Academy was technically a cult, which could not sensibly be denied on the assumption that registration as such was required (even though it could, of course, be rejected together with the assumption in question). The debate, given the assumption, must be about whether the technical qualification is sufficient for the inferred characterization. If registering oneself as a devotee of Artemis were the only way to obtain a hunting license, would the registration itself make the registrant a devotee of Artemis? Would not a person unmoved by the goddess still be able to register as required just to obtain the legal permission to pursue wild game?

And a question for the opposite camp might be this: Even if registration as a *thiasos* was not required, so that no Athenian secondary school of the relevant period was ever a cult simply by default or definition, could the Academy not have been a cult anyway? Could it not have been a cult by choice? More generally, is this not possible even in the complete absence of evidence? Even if every school had a shrine to the Muses in its backyard, an altar of Zeus up front, and a bust of Apollo in every room, is it not possible that Plato took his own idols just a little bit more seriously than everyone else did theirs? Or, leaving aside the levity, is it not possible that even this exaggerated scenario reflects, whether in the person of Plato or in that of others, sincere sentiments and sober interests rather than a hollow cultural charade? Just because a certain practice is culturally ubiquitous does not mean that people are merely going through the motions rather than participating with conviction and devotion.

While it is true that reflecting harder on a problem is hardly ever a waste of time, the present impasse here is in making too much of the clues. We do not have conclusive evidence that the Academy was any kind of cult. Yet this shortcoming does not prove that it was not. Further debate always holds promise, but until a resolution, or a breakthrough of any sort, is reached, the best course would seem to be to embrace indeterminacy as a common ground, expanding the discourse through evidentiary addition or clarification rather than through generalization.

As a first step, we ought to acknowledge that even if the Academy were nothing like a cult, it also might not have been much like a university. Although the school has been hailed as the prototype of modern institutions of higher learning, the popular analogy begs for elaboration and qualification. This is the case independently of any questions regarding a religious origin or history. Rejecting the analogy is now more fashionable than making it, primarily due to increasing acknowledgment of a lack of evidence, but the fact remains that it is an early example of education beyond the minimum required by law and arranged by custom. Indeed, the Academy was not a university in the modern sense, arguably not even in the medieval sense. Nor was Plato's tutelage comparable to that of a typical professor. But the Academy was a place where one could engage in learning beyond the compulsory level.

1.6.3. Pedagogical Profile

The modern institutional division between faculty and students would not be the best way to visualize the fluid Academic collaboration between advanced and fledgling philosophers, all equally dedicated to the pursuit of truth, and, eventually, the attainment of wisdom, with the senior members guiding the junior, but not indoctrinating and evaluating them. Nor was the Academy, as is sometimes claimed, often merely because it seems poetically appropriate, an implementation of the educational model of the *Republic* (Cherniss, 1945, pp. 66–81).

What was going on is better characterized as learning than as teaching. Plato had a major role in shaping and executing that process, no doubt, enjoying the greatest influence, but he was neither the only instructor nor the only administrator. The romantic vision of a curriculum conducted entirely through the transmission of information from Plato to an awestruck audience has no basis in reality. The Academy was certainly not a gathering place for groupies hanging on Plato's every word.

As might be expected, Plato had a special status, being both the founder and the head of the school, but his rank among the faculty, so to speak, was that of a "first among equals" (πρῶτος μεταξύ ἴσων, or, "primus inter pares," in the iconic Latin version more familiar today), more like a prime minister than a king, or, in the religious terms that the phrase conjures up, more like the ecumenical patriarch of the Eastern Orthodox Church than the supreme pontiff of the Roman Catholic Church. Despite the anachronistic analogies, the basic distinction is not a modern speculation or reconstruction but a report of Plato's own assessment of his place in the Academy, an assessment which appears to have been shared by other senior members, none inclined to admit to an inferior standing as a scholar or philosopher, though all prepared ultimately to defer to his authority in administrative matters (Cherniss, 1945, p. 65; Lynch, 1972, p. 55; Wallach, 2001, p. 67).

The heads of the school were known as "scholarchs" (σχολάρχης), and, the headship, as the "scholarchy" or "scholarchate." We do not know much about the details of the succession process. The scholarch was evidently an elected official, as we have testimonial confirmation to that effect. Specifically, what we have is sporadic references to the election of one scholarch or other, not a complete record of election results tracing the entire chain of scholarchs. And the evidence available is not without contradiction, or, what is less forbidding, exception, such as the anomalous cases of ascension without election and of administration by coalition. For example, we know at least that Speusippus, the first scholarch after Plato, was appointed or nominated by Plato rather than elected in open competition, that Xenocrates, the next scholarch, was indeed elected against opposition, and that, somewhere down the line, Telecles and Euander held office as joint heads of the school.

No matter how the office was filled, the scholarchy was a position of considerable influence. Whether in the person of Plato or in that of any other, the post came with an obvious liberty, and, in fact, proven tendency, to implement a vision. Scholarchs certainly left their mark, some more boldly than others, but none so overbearingly as to replace dialogue with doctrine, or education with inculcation. To be sure, grand ideological turns in the history of the Academy evince, at least to a degree beyond outright denial, the absorption of the individual by the institution, for such collective turns would be impossible without individual compliance or cooperation. Nevertheless, even these defining moments, or, more likely, transitional processes, were more about philosophy than they were about pedagogy.

Notwithstanding specific ideological differences between different periods in the history of the Academy, the general pedagogical platform of the school favors epistemic discovery over dogmatic instruction. The approach followed seems to have left no room for the rigid and regimented instillation of sacrosanct tenets, not even in decidedly Platonic matters, such as the notorious notion of forms. No ideas or persons were beyond question or challenge, as perhaps best evidenced by the rise of Speusippus to the scholarchy despite his open opposition to Plato's views on the forms (Cherniss, 1945, pp. 81–82). Although we are not comfortably clear on how exactly the Academy worked, we are fortunate enough to be able to rule out some misconceptions. Cherniss (1945, p. 81) provides important interpretive boundaries in a classic statement: "All the evidence points unmistakably to the same conclusion: the Academy was not a school in which an orthodox metaphysical doctrine was thought, or an association the members of which were expected to subscribe to the theory of ideas."

As for its curricular range, the Academy, at least in Plato's day, is more likely to have emphasized method over conclusion, focusing more on the demonstration and critique of modes of reasoning than on the presentation of facts and theories. This, of course, is not to deny the consideration and communication of factual information as part of the program. Even though dialectic reigned supreme, the Academy was not a breeding ground for abstract discussion. The curriculum was adequately diversified, but the diversity was manifested in electives rather than imposed through requirements. The central subject was mathematics, including not only the study of numbers and shapes, but also applied fields, such as astronomy and music.

The concern with mathematics was so dominant as to give rise to the legend, now widely thought to be an embellishment, that an inscription above the entrance to the school barred entry to anyone not versed in geometry: *Ageōmetrētos mēdeis eisitō* (Αγεωμέτρητος μηδεὶς εἰσίτω). The standard translation is: "Let no one ignorant of geometry enter." It can also be found translated as: "Let no one who is not a geometer enter." The latter is more restrictive, but neither is intended to declare the Academy an exclusive lodge for geometers. The sign, whether real or imagined, seems to have been a playful variation on an actual dictum customarily displayed above the entrance to sacred places, stipulating that unfair or unjust persons (basically, anyone immoral) may not enter. Geometry being the science of proportion, and justice being, at least for Plato, a matter of proportion, the derivative maxim associated with Plato actually says pretty much the same thing as the original dictum. The clever switch represents the unjust person as the "ungeometrical" person, which might even be a better translation than one invoking a lack of skills or knowledge in geometry.

This explanation is, of course, no more certain, or scientific, than the account it purports to explain. Competing explanations abound: One of them holds that the focus is on geometry simply because it represents the most fundamental training for the intellect, which cannot handle philosophy if it cannot handle geometry. Another holds that the reference to geometry did not then carry the exclusive sense it does today, originally including far more than the branch of mathematics dealing with the relational properties of space. The first explains why the inscription is exclusive, the second denies that it is. Neither has a greater claim to veracity than the other. Nor do they trump the creative identification of geometry with justice. In any case, we are speculating on a legend. Since the legend itself cannot be substantiated in fact, the interpretive scenarios need not be either. Sensibility thus emerges as a sufficient criterion, and, on this count, the legend and its various explanations seem not only agreeable but also rather fitting for the context.

What makes this a legend rather than a report or anecdote is not only the distance between Plato and the earliest extant records, but also the variability of the records, giving mutually inconsistent coordinates for the physical location of the inscription, claimed variously to be at the Academy, at the *mouseion* (the shrine to the Muses), and even at Plato's home. Our sources for the legend date back no further than the middle of the fourth century, where we find an annotation by the rhetorician Sopatras in his commentary on Aelius Aristides (117–181). To be precise, the source is actually an anonymous scholiast thought to be Sopatras. The annotation in question places the inscription at the front of Plato's school, identifying it specifically as a variation on the traditional motto directed at "unfair" or "unjust" persons, here becoming the "ungeometrical" person.

The basic elements are repeated by Alexandrian scholiasts of the sixth century, who relate the story in their commentaries on Aristotle: John (Joannes) Philoponus (alternatively: John the Grammarian or John of Alexandria) in his *Commentary on Aristotle's De Anima* ([CAG 15] 117.29); Olympiodorus in his *Prolegomena and Commentary on Aristotle's Categories* ([CAG 12.1] 8.29–9.13); Elias (sometimes identified as pseudo-Elias or replaced altogether with David) in his *Commentary on Aristotle's Categories* ([CAG 18.1] 118.18–19). The Alexandrian tradition keeps the inscription exactly as it is in Sopatras, but transfers it from the entrance of the Academy to the entrance of the *mouseion*. Not everyone treats the Alexandrians uniformly in this regard. That is, not everyone has them all perpetuating the same legend. The stability of the inscription is widely acknowledged, but the move from the school to the shrine is not confirmed universally. For example, Gutas (in Fortenbaugh *et al.*, 1985, p. 118) excludes Philoponus and considers the Alexandrian "fabrication" of the legend to start with Olympiodorus, to be preserved by Elias and successors.

The location of the inscription appears to shift once again, later in the Middle Ages, this time from the *mouseion* to Plato's home, somewhere visible immediately before entry. Responsibility for this move rests with Johannes Tzetzes (c. 1110–1180), a twelfth century Byzantine scholar, who places the inscription over the main doorway to the house (*Chiliades* 8.974–977). This, for a while, was the most widely quoted source for the anecdote, enabling its transmission and shaping its form well into modernity.

The shifting location is not very important. But it is a fact, and deserves noting for that reason alone. Moreover, it helps explain why tertiary references fixated on one or another of the locations, while fully ignoring the others, often contradict one another on where the inscription was displayed. They usually contradict one another in silence, but sometimes they also correct one another, as if competing accounts had simply misquoted or misunderstood the only available reference, or the only authoritative one, as opposed to tapping one of several possibilities at the source. To adopt a pragmatic spin, this may not technically count as a contradiction if the school, the *mouseion*, and Plato's house can all be said sensibly to be on the grounds of the Academy, which, as nebulous as it is, might qualify as a single location. Yet this is also a bit of a cheat, as there really is a difference between the entrance to one building and that to another, which better reflects the discrepancies we encounter in tracing the history of the story. If one of the three locations had to be picked, the entrance to the school would be a fitting choice for obvious reasons. Precisely where this would be is not immediately clear, as school was, evidently, all around. But perhaps we might be justified in imagining a main building. We might even think of this as the Academy proper, because an edifice of some sort is, after all, rather than an open field, or the shade of an olive tree, the image conjured up in our minds when we hear a reference to Plato's Academy. And the second choice, no doubt, would be the *mouseion*, an appropriate locality indeed to keep unjust people out.

1.6.4. Legendary Longevity

Another embellishment regarding the Academy is the customary dramatization of its longevity. Its endurance for close to a millennium is often touted as the foremost sign of strength, whereas what is in question is the identity or individuality of the very entity thus enduring. While the Academy was still in existence well into the sixth century, it had long before then quit being the place established by Plato. Being governed by the will and vision of its scholarchs rather than by the guidelines and requirements of an institutional charter, the school went through drastic changes in its strategic vision and philosophical outlook. No institutional continuity can be claimed for it, and its physical continuity is also suspect, particularly in connection with a silent period in historical records pertaining to the school during imperial developments culminating in the establishment of the Roman Empire and throughout the nascency of that emerging world power. This silent period is consistent with a physical interruption of roughly two centuries starting sometime around the siege and sack of Athens in 86 BC by Roman forces under Sulla (Lucius Cornelius Sulla Felix) and the death in or about 84 BC of the scholarch, Philo of Larissa. The known facts do not confirm actual termination and resurrection, but the missing facts make the assumption of continuity tenuous at best.

The level of extrapolation in Academic history is high enough to encourage alternative constructions. Even Plato's founding role could be interpreted in terms of a milestone instead of an ultimate beginning, with Cicero, for one, speaking of a single tradition extending as far back as Democritus, and assigning Socrates a particularly prominent presence (*Academicae Quaestiones* 1.12.44, 2.5.14). Cicero, in fact, seems just as comfortable merely including Plato in this tradition

(*Academicae Quaestiones* 1.12.46) as he does in declaring him the founder of a philosophical system (*Academicae Quaestiones* 1.4.17). This is not to say that Cicero considers Democritus the first scholarch of the Academy, followed by several others, including Socrates, before finally arriving at Plato, but he does recognize a unity of purpose if not of thought and method. Neither this nor any other suggestion ever gained lasting credence as a viable alternative to the standard chronicle of an institutional inception with Plato, but the rumination itself is evidence of room for exploration, confirming at least the plasticity of antiquity's experience and experiment with schools. An institutional lifespan exceeding that of most empires will naturally invite additions and even revisions to its history, especially the further back it is from the time of consideration. The chronology of the Academy is neither exceptionally problematic nor incontestably stable in this regard.

Our current information is not grounded directly in official records, but it is also not severed from reality. This tends to leave us at odds about precise dates in the schedule of succession of scholarchs, but not without a broad base of agreement. The following chronology developed by Dorandi (1999, pp. 31–35, 53–54) represents a solid anchor in contemporary reckoning:

Heads of the Academy: Dorandi

	Start	**End**	**Years**
Plato of Collytus	388	348/347	40
Speusippus of Athens	348/347	339/338	9
Xenocrates of Chalcedon	339/338	314/313	25
Polemo of Athens	314/313	270/269	44
Crates of Athens	270/269	268–264	2-6
Arcesilaus of Pitane	268–264	241/240	23-27
Lacydes of Cyrene	241/240	226/225/224	15 or 16
Telecles & Euander of Phocis	226/225/224	167/166	58 or 59
Hegesinus of Pergamon	167/166	167/166	1
Carneades I of Cyrene	167/166	137/136	30
Carneades II	137/136	131/130	6
Crates of Tarsus	131/130	127/126	4
Clitomachus of Carthage	127/126	110/109	17
Philo of Larissa	110/109	84/83	26

Notes: All dates are B.C. The number in the last column, representing the approximate duration of the term in years, is the difference between the first number stated for the start and the first for the end for each scholarch.

Source: Tiziano Dorandi: "Chronology": *The Cambridge History of Hellenistic Philosophy* (1999): pp. 31–35, 53–54.

Covering roughly three centuries, Dorandi's work accounts for less than a third of the lifespan traditionally claimed for the Academy. The restricted scope is a reflection of the current practice of ending the succession with Philo (84 BC) as opposed to pursuing a dubious timeline all the way through the edict of Justinian I (529). Although the difference adds up to more than half a millennium, the sheer volume does not make the portion left out any more relevant.

Stepping back from this relatively tight focus to review the full picture in its traditional panoramic splendor is still possible. The following chain of succession put together by Ueberweg (1872, pp. 485–487) is a typical rendition:

Heads of the Academy: Ueberweg

Before Christ	**After Christ**
Plato of Collytus	Ammonius of Alexandria
Speusippus of Athens	[?] Aristodemus of Aegium
Xenocrates of Chalcedon	Calvisius Taurus of Berytus or Tyre
Polemo of Athens	Atticus
Crates of Athens	Diodotus or Theodotus
Arcesilaus of Pitane	Eubulus
Lacydes of Cyrene	[?] Theodorus of Asine
Telecles & Euander of Phocis	[?] Euphrasius
Hegesinus of Pergamon	[?] Chrysanthius of Sardis
Carneades of Cyrene	Priseus of Molossi
Clitomachus of Carthage	Plutarch of Athens
[?] Charmadas	Hierius and Asclepigenia
[?] Aeschines of Neapolis	Syrianus of Alexandria
Philo of Larissa	Proclus the Lycian
Antiochus of Ascalon	Marinus of Sichem (with Zenodotus)
Aristus of Ascalon	Isidorus of Alexandria
Theomnestus of Naneratis	Hegias
	Damascius of Damascus

Notes:

1. Dates, where given by Ueberweg, omitted here.
2. Question marks from the original.
3. To avoid any confusion: the Aeschines listed here is neither the one associated with the emergence of Socratic dialogue as a genre nor the one hailed as one of the ten Attic orators of the Alexandrian tradition; the Ammonius listed here is not the one credited with founding Neoplatonism; the Plutarch listed here is not the famous biographer marking the pinnacle of Middle Platonism.

Source: Friedrich Ueberweg: *History of Philosophy: From Thales to the Present Time* (1872): pp. 485–487.

Compared to Dorandi, Ueberweg misses Carneades the Younger and Crates of Tarsus between Carneades the Elder and Clitomachus of Carthage. He also inserts two scholarchs between Clitomachus and Philo, the final two considered by Dorandi, and adds more than twenty fresh names after that.

In Ueberweg, we have a fuller history, but the more it includes, the more it resembles the Ship of Theseus, with different teachers teaching different students at different times, all under the name of ostensibly the same school. No doubt, every ship is a bit like that of Theseus, becoming more so with time, and schools are not much different. For example, the University of Oxford today is not operating with the same people it was a hundred years ago, be it faculty, students, administrators, or groundskeepers. It may have some of the original bricks, but that cannot last forever. It is, of course, still processing applications at the same address, but even this may change in time, especially with the prospect of technological advances ushering in a paradigm shift in our educational system.

What ultimately sets Oxford apart from the Academy is an uninterrupted and uncontested succession of human resources keeping each position functioning and the organism alive. In contrast, the restarts, revivals, and relocations of the Athenian prototype are not indicative of any greater cohesion or continuity than can be had by a group of Platonists banding together today to reopen the Academy, this time perhaps in Istanbul.

Redirection, however, is another matter altogether. A recalibration of core values, convictions, or processes may be telling in many ways, but it is not necessarily indicative of a disruption of continuity, at least not to the extent of destroying institutional identity. Indeed, Academic history, both within the specific stretch studied by Dorandi and in the greater context unrestricted by anything except the legal terminus, bears witness to several ideological realignments. In fact, the historical profile of the school is traditionally presented in phases corresponding to such shifts in ideology. Curiously, the approach is not bound by a single tradition. For example, Cicero recognizes two distinct Academies, Diogenes Laërtius, three, and Sextus Empiricus, five:

- Cicero acknowledges only two divisions, the Old Academy and the New Academy, placing the break at the scholarchy of Arcesilaus, universally agreed to have introduced a transformation from dogmatism to skepticism (*Academicae Quaestiones* 1.12.43–46).

- Diogenes Laërtius embraces three divisions, noting the same skeptical turn as Cicero but breaking up what follows, as he starts the Old Academy with Plato (*Lives* 3.5, 3.7), the Middle Academy with Arcesilaus (*Lives* 4.28), and, the New Academy, with Lacydes (*Lives* 4.59).

- Sextus Empiricus reports five divisions: the Old Academy of Plato, the Middle Academy of Arcesilaus, and the New Academy of Carneades and Clitomachus, followed by a Fourth Academy under Philo and Charmadas, and a Fifth Academy under Antiochus (*Outlines of Pyrrhonism* [PH] 1.220).

The intersection of the three ancient overviews corresponds precisely to the stretch of time examined by Dorandi, namely, Plato through Philo, with Sextus tacking on an extra school at the very end. Actually, Sextus himself seems to endorse only the first three divisions he reports, while merely communicating the last two as part of the prevailing story, to which he apparently does not subscribe fully. Diogenes, in turn, is in general agreement with the primary account of Sextus. As for Cicero, while his recognition of two divisions is in conformity with the common perspective of a skeptical turn, he maintains that the New Academy (skeptical) is not so new after all, given that a tradition including Plato himself (*Academicae Quaestiones* 1.12.46) and extending back even beyond Socrates (*Academicae Quaestiones* 1.12.44–45) confirms the existence of a skeptical mindset from the beginning and precludes its emergence as a strictly later development, especially as an innovation.

Cicero's perspective on continuity clearly transcends the Academy as we know it, as he glorifies a single tradition minimizing, and ostensibly even eliminating, any differences between the schools of Plato and Aristotle (*Academicae Quaestiones* 1.4.17–18), and finding substantial harmony, or at least a considerable common denominator, between an otherwise diverse range of philosophers: Empedocles of Acragas (Agrigentum); Anaxagoras of Clazomenae; Democritus of Abdera; Parmenides of Elea; Xenophanes of Colophon; Plato of Collytus; Socrates of Alopece (*Academicae Quaestiones* 2.5.14, listed in this order; list partially anticipated in 1.12.44). In short, Cicero conceives of scholarchs following Plato as preserving a tradition preceding Plato (*Academicae Quaestiones* 1.9.34; *De Legibus* 1.38–39).

Leaving tradition aside, the contemporary conception of the Academy is restricted to the temporal framework of Dorandi, starting with the momentous initiative of Plato and ending with the fateful scholarchy of Philo. The divisions in this period may or may not be recognized precisely as they were by the ancients, or at all, but later developments, including the final break acknowledged rather reluctantly by Sextus, are certainly excluded from consideration as part of a cohesive whole. What remains outside, however, can seem confusing, with designations there appearing no less Platonic than the divisions recognized within the Academy proper. Chief among these are Middle Platonism and Neoplatonism:

- Middle Platonism is a departure starting with Antiochus, who broke away from the Academy of Philo around 90 BC in rejection of the prevailing skeptical philosophy and in advocacy of a return to a dogmatic platform recognizing the possibility of knowledge, championed by an overarching initiative to develop Platonism along eclectic lines broadly consistent with Peripatetic and Stoic traditions.

- Neoplatonism is a later development, absorbing Middle Platonism, but becoming even more eclectic in drawing inspiration from Neopythagoreanism and oriental mysticism in addition to the existing strands of Peripatetic and Stoic philosophy. Generally considered to start in the third century with the Alexandrian philosopher Ammonius Saccas, it actually finds impetus with his student Plotinus (204–270).

Any standard reference work should suffice for a basic overview of these developments, though each is far too complex to summarize in passing, here or elsewhere. The relevant point here is to note their mercurial position as a part of Platonism separate from the Academy.

Their exclusion as such can seem arbitrary, as the distinction is conventional rather than natural. Both the separation as well as the accompanying names are modern inventions. Middle Platonism, for example, is the reclassification, or simply redesignation, of what Sextus (PH 1.220) recognized as the Fifth Academy. To repeat a rather hackneyed but nonetheless informative caveat, neither the Middle Platonists nor the Neoplatonists actually considered themselves anything but Platonists. The Middle Platonists certainly were not aware that they were in the middle of anything, and the Neoplatonists made no claim to anything new, instead introducing the new as already present in or anticipated by the old.

Yet even such generalities run the risk of distorting the facts, especially when the facts are spread across multiple scholars and several centuries. The Neoplatonism of Plotinus and any random successor can differ as widely as the Platonism of Plato and any random successor. Even so, some framework or other is required for intelligent discussion. Learning and even adopting the prevailing one is important, in fact, required, if only to challenge it.

1.6.5. The Star Student

The greatest claim to fame of the Academy, next to its founding and administration by Plato, is its inclusion of Aristotle in the student body. Aristotle arrived at the school in 367 BC at the age of seventeen, remaining there, according to most accounts, for two decades through the death of Plato, though possibly departing the year before that. His arrival coincided with Plato's second trip to Syracuse, during which Aristotle's education was the responsibility of Eudoxus of Cnidus, the acting head of the school in Plato's absence, but Plato is known to have taken a personal interest, upon returning to Athens, in the young philosopher's development. Aristotle eventually became a lecturer at the school, but never rose to its headship, with his departure often attributed, though on little more than sensible conjecture, to being passed over for that position by Plato, who instead nominated his own nephew, Speusippus, in an apparent act of nepotism.

We cannot be sure that nepotism is the operative motive here, even if the context constitutes a classic example. The room for hesitation is not sentimental but rational. The danger is not only in prejudging the integrity of Plato, or in judging it by contemporary standards, but also in underestimating the intellect of Speusippus. Removing the qualification "apparent" in describing the act as nepotism would be unfair, not just to Plato but even more so to Speusippus. The fact that Aristotle has withstood the test of time better than Speusippus gives us an unsporting advantage in comparison. And it does not guarantee that Aristotle stood as the better philosopher in 347 BC, the year the choice was exercised. Nor does it suggest that Aristotle had demonstrated greater promise than Speusippus in the two decades before that, a period preceding his maturity. In fact, Aristotle (384–322 BC) at seventeen must have been decidedly less impressive than Speusippus (408–339/338 BC) at forty-one, which is how they stood the year Aristotle arrived at the Academy. This may have changed by the time Plato died, when Aristotle was thirty-six or thirty-seven, and Speusippus sixty or sixty-one, but we still cannot say whether Aristotle was the better candidate then, as the comparison is between two adult philosophers, whereas we know that he was not the better candidate at the time of his arrival, where the comparison is between an experienced philosopher and an adolescent apprentice. Somewhere in between, the gap must have closed considerably, if not entirely, possibly even reversing itself, but there is something to be said for tenure as well. Be that as it may, we can rest assured that kinship with Plato was not the sole qualification of Speusippus. In our eagerness to admire past masters, we have to keep in mind that the people closest to them were often eminent philosophers in their own right, not minions responsible for keeping the papyrus rolls organized and free of mold and mildew.

That said, Aristotle is indeed a star in the history of philosophy. Even if Plato himself had not risen to a level of superlative eminence as a philosopher, his contribution to the field would have been invaluable in having mentored someone who did. Alfred North Whitehead's (1929) memorable characterization of the history of Western philosophy as a series of footnotes to Plato might have seemed far less hyperbolic had it not been for the existence of Aristotle, especially in such close temporal proximity to Plato. (Although Whitehead's actual reference is to the "European philosophical tradition" (1978, p. 39), the exclusion of the rest of the Western world is not a denial of the adequacy of philosophy in the Americas but a reflection of the relative brevity of the history of philosophy there.) Perhaps it is only the rare combination in time and in mind that so inspired Raphael to immortalize his conception of the Academy, or, what is more likely, to project the emerging ideal of the modern university onto the legendary setting of the School of Athens, with the two philosophers par excellence at the center.

1.7. Plato's Legacy

The material goods Plato left behind are itemized by Diogenes Laërtius (*Lives* 3.41–43). We should be hard pressed to find anything of this today, and unlikely to recognize anything thereof even if we happened to stumble upon it. The intellectual goods he left behind are, no doubt, far more important for us. We are fortunate to have nothing missing in this category, that is, if we equate his intellectual legacy with his written work.

On the other hand, we may also count in this category his pupils. Students do not always agree with their teachers, but they are influenced and inspired by them, usually to a far greater extent than may be apparent. The bond is reducible neither to doctrine nor to method, instead incorporating and transcending both in a dynamic process of mutual education.

Influence and inspiration within the Academy appears to have flowed in both directions, benefiting master and pupil alike, perhaps not with equal force, but certainly with comparable receptivity. Plato was not a sage beyond improvement but a philosopher in pursuit of wisdom. This was a joint initiative. He taught, but he also learned. Moreover, as already mentioned, not everyone around him was a student or a neophyte. In his role as a "first among equals," Plato was not even the only senior guide. He was surrounded by full-fledged scholars and first-rate philosophers.

This makes it all the more important to take a critical look at those around him and those surviving him. Any insight into the mindset he helped produce is no less an example of the forces shaping his own development. And the combination constitutes the core of the intellectual energy shaping the Western intellectual tradition. Hence, the legacy of Plato is felt not only in direct offshoots such as Middle Platonism and Neoplatonism, but also in standalone systems of grand practical significance, for example, in the historical evolution of exegetical trends in the Abrahamic religions, mostly in Christianity and Islam, but also in Judaism, the last in a reciprocal interplay of interpretive inspiration. To be sure, we cannot gather all this from a membership roster of the Academy, but it would be a good place to start, or at least a profitable point of reflection.

We do not know everyone associated with the Academy during the time of Plato. Even the reference to the "time of Plato" blurs the picture, as it covers four decades, where the membership roster on any random day is not certain to be duplicated on another. Yet with some tolerance in accuracy and exhaustiveness, a fairly reliable idea can be developed. The main sources are the following:

- Philodemus: *Academicorum Philosophorum Index Herculanensis* (=Papyrus Herculanensis 164: F12 [T3a]; 1021: col. 6 [T3b]).
- Plutarch: *Adversus Colotem* (*Against Colotes*) 32: 1126c.
- Diogenes Laërtius: *Lives and Opinions of Eminent Philosophers* (3.46–47).

These are neither identical nor contradictory in content, as none professes to be exhaustive. There is significant overlap. Yet a comprehensive picture is not guaranteed even if we merge all three accounts, and a veridical one is not likely if we do so uncritically.

The standard approach is to start with, or, in fact, to be fully contented with, the report of Diogenes, who names more people than any other source. While we can also scour scattered references to individuals, whether in Diogenes or elsewhere, the most convenient source is a list already prepared in his *Life of Plato* (*Lives* 3.46–47). The central information can be summarized as in the following table:

Disciples of Plato (As Reported by Diogenes)

Main List (17 people)		**Addenda (6 people)**
Speusippus of Athens	Timolaus of Cyzicus	Lastheneia of Mantinea ♀
Xenocrates of Chalcedon	Euaeon of Lampsacus	Axiothea of Phlius ♀
Aristotle of Stagira	Python of Aenus	Theophrastus of Eresus
Philippus of Opus	Heraclides of Aenus	Hyperides the Orator
Hestiaeus of Perinthus	Hippothales of Athens	Lycurgus of Athens
Dion of Syracuse	Callippus of Athens	Demosthenes of Athens
Amyclus of Heraclea	Demetrius of Amphipolis	
Erastus of Scepsis	Heraclides of Pontus	**Anonymous**
Coriscus of Scepsis		"Many others"

Notes:

1. Names are listed in the order of the original.
2. Erastus and Coriscus of Scepsis are listed as being from "Scepsus" in the Hicks translation and "Sceptos" in the Yonge translation.
3. Diogenes cites the following sources for the "addenda": The two women, Lastheneia and Axiothea, are reported by Dicaearchus to have worn men's clothes. Hyperides and Lycurgus are listed on the authority of Chamaeleon with the further confirmation of Polemo. Demosthenes is listed on the authority of Sabinus quoting Mnesistratus of Thasos. His discipleship is not universally acknowledged, though it is confirmed at least by Suidas, Cicero, and Quintilian.

Source: Diogenes Laërtius: *Lives* (3.46–47).

Diogenes professes to be listing disciples of Plato, not members of the Academy, but equating one with the other should be no crime. After all, Plato is not likely to have had very many disciples before establishing the Academy, and even less likely, after having done so, to have lost the ones he had. As informative as it is, the report would have been infinitely more telling had it not included the qualification that there were "many other" disciples besides the ones listed by name.

Diogenes lists a total of twenty-three people. He divides the report into two unequal parts, the first listing seventeen disciples without invoking a single source, and the second adding six more with various references, sometimes doubling up on a single entry. The division is introduced by ending the primary list with a blanket reference to "many others," which the subsequent six names are supposed to instantiate as representative examples. Two of these are women, which might speak for the progressive character of the Academy, save for the additional remark that they reportedly wore men's clothes, presumably not entirely by choice, or at least not to make a fashion statement. The auxiliary list is not in any way inferior to the primary list, as it includes highly influential people. While it is not clear how much distinction any of them had achieved during Plato's lifetime, their celebrity beyond that is a matter of record. Thirteen years younger than Aristotle, Theophrastus was no more than twenty-four when Plato died, but turned out to be a prominent philosopher, succeeding Aristotle as the head of the Lyceum. Hyperides, Lycurgus, and Demosthenes were critically acclaimed orators and logographers, each posthumously earning a place in the Alexandrian Canon of Ten Attic Orators. Demosthenes was more highly regarded than the other two, not to mention the remaining seven, and also left a mark as statesman.

The primary list, of course, speaks for itself, especially the first column in the table above. Biographies of some of the more prominent ones abound as standalone works, and, of the lesser celebrities, at least in encyclopedias. Guthrie (1978, pp. 446–492) devotes a chapter to a selection of the disciples, with a view to paving the way for his book on Aristotle (1981) in the same series (*A History of Greek Philosophy*).

Modern efforts to expand the list of Diogenes (e.g., Dillon, 2003, pp. 13–15; Marrou, 1956, pp. 64–65) invariably invoke either the records of Philodemus or the overview of Plutarch.

- Philodemus (Papyrus Herculanensis 164: F12 [T3a]; 1021: col. 6 [T3b]) seems to offer at least seven fresh names: Heraclides of Heraclea; Amyntas of Heraclea; Menedemus of Pyrrha; Chaeron of Pellene; Hermodorus of Syracuse; Calligenes; Chion of Heraclea. But Dillon (2003, p. 13, n. 25) suspects that the first two actually refer respectively to Heraclides of Pontus and Amyclus of Heraclea in the list of Diogenes.

- Plutarch (*Adversus Colotem* 32: 1126c), focusing exclusively on statesmen coming out of the Academy, lists a total of eleven names, duplicating five in Diogenes: Dion of Syracuse; Python of Aenus; Heraclides of Aenus; Chabrias of Athens; Phocion of Athens; Aristonymus of Megalopolis; Phormion of Elis; Menedemus of Pyrrha; Eudoxus of Cnidus; Aristotle of Stagira; Xenocrates of Chalcedon (listed in the order of the original).

Merging the three lists is not merely a matter of eliminating the redundancy in the overlapping parts. Actually, it is, but the problem is that the inherent redundancy may not be limited to the apparent overlap: Names in one list can easily be confused in another, and apparently different names could actually belong to the same person, as demonstrated, for example, in Dillon's (2003, pp. 13–15) careful comparison of certain entries in Philodemus and Diogenes. Useful comparisons, again, of Philodemus and Diogenes, are also available in Gaiser (1988, pp. 443–449) and Lasserre (1987, p. 436), while Plutarch's focus on the Academy's production of statesmen might best be read in the light of the commentary by Zeller (1876, pp. 30–32, n. 64) and the assessment by Chroust (1967, pp. 25–40).

But why should the lists differ in the first place? The most intuitive explanation is that they differ largely in proportion to the access each compiler must have had to what would naturally be the same actual facts, quite likely also showing some variation in accordance with any theme each might have wished to emphasize therein, as in the case of the political perspective provided by Plutarch. Given that we do not have the original records to confirm or deny any differences between these sources, and, more important, to weed out with certainty genuine redundancies lurking behind mistaken and misleading variations, merging the lists is not guaranteed to enhance the quality of our information even if it produces a longer string of data.

Fortunately, the reports are sufficient as they are, severally or jointly, to shape our thinking about the Academy. A particularly useful bit of insight afforded is the geographic diversity of the membership profile. This is especially apparent in the coverage by Diogenes, where only five of the twenty-three people listed turn out to be Athenians, a testament to the ability of the school to attract students from outside Attica. The Academy, it seems, even in Plato's time, was well on its way to becoming a Panhellenic institution rather than struggling as a local presence with a local reputation.

The next chapter focuses on the thought of the man attracting the top minds of his world to come philosophize with him.

Two

THOUGHT OF PLATO

The greatest obstacle to a healthy introduction to the thought of a philosopher is the thought of someone else on what that is. The superlative here may be an exaggeration, but the rest of the statement is not. Too often, the first impression one gets of a philosopher is through the current interpretive paradigm: the set of instructions and discussions constituting the received view at any time. Abandoned interpretations can be just as intrusive, but they are seldom available to a newcomer. Prevailing perspectives usually prevail for good reasons, and are often indispensable in intermediate and advanced studies, but they will stand in the way of the objective formulation of initial impressions, and they will prejudice any attempt at a critical assessment. Possibly the worst introduction to any philosopher, then, is through a formulaic approach expressing the relevant positions in other words.

By the same token, the healthiest path would seem to be to access the thought of philosophers directly through their own work. No doubt, all philosophical writing will not be equally accessible. Particularly difficult pieces will require support from the outset. For example, it is difficult to work through the *Critique of Pure Reason* unaided. The point, however, is not that the initial effort should be unassisted, but that it should be unbiased. An understanding of the output should shape an interpretation of the philosophy, not the other way around.

Plato is a rare exception, not in the sense that just the opposite is required in his case, but in the sense that the relationship between his output and his thought constitutes a special problem not to be glossed over by generalized advice on how best to do or read philosophy. While it is generally true that interpretive intermediation can be an obstacle, Plato is perhaps the single greatest example of what can go wrong either way: Both avoiding and seeking out exegetical guidance comes with complications, placing a heavy burden on Plato's readers. This is because the accessibility of his thought through his writing is precisely what is at stake at the most general level of debate dividing scholars.

In its simplest form, the question is whether Plato's philosophy is contained in Plato's dialogues. The suspicion is not that someone else's philosophy masquerades as Plato's, but that his own is not to be found there. The further question whether the philosophy of Socrates appears alongside the philosophy of Plato is also relevant, but that is an entirely different problem, one readily assuming that the corpus contains a philosophy, and questioning if we know precisely where the credit is due. No one would deny Socrates a role of influence. And hardly anyone suspects that it is all Socrates. But the prior concern is whether Plato reveals his own thoughts at all, not whether we can weed out what belongs to Socrates, or to anyone else, for that matter. Even this does not quite capture the root of the issue. At the conceptual bedrock of its perplexity, the debate is about whether the Platonic corpus houses a philosophical system in the first place, whosever it may be.

This is an unusual problem to encounter in a philosopher. The reason for the complication is Plato's *modus operandi*: He tells stories instead of defending positions. The problem is not that the stories he tells are difficult to follow in the manner that the statements Kant strings together are difficult to follow, but that they are stories rather than successions of statements. Fortunately, they are clearly organized, highly intelligible, and often entertaining stories. They are dialogues, arguably the most appropriate form of fiction for philosophy. Still, the result is fiction. And fiction conceals conviction. Worse, Plato never appears as the hero. Nor is any hero readily identifiable with Plato. Still worse, no hero ever gets the girl, or rides into the sunset.

So, the first problem is that Plato's thought is not immediately discernible in or through his work. The second is that his work is not expressly dedicated to a particular conclusion. It is not reducible to any particular ideology. Even the most rigorous arguments are provisional, even the most passionate speeches, tentative.

Plato says many things, but never as Plato, except, of course, for the letters, and never with authority, or without reservations and a back door to revision. He communicates through his characters, often with imagery and metaphor instead of pure dialogue. His work does not leave the reader with the satisfaction of having gained insight into his deepest convictions, or even of having encountered a philosophical system, his own or anyone else's.

The question to ask is this: Do Plato's dialogues advance a philosophical position? Do they hang together as part of a philosophical system? On one side of the debate, the "dogmatic" or "doctrinal" interpretation is that they do; on the opposite side, the "skeptical" interpretation is that they do not. The dogmatic interpretation derives its name from the attribution of a definite position to the works of Plato, while the skeptical position gets its name from the attribution of a skeptical position. This may already be clear from the names, but the best place to avoid a misunderstanding is the beginning: The dogmatic interpretation portrays Plato merely as having opinions and convictions, not as refusing to consider alternatives, nor, therefore, as having a closed mind or an aversion to rational discourse. And the skeptical interpretation is not a skeptical stance about whether Plato advocates any particular philosophical position; it is a categorical claim that Plato himself embraces a skeptical stance, thus advocating no particular position at all. Alternatively, shifting the focus from the person to the work, the dogmatic interpretation depicts the dialogues as reflecting identifiable convictions, while the skeptical interpretation denies that they stand for anything in particular, except possibly indirectly as a demonstration of the inevitability of skepticism. This is the most fundamental division in the interpretation of Plato.

No matter the answer, the question itself, to repeat, whether Plato's dialogues advance a philosophical position, is not immediately clear. It seems to introduce, or conceal, an ambiguity between distributive and collective predication. This calls forth another question: Are the dialogues to be tested for philosophical content individually or as a whole? Or are both tests required, just for good measure, and, ideally, with mutually consistent results? Must all the dialogues bend in the same direction, turning out to be either all dogmatic or all skeptical? The debate seems to allow no room for the possibility that some dialogues might fall into one category and some into the other. They either each serve the same core philosophy, or they are, one and all, independent of centralized ideation.

The problem is superficial. The question concerns the corpus as a whole. So should the answer. The locus of the debate on dogmatism versus skepticism is not this or that particular dialogue but the whole body of them handed down as the philosophical output of Plato. The dogmatic position, after all, is not that every dialogue is a conduit for the transmission of a central philosophy. And the skeptical position is not that no character in any dialogue ever utters anything that can properly be considered a philosophical statement or explanation. To require a central doctrine or set of doctrines to be present in every dialogue is too strong a requirement for a dogmatic interpretation of the whole. Likewise, to require the complete absence of philosophical claims or perspectives is too strong for a skeptical interpretation of the corpus, or of Plato. The assessment must extend to the level of the dialogue, but, in the final analysis, the proper focus for a judgment is the corpus. The collective evidence must be sufficient for a conclusion one way or the other. This certainly requires examining the dialogues, but not with a view to anchoring the conclusion to any single one of them.

The question of the proper approach hangs on the distance between Plato and his audience. A closer look at that distance should be the first step in any examination. Inspection will not eliminate the distance, but familiarity might make it more navigable.

2.1. Barriers to Access

The immediate problem in discussing Plato's thought is the uncertainty of what that is. Reading his works, even all of them, will not take us inside his mind. In all likelihood, it will take us somewhere near, but we can never be sure, and, perhaps worse, we may not all end up at the same place. This is not because Plato is difficult to understand or interpret, but because he hides his views from his readers. He does this by putting everything into the mouths of dramatic characters debating or exploring a philosophical issue, which he thus presents without taking a side. Not only does he not take sides, but he simply does not express any opinions whatsoever as author. He leaves the readers with the characters, preferring to remain outside the engagement altogether. The dialogue form guarantees a comfortable distance of this sort. Indeed, the voluminous body of his extant works, thought to include everything he wrote for publication, and in that regard representing an unusually large collection for manuscripts surviving since antiquity, consists almost entirely of dialogues.

Plato's scholarly output merits separate consideration best undertaken in a discussion isolated from other problems, as in the following chapter dedicated exclusively to a skeletal survey of his works, but some of the basic intricacies of that output are also relevant to a general overview of his philosophy, where we must note at least the presence of barriers to access. Plato apparently relishes such barriers, as he sets them up personally, the primary one through his choice of literary form, the others through the way he molds that form. The problem, then, is not in following Plato's writing, but in determining how much of it, if any at all, reflects his own philosophical convictions. Locating the philosophically strongest position, or, what is the same, the dramatically favored viewpoint, among the characters is usually easy enough, rarely taking more than one reading. Such a vantage point is not merely available but readily identifiable in the typical dialogue. One often need look no further than the dramatic persona of Socrates, immortalized as the protagonist in most of what Plato wrote. By the same reasoning, where Socrates is absent, or in the background, one might turn to the pinch hitter for the word of Plato.

Who speaks for Plato? This is a simple question with a complicated answer. It was not always so. The answer used to be just as simple. Diogenes Laërtius, for example, saddles Plato with every view put forward by the central figure in every dialogue. All told, he gives Plato four mouthpieces:

> His own views are expounded by four persons, Socrates, Timaeus, the Athenian Stranger, the Eleatic Stranger. These strangers are not, as some hold, Plato and Parmenides, but imaginary characters without names, for, even when Socrates and Timaeus are the speakers, it is Plato's doctrines that are laid down. To illustrate the refutation of false opinions, he introduces Thrasymachus, Callicles, Polus, Gorgias, Protagoras, or again Hippias, Euthydemus and the like. [Diogenes Laërtius: *Lives* 3.52; Hicks translation; footnote reference markers omitted]

Diogenes is representative of a long tradition preceding and following him. He or anyone else in that tradition might unsurprisingly have added Parmenides to the list as a character speaking for Plato, but the common ground is not so much what belongs on the list as it is that there is such a list. Against a considerable history of making these characters dramatic mouthpieces for Plato, recent scholarship, as illustrated in a collection of essays edited by Gerald Alan Press (2000), is shifting away from assigning a spokesperson to Plato. Commentators have been growing especially wary of assuming the various Socratic performances to be nothing more than the dramatic expression of Platonic philosophy. This is, on the whole, sensible, but, carried to an extreme, as in the position that no character in Plato ever says anything held by Plato himself, it runs the risk of representing Plato as unable or unwilling to impart any philosophical wisdom, or, worse, as hiding chunks of it in an inscrutable dramatic maze.

This issue is passionately debated in the secondary literature, but a resolution is not crucial to settling, or even understanding, the prior dispute: Identifying Plato's dramatic mouthpiece, or establishing that he does not have one, would not vindicate either the dogmatic or the skeptical interpretation over the other. There are easy answers. For example, every leading protagonist may be speaking for Plato, just as Diogenes proclaims, and the rotation between spokespersons may simply mark changes in view, each promulgated through a different character. Still, the problem remains, as the sum of the strongest positions throughout the corpus does not constitute a coherent philosophical system. On the contrary, it includes notable contradictions, at least on the surface.

This suggests another easy answer: Perhaps Plato has no positive views, or does not wish to share them, thus offering the dialogues not so much as his considered opinions on philosophical issues but more so as intellectual exercises demonstrating how to do philosophy. The problem becomes more and more difficult as the easy answers multiply. And even if the entire corpus were philosophically consistent, we can never be sure whether we are receiving Plato's views, regardless of what we might be receiving through this or that character.

As a matter of fact, far from solving the problem, the presence of Socrates as the central figure in the dialogues exacerbates it. The fact that Socrates is himself an eminent philosopher introduces the possibility that Plato is reporting the actual views of the master instead of merely honoring his memory through drama. The consideration that Socrates wrote nothing at all lends additional credence to the possibility of a reporting role by Plato. The full range of possibilities in this respect includes endless combinations between a complete absence of Socratic contribution and a complete absence of Platonic originality. Put differently, the Platonic corpus may be entirely Platonic, with Socrates merely a dramatic character, or it may be entirely Socratic, with Plato merely a recording scribe, or it may be something in between, with virtually infinite possibilities for the precise ratio of their respective contributions. The Socratic extreme has no proponents in print, while the Platonic extreme finds at least moderate support among scholars, though still leaving some sort of combination as the reigning view.

Ironically, the closest thing we have to an advocate of the Socratic extreme is Plato. This constitutes a fascinating exception to the absence of published proponents of the Socratic extreme, with Plato professing, and *ipso facto* proving, quite the opposite in a letter to Dionysius II:

> The best precaution is not to write them down, but to commit them to memory; for it is impossible that things written should not become known to others. This is why I have never written on these subjects. There is no writing of Plato's, nor will there ever be; those that are now called so come from an idealized and youthful Socrates. [*Second Letter* 314b–c; Morrow translation, with the omission of a footnote reporting "modernized" as an alternative for "youthful."]

Such a sensational statement begs for explanation. A natural reaction is to question whether Plato might not have written the letter before he wrote anything he considered substantially different from what Socrates had to say. Another possibility is that the statement is an example of hyperbolic deference to a master, common in ancient cultures, though outdated in modern times, especially in Western civilization. Either possibility would explain the generous attribution to Socrates, and they would also be compatible in a joint explanation. Neither would explain the pledge never to write anything, but here a comparably natural explanation suggests itself: Plato may have simply decided not to follow through with the pledge, possibly upon realizing that he had much to say that had not been said before, or that had not been said adequately, whether by Socrates or by anyone else.

None of these considerations will do. The reason is that they all come with a presumption of early composition for the letter. Reputable efforts to date the letters place the entire batch in the last two decades of Plato's life, when he would have long been aware of any contributions he might be able to make better than his predecessors. A further possibility is that the letter is a forgery. Indeed, it attracts more rejection than acceptance among experts considering its authenticity. However, this is not a sound basis for denying that Plato objects to writing, as a letter in great favor with specialists studying the authenticity of the canonical works repeats the same considerations, though, this time, without attributing anything, let alone the entire corpus, to Socrates:

> There is no writing of mine about these matters, nor will there ever be one. For this knowledge is not something that can be put into words like other sciences; but after long-continued intercourse between teacher and pupil, in joint pursuit of the subject, suddenly like light flashing forth when a fire is kindled, it is born in the soul and straightaway nourishes itself. [*Seventh Letter* 341c–d; Morrow translation]

This passage is from an open letter addressed to the associates and friends of Dion, apparently soon after his assassination in 354 BC, which places it six or seven years before Plato's death. If authentic, as it is widely believed to be, its apparent date of composition leaves no doubt that Plato, at least up until the last six or seven years of his life, remained opposed to communicating his philosophy in writing. Specifically, the opposition concerns the forms. The otherwise vague reference to "these matters" is actually an allusion to the forms, as the greater context makes clear, though without using the exact words ("eidos" or "idea") for them.

The focus on the forms is especially perplexing because they figure prominently in what are considered Plato's central dialogues, and arguably in many places besides. Yet these are not discussions *of*, *on*, or *about* the forms, but discussions that happen to invoke them. This leaves room for a reconciliation between the denial in the letter and its apparent contradiction in the dialogues.

The *Parmenides* presents a notable exception, since the discussion there is precisely about the forms, but, even there, the absence of a clear and enlightening conclusion is consistent with the position that Plato did not publish or publicize his views on these matters. In other words, since the *Parmenides*, raising many important issues without settling any, brings us no closer to understanding what Plato thought about the forms, particularly in comparison to where we might be without having read the dialogue at all, it does not really count as an exception to the spirit of what is repudiated in the letter.

Nevertheless, a reconciliation of this sort is not altogether satisfying. The letter goes on to denounce writing itself in no uncertain terms, demonstrating a general condemnation of the medium rather than a specific opposition to it in regard to forms:

> For this reason anyone who is seriously studying high matters will be the last to write about them and thus expose his thought to the envy and criticism of men. What I have said comes, in short, to this: whenever we see a book, whether the laws of a legislator or a composition on any other subject, we can be sure that if the author is really serious, this book does not contain his best thoughts; they are stored away with the fairest of his possessions. And if he has committed these serious thoughts to writing, it is because men, not gods, "have taken his wits away." [*Seventh Letter* 344c–d; Morrow translation, the original text of which includes a footnote identifying the terminal expression as coming from the *Iliad*: 7.360]

The "high matters" mentioned in the passage, as far as Plato is concerned, can still be taken as nothing other than the forms, but the generalization introduced therein recognizes the possibility of a variety of comparable matters for other serious thinkers, who are, one and all, warned against putting their own cherished ideas into writing, thus confirming that the problem, whatever it is, is not just about the forms.

The intensity of the epistolary stance against publication rivals that of the corresponding dialogic opposition laid out in the *Phaedrus* (274c–275e, 276c), where the written word turns out to be valuable only as a reminder, and not so much even then, as it is practically dead: Writing, we are told in the *Phaedrus*, is unable to edify or to respond to questions, and it is counterproductive in its tendency to promote intellectual lethargy as excessive reliance on the text turns into an aversion to exercising memory.

The collective evidence leaves us with an apparent contradiction: Plato seems strongly opposed to the written communication of rational reflection on serious subjects, so strongly as to issue a warning against it, while himself producing a considerable collection of writing widely regarded as the most influential in the history of philosophy. Since one component of the apparent contradiction is a fact, any exegetical effort must focus on the other. In other words, since Plato has in fact published the dialogues, any explanation must be restricted to the warning and personal reservations that should have kept him from doing so.

One possibility is that Plato considers the dialogues exempt from his own warning, conceivably because he finds the genre so dynamic and interactive as to sidestep the problems of inertia and rigidity typically encountered in writing. Or perhaps the dialogues do not even qualify for the warning, say, because they do not contain his final conclusions or the critical reasoning taking him there, whereas the warning is expressly about considered opinions offered in earnest. A third possibility is that the warning applies no less to talking about these matters as it does to writing about them, being instead directed against their verbalization in any form, written or spoken. This can be invoked either to exonerate the dialogues, as in the first possibility, specifically, on the grounds that written dialogues qualify for the same exemption as oral discourse, or, failing that, to condemn all oral efforts along with the written. Still far from enjoying mass appeal, the third scenario has been gaining adherents, including, for example, Wieland (1982), Sayre (1988, 1993a, 1993b), Williams (2006, see especially p. 179), and Gonzales (2002, pp. 31–83, especially pp. 48–51), the last three comparable in this regard to Wieland and to one another, and covered in some detail in the final section (§ 2.6) of this chapter, though primarily in connection with their standing on another matter.

To return to the problem of distance between author and audience, taking the central character as some sort of bridge is only natural, but the path is more tortuous than such a linear solution may suggest. A portrayal of Plato as a mere philosophical conduit for Socratic principles and practices can hardly be defensible. At the other extreme, Plato's decision to honor the master might in fact have gone no further than naming his own protagonist after the historical Socrates, but nearly everyone engaged in Platonic philosophy makes room in there for something of Socrates besides the name. A traditional interpretation, though no longer uncontested, is that some of the dialogues, those written early in Plato's career, are distinctly Socratic, while the rest reflect Plato's own philosophical outlook.

Constituting the basis of what is known as the standard view, or standard account, the distinction is not merely biographical but also bibliographical. It is, at any rate, temporal, or, to be specific, chronological. Supposedly, the Socratic period comes first, with the true Plato emerging later, though the latter part is further subdivided into two or three distinct groups. The chronological nature of the distinction makes it just as much about the corpus as it is about the philosophy. This can be significant in such a peculiar context where the work of the thinker is not necessarily the same as the thought of the thinker. Accordingly, the standard view is taken up more fully in the next chapter, where the focus is primarily on the works and only incidentally on the philosophy. Be that as it may, certain thematic elements of the distinction are relevant here as well, and can fruitfully be examined without invoking the chronological dimension, best studied in conjunction with the layout and intricacies of the corpus.

The basic distinction can be parsed further: Do the so-called Socratic dialogues reflect a phase in Plato's intellectual development where his views coincided with, or were at least roughly aligned with, those of Socrates, or do they reflect a period when he deliberately suppressed his own views in order to report those of Socrates? Any choice between the two possibilities would be underdetermined by the evidence, while an alternative, especially one drawing on the two and remaining in between, may be just as reasonable.

We may never know the whole story, but we can rest assured that any reporting by Plato is philosophical rather than purely journalistic, or historical, depending on the frame of reference, and that the drama is a literary vessel for the message rather than a record of actual events. A notable exception is the *Apology*, where we become privy to Socrates's fateful defense in court, an actual event confirmed by external evidence, though, even there, Plato's role is not strictly that of a court stenographer. Other than that, Socrates may or may not have actually run into Euthyphro before the trial, had long talks with Crito while in prison, and spent time in conversation with his friends and disciples on his last day, as depicted, respectively, in the *Euthyphro*, *Crito*, and *Phaedo*, but these all differ from the *Apology* in that nothing of their drama has a confirmed basis in fact and that the conversations they recount are almost certainly wholly imagined. Even in the *Phaedo*, all we can be certain of is the death of Socrates, not its occurrence exactly as depicted in that dialogue. The verisimilitude in these, and in everything other than the *Apology*, goes no further than the possibility of convergence between peripheral plot elements and reality. In general, we can be reasonably confident, first, that the Socratic dialogues do not attempt to describe events precisely as they occurred, and, second, that they successfully capture how they might have occurred, thus offering a realistic account of Socrates in action, without being slavish to the facts.

We can be confident in this because the genre at large operates with a presumption against assuming what is said by the character Socrates to have actually been held by the historical Socrates. This is not to say that the character affords no insight into the person characterized, but that the insight therein is not equivalent to a reliable biography. Authors of the period are allowed considerable leeway in what they make Socrates the character do or say, so long as they do not make him do or say things wholly unlike what the real one might have done or said. Hence, the anecdotal information we are left with, whether in Plato or in any other disciple of Socrates, has representative rather than documentary authority. (See, for example, Kahn, 1995, pp. 26–35; 1996, pp. 1–4, 34–35.)

How does such artistic freedom relate to the debate on Socrates as Plato's mouthpiece? It obviously promotes the mouthpiece scenario if only because it allows room for the possibility. It does not, on the other hand, confirm the scenario. It does, of course, undermine the position of dissenters rejecting the scenario purely on the grounds that anything put into the mouth of Socrates the character ought to respect the fact that Socrates the person was a philosopher of first rank, whose ideas deserve perpetuation without corruption and whose persona deserves preservation without adaptation. As venerable as Socrates may have been, this evidently did not create an obligation to be factual in characterization, possibly encouraged by the fact that the man himself put nothing into writing. Veneration manifested as textual realism goes against the general practice, which is open to the mouthpiece scenario, closed to its rejection out of hand, but inconclusive in the end, especially in accommodating, at least theoretically, a third possibility midway between the apparent alternatives: (1) If Plato or any other Socratic were bound by the genre to make the character Socrates as close to the real Socrates as possible, this would preclude the mouthpiece scenario. (2) Given that practitioners are allowed and even encouraged by the genre to take liberties with the character, this creates ample room for making that character a mouthpiece. (3) Still, the character could quite conceivably stray from the real Socrates without representing or delivering the thoughts of the author, thus remaining at an equal or comparable distance from both, though it is difficult to imagine what purpose would be served, other than entertainment, by a character that acquaints readers with neither the person characterized nor the person doing the characterization.

The identification of this common literary dimension, prematurely albeit unavoidably ushering in the concept of genre to introduce the inherent flexibility of Socratic characterization, now necessitates a brief clarification in regard to terminology: Strictly speaking, any reference to "Socratic dialogue" is vague unless connected with an author, either explicitly by name, or implicitly as above in the contextual connection with Plato. Otherwise, the reference remains indeterminate between a multitude of authors in the same genre. While the genre itself is a topic for discussion in the next chapter, as it deals primarily with the works rather than the thought of Plato, the caveat is just as relevant here because of a potential ambiguity between the dialogues of Plato in his own "Socratic period" and the works of anyone else engaged in the same genre. Any ambiguity, however is purely theoretical, as Plato is the only Socratic discussed here.

Having made that clarification, the dialogues of Plato in his Socratic period have some distinctive features, that is, characteristics that set them apart from his other work. Chief among these shared properties is sharp and lively dialogue directed at the exploration of the nature of a particular concept, typically a moral one, such as virtue (*Protagoras*), piety (*Euthyphro*), friendship (*Lysis*), courage (*Laches*), or temperance (*Charmides*). A related common attribute is the pursuit of definition as the key element in the conceptual study on hand: What is virtue? What is piety? And so on. The search for a definition usually unfolds as a debate between Socrates and a main antagonist who is a supposed, usually self-proclaimed, expert on the matter under consideration, but it is also amenable to dramatic treatment as a joint effort carried out by the main characters. Another defining quality is that the discussion ends without a definition, or without even a resolution, though producing substantial conceptual clarification. A typical ending depicts the antagonist rushing off (as in the case of Euthyphro, who urgently takes his leave to keep another appointment he just happened to have remembered) after a stupefying and humiliating battle of wits with Socrates, who tears down every definition and perspective offered.

Plato's other dialogues, those that are not Socratic, are more constructive than destructive. While this is true, labeling the distinction in these terms runs the risk of confusion with a more prominent division between a so-called "critical" period and a "constructive" one, jointly exhausting the dialogues that are not Socratic. Perhaps, then, it is better to express the difference in reference to the more amicable circumstances featuring more cooperative characters in the dialogues that are not Socratic. These are more harmonious and collaborative than polarized or combative. In other words, they focus more on developing a viewpoint than on demolishing competing ones. Even where they are dedicated to analysis rather than development, they are more positive than negative. This being so, the characters interacting with the protagonist tend to be supportive rather than antagonistic, especially in comparison to the Socratic dialogues driven by a protagonist bedazzling a main antagonist.

These distinctions and others like them add up to a generally prominent difference between dialogues that are Socratic and those that are not, thus frustrating the search for an overarching philosophical system governing the entire corpus, not to mention complicating the problem of discerning Plato's view in all that is said.

What Plato says is usually perfectly clear. The difficulty arises because we cannot be certain whether what he says is his own view, so long as he chooses to say it through characters in a drama. This is not a unique choice among the contemporaries of Plato, whether they be engaged in philosophical or nonphilosophical literature. But it is with respect to Plato that we are most likely to regret being deprived of direct intellectual access as might be found in treatises. As it is, having opted for dialogues instead of treatises, Plato severs himself from the audience. The dialogues are even thought by some scholars to be intended as pedagogic devices to stimulate the thinking of students on certain issues instead of as expressions of Plato's own conclusions on such issues.

Regarding his lectures, where he would indeed have shared his personal convictions, experts are divided: Some say that none of his lecture notes survived, while others claim that he did not lecture from notes, which, therefore, were not lost but never existed. Either way, the problem would have been circumvented by the preservation of class notes by students, but we are deprived of these as well, leaving us with nothing conclusive regarding his convictions.

External testimony, for example, that of Aristotle (*Physics* 209b11–15) in a parenthetical reference to a point of divergence between what Plato writes in the *Timaeus* and says in person, raises the possibility of an unwritten teaching, shared face to face with disciples but never published. This would mean not only that Plato himself avoided publication, but presumably also that either his disciples were sworn to secrecy or their class notes were lost, possibly both. Evidently, any confidentiality agreement could not have been entirely effective given the sheer existence of the legend, a believably documented one, albeit with testimony rather than direct records.

Even if any or all of this is true, we can hardly rest assured where we stand. This is because the possibility of an unwritten teaching, no matter how plausible, actually serves as a gateway to an alternative interpretation rather than as a means to enhance and enrich the prevailing effort to understand what we have on hand. While this deserves fuller consideration, provided later on (§ 2.3, § 2.4), suffice it to say here that the unwritten teaching is normally invoked in opposition to the mainstream effort rather than in support of it. The words allegedly uttered by Plato in private do not match, explicate, or entail the ones recorded in the dialogues. The difference is not one of diametric opposition, but of inconsistency, wherein what is in the dialogues could be reinterpreted to accommodate the oral tradition, which makes it possible to use the latter to understand the former. The reverse, that is, the possibility of reinterpreting oral tradition to accommodate what is in the dialogues, might also be true, but it is irrelevant, given that the point is not to draw on the dialogues to improve our understanding of the testimonial evidence, which has never been in serious need of clarification, especially not from a source itself controversial in meaning, but to proceed in the opposite direction. This being so, scholars interested at all in the unwritten teaching are usually interested in it as the definitive guide to understanding Plato, resolving any conflict between the reported oral tradition and the *ipsissima verba* of canon in favor of the testimonial evidence.

Fortunately, obstacles to determining Plato's true views, preferably though not practicably with certainty, do not detract from the value of discussing the contents of the dialogues handed down as belonging to Plato, regardless of whether they all represent his philosophy or some are his reports or interpretations of the philosophy of Socrates, or of other influences. It is, after all, what passes as philosophy in these dialogues that Plato is famous for. We might need to ponder and elucidate what we find there, and possibly even to unscramble it, but we need not abandon it altogether. We certainly need not second-guess it on the authority of fragments of external testimony that may or may not lead us toward the truth. This is not to deny the reliability of external testimony but to fear the risk of being diverted from the right path by the promise of being directed toward it. Failing to understand Plato's words is one thing, but trading them for somebody else's is quite another. Inside information of this sort might indeed be useful, even indispensable, but its standard utilization in supplanting rather than supplementing the information already in hand should raise some flags. There might well be something missing in the picture. Then again, we could be looking for a missing link that never existed to begin with. Worse, we just might find it. The prospect, with or without success, should not blind us to the reality: What we have to work with is impressive enough as it is.

On the other hand, this is not a license to ignore reasonable reservations on whether what we have is truly a link to the mind of Plato. Nor should anyone rest comfortably without at least considering the possibility that what we have in the dialogues is not even a philosophical system, if that is understood as anything like an integrated set of positive doctrines. None of this keeps us from working on, and with, what we have. The skeptical challenge is not against taking what we have seriously but against treating everything else as irrelevant. To be fair, it does not ask us to abandon what we have in hand but to reconsider canon in view of other evidence, indeed, overriding and even revising it where necessary, but not simply brushing it aside, nor trading it on a whim. Describing it as abandoning the dialogues might not be fair since its mission is in fact to explain the dialogues. We can reject the approach, but we ought not to ignore the evidence.

2.2. Approaches to Plato

2.2.1. Primary Divisions

Labels abound in the interpretation of Plato. They almost invariably come in pairs, and, in that case, usually with deep institutional divisions. The leading ones, those at the most fundamental level of analysis, may be laid out as follows:

- dogmatic versus skeptical;
- unitarian versus developmental;
- continental versus analytic.

A brief description of each of these in itself might be helpful before a comparative assessment. While these divisions do not exist in isolation from one another, understanding the ways in which they tend to intersect requires understanding the tension peculiar to each. This will help in developing a general classification, or at least in appreciating efforts to do so, given that multiple vantage points are a natural temptation to look for the big picture (§ 2.2.3), whether or not it exists.

- The first of the three basic divisions, contrasting a dogmatic approach with a skeptical one, represents disagreement about whether the corpus is a gateway to indoctrination in Platonism, whatever that may be. Already introduced in the beginning of this chapter, the essential dispute here is about whether the dialogues impart doctrine, the alternative being that they exercise the intellect in critical thinking, without inculcating a specific conclusion or imposing any particular creed, though possibly manipulating the general educational program in a particular direction, any direction, as opposed to nowhere at all.

  Technically, a true division in this context would have to be between dogmatism and nondogmatism, the first holding that the dialogues impart doctrine, and the second that they do not, thus having no bearing on whether they advocate skepticism instead. This is indeed the modern formulation. Yet the original division was in fact between dogmatism and skepticism, the latter representing the *de facto* alternative to advocating positive views, and contemporary discussions still tend to use the same terminology, often in full awareness that skepticism is not the only alternative to dogmatism.

The actual choice of terms does not matter as much as the realization that opposing views do not necessarily force a choice on us. In this particular case, we can consistently reject both alternatives in the opposition between dogmatism and skepticism, but we cannot sensibly reject both dogmatism and nondogmatism. Not being a dogmatist does not automatically make Plato a skeptic. He was probably neither. Nevertheless, the terminology of the original distinction need not be avoided just because it is silent on the third possibility. It does, after all, represent an actual, historical opposition. Using the term "nondogmatism" to cover skepticism, and more, would be correct, but it would also bury some relevant detail. Such a switch in terminology is best reserved for arguments on how to interpret Plato rather than for reviews of how he has been interpreted.

- The second division, pitting the unitarian against the developmentalist, represents disagreement about whether the entirety of the work originates from a fixed philosophical and literary outlook, as opposed to evolving over time with major shifts in thought and style. This is the difference between producing everything from a mature perspective and growing with one's work. The disagreement, though, is not about whether the corpus shows signs of internal conflict, but about how to explain it, given that it exists. In other words, unitarians do not deny the apparent ideological heterogeneity any more than developmentalists try to prove it. Both deal with it as is, unitarians by positing a unity underlying apparently disparate viewpoints, developmentalists by embracing these as actually incongruous and arranging them in groups purportedly reflecting intellectual growth.

- The third division, juxtaposing the continental and analytic traditions, represents a divergence in textual analysis, roughly between emphasizing the drama and emphasizing the logic, though these are by no means mutually exclusive possibilities. This is about whether it is better to favor the dramatic clues or the philosophical arguments in interpreting any particular dialogue, the first alternative representing the continental approach, and, the second, the analytic. Although a choice is not necessary, a joint focus on drama and logic being not only conceivable but practicable and desirable as well, the debate is obviously between those who find the choice unavoidable, with each side finding the basic principles of the other an impediment to the fullest pursuit of its own agenda.

2.2.2. Secondary Divisions

The divisions just introduced do not bring out all the schools of thought, but they do exhaust the interpretive possibilities at the most general level. A few comparably popular divisions are associated with proper names. Among such approaches, we may count the Straussian platform, so-called because of its origination with the interpretive strategies of the philosopher Leo Strauss (1946, 1952, 1964, 1983), who made the recovery of hidden meaning the primary aim of literary criticism, based on the guiding principle that the deepest convictions of great philosophers never make it into print as unambiguous declarative sentences strung together in a forthright address aiming at full disclosure. We may also count here, that is, among proper names with a claim to fame, though entirely independently of Straussians, the Milan-Tübingen paradigm, named for the cities representing the locus of academic activity by scholars locating the deepest convictions of Plato in the unwritten teaching, either exclusively or primarily, thus leaving the written work either devoid of definitive doctrine or mottled with incomplete reflections of the original creed and derivative bits and pieces thereof. Neither approach, by design, rewards a propensity for probing deep into the logic of arguments, each instead nurturing an awareness of the dramatic context.

Both fall under the category labeled "continental" in the short list above (§ 2.2.1). They can also be classified as "esoteric" approaches, and indeed are, perhaps even more often. This brings up yet another major designation, but not necessarily another division. In fact, the epithets "continental" and "esoteric" are often used interchangeably in the context of interpretive approaches to Plato. The term "continental" is often reserved for emphasizing the precedence of dramatic over logical elements in textual interpretation. The term "esoteric" also has that connotation, but it carries the emphasis one step further, not merely shifting the focus from the argument to the drama, but going beyond the text altogether, typically to bring in the interpretive framework of the oral tradition, in an effort to test the actual words against the allegedly actual thoughts. The choice of nomenclature is strictly a matter of emphasis. One and the same interpretation can be found labeled "continental" as often as it is designated "esoteric," depending on who is doing the reviewing, without, however, anyone missing the mark in diagnosing the actual affiliation.

That said, "continental" and "esoteric" are not synonymous terms, certainly not in a lexical sense, but also not when the context is restricted to philosophical traditions, or when it is confined even further to literary criticism. In fact, each of the terms, particularly "continental," may suggest different things when considered generally as a school of philosophy and when predicated specifically of the interpretation of Plato. They are synonymous only because, and when, they are used synonymously. This leaves plenty of room for disagreement over usage, but only in the sense of a coexistence of different preferences, not in the sense of a clash between right and wrong. Hardly any ground is available for quibbling sensibly or usefully over whether a particular approach to Plato is continental or esoteric.

Given that "continental philosophy" is not a geographical designation but a methodological one, following the reference should simply be a matter of delineating characteristics common and unique to the corresponding philosophical tradition. Yet what is simple is not *ipso facto* helpful. What are the defining characteristics of continental philosophy? The answer is typically no more enlightening than absurdly taking the reference in a geographical sense as denoting philosophy done in the European mainland. The geographical conception would indeed be a confusion, but it would be no more misleading than the proper methodological sense whose stock specifications project such an infallibly high level of generality as to cover at once areas as widely divergent as deconstruction, existentialism, phenomenology, and structuralism. The proper extension of the term reveals such loosely connected elements that the preferred route often turns out to be a negative definition, drawing a contrast with analytic philosophy.

Since analytic philosophy is commonly conceived as proceeding with a rigorous preoccupation with analysis, continental philosophy might be thought of as proceeding without one. But how helpful is this? And is it true? Such recourse to a negative definition of continental philosophy can be only as useful as the positive definition of analytic philosophy. The essence of the analytic tradition is the treatment of philosophical problems with conceptual solutions, promoting the clarification of concepts as clearing the way for an analysis of issues, and the entire process relying heavily on the tools of formal logic. Drawing out the contrast with continental philosophy, however, is a delicate matter. Associating one with logical analysis basically requires distancing the other from it. This can easily turn into an invective against the value of the continental tradition, as if logic and rationality were alien to it. Repudiating analytic methods does not push the continental approach outside the domain of "real philosophy" any more than meeting at the Café Central at the old Bank- und Börsengebäude in the heartland of Europe places the logical positivists of the Vienna Circle in the continental tradition.

This does not mean that it is impossible, or even all that difficult, to distinguish between continental and analytic approaches, which can, quite to the contrary, be easily told apart, especially if a specific frame of reference is in question. The functional distinction in the context of Platonic studies, as already mentioned above, is between following the dramatic clues, as done in the continental approach, and dissecting the arguments, as done in the analytic approach. What makes the continental approach esoteric at the same time is the acknowledgment of the permissibility, the desirability, and, as the case may be, even the necessity, of going beyond not just the arguments but the whole dialogue, whether by reading between the lines to uncover messages best not put into so many words, lest the author be persecuted or prosecuted for them, or by seeking a concordance between the text and the unwritten teaching.

What truly divides scholars on this issue is not so much the differential emphasis on drama versus argument, but the value assigned to what is not readily in the text, be it drama or argument. Otherwise, no esotericist ignores arguments that are at once clear, sound, and relevant, merely out of an eccentric fascination with what can instead, or in contradiction, be gleaned through the dramatic elements. And, likewise, one of the safest bets around is bound to be that not even a direct descendent of the logical positivists will be so artless and obtuse as to miss a particularly arresting and revealing dramatic subtext in a rush to get on with the logic-chopping. The two camps are coming closer together in emulating each other's strengths. The esotericists no longer shrink from schematizing syllogistic chains or filling out enthymemes to make a point, and the analytic philosophers are no longer embarrassed to include symbolism and metaphors as integral parts of their analyses. What still divides them, however, and what will continue to do so indefinitely, is their attitudes toward the text itself. They can never merge completely so long as one refuses to be bound by the text and the other to depart from it.

2.2.3. The Big Picture

How does everything fit together? Or does it? Do the prevailing approaches to Plato admit of a general classification resembling anything like a big picture? Certainly, a thread of reasoning, or chain of connections, presents itself, but is it there by design, or is it the result of the natural tendency to perceive order in, or to impose order on, what otherwise lays in chaos? Equally important, are the links laid out in a linear chain of connections, or are we dealing with some sort of mesh pattern? It is difficult to tell before following the leads, at least the obvious ones.

We might pick up the thread, or chain, at the tension between continental and analytic approaches, a tension which spills over into the distinction between dogmatism and skepticism, thereby cascading further into the one between unitarianism and developmentalism. Or perhaps it spills over into these two distinctions separately, and not through one into the other. But surely the absence of any links in any direction would be more difficult to establish, and less likely to appeal to our intuitions, than the presence of one or another. The fact of the matter would seem to depend on whether unitarianism and developmentalism are ways of being dogmatic, or whether they can be classified instead, or, more interestingly, at the same time, under the skeptical perspective, or, in the least exciting scenario, and fortunately the least tenable one, whether no significant correlation can be established.

Is the esotericist a resourceful dogmatist refusing to be frustrated by the inadequacies of the obvious? This is certainly a possibility. It would make the prototypical representative predisposed either to transcending, and even contradicting, the realm of literal meaning in search of hidden meaning, as in the case of Straussians, or, to going outside the corpus altogether in search of unwritten doctrines, as in the case of the practitioners of the Milan-Tübingen model. By way of contrast, the obvious role of opposition left for the analytic philosopher is that of a skeptic (nondogmatist) who denies that a unifying doctrine is to be found within the dialogues, and cares little for what goes on without, characteristically chalking up any and all internal inconsistencies to changes in view, instead of thinking outside the box in any way to figure out what is not inside.

This is a generalization polarizing the interpretation of Plato into one big disagreement instead of several smaller ones. It does not, by any means, reflect an academic consensus on the state of Plato scholarship. It is a deliberate oversimplification for the sake of exploring plausible possibilities. It might even be outright wrong in certain respects, distorting some details and ignoring others. But the various divisions in the interpretation of Plato are not inherently discrete or disparate, and seeking out the big picture will hardly obscure issues that are already unresolved. We may end up with more than one big picture, or, more sensibly, with different renditions of the same panorama, but this should not leave us any worse off than where we stand with none at all.

The three divisions in the original list are related, or, perhaps more accurately, correlated, if not causally or essentially, then certainly statistically. The short list in the beginning of the section (§ 2.2.1) can be rearranged along the threads of methodological and interpretive affinity cutting across the debates:

- dogmatic (doctrinal) ↔ unitarian ↔ continental (esoteric)
- skeptical (nondogmatic) ↔ developmental ↔ analytic

This is basically the same list with the underlying matrix structure transposed to create a new row bringing together the first terms in the original three lines, set against another new row drawing on the second terms in the original three lines.

The arrows are not intended to propose a flow or direction. They merely represent connections, left rather vague, possibly even with added confusion through the use of double-ended arrows, adopted specifically to avoid the unwarranted determinacy and restriction of the traditional ones that point only to the right. And the linear alignment is not intended to suggest that only the middle term is linked with both of the other two, the others being limited to a single link each, in either case with the middle term. The succession need not be thought of as linear, nor as starting or terminating at a specific point.

Perhaps triangles would have worked better than lines. But that configuration would have signaled commitment to a full triangular relationship, whereas the reality is just not that clear, not clear enough, that is, for commitment to every permutation implied by the form. Although the line schema might fare no better in this regard, replacing it with a triangular model would be a pretentious refinement bringing no additional clarity or accuracy. Even so, if need be, a Platonist will surely be able to imagine a triangle without actually seeing it on the page.

The point, in any event, is to determine the pattern, if at all discernible, in scholarly tendencies across the issues. This particular rendition of the big picture assigns the dogmatist a unitarian view of Plato's philosophy, grounded in, or explored through, a continental, or, what is the same, esoteric, interpretation of the corpus. The skeptic, in contrast, finding the corpus wanting in philosophical uniformity, not to mention unity, swears by developmentalism, pursuing the analytic approach to interpreting the dialogues.

Not everyone will agree to this breakdown. Rowe (2003a, pp. 98–124), for one, does; at least partly. In one of his several masterly introductions to Plato, the one for a broader historical compendium by Cambridge, he connects dogmatism with the continental tradition, and skepticism with the analytic, except that in the former case, he refers specifically and separately to esoteric and Straussian strands, indicating that he identifies esotericism exclusively with the Milan-Tübingen school in contradistinction to the Straussian perspective, which he simply recognizes as what it is without classifying it as esoteric (Rowe, 2003a, pp. 119–120). His emphasis on the particular distinction does not overturn his general agreement with the bipolar alignment of tendencies sketched above. The first line of the schema above includes both the Straussian and Milan-Tübingen perspectives under the "continental" heading, taken to be contextually synonymous with "esoteric." Rowe's preference for separating them can only be applauded, as no two schools of literary criticism can be more different, but this does not change the fact that both can be deemed esoteric in the fullest sense of the word even if they are esoteric in entirely different ways. In each case, the guiding principle is that Plato's considered opinions, his deepest convictions, are not out in the open for all to see. Each party thus recommends an esoteric interpretation, the Straussians in elevating hidden meaning above the given meaning, and the Milan-Tübingen scholars in promoting the unwritten teaching over the written words. The main difference is that the Straussians need little more than the canonical manuscripts to reach their conclusions, as the point is precisely to mine the text itself for hidden meaning, while the others have to leave the realm of canon to reach theirs, drawing as they do on the testimonial evidence of an oral tradition. Each one thereby promises privileged insight into the real Plato, a literary recluse not easily captured through conventional means.

At any rate, the precise classification of the Straussian and Milan-Tübingen models has no bearing on the organizational breakdown of Platonism at the broadest level. The two approaches belong in the same general division as varieties of esotericism, at least from the negative perspective that neither one reduces the interpretation of Plato to a straightforward reading of the dialogues.

To return to the broadest level of analysis, the schematic classification above is a reasonable scenario, showing a natural alignment of preference patterns. Yet the connections therein are neither unassailable nor complete. They are not even the results of actual surveys or sampling studies among scholars, except, as mentioned, for the partial support of Rowe (2003a, pp. 119–120), among any number of other advocates. They are simply the results of reflection on what a specific commitment or inclination in one dimension might push a sensible person toward in another. This need not always pan out as sketched above. For example, the unitarian is depicted as a dogmatist because it is difficult to be a unitarian about anything without a corresponding set of doctrines, or at least one. But the developmentalist can also be a dogmatist, given that development can proceed with the replacement of one doctrine by another, instead of being indicative of the absence of a doctrine to begin with. From these two relationships, it follows that the dogmatist can technically be either a unitarian or a developmentalist, inasmuch as dogmatism is about having opinions as opposed to not having them, and is entirely indifferent to whether the commitment in question reflects a fixed position or evolves as a changing viewpoint.

As for the skeptic (nondogmatist), the sketch on hand already acknowledges developmentalism as a possibility, in fact, as the expected complement, but is unitarianism thereby denied as an alternative outcome? Although it is not intuitively appealing, scholars do not rule out the possibility. How can an interpretive perspective supporting a unitarian organization also support a developmental formation? This seems to be the intuitive obstacle in the case of skepticism. But if dogmatism can support both unitarian and developmental renditions, why might not the same hold for skepticism? For example, skepticism might lead perhaps to developmentalism, as already discussed, or possibly to unitarianism, presumably in consistently withholding assent to any positive doctrines, though it is sometimes difficult to see how this would be unitarianism, as consistently assenting to no view at all sounds too much like the opposite of consistently holding the same view, which is the essence of unitarianism. Such contradictions, however, tend to be merely apparent. This one, in fact, is: If the defining feature of unitarianism is the holding of a single fixed viewpoint, then to question whether that requirement is satisfied by consistently withholding assent to any positive doctrine is actually to question whether the consistent withholding therein constitutes a viewpoint, not whether it is singular as opposed to plural, nor whether it is fixed as opposed to variable, and even less whether it is held as opposed to not held. Even if this presents a logical problem, it is not accompanied by a psychological problem, the absence of which allows for doxastic consistency in the skeptic's being a unitarian.

The problem might simply be in polarizing the issues beyond necessity, beyond, that is, the intensity actually indicated by a plurality of viewpoints. Alternatives need not be diametrically opposed to accommodate different possibilities. Along the same lines, in another of his generalist introductions, one appearing in a multiple-author companion dedicated exclusively to Plato, Rowe recognizes that "'developmentalism' is as much a strategy for *maintaining* a kind of 'unitarian,' or at least unifying, approach, as it is an alternative to it" (2006a, p. 16; Rowe's emphasis). To cite another example, Wolfsdorf (2008, pp. 3–28, especially p. 6, n. 9) sees no problem in connecting either a unitarian or a developmentalist perspective with either a dogmatic or skeptical perspective, acknowledging the full range of combinatorial possibilities.

These two examples demonstrate scholarly opposition to slavish dedication to any configuration. They embrace the possibility of various renditions of the big picture in the study and interpretation of Plato. Hence, their counsel is both general and negative.

A specific alternative to the unifying picture sketched above may be found in Beversluis (2006, pp. 85–111), who treats unitarianism and developmentalism as varieties of dogmatism, or as a division within dogmatism. Specifically, he takes dogmatism as the thesis that Plato advances philosophical doctrines in the dialogues, wherein unitarianism holds that the corpus reflects the progressive revelation of a viewpoint already held in fully developed form before the first piece published, and developmentalism presents the alternative that the corpus is the product of a changing viewpoint as opposed to the piecemeal disclosure of a fixed one. In contrast, he takes skepticism, which he prefers to call "nondogmatism," to be the view that Plato does not advance philosophical views or doctrines in the dialogues, either because he held none, as advocated, for example, by Press (2000, pp. 27–38), or because he shared none in writing, as advocated, say, by Nails (1995, pp. 229–230; 2000, pp. 15–26). Whether or not Beversluis has got it right, the point here is that this would not necessarily make someone else wrong. The pieces obviously fit together in more ways than one.

The big picture is like a kaleidoscope, hardly ever turning up a disagreeable combination. This includes the distinction between the continental and analytic traditions. As touched upon earlier, the model on hand aligns the continental, or esoteric, with dogmatic and unitarian perspectives, and, the analytic, with skeptical and developmental perspectives. But this is not set in stone. It can go the way of the shuffle apparently apposite to the other divisions.

One thing that precludes a unique and unexceptionable solution to integrating the various divisions, that is, restriction or reduction to exactly one definitive formula, is the variety of ways of being in one camp or the other in any division, particularly in the opposition between dogmatism versus skepticism. Choosing between dogmatism and skepticism, for example, is a matter of taking a position either in reference to the dialogues severally or in reference to the corpus collectively or in reference to both at once.

To illustrate, with respect to the dogmatic approach, the position that each dialogue advocates a well-defined doctrine, or that such a doctrine may be identified in each dialogue, no matter what may be said of their collective consistency, is different from the position that the corpus as a whole advocates a well-defined doctrine or set of doctrines, or a central creed. Both positions demonstrate the dogmatic or doctrinal strand. (The latter, the one pertaining to the corpus as a whole, may be considered unitarianism, which would, in this case, make it a type of dogmatism, though it would not thereby restrict dogmatism to unitarianism, nor unitarianism to dogmatism). Either one may be maintained. And both at once may be held, or even required, in a particularly strong brand of dogmatism.

At the opposite end, comparable prospects await the skeptical approach. The nature of the skepticism in question may be that the dialogues do not severally advocate any particular doctrine, or that the corpus as a whole does not constitute a philosophical system, being instead composed of loosely, if at all, connected conclusions, which are drawn in the first place for the sake of the logical exercise they afford rather than toward the advancement of a particular viewpoint. The skeptic, that is, may be skeptical of the didactic intent or content of each dialogue, or of the corpus, or of both. Or even of Plato himself.

Given the range of possibilities, a dogmatist and a skeptic need not even be in direct opposition, though they most often are. A dogmatist affirming only that each dialogue defends a definite position could get along quite well with a skeptic denying merely that the corpus as a whole does not offer a unified philosophical viewpoint.

A similar reconciliation, though partially, not fully, may be struck, as mentioned earlier, between the continental and analytic traditions. Esotericism can become too rigid in denying that anything at all of Plato's philosophy is to be found in the dialogues. At the other extreme, no greater flexibility awaits in the view that the dialogues afford full access to the mind of Plato, or that they afford the only possible access, full or otherwise, nothing else being useful even in a supplementary capacity. Fortunately, neither esotericists nor analytic philosophers are all extremists. Assessing Plato's literary *modus operandi*, Hyland (2004, p. 90) contends that "the expression of his views could not have been the guiding intention of his writing dialogues." He also suggests that, if this is true, finding out Plato's views should not be our guiding intention in reading his dialogues. This displays a moderate esotericism, far from holding Plato's work to be sterile with respect to his thought. The claim is not that we will find nothing of Plato in the dialogues, but that we will not find everything there. But so long as we do not make it our "guiding intention," and, in fact, even if we do, we may reasonably expect to find something there, as Hyland fully admits.

Indeed, there must be better ways to transmit dogma than to weave it into drama, but the choice does not prove the exact opposite intention. To be more specific, the entirely sensible position that "the expression of his views could not have been the guiding intention of his writing dialogues" does not, in turn, imply that "the concealment of his views must have been the guiding intention of his writing dialogues," an aim best served by writing nothing at all.

The dialogue form is naturally suitable for doing philosophy, and its utilization need not imply anything about hiding or disguising convictions. These are, no doubt, sensible inferences, but they are not conclusive. Yes, dramatic conversation affords the author incomparable opportunities for concealment. But this is not the only possible explanation for the choice, especially with the Socratic dialogue constituting a *bona fide* literary genre rather than an idiosyncrasy of Plato. Nor is that genre known for its popularity with subversive philosophers, nor with subversive writers who are not philosophers, nor even with philosophers who are not subversive. Thus, dialogic expression is not proof of fearful concealment, though it is indicative to a degree worth exploring. It just is not conclusive. In fact, any concealment, if deliberate at all, need not even have been fearful. It could be explained just as well through pedagogical assumptions. Plato might simply have been inclined to demonstrate philosophy in action without indoctrination, that is, attempting to teach without inculcation, thus putting everything in the mouths of characters instead of declaring anything in the first person. This, in turn, does not imply or require a meticulous effort to keep his every conviction out of print.

2.2.4. Historical Context

The next chapter, dedicated entirely to the works of Plato, specifically from a structural and organizational standpoint, discusses the analytic perspective in detail, especially in its contribution to the standard developmental model for interpreting the intellectual output of Plato. Focusing more here on the alternatives, including a bit of the historical background, at least with a slant toward recent history, might contribute to more balanced coverage overall.

What is particularly engaging in this respect is the esotericism of the Milan-Tübingen school. This is not to say that the Straussian perspective is not worthwhile, but that it is not unique to Plato. The Straussian model of reading the text closely to uncover its hidden meaning can be applied in any context. Although it is especially appropriate to Plato, and specifically applied to it both by Strauss and by his disciples, this does not change the fact that it is universal. It is not about Plato; it is about interpretation. It works comparably well with, and is just as pertinent to, Hobbes, Locke, and Rousseau, to name a few of the other sources of great books attracting the interpretive interest of Strauss and Straussians. In contrast, the Milan-Tübingen school is exclusively about Plato.

Straussianism holds additional complications. For one thing, it has not been a unified school of thought since the death of Leo Strauss in 1973. A rift between followers situated in the opposite coasts of the continental United States has been definitive, with the West Coast Straussians originally led by Allan David Bloom at the University of Chicago and the East Cost Straussians associated with Harry Jaffa at Claremont McKenna College in California diverging as much from each other as from ideologies that are not Straussian. A further problem, a practical one, is that the Straussian perspective, no matter whose, is difficult to discuss intelligently because Straussians are often prejudged on the merits of how Straussianism is perceived in its political and polemical dimensions. It would be counterproductive if not outright misleading, at this point and in this context, to tiptoe around the *ad hominem* rejection of Straussian interpretations of Plato primarily in reaction to connotations of the general sociopolitical outlook typically associated with Straussianism. Cutting through the diatribe and moving past the prejudice often turns out to be difficult for both sides. Straussian interpretations of Platonic dialogues tend to be rejected as often in sweeping reaction to the neoconservative ideology associated with the platform as they do on the basis of a point-by-point disagreement with the accuracy of the reading of the corresponding passages. None of this is an excuse to ignore the alternative. The fact that it transcends Plato, however, is a reason to direct the reader to the original sources

(Strauss, 1946, 1952, 1964, 1983) instead of proceeding deeper into exegesis and commentary, especially in a broad survey such as this.

As for the Milan-Tübingen school, the debate always revolves around Plato. Objections are no less passionate, but they are free of political undertones. The central paradigm, named after the geographical focal points of a single school of thought, constitutes the leading alternative to the transparent Plato of the analytic tradition. Put simply, the alternative is that Plato's dialogues do not transmit Plato's doctrines, which are instead reserved for an inner circle of students and colleagues, and, even in that context, revealed and discussed only orally. To be sure, the dialogues do put some views out there, as the corresponding discussions readily demonstrate, but the claim is that these are not Plato's true convictions. This does not mean that they are the opposite of, or inconsistent with, what he believes, but that they are not fully representative of it. They cannot be stitched together to identify his philosophy, at least not clearly enough for a thorough understanding. Accordingly, penetrating the surface requires not just close reading, substituting this for that in an effort to uncover a hidden message, but reaching all the way through to the unwritten teaching. The truth to be discovered is not a secret message encrypted in the text but an entire creed intimated external to it. The unwritten teaching may, in turn, reveal to us messages previously hidden in the text, or appearing so for a lack of proper orientation, but the sequence of discovery starts outside the corpus.

Despite the order of its compound name, "Milan-Tübingen," the approach originates in Tübingen, later expanding to Milan. The Tübingen component derives from the Eberhard Karls Universität Tübingen, one of Germany's oldest universities, founded in 1477 and situated in the city of Tübingen in Baden-Württemberg. Among its many international distinctions, it is the birthplace of a unique strand of esotericism in Plato studies, or, more accurately, the place of rebirth, given that the rudiments of the approach, or at least the inspiration for it, can be traced all the way back to Aristotle. The modern inception was a seminal doctoral dissertation by Hans Joachim Krämer in 1959, arguably one of the most resounding dissertations in philosophy in the twentieth century. Prominent proponents of the platform also include Konrad Gaiser (1963, 1980) and Thomas Alexander Szlezák (1985, 1993, 2004), both responsible as much for shaping Tübingen esotericism as for advocating it. The Milan component owes its place in the geographical designation to the efforts of Giovanni Reale, originally hailing from the Università degli Studi di Parma, later moving to the Università Cattolica del Sacro Cuore in Milan, where he established a Center for Platonic Studies, subsequently joining the Università Vita-Salute San Raffaele, also in Milan. Reale is best known for his contributions to the history of ancient philosophy (1975–1980), attracting a particular following worldwide with his work toward the development of a new model for the interpretation of Plato (1984).

While the approach is less popular in the Anglo-American world, its introduction there dates back to a momentous reaction to Krämer by Gregory Vlastos (1963). What makes this a milestone is not so much the specific nature of the reaction as it is the analytic camp's recognition of the esoteric alternative as a serious challenge. Vlastos, however, is not the point of origin of the opposite camp. Given that, at least in modern times, the esoteric interpretation is a reaction to the dogmatic interpretation, rather than the other way around, Harold Fredrik Cherniss (1945) precedes Vlastos on the analytic front. Be that as it may, esotericism has been finding a voice in the Anglo-American world not only through translations of the output of the Milan-Tübingen school, where German and Italian reign supreme as the languages of Platonism, or rather, of Plato studies, but also through work originally in English by the likes of John Niemeyer Findlay (1974).

Of course, the opposition between the continental and analytic interpretations of Plato does not originate in an intellectual vacuum. These are, as Rowe (2003a, pp. 119–120) says, the modern analogues of an ancient debate. For example, the dogmatic perspective starts with the Academy immediately after the death of Plato, giving way, within a few generations, to the skeptical perspective. Thus, the question of interpretation is nearly as old as Plato.

Still, the modern formulation of the interpretive debate, specifically as an opposition between unitarianism and developmentalism, can be located in the nineteenth century, fully maturing in the twentieth.

Unitarianism dates back to the work of Friedrich Daniel Ernst Schleiermacher, whose translations (1804–1828) of the dialogues were prized at least as much for the introductions appended, with particular interest aroused by the framework principle that the corpus is the result of the progressive revelation of a fixed outlook, laid out in a particular order for pedagogical reasons. Proponents of unitarianism in its heyday include Hans Friedrich August von Arnim (1896, 1912), Paul Shorey (1903, 1933), Paul Friedländer (1928–1930), and Werner Wilhelm Jaeger (1933–1947).

Developmentalism starts with Karl Friedrich Hermann (1839), who was the first to identify a Socratic period in Plato's works, insisting that the implied development, that is, the intellectual development evident in the corpus, is due to actual development in the thought of the philosopher. Like many other interpretive trends, the honor for the origin of this one can be assigned to Aristotle, who treats the Socratic dialogues differently from the rest of Plato's works, but Hermann can safely be regarded the first to articulate the difference as a theory, including, for instance, the thesis that the first book of the *Republic* was composed separately as a standalone work predating the rest of the dialogue (1839, pp. 538–540). Faring better in anglophone circles than did unitarianism, developmentalism flourished with the input of George Grote (1865, pp. 246, 272–273), William Keith Chambers Guthrie (1975), and Gregory Vlastos (1991). It still tends to be associated more with Vlastos than with anyone else. This is largely because he is at the intersection of developmentalism and the analytic tradition, making him the prime target of contemporary esoteric reactions.

Possibly the best way to decide between opposing approaches to Plato, particularly between esoteric and analytic interpretations, is to go to the source of the controversy: the unwritten teaching. This is not the only issue dividing them. And they differ as much in style and methodology as they do on assumptions. But this is the heart of the controversy. So, a basic understanding of the unwritten teaching is essential to the formulation of an informed and intelligent judgment regarding the opposition in and around Plato.

A basic understanding of the written teaching is, of course, no less important. And it might be strange in a chapter dedicated to the thought of Plato to discuss his unwritten teaching before his written teaching, in fact, largely instead of it. But there is a natural presumption that a reader of secondary literature will be familiar with the corresponding primary literature. This book should not be one's first encounter with Plato. Moreover, the sense in which this chapter is dedicated to the thought of Plato is not so much as an explication of his thought, but more so as a guide to and demonstration of the issues involved in accessing or even identifying it. Just as the next chapter is dedicated to the works of Plato from the perspective of the entire corpus, this one is dedicated to the thought of Plato from the perspective of his overall philosophy. He may not even have one. But settling that one way or the other will surely enrich any effort to discuss his specific positions on various issues.

Plato expressed an opinion on everything. He is not primarily an epistemologist, or primarily a metaphysician, or primarily an ethicist, or primarily an aesthetician. He is all of these things, and more. He is primarily a philosopher. If there is any possibility that he is profoundly committed to a central doctrine or doctrines, written or not, then that possibility deserves consideration before everything else, or at least as much as anything else.

Any effort in this direction may well start with the esoteric perspective, specifically the Milan-Tübingen paradigm, if only because its proponents are united in what they nominate in this regard. Their emphasis on the unwritten teaching constitutes a unified proposal for a specific candidate for the philosophical foundation in question. In contrast, commentators on the written work remain divided in their opinion of what, if anything, takes precedence over everything else. Still, even in a range of options, the forms stand out as the central focus in any initiation into Plato. Accordingly, the remainder of the chapter is devoted to a basic overview of the unwritten dimension of what allegedly makes Plato tick, followed by a discussion of the forms as taking on a comparable role in the written work. The point of the specific combination is not to establish precise analogues in the oral and written traditions, or even to forge methodological links between the unwritten teaching and the canonical corpus, but to consider the inspirational counterparts at the most fundamental level of the thought of Plato, separately according to testimony and as a matter of record.

2.3. Unwritten Doctrines

Esotericism has been in the backdrop of Platonic studies since Aristotle. It can be traced back to him at least in the fabled form of an unwritten doctrine or doctrines. The illustrious protégé was the first to compare Plato's written and oral teaching, referring to the latter as "agrapha dogmata" (ἄγραφα δόγματα), literally, "unwritten dogmas (or doctrines)" (*Physics* 209b11–15). Never quite able to compete with the undisputed word of Plato in the transmission of his written work, or, strictly speaking, setting aside any implications of certitude about authorship, never even able to compete with the manuscripts handed down as the Platonic corpus, the perspective of the unwritten doctrine took on a legendary status throughout history, often consulted and cited in an auxiliary capacity, but never growing into a primary role in Platonic interpretation, except for sporadic command performances severally attracting critical acclaim but collectively falling short of a mainstream paradigm shift. Neoplatonism may be considered a grand exception, as it brought out certain themes with greater emphasis than warranted by the manuscript tradition alone. And a second wind emerged in the twentieth century as more and more scholars started to assign definitive importance to the unwritten doctrine, or doctrines, as the case may be, even elevating it above the actual text in the event of a contradiction with canon. A watershed in the history of interpretation, or at least an emblematic milestone in that regard, was Gaiser's (1963) initiative to collect all the relevant sources, publishing them as an appendix to his pioneering work on Plato's unwritten teachings.

The first question that naturally comes to mind is about content: What is this unwritten doctrine? Or, if there is more than one, what are they? Only one answer can be entirely accurate: We do not know. The man whose doctrine it was never wrote it down. Hence, the name "unwritten doctrine." In fact, according to the logic of any esoteric perspective grounded in the existence of an "unwritten doctrine," no matter what that may be, we should be able to expect that Plato's reason for keeping it secret should have been binding on all his disciples, with the doctrine or doctrines in question never seeing the light of day. We simply should not know about this. Yet security leaks date as far back as Aristotle. This means either that Aristotle was a traitor or that the so-called "unwritten doctrine" was not so hush-hush to begin with.

Indeed, the sensible esotericist insists not that Plato wanted to keep the general public ignorant of his deepest convictions, which he discussed only within his circle of disciples, but that he did not publish or publicize his every thought in the precise way or moment he thought it. To think otherwise, that is, to think of Plato as attempting to keep the general public from finding out what he really thinks, would be to construe the Platonic corpus as deliberate disinformation, as opposed to an inadequate reflection of available information. Thus, the focus has to be on why? Why is there even room for an unwritten doctrine between what Plato thought and what he wrote? Given that he loved to write, if the volume of dialogues is any indication, why did he not write what he believed? To be more specific, why did he not share in writing his understanding of "the truth, the whole truth, and nothing but the truth"?

His mistrust of the written word is a stock answer, but it has little explanatory power since he did in fact resort to the written word just as much as the next philosopher, possibly even relishing it more than any other. Hence, the standard appeal to passages in letters (2.314b–c, 7.341c–d, 7.344c–d) or dialogues (*Phaedrus* 274c–275e, 276c) where Plato disparages and discourages writing does not explain why he put so much into writing, taking care to do it so beautifully. And it certainly does not explain why he would keep the good stuff secret, spending, actually wasting, a lot of time on lesser thoughts, basically, promulgating either lies or garbage.

We are all agreed that the *Republic*, at least, is not garbage. The same may safely be concluded about the *Phaedo*, *Symposium*, and *Phaedrus*. And we might find widespread agreement to the same effect regarding lesser masterpieces and even works that are not quite masterpieces. In fact, the entire corpus should pass the strictest of quality control mechanisms, easily so in accordance with the standard we have come to expect from subsequent contributions to the history of philosophy.

The possibility of deliberate deception is even less likely because, if the aim were to conceal the philosopher's considered opinions, this might have been achieved more efficiently by publishing nothing, or by placing an embargo on doctrinal discussions and keeping printed matter circulating internally, rather than by producing a large volume of good literature that demonstrates serious philosophy, without revealing the party line, so to speak. To get to the truth of the matter, we need to go to the source, that is, the actual oral teaching. Fortunately, we are not entirely without recourse, despite what the name "unwritten" might suggest.

Plato's "unwritten doctrine," or, perhaps more appropriately, his "unwritten teaching," since what is at issue is not necessarily a solitary formula but a body of knowledge, or at least of information, refers to anything he might have taught but not published. This is basically the difference between what he might have taught at the Academy and what he wrote in the dialogues. Scholars are not holding their breath for Plato's lecture notes to be eventually uncovered or recovered. The consensus is that no such notes existed in the first place. The next best thing would be notes taken by those in attendance. These, however, are lost. What we do have is the later reflections rather than the simultaneous notes of witnesses. These might be supplemented by the accounts of those tutored by those in attendance, that is, the records of the students of students of Plato. Our best bet, in the end, is Aristotle.

What we learn from Aristotle in this regard is not expanded or elaborated elsewhere to any significant degree, but it is also not contradicted elsewhere. It is thus largely reliable, despite Aristotle's reputation for being a bad historian, often for misunderstanding and misrepresenting Plato, or worse, for misrepresenting

Plato without misunderstanding him. What we get from Aristotle, or from anyone else, is not in the form of a systematic distinction between what Plato taught at the Academy and what he put into writing, but a conspectus, again, not particularly systematic, of his basic philosophical outlook, irrespective of whether it might be privately held, closely guarded, or publicly declared. The bulk of this comes in the first book of the *Metaphysics* (1[A].6), where Aristotle undertakes an exposition of Plato's philosophy (*Metaphysics* 987a29–988a16), without any regard to the distinction between inside information and public knowledge, otherwise implicit in the reference in the *Physics* (209b11–15) to *agrapha dogmata*.

Specifically, Aristotle tells us that Plato's metaphysics is built on two fundamental principles: the "one" and the "indefinite dyad." The indefinite dyad, indefinite because the definite dyad would be the number two, and because an unqualified reference (just plain "dyad") would be at best ambiguous, is also called the "the great and the small." It is the material substratum of reality, representing plurality, or, strictly speaking, duality, open in either direction, thereby accommodating extensibility and divisibility *ad infinitum*, in contrast to the rigidity of unity inherent in the concept of the one. These two principles together account for everything else, that is, for every other aspect or element of existence. For instance, the forms are generated from the one and the indefinite dyad, while sensible things are generated from the forms and the indefinite dyad (*Metaphysics* 987b19–22, 988a10–15). This means that, ultimately, the one is the cause or essence (or the cause of the essence) of the forms, while the forms are the cause or essence (or the cause of the essence) of all other things (*Metaphysics* 988a10–11, 988b4–5).

This is not all there is to the unwritten teaching, but it is the gist of the matter. A proper overview would have to take stock, additionally, of the explicit positioning of mathematical objects between the forms and sensible matter, thereby completing the picture of reality offered (*Metaphysics* 987b14–35). And the causal relationships, no doubt, require explication. But the foundation of the unwritten teaching, what separates it from the written work, is the two metaphysical principles, the one and the indefinite dyad. The debate, then, is about how seriously we are supposed to take this metaphysical foundation. Classic discussions describing and analyzing the unwritten teaching dispassionately, that is, without aiming primarily to recommend or reject its adoption as an interpretive platform on Plato, although dated from the perspective of the specific arguments on either side of the debate, can still be rewarding in developing a balanced perspective of precisely what is at risk and in determining the strength of the relevant evidence: Burnet (1914, pp. 312–332); Findlay (1974); Guthrie (1978, pp. 418–442); Ross (1951, pp. 142–153); Sayre (1983, pp. 75–117; and not so dispassionately in 1993a, pp. 167–184); Taylor (1960, pp. 503–518).

2.4. Lecture on the Good

The typical highlight of discussions on the unwritten teaching is a notorious lecture by Plato on the good. This is ironic. On the one hand, it fits the concept of unwritten doctrine so well as to constitute prime evidence in that regard, because it is a lecture, and thus spoken, not written, and, more important, because the reported content is absent from the written works, which are bereft of at least that particular presentation, if not of all oral doctrine. This is not to deny that the written might reflect the unwritten, especially given clear signs of convergence, for example, in the *Republic* (6.504e–509c, 7.522b–534c) and in the *Philebus* (65a), but were there no difference, there would be no distinction. On the other hand, it contradicts the concept of unwritten doctrine because it is a public lecture, whereas secrecy, for whatever reason, plays a major role in that very concept. Secrecy is why the unwritten doctrine is unwritten in the first place. The point is not so much that the doctrine is spoken rather than written, but that it is concealed rather than revealed. What breaks the mold in the example of the notorious lecture is not that it is spoken, but that it is public. Here we have an open session on what is otherwise supposed to have been whispered in closed circles rather than shared with everyone. This is not far from putting it in a book intended for general circulation. The anecdote thus looks as much like a counter-example as it does like a confirmation of the existence of an unwritten teaching, or, to be precise, the existence of a significant or definitive unwritten doctrine.

Commentators disagree on whether this was an unusual occurrence, perhaps even a unique one, never to be repeated, or merely an episode in a series, providing a glimpse into a routine practice. If it was indeed a singe lecture, this would be a mitigating factor in the otherwise puzzling disclosure of "inside information." This is the possibility that the lecture was a solitary exception intended to "shock and mock the curious Athenians, making it plain to them that the question of what is 'good' is altogether too difficult for a couple of hour's treatment in public" (Thesleff, 1993, p. 39; see further: Gaiser, 1980, pp. 5–37). If, on the contrary, it was repeated regularly, particularly as part of an established practice, this would then make the public disclosure all the more curious, or the scenario of unwritten teaching all the more contradictory. This is the possibility that the lecture we know about was a representative example of a series of lectures rather than a single presentation, and probably a series of connected lectures as opposed to a standard performance repeated over and over, thus resembling a course more than a single lesson (Ross, 1951, especially pp. 148–149). A third possibility, a kind of hybrid of the other two, is the scenario that the "famous public lecture" was a unique event whereas "lectures on the good" were indeed standard practice in the Academy, with the single public lecture, even if intended to "shock and mock" the uninitiated, drawing on the academic course.

The lecture itself is lost. Among the surviving reports on it, the standard reference is the account of Aristoxenus of Tarentum, relating what he heard from his teacher Aristotle, who, in turn, personally attended the lecture in question. The highlights of what we get through Aristoxenus (*Elementa Harmonica* 2.30–31) is as follows:

> It is surely better to begin by stating the nature of the inquiry, and what it involves, so that with this foreknowledge we may proceed more easily on our chosen way, and recognize what stage we have reached and not unwittingly deceive ourselves about the matter.
>
> As Aristotle was wont to narrate, this was what happened to the majority of the people who heard Plato's lecture On the Good. Each came expecting to learn something about the things which are generally considered good for men, such as wealth, good health, physical strength, and altogether a kind of wonderful happiness. But when the mathematical demonstrations came, including numbers, geometrical figures and astronomy, and finally the statement, Good is One it all seemed to them, I imagine, utterly unexpected and strange; hence some belittled the matter, while others rejected it.
>
> And what was the reason? They did not know what was coming but went along, like argumentative people, at the mere word. But if someone begins with a summary of his lecture, then, I hold, everyone who came to listen is free either to give up, or, if he likes, to stay, with the understanding he has already gained.
>
> Hence Aristotle himself, for these very reasons, as he said, used to give his prospective audience a summary of what he intended to say, and in what manner. Likewise it seems to me better, as I said at the beginning, to have foreknowledge. [Gaiser, 1980, p. 5; footnote reference markers and parenthetical Greek annotations omitted]

Writing nearly nine hundred years later, Simplicius notes that, among others, those present at the lecture included Speusippus, Xenocrates, Hestiaeus, and Heraclides of Pontus (*Commentary on Aristotle's Physics* [CAG 9] 1.4.187a, 3.4.182b).

The context of the Aristotelian account we get through Aristoxenus is obviously not one of admiration or appreciation but censure. Moreover, the criticism is not even about the subject matter. It is about the presentation. In fact, it is not about the presentation itself but the public relations work preceding the presentation. Aristotle evidently condemns Plato, as does Aristoxenus, for failure to prepare the audience adequately for the lecture, leaving people in the dark on what to expect. Nevertheless, even this brief and negative overview is informative enough, attesting to Plato's predilection for a mathematical account of the good.

The lecture reinforces the readily demonstrable, and, in fact, well-documented, preoccupation with the good, and points thereby to a possible reconciliation with what is a matter of record. The most salient discrepancy between the so-called unwritten teaching and the received manuscripts is the two fundamental metaphysical principles of the oral tradition versus only one in the Platonic corpus.

Worse, the principle in the corpus cannot simply be assumed, and possibly not even demonstrated beyond question, to be one of the two in the legend. In fact, the comparison itself bears two different interpretations, one focusing on the forms, the other on the good. A tempting approach is to take the fundamental metaphysical reality posited in the written work to be the forms. But the good also presents itself as the ultimate source of reality, unless we are prepared to ignore the *Republic*, in the course of the grand folly required to look elsewhere for a metaphysical first principle.

Either way, we are left with a singular force that does not seem to be, at least on the face of it, identical with either of the two in the unwritten teaching. Part of the problem is superficial. In the case of the corpus, what we are looking for is the good, not the forms, which, after all, can be accounted for by the good, thus making it the first principle from the canonical perspective. The proper comparison, then, is between the good, as explicated in the written work, and one of the two principles embraced in the unwritten teaching. The obvious choice is to equate, or at least associate, the good with the one.

This is defensible if only because these are the supreme ontological and metaphysical realities in their respective realms, written and oral, both of which belong to Plato, but which cannot simultaneously be attributed to the same sane philosopher unless the respective supreme realities are one and the same, or very nearly so, or unless they are, at the very least, sufficiently related to remove an otherwise mad or duplicitous contradiction. There is also independent evidence. Unfortunately, it is not conclusive. The prime evidence is the legendary lecture itself (Aristoxenus: *Elementa Harmonica* 2.30–31), allegedly declaring unequivocally that the good is one, which finds corroboration in the written work (*Republic* 6.507b–511e; 7.514a–520a; *Philebus* 65a). Additional support is available in Aristotle's portrayal of Plato as associating the one with good, and the indefinite dyad with evil, though the portrait, skeletal as it is, might have benefited from sharper lines (*Metaphysics* 988a14–15, 1091b11–15). The association is undeniable, but also unclear.

A more sophisticated connection between the written and unwritten teaching is sometimes sought in the fourfold ontological classification of the *Philebus* (23c–27c): limit; the unlimited (*apeiron*); their mixture; the cause of the mixture. The connection advocated here is that the one corresponds to the limit, and the indefinite dyad to the unlimited (Hackforth, 1972, pp. 37–43; Sayre, 1983, pp. 95–117, more extensively at pp. 118–186). This interpretation is more than modern speculation on a felicitous fit. It goes back to Aristotle's testimony that Plato equated the indefinite dyad with the unlimited, explicating both severally, and therefore either indifferently, as the great and the small (*Metaphysics* 987b20–27). This, of course, is a return to the level of testimonial evidence. Although modern studies, such as those, just cited, by Hackforth (1972) and

Sayre (1983), elevate us above this level, they do not take us beyond the scope of reasonable disagreement.

The case is simply not compelling in either direction, leaving enough room for the emergence and maintenance of a tradition of esotericism, and, alternatively, for rejecting all testimony contradicting the corpus, and thereby denying an oral tradition altogether. Where difficulties arise, however, is not so much in privileging internal versus external evidence, but, ironically for a study of Plato, in avoiding a dialectic between the two. The esoteric position, after all, is censured less for placing faith in the alleged words of Plato outside the corpus than for refusing to do the same for his authentic words within the corpus. Likewise, the analytic position is denounced less for what it finds on the inside than for what it ignores on the outside.

The fundamental problem is that what is on the inside is not consistent with what is on the outside, at least not readily so. This, in turn, is a prime opportunity for dialectical exploration. There is, to be sure, a massive ongoing debate, but polarization into two opposing camps hardly counts as dialectic, at least not in the sense required for Platonic progress. What is required is the contribution of parties willing and able to devote disinterested attention to both sides of the issue. Even then, a solution may not present itself, but only then will the effort have been fit for Plato.

2.5. The World of Forms

Plato is perhaps best remembered for his theory of forms. Oddly enough, the theoreticity of that theory is in dispute. The alternative, rarely pursued positively, or even supplied explicitly, is presumably that it is something less serious and less impressive than a theory, more like an opinion. Indeed, calling it a "theory" without addressing the dispute might be presumptuous. On the other hand, this is no excuse to mark up a page with unsightly scare quotes, making the issue appear more frightful than it actually is. The prevailing debate is important enough to deserve and extraneous enough to require separate treatment, provided in the next section (§ 2.6). Any reference to "theory" outside that context, whether preceding or following the relevant section, is merely conventional rather than argumentative. No judgment is intended where one is not announced.

Having said that, it should be safe, even at this point, and, in fact, at any point, to assert that Plato is perhaps best remembered for introducing us to his world of forms. The forms are intelligible templates for what we perceive in the sensible world. Conversely, what we perceive around us is the sensible reflection of a supersensible reality, a realm that can be grasped only by the intellect, not by the senses. Yet being accessible through the mind alone instead of registering as sensory inputs does not mean that the forms exist only in the mind. They exist in fact. They are not subjective constructs. They have objective reality. Not only do they exist, they represent the highest level of reality, that which is not confined by the boundaries of space and time.

Such positions border on philosophical doublespeak: The question intended is whether something, whatever is being discussed, exists in space and time. The answer given is that it exists outside space and time. The real controversy, in the meantime, is whether it exists at all, a problem buried in the disagreement over whether the meaning of existence is fixed to space and time.

This is not to say that the question has not been answered. The answer may even be legitimate, but it is not clear, nor even comprehensible, at least not without substantial elaboration. We simply do not understand what it means for anything to exist outside space and time. It not only contradicts convention, but it taxes the imagination as well. We cannot conceptualize it. We can certainly think and talk about it, but rarely with a clear notion of the nature of such transcendent existence. The closest we come is in our thinking of numbers and universals. These are things whose existence we debate. But the same metaphysical quagmire, ontology without space and time, also includes everything we pretend to exist without really believing it. Elves and fairies and various other sprites come to mind. These are things whose existence we reject. Where do the forms fall? It is not clear. Obviously, Plato assigns them a superlative claim to reality, far from fairyland. How, then, do we evaluate his position? We certainly cannot get very far scientifically. We should be happy just to understand the position. But we cannot properly evaluate it, if this means anything like verifying its accuracy.

Fortunately, this is not a difficulty unique to Plato, as can be confirmed by anyone who has ever debated or even considered the existence of God. The analogy is not a call for faith in the existence of the forms. It is merely a suggestion that the best we can do is not to prove their existence but to understand the implications of that possibility. Ignoring the finer points of the semantics of existence, we may rightly adopt the following position: The forms, being intelligible, are immutable, and, being immutable, perfect, whereas we live in a world of appearance constituting an imperfect approximation to reality.

This, then, is the basic concept as well as the theory. In other words, a description of the concept is all we get by way of theory. This is complemented by illustrations of its application in various dialogues, where each demonstration may inspire us to flesh out the theory further. But, on the whole, Plato leaves us wanting for detail in an exegetical puzzle comprising scanty and scattered statements on what the forms are, copious references to various different forms with no further elaboration on the general concept, and plenty of coverage in arguments using the forms to shed light on something else rather than the other way around. This being so, a definitive exposition of the theory is not to be found in Plato's own words. Worse, he seems to be uncomfortable with the theory, questioning it, revising it, gradually reducing philosophical reliance on it, and arguably even abandoning it over time. One might do well to consult the *Phaedo* and the *Republic* for an understanding of the theory, study the *Parmenides* for a critique, and examine the *Sophist* for redirection.

This does not mean that the rest of the dialogues can safely be ignored in this regard. Most any of the remainder will help round out the picture, but none is crucial by itself. Many invoke the theory, making full use of it toward the establishment of a particular thesis, without thereby expanding it. Even the early dialogues in pursuit of definitions unifying a multiplicity of instances (or examples) of a single concept, usually a virtue, are thought to be either rudimentary versions of the theory or the Socratic anticipation of forms, or possibly a combination of influence by the master and inspiration by the pupil. Plato gets a lot of mileage out of the theory in the works of his middle period, including, in addition to the two already mentioned, most notably, the *Cratylus*, *Phaedrus*, and *Symposium*, and the prominence of the forms in a dialogue as late as the *Timaeus* frustrates views that he abandoned the theory in old age.

These considerations already infringe on another taboo in Plato studies: prejudging the order of composition. The chronology of the dialogues, together with the contentious problems involved, is taken up in detail in the next chapter (§ 3.3), but the *Parmenides* and the *Timaeus* are so central to discussions of the fate of the forms that separate coverage here becomes inevitable rather than premature. Put simply, their joint significance, ignoring, for the sake of expedience, the entire debate on chronology, is that the *Parmenides*, coming at the end of the middle period, challenges the forms, while the *Timaeus*, coming near the end of the late period, continues to embrace them. The late presence of the forms makes their earlier abandonment *prima facie* unlikely. While this description is in terms of the standard developmental account, examined fully in the next chapter, it is more or less substantiated by the evidence of stylometric studies, also covered in the same chapter. This means that scholars eager to disagree on chronology, not merely on the actual sequence but on the very possibility of determining anything in that regard, nevertheless agree that the *Parmenides* predates the *Timaeus*. No doubt, there are exceptions. But even general agreement is significant. If the *Parmenides* and the *Timaeus* actually belong where they are customarily placed in the development of the corpus, Plato cannot have given up the forms. This is why the late position of the *Timaeus* is a favorite reference for anyone denying that the *Parmenides* kills off the forms, or requires their modification beyond recognition, and a challenge to anyone claiming that the forms die with the *Parmenides*, or shortly thereafter.

Invoking the presence of the forms in the *Timaeus*, however, does not automatically settle the issue. Two objections are at least conceivable. The first is a direct denial: no forms in the *Timaeus*. The second is an indirect challenge: no *Timaeus* in the late period. The first would have to be in the form of the typical scholarly dispute proceeding with mutually contradictory interpretations of exactly the same passages. The second is more interesting, if only more inspired and provocative. The first would be no less pertinent to philosophical progress, but it is hardly defensible unless recast less outlandishly as a rejection of the equivalence of what passes as forms in the *Timaeus* and the middle period, as opposed to absolute opposition to the presence of any forms at all in the *Timaeus*.

The second, more interesting debate flourished in the 1950s, and continues to engage scholars. The roots are in an exchange between Owen and Cherniss:

Specifically, Owen's (1953, pp. 79–95) appeal to the philosophical community to reconsider the chronological position of the *Timaeus* in the Platonic corpus has its historical counterpart in Cherniss's (1957, pp. 225–266) exhortation to preserve the place of that dialogue in the late period. Owen's break with tradition, though not the first revisionist move in this area, proves radical enough to agitate the preservationist stance, finding fresh impetus in the response of Cherniss. Aiming to put the forms to rest for good, Owen transfers the *Timaeus* from the late to the middle period, dubbing it "the crowning work of the *Republic* group," and placing it, together, of course, with the *Critias*, just before the *Parmenides*. This vitiates the thesis that Plato retains the forms after the *Parmenides*, given that the thesis is grounded almost entirely in the supposition that he retains them in the *Timaeus*. Cherniss (1957, p. 226, n. 3, n. 4) notes that Owen is not the first to place the *Timaeus* before the *Parmenides*, but he responds directly to Owen anyway.

The matter has been under discussion ever since. One of the more interesting contributions comes from Sayre (1983, pp. 15–16, 256–267), who is roughly aligned with Owen, thus agreeing that the *Timaeus* comes before the *Parmenides*, though not necessarily before the entire dialogue. Sayre insists that the *Timaeus* predates the second part of the *Parmenides*, and possibly the first as well, but he is not uncomfortable with placing it between the two parts (presumably somewhere around 135c, depending on the recognition and placement of transitional material belonging no more to one part than to the other). There is virtually no end to interesting highlights in the ongoing debate. Further details are not relevant here, and the essential issue is clear enough in the historical exchange between Owen and Cherniss. A concise overview covering later developments as well as the original dispute is available in Zeyl's (2000, pp. xvi–xx) introduction to his own translation of the *Timaeus*.

The position of the *Timaeus* in relation to the *Parmenides* has a cascading significance. The discussion is typically anchored to composition order but it is just as relevant to dramatic order. This, of course, is not a substitute for settling the question of chronology. In fact, it has no bearing at all on that question, but it has some interesting implications of its own. The main difference is that the dramatic context, in contrast to the chronological, has little if any room for debate.

First, consider the nature of the experience in the typical encounter with the *Parmenides*. Reading the *Parmenides* is like finding out there is no Santa Claus. The analogy is not perfect, but the disappointment is undeniable in either case. Just as those growing up with presents from Santa every Christmas find out sooner or later that the reality had all along been far less splendiferous, those introduced to Plato in the standard fashion sooner or later come across the *Parmenides*. We are first enchanted by the powerful imagery of the forms, mesmerizing us in dialogue after dialogue, only to be thrown abruptly into a state of confusion, suspicion, and disillusion. Admittedly, this scenario assumes that one reads the dialogues in a certain order. But one almost always reads the dialogues in that certain order. They are presented that way. Whether in high school or in college, classes either do not bother with the *Parmenides* at all, or they pick it up only after covering the central dialogues. Independent reading is also guided toward this sequence by the standard arrangement of collected works, with the notable exception of the Hackett edition. Belief and even indoctrination in the forms precedes reservations regarding their existence.

Now, imagine a different approach. What would happen if we were to read the *Parmenides* first and the central dialogues immediately afterwards? Suppose we read the *Parmenides*, *Symposium*, and *Phaedo* in that order, possibly even making room for the *Republic* and the *Phaedrus* anywhere between the first and the third. We might even add the *Timaeus* just before the *Phaedo*. What is the story arc we would encounter in this sequence? One possibility, if we assume that the dialogues feature the same character Socrates, as opposed to five or six different heroes each of whom happens to be named Socrates, is that a philosophically oriented young man starts out in life with some passionate albeit confused ideas about the forms, encounters a sagely old philosopher convincing him to keep questioning that outlook toward greater clarity, and eventually dies at a fairly mature age with even greater passion about apparently the same basic set of beliefs.

The outcome here would seem to be that the young man has worked the problems out to his own satisfaction, and possibly to the satisfaction of the author, despite never revealing that solution to the audience of the dialogues. The early encounter with the old philosopher has taught the young one to keep challenging himself on convictions short of certitude, never brushing aside difficulties, yet never letting them overturn what seems right otherwise. This leaves no room for developments inimical to the forms.

This is not a contrived thought experiment. It is not an unreasonable scenario. It is precisely the order in which the story unfolds if the dialogues are read in dramatic order.

If dramatic context is to be assigned any relevance at all, the relative dramatic date of the *Parmenides* is a nagging curiosity, especially on the interpretation that the dialogue questions or rejects the theory of forms: Why would the youngest dramatic Socrates (*Parmenides*) throughout the entire corpus be assigned to a dialogue challenging that which the oldest dramatic Socrates (*Phaedo*) still obviously maintains on the day of his death? The dramatic order of the dialogues is covered in greater detail in the next chapter (§ 3.5), but even knowing only that the sequence starts with the *Parmenides* and ends with the *Phaedo*, an uncontroversial fact, is suggestive enough in regard to the question whether the forms survive the *Parmenides*.

Notwithstanding the overwhelming tendency to focus on the *Timaeus*, the case admits of other clues to the same effect. For example, Guthrie (1978, pp. 57–61, especially pp. 59–60, n. 3) finds an abundance of evidence for the presence of forms, and, thereby, against the abandonment reading, in a host of references in dialogues commonly accepted to be later than the *Parmenides*, with the list including the *Sophist* (248e–249d, 254a, 256a–b), the *Statesman* (269d, 285e–

286a), the *Philebus* (15a–b, 58a, 59a–c, 61d–e, 62a), and the *Laws* (859e). Just as important, the turning point itself, where the theory is supposedly repudiated, remains committed to the forms, as the *Parmenides* ultimately and expressly embraces and endorses the theory despite all the difficulties exposed therein. This comes out in the transition between the two parts of the *Parmenides* (particularly 134e–135c), where the call is not to abandon the forms but to study them. The assessment of the sagely Parmenides is not that the forms do not exist but that knowledge of them requires extraordinary intellectual gifts (*Parmenides* 135a–b), which should then be developed through training in dialectic (*Parmenides* 135d). This combination of talent and training is both necessary and sufficient for understanding the forms and instructing others in turn. This much is explicit in the text. The implication, at least in the way the drama unfolds, is that Socrates already has the gift and would thus benefit from the dialectical training, as demonstrated throughout the second part of the dialogue (*Parmenides* 135e–166c).

At any rate, the absence of a dedicated presentation, laying out the entire theory in a single session as opposed to revealing bits and pieces of an account evolving over a substantial period, if not a lifetime, has forever precluded agreement regarding the nature of the theory of forms, as well as its place in Plato's philosophy.

The literature is vast, even where the scope of consideration is limited to book-length treatments of the topic: Ross's rendition in *Plato's Theory of Ideas* (1951) is an indispensable classic. This can be supplemented profitably by a more recent treatment such as Dancy's study of how the theory takes shape between the early and middle dialogues, a process he discusses in *Plato's Introduction of Forms* (2004). Any examination of the earlier theory would benefit from Allen's insight, which he shares bundled together with his translation of an early dialogue, released in a single package as *Plato's "Euthyphro" and the Earlier Theory of Forms* (1970).

The notorious crisis at the end of the middle period is a favorite subject. Respected work in this area includes, though is by no means limited to, studies by Meinwald (1991), Pelletier (1990), Rickless (1997), and Sayre (1983, 1996).

A common pedagogical practice is to introduce the theory together with the reaction of Aristotle. Anyone having missed that opportunity, or wishing to deepen the experience, would do well to consult Fine's perspective laid out in her book *On Ideas: Aristotle's Criticism of Plato's Theory of Forms* (1993).

The list of secondary literature on the forms can be extended far enough to exhaust the curiosity, and even the patience, of the most voracious reader. For an appreciation of the diversity of thought, the entries mentioned might usefully be rounded off by the collection of essays edited by Welton as *Plato's Forms: Varieties of Interpretation* (2002).

2.5.1. Philosophical Significance

Despite disparate views on matters of interpretation, the philosophical legacy of the forms is celebrated unanimously as a momentous contribution in at least two respects:

- First, the appeal to forms marks one of the earliest and most famous statements of metaphysical dualism, separating reality and appearance with a division constituting a benchmark for ontology throughout the subsequent course of Western philosophy, and becoming a source of philosophical inspiration for Christian as well as Islamic theology.

- Second, Plato's identification of the realm of forms with permanence, and, the sensible world, with change, represents a resourceful solution to an age-old problem regarding the possibility of stability in a world of flux, previously dividing philosophers in a debate often narrated in contemporary classrooms in reference to the ever-changing world of Heraclitus and the permanent one of Parmenides.

Plato's dualism is not limited to a distinction between the intelligible realm of forms and the sensible realm in which we operate. He distinguishes just as forcefully between the soul and the body, making insight into the intelligible world more than an empty possibility, with the soul able to grasp that which the body cannot detect. This is not necessarily a simple division: The soul is sometimes an indivisible entity, as presented in the *Phaedo*, and sometimes a composite one comprising reason (mind or intellect), spirit (will or volition), and appetite (desires and emotions), as presented in the *Republic*, and even more graphically in the *Phaedrus*, where reason is the charioteer of a carriage drawn by spirit and appetite. However, its precise constitution does not change the fact that the soul, whether atomic or divisible, stands in sharp contrast to a material body, and that it is this incorporeal part of us that has access to the supersensible realm of forms. Plato's views on the soul are taken up in detail in chapter seven, dedicated primarily to the account of immortality in the *Phaedo* (§§ 7.1–7.12), and secondarily to the treatment of the same concept elsewhere (§ 7.13), supplemented by a broader sketch of a comparative psychology independently of the question of immortality (§ 7.14).

This still does not do justice to Plato's dualism. Neither the form-particular distinction nor the soul-body distinction is the end of the story. The model is rich, and the possibilities vast, apparently bounded only by the imagination. Thesleff (1993, pp. 17–45; 1999, pp. 14–25; 2009, pp. 397–410), for one, identifies and discusses ten different contrasts in this connection: divine/human; soul/body; leading/being led; truth/appearance; knowledge/opinion; intellect/senses; defined/undefined; stability/change; one/many; same/different. He both states and demonstrates that the list is illustrative rather than exhaustive, though his chief concern is not the range, but the essence, of the inherent dualism: He does not even call it a "dualism," preferring instead to speak of two levels of the same universe, which he examines in his *Studies in Plato's Two-Level Model* (1999; anticipated in 1993; reprinted in 2009). The basic idea is that the distinctively Platonic contrast is not polar but complementary. As such, the paired elements are constituents of a single world, not principles of division, or forces of repulsion, between two separate worlds. One element is dominant, for example, the first item listed in each pair above. Although this marks the primacy of one level over the other, both are fully contained in the same reality. Not only is the contrast grounded in a single world, it is positive rather than negative: The emphasis is not on the difference but on the correspondence, the reciprocity, the harmony. This is the sense in which Thesleff interprets the relationship between forms and particulars, a distinction in fact subordinate to the fundamental paradigm of two levels, but historically elevated to a more prominent position, owing mostly to excessive critical attention dating back to Aristotle.

As for the reconciliation of permanence and change, this was a much-needed development, a necessary condition for serious engagement in philosophy, placing the enterprise on a sure footing, particularly as it pertains to an investigation of knowledge and critical reflection on morals. In epistemology, the forms provided the stability needed for constructing a fertile philosophical system in and about a field otherwise in inscrutable flux and allowing no greater insight than the possibilities represented by subjectivism. As a corollary, the forms supplied the anchor required for a defense of absolute values and universal principles in ethics, without either succumbing to or necessarily denying the central observations of cultural relativism, and thereby enabling the development of a viable position on ethical objectivism. Similar benefits accrue in all areas where the prospect of constant flux discourages the initiation and orientation of a philosophical position, and that of permanence frustrates analysis and progress. Hence, the forms do not so much constitute a philosophy as they do a tool for doing philosophy.

The transliteration of the term Plato uses for the indigenous elements of this mysterious platform for philosophy is "eidos" (εἶδος), or, less commonly, "idea" (ἰδέα), the connotation in either case being something that is seen, as governed by the root verb "to see." We cannot, of course, "see" the forms literally, but etymology need not always be felicitous to be informative. The term was initially rendered into English as "idea," owing to the compelling visual resemblance to the Greek, but later preferences leaned toward "form," primarily to avoid the natural, but in this context misleading, association of "idea" with that which exists in the mind alone. Current usage still favors "form."

The terminology in contemporary discussions, particularly in English, is firmly anchored to a contrast between forms and particulars, nomenclature fashioned after the distinction between universals and particulars. Indeed, the theory of forms can be considered Plato's anticipation of universals in a scientific context grappling with the distinction between things and their properties. The absence of such a distinction in Ionian science, with a lack of insight into the matter even in Socratic Athens, makes the theory of forms all the more impressive. It also helps excuse ambiguities in what exactly the forms are, as well as a variety of derivative problems and unanswered questions, including whether souls and numbers and geometric figures are forms.

The forms are not identical with universals, which, though themselves far from uniform in treatment, are commonly subdivided into types (vs. tokens), properties (vs. substances), and relations (relative positions). The list might, with considerable disagreement, be expanded to include concepts, events, states, words, propositions, sets, numbers, geometric figures, and, in short, all abstractions, without regard to whether any of these are proper universals. Even then, the forms would not be exactly the same as universals, or abstractions, as they might be called, depending on how the list is filtered. For one thing, the existence of the forms is objective and absolute: They have objective reality in that their existence is not dependent on perception, and, from a purely internal perspective, in that they are not mere mental constructs. Their existence is absolute in that their reality is not in any way comparative, conditioned, contingent, dependent, derivative, qualified, or relative. Moreover, the forms have a causal relevance, which is generally denied universals or abstractions in contemporary discussions in metaphysics and the philosophy of language. In other words, the forms factor into reality as causal explanations, whereas universals or abstractions are generally considered in the current academic study of philosophy to be causally inert.

Due to the ongoing development of the theory of universals as an active concern, in contrast to the static historical context of the theory of forms, numerous other differences may be sought in areas left unexplored by Plato. However, the objective and absolute reality and causal relevance of forms stand out as the defining features in this regard.

2.5.2. Causal Explanation

The way the theory reconciles permanence and change in the distinction between a stable reality and a changing appearance is by making the thing in itself the causal explanation for the thing as it appears. Specifically, it removes the inherent tension, whether in different worlds or in different levels of the same world, through a causal explanation grounding appearance in reality. The form for anything is the reason why it is the way it is. Historians of philosophy are reluctant to speak of a causal theory prior to Aristotle, but this is Plato's answer to what makes anything what it is, ostensibly falling under what Aristotle considers a formal cause, but actually invoked, rather unsuccessfully, according to Aristotle, to explain a great deal more.

As a matter of fact, Aristotle reports Plato as covering both material and formal causes (*Metaphysics* 988a8–16), assigning the role of material cause to the indefinite dyad, while specifically classifying the forms as formal causes (*Metaphysics* 988b1–5), though acknowledging that the forms themselves are dependent on the indefinite dyad as a material cause and on the one as a formal cause (*Metaphysics* 987b19–22, 988a10–15). This characterization alone would limit Plato's account of causation to the causal dimension of being, which is satisfied by material and formal causes, as opposed to that of becoming, which calls for efficient and final causes. Aristotle does recognize a more ambitious aim in the Platonic project, but finds it unfulfilled in execution. Although he admits that Plato considers the forms to be causes in a comprehensive sense, covering both being and becoming, he finds the attempt wanting at least because the forms do not constitute a sufficient causal explanation without the addition of an efficient cause (*Metaphysics* 991b3–8).

While we may be informed by Aristotle's testimony on Plato's views, and educated by his judgment on the same, this should not be a substitute for a more direct route to both information and judgment. In that regard, textual evidence does not patently bear out or contradict Aristotle's interpretation. This is partly because Plato brings out different aspects of the theory in different places, and partly because Aristotle is not always clear on whether he is reporting or evaluating, nor on whether he is thinking about a specific written reference or his own privileged access to Plato's philosophy.

A safe general interpretation of information at the source would be that each form determines the essential nature common and unique to everything of which it is a form, so as not only to enable but also to give substance to designations identifying all and only things subsumed under that form. Forms are the referents of general terms, whether denoting types (e.g., horse, fire, circle), properties (e.g., white, hot, round), or relations (e.g., over, under, around). To cite an example offered by Plato himself, there are many beds, but only one form of bed, which is the same for each and every bed, and by virtue of which all beds are beds (*Republic* 596a–597d). This is intended to illustrate the principle that a unique form corresponds to a multitude of things of a certain kind, and derivatively that the singularity of forms accounts for the diversity of phenomena.

The relationship points to both causation and explanation. It affords a type of causal explanation, but the link between cause and effect, or between explanans and explanandum, is not entirely clear. Plato readily acknowledges substantial uncertainty in the matter, if emphatic hesitation by Socrates as a dramatic character counts as such acknowledgment (*Phaedo* 100d). To be sure, he does not leave us in the dark. He elucidates the relationship in several ways, but the multiplicity lends itself to contradictory accounts undermining the effort rather than complementary outlets fortifying it. For example, he speaks of the "presence" of the form in its earthly manifestations, and, just as vaguely, of a "communion" between the two. He also considers the objects of our experience as "participating" in their respective forms, and the forms as somehow "inhering" in the phenomena with which they are associated. At one end, the forms are paradigms, models, patterns, templates, blueprints, molds, causes, and reasons. At the other end, their empirical counterparts are copies, images, examples, manifestations, instantiations, reflections, effects, and results.

The inherent dualism inevitably runs into problems regarding the purported connection, causal or otherwise, between two discrete realms that are essentially incompatible. How can something incorporeal be a "model" for anything with spatial and temporal dimensions? In what sense can empirical phenomena "participate" in transcendent reality? Both questions are, in essence, demands for an account of the connection between the two realms. And the answers become no more obvious or authoritative when we take these realms as different levels of the same world than they do when we construe them as altogether different worlds. The problem does not turn on what is meant by "realm" in this context. Perhaps "venue" would be an even better term if what is desired is neutrality between "world" and "level."

In any case, the challenge is not so much about the locus of activity as it is about the agents involved. Even if the two-worlds interpretation were to be decisively supplanted by a two-levels interpretation, as suggested, for example, by Thesleff (1993, pp. 17–45; 1999, pp. 14–25; 2009, pp. 397–410), the same questions would then straddle two discrete levels of reality that are essentially incompatible. The difficulty is not that the forms and the particulars exist in entirely different worlds but that they are themselves entirely different kinds of things, representing ontological incompatibility, whether in different worlds or in different levels of one and the same world. This is not to glorify the difficulty but merely to define it. It is what it is whether it has an easy solution or none at all.

2.5.3. Self-Predication

A notorious problem discussed in the context of the connection between the intelligible and the sensible is the tenability of considering a form in terms of what it is a form of. Is the form of horses a horse, the form of fire, a fire, the form of circle, a circle? Derivatively, does the form of horses run a good quarter-mile, is the form of fire hot, is the form of circle round? Such questions illustrate what is commonly known as the problem of "self-predication" in forms, following terminology introduced by Vlastos (1954).

Plato revels in self-predication. He typically sticks with conceptual cases rather than tangible items. He does not often place himself in the position of making forms out to be farm animals. However, this makes little difference, as the practice seems no less counterintuitive in abstract than in concrete entities. We may find greater absurdity in considering a form to be a horse, but we would still find it sufficiently incredible that justice should be just, or piety pious, and so forth, which is precisely what Plato serves up (e.g., *Protagoras* 330c–e). This is not to say that no form can escape absurdity in self-predication. For instance, the form of invisibility would have to be invisible. Examples abound, all in the same vein: The form of perfection might reasonably be said to be perfect, the form of eternity is, no doubt, eternal, and the form of forms would have to be a form.

However, the possibility of self-predication without absurdity does not preclude a firm stance behind the negative reaction to classifying forms as perfect versions of the particulars of which they are forms, which would require their being essentially the same kind of thing as their particular instantiations. The pertinent question in this regard is whether the forms necessarily embody the characteristics defining their empirical counterparts. The question, in other words, is whether they must do so, not whether they can or might do so under special circumstances. The response is firmly negative. The affirmative cases (invisibility, perfection, eternity, formness, and so on) are all accidental, each concerning a general attribute a form has by virtue of being a form, and not a specific attribute it has by virtue of being the form of that attribute or of something with that attribute.

The denial of self-predication is not the way out. Even full repudiation still leaves a problem. In fact, it is half of the very problem intended to be exposed by questions probing into self-predication in forms. The point of such questions is to pose a dilemma construing the theory of forms to be either absurd or internally inconsistent: If the form of beds is taken to be a bed, the theory is absurd, and if it is not, it is unworkable, ostensibly because that which is not a bed cannot be a paradigm of it.

One way out is to take the dilemma by the horns, acknowledging that forms are indeed essentially different from what they are forms of, without giving up the claim to a workable theory. The dilemma is essentially a special version of the general question regarding the cosmological possibility of a connection between the world of forms and the one we experience around us. All such questions carry a bias in favor of the realm of experience, and against anything remaining outside, with their very construction conforming to the mental categories used in the conceptual organization of sensory inputs, and any difficulty or peculiarity laid on the doorstep of the forms. The challenge to demonstrate the connection between the two realms is actually something of a push for a commitment to a point or region of intersection, or, as the case may be, a moment or juncture of interaction, that is open to perception or observation or any other means of empirical verification.

Would the challenge be more reasonable, and, the theory, less problematic, if we were to pursue the dualism as two levels of a single world, say, in the manner of Thesleff (1993, pp. 17–45; 1999, pp. 14–25; 2009, pp. 397–410), rather than explicating it as two separate worlds? Under that scenario, instead of the form causing a phenomenon, or being the finest example of it, the phenomenon is how the form is manifested as an object of perception. How, if at all, does this change the situation? The immediate impression is that some sort of ontological continuity seems to be established. Perhaps the form of a horse does not have to be a horse any more than the actual animal inspiring an equine painting has to be a painting. This is a promising response to the problem of self-predication, but it is not the result of replacing the two-worlds model with a two-levels model. What is promising here is the delineation of the minimally required relationship between an original and its copy that still accounts for the fact that one is the original, and, the other, the copy, and that promise can be fulfilled just as well under the assumption that the original and the copy are in two different worlds. The obstacle never was the distance between the two but the difference between them.

Although the emerging solution, or, more accurately, the response identified above as promising, is not a function of switching interpretive paradigms, the opposite may indeed be practicable, with this particular approach finding a more natural setting in the two-levels model than in the two-worlds model. A still better model may be available: Perhaps this is not a question of two levels of the same world but two aspects of the same reality. Uniting forms and particulars as two aspects of the same reality seems to leave fewer loose ends than placing them in two levels of the same world. This, of course, assumes that the former yields one thing, and, the latter, two things in one place. If, on the other hand, the two levels are intended, not as divisions of the world hosting forms and particulars, a world bringing them together in the same place, but as the forms and the particulars themselves, each constituting one of the two levels rather than merely existing in one or the other, then the two-levels model is no less fitting under the circumstances than the two-aspects model. The model is irrelevant so long as the problem is understood to be about the things rather than their locations. The two-levels model is not necessarily inconsistent with this, but the two-aspects model captures it without ambiguity. Still, the proper interpretive paradigm is suggested by the potential solution rather than the other way around.

To return to the approach adumbrated above, the possibility of a minimally required relationship is well worth pursuing on its own, that is, with full indifference to whether the underlying assumption is of two worlds or of two levels or aspects of the same world. In fact, regardless of whether the analogy moves from the original to the copy or the other way around, the association does not require equivalence in kind: Rodin's *L'Âge d'Airain* need not be a man, and the Belgian model posing for it need not be made of bronze; the map of Canada need not be a country, and Canada itself need not fit in the glove compartment of a car; my image in the mirror need not be a human being, and I need not myself be a mere reflection sustained by light alone.

To object that disparity in kind precludes the possibility of a connection is tantamount to the denial of a link between cognitive content or processes, on the one hand, and intellectual output, on the other, as if theorems, poems, and songs were not extensions of mental states, which, extended and disseminated as such, become open to repeatable individual and collective experience. Hence, to go through the exercise one more time, the instantiation of a form as an object of experience is no farther to reach than the manifestation of thoughts in the mind as a book, a stream of consciousness as a story, or the "spontaneous overflow of powerful feelings" as a poem in the manner of the vivid Wordsworth description.

This is not, however, Plato's solution. He would be neither eager nor willing to disown self-predication. This is not his solution because he does not see a problem.

The alternative to repudiating the self-predication of forms is to deny its absurdity. One way of doing this is to construe Plato's relevant declarative statements, namely, those evincing self-predication of forms, as identity claims rather than attributions, characterizations, or descriptions. This is to take a statement such as "justice is just" to be saying that justice is what is just, and that what is just is justice, so that justice is precisely what it is to be just, thus identifying the referent of the noun naming the concept with the quality ascribed by the adjective, that is, claiming a direct correspondence in identity between the two, rather than proclaiming that justice is something that is just and thereby attributing the quality of justness to justice.

This approach originates with Meinwald's (1991) application of a distinction between two kinds of predication in Plato's *Parmenides*: *pros ta alla* ("in relation to the others"), wherein the subject, whether a form or a particular, is characterized by the predicate, as in "three is odd," and *pros heauto* ("in relation to itself"), wherein the subject, always a form, is identified with the predicate, as in "the odd is odd." She finds her own approach to be anticipated in Frede's (1967) distinction between the *pros allo* and *kath' hauto* uses of the copula "is" and in Owen's (1965, 1970) distinction between identity and predication (Meinwald, 1991, p. 75, n. 18; 1992, pp. 395–396, n. 29), but it is her work that is widely acknowledged as a seminal contribution to the interpretation of predication in Plato and hailed in particular for its application toward the solution of problems in the *Parmenides*.

Meinwald's innovation continues to motivate a stream of studies either rejecting it or carrying it forward or simply drawing inspiration toward new directions. However, these all rest on close scrutiny of the original text in Greek, thus making the issue the exclusive venue of Plato scholarship, not fully accessible to mere philosophers, whether students or teachers of philosophy. The distinction in predication can be understood and examined in contemporary English as well, but its value as a definitive solution to the problem cannot be confirmed in translation. As far as English translations are concerned, the differentiation advocated between modes of predication still looks like a viable solution to apparently problematic instances of self-predication in forms, even if it is not unassailable as a description of what Plato seems to be doing. Not every instance of self-predication in forms can reasonably be attributed in standard English editions to identity claims. Some instances seem like Plato is really characterizing a form by what he is predicating of it. Perhaps the most vivid example of this is his characterization of the form of beauty as beautiful (*Phaedo* 100c, *Symposium* 210e), though the justness of justice is also memorable (*Protagoras* 330c). Moreover, the interpretation of self-predication as an identity claim is not as intuitively appealing in cases where the particular associated with a form happens to be a physical entity, such as a horse or a bed. Fortunately, Plato tends to stay away from these.

2.5.4. Third Man Argument

The problem of self-predication in forms plays a central role in a larger problem discussed as the "Third Man Argument," a phrase coined by Aristotle (*Sophistical Refutations* 178b37–179a10; *Metaphysics* 990b15–17, 1038b35–1039a3, 1059b5–9, 1079a11–13). A hyphen is required by grammar but omitted by convention. Happily, it becomes immediately clear in any discussion, even technical ones among specialists, that what is in question is not the third argument in a series of "Man Arguments" but the one and only argument about a "Third Man." This is a reference to a specific argument appearing in the first part of the *Parmenides* (separated from the second part at 135c, or a bit earlier, depending on the allowance for a transitional stage, either way, corresponding to roughly one-fourth of the dialogue), where Plato undertakes self-criticism focusing exclusively on the theory of forms. The relevant passage (*Parmenides* 131e–133a, especially 132a–b) is an exchange between a young and naive Socrates and an elderly and wise Parmenides. Parmenides contends that the position held by Socrates, that all large things are large by participation in the form of largeness, is open to the objection that this form of largeness and all the large things subsumed under it would then together need an additional form of largeness in which to participate in order to have a claim to largeness themselves, and then the entire batch described would need yet another form of largeness, and so on, thus forcing an infinite regress. The regress is caused by the interminable quest to unify, under a single causal explanation, the largeness of everything that is large, wherein the unifier always presents itself as an additional element to be unified with the batch of things subsumed under it.

The objection by Parmenides could just as well be called the "Third Largeness Argument," which would, in fact, be more accurate, but Aristotle's terminology stuck as he invariably replaced the example of largeness with that of man in his discussions of and references to the argument, though none of his extant works includes a full expository or critical account with explicit references. The problem of self-predication in the Third Man Argument, while not identified as a separate problem there, either by Socrates or by Parmenides, is contained in the implicit assumption that the form of largeness is itself large, as it is part of the original group requiring participation in an additional form of largeness. Although the regress proceeds at each step with a batch of items consisting of a form of largeness and whatever is subsumed under it at that level, the objection could, it seems, have been freed of excess baggage and directed exclusively at the form of largeness, which, if itself large, must be so by participating in another form of largeness, thus confirming that it cannot participate in itself, and focusing the regress specifically on the form of largeness. This would be to explain the problem in terms of a simpler conflict: Participation in the form of largeness is a necessary condition of largeness (being large) but a meaningless prospect for the form itself, which needs a higher-order form of largeness to validate its own claim to largeness (being large), and so on *ad infinitum*. Perhaps more perspicuously, participation in the form of largeness is a necessary condition of being large but a null event for the form representing that condition, the satisfaction of which by that form is either impossible or regressive, thus initiating an infinite series of iterations of an overarching form of largeness.

This is precisely where approaches such as Meinwald's (1991, 1992) come into play, removing the internal contradiction by differentiating between modes of predication for forms and particulars. Hence, the scholarly concern with self-predication in forms is not so much with the possibility of intuitively silly instantiations, such as the form of largeness being large, as it is with the possibility of a systemic inconsistency in the theory of forms.

Many solutions have been proposed for the difficulty presented by the Third Man Argument, but none has found universal acceptance in the community of Plato scholars studying the issue. Not all commentators agree that a solution is available. Then again, some deny the existence of a serious problem to be solved, invoking the fact that the forms exist in a separate realm, or constitute a different reality, that we do not understand, and claiming simply that the apparent difficulty here cannot be assumed to be a difficulty there as well. Despite the absence of a standard solution, a conventional mode of discussion has emerged. Contemporary presentations and debates are shaped by a seminal analysis by Vlastos (1954), whose terminology has become common parlance among philosophers interested in the argument. The analytic breakdown he offers for the argument, or, to be more accurate, the main principles underlying the argument, can be summarized as follows, including his own appellations for the principles:

- One-Over-Many (OM): Any multitude of things recognized as having a predicate in common must be acknowledged to share that predicate by virtue of participation in a single form corresponding to it. To spell it out in the standard notation, if a number of things, *a*, *b*, *c*, etc., are all *F*, there must be a single form, *F-ness*, participation in which makes them all *F* (Vlastos, 1954, p. 320).

- Self-Predication (SP): Any predicate common to a multitude of things can also be predicated of the form by virtue of participation in which those things have that predicate in common. That is to say, the form, *F-ness*, participation in which makes things *F*, is itself *F*. Put simply, though somewhat cryptically, any form can be predicated of itself (Vlastos, 1954, p. 324).

- Non-Identity (NI): Nothing taking on a predicate through participation in a form is identical with that form. The form by virtue of participation in which a multitude of things are all *F* is not itself one of those things, nor can it sensibly be considered to be. Stated briefly, forms do not participate in themselves (Vlastos, 1954, p. 325).

The nomenclature for the three principles, together with their acronyms, if not also the precise notational exposition, constitute the standard jargon in current studies, even if only to mark a point of departure or to declare complete repudiation. The original intention was to show that the principles are severally necessary but jointly inconsistent, thus undermining the plausibility of causal explanation through the theory of forms. Subsequent debates have focused largely on the question of mutual compatibility, though the position on separate necessity has not gone unchallenged. Since only so much can be done with exactly the same set of principles, such debates usually revolve around interpretations, qualifications, or modifications, not to mention rejections, replacements, and additions.

2.5.5. Symmetry and Exhaustiveness

The tension between the self-predication and non-identity principles receives the greatest attention in discussions of the Third Man Argument. Yet the one-over-many principle gets ample coverage independently of the other two, especially in a generalized variant positing a form for everything. Presumably, the principle states that there is only one form that corresponds to each category of things of the same kind, but it also tends to attract stronger interpretations turning the quota into a requirement, as if the principle declared that nothing is without a form. The original emphasis is on limiting the number of forms applicable to each category of things of the same kind, specifically, by identifying exactly one such form per category, thereby ensuring the unification of all the things in each category. Evidently, it is an inviting leap, unwarranted though it may be, from a single form for everything of a kind to a form for everything.

Do all particulars have a form? Put differently, can there be a particular without a form? This question, in either formulation, is the center of a long-standing debate. Due regard for consistency would seem to require a form for each kind of particular. The restriction to a kind, or type, is required to avoid postulating, for example, a separate form for each campfire ever built, or even for each fleeting flame in every fire, as opposed to one form covering fire in general.

Aristotle recognizes the supply-side pressure on forms. His reading is that there are at least as many forms as there are types of particulars (*Metaphysics* 990b4–8). He finds the theory to maintain that each category of particulars, whether physical substances or other things, has a form of the same name and exists separately from the particulars (*Metaphysics* 1079a1–4). Yet the young Socrates defending the theory of forms in the *Parmenides* (130b–c) denies the existence of forms of hair, mud, and dirt, and is ambivalent about the existence of forms of man, fire, and water, while affirming the existence of forms of likeness, unity, plurality, rightness, beauty, and goodness. The demands of consistency add further uncertainty as Socrates considers whether he may reasonably distinguish between things that do and do not have forms, or must instead affirm (or deny) the existence of forms for everything (*Parmenides* 130d).

The ambiguity in the *Parmenides* precludes easy answers to the question regarding particulars without forms, but the obverse is just as interesting: Can there be a form without a particular? As far as textual evidence is concerned, neither formless things nor empty forms seem to be ruled out. However, this is not an intentional allowance but a fuzzy area underlying uncertainty. In other words, it is not a positive feature of the theory but a corollary of what it leaves open. What is at stake is not merely the plausibility of the theory but also the clarity of its creative origin, the actual process of psychological discovery: The greater the hesitation on fundamentals, the greater the temptation to take the forms to be fashioned after particulars rather than the other way around. Nevertheless, for better or for worse, the universe Plato leaves us with is not necessarily symmetrical between forms and particulars, thus making each possible without the other.

Another fuzzy area is whether the distinction between forms and particulars is exhaustive, that is, whether the universe consists of nothing but forms and particulars. Again, Plato makes no commitment either way. However, the nature and purpose of the contrast suggests that it does not exhaust the universe: The division between forms and particulars distinguishes not between being and nothingness, in other words, between what does and does not exist, but between reality and appearance. The aim of the distinction is not to construct a definitive and comprehensive ontology by weeding out things that do not exist or are not real. Instead, the aim is to develop a theory of how reality manifests itself. This comes with a distinction between reality and appearance, but even here the emphasis is not so much on the difference as it is on the connection. And even if we were to shift our attention to the difference, what we find is not a filter for what exists but a mirror for what is real.

Plato never claims that particulars do not exist or that they are not real. He maintains merely that they are imperfect instantiations of the forms. This does not make them any less real. To be sure, it makes them less authentic instances of what they instantiate, but it does not make them less real in themselves. They are no less real as copies than the forms are as models. They may represent a lower level of reality, a derivative or contingent existence, but they are real nonetheless, and they exist all the same.

Had the distinction been between that which does and does not exist, then the underlying ontology would have been exhaustive, but the interpretation in terms of reality and appearance accommodates external possibilities: To classify particulars as the phenomenological manifestations of the forms is not a denial of their reality, much less of their existence, but a description or explanation of their ontological status. Nothing in the prevailing ontological scheme requires a restriction of the universe to forms and particulars. Being neither a form nor a particular is at least a possibility that is not rejected or contradicted in the Platonic corpus.

2.5.6. Ontology of Mathematicals

The leading candidate for what might be found in limbo between forms and particulars is mathematical objects, that is, numbers and geometric figures. For example, it is not clear whether the number three simply is a form or whether it instead has a form. It is clear, of course, that the number three is different from a group of three things. What is not clear is whether it is this number that is the form, or yet another construct, one further removed from appearance and subsuming the number under it. The same holds for a circle or a square, and, in short, for all numbers and geometric figures.

Aristotle offers some insight here. The gist of what we get through Aristotle is that Plato takes the objects of mathematics to occupy an intermediate position between forms and particulars, resembling the forms and differing from particulars in being eternal and immutable, and resembling particulars and differing from the forms in being plural (*Metaphysics* 987b14–17, 1059b5–14).

This is not all that Aristotle has to say on the subject, but it is the most important part. It might be appreciated better in the greater context of his distinction between different senses of number. This is where he summarizes what he takes to be all possible conceptions of number, that is, from a certain perspective, followed by an assessment of the tenability of holding these conceptions, which is where he purportedly explicates Plato's position.

The entire process unfolds in a few pages in the thirteenth book of the *Metaphysics* (13[M].6–7), though these are not Aristotle's only relevant references in this regard. Specifically, with an overarching understanding of numbers as consisting of units, Aristotle lays out three different possibilities regarding whether and how these units can be combined with one another (*Metaphysics* 1080a15–30): (1) every unit as combinable with every other; (2) no unit as combinable with any other; (3) units as combinable within the same number but not between numbers. The first scenario illustrates what he calls "mathematical numbers," and the third corresponds to what he calls "formal numbers" (or "ideal" or "eidetic" numbers), while the second seems to be there just to exhaust the possibilities, as he admits that no one actually holds this rather unreasonable view (*Metaphysics* 1080b8–10). He associates Platonism with the third scenario, though without specifically naming Plato or anyone else in particular (*Metaphysics* 1080a23, 1081a23–25). He also suggests that Platonism is consistent with the unworkable prospects in the second scenario, but he is careful to acknowledge that Platonists do not in fact subscribe to this position (*Metaphysics* 1081a35–b1).

We may safely limit our attention to the first and third possibilities, since Aristotle himself declares the second one irrelevant. The distinction between mathematical and formal numbers is that the former are amenable to mathematical operation whereas the latter are not. Formal numbers can be neither combined nor compared, because they are, in essence, forms. Mathematical numbers can indeed be combined or compared, corresponding as they do to our own ordinary notion of number, for example, when we assert that one plus two equals three.

They are neither forms nor particulars. They reveal something of a hybrid nature, being eternal and immutable like forms yet plural like particulars (*Metaphysics* 987b14–18, 991a4–6, 1079a35–36): For instance, the number three is eternal and immutable in that it does not change over time in the fashion of developing or decomposing organic matter; instead, it continues to be precisely what it is, which is what marks its affinity to the forms. On the other hand, it is not unique, as there is no logical or mathematical limit on how many threes might exist, which evinces a plurality characteristic of particulars in contradistinction to forms. This explains how mathematical numbers could ontologically rank somewhere between forms and particulars.

This is a fair introduction to an Aristotelian interpretation of Plato's theory of numbers, or, more generally, of mathematical objects, thus including geometric shapes. But enthusiasm is best tempered with caution before proceeding any further. While the foregoing encapsulation appears plausible enough, Aristotle says such bizarre things about Plato's mathematical orientation that suspicion creeps in regarding his overall guidance in the area. For example, if we had nothing to go by except the testimony of Aristotle, we would be burdened with an impression of Plato as holding that (1) all forms are numbers (*Metaphysics* 991b9, 1081a12; *De Anima* 404b24–25) and that (2) numbers (of things in themselves) go up only to ten (*Physics* 206b27–33: in direct reference to Plato; *Metaphysics* 1084a12–15, 1088b10: in reference to "some who say"). These just do not sound right.

Wonder as we might whether Plato considers numbers to be forms, here we have Aristotle telling us the converse, namely, that Plato takes forms to be numbers, reportedly holding universally that all forms are numbers. Given that this allows room for the possibility that some numbers are not forms, it is consistent with the distinction between formal and mathematical numbers. The problem, however, is that it is difficult to interpret without further information. It becomes all the more incredible in connection with the second claim that Plato recognizes only the numbers one through ten: While this is rather unbelievable as it is, it has the unfortunate consequence of severely limiting the number of forms, given that all forms are numbers, and that there are only ten numbers. Aristotle probably means either or both of these assertions in some other way, but this is all that he shares.

This does not necessarily mean that Aristotle's guidance here is unreliable. The problem might instead be that, missing something obvious to Aristotle and his audience, we fail to appreciate certain abbreviations and shortcuts. The aim, of course, is not to assign blame but to remedy the problem.

Unfortunately, the problem is too generalized to admit a specific solution here. A common assessment is that Aristotle's eagerness to challenge the master sometimes gets in the way of a reliable report or accurate exegesis, leaving us instead with highlights of the most objectionable points, liable thereby to be misinterpreted as the whole story, or mistaken for a serviceable summary. This has a ring of truth to it, but it may also be a bit unfair. Aristotle, after all, is not a mere chronicler. His reputation as a philosopher is comparable to that of Plato. He may certainly restrict exposition of a particular position strictly to whatever would serve his needs to challenge that position. But even if he is entirely justified in this approach, it is still a problem that we are none the wiser about what is going on.

An additional difficulty, one that is easily overlooked, is that Aristotle is competing, not with Plato, but with Platonists. Whenever he ascribes any view to Platonism, or to Platonists, without specifically naming anyone, which happens more often than one might expect, he is talking about the party line current at the Academy at some indefinite time after Plato's death and before his own. His direct competition in the Academy is represented first by Speusippus, who was scholarch for eight years immediately after Plato's death, and next by Xenocrates, who took over for the next twenty-five years. Thus, anytime we think we are getting Plato's views, we might well be getting those of Speusippus or Xenocrates instead. This being so, the possibility of misunderstanding looms large even on the assumption that Aristotle is a faithful and careful reporter of views with which he does not agree.

Yet if we restrict our use of Aristotle to just those passages where he names names, we would not be able to use as much of his work as we actually do in formulating our understanding of Plato. Among the tamer passages in the foregoing overview on numbers, the only thing Aristotle says about Plato by name is that he makes numbers intermediate between forms and particulars (*Metaphysics* 987b14–17, repeated without a name at 1059b5–14). This is not much to work with, but it can be expanded fruitfully, though only with due vigilance. Hence, developing a sense of the judicious use of Aristotle in the interpretation of Plato promises substantial returns for the classical scholar.

Aristotle's testimony is best used to supplement rather than supplant conclusions based on a direct study because he rarely announces whether he is offering his own interpretation or sharing objective information comparable to an interview with Plato. Since we cannot corroborate the latter, nor distinguish it from the former, we need not be particularly eager to give up our considered opinions on Plato in favor of anything said by Aristotle. The choice is not always between supplementing and supplanting prevailing conclusions. Oftentimes, fresh insight is required instead. In that event, we would obviously do well to follow Aristotle's lead where it is clear and sensible, and even better to ignore it where it is not.

2.5.7. Credit for the Approach

The theory is invariably called *Plato's* "theory of forms" (or *his* "doctrine of ideas" or some variation thereof), whereas the context in dialogues dealing with the forms tends to show that Plato is not introducing concepts previously unheard of but drawing on what is already at least somewhat familiar. For example, members of the dramatic audience of the *Phaedo*, particularly Simmias and Cebes, seem to be acquainted with the concept of forms, and generally receptive of the associated theory. This in itself may not prove that the invention does not belong to Plato, but it does rule out the *Phaedo* as his introduction to the concept or the theory. The further fact that none of his other works can be considered an introduction to the forms, or, conversely, that the forms never receive a proper introduction in the entire Platonic corpus, suggests that the theory might have its origins elsewhere, at least in rudimentary form.

The forms are prominent enough in Plato's philosophy that he might reasonably have been expected to make room for a thorough if elementary exposition in one of his dialogues had the theory been entirely alien to his audience. Perhaps the first part of the *Parmenides* comes closest in that respect, despite the status of that dialogue as a critique of the theory in question. But that does not make for a terribly enlightening introduction.

None of this shows that Plato merely advocates or utilizes the theory of forms instead of creating it. Alternative explanations are no less tenable: He might have deliberately refrained from a formal introduction in writing due to dramatic considerations, or perhaps simply because he was already satisfied with a verbal promulgation of the theory, or for some other reason. To generalize, he could conceivably have chosen not to dramatize a dedicated pedagogical account, even if he had invented the forms from scratch, with no intellectual debt in the effort.

Moreover, the familiarity of Plato's dramatic audiences with the forms is a matter of interpretation, not fact, even in the *Phaedo*, where the indications are the strongest. Such a reading seems to originate, at least in English publications, with Burnet (1892, p. 354 ff.; 1911, p. xliii ff. and notes *passim*; 1914, p. 154 ff.; as cited by Grube, 1980, p. 291), though it does not by any means end there as well. Grube (1980, pp. 291–294) vehemently rejects this perspective, arguing that the relevant passages in the *Phaedo* show a progressive introduction of the theory, which, he claims, cannot sensibly be interpreted as being familiar enough not to require the very introduction being provided. Burnet seems to overemphasize the apparent familiarity of the audience, whereas Grube dismisses the same elements too easily.

These are not the only two proponents of the opposing interpretations, but they are sufficiently representative of the debate. Although it remains unresolved, the debate need not be interpreted to reflect irreconcilable views: A concept or theory may be explained systematically even if it is familiar, with neither possibility ruling out the other. Hence, it is at least conceivable that the *Phaedo* provides an introductory exposition of a familiar theory. The theme of familiarity may even serve a purely dramatic purpose rather than signifying anything about authorship.

The safest outlook to maintain, especially in the absence of conclusive evidence to the contrary, is one giving full credit to Plato. Nevertheless, a search for sources of influence and inspiration promises intellectual rewards. In terms of internal evidence, a clue to orient such a search may be found in the *Parmenides* (130b), where the eponymous hero of the dialogue is intrigued not by the fact that the character Socrates believes in the existence of the forms but by the fact that he separates them from the things participating in them. The question there is not whether Socrates himself has come up with the concept of forms, but whether Socrates himself has come up with a conception of forms as distinct from what participates in them. What impresses the sagely Parmenides about the ideas of the young Socrates in the dialogue is precisely the breakthrough attributed to Plato in reality. The standard view is that the focus on universal definitions in the early dialogues anticipates the development of the forms as separate entities in the middle period, with the common assumption that the division corresponds to that between the philosophies of Socrates and Plato.

This is yet another controversial issue among Plato scholars. Not all interested parties would agree to this way of dividing up the corpus. Many would object that it is all Plato, whose intellectual development may thus be interpreted to be mapped out throughout the received manuscripts. Yet the assessment goes as far back as Aristotle, who finds Socrates the most important source of inspiration as well as the most significant point of departure for Plato. Specifically, Aristotle reports that Plato's intellectual heritage includes, in no apparent order, the Pythagoreans, Cratylus, Heraclitus, Parmenides, Empedocles, Anaxagoras, and Socrates (*Metaphysics* 987a29–988a16). He depicts Plato as building principally on the Socratic practice of seeking universal definitions of ethical concepts, with a novel approach of universalizing the form instead of the sensible thing, and thus driving a conceptual and ontological wedge between the two (*Metaphysics* 987b1–10). According to Aristotle, Socrates had already focused attention on universals, but the separation of forms begins with Plato (*Metaphysics* 1078b7–32, 1086a30–b12). The influence of Socrates seems indubitable, but the separation of the forms from the particulars of which they are forms is at least as important an advancement as the development of the concept. The contribution here is not merely an ontological nuance but a revolutionary new outlook recognizing a distinction between substance and property.

Socrates is not the only candidate for an alternative origin for the theory of forms, or for the basic notion, principles, or intuitions underlying the theory. Pythagoras is another candidate. And Parmenides is yet another, at least as an inspiration if not as a model.

The assignment and denial of credit is risky business, not just in relation to the theory of forms, but in connection with the general development of the history of ideas. It becomes increasingly tricky with the age of the subject and the scarcity of documentation. The possibility of error becomes substantial as one ventures back to antiquity, where both factors stand as obstacles. For example, the fact that Pythagoras and Parmenides predate Plato does not necessarily mean that any Pythagorean or Eleatic strands in Plato's philosophy must have been borrowed from or inspired by these predecessors. The scant writings surviving the founders and early members of these schools of thought leave open the possibility that apparent influences on Plato are instead Platonic influences on later Pythagoreans or Eleatics, conceivably drawing from Plato doctrines subsequently misidentified as originating with their schools rather than with Plato. Any such distortion along the way may or may not be deliberate, but it will be permanent. This, in short, is the possibility of Plato's intellectual legacy being disguised as his inheritance. This is not to say that the flow of information and inspiration must have been from Plato to elsewhere, simply because he was a great philosopher, but merely that chronological order alone is not sufficiently compelling to prejudge the issue against Plato. The greater danger, as Hare (1982, p. 10) warns, is not in ignoring a possible source of inspiration for Plato, but in robbing him of rightful recognition in innovation.

2.6. Does Plato Have a Theory of Forms?

The most interesting debate on Plato's theory of forms is whether or not there is such a thing. Perhaps a bit on the strange side, especially for the uninitiated, the question is not whether there is such a thing as a form but whether there is such a theory: Is the theory famously ascribed to him in textbook exposition really a theory in Plato? The question should hold interest at least because it is foundational.

Nothing about the theory can possibly be more relevant. It is of little use to discuss, say, whether the forms exist, unless we agree that the theory exists. We have to be able to show that Plato holds the theory, if we are going to challenge him in regard to what he says in it, and particularly if we are going to charge him with being wrong in it.

What is interesting here is not so much the question itself as the occasion for it, in other words, that any doubt should arise in the first place. The reason for suspicion is that we cannot turn to a specific passage in any of Plato's works to learn about the theory of forms in the way we turn to passages in Bentham or the Mills to learn about utilitarianism. And the difference cannot be reduced to that between dialogues and essays. The dialogue form may be a literary boon for hiding the author's deepest convictions, but it certainly is not a hindrance, literary or otherwise, to expressing them.

The debate is not over whether Plato expresses his theory with the clarity in which Bentham and the Mills express theirs but whether Plato says anything at all that can reasonably count as a theory of forms. Few people would want to dispute that Plato is as openly passionate about the forms as Bentham and the Mills are about utilitarianism, but many who decline would be willing to challenge whether the object of Plato's passion is manifested in a theory. He is evidently not trying to conceal anything, given that his characters exhibit an obvious fascination with the forms, both in glorifying them, as in the *Phaedo*, and in questioning them, as in the *Parmenides*. The question, rather, is whether the sum of all that he says about the forms amounts to a theory of forms, or, more specifically, to the very theory we find ascribed to him in the secondary literature, to give it a name, the "classical theory of forms."

The problem is sometimes conflated with what goes on in the *Parmenides*. But these are separate issues, and they are best kept that way. The *Parmenides* is indeed important for those who insist that Plato subscribes to the theory of forms. They have to be able to establish that the critique of the *Parmenides* does not convince Plato to abandon the theory, or to transform it into something decidedly different. Yet the same dialogue is not nearly as important to those who deny that Plato subscribes to the theory of forms. Their denial is not based on the premise that he abandons the theory upon finding too many holes in it, as demonstrated, at least on the level of suspicion, in the *Parmenides*. Instead, they argue simply that he never holds the theory to begin with. The objection is usually that what passes for theory is more like a loose collection of premises than like a theory, or that Plato is too distant to dogmatic solutions to have a theory of any sort. Some other route may be followed instead, or in addition, but the common point in an overwhelming majority of the cases will be rejection independently of what goes on in the *Parmenides*.

This is not to deny that scholars are divided over the fate of the forms before and after the *Parmenides* but to recognize the independent possibility and reality of questioning whether Plato's talk of forms constitutes a theory in the first place. In other words, only the first two of the following three positions are relevant to the debate: (1) Plato has a theory of forms; (2) Plato does not have a theory of forms; (3) he does before but not after the *Parmenides*. The third is an entirely respectable position, but it is not what people argue about when they discuss whether Plato has a theory of forms. The debate is no more about the *Parmenides* than it is about, say, the *Charmides*. Just as the point is not to determine whether the theory is anticipated in the *Charmides*, it is not to determine whether it is undermined by the *Parmenides*.

There is no question that talk of the forms, positive, passionate talk, is concentrated in a few dialogues: *Cratylus*; *Phaedo*; *Symposium*; *Republic*; *Phaedrus*. This is the battleground. The point is to settle the debate right here. The question is whether this handful of dialogues shows that Plato has a theory of forms. It matters not what happens outside, whether in presumably earlier dialogues, where the theory has ostensibly not yet been formulated, or in presumably later ones, where it has possibly been abandoned or otherwise altered beyond recognition. No doubt, the additional points are well worth discussing, and might even be indispensable to a general overview of Plato's thought, but they are not pertinent to the central question here.

That said, the central question can be formulated in two different ways, both recognized in the foregoing discussion, but not properly distinguished therein. The first is the question whether Plato subscribes to the classical theory of forms. This, to spell it out, is to ask whether the theory of forms commonly attributed to Plato is actually held by Plato. The second is the question whether Plato subscribes to any theory of forms, or even to any theory about the forms. This is to ask whether any theory explaining, employing, or concerning the forms, no matter the content, can sensibly be attributed to Plato.

These are entirely different questions. The difference itself is not critically important, but it is important to note that there is a difference. This certainly is not the moment of truth in the debate, as if everything were hanging on the distinction, which, once drawn, could settle the matter. But perspicuity is a minimum requirement in any discussion. What is important, therefore, is to recognize that these are different positions, mainly so that we are all clear on what is at stake, thus agreeing at least on what it is that we disagree on. Otherwise, the distinction neither defines nor settles the prevailing debate, which is typically about whether Plato subscribes to the classical theory of forms. Those who affirm this could not care less whether he has other theories as well, and those who deny it do not argue that he holds some other theory instead. Where the second formulation comes into play at all is in the negative camp, where interested parties are rarely shy about denying that Plato has any theory whatsoever about the forms. This, however, does not create any additional pressure on opponents in the positive camp. On the contrary, it eases the burden of proof to the point where any theory of forms will do, but the focus in the positive camp usually remains fixed on the classical theory of forms.

This is not to rule out the possibility of a weaker claim in the positive camp but to point out the reality of the stronger claim, or rather, the precise claim. The ongoing debate on the matter is the result of a reaction to the interpretation of Plato as working with the classical theory of forms. The positive camp, as it is the first to be set up, is categorically about this theory. The negative camp, set up in direct opposition to this, may contradict it specifically, or go beyond it to deny any theory of forms in Plato, or, for that matter, go all the way, as is often the case, to the extreme of denying any theory at all in Plato. Yet the primary aim in opposition is to contradict the original position. More important, defending that position does not require defeating every thesis advanced in competition, but only those advanced in direct contradiction. This is why the debate remains focused largely on the classical theory of forms. The negative camp does not force it off that axis, and the positive camp, being already entrenched there, is perhaps too comfortable to carry it elsewhere, even if that means an easier defense.

It is, of course, possible to recast the discussion without restriction. In fact, more and more scholars in the positive camp are repositioning the last line of defense at *any* rather than *the* theory of forms, arguing that what Plato says about the forms can sensibly be interpreted as a theory even if it is not in fact identical with the classical theory. Such diversification of the defense is a result of the maturation process in the debate. As initial reactions to the positive camp begin to mature, the positive camp itself finds a definable position to oppose, and starts asserting its own position as a reaction to the negative camp. Or, from a different perspective, the original positive camp, still concerned exclusively with the classical theory of forms, finds an ally in an entirely new camp comprising parties joining the debate specifically to contradict the negative camp. The reality is probably somewhere in between.

Either way, these differences come out in individual arguments. They are not organized in definable schools of thought on the matter. Instead, they remain scattered in provocative calls for denial in brilliant moments of doubt. Going through them all is hardly necessary, nor even particularly helpful, but some are not to be missed.

Fortunately, the effort can safely be restricted to the negative camp. The negative views are more informative if only because the positive position is the standard one. If the question were ever to arise whether Bentham or the Mills truly do subscribe to utilitarianism, it would be infinitely more interesting, not to mention entirely sufficient to an understanding of the debate, to focus on the negative arguments. This is not because Bentham and the Mills definitely are utilitarians, which, indeed they are, but because we are already familiar with that side of the debate. Not only are we familiar with it, but we are indoctrinated in it without restraint or reservation, as if an alternative were inconceivable.

This is roughly where we stand with respect to a theory of forms in Plato. We believe not only that he has such a theory, but also that we know precisely what that theory is. This is one of the first things we learn about him. We are likely to hear about it even if we read nothing he actually wrote. Thus, it is well worth confirming. The best way to do that is to understand the challenge.

The opposition can be formidable. Exceptional representatives include, though are not limited to, the following: Julia Elizabeth Annas (1981, pp. 217–241; 2003, pp. 83–87); Francisco J. Gonzales (2002, pp. 31–83); Drew A. Hyland (2002, pp. 257–272); Kenneth M. Sayre (1983, 1988, 1993b, 1995, 2002); Bernard Arthur Owen Williams (2006, pp. 148–186, especially p. 154).

2.6.1. Julia Elizabeth Annas

Annas (1981, pp. 217–241) contributes to the debate through her celebrated introduction to the *Republic*, denying therein that what Plato does with the forms constitutes a theory in the conventional sense. In addition to denying that the bits and pieces of apparently doctrinal discussion in the *Republic*, often made out to be a handbook on the forms, hang together as anything like a coherent theory on the forms, let alone the very theory of forms occupying scholars, she affirms that the dialogue provides "no open treatment of what they [the forms] contribute to the argument" (Annas, 1981, p. 217). She recognizes neither an intention nor a motive to set up the forms as an analytic or methodological tool "analogous to a scientific theory that explains phenomena in a way removing puzzles about them" (Annas, 1981, p. 233). She grants that Plato's beliefs about the forms constitute an interconnected whole as opposed to a disjointed collection, but she is not impressed by the degree or the kind of interconnection evident (Annas, 1981, p. 235).

Not only does she consider the treatment of forms unlike a proper theory, but she also regards the forms themselves unlike theoretical constructs. The crucial point on both counts is that the existence of the forms is to be perceived rather than demonstrated, not so much in the sense that this or that form is to be perceived, thereby confirming their existence severally, but in the sense that the "existence of the forms" as a truth is something to be perceived rather than proven (Annas, 1981, pp. 237–239). The forms can be known, but not through observation or argument. Specifically, "knowledge of them is part of the *good* person's understanding" (Annas, 1981, p. 237, her emphasis). This makes reason alone insufficient, and, virtue, essential, for insight into the matter. And this, in turn, is not the kind of condition stipulated in a standard scientific theory. Annas (2003, pp. 83–87) maintains a similar position in her *very short* generalist introduction to Plato, where she repudiates the tendency to make any sort of theory out of the forms.

The focal point of Annas is the inclusion of virtue in the epistemic requirement for perceiving the "existence of the forms" (1981, pp. 237–239). To be sure, we do not normally require this of scientific theories, but does this really vitiate the claim that Plato has a theory of forms? If the putative theory reflects all the standard characteristics, that is, conditions necessary and sufficient for any set of propositions to qualify as a theory, whatever the actual criteria may be, does the presence of one extraneous feature overturn its status in this regard? If anything, the extra requirement may be said to make it more than just a theory rather than something resembling a theory but falling short. Nevertheless, this does not prove Annas wrong on the whole. Her two claims, or arguments, here are mutually independent: She argues separately that Plato's conception of forms does not constitute a theory and that Plato makes virtue an epistemic condition as described. She does take the latter as supporting the former, but not as constituting the sole evidence for it.

Another objection may be that knowledge of the forms, either the forms themselves or the "existence of the forms," whether through virtue or in some other way, is irrelevant to the theory itself, which need not be proven true to qualify as a theory. By way of analogy, knowledge of strings, or, to adopt the formulation of Annas, perceiving "the existence of strings," put simply, quantum vibrations of threadlike structures representing the most basic level of reality, would be celebrated by theoretical physicists the world over, but this would be conclusive proof of string theory, which, on the other hand, is no less a theory without such proof. Here, too, Annas can fall back on the mutual independence of the questions whether Plato has a theory of forms and whether he resorts to extraordinary epistemic treatment of his conception of the forms. In other words, since she has other objections to the theoreticity of the so-called theory, she can give up, or keep separate, her objection to its reliance on the perception of a good person, or, for that matter, of any person.

Moreover, the fact that Plato's forms have metaphysical, epistemological, and ethical dimensions, unlike strings, which do not even have all three spatial dimensions, let alone all the extra philosophical ones, is really a problem about Plato, not about the account of Annas on Plato. The classical theory of forms, whether or not it really counts as a theory, and independently of whether Plato subscribes to it, lies at the intersection of epistemology, metaphysics, ethics, and aesthetics. In terms of ambition, even the elusive "theory of everything" in physics pales in comparison, as its scope is limited to physical phenomena, despite the apparently exhaustive reference to "everything," which is actually quite specific to the context, whereas the theory of forms discussed in connection with Plato is a "theory of everything" pretty much about everything. Plato's coverage of the forms may or may not count as a theory, but this does not change the fact that Annas has captured a sense of what sets it apart from any other theory, or, more to the point, from what we normally consider a theory.

2.6.2. Francisco J. Gonzales

Gonzales (2002, pp. 31–83) finds the theory of forms to be a product of scholarly reconstruction that goes beyond the text. This is in contrast to an extraction, perhaps with a bit of synthesis and extrapolation, of what is already there in explicit terms. He argues that what circulates in secondary literature as the theory of forms is such a critical component of the outlook presumably built on it that Plato would have had to lay it out in full detail had he really held such a theory. He finds it especially telling that the dialogues are either severally ambiguous or mutually contradictory, if not altogether silent, on what forms are (the nature of forms), what forms there are (the range of forms), and how they are related to the world around us.

These are not his only questions, nor does he ask them precisely in this way or in this order, but he finds them compelling in the case against the existence of a theory of forms by Plato. Supplementing the negative observation, that is, the absence of such a theory in the dialogues, he invokes the *Seventh Letter* (especially 341c–d) as positive evidence that Plato finds the forms unsuitable for articulation in words, or, conversely, that he finds rational discourse insufficient for understanding the forms (Gonzales, 2002, pp. 48–51). His conclusion is that the forms are to be intuited as and through the discursive process of dialectic, not as a result, but in the very activity, the engagement itself, as opposed to being understood as or through a theory in any sense (Gonzales, 2002, pp. 62–64). He contends that interpreting them as a type of rational intuition has the additional advantage of accounting for their normative character, usually missed by attempts to reconstruct them as a theory, where their typical designation as "ideals" invariably requires knowledge of the good, or at least an understanding of what is good (Gonzales, 2002, pp. 63–64).

Here, Gonzales seems to confirm what Annas has to say about the matter. The main thrust of their respective positions appears to converge on virtue. This would suggest that the portion of the preceding discussion pertaining to the diagnostic climax of Annas's account may be taken up in connection with that of Gonzales as well. But this is not specifically emphasized in context. In point of fact, Gonzales thrice cites Annas, but not to express approval or even to acknowledge a debt of inspiration (2002, p. 67, n. 15, n. 21; p. 75). On the contrary, he recognizes a mutual divergence rather than agreement. He sees himself as denying that there is a theory of forms in Plato even if we adopt such a weak definition of "theory" as to allow relatively loose or nebulous doxastic structures to qualify as a theory. In contrast, he sees Annas as making that denial on the basis of a stronger definition, which, he contends, includes too much in the concept and excludes too little in Plato. Or, from a different perspective, Gonzales denounces Annas for her willingness, on a weak enough interpretation of the concept of "theory," to acknowledge that Plato has a theory of forms.

This does not reduce the problem to a strictly relative matter. Gonzales is careful not to leave the reference to strength and weakness vague. Specifically, he anchors his understanding of a strong definition of "theory" to inferential integrity, invoking criteria laid out by Sayre for a propositional system designed for deductive explanation (Sayre, 1993b, pp. 175–176; cited by Gonzales, 2002, p. 66, n. 15). He specifies his understanding of a weak definition of "theory" with another reference, that of Griswold responding to Sayre, wherein a theory becomes "an argument in favor of propositions or general principles that illustrate the principles of a subject, or that establish the defining characteristics of some set of entities" (Griswold, 1993, p. 203; quoted by Gonzales, 2002, p. 66, n. 15). The most salient difference is in the requirement of systemwide deductive functionality under the strong definition and the absence of this under the weak definition. This basic framework is supplemented by tacit quality restrictions, presumably a ceiling on the strength of the strong definition, and obviously, albeit still implicitly, a floor on the weakness of the weak definition. The ceiling should be low enough to make sure standard theories are not disqualified, and, the floor, high enough to make sure random musings are. On this basis, Gonzales is prepared to deny that Plato has a theory of forms on either interpretation. And he charges those who are not thus prepared, specifically, those who, like Annas, are willing to concede that Plato has a theory of forms in at least some loose sense, with diluting the concept of "theory."

2.6.3. Drew A. Hyland

Hyland (2002, pp. 257–272) takes the strongest stance conceivable against encumbering Plato with a theory of forms, not just the classical theory, but any theory. He does not even wait for the opening paragraph to state his position, which is clearly revealed in the title: "Against a Platonic 'Theory' of Forms." In fleshing out his thesis, he aligns himself with what he describes as a growing reaction to the standard practice, specifically mentioning Wieland (1982), Sallis (1975), Rosen (1983, 1988, 1991), and Griswold (1988, pp. 143–167). Setting up his own assessment of taking Plato to have a theory of forms, he disputes both the evidence and the result, the first as lacking, the second as misleading.

Thus, he issues two separate challenges. His first challenge is a comprehensive rejection of the evidentiary basis for a theory of forms in Plato, denying any internal corroboration in the corpus as well as any external confirmation in testimony. He rejects both developmentalism and esotericism insofar as they are united in a shared assumption, that is, the scenario that "Plato *intended* to present a consistent theory of forms, either in the dialogues or in the Academy" (Hyland, 2002, p. 264, his emphasis). What is especially noteworthy here is his denial that Aristotle considers Plato's discussion of forms to constitute a "theory," which, according to Hyland (2002, p. 259), is a common misperception perpetuated by erroneous albeit popular translations of what Aristotle in fact refers to as an "opinion" (*Metaphysics* 1078b9–12).

Hyland's second challenge is against the utility of the interpretive model, namely, the model of Plato with a theory of forms. This is independent of his objections to the accuracy of the model. He simply sees no benefit in making Plato out to be a theoretician. In fact, he finds harm in it. He denies, in other words, that the model is a useful guide, even for basic insight into what would otherwise have to be gleaned from several different works. He opposes this as a standard spin on the model. He considers it to be little more than a standing safety net for failure to establish the historical accuracy of the model, whereupon the fallback procedure is to claim heuristic utility. He submits, to the contrary, that the approach is harmful, not merely missing the truth, but grossly distorting it.

He finds all talk of theory anachronistic, not just with respect to Plato, but, quite generally, in association with classical Greek thought. He maintains that the anachronism, originating in the nineteenth century, distorts Plato by imposing on his thought and work four assumptions essential to the concept of "theory" but not to be found anywhere in the corpus, whether specifically in regard to his discussion of the forms or regarding the entirety of his intellectual output: (1) comprehensiveness; (2) provability; (3) consistency; (4) confirmation, understood not as full confirmation in fact but the demonstrable possibility of such, as evinced by the presence of actual corroborating instances (Hyland, 2002, pp. 260–261). He claims both that Plato's account does not answer to this description, and, more importantly and urgently, that it is not designed to do so.

Echoing his earlier, book-length treatment (Hyland, 1995, pp. 165–195), his suggestion is that the "'existential' teaching of the dialogues," by which he means the dependence of the human condition, and therefore of philosophy, on context (the specific circumstances in any situation), precludes the possibility of a theory of forms, primarily because we can never fully transcend the immediate context toward an absolute generality to arrive at universal answers or patterns (Hyland, 2002, pp. 266–270).

This is a definitive impasse. The universal is simply out of reach, except, of course, through its instantiation, which, nevertheless, still leaves us at the level of experience, which, again, is restricted to the context. But Hyland is at pains to repudiate, on behalf of Plato, any implications of situational relativism. He insists that Platonic truth is not necessarily defined by the context but merely manifested in it. He allows room for transcending the existential framework but not for leaving it behind entirely. Any transcendence is necessarily limited. We do generalize from experience, and this may be immensely useful, but we do not, and cannot, experience the general. The universal has no context.

Hyland's point is well taken. A tempting objection is that context-dependence establishes only that separately existing forms cannot be intelligible as stipulated by the classical theory of forms, and not, in addition, that Plato does not subscribe to this particular view or to the entire theory. However, Hyland never claims that one implies the other. He invokes specific evidentiary grounds for rejecting Plato as a theoretician of forms, whereupon he fills the absence of a theory with an account of what Plato actually does with the forms. That account is fleshed out more fully in his earlier work, likewise denying that Plato anywhere attempts to universalize the context or contextualize the universal, but embracing the possibility that Plato himself "has had a noetic experience of the formal structure of the intelligibility of things" (Hyland, 1995, p. 187). This, Hyland contends, is what gives Plato the confidence he apparently has in what he says, yet without thereby moving him to formalize it in or as a theory, on the contrary, convincing him that this is not the way to go.

The postulated noetic experience is not reducible to a descriptive account. Nor can the resultant understanding be instilled in others through inculcation or indoctrination. It must instead be repeated by others, again, in the form of a personal noetic experience, which simply cannot be replaced by a set of principles or instructions.

This is not, however, a suprarational event, dependent, as it were, on mystical enlightenment. It is a dialectical process (Hyland, 1995, pp. 185–187): Our noetic awareness feeds on discursive confirmation, always incomplete but never irrelevant. In turn, our dialectical exercises are framed by our rational insights or intuitions about the world. This points to a symbiotic relationship between *noesis* and *dianoia*. But Hyland adds an animating principle, a sort of catalyst keeping the epistemic process in motion. The catalyst is "trust" (*pistis*). This is not the sort of trust associated with faith but the kind grounded in experience. We learn from experience to trust experience, while acknowledging all along that it is irrevocably open to question. Thus, what is in question is not a leap of faith but an accrual of reliability.

One might object that Hyland's account of what Plato does with the forms, ostensibly in the absence of a theory of forms, still looks suspiciously like a theory, if not of forms, then of reality and of what we can be justified in saying about it. It does, for example, lay out a coherent descriptive framework for Plato's considered opinion on the nature of reality and the acquisition of knowledge. The objection, then, would be that the fact that this does not turn out to be the classical theory of forms attributed to Plato does not show that no theory of forms can be attributed to him. At least, it seems, the one outlined by Hyland can.

But this would be to mistake exegetical skills in Hyland for a theory in Plato. Hyland cannot truthfully deny having uncovered Plato's *modus operandi* and laid it out in a systematic manner apposite to contemporary scholarship, but he can, and does, faithfully deny that he has found any theoretical development therein. Any elements that resemble the ingredients of theory can be attributed to the systematic nature of good exposition. Moreover, even if Plato himself were to rise from the dead and endorse Hyland's account as a theory of his own, this is neither the theory of forms nor a theory of forms. It is simply a philosophical outlook that happens to include talk of the forms.

On the other hand, a comparable objection may be pursued in connection with two mutually incompatible points in Hyland's assessment of the situation. One is his report that Aristotle twice refers to Plato's conception of forms as an "opinion" (*Metaphysics* 1078b9, 1078b12), mistranslated or overtranslated both times either as "theory" or, less egregiously, as "doctrine" (Hyland, 2002, p. 259). The other is his claim that the concept of "theory" was entirely alien to the classical Greek mind (Hyland, 2002, p. 260). As it happens, Hyland's position regarding the strangeness of the concept undermines the relevance of his observation that Aristotle considers the forms an "opinion" rather than a "theory" of Plato. Given that Aristotle, being a Greek of the classical period, would not, under Hyland's own scenario, have an understanding of "theory," he cannot speak of any "theory of Plato," no matter the content, thereby making it irrelevant that he does not designate the forms a "theory," and equally irrelevant that he uses some other term instead. What is relevant is that Aristotle's evaluation of Plato's forms can be on a par with what might be expected of one scholar appraising a theory by another, even if the term "theory" does not appear anywhere in the appraisal.

The minimum platform for agreement here is that Aristotle tackles Plato's views on the matter with a profound frustration that would be out of place in reaction to mere opinion. He takes such pains to refute whatever can be made of Plato's talk about forms, and shows such intellectual comfort in the thought of having achieved this aim, that he can sensibly be interpreted as dealing with more than an opinion, quite possibly with a theory, or at least with something anticipating and even approximating our modern conception of a theory as clearly and as fully as it would have been possible to do so then.

While it might be unfair to fault Hyland for an overly systematic exposition of Plato, it is not unfair to press him on what he makes of Aristotle's treatment. Hence, even if a theory cannot fairly be said to be lurking beneath Hyland's reconstruction of Plato, one can reasonably be claimed to be motivating the reaction of Aristotle. This possibility certainly does not make or break Hyland's presentation, but it would seem to leave some room for theoreticity in Plato.

2.6.4. Kenneth M. Sayre

Sayre is a prolific contributor to scholarship on Plato's late period, with a particular interest in metaphysical issues. His presence in the movement to strip Plato of the classical theory of forms falls in two fronts: The first is a destructive response, a direct denial of a theory of forms in Plato (1988, 1993b, 1995). The second is constructive work explicating Plato's ontological dialectic, which, as it turns out, cannot be captured by such a theory (1983, 2002).

The best representative of his work in the first group is an essay with a bold title, no less forceful than that of Hyland (2002, pp. 257–272): "Why Plato Never Had a Theory of Forms" (Sayre, 1993b, pp. 167–193). With a specific understanding of "theory" (Sayre, 1993b, pp. 175–176) as a coherent set of general propositions held together by the rules of deductive inference and collectively constituting an explanatory platform, the essay denies that anything Plato has to say about the forms answers to this description.

On the face of it, this seems entirely appropriate. The first few actual theories that might pop into one's head will probably fall neatly in the scope of Sayre's general conception. Examples include the theory of relativity (general or special), the big bang theory, and the theory of evolution. The list may be extended, though with some effort, as not too many theories tend to "pop" into one's head. Either way, the point is the same: Sayre's approach seems fairly representative of real theories. The potential problem, however, is that his conception of "theory" might be too strong, which, if so, would leave open the possibility of giving Plato a theory of forms under a weaker sense of "theory."

Indeed, Sayre's formulation is precisely what Gonzales (2002, p. 66, n. 15) classifies as a "strong definition of 'theory'" (though himself favoring a weaker one, not to sneak the theory in, but to make the denial more meaningful), and it is what Griswold (1993, p. 203) criticizes as prejudicing the issue with an unjustifiably loaded sense of the concept in question. Surely, we do not want to strip Plato of a theory of forms by resorting to unreasonably strict requirements for what counts as a theory, but, by the same token, we should not want to relax the definition just so we can saddle him with the theory, or, as the case may be, just to make the denial more meaningful or more powerful. We should want simply to get it right. This requires some sort of balance between strong and weak formulations, given that we are not all of one mind on this. What we mean by "theory" is not as straightforward as what we mean by "proposition" or "conclusion." It is more flexible, that is, amenable to modifying the qualifications without changing the meaning, and the top priority is to guard against unreasonable extremes. As it is, the differences between Plato scholars seem to be a matter of reasonable disagreement rather than oversight or impropriety on the part of the parties contemplating whether Plato can be said to be working with a theory of forms.

To return to Sayre's denial in the essay with the daring title (1993b, pp. 167–193), his opposition combines the negative claim that nothing of the sort is actually to be found in the corpus with the positive claim that Plato himself is decidedly against the feasibility and even the possibility of a theory of forms. The negative claim goes though the passages typically invoked in the literature dedicated to the construction of the classical theory of forms, with Sayre arguing instead that the best evidence falls short of establishing a theoretical position. The primary focus here is on the definitive methodological turn in the *Phaedo* (100a–107b), the one recommending logical inquiry into propositions as an alternative to empirical inquiry into physical phenomena. The negative claim is grounded in the evidence of the *Seventh Letter* (341c–d, 344c–d) as a repudiation of any attempt to systematize the forms in or as a theoretical framework. This is complemented by earlier work dedicated exclusively to the proper interpretation of the epistolary caveat concerning writing: "Plato's Dialogues in Light of the *Seventh Letter*" (Sayre, 1988, pp. 93–109). Sayre's concern in this essay finds its fullest expression in a book-length treatment of the topic in *Plato's Literary Garden* (1995), borrowing the horticultural metaphor of dialectic in the *Phaedrus* (276d), while drawing heavily on the *Seventh Letter*, to demonstrate that Plato intends the dialogues as teaching instruments, not as doctrinal proclamations.

Sayre's work on the second front (1983, 2002) is concerned essentially with what can be said of the ontology of Plato, and only incidentally or derivatively with whether this leaves room for a theory of forms. His classic statement on the issue is *Plato's Late Ontology* (1983), an attempt to demonstrate that Aristotle's presentation of Plato, often found to be at odds with Plato's own work, can actually be substantiated directly through the Platonic corpus, particularly the late period. This provides an alternative to looking for corroboration of Aristotle in "unwritten teaching" by Plato, as practiced by the esoteric tradition of the Milan-Tübingen school, as well as an alternative to denouncing Aristotle for having misconstrued Plato, as supposed, for example, by Cherniss (1945). The middle ground Sayre offers is an interpretation of the late period as largely vindicating Aristotle's account without having to turn to the unwritten teaching, which Sayre replaces primarily with the written one he finds in the *Philebus*.

The upshot of all this for the classical theory of forms as separately existing yet directly knowable ideals is that, independently of whether anything said on the matter would qualify as a theory, most of what is said on the matter is confined to the middle period, the essentials of which are abandoned in the late period through a process starting as early as the *Parmenides* and culminating in the *Philebus*. This means that Sayre cannot afford to leave the *Timaeus*, where there is still fairly enthusiastic talk of forms, in its customary chronological position near the end of the late period. The further it lies from the *Parmenides*, the worse it is for Sayre's thesis. Indeed, he draws it in closer to the center, willing even to insert it smack in the middle of the *Parmenides*, that is, with respect to the temporal dimension of the work. But pursuing this move any further would be an unnecessary digression at this point, especially since Sayre is not alone in favoring an earlier date for the *Timaeus*. (Compare, for instance, Sayre [1983, pp. 15–16, 256–267] with Owen [1953, pp. 79–95].)

The central problem is with the notion of separately existing forms. The reconciliation of ontology and epistemology is achieved by rejecting the two-worlds paradigm of the middle period cutting us off from the realm of forms and thus making knowledge (of them) impossible. The epistemic barrier disappears as Plato gives up the total separation of the forms, instead making the indefinite dyad a common denominator in the ontology of forms and particulars: The forms are generated through the one and the indefinite dyad, while the particulars are generated through the forms and the indefinite dyad. In the process, the forms lose any claim they may have otherwise had to representing the fundamental principle of reality. While this is not a direct statement about whether Plato has a theory of forms, nor even specifically about whether he holds the one commonly ascribed to him, the implication is that he does neither.

Sayre has so much to say, both directly and indirectly, that he might perhaps be questioned for explaining both at once "Why Plato Never Had a Theory of Forms" (1993b) and why he abandoned the theory of forms (1983, 2002). This, however, would be unfair. Although Sayre does hold that what Plato does with the forms in the middle period differs from what he does with them in the late period, this does not commit him to the view that Plato has a theory of forms in either period. What Sayre is really against is reducing Plato's ontology to the classical theory of forms, which, he contends, defines Plato neither in the middle period nor in the late period. This, in turn, does not require denying that some dialogues, specifically, those clustered in the middle period, contain elements of the classical theory of forms, which, after all, is not pure fiction but an account at least inspired by canon if not deduced from it.

2.6.5. Bernard Arthur Owen Williams

Williams is not a Platonist, nor even a Plato scholar. He is foremost a moral philosopher. But he is also one of those rare thinkers defying classification, with work that is as diversified as it is definitive. Attesting to the breadth of his expertise, it is his contribution that represents the entry on Plato in an ambitious series on the Great Philosophers (1998 [=2006, pp. 148–186]). This is where we find his reservations regarding the standard interpretation of Plato as working with a theory of forms.

Williams is not especially concerned, as many others are, with conceptual points regarding what constitutes a theory and whether the so-called "theory of forms" qualifies as one, questions jointly defining the typical analytic substructure for assessing whether Plato holds such a theory *qua* theory. His own denial that Plato has a theory of forms is grounded in his more basic denial that Plato has a system. Rather than representing a component in an integrated whole, "each dialogue is about whatever it is about" (Williams, 2006, p. 154). To be sure, each dialogue is a part of the corpus, and the dialogues collectively define the canon, but they do not hang together as a system. They do not constitute an organic whole. In effect, Williams finds it simply too dissonant to ascribe a theory of forms to Plato.

As his essay is not dedicated exclusively to this point, he lays out his thoughts on the matter in the course of a broader assessment of Plato's impact on Western philosophy. His viewpoint on the historicity of the theory of forms comes out in the process of defining his own position on the interpretation of Plato's thought and work, specifically, in relation to developmentalism and esotericism (Williams, 2006, especially pp. 152–154, 179). Demonstrating what is always a refreshing perspective in any polarized issue, he objects to all parties concerned, in this case, both to developmentalists and to esotericists.

Against the developmentalists, while finding "some truth" in their biographical division of the corpus, Williams argues that grounding the entire enterprise on the theory of forms is precarious because there is "no theory of forms," by which he means to deny, of course, only that there is one in Plato (2006, pp. 153–154). He notes that the common practice of anchoring the middle period to the theory of forms inevitably leads to the question whether and when Plato gives the theory up, as is invariably asked in the face of the grand critique in the *Parmenides* and new directions in the *Theaetetus*, *Sophist*, and *Statesman*. He finds the question rather loaded, ostensibly like asking someone about giving up drugs without having first established an addiction, the philosophical analogue of which, he suggests, has not been established in Plato. Or, without putting metaphors in his mouth, his assessment is that the interpretive framework of the developmentalist assumes too much.

Against the esotericists, Williams argues that Plato's reservations regarding writing, particularly in the *Phaedrus*, neither denounce writing about philosophy nor glorify talking about it instead. They clearly favor the spoken word over the written, but not as an absolute rule. In fact, the preference is severely qualified, though not explicitly. The underlying assumption is that the spoken word would be part of a dialogue, which can be kept alive indefinitely, unlike the written word, which is bound and gagged by the intellect of the author, even in dialogic form, not to mention its entirely lifeless presence in treatise form. Otherwise, an oral speech fares no better than a written treatise, and presumably worse than a written dialogue, on the criteria laid out by Plato. It is in this spirit that Williams maintains first that Plato's famous critique of writing is not strictly prohibitory, instead merely imposing limitations on writing, and giving the philosopher a reason to write rather than taking it away (2006, pp. 151–152), and second that any objection or difficulty associated with the possibility or feasibility of a written doctrine holds just as well against an oral doctrine (2006, p. 174).

In sum, Williams rejects what is central to both positions, censuring developmentalism for excessive reliance on the theory of forms as a theory in and of Plato, while denouncing esotericism for misreading the critique of writing. Interpreting Plato as valuing philosophy for its activities rather than for its conclusions, he takes him to be engaged in theory without advocating any particular theory (Williams, 2006, p. 179). Plato, in short, trusts no theory for delivering the truth, but considers the general pursuit conducive to obtaining it, or, with due restraint, to obtaining a glimpse of or into it. As Williams puts it, Plato's dialogues are "not intended to control the minds of his readers, but to open them" (2006, p. 179), which leaves no room for indoctrination in a specific theory, particularly one so silencing as a theory of forms would be, but leaves ample room for dialectical training in search of the truth. Even where the training in question is fully immersed in talk of forms, this does not constitute a theory of forms.

What is most directly relevant to the case under consideration is the position of Williams against the developmentalist. But is he entirely fair in this regard? He objects to developmentalism because it bets too heavily on Plato's having held a theory of forms, actually, on his having held the theory of forms commonly circulated in philosophy textbooks. He finds no sense in asking whether or when Plato gives the theory up because, so he claims, Plato never holds it in the first place. But is this true? Is the question really analogous to asking someone about giving up drugs without having first established an addiction? Does Plato's documented engagement with the forms have no indicative bearing on the case? Indeed, he may not be comparable to the incorrigible crack addict who has been in and out of prison for possession, distribution, and trafficking. But is he instead comparable to the model citizen who would not know cannabis from lettuce if both were dried up, chopped up, and rolled up in paper? Or is he somewhere in between? Did he perhaps have a drug habit for a while, eventually giving it up? Does he still get high every now and then, without actually feeling compelled to do so? Is there, in short, some middle ground where he might be said to have taken puffs without effectively inhaling the smoke, or inhaled it without holding it in long enough to get high, or having gotten high without making a habit of it, or having developed a habit without letting it get out of hand?

The aim of the barrage of questions is not a wholesale rejection of Williams but a partial defense of the developmentalist. Williams is certainly right to claim that the developmentalist is not on firm ground. He may also be right that Plato has no theory of forms. And he need not positively establish the latter in order to demonstrate the former. Reasonable doubt is sufficient. But this works both ways, if anything about it can seriously be said to be working at all: The developmentalist need not positively establish the presence of the theory to proceed sensibly with a position affirming it. Evidentiary extrapolation is sufficient, perhaps not for the last word on the matter, but certainly for a respectable statement on it. The evidence just does not add up to a black-and-white case. The grey area is large enough to construct the developmentalist model, and, the foundation, shaky enough to condemn the building.

2.6.6. General Evaluation

As the common adage has it, there are two sides to any debate. And this one is no exception. Yet we already know the two sides here. Although the foregoing survey is dedicated exclusively to the negative camp, the positive camp requires no introduction. Being the default perspective, "Plato's theory of forms" need not be instantiated or explicated beyond the prevailing generalities in order to be understood. Accounts of it abound in the literature, and specific references would be largely superfluous.

Nevertheless, it might be practical to look at a few examples of enlightened advocacy against dissenting opinion, that is, demonstrations of an ongoing resolve to attribute a theory of forms to Plato despite awareness of reasoned arguments against the practice. These might, for example, fruitfully include Rickless (1997), who concentrates specifically on the *Parmenides* to show not only that there is such a theory, but also that it survives its greatest critic, and Gerson (2002, pp. 85–109), who argues more generally that Plato has a theory of forms, and that it, in fact, constitutes the basis for the chronological divisions in the standard account of developmentalism.

Evidently, although the positive perspective hardly requires an example, it may now require a defense. This, however, need not be pursued through specific examples from the literature as done to illustrate the negative position. Laying out the negative position in this way provides insight into the anarchistic flavor of the reaction, proceeding, as it does, with unpracticed and, therefore, distinctive observations, rather than arguments designed to explain or defend a party line along a predefined course. Not only would this be less apposite to the positive perspective, where the course in response is in fact largely predefined by the attack of the negative perspective, but it would also leave no room for organizing the salient points of the debate. The goal is not to determine the winner, but to make sure both sides are clearly understood. This, in turn, does not require giving equal time to the two sides, but, even if it did, the foregoing disparity in favor of the negative side is surely canceled out by the head start the positive side has already had.

Two issues stand out, one concerning the theoreticity of the theory, the other concerning the disposition of the theoretician. Both are defined by the negative camp. They are not emphasized, nor even specifically considered, in the inaugural presentation of the positive camp. Each one originates as a challenge rather than a constructive proposition. The first is the challenge that Plato's views on the forms do not constitute a theory. To be perfectly clear, and to avoid judging the further question whether he even has views on the matter, a more felicitous formulation might be that Plato's remarks about the forms, that is, what is written about them in the dialogues, do not qualify as a theory. They fall short. They simply do not fit together in a way that matches our conception of theoreticity. The second challenge is that a dogmatic approach of any sort is so alien to Plato that he could not have possibly held a theory of forms, be it the classical one or any other. The strategy here is to establish a general position precluding the consistency, and, therefore, tenability, of characterizing Plato as subscribing to the classical theory of forms: Holding no theory at all, he holds none about the forms, and he therefore holds not the one typically ascribed to him.

On both counts, the forms may exist, Plato may believe this, and he may even be fascinated by it, but he does not have a theory about it. There are other points of interest, but the discussion cannot be laid to rest without a meeting of the minds on these two issues. The negative side is sufficiently represented in the foregoing survey, and the positive side hardly requires special representation, but a recapitulation may help form a final judgment. Any bias therein toward the positive camp is to make up for giving the negative camp a definite voice while leaving the positive camp generalized as a silent original position. This being so, weaving in rebuttal options for the traditional perspective should enhance rather than undermine the fairness of any recapitulation at this point.

What is required, above all, is clarity. Is too much of it possible? Probably not of genuine clarity, but quite so of assumptions, stipulations, and arguments disguised as clarification. This is a prime strategy in the focus of the negative camp on theoreticity. To be fair, it is no less prominent in the response of the positive camp. The only place it is absent is in the original position, where the early history of reference to the "theory of forms" is almost certainly grounded in the need for a heuristic shorthand as opposed to a deliberate attempt to claim a precise scientific designation for Plato's position on the forms. What was originally identified by the positive camp, then the only camp, as "a theory of forms," and introduced thereby as "the theory of forms," is now challenged on its qualification as a theory.

This is not to deny the coexistence of an alternative designation as "doctrine of ideas," but its gradual replacement with reference to "theory of forms," ignoring the shifting preference from "idea" to "form," is a move away from the picture of a dogmatic Plato embracing a doctrine rather than a move toward the picture of a scientific Plato formulating a theory. Put simply, the development of the nomenclature is not indicative of a deliberate redefinition of Plato as a scientist. Indeed, it may have been inspired by nineteenth century developments in science, giving impetus to paradigm shifts in the philosophy of science. But the reflection in Plato amounts to little more than fresh insight into the unity of his thought and the coherence of his method, which is the same thought and same method no matter what new names we come up with. Yet we still remain engrossed in definition and clarification as if facing an unfamiliar concept or unique problem.

The intensity of the present focus on definition borders on reducing the inherent disagreement to semantic differences. We are not far from recasting the debate as a merely verbal dispute. Yet we should have recognized by now that a merely verbal dispute would not have survived such persistent efforts at clarification. Either the dispute is not merely verbal or clarification efforts have not been dispassionate. Curiously, both sides remain focused on ironing out conceptual confusion, as if winning the debate were a matter of adding one final touch of the subtlest semantic refinement to previous efforts. On the contrary, analytic efforts from here on out might best be directed not at fine-tuning our conception of theoreticity but at weeding out unhelpful distinctions and tangents introduced along the way in creating the current platform of discussion.

For example, denying Plato's talk of forms to constitute a theory in a strict sense while affirming it under a relatively relaxed definition risks introducing greater sophistication into the debate than warranted by the actual facts of the case. Worse, it might not really answer the question. Worse still, the question might not be the right one. Asking whether the definition is too strong or too weak, or strong enough or weak enough, just might beg the question of whether it is open to such calibration in the first place, that is, whether we are still talking about the same term, or concept, in the face of such variability, and, therefore, whether we are still disagreeing about the same issue. If the definition is so flexible as to allow the same person, with basically the same answer, to take either of opposite sides on the same issue, then the question has not been answered, the answer has to be questioned, and either or both might be duplicitous or misformulated. This is what happens when the same passages from the same dialogues collectively pass for a theory under a relatively weak conception of theoreticity while failing under a stronger conception.

What we really want to know when we ask if Plato's statements on and about the forms count as a theory is whether or not they instantiate the standard notion in our cumulative experience. What counts as a theory? Are Plato's statements about the forms *ad hoc* doxastic accretions or do they constitute an integrated explanatory system? Is the difference a matter of degree? Our intuition is that it is not. Yet we blur the distinction when we make it a function of the strength of the definition of "theory." And we do the same when we keep realigning it with the prevailing conception of theoreticity, somehow always in need of an update.

An unfortunate ramification of this is a tendency to treat the absence of evidence as the evidence of absence. The negative camp may be right in claiming that there is no conclusive evidence for the existence of a theory of forms, but this, in turn, is not evidence to the contrary. Not only is it not *conclusive* evidence to the contrary, it is not even *indicative* evidence to the contrary; it is as good as absolute silence, complete cluelessness.

This is so, even if theoreticity as a concept would be anachronistic in context, as maintained, for example, by Hyland (2002, p. 260). In fact, this additional information adds nothing to the interpretive possibilities. In a sense, denying that Plato holds a theory of forms, or of anything else, may be just as anachronistic as insisting that he does. If the concept is alien, it can no more be repudiated than embraced. Declaring its presence impossible makes its absence meaningless. What would be telling is if Plato were to share our concept of "theory," even if not our particular conception of theoreticity, without himself holding a theory of forms. Perhaps more perspicuously, this is the scenario of Plato having a notion of theory but not a theory of forms. If, on the other hand, the concept of "theory" were entirely alien to his mindset, then he could not have deliberately avoided it, and anything looking remotely like a theory holds interest precisely for being like it than for falling short.

Any hesitation in this regard tends to be exacerbated by the fear that equipping Plato with a theory of forms reduces the forms to theoretical entities. This, so the hesitation brews, would then be in conflict with the conviction he demonstrates in regard to their existence, and with how much he lets hang on what would in essence be an uncertainty. But theoreticity diminishes neither the forms themselves nor Plato's faith or trust in them. The physicist is no less convinced that quarks exist than Plato is that the forms do. And both go on to build entire universes out of what they have.

With regard to the forms, the point is rarely to corroborate their existence. Quite the opposite, as soon as it comes up, the question of their existence is quickly internalized as a necessary assumption that ought to be verified later, though somehow never pursued in the moment when it is most relevant. The point, rather, is almost always to employ that assumption in the exploration of an altogether different issue, usually a fundamental problem otherwise defying a satisfactory solution. The *Parmenides* is obviously an exception, but the generalization stands. How is it different, then, from what is done with quarks?

What we have, in the end, is not the absence of a theory, not even the absence of evidence for a theory, but the absence of conclusive evidence for it. And we have allowed an entire enterprise to flourish around this deadlock. Yet the evidentiary vacuum is no less adequately filled by the assumption that Plato is merely refraining from indoctrination than it is by the assumption that he has no theory of forms. The first is consistent with other things we may confidently say of the Platonic corpus, especially given the notorious distance between Plato and his audience, but the second clearly is not, instead remaining an isolated and even outlandish judgment unto itself. What makes the second judgment isolated is simply that it is not related to anything else about the corpus; what makes it outlandish is that its isolation is juxtaposed with an abundance of talk about the forms and serious use made of them.

Can we, then, consistently claim that the canonical references to the forms do not add up to a coherent platform of ratiocination capable of aiding explanatory or exploratory projects in a way that significantly expands or enriches the prevailing web of belief? The reference here to the "significance" of the expansion is not an attempt to sneak some plasticity into theoreticity, certainly not after having impugned open efforts to do the same thing. It is merely a makeshift provision to exclude trivial expansion, thereby ruling out at least internal contradiction and any conjecture other than what is already inherent in the theory itself. It can be further elaborated in any sensible way. That said, how are we to answer the question? Do we expect anything more of a theory? And, more important, does Plato's talk of forms not add up to this?

What might possibly stand in the way? Surely, it is not that the entire theory is not laid out as it would be in a textbook. Nothing in Plato ever is. The typical complaint, rather, is that we are not warranted in reconstructing the classical theory of forms from what is said in the dialogues, not because it contradicts anything there, but because it goes beyond it. Thus, the objection is not that the theory is not explicit in the text, but that it is not even implicit there, not fully anyway. But this is a moot point, since it is the nature of reconstructive work to end up with more than what is available prior to reconstruction.

A second complaint is that the finished product, even granting a flawless reconstruction process, is not theoretical enough. The end result is simply not a theory. This turns out to be a judgment requiring a special definition of theoreticity, and possibly begging the question. It might, in fact, beg the question in both directions, offering no special advantage to the positive camp either, but this still leaves the negative camp with an unsubstantiated challenge.

The first two complaints are not even mutually compatible. They are usually brought up in separate efforts because it is not sensible to charge the positive camp both with creating a theory where none exists and with failing to end up with a theory. The charge would then be about failure to produce a theory while attempting to do so, hence, about incompetence, but this assures consistency at the cost of believability. The point, presumably, is that the positive camp is wrong, not stupid.

A third complaint is that Plato never even attempts, or, evidently therefore, intends, to use the forms as a theory. The objection here is not only that Plato does not present a theory of forms, explicitly or implicitly, but that he has no such intention, and probably no such notion, leaving us nothing from which to reconstruct a theory that might otherwise be at least implicit. This is perhaps the weakest claim in the negative camp. Plato demonstrably invokes the forms, not merely in passing, but at critical junctures throughout the middle period, where most turning points start with the character Socrates ushering in the concept of forms, perhaps not in the proper configuration of a theory but definitely toward the systematic formulation of an answer to a problem otherwise defying a solution. What is thus introduced, even if it fails to meet formal criteria for theoreticity, is in fact employed in a systematic problem-solving capacity. Hence, the intention, if anything at all may be said about it, is more evidently there than not.

In spite of all this, or rather, as the common denominator there, the negative camp has an ironclad diagnosis: The evidence is not sufficient to conclude with certainty that Plato has a theory of forms. No matter the individual arguments, for or against, this much is clear. This does not mean that Plato has no theory of forms. Nor does it mean that believing that he does is unreasonable. It means only that denying that he does is reasonable, though no more so than affirming it.

As philosophers of science are wont to remind us, albeit not unanimously, all theories are underdetermined by the evidence. That is, every theory is underdetermined by the evidence for that theory, not because something is wrong, but because that is the nature of the relationship between theory and evidence. What sets the theory of forms apart, rather comically, is that it is not just the substance of the theory but its very existence that is underdetermined by the evidence. In other words, not only is the theory of forms questionable, but so, too, is the theory, or hypothesis, that Plato has a theory of forms. We have no better recourse than the dialectical process to settle our differences. This, in turn, is precisely where we are in the ongoing debate. Hence, quite ironically, we find ourselves engaged in the Platonic art of dialectic, debating whether he practices it the way he does, with the theory of forms at the center.

Three

WORKS OF PLATO

Most of Plato's works are in the form of dialogues. The only exceptions are letters, definitions, and epigrams, collectively amounting to relatively little in bulk or in substance, and often dividing scholars on the issue of authenticity. Everything else is a dialogue, at least technically. Some of these unfold as long speeches with barely enough interlocution to justify classification as a dialogue as distinct from a monologue, but, strictly speaking, even one interruption is enough since the distinction between dialogue and monologue cannot be held to a quantitative standard beyond just the one exchange that breaks an otherwise solo performance. More important, the decisive factor in classification is a broad fit with the genre rather than adherence to a precise number of speakers, or attention to an equitable distribution of speaking parts. Plato's approach, on this interpretation as well, is unmistakably dialogic.

The decision to proceed with dialogues may have been motivated by the inherent advantages in mass appeal, especially if people back then, as they do now, preferred drama over disquisition. The approach is also pedagogically rewarding as a tool for stimulating thinking without indoctrination. However, these are unlikely to have been the only considerations behind Plato's choice: He does not treat the dialogue form as a mere delivery channel for thoughts. He shows at least as much concern for the channel itself as for the ideas transmitted therein. As a result, his dialogues are praised no less for their literary value than for their philosophical contribution. The dramatic elements are often as important as the logical ones. Plot, setting, and character are never merely incidental or instrumental to argument; they complement the argument while presenting it, that is, in the very act or process of presenting it, and, as such, they constitute an essential part of the philosophy. In this regard, Plato's utilization of the dialogue form stands alone in the history of Western philosophy, not because no one else has written philosophical dialogues, but because no one else has done it so well, shaping and perfecting the literary genre as well as the field of study taken up through that genre.

Plato did not invent dialogic prose. Setting aside the dialogue form in general, even the Socratic dialogue, as a distinct literary specialty, is not exclusively Platonic. The genre of the "Sōkratikos logos" (Σωκρατικὸς λόγος), literally denoting the "word of Socrates," but in fact referring to "Socratic discourse," is commonly known in English translation as the "Socratic dialogue," for which the direct equivalent in Greek would actually be "Sōkratikos dialogos" (Σωκρατικὸς διάλογος). Be that as it may, the name that has been handed down is "Sōkratikos logos," and the standard English designation is "Socratic dialogue." The genre originates in dramatic or narrative prose featuring Socrates and written by his disciples, or "associates," as he calls them. These include, but are not limited to, Aeschines of Sphettus (a.k.a. Aeschines Socraticus), Antisthenes of Athens (Antisthenes II, Son of Antisthenes), Aristippus of Cyrene, Euclides of Megara, Phaedo of Elis, and Xenophon of Athens, in addition to Plato. The definitive source for the originals is the four-volume compendium edited by Giannantoni (1990), but a basic orientation can be had through surveys such as those by Clay (1994, pp. 23–47), Döring (2011, pp. 24–47), and Kahn (1996, pp. 1–35).

The name of the genre derives from Aristotle (*Rhetoric* 1417a20; *Poetics* 1447b11), though the textual context shows him not so much proposing a name for the genre as pointing out that it has no name. Else (1957, pp. 39–67), for example, objects with passion and erudition to construing Aristotle's reference as an act of naming, but a name can nevertheless originate somewhere without a deliberate attempt at naming, or without a formal proposal for a name.

Aristotle also reportedly identifies Alexamenus of Teos, in a work now lost (*On Poets*), as the creator or originator of the genre, that is, as the first person ever to write Socratic dialogues, but the attribution is in dispute.

We do not have much to go on, yet we are all clear on what that is: Aristotle's reference to Alexamenus is substantiated by fragmentary evidence from *On Poets* (fr. 72 Rose = Athenaeus 11.505c) and corroborated by Diogenes Laërtius (*Lives* 3.48) citing Favorinus. The facts of the matter being so few, they make their way into every discussion or reference: Else (1957, p. 41, n. 154); Haslam (1972, pp. 17–18); Thesleff (1982, p. 56, n. 12 [=2009, p. 203, n. 138]); Janko (1984, p. 147); Clay (1994, p. 34, n. 22, invoking Haslam, 1972); Nails (1995, p. 11, n. 8, citing Thesleff, 1982); Dorion (2011, p. 7, n. 21).

The problem is not just that the evidence comes from fragments of a lost work, making it difficult to be certain about what was meant, nor that the corroborating testimony is by a source eager to report anything and everything available to him in writing, but at least partly also that all this is at best confirmation that Aristotle actually said such a thing, asserting the primacy of Alexamenus as a literary innovator, and not, in addition, that it is true. Any room for doubt is amplified by the several other names nominated for the distinction but even more so by the reality that just about any of its practitioners, whether on record anywhere as the first, or the last, or at all, could in fact have been the first to use the form in question.

The genre, however, involves more than making Socrates the central figure, and excludes, for example, comic work, such as that of Aristophanes. Moreover, making Socrates the central figure creates no obligation to be slavish to the memory of the historical Socrates. The *Sōkratikos logos* is not concerned with the dissemination of information about Socrates. Nor is its *raison d'être* to promulgate Socratic doctrines, which might have been preserved more accurately and transmitted more effectively through a manifesto of basically any form other than fiction, and which the man himself might have done well to transcribe or dictate personally, or at least to commission or authorize, in his own lifetime. Like the Greek biographical tradition, the Socratic dialogue attempts to capture personality rather than reality, with little concern for historical accuracy, or even for chronological possibility. This is why Plato does not hesitate to place everything in the world of yesteryear instead of in his own time, thus tapping his imagination more than his experience. Taking advantage of the genre's inherent exemption from veridical dramatization and characterization, he confidently introduces his audience to people he himself never met. (See, for example, Kahn, 1995, pp. 26–35; 1996, pp. 1–35.)

This is how we meet the famous Eleatics, Parmenides and Zeno. Parmenides was already dead when Plato was born. Zeno, at that point, did not himself have very many years left. In the same manner, we are artfully made witness to the rising tide of the itinerant teachers of *aretē* (ἀρετή), encountering Protagoras of Abdera, who must have been dead before Plato ever made the transition from wrestler to philosopher, and Gorgias of Leontini, who might actually have performed in the presence of Plato, though that possibility is grounded, more than anything, in the reputation of Gorgias as a centenarian, or perhaps even supercentenarian. And we find all of these characters in heated debate with a Socrates depicted at different stages in his life, as if Plato had been his shadow the whole time.

Although Plato's extraordinary talent transfers us to the scene of discussions between Socrates and first-generation Sophists, this should not fool us into thinking that we are privy to the actual words spoken between them, if such meetings ever in fact took place. We do not get to know either Protagoras or Gorgias in reading Plato. And hardly any greater reliability need be assigned to what we find out about Socrates in the same way. This is not to say that Plato's portrait of Socrates is not to be trusted, but that it is not to be treated as a modern biography. It is most assuredly not wholly fabricated or particularly mendacious, but it is also not intended as a precise representational sketch. Plato is thus no exception to the Socratics, all writing about Socrates, none with a view to recording facts for posterity.

Few of the Socratic dialogues outside Plato have survived intact. Specifically, only those by Xenophon have. Xenophon's Socratic work includes the *Apology*, *Memorabilia*, *Symposium*, and *Oeconomicus*, and possibly also the *Hiero*, if the protagonist need not be Socrates for the work to count as Socratic. None of the other Socratic dialogues is available in its entirety, but fragments abound, except for the work of Aristippus, for which we have to rely on anecdotal evidence. Nevertheless, testimonial evidence regarding the genre is abundant, compelling, and informative.

Fortunately, we have far more than testimony in the case of Plato. All of his writings are believed to be extant. The basis for this belief is that all the works attributed to him throughout history are still in existence today, with the exception of spuria readily exposed as such in classical times but long lost now. He has always been a central figure in philosophy, followed zealously, opposed just as passionately, but never neglected. Because of this, the fact that millennia of uninterrupted discussion on Plato does not include a single reference to a work of his that is no longer in existence constitutes strong evidence that all his work has survived to date. In fact, the key question regarding Plato's work has long been, not whether any of his writings have been lost, but whether all that are attributed to him were in fact written by him. Some were recognized even in ancient times as spurious, whether outright forgeries or merely erroneous attributions, but nothing new, be it genuine or apocryphal, has surfaced afterwards. Specifically, Diogenes (*Lives* 3.62) reports ten dialogues that were confirmed as spurious in his own time, hence, at least as early as the fifth century and probably hundreds of years before that: *Axiochus*; *Demodocus*; *Eryxias* (or *Erasistratus*); *Halcyon*; *Sisyphus* (or *Acephali*); *Chelidon*; *Epimenides*; *Midon* (*Horse Breeder*); *Phaeacians*; *Seventh Day*. The first five in listing order have survived; the rest have been lost. The surviving five dialogues, together with two other works verified by the ancients as spurious, but not mentioned by Diogenes, namely, *On Justice* and *On Virtue*, have traditionally been a part of the Platonic corpus. Anyone interested in the spuria, including those reported by Diogenes, as well as those missed by him, would do well to consult Taylor (1960, pp. 521–555) for an overview.

3.1. The Platonic Corpus

The following table illustrates the Platonic corpus. It covers everything, genuine or spurious, ever attributed to Plato and still in existence. Thus, it excludes that which is no longer in existence. Fortunately, whatever is no longer in existence, to the best of our knowledge, is not actually by Plato. This, then, is the received wisdom. This is what we have: Everything Plato ever wrote, plus some things he did not write. It is all transmitted together in the collection of manuscripts handed down as canon. The distinction between his work and everything else in the bundle is, however, a matter of contention rather than convention. There are easy cases, and there are hard debates. The current state of opinion is far from anything resembling a consensus, but it also bears a safe distance to what might count as chaos. The table reflects a fairly typical position on the breakdown of authenticity, which is to say, it might not please everyone, but it certainly will not alienate very many people. It should, at any rate, surprise no one.

The Platonic Corpus
Historically Exhaustive List of Works Attributed to Plato and Still in Existence

Dialogues (Alphabetical Order)				Other
Genuine (24)		**Dubious (6)**	**Spurious (12)**	**Work**
Apology	Meno	*Probably*	Alcibiades 2	Letters
Charmides	Parmenides	*Genuine*	Axiochus **	Definitions
Cratylus	Phaedo	Hippias Major	Clitophon	Epigrams
Critias	Phaedrus	Ion	Demodocus **	
Crito	Philebus	Menexenus	Eryxias **	
Euthydemus	Protagoras		Halcyon **	
Euthyphro	Republic	*Probably*	Minos	
Gorgias	Sophist	*Spurious*	On Justice *	
Hippias Minor	Statesman	Alcibiades 1	On Virtue *	
Laches	Symposium	Epinomis	Rival Lovers	
Laws	Theaetetus	Hipparchus	Sisyphus **	
Lysis	Timaeus		Theages	

Notes:
1. The items listed under "other work" are generally considered spurious, or otherwise insignificant, except for the *Letters*, several of which are widely accepted, all thirteen of which are disputed, and none insignificant.
2. The spurious dialogues marked with an asterisk were recognized as such even in ancient times, with a second asterisk indicating mention by Diogenes Laërtius (*Lives* 3.62).

All told, the dialogic portion of the corpus includes forty-two dialogues, with the degree of expert agreement regarding their authenticity varying over time. Although the number of dialogues considered authentic dwindled to the single digits in the nineteenth century, this was a historical aberration that has since rebounded decisively, stabilizing around a couple of dozen genuine works, another dozen spurious works, and a handful of debatable works. With respect to lost spuria reported by Diogenes Laërtius, we are stuck with the original appraisal of them as spurious, but this is not worrisome given the complete absence of historical evidence suggesting that any of the corresponding works might be authentic. Another mitigating factor in this respect is the fact that nothing the ancients deemed spurious, whether still existing or now lost, is currently considered authentic, whereas several works they accepted as genuine are now universally rejected, showing that the ancients were easier to satisfy, which is comforting with respect to the rejects they failed to pass on. In other words, given that the judgments of the ancients have never been revised to reverse a rejection, but only to reverse an endorsement, it is a boon that all the lost works happen to be what they already considered spurious.

Corpus math is still far from standardized. The preceding table is in broad agreement with what is known as the "standard view," which, however, might well qualify as the least popular or most widely challenged standard in any context. Actually, the "standard view" is only derivatively relevant to the difference between genuine and spurious works. Instead, it pertains specifically to the arrangement of the genuine works in the order of composition, at least in terms of productive periods if not in a strict chronological sequence, either one of which presumably reveals the progression of Plato's philosophical and literary development. The table is intentionally silent on chronology, because this is a controversial issue requiring independent consideration, but it may still be said to reflect the standard view as far as authenticity is concerned. Ironically, the standard view is not all that standard, even in itself, that is, even upon ignoring opposition, because its proponents are engaged as much in correcting one another as they are in convincing skeptics and refuting opponents, but any details in this regard are best reserved for a separate discussion (§ 3.3.3).

Despite the strength of the outright departure, or that of the internal discord, any view that deserves characterization as "standard" must be capable of expression in a fairly representative formulation. In this case, dissension and hesitation aside, this is the view that among the forty-two surviving dialogues, more than half can be attributed to Plato with near certainty, and several more on top of that with reasonable confidence, with the resulting canon amenable to chronological arrangement. Specifically, the standard view embraces a core of two dozen dialogues as authentic and rejects another dozen as spurious. Thus, thirty-six of the forty-two dialogues associated with Plato come with a definite verdict regarding their authenticity. This leaves six dialogues that are neither universally accepted nor universally rejected: Three of these are considered genuine by most scholars and bogus by some, while the other three are considered genuine by a few experts and bogus by most. The three works that are widely accepted are *Hippias Major*, *Ion*, and *Menexenus*; the three that are widely rejected are *Alcibiades* 1, *Epinomis*, and *Hipparchus*.

Plato's intellectual legacy outside the dialogues is limited to thirteen letters, a book of definitions, and a small collection of epigrams. The letters, offering, if genuine, the only direct insight we may have into Plato's life, with particularly detailed accounts of his involvement in the politics of Syracuse, are far more important than the other two items. The definitions have been handed down collectively as a compendium of 185 entries apparently compiled from two distinct collections characteristic of Academic work but not necessarily identifiable as the work of Plato. The epigrams, eighteen in all, are short poems in the form of elegiac couplets, most comprising exactly two lines, five doubling that length, and one reaching six lines. Expert opinion is divided over the authenticity of the letters, but the definitions and epigrams are widely rejected and philosophically inconsequential. The letters are indeed informative, even uniquely so, but not everyone agrees that they were written by Plato. The verdict on their authenticity tends to be piecemeal as well as wholesale, with some scholars accepting some letters while rejecting others, and other scholars arriving at uniform judgments on all thirteen letters, thus formulating a blanket opinion one way or the other, though not necessarily agreeing yea or nay among themselves.

Letters Attributed to Plato in the Traditional Corpus

Name	**Date**	**Recipient**
Letter 1 (5)	≥ 360	Dionysius II of Syracuse
Letter 2 (6)	> 360	Dionysius II of Syracuse
Letter 3 (9)	≥ 357	Dionysius II of Syracuse
Letter 4 (10)	≥ 357	Dion of Syracuse
Letter 5 (4)	365–360	Perdiccas III of Macedonia
Letter 6 (13)	± 350	Hermias of Atarneus, Erastus of Scepsis, Coriscus of Scepsis
Letter 7 (11)	> summer 354	Friends of Dion of Syracuse
Letter 8 (12)	> 353/352	Friends of Dion of Syracuse
Letter 9 (1)	> 383	Archytas of Tarentum
Letter 10 (8)	> 360	Aristodorus of Syracuse
Letter 11 (7)	> 360	Laodamas of Thasos
Letter 12 (2)	> 383	Archytas of Tarentum
Letter 13 (3)	≥ 365	Dionysius II of Syracuse

Note: The numbers in parentheses indicate the position of the letters in a ranking in the chronological order proposed by Debra Nails.

Source: Debra Nails: *The People of Plato* (2002): pp. 329–330.

Guthrie (1978, p. 401) shares an interesting opinion poll, which, though outdated since his effort to communicate it, and admittedly not definitive to begin with, approximates a probability distribution of epistolary authenticity, graphically demonstrating how controversial the letters have been and can still be among Plato scholars. The most widely rejected seem to be the *First*, *Second*, *Fifth*, *Ninth*, and *Twelfth Letters*. Fortunately, the most valuable ones, specifically, the *Seventh* and *Eighth Letters*, happen to attract the greatest expert agreement regarding their authenticity, followed by the *Sixth* and the *Third Letters*. The value of the *Seventh* and *Eighth Letters* is grounded in the contribution they make to the historical record of primary sources on the life of Plato, though coverage is limited to his visits to Syracuse and his dealings with those in and around power there. In this regard, they are complemented by the first four letters, the first two of which are unlikely to be authentic, and by the last. Despite ongoing debates, Guthrie was able to detect, even in 1978, that the critical approach to the letters was, generally speaking, shifting from rejection to acceptance, indicating the emergence of a positive outlook that continues to prevail today.

Another fortunate tendency in scholarly approaches to the letters is the separation of the issue of authorship from that of accuracy. Put simply, this is the recognition that a forged letter need not be inaccurate, especially since the very purpose of any forgery is to appear so much like the original as to be indistinguishable from it. In terms of insight into the life of Plato, the difference between a genuine letter and a spurious one seems, in essence, to be that between autobiographical and biographical information.

On the whole, nothing that is rejected, whether among the dialogues or in the comprehensive corpus, is a masterpiece of literature or a jewel in the annals of philosophy. This makes both past and present debates regarding authenticity less significant than they might have been otherwise. Although a division between genuine and spurious works that just happens to embrace the good stuff while rejecting the lesser works may seem suspiciously convenient, such a breakdown is apposite to Plato's position as one of the greatest philosophers and writers of all time, and it is just as likely to be a direct causal result of this position as it is to be a reflection of respect for it, though separating the two is difficult.

Plato is not thought to have produced any other written work, be it dialogues, formal treatises, or even lecture notes. More accurately, he is thought not to have produced any other written work. This view is not a tentative conclusion drawn exclusively from a lack of evidence for his having left behind any other work; rather, it is a positive conviction based on evidence for his not having left any behind. At any rate, nothing crucial hangs on the balance, as the corresponding intellectual heritage can hardly be made any greater than it already is. Moreover, the known work is so broad and abundant that anything lost is more likely to be correlated closely with something extant, and therefore long recognized and digested, than it is to be unique in any significant way, especially in regard to philosophy if not also to literature.

3.2. Structure of the Corpus

It is human nature to impose a structure on any volume of work, even on a single tome. This is perhaps because it is also human nature to compose or produce in this way. No matter the reason, an output as voluminous as Plato's is better considered in some sort of order than with none at all. Any order can, by definition, be expected to be a sensible one, though none will satisfy everyone, nor will any be guaranteed to be serviceable forever.

Two classification schemes handed down from antiquity are trilogies and tetralogies. The account of Plato by Diogenes Laërtius includes specific sources for both of these approaches. The emphasis in either case is on how the dialogues ought to be read, or on how Plato intended them to be read, that is, on good or intended combinations of dialogues for reading or study. This may well turn out to match the order in which they were written or published, but the presentation does not make the actual order of production as great a concern as the proper order of study.

The oldest known classification, on one interpretation of the evidence, is an arrangement by trilogy, an approach which Diogenes (*Lives* 3.61–62) reports as common, though specifically identifying only one source, Aristophanes of Byzantium (c. 257–180 BC). Not to be confused with the comic poet predating him by more than a century, this Aristophanes was a Greek scholar, most notably a grammarian, and held the distinguished post of head librarian at the Royal Library of Alexandria. The trilogy classification attributed to him may be summarized as follows:

Plato's Trilogies: Aristophanes of Byzantium

1	Republic	Timaeus	Critias
2	Sophist	Statesman	Cratylus
3	Laws	Minos	Epinomis
4	Theaetetus	Euthyphro	Apology
5	Crito	Phaedo	Letters

Source: Diogenes Laërtius: *Lives* (3.61–62).

This scheme covers fewer than half the dialogues in the corpus, though it still recognizes the remainder as individual works. For this reason alone, that is, for its narrow taxonomic scope, it is not as appealing or as useful as the nine-by-four tetralogical classification superseding it, even if other considerations were to favor groups of three over groups of four.

Diogenes cites Thrasyllus as his source for the tetralogical scheme (*Lives* 3.56), but he also indicates, without identifying anyone in particular, that others could be credited for the same approach (*Lives* 3.61). Although the reference to Thrasyllus includes nothing beyond the bare name, this source is believed to be Thrasyllus of Mendes (d. 36), an Egyptian grammarian responsible for putting together one of the first complete editions of Plato's collected works. He also tends to be identified with Tiberius Claudius Thrasyllus, a mathematician and astronomer serving as the astrologer of Emperor Tiberius (42 BC–AD 37; reign: AD 14–37), after befriending him in exile in Rhodes prior to the emperor's rise to power. Any biography drawing on both traditions at once will obviously be richer, but these may well be two different people, in which case Thrasyllus of Mendes would have to be credited with editing Plato's works, which would make Tiberius Claudius Thrasyllus a court astrologer with no particular expertise in Plato. It is hard to say which is the more enviable position, but, if these really are two different people, the Platonist may have been far more influential regarding the development of Platonism than is acknowledged by Diogenes. At least one major reassessment in modern times (Tarrant, 1993) assigns Thrasyllus greater prominence in the history of Platonism, but the profile available in Diogenes is still a good place to start.

Diogenes (*Lives* 3.56) reports Thrasyllus as taking no credit for the arrangement in tetralogies, giving none to anyone else, and claiming instead that Plato's original output was already laid out as such. This would mean that the tetralogical scheme precedes the trilogical scheme, rather than the other way around as might otherwise be suggested by the attribution of the trilogy approach to Aristophanes (Diogenes: *Lives* 3.61–62), who flourished a couple of centuries before Thrasyllus. The way out depends at least partly on whether Thrasyllus was an innovator or reporter in this regard. It cannot be true both that Plato arranged his own work in tetralogies and that this somehow came after a generally established systematic preference for organizing that same work in trilogies, especially as the inception of the latter effort is attributed to someone born nearly a century after Plato died. It also cannot be the case that Plato arranged his own work in tetralogies while this was completely unknown to Aristophanes in introducing the schema of trilogies no more than 150 years or so later. One answer might be that Plato himself had no particular preference for organizational structure, while Aristophanes favored trilogies, and, Thrasyllus, tetralogies, the latter eventually prevailing.

However, not everyone agrees that trilogies come before tetralogies in the history of structural perspectives on the Platonic corpus. Philip (1970, pp. 296–308), for one, makes a strong case for just the opposite: Having twice announced intended tetralogies, one being the *Republic-Timaeus-Critias*-[*Hermocrates*], the other, the *Theaetetus-Sophist-Statesman*-[*Philosopher*], in each case, the bracketed final element never delivered, evidently, never even started, Plato himself may have been the original inspiration for the tetralogical classification, which may be why Thrasyllus attributes the ordering to Plato.

Yet going purely by the math involved in the actual output, the same evidence could just as well be cited in favor of the primacy of the trilogical scheme, given that both series supposedly supporting the tetralogical perspective are in fact trilogies, not tetralogies as presumably intended. On the other hand, as Philip (1970, p. 301) points out, one of these two series can be recast as stringing together the *Cratylus-Theaetetus-Sophist-Statesman*, dropping the unwritten *Philosopher* and adding the *Cratylus* to form a "natural tetralogy," thereby presumably salvaging the thesis that the tetralogical scheme might originate with Plato.

This, in itself, may be a respectable position, but the extended argument, that is, the overarching perspective including the convenient transition from "intended" to "natural" tetralogies, might appear a bit crafty, not to mention that it could just as well be said to commit the proponent to a classification by pentalogy (adding the *Cratylus* without dropping the *Philosopher*, and thus exemplifying what would be an "intended" pentalogy). Then again, the Socratic series joining the drama in the *Euthyphro-Apology-Crito-Phaedo* sequence may count as another "natural tetralogy," and, therefore, as an additional clue in favor of the tetralogical classification. The evidence can be stretched in one direction or the other, but it is, in the final analysis, inadequate to establish with certainty that Plato either used or favored any particular arrangement.

Fortunately, we have good guides for what can be done with the evidence available. While the trilogy/tetralogy distinction alone hardly requires or constitutes a particular specialization, or merits exclusive attention, a representative list of introductory surveys of the Platonic corpus from a structural perspective might include the following: Cooper (1997, pp. vii–xxvi); Field (1930, pp. 64–76); Irwin (2008, pp. 63–87); Rowe (2003a, pp. 98–124; 2003b, pp. 17–32; 2006a, pp. 13–24; 2006b, pp. 159–170; 2007, pp. 1–51). But we do not have to consult any details, here or elsewhere, to conclude that the tetralogical scheme triumphs over the trilogical one, if only because it is far richer, affording greater interpretive and organizational possibilities. We may not know whether it came before or after the arrangement by trilogy, but we do know it survived it.

According to the tetralogical tradition, Plato gave two titles to each dialogue, one usually a proper name designating the principal character (excluding Socrates), and, the other, a brief description of the subject matter, and he published them all in tetralogies. Exceptions to using a proper name for the main title make up one-fourth of the works in question, eight of thirty-six: *Apology*; *Laws*; *Letters*; *Republic*; *Rival Lovers*; *Sophist*; *Statesman*; *Symposium*. The following table illustrates the full details of the Thrasyllan classification as laid out by Diogenes (*Lives* 3.56–61):

Plato's Tetralogies: Thrasyllus of Mendes

		Standard Title	Descriptive Title	Type
1	1	Euthyphro	On Holiness	tentative
	2	Apology	Apology of Socrates	ethical
	3	Crito	On What Is To Be Done	ethical
	4	Phaedo	On the Soul	ethical
2	1	Cratylus	On Correctness of Names	logical
	2	Theaetetus	On Knowledge	tentative
	3	Sophist	On Being	logical
	4	Statesman	On Monarchy	logical
3	1	Parmenides	On Ideas	logical
	2	Philebus	On Pleasure	ethical
	3	Symposium	On the Good*	ethical
	4	Phaedrus	On Love	ethical
4	1	Alcibiades 1	On the Nature of Man	obstetric
	2	Alcibiades 2	On Prayer	obstetric
	3	Hipparchus	The Lover of Gain	ethical
	4	Rival Lovers	On Philosophy	ethical
5	1	Theages	On Philosophy	obstetric
	2	Charmides	On Temperance	tentative
	3	Laches	On Courage	obstetric
	4	Lysis	On Friendship	obstetric
6	1	Euthydemus	The Eristic	refutative
	2	Protagoras	Sophists	critical
	3	Gorgias	On Rhetoric	refutative
	4	Meno	On Virtue	tentative
7	1	Hippias Major	On Beauty	refutative
	2	Hippias Minor	On Falsehood	refutative
	3	Ion	On the Iliad*	tentative
	4	Menexenus	The Funeral Oration	ethical
8	1	Clitophon	Introduction	ethical
	2	Republic	On Justice	political
	3	Timaeus	On Nature	physical
	4	Critias	Story of Atlantis	ethical
9	1	Minos	On Law	political
	2	Laws	On Legislation	political
	3	Epinomis	Nocturnal Council (or Philosopher)	political
	4	Letters	Letters	ethical

Notes: The descriptive titles marked with an asterisk require comment.
3.3: The *Symposium* is actually about love, not "the good" as above.
7.3: The proper descriptive title for the *Ion* is "On the Rhapsode's Art."

Source: Diogenes Laërtius: *Lives* (3.56–61).

Thrasyllus reportedly presents Plato as having been inspired by the organizational principle behind staging plays in groups of four at literary festivals in ancient Greece. This is a reference to the common theatrical practice of combining a comedy with three tragedies. Thus, Plato ostensibly organizes his work in an analogous manner, which would require grouping together a dialogue of one type with three of another. Philosophical dialogues being rather resistant to classification as comedy or tragedy, the candidates for relevant categories in this case are as follows: critical (detective); ethical (moral); logical; obstetric (maieutic); physical; political; refutative (eversive); tentative (Diogenes: *Lives* 3.58–61). A straightforward analogy would seem to require combining three dialogues falling under one of these eight designations with a fourth dialogue falling under a different designation. This is what happens in five of the tetralogies (1, 2, 3, 5, 9), but the rest break the pattern (4, 6, 7, 8), which suggests that the analogy might be more complex than a strict three-plus-one formula. Perhaps the eight categories are intended to be grouped in a certain way whereby the analogy could be fulfilled through a tetralogy's representation of certain sets or groups of categories and not necessarily of the individual categories. Or perhaps the analogy is not more complex but simpler, requiring merely that four dialogues be brought together in any combination so long as they are not all of the same type, or possibly even without this stipulation, and, thereby, regardless of how many of each type is included in any given tetralogy. At any rate, the precise correlation with theatrical practice is not obvious, beyond, that is, the total adding up to four.

The parallel drawn between Greek theater and Plato's scholarly output is nothing if not colorful, forceful, and especially appropriate for the historical context. However, the current view is that the classification originating with or transmitted by Thrasyllus is not one that was presented or intended by Plato. A glaring defect in the tetralogical classification illustrated in the preceding table is the presence of dialogues now considered spurious. Another weakness is that dialogues tend to be grouped together despite apparent discord, so much so that some of the tetralogies are comparable to multiple choice questions asking which item does not belong in a certain group (e.g., the third and eighth tetralogies). A third difficulty is that the organizational effort attributed to Plato is not accompanied by a convincing motive for the structural strategy, unless one is fully satisfied with the adoption of theatrical practice as sufficient motivation in itself. Perhaps most important, no evidence can be adduced, beyond the alleged testimony of Thrasyllus, to show that Plato himself actually worked with a superstructure, whether it be the one purportedly reported by Thrasyllus or an altogether different formula based on pairs, trilogies, or tetralogies.

That said, the Thrasyllan scheme is superior to the classification by Aristophanes, at least in covering more than double the material, while leaving nothing but spurious work outside the grand structure. Despite some overlap, the two arrangements are incompatible: Each of the first three Aristophanic trilogies is a subset of a Thrasyllan tetralogy, but the remaining two trilogies are not. An interesting note in this regard is that Diogenes (*Lives* 3.61–62) describes the

Aristophanic classification as an "arbitrary" arrangement, whereas more than half of it coincides with the Thrasyllan scheme supposedly originating with Plato himself in accordance with a plan. Still, the two classification schemes as reported cannot both be followed at once, even as a packing list, let alone as a suggestion for reading order. However, while they are mutually exclusive, they are not jointly exhaustive. The prevailing view is that neither approach can be linked directly to Plato himself, that nothing is gained by following one rather than the other, and that neither one offers any advantage over reading the dialogues in any other rational sequence or possibly even in random order.

Nevertheless, the tetralogical classification, representing the prevailing standard during the life of Thrasyllus, and, apparently, firmly sacrosanct as canon by the time of Diogenes, remained largely unchallenged through the eighteenth century, but crumbled in the nineteenth, with a great deal of controversy regarding not only proper classification but also authorship. The twentieth century brought renewed respect for the traditional corpus in regard to authenticity but not in regard to classification, as chronological division into three main periods of intellectual activity became the dominant view.

Still reigning, at least in Anglo-American circles, as the "standard view," or, to be more specific, as the "standard developmental account," and sometimes even expressed in full detail as the "standard chronological account of three productive periods," this is the position that Plato's work falls into three distinct periods: early, middle, and late. The division into three periods constitutes the leading version of the developmental interpretation of Plato, but common variations include a transitional category between the first two periods, or between the last two, or sometimes both. In either formulation, the central claim is that Plato's philosophical outlook and literary skills continued to develop as he produced the corpus, this constituting the main alternative to the opposing ("unitarian") interpretation that the entire corpus represents an undertaking from the standpoint of a fully developed outlook and set of skills.

Developmentalism and unitarianism do not exhaust the interpretive possibilities. Rejecting one does not require adopting the other. But the remaining option is to take Plato's work to be entirely disjointed. All that is left is the portrait of a Plato who writes discrete pieces with no regard or responsibility in one for what he says in another. This is atomism.

Thus, the interpretive choice at the most general level is between a holistic and an atomistic perspective of the corpus. The polarity between developmentalism and unitarianism becomes relevant only upon the rejection of the atomistic perspective. The "atomistic" perspective might alternatively be described as "pluralism," this being a direct contrast with "unitarianism," thereby juxtaposing the possibility of multiple first principles, or multiple sets of them, conceivably as many as the number of dialogues, with the restriction to just one such principle, or to one set. In this case, the broadest division would be between pluralism and unitarianism, with developmentalism relegated to the position of either (1) a type of pluralism with the distinct views showing a linear pattern rather than a chaotic distribution, or (2) a type of unitarianism with the single view in question discernible only in the whole rather than in any particular dialogue.

None of the three perspectives actually requires subordination to any of the others. The search for a precise classification can, in fact, get tedious and might even be futile. The important point is that three methods compete for insight into Plato's work. Two of these, developmentalism and unitarianism, are more interesting than the third, atomism or pluralism, an outlook which assigns no greater unity to the Platonic corpus, or expects no greater unity from it, than might be found between the works of different philosophers from rival schools of thought.

The key issue between developmentalism and unitarianism is whether the corpus reflects a dynamic view or a static view. This is the difference between taking the entire collection as one giant work in progress and taking it as episodes of a predetermined position. Although both philosophical outlook and literary style are inherently relevant to the kind of scholarly growth under consideration, the debate is more about the outlook than about the style.

The fundamental disagreement regarding outlook is not about whether some dialogues tend to affirm what others deny. Both the developmentalist and the unitarian agree that this is the case. The difference is that the developmentalist interprets this as a changing viewpoint while the unitarian explains it as the progressive revelation of a fixed viewpoint, fully developed from the outset but laid out piecemeal to accommodate the special needs of each dialogue and to promote the best reception of the whole.

The motivation for the developmental perspective is the explanation of apparent inconsistencies, such as (1) the simple soul of the so-called "early" dialogues in contrast to the tripartite soul emerging in the "middle" dialogues, and, parallel to this, (2) the repudiation of even the possibility of *akrasia*, roughly speaking, "moral backsliding," or, as it is often translated, "weakness of the will," in the early dialogues, as opposed to its acknowledgment in the middle dialogues, and, perhaps most striking, (3) the confinement of such a rich conceptual platform as the world of the forms to the middle dialogues. The motivation, then, is to explain such inconsistencies, if that is what they are, as the natural stages of a view in progress.

To be sure, the alternative is not necessarily to be stuck with inexplicable inconsistencies. Unitarianism, in turn, is no less plausible as it pushes the scenario of a philosophical dissemination program planned in advance and executed inadvertently yet unavoidably with particular inconsistencies that turn out to be merely apparent rather than genuine in the context of the whole. This is to evaluate consistency at a collective rather than distributive level. Another way out is available, for example, in the equally simple explanation that apparent inconsistencies are manifestations of different approaches impressing different perspectives upon different audiences, the hallmark of an interpretive framework, such as atomism, or, what is the same, pluralism, rejecting a systematic Plato and an organic corpus. Yet what is appealing about the developmental interpretation, and about the standard view in particular, is not only that it irons out the apparent inconsistencies, but that it tells a story.

We all love a good story. This one is about a young Plato starting out with an early period of work reflecting the influence of his mentor Socrates, flourishing into a middle period introducing independent and memorable ideas, and maturing into a late period having either abandoned or digested his earlier views, particularly those of the middle period, ostensibly toward refinement, with the benefit of the kind of wisdom that comes with experience. This is not the only possible instantiation of the developmental interpretation, where any temporal structure would work so long as some intellectual growth is acknowledged during the production of the corpus. In fact, the same three divisions tend to be described as "Socratic," "critical," and "constructive" by those wishing to avoid the chronological commitment involved in distinguishing between early, middle, and late periods. The label "Socratic" comes with its own problems, as it could refer to dialogues representing the philosophy of the historical Socrates, or to dialogues representing the views of Plato under the influence of the historical Socrates, or simply to dialogues where the character Socrates, whomever he may represent, has a battle of the wits with various antagonists or dominates the scene in some other way. An additional problem with this label is that dialogues as "late" as the *Theaetetus* or the *Philebus* might also answer to the characterization of "Socratic," thus making it a poor substitute for the designation "early." Finally, the most general difficulty is the possibility of confusion due to the fact that the same name is used for the genre of Socratic literature, including not only the works of other writers, but also, by definition, nearly all of Plato's works, not just the ones hypothesized to be earlier.

Altogether different labels may be used, including "elenctic" and "aporetic," though preferably not solely as a means to sidestep other designations. The first label is a reference to the Socratic "elenchus," the master's customary method of inquiry and debate through a rapid succession of questions and answers employed in a dialectical search for the truth. The second label derives from the frustrating "aporia," a kind of logical impasse, typically resulting from an elenctic examination proving the antagonist wrong without establishing what is right. One is not far when the other is around. The elenchus has been known to be successful, in fact, more often than not, but, when it is not, or before it is, aporia is a likely outcome. More succinctly, the elenchus may or may not produce aporia, but aporia rarely develops in any other way. The term "aporia," in this context, is associated as much with the psychological result, some sort of perplexity or bewilderment, as it is with the logical condition, the elenctic deadlock responsible for the confusion.

Although elenctic and aporetic dialogues overlap with the early dialogues, they merely pick out a subset therein without converging completely. Not all of the early dialogues conduct philosophy through the elenchus. Nor do they all end in aporia. These two labels may be useful, but not necessarily as a replacement for any others. Moreover, those who object to the standard account object to its divisions, not to the particular names used for those divisions. The actual divisions, that is, the contents by dialogue, do not vary with nomenclature, which, whether temporal or descriptive, pertains to naming the distributive arrangement resulting from the organizational principle represented by the standard account. The divisions do tend to vary with the scholar doing the division, but not because of the names chosen for the periods.

In any case, the stylistic development, parallel to the intellectual, proceeds with the early period's swift and clever exchanges designed to tear down prevailing positions, typically with Socrates outwitting opponents, followed by the middle period's elaborate dramas serving as the breeding ground for more fully developed arguments, pursued as much in collaboration between interlocutors as against opposition, and concluding with the late period's extended speeches delivered with relatively little opposition and a bare-bones dramatic backdrop.

Despite the intuitive appeal of the story, the twentieth century ended and the twenty-first opened with strong reactions to the developmental approach, particularly to the standard view, instead typically embracing the alternative of production from an omniscient perspective and categorization through a pedagogical rather than chronological orientation. The primary focus of reactions has been the circularity of inventing a story to organize the corpus in chronological order, which then constitutes the sole evidence for the story. Emerging alternatives, whether newly conceived or newly reinvigorated, have yet to topple the established breakdown of Plato's productivity in three to five periods from youth to old age. They are gaining ground, especially among continental philosophers, but not with a consensus on a new paradigm.

Scholars rejecting the standard account are also careful to avoid its terminological apparatus, namely, designations as "early," "middle," and "late." Retaining the chronological framework for convenience in reference, as done here, should not be taken as an endorsement of that perspective, or as a challenge to any alternative, as the entrenched terminology is familiar enough with or without a commitment to its interpretive origin.

There is no single standard for studying the structure of the corpus. Knowing the order of composition would be helpful for obvious reasons. But alternatives need not stand in contradiction or even in competition with this. Chronological order is not the only or foremost consideration in efforts to systematize the study of Plato. The dialogues can be grouped in other ways as well. For example, a classification scheme according to subject matter may afford some convenience, and possibly some insight, as might a categorization in terms of correspondence with the basic divisions of philosophy. Many scholars have their own theories on the complete chronological order, which may or may not corroborate the standard account. Many again demonstrate other meaningful ways that the dialogues can or should be grouped together. One way that comes to mind is the order in which Plato intended the dialogues to be read, or, independently of that, the order in which the dialogues ought to be read (would best be read). Another possibility is the order in which the dramatic settings of the dialogues line up in the corpus, which might itself be usefully scrutinized for a unifying dramatic substructure.

Whole books can easily be devoted to any one of these considerations, and, in fact, many have been, but neither the generalist nature of the present effort, nor the corresponding limitation of space, is reason enough to skirt the issue here. The questions are too fundamental, and, the stakes, too high, to entrust to summary judgment, especially in a study that purports to be a guide or companion to Plato rather than a commentary on a special topic. A lot hangs on chronology, not only on how it goes, but on what it indicates. Hence, a chronological appraisal of the corpus, together with all the assumptions, implications, and controversies connected with it, is essential to any survey of the prospects for a structural exegesis of Plato. This might fruitfully be combined with a consideration of some of the more interesting attempts at identifying such a structure in his works, or, as the case may be, imposing such a structure on them. At the very least, chronological order, both in general and in its implementation as the standard developmental view, should be compared with the rising alternatives, including pedagogical order and dramatic order. These are taken up in turn over the next few sections.

3.3. Chronological Order

What is meant by "chronological order" in this context is almost invariably the order of composition. While this explanation may seem superfluous, misunderstanding tends to creep in where understanding is taken for granted. Strictly speaking, the term "chronological order" can be ambiguous here because it is just as apposite to the sequential order of the dramatic settings as it is to the order of composition. Technically, even the order of intended or recommended study can be said to be chronological, or at least sequential, and, in that case, by implication, chronological, since one work must come first, another second, and so on. But the main risk, small though it may be, is confusion between production and drama. Even though a reference to chronological order is not liable to be mistaken for anything other than the order of composition, especially while actually discussing the order of composition, there is nothing less chronological about the temporal progression of the dramatic settings. The most precise treatment would be to call one of these "composition order" and the other "dramatic order," avoiding the term "chronological" altogether. However, the reference to chronology is so embedded in the literature that its absence might be more awkward than its presence would be confusing. This being so, it is best to restrict and specify its scope of application, which, following convention, means that it refers only to the order of composition, and not to the dramatic order, nor to any other conceivable arrangement.

With terminological clarification out of the way, the reader may wish to move on to the principal sources. Anyone interested in the history of attempts to determine Plato's order of composition would do well to consult Brandwood's *Chronology of Plato's Dialogues* (1990), Nails's *Agora, Academy, and the*

Conduct of Philosophy (1995), Thesleff's *Studies in Platonic Chronology* (1982), or the reprint in his *Platonic Patterns* (2009), plus his "Platonic Chronology" (1989), and Young's "Plato and Computer Dating" (1994). Any survey is destined to be outdated, even a historical one, but building on a reliable foundation is easier than starting from scratch each time. Such a foundation is within quick reach in any of these studies, each one alone sufficient for a solid historical orientation, and all of them together certain to impart and promote general expertise.

That said, a serviceable overview of the central issues in Platonic chronology need not be directly parasitic on these or any other particular studies. While a serious study dedicated exclusively to this problem cannot afford to ignore these works, a basic overview can go to the heart of the matter without necessarily projecting their specific contents or even adopting the basic blueprint. The major issues, after all, are still the same, no matter how well they may have been analyzed in previous efforts.

3.3.1. Dating Methods

The chronology of the dialogues is a major source of controversy among Plato scholars in general. The discord is much greater here than in debates over authorship, which might count as fully settled in comparison. The chronology question also carries more at stake for specialists studying the order of composition, either for its own sake or in connection with a key issue other than the order itself, perhaps in support of a grand theory on Plato. Even those dedicated to working out the chronology as an independent project, worthwhile in itself, are unwittingly serving other ends pursued by other scholars. By and large, knowing the precise sequence would have precluded or mitigated important disputes prevailing today in regard to Plato's considered opinion or final position on a particular topic, and, in some cases, on an entire division of philosophy.

This is precisely what is at stake in the pursuit of a production timeline. Plato's deepest convictions, already veiled behind the dramatic cloak of the dialogue form, are obscured even further in the absence of chronological insight into a corpus possibly spanning more than half a century. The suspicion is that such a long period of intellectual activity must have included changes in view, which might be brought to light by determining the order in which the works were produced.

Fortunately, we are not completely in the dark. Several options are available for probing into the order of production. Any approach also benefits from the presence of a temporal anchor serving as a common starting point and from several sturdy signposts along the way.

For example, the *Laws* is traditionally accepted to be the final dialogue, and is still widely considered to be so, though the *Critias* is sometimes nominated for this position due to its standing as an incomplete work. One or the other can safely be taken as the terminus, from which point relevant clues can be followed backward to establish the chronological development. As it happens, the standard practice is to work back from the *Laws*. This is partly in deference to the testimony of Aristotle (*Politics* 1264b26–27) that the *Laws* comes after the *Republic*. While this alone is not sufficient to place the *Laws* at the end of the line with any certainty, or even to place it confidently in that general area, the evidence is strengthened by the reports of Diogenes (*Lives* 3.37) and Olympiodorus (*Anonymous Prolegomena* 24.13–19) that the text of the *Laws* had yet to be transcribed from wax tablets at the time of Plato's death.

The combined evidence is better, but its strength comes from the wax story, which, if true, says a lot, whereas Aristotle's testimony, establishing nothing more than the production sequence of two works in relation to each other, does not take us very far. Unfortunately, the imagery of a major work left unfinished, no matter how close to completion, no matter how far, is a perfect metaphor for a productive life, a metaphor which surely holds all the motivation required for disciples to invent such a story, especially with inspiration from the master himself, who left them with the vivid example of the tailor of Cebes perishing before his last cloak (*Phaedo* 87a–88b).

Still, we need not give up the evidence. For one thing, it is just too useful. But to submit a more substantive plea, Plato did in fact lead a productive life, and even if the wax story was invented just to drive that point home, it would have made more sense to invoke the work that really was the latest instead of naming one at random. Even if this does not clear the anecdote of all traces of fabulosity, it does restore the sensibility of imagining the *Laws* at the end of the line. It still taxes the imagination to picture the amount of wax required to hold the entirety of such a long composition, not to mention the cavalier attitude required to have the only copy of such a precious intellectual investment sitting in wax, which is just a step up from scribbling it in the sand, but a fully fabricated story would surely have been designed with fewer dampers on believability. The basic scenario was probably true, or very nearly so. The anecdotal flavor, then, may simply have been an allegorical or hyperbolical reflection of the rough state of the actual product left behind. (See, for example: Morrow, 1960, pp. 515–516; Dillon, 2003, p. 182, n. 14.) At any rate, the choice of the *Laws* as the philosopher's final contribution, fact or legend, is consistent with the appearance of the work as less refined and less polished than the other dialogues, suggesting death before completion, or indicating at least that Plato might have never had an opportunity to bring it up to his usual standard.

It is also consistent with a conscious effort in old age to get out as much philosophy as possible without worrying about making each unit a literary masterpiece. But this holds, if at all, for the entire late period, and not just for the *Laws*. In fact, the distinction between the *Laws* and most everything else in the Platonic corpus runs deeper than the refinement of prose. Experts, for example Nails and Thesleff (2003, pp. 14–29), argue that the work is not just rough from a literary standpoint but also unwieldy from a philosophical perspective, specifically, that it is internally inconsistent, so much so as to be indicative of patchwork production. This is the possibility that the dialogue is either partly or wholly the work of someone else, that it was either composed or finalized by a member of the Academy other than Plato, or possibly even that it was a community project begun in Plato's lifetime but finished after his death (Nails and Thesleff, 2003, pp. 14–29).

This, of course, does not invalidate the assignment of a late position to the *Laws*. On the contrary, it may even be said to corroborate such an assignment, given that the thrust of the argument is that Plato, having just died, was not around to sort out the contradictions between the separate contributions to the community project, eventually handed over to a solitary editor whose efforts at unification still left telltale signs of contradiction between disparate portions of the whole. This is not a challenge to when we think the *Laws* was written but to how we think it was written.

Although the challenge does not require us to change the place traditionally assigned to the *Laws* in the order of composition, it may require something even more frustrating. It may require us to throw out the *Laws* altogether in our effort to determine a chronology, thereby leaving us without an anchor. Yet to listen to Nails or Thesleff, we would have to throw out a great many works besides, and we would, moreover, have to abandon developmentalism itself. This may, indeed, turn out to be the way to go, but not yet, at least not before completing the survey, in progress, of structural interpretations of the corpus as a whole. To give in to Nails and Thesleff now would be to skip over a good bit of deal of detail regarding what else may be wrong with developmentalism, and, perhaps, even of what may be right with it. More to the point, it would require terminating or disrupting a methodological survey, the point of which is not to champion any one method or platform but to discuss them all.

To return, then, to the special position of the *Laws*, the dialogue is the mainstay of traditional dating efforts. While not everyone agrees that the *Laws* is Plato's final work, hardly anyone who disagrees rejects the possibility, instead objecting merely to the necessity perceived in the evidence available. The most forceful bit of evidence is the account of the draft found in wax at the time of Plato's death, but the veracity of that story could, as conceded above, go either way, either the way of legend perpetuated without confirmation or the way of hyperbole intended to embellish a basically true story. Both agreement and disagreement is defensible. Accordingly, challenges to the traditionally accepted position of the *Laws*, as in Owen's (1953, pp. 79–95, especially p. 79, n. 4; p. 93, n. 3) seminal assessment of the place of the *Timaeus*, tend to deny the strength of the evidence available rather than the accuracy of the assignment. What is in question is the inferential reliability of the conclusion, not its possibility as a matter of fact.

Indeed, the position of the *Laws* is inconclusive, not because the evidence for and against the work's being Plato's last is equally balanced, but because the facts, despite favoring the traditional assignment, are not certain. Even if the collective evidence falls short of conclusive confirmation that the *Laws* comes after everything else in the corpus, it provides reasonable grounds for taking the work as being among the last and, thereby, as representative of what might be expected philosophically and stylistically of Plato's intellectual output in that period, though bearing in mind that the output might, as argued by Nails and Thesleff (2003, pp. 14–29), be diluted or infested with foreign elements. This, in turn, is all that is required of an anchor, especially if the goal is to determine broad divisions in the corpus corresponding to the general development of the philosopher, as opposed to the more ambitious and less promising task of determining the precise chronological position of each and every dialogue.

A whole article can be devoted to the chronological position of a single dialogue, and entire books are available on the production sequence of the complete body, or on a particular method of determining that sequence, but the overviews by Guthrie (1975, pp. 41–56) and Allen (1984, pp. 6–25), and even the master generalist Copleston (1946, pp. 135–141), still stand as rewarding nontechnical introductions to the general endeavor. The common ground in their accounts of the leading approaches to the timeline of Platonic production can be summarized as follows:

- Biographical extrapolation: ranking the dialogues in terms of the level of philosophical and literary development they represent in Plato's life as a scholar, basically on the assumption that the naive must predate the sophisticated.

- Stylometric evaluation: ordering the dialogues in accordance with variations in writing habits determined through test variables measuring specific aspects of an author's approach to language.

- Internal references: working out the temporal primacy relations between dialogues according to their references to one another.

- External anchors: using dramatic references to actual events as evidentiary markers for the earliest possible composition dates of the corresponding dialogues, and, where applicable, going in the opposite direction to take stock of any external testimony regarding any dialogue (e.g., Aristotle's report that the *Republic* precedes the *Laws*).

The first thing to note here, before fleshing out these synoptic descriptions, is that there really is no such thing as the "biographical extrapolation approach." The approach itself is entirely familiar, but the title attached to it is not. The name is not in common parlance, not even among Platonists. The point in giving it a name is obvious: convenience in reference. The point in giving it this particular name may not be. The name is an allusion to the way that the method extracts a presumably implicit intellectual biography from the common philosophical and literary features of the dialogues, while using that biography to structure the corpus, whether in groups or in full chronological order. It might just as well have been called "bibliographical extrapolation" instead of "biographical extrapolation," since these represent opposite perspectives of the same circular process, revolving around the skeletal intellectual biography extracted from, and read into, the distribution of themes and treatments across the dialogues. Neither may be the best name for it, but both adequately capture the essentials. "Biographical extrapolation" sounds better if only because it is shorter.

The leading alternative in the secondary literature seems to be not to name the approach at all, instead describing it once, somewhat as above, and picking a truncated version of the description to refer to it thereafter. But this is the leading alternative only because those who do use a name do not agree on one. The "biographical extrapolation approach" corresponds roughly to the combination of what Guthrie (1975, pp. 42–48) discusses under the rubrics of "literary criticism" and "philosophical considerations." That same combination could have been called "scholarly development," a name which has greater intuitive appeal than "biographical extrapolation," but any designation incorporating the word "development" runs the risk of confusion with the standard developmental account or even with developmentalism itself as the general perspective that Plato wrote from an ever developing viewpoint as opposed to a static viewpoint. Hence, the name "biographical extrapolation" reflects a negative choice more than a positive one, and is not, in any case, an attempt to coin a phrase just for the sake of it.

Although the biographical extrapolation approach represents the essence of the standard developmental account, it is neither identical with nor methodologically exhaustive of that account. The other three are also relevant to the standard developmental account, though not necessarily all in a supporting capacity. The biographical extrapolation approach is simply the inspiration for the standard account, proponents of which can and do invoke any of the other three approaches, or something else altogether, for support or confirmation, though on a selective basis weeding out anything that may constitute a direct contradiction, as is the case with stylometry. The reason that the standard account figures prominently in any discussion of chronology is not that no other arrangement could possibly fit the data, but that the standard account is more memorable than sterile permutations that do not tell a story. For this reason, any chronological study, even if it proposes an entirely new timeline, is inevitably a commentary on the standard account.

Before moving on to an examination of each approach in greater detail, it is also important to note that these are not alternative approaches supporting competing arrangements. They might in fact support different conclusions, but not because they represent mutually inconsistent strategies by design. On the contrary, the hope is that they would be more helpful in combination than in isolation. These are widely used tools to determine the order of composition, and they are probably the only effective ones available toward that end. None of them is conclusive alone, and all of them together might still fall short of achieving the desired end, but they are more enlightening jointly than severally. The only impediment to synergy is a clash between the results of the first two approaches, as the standard account, inspired by the biographical extrapolation approach, is at least partially but quite consistently undermined by stylometric tests. While this does not mean that the methods are antithetical, the results certainly can be.

3.3.1.1. Biographical Extrapolation

Can the chronological order of John Stuart Mill's works be determined from his development as a thinker and writer, and, conversely, can his development as a thinker and writer be diagnosed through a chronology of his works? Perhaps. Mercifully, we do not have to try. We already know the publication dates of Mill's works. And Mill was thoughtful enough to leave behind a fairly detailed *Autobiography*. We do not have to wonder whether he was influenced by Jeremy Bentham, Auguste Comte, or Harriet Taylor in order to date any of his works, and even if we were to need that information for whatever reason, it is right there in the *Autobiography*. We are well informed on all counts: life, thought, and works. This being so, we can take our definite knowledge in one area to corroborate our definite knowledge in another area. This might be an entirely pointless exercise, but it would be both possible and reliable.

Can the chronological order of Plato's works be determined from his development as a thinker and writer, and, conversely, can his development as a thinker and writer be diagnosed through a chronology of his works? Here, the exercise would not at all be pointless, but even if it were possible, it might not be all that reliable. What accounts for the difference? For one thing, we do not have an autobiography of Plato. The closest we come is a few letters of doubtful authenticity and limited coverage. We also lack a reliable biography by anyone who knew him personally. Nor can we claim any certainty regarding his convictions, since he hides them behind the mask of drama and dialogue. Finally, we have no idea when he wrote anything. We might still be able to work something out with what little we know, but there is no way to double-check the answers as in the case with Mill.

This is where we stand with the biographical extrapolation approach to the Platonic corpus. While it is reasonable to expect philosophical and literary growth to be reflected in intellectual output, reflection of any kind is rarely a substitute for direct illumination, and almost always leaves room for interpretation. The evidentiary relationship between scholarly growth and output is opaque and circular rather than clear and linear. A shift in philosophical or artistic outlook need not be identifiable in every single work belonging to one period or the other on either side of the shift, and differences in methodology or style need not always be associated with a change in outlook, but correlations are plain to see after the fact. For example, a painting already known in fact to have been produced by Raphael in a certain year can be proven over and over to belong to the corresponding period in Raphael's life through a plethora of interpretive details connecting the work and the artist, but the same set of interpretive details, without the actual matter of fact it corroborates, that is, taking away the assumption that we already know, for example, that the painting was done by Raphael in 1510, may not suffice to place the work in any particular period, let alone to date it with certainty. That said, such evidence can certainly be useful, and, all else remaining the same, opinions are best formulated in conformity with the clues available instead of in contradiction or ignorance of them.

Greater wisdom and experience can reasonably be expected to show up as improvements in works, just as the enhancement or deterioration of skills might plausibly be said to be detectible in them. Even differences manifested merely as differences, neither better nor worse, should in general help mark out distinct periods in a thinker's or artist's life and work in terms of outlook and style. In fact, such signs are naturally cumulative so that the collective evidence may be compelling even where no single work is telling. In regard to Plato, an appeal to intellectual growth can be convincing in establishing temporal clusters of work, but it cannot be trusted as the sole or deciding factor in a complete arrangement of all the dialogues or as the only argument for the position of a particular dialogue.

Plato's intellectual or scholarly development has two dimensions, one philosophical, the other, literary. Presumably, the two run parallel courses, in the same direction, at comparable paces. With respect to the philosophical dimension, one of the strongest clues in grouping dialogues according to their dates of composition is the position taken in each with respect to the forms. Those where the forms are at center stage can readily be distinguished from those where they are not, and the latter group can convincingly be divided in accordance with whether the theory of forms has yet to emerge or has left the limelight to other methodological constructs. For example, the forms figure heavily in the *Phaedo* and the *Symposium*, are not yet present in the *Laches* and the *Lysis*, and seem abandoned in the *Sophist* and the *Statesman*, which instead showcase the method of collection and division, already praised in the *Phaedrus* (265c–266c), as the dialectical tool of choice, leaving the theory of forms behind at least in terms of periodic popularity. In contrast, some dialogues feature neither the theory of forms nor the method of collection and division as the central focus, or even in an auxiliary capacity. The point, however, is that dialogues with a common philosophical orientation represent distinct periods in Plato's philosophical outlook, in other words, that they are connected temporally, not merely related thematically or methodologically.

Evidence of intellectual or scholarly growth can plausibly be sought as much in literary style as in philosophical outlook. This seems especially relevant to a masterful writer like Plato, a full appreciation of whose works requires a balanced combination of literary criticism and philosophical analysis. A popular consideration in connection with the literary leg of biographical extrapolation is that the dialogues become less dramatic over time, with Plato devoting less energy, as he matures, to the setting, characterization, and plot development, and gradually phasing out the punchy exchanges of the early works in favor of longer speeches by the protagonist. This, in short, is literature making room for philosophy, sometimes even said to be leaving the stage entirely to philosophy.

The conformity of a work with this description might have counted as an official stamp of production date had it not been for Plato's playful genius. Any of his literary and artistic habits may have been common to certain periods, but were rarely restricted to one or another, and his skills, though naturally developing over time, were so high to begin with that a distinction can hardly be drawn between mediocrity and excellence. This still leaves open the possibility of a workable distinction between periodic preferences for one style over another, so long as this is not taken by itself as conclusive evidence of a work's composition in a certain period. Any revisionary tendencies by Plato are liable to throw off such conclusions, especially upon confirmation of the tendencies, and they would be sufficient at least to introduce reasonable doubt, even if they were to remain unconfirmed and merely possible.

Another example of attempts to date Plato's works by tracing his literary development is appeals to the changing nature of the overarching structure separating the audience from the dialogue. Most of the works are in the form of direct conversations, but some are narrated. The narrated exceptions, widely considered literary masterpieces, include the *Republic*, the *Phaedo*, and the *Symposium*. The narrative approach affords the advantage of having the narrator smoothly direct and redirect the dialogue while pumping it as needed with information in the guise of dramatic detail. Dialogues in this style are traditionally grouped together as belonging to the same period, with Plato taken to have later abandoned the approach. Precisely when and where, that is, in which dialogue, Plato first embraced this approach is not certain, but the point of transition away from this style is taken to be the *Theaetetus*, a dialogue where the narrator, Euclides, familiar in reality as a disciple of Socrates, one of several fleeing Athens upon the execution of the master, explicitly announces that he has transcribed an actual conversation without narration so as to avoid disruptive dialogic markers such as "I said" and "he agreed" (*Theaetetus* 143a–c). Here, too, one would do well to bear in mind the caveat regarding Plato's tendency to defy categorization in his quest to find the best match between subject matter and approach. However, the stylistic shift is helpful at least in corroborating distinctions drawn on other grounds between earlier and later dialogues, as it is in general agreement with those.

3.3.1.2. Stylometric Evaluation

Usage patterns in relation to certain linguistic elements, usually quantified specifically in terms of the occurrence per page of those elements, invariably point to similarities and differences between dialogues, which can then be grouped or even ranked on this basis. The emphasis on stylistic elements is not to be confused with the literary component of the first approach, the one focusing on biographical extrapolation. The difference is that the stylistic focus here is exclusively on the usage of language as manifested in grammar, syntax, vocabulary, and so forth. The greatest advantage is quantifiability, while the primary difficulty is, again, Plato's ability and willingness to vary his style at will. He is all too likely, in any period, to produce a dialogue that looks or reads like it belongs in an altogether different period. This may be overcome to a certain extent by concentrating on stylistic variations that are unconscious rather than deliberate, if such a distinction can be drawn reliably. At any rate, the result, a pattern of similarities based on a set of test variables, is circular in itself, requiring a fixed point of reference to unfold into a linear temporal sequence. That point, notwithstanding the reservations mentioned earlier, is generally agreed to be the *Laws*, everything else being laid out in accordance with its distance from this *terminus ad quem*.

The correlation between dialogues in terms of frequency distributions of this sort became a particularly important and useful consideration with the advent and proliferation of computers in the second half of the twentieth century, but the method itself can be traced back to Campbell's comparison of the *Sophist* and the *Statesman* in 1867, and was already well-defined by the end of the nineteenth century, owing both to partial applications covering clusters of dialogues and to exhaustive ones covering the entire corpus. Independent pioneering work by Dittenberger (1881) and Lutoslawski (1897) was complemented by an innovative twist by Ritter (1910), who applied the method to the works of Goethe, an author whose publication chronology was already known, thus enabling a demonstration of the reliability of the stylometric method of dating.

3.3.1.3. Internal References

One work's reference to another within the Platonic corpus constitutes the strongest evidence possible for chronological sequencing studies, but such references are rare and often indirect. One of the most unequivocal examples is a dramatic thread running through the *Theaetetus*, *Sophist*, and *Statesman*: The *Theaetetus* (210d) ends with an agreement to reconvene on the following day, while the *Sophist* (216a) opens with an acknowledgment that the drama unfolding constitutes fulfillment of that agreement, and the *Statesman* begins (257a) with an unmistakable reference to the general dramatic setting of the *Sophist*, and includes an additional reference to it midway (284b) through the dialogue. The *Theaetetus* (183e) and the *Sophist* (217c) also contain references to the *Parmenides*, which can, on that basis alone, be placed prior to those two dialogues, though not necessarily immediately before them, that is, immediately before the earlier of the two. Another connection can be found in the opening of the *Timaeus* (17a–19a) with a summary of parts of the *Republic*. Arguably the most prominent internal link is the continuation of the storyline extending smoothly from the *Timaeus* to the *Critias*. Such evidence points to incontestable connections, but it is too sparse to trace the production history of the entire corpus from start to finish.

That said, the direct reference of one work to another is a special kind of evidence, not generalizable to all possible dramatic links between the dialogues. Not all internal evidence carries the authority of internal reference, which must be distinguished especially from the incidental unity or continuity of dramatic elements across dialogues. Sorting the dialogues in accordance with a dramatic timeline to be constructed from, say, the adventures of Socrates the character, even if the dramatic dates could be identified across the board, or at least put in relative order, would not give the production sequence of Plato the author. For example, the *Euthyphro*, *Apology*, *Crito*, and *Phaedo* show dramatic continuity, following Socrates from indictment to execution, but the *Phaedo*, often placed in a different period in Plato's life, clearly stands apart from the other three, both as a philosophical tour de force and as a literary masterpiece. Moreover, apparent dramatic continuity, wherever it lacks a direct reference, does not guarantee that the earlier dramatic setting is actually the earlier production, as in the example of the *Euthyphro*, which is generally considered to be a later undertaking than the *Apology* and *Crito*.

Perhaps the best demonstration that the temporal precedence of dramatic events is not in itself a reliable guide to the order of composition is the extraneous and deceptive dramatic continuity between the *Theaetetus* and the *Euthyphro*, wherein the former ends with Socrates on his way to the precise setting described in the latter. The drama of the *Euthyphro* unfolds between the events of the *Theaetetus* and the *Sophist*, without any thematic, stylistic, or philosophical correspondence to these two dialogues, invariably classified as much later works. Placing Socrates at the porch of the king-archon where he awaits arraignment toward the fateful trial, the *Euthyphro* opens like an otherwise incongruous sequel to the *Theaetetus*, which, as the later production, stands as the source of the curious anachronism, and, thereby, as a warning against automatically taking all dramatic details to be the footprint of the production schedule.

Theoretically, even direct references could be misleading. For example, the dramatic thread blending the end of the *Theaetetus* (210d) into the beginning of the *Sophist* (216a) could conceivably have been an afterthought. It is entirely possible, unlikely though it may be, to start with one work (*Sophist*), follow it up with a prequel (*Theaetetus*), and subsequently revise the original with deceptive references to the prequel, so that the prequel no longer reads like a prequel but like the actual beginning. This is not to cast aspersions on the *Theaetetus-Sophist-Statesman* sequence, the rejection of which would be unreasonable, but to suggest that even the strongest dramatic link does not constitute conclusive proof of relative production dates. There is no reason to doubt that particular sequence, but should others admit of reasonable doubt, they ought not to be followed blindly but evaluated critically. Fortunately, all the reasonable doubt still leaves room for comfort in the conclusions we draw regarding the order of composition from the cross-references in the corpus.

3.3.1.4. External Anchors

The relationship between drama and reality can be pursued in both directions. From the inside out, Plato's references to historical events can be verified wherever the dates are known with certainty. These might be battles, conquests, religious ceremonies, sporting events, festivals of the arts, or other landmark events or developments in the social, political, or military milieu of the classical world. The operating scope is virtually inexhaustible, including milestone achievements in literary work, artistic expression, and scientific thought, but most clues fall in the realm of military activity. Examples include a reference in the *Theaetetus* (142a–c) to a clash in or near Corinth and references in the *Laws* (638b) to military victories by Syracuse over Locri and by Athens over Ceos. One outside the military realm includes a reference in the *Symposium* (173a) to the tragic poet Agathon's first literary victory at a public competition.

Had all the dialogues been sprinkled with an abundance of temporal anchors to reality, dating them, possibly even in absolute terms as opposed to relative positions, would have been easy enough. As it is, external references of this sort are few and far between. Still, the earliest possible dates of composition suggested by such clues can be used in conjunction with other evidence to establish a chronological order for strings of dialogues, though unanimous agreement on the entire sequence from beginning to end is unlikely.

In the opposite direction, leads of external origin can be valuable, particularly if originating in the commentaries of notable philosophers or historians from that period, for example, direct testimony in the works of Aristotle. Actually, the surviving works of Aristotle are more useful in confirming Plato's authorship of certain dialogues, none of them controversial anyway, at least at present, than in establishing their order of composition. Nevertheless, the general point stands: The proper appeal to authority here concerns the contemporaries of Plato, not all historians of philosophy through the ages up to the present time.

For example, the reason we trust anything Copleston has to say is not that he is a fountainhead of privileged information but that we trust him to be a reliable collator and interpreter of privileged information. Going back fifteen, sixteen, or possibly seventeen centuries, the same can be said of Diogenes, a far less discerning and meticulous source than Copleston, whose own reliability, however, depends, somewhat paradoxically, at least partially on that of Diogenes and others like Diogenes. We must have reliability at the source, and the closer we are to the source, the greater are our chances of exposure to accurate information. What is relevant in this case, then, is the word of people who are known to have personally interacted with Plato, or are likely to have done so, or at least to have been in contact with those who have done so. Anything beyond that falls under reporting rather than testimony. However, as desirable as it may be, testimonial evidence is only as reliable as the source, while suffering from the same problem of scarcity as the external references from the inside out.

3.3.2. Prospects for a Joint Solution

Efforts in all four directions have been fruitful, but not to a point inspiring the kind of confidence associated with unequivocal deduction. The entire project, regardless of the angle, resembles reverse engineering. Although knowledge of the exact order of composition would have provided great insight into Plato's development, both philosophical and literary, this is not a reciprocal relationship: Insight into Plato's development does not establish the exact order of composition, especially as different experts tend to offer differing and sometimes opposing streams of insight. No insight, in the end, is guaranteed to be aligned with the historical circumstances.

The most basic problem with the developmental perspective, including philosophical and literary considerations as well as stylometric analyses, is the very assumption of sequential production over a career spanning roughly half a century. As a possibility, even if purely theoretical, Plato might have composed everything in his maturity as a philosopher and writer, squeezing the entire effort into less than half the typically assumed length of time. This does not even have to be envisioned as a significant constraint on the professionally active portion of his life. He might simply have matured early, say, in his late thirties, thereafter writing everything with the same mindset and skills at a leisurely pace.

To be sure, the possibility of his having written everything from a mature viewpoint does not rule out sequential production, which would still be the most reasonable expectation, given that writing one piece after another is a more natural approach and manageable undertaking than tackling many or all at once, but it does rule out the possibility of developmental progress in the corpus, and, therefore, of grouping the works in accordance with the corresponding stage of development in the author's life. More and more scholars are denying developmental connections. The alternative is to hold all works to be the product of an equally or comparably developed intellectual outlook.

This is a reasonable interpretation except perhaps in an extreme form insisting on a perfectly static philosophy showing absolutely no variation from dialogue to dialogue. One would then have to contend at least with the assault of the *Parmenides* on the world of forms, which the dialogue leaves crumbling under its own weight, presenting a stark contrast to the glorification in dialogues such as the *Republic*, *Phaedo*, and *Symposium*. Distinctions between earlier and later works have been drawn on this basis alone, and while such distinctions are by no means incontestable, they cannot be dismissed without argument. Even the positioning of the forms, that is, where they are concentrated in the corpus, can be explained away if one interprets the apparent philosophical development from one dialogue to another as a pedagogical tool intended only to help readers advance in their own development rather than reflecting any such development in the author. However, that, too, requires greater evidence than its mere possibility.

Another challenge to the developmental perspective is the likelihood of overlaps in composition. The fact that the dialogues vary substantially in length underscores the possibility of finishing several short ones while producing a longer one. For example, the *Phaedo* is more than four times the size of the *Crito* or the *Hippias Minor* but less than one-fourth the size of the *Republic* or the *Laws*. Such big differences in length are significant, even if Plato never worked on more than one dialogue at a time, thus cranking them out without interruption regardless of length. This is because the operating principle of the developmental perspective makes a longer work likely to show as much variation internally as found between several shorter ones of comparable total length, provided that the production time is roughly the same in both cases.

To object that Plato would have revised the longer work toward uniformity in thought and style is to welcome a revisionary interpretation of the entire corpus, which might, on the same grounds, be said to have been revised so extensively as to defy dating on the basis of any sort of philosophical, literary, or linguistic development. In fact, this is consistent with certain historical accounts of Plato as a perfectionist of sorts, constantly revising and polishing his works, a legend which, if true, vitiates the basis for the modern search for order, especially in connection with studies of biographical extrapolation and stylometric evidence.

Dionysius of Halicarnassus, flourishing during the time of Christ, presents Plato as such a revisionist, supplying the anecdote that a tablet containing several different versions of the opening sentence of the *Republic* was discovered among his belongings upon his death (*De Compositione Verborum* 25). Quintilian (*Institutio Oratoria* 8.6.64) relates the same story no more than a few generations later. Diogenes (*Lives* 3.37) subsequently provides confirmation, citing as his sources the poet and grammarian Euphorion of Chalcis (born c. 275 BC) and the Stoic philosopher Panaetius of Rhodes (c. 185–110 BC). Guthrie (1975, p. 51, n. 1) discounts the reports, apparently in disappointment with the quantity rather than the quality of ancient sources, but it only takes the one to discover and transmit the truth, which hardly improves with repetition. The evidentiary difference between a single report and none at all is far greater than that between a single report and many. Moreover, even the bare possibility of a revisionist or perfectionist bent in Plato, without any testimony to that effect, stands as a nagging weakness in the developmental perspective.

Both the possibility of production from a revelatory as opposed to evolutionary position and the possibility of constant revision cast doubt upon the developmentalist conclusions supported severally or jointly by biographical extrapolation and stylometric evaluation, but these theoretical problems still leave us with respectable evidence in favor of the developmental perspective. Although signs of philosophical and literary progress between dialogues may not be definitive indicators of scholarly growth, possibly having been feigned for the educational benefit of the reader, or, put differently, possibly reflecting deliberate pedagogical choices unrelated to personal growth in the educator, the room for doubt created therein does not make such clues altogether unreliable or irrelevant. The developmental evidence available still constitutes an acceptable platform for working out a chronology. What is called into doubt is the certitude of the perspective, not its tenability.

Be that as it may, difficulties are not limited to the first two approaches to dating or ordering Plato's dialogues. Attempts to capitalize on internal references and external anchors are also not infallible. References between dialogues are generally reliable, but they cannot all be followed indiscriminately. For example, in a sequence mentioned earlier, the dramatic setting at the end of the *Theaetetus* (210d) leaves Socrates on his way to the courthouse to hear the charges eventually leading to his conviction and death, and the opening of the *Euthyphro* places him immediately outside that courthouse as he awaits the indictment, but the established view on the actual order of production is in the opposite direction, with plenty of papyri separating the two works. With respect to external evidence, a comparable obstacle may be encountered through anachronisms and irreconcilable dramatic references. An example of this may be found in the reference in the *Symposium* to Agathon's victory in a literary festival (173a), which is often found to be historically incompatible with the reference in the same dialogue to Spartan intervention in Arcadia (193a). This is not universally acknowledged to be an anachronism (Guthrie, 1975, p. 365, n. 3), but it is a good reminder of the fact that Plato has a dramatic license to play with historical events. An example that is not open to debate is an internal contradiction regarding the relative ages of Alcibiades and Agathon in relation to Apollodorus and Glaucon: The first two are much older than the latter two in the *Symposium*, but much younger than the same two in the *Theaetetus*.

Where does all this leave us? Even a rough overview as the foregoing shows that the possibilities are limited in the latter two approaches, one checking cross-references between dialogues, and, the other, dropping anchors to external reality, either through dramatic references to reality or through real references to the drama. Even if these two approaches were flawless, both could be exhausted without achieving anything near a full chronology. They must be supplemental to a primary method, either corroborating or falsifying it, but not replacing it. Perhaps the same could be said of the first two approaches, but they at least promise a fuller picture if correct. The first approach, biographical extrapolation, has the advantage of forming, or at least framing, such a full picture, namely, the one in the standard account of three main productive periods, sometimes fleshed out as a total of four or five periods, and occasionally laid out in a complete chronological order of the dialogues, with or without periodic divisions. The second approach, stylometric evaluation, likewise offers a full picture, also typically in three periods, arguably in just two, but in either case, sometimes with the entire series in order. The best way to proceed would then seem to be to take a closer look at these two approaches.

Of course, two approaches, each sufficient if correct, are still not jointly conclusive unless the results are mutually consistent. Unfortunately, stylometry contradicts the standard developmental account, which is the claim to fame of the biographical extrapolation approach. The contradiction is only partial, or localized, accompanied by equally impressive partial confirmation, but the slightest contradiction precludes the consistency of the whole, whereas partial consistency does not remove a contradiction. If one is right, the other must be wrong.

What two things exactly are we talking about? Specifically, the contradiction applies to the findings of the two approaches, that is, to the typical results, rather than to the assumptions, methodology, or implications, or to any other feature having to do with the approaches themselves. This, then, should be the focus: the standard account versus stylometric patterns.

Having already covered much of the biographical extrapolation approach, not to mention the standard developmental account supported by it, this part of the discussion can safely be limited to an overview of representative conclusions in this area. This is the theme of the next section (§ 3.3.3). The stylometric approach, on the other hand, has the advantage of a reasonable claim to being scientific. This makes it the critical element in any contest, and it deserves closer scrutiny, not only in itself, but in direct comparison with the standard account. This is the theme of the section immediately following the next (§ 3.3.4).

3.3.3. Standard Developmental Account

Despite growing opposition, the standard account of the developmental perspective is still the leading organizational platform for the Platonic corpus. This may be partly because the opposition tends to be more destructive than constructive, hence, attempting to tear down the standard account without offering anything in its place. It may also be because the opposition, even where it is constructive, is too fragmented, with critics agreeing that the standard account is untenable, without agreeing on what is tenable. Either way, the standard account still has a respectable following, quite likely to be greater than any other single perspective on the matter.

As regards internal harmony within the standard account, no two views are identical. This, however, is as it should be, considering the difficulty of publishing a piece identical to one already in print. Although no two views are identical, no two are so different as to be unrecognizable as instantiations of the same general outlook. No study to date has united experts in a precise chronology, but specific areas of agreement have been sufficient to sustain a common platform. There is a strong consensus on where many of the dialogues belong in a chronological listing, though the agreement falls short of a complete sequence from end to end. The agreement at the most general level is that Plato's works correspond to three periods in his scholarly development: early, middle, and late. Sometimes, this is extended to four and even five periods, but what is central to the standard account is the trio.

The leading proponents rarely agree on all the dialogues to be listed under each period; nor do they agree on the order of the dialogues which they do attribute to the same period. However, the overlap is greater than the divergence, and the result is a statistically significant, heuristically useful, and intellectually edifying pattern.

Cornford's classification is a popular example of attempts to organize Plato's output in categories corresponding to his scholarly development (1927, pp. 310–332):

Standard Developmental Account
Francis Macdonald Cornford
27 Dialogues (Chronological Order)

Early Period (11)	**Middle Period (8)**	**Late Period (8)**
Apology	Meno	Parmenides
Crito	Phaedo	Theaetetus
Laches	Symposium	Sophist
Lysis	Republic	Statesman
Charmides	Phaedrus	Timaeus
Euthyphro	Euthydemus	Critias
Hippias Minor	Menexenus	Philebus
Hippias Major	Cratylus	Laws
Protagoras		
Gorgias		
Ion		

Source: Francis Macdonald Cornford: "The Athenian Philosophical Schools": *The Cambridge Ancient History* 6 (1927): pp. 310–332.

The basic pattern, whether in Cornford or in others, is not grounded solely in a speculative consideration of how certain themes in the corpus can be distributed to give Plato's intellectual and scholarly activity an intelligible structure. It is grounded primarily in this, supported by major clues from other approaches. Specifically, it is the result of combining the biographical extrapolation approach with the evidence of internal references and external anchors, in short, signifying a combination of everything other than stylometry.

Cornford's proposal is by no means the only or even the standard division into three groups. Allen's classification, proposed more than half a century after Cornford's, demonstrates how much scholarly opinion can vary around a common core of consensus. Allen's approach can be illustrated as follows (1984, pp. 13–15):

Standard Developmental Account
Reginald E. Allen
28 Dialogues (Chronological Order)

Early Period (12)	**Middle Period (10)**	**Late Period (6)**
Apology	Meno	Sophist
Crito	Gorgias	Statesman
Laches	Menexenus	Timaeus
Ion	Cratylus	Critias
Hippias Major	Symposium	Philebus
Hippias Minor	Phaedo	Laws
Charmides	Republic	
Alcibiades 1	Phaedrus	
Lysis	Parmenides	
Euthyphro	Theaetetus	
Euthydemus		
Protagoras		

Source: Reginald E. Allen: *The Dialogues of Plato*: Volume 1 (1984): pp. 13–15.

The most salient difference between the two approaches is Allen's enlargement of the Platonic corpus through the inclusion of *Alcibiades* 1, not trusted to be authentic by Cornford. In addition, Allen reassigns four dialogues to different groups: He bumps up the *Gorgias* from the early to the middle period, while pushing back the *Euthydemus* from the middle to the early period. He also transfers the *Parmenides* and the *Theaetetus* from the head of the list in the late period to the bottom of the list in the middle period, but this does not constitute a disagreement in the overall chronological sequence.

Similarities and differences can be explored through other examples. Yet the multiplicity of approaches still leaves a viable central consensus, and shows differences to be concentrated in clusters rather than distributed evenly across periods. The three groups representing Plato's scholarly development are not equally stable in terms of the number and order of dialogues placed in them, or detected therein, by experts. Many scholars find the first two groups to be far less cohesive than the third, and claim that dialogues in these two groups are better examined in three distinct categories, thus working with a total of four groups.

The underlying motive in this case is not so much to supplant the traditional perspective of three periods in Plato's thought as it is to facilitate the search for the actual order of composition by providing an extra chronological division to relieve the pressure on the first two groups.

Copleston offers a classic example of a classification alternative with a total of four chronological divisions. Copleston's approach, with three categories jointly covering Plato's early and middle periods, can be summarized as follows (1946, pp. 138–140):

Standard Developmental Account
Frederick Charles Copleston
28 Dialogues (Chronological Order)

Socratic Dialogues (9)	**Transitional Dialogues (7)**	**Works of Maturity (4)**	**Works of Old Age (9)**
Apology	Gorgias	Symposium	Theaetetus
Crito	Meno	Phaedo	Parmenides
Euthyphro	Euthydemus	Republic 2–10	Sophist
Laches	Hippias Minor	Phaedrus	Statesman
Ion	Hippias Major		Philebus
Protagoras	Cratylus		Timaeus
Charmides	Menexenus		Critias
Lysis			Laws
Republic 1			Epinomis

Note: The total indicated in the title of the table, giving the actual number of dialogues under consideration, does not match the sum of the totals for the groups, because the *Republic* is listed twice.

Source: Frederick Charles Copleston: *A History of Philosophy*: Volume 1 (1946): pp. 138–140.

The essential difference here, compared to the first two classifications, is the presence of a transitional category between the early and middle periods in the standard division into three chronological groups. This helps stabilize the lists for the early and middle periods because it serves as a receptacle for all the dialogues otherwise shifted back and forth between these two categories as scholars debate their correct placement. The transitional category thus accommodates the dialogues most frequently and emphatically denied a place among the defining works of the early and middle periods.

Copleston's personal touch includes a few additional differences with the first two perspectives: He makes room for the *Epinomis*, ignored by both Cornford and Allen, while he disregards *Alcibiades* 1, also ignored by Cornford but embraced by Allen. Another notable difference is that Copleston considers the first book of the *Republic* separately from the remainder of that work, placing these two parts in entirely different categories, with a buffer zone in between further emphasizing the difference. This is a fairly common conception of Plato's most popular work, the first book of which is often considered a separate and introductory dialogue titled *Thrasymachus*, though not without strong dissent (for example, Kahn, 1993, pp. 131–142).

Vlastos likewise offers an alternative with a total of four groups, but he differs from Copleston in subsuming the transitional category specifically under the early period, instead of leaving it as a neutral zone between the early and middle periods. The following table illustrates the divisions espoused by Vlastos (1991, pp. 46–47; 1994, p. 135):

Standard Developmental Account
Gregory Vlastos
27 Dialogues (Alphabetical & Chronological Order)

Early Period (15)		**Middle**	**Late**
Elenctic (10)	**Transitional (5)**	**Period (7)**	**Period (6)**
(alphabetical)	(alphabetical)	(chronological)	(chronological)
Apology	Euthydemus	Cratylus	Timaeus
Charmides	Hippias Major	Phaedo	Critias
Crito	Lysis	Symposium	Sophist
Euthyphro	Menexenus	Republic 2–10	Statesman
Gorgias	Meno	Phaedrus	Philebus
Hippias Minor		Parmenides	Laws
Ion		Theaetetus	
Laches			
Protagoras			
Republic 1			

Notes:

1. The total indicated in the title of the table, giving the actual number of dialogues under consideration, does not match the sum of the totals for the groups, because the *Republic* is listed twice.
2. The list is from *Socrates, Ironist and Moral Philosopher* (Vlastos, 1991, pp. 46–47). It is essentially same as the later classification in *Socratic Studies* (Vlastos, 1994, p. 135), which lists the works of the early period in a single alphabetical sequence, subsequently taking up their chronological order, instead of starting out with two subdivisions as above. The later effort picks out the same five works listed as "transitional" above to follow all of the works listed as "elenctic," placing the *Gorgias* at the end of the elenctic period, and, the *Meno*, at the end of the transitional.

Sources: Gregory Vlastos: *Socrates, Ironist and Moral Philosopher* (1991): pp. 46–47; *Socratic Studies* (1994): p. 135.

Vlastos rejects both *Alcibiades* 1 and the *Epinomis*, and follows the same general template as Cornford in quantitative as well as qualitative terms. He divides the *Republic* in the same way as Copleston.

Kraut is in broad agreement with Vlastos, differing specifically on the positions of three dialogues: He bumps the *Gorgias* and *Republic* 1 from the first to the second division in the early period, and, the *Meno*, from the second division of the early period to the top of the list in the middle period (Kraut, 1992, p. 46, n. 57):

Standard Developmental Account
Richard Kraut
27 Dialogues (Alphabetical & Chronological Order)

Early Period (14)		**Middle**	**Late**
Elenctic (8)	**Transitional (6)**	**Period (8)**	**Period (6)**
(alphabetical)	(alphabetical)	(chronological)	(chronological)
Apology	Euthydemus	Meno	Timaeus
Charmides	Gorgias	Cratylus	Critias
Crito	Hippias Major	Phaedo	Sophist
Euthyphro	Lysis	Symposium	Statesman
Hippias Minor	Menexenus	Republic 2–10	Philebus
Ion	Republic 1	Phaedrus	Laws
Laches		Parmenides	
Protagoras		Theaetetus	

Note: The total indicated in the title of the table, giving the actual number of dialogues under consideration, does not match the sum of the totals for the groups, because the *Republic* is listed twice.

Source: Richard Kraut: "Introduction to the Study of Plato": *The Cambridge Companion to Plato* (1992): p. 46, n. 57.

Controversy abounds against a backdrop of general agreement on three or four groups, sometimes five, adding a transitional division between the middle and late periods. The contemporary debate is generally focused on the same few dialogues, though individual studies attracting attention to an otherwise unproblematic work tend to reorient the overall effort from time to time. The center of attention is the early period, as demonstrated by initiatives to examine it in two distinct categories. However, unresolved disputes are also attached to a few dialogues outside the early period. For example, the *Parmenides* and the *Theaetetus* are sometimes placed in the middle period and sometimes in the late period. The positions of the *Timaeus* and the *Critias* are also often disputed, but not in relation to one another, and typically not so much as to be banished from the group of dialogues belonging to Plato's maturity, though exceptions have been resounding (Owen, 1953, pp. 79–95; Sayre, 1983, pp. 15–16, 256–267; both discussed briefly in the opening pages of § 2.5). All in all, the specific disagreements help define and refine the general agreement, as particular dialogues find a firmer position in the chronology while others may be uprooted for closer study in a new debate.

3.3.4. Stylometric Evaluation

Although alternative chronologies for the corpus are being proposed through a steady stream of inspiration, nothing short of unearthing hard evidence is liable to be impressive enough to settle the issue. The ongoing debate seems to have reached a point where the possibility of agreement now depends more on literally digging up new evidence, say, in the course of an archeological excavation, than on rehashing old evidence in the course of an academic symposium. As for efforts above the ground, hardly any progress can be expected outside stylometric evaluation, since we should well have exhausted what can be accomplished through other methods, those that did not have to wait for the advent of computers to reach their greatest potential. Yet further improvements in information technology are unlikely to strengthen stylometric tests, which have already reaped the benefits of computerization, and are not in the least being held back by technical difficulties, such as inadequate processor speed, insufficient memory, or limited storage capacity.

Ledger was able already in 1989 to step up the possibilities, from experimenting with whole words, to tracking patterns in single letters. More accurately, the frequency measured was still that of words, but the selection criteria was the occurrence of certain letters, thus counting the occurrence of words that have a certain combination of letters. Even this was not the result of advances in computers but insight in methodology, moving from selecting words based on their meaning and grammatical function to selecting them based on their orthographic content (Ledger, 1989, p. 2).

However that may be, any improvements, whether grounded in better computers, better statistics, or better assumptions, will continue to be undermined by the nagging possibility of a basic design flaw: the assumption of unrevised output from a style evolving at a uniform rate. Stylometric studies study the style of the text handed down to us, necessarily proceeding on the assumption that it has no history, thereby failing by design to account for possible revisions. Nor can they compensate for any distortions due to individual production times that must have been substantially longer (e.g., *Republic*) and substantially shorter (e.g., *Crito*) than the average for the corpus. Ledger (1989, p. 85) himself admits that "it is quite possible that the longer dialogues took several years to write, especially the *Republic* and the *Laws*, and their completion may have been delayed while other dialogues of less moment were attended to."

The possibility that stylometric studies are the last hope, save for digging in the earth for a lost personal log by Plato, does not mean that the answer is left up to statisticians rather than philosophers. For one thing, the statistical expertise required for a stylometric study is not so advanced as to forbid a primary specialization elsewhere, such as philosophy or philology. More important, stylometrists working on the Platonic chronology, regardless of their primary areas of expertise, tend to be at least as knowledgeable about Plato's works as are Plato scholars not particularly interested in the chronology.

A thorough analysis of all major stylometric studies is not necessary for a basic orientation, which is greatly facilitated by the presence of common features and conclusions. Being up to date may not even count as a particularly pressing concern in this regard. Kahn (1996, p. 44), for one, finds "Platonic chronology since 1896" governed by "confusion, not progress," with the year in question representing the publication date of seminal stylometric studies by Campbell and von Arnim, both invoked by Kahn largely in reference to survey work by Brandwood (1990) and Lutoslawski (1897). His own contribution appearing exactly a hundred years later, Kahn dismisses the century in between as unproductive, opposing the groundbreaking stylometric innovations by Ledger no less than the familiar formula of the standard developmental account. Kahn's perspective is interesting enough to deserve serious consideration, particularly as his effort, neither developmental nor stylometric, represents an altogether different category, examined later, specifically, in the next section (§ 3.4), as pedagogical.

As for stylometry itself, a basic orientation, pace Kahn, ought to take account of developments beyond the pioneers of the method, even if on a selective basis, and perhaps also of possibilities likely to be realized by future analysts. The work of Ritter (1910, 1933), though not inaugurating the approach, is an enlightening gateway to early efforts, all representative of the initial excitement of providing a scientific basis for a previously chaotic discussion built on untestable speculation. This may fruitfully be combined with a retrospective review, say, that of Rowe (2003a), whose assessment well over a century after the inception of the method confirms the reliability of core conclusions. Finally, Ledger's work (1989), aiming to tap new dimensions from the vantage point of a solid platform, commands interest both for the achievements it claims and for the possibilities it exposes.

3.3.4.1. Classical Stylometry: Constantin Ritter

Ritter's contribution has a history not easily captured in a single diagram. His understanding of the organizational scheme warranted by the stylometric evaluation of the corpus evolves over time with refinements introducing increasingly greater structural detail while reflecting growing confidence in the method. Yet the following table is a fair summary of his considered opinion:

Stylometric Classification of the Platonic Corpus Constantin Ritter 26 Dialogues (Chronological Order)			
Early Period (16)		**Middle Period (4)**	**Late Period (6)**
Group 1 Hippias Minor Laches Protagoras Charmides **Group 2** Euthyphro Apology Crito Gorgias	**Group 3** Hippias Major Euthydemus Cratylus Meno Menexenus **Group 4** Lysis Symposium Phaedo	**Group 5** Republic Phaedrus Theaetetus Parmenides	**Group 6** Sophist Statesman Timaeus Critias Philebus Laws

Notes:

1. Ritter notes that the groups indicate definite lines of demarcation while the order within them is less certain.
2. His only uncertainty regarding whether a dialogue belongs to its assigned group is the *Hippias Major*, which he suspects might instead come at the end of the first group.
3. He has several reservations about order within the groups, allowing for the interchangeability of the following: Group 1: *Laches*, *Protagoras*, *Charmides*; Group 3: *Euthydemus*, *Cratylus*; Group 4: *Lysis*, *Symposium*, *Phaedo*; Group 6: *Timaeus*, *Critias*, *Philebus*.
4. He suggests that the *Menexenus* could be moved one place in either direction, though if moved forward, it would be in an entirely different group.
5. Ritter's *Platon* (1910, p. 273) predates this scheme with a classification using just the three periods, the first corresponding to the first four groups above, the second, equivalent to the fifth group, and, the third, matching the sixth group.

Source:
Constantin Ritter: *The Essence of Plato's Philosophy* (1933): pp. 27–28.

Ritter's investigation yields three basic divisions, the first of which is divided further into four subdivisions. The distinctions, at any level, are essentially stylistic, but the results are also couched in temporal terms. A fundamental question, then, regardless of the organizational level considered, is whether these are stylistic or chronological divisions. A common cause for hesitation is that the stylometric method's claim to scientific reliability is based on its exclusive focus on objective properties of style, whereas its findings are often expressed in terms of a succession of parts of the corpus, no less chronological than the standard account of the developmental approach dividing scholars. Any such hesitation is grounded in confusion. There is nothing objectionable about exploring the temporal precedence between stylistically distinct parts of the corpus. What is objectionable, though not necessarily indefensible, is adopting a chronological scheme derived from a speculative story regarding the production of the corpus while using the resultant timeline to sustain the very story inspiring it. Although stylometry itself does not provide temporal insight, the method being limited by design to purely stylistic conclusions, its findings as such can consistently, that is, at least without self-contradiction, be dated according to other considerations.

Divisions can be both stylistic and chronological at once. This means not merely that dialogues displaying differences in style might have been composed at different times, as must have been the case in any two works that were not strictly simultaneous, whether or not they were stylistically similar or divergent, but that they might have been composed during different developmental periods in the author's life or career. Accordingly, the point is not just that divisions can be both stylistic and chronological at once, but also that they can be both stylistic and developmental at once. While a stylometric test would not in and of itself reveal which of two different texts is earlier, once the basic stylistic distinction is made, independent evidence may be invoked for the temporal order.

For example, one style may simply be more sophisticated than the other, possibly being amenable to fruitful comparison against a paradigm for literary development. Even if writers do not everywhere and at all times follow precisely the same stages of development, some elements of style might reliably reflect greater maturity, experience, competence, and the like, attributes useful for chronological and developmental distinctions. And even if such features do not transcend place and time, certain clusters of them may be particularly indicative in a certain region in a certain period. A striking feature in a group of Plato's works may, for instance, coincide with signs of maturity common and unique to Attic prose writers flourishing after Socrates, even if the feature would be unhelpful and the correlation meaningless in other contexts. This would then help identify works of Plato's maturity as distinct from those of his youth.

Even better, a correlation of this sort might be identified between a group of Plato's works and a known stylistic trend among his contemporaries, which might then justify, or even require, aligning that group with the readily datable works of someone else. The avoidance of hiatus by both Isocrates and Plato comes to mind. The relevance of such appeals, of course, depends on whether the stylistic elements in question are purported to be conscious or unconscious. Measuring distinctions grounded in unconscious elements of style avoids the common criticism that conclusions may be undermined by Plato's ability to vary his style at will, a perennial protest against using stylometry in Plato, but it also weakens the grounds for pursuing connections with conscious choices by other writers of the period. In other words, a study boasting the purity associated with stylistic patterns that are not deliberate cannot at the same time claim to expose Plato's emulation of this or that writer, except perhaps in the sense of probing an unconscious influence. Note, however, that an inference in the other direction is not as objectionable, since a writer whose works are datable may have been influenced by stylistic characteristics unique to a particular period in Plato instead of having inspired them, and the connection might turn out to be serviceable toward a chronology whether or not the features identified and adopted by the other writer were developed consciously by Plato.

In one way or another, stylometric conclusions, even though they do not come with dates, can consistently be combined with other considerations in an effort to identify a temporal structure and developmental precedence. No doubt, the choice between conscious and unconscious stylistic features is relevant, but the results, in either case, can usefully be linked with independent chronological clues despite the natural temporal sterility of stylometry itself. The stylistic distinctions will not be blurred or impaired by any fault in the dating. For example, purely stylistic conclusions can be processed further with the benefit of chronological information peculiar to the corpus. Any indication regarding the position of even a single dialogue can be immensely useful in such a case, with the corpus already divided into groups on the independent scientific grounds afforded by stylometry. Thus, knowing the position of a single dialogue in the production sequence of the corpus may not go far toward laying out the full sequence, and knowing that certain dialogues belong together stylistically may not be much better as an isolated clue, but the combination could be quite useful, at least substantially more so than the insight afforded by two otherwise inconclusive pieces of evidence.

None of these particular points is peculiar to Ritter's perspective, but they are all relevant to it. And since his work is not only representative of the early application of stylometry to Plato, but also essentially unfalsified, at least with respect to a common core of conclusions confirmed many times over, it is best taken up together with any principles and provisions attached to the general approach.

The most stable conclusion in this respect is the identification of a stylistic affinity between dialogues also considered related on other grounds. This is a group of dialogues commonly considered "late," with the temporal reference applying both to style and to viewpoint. Given that the standing aim is to use style to confirm viewpoint, any assessment of the prospects for success may benefit from a vantage point bringing together the best of subsequent scholarship in both areas. Rowe offers such insight in multiple works (2003a, pp. 98–124; 2003b, pp. 17–32; 2006a, pp. 13–24; 2006b, pp. 159–170; 2007, pp. 1–51), the most explicit being a highly accessible conspectus in his contribution to *The Cambridge Companion to Greek and Roman Philosophy* (2003a).

3.3.4.2. Stylometry vs. Standard Developmentalism: Christopher J. Rowe

Rowe's (2003a) approach is educational rather than argumentative. He lays out separately, first what he considers to be a representative sketch of the standard account in the developmental view, and next the consensus withstanding the test of time in stylometric evaluation, thus clearly exposing the areas of convergence, and thereby enriching the prospects for analysis and discussion.

His overview of the standard account of Plato's scholarly development rests on the classic template of three distinct productive periods. Specifically, he identifies the following distribution of dialogues as representative of this scheme:

Generic Profile of the Standard Account
Christopher J. Rowe
27 Dialogues (Alphabetical & Chronological Order)

Early Period (15)		**Middle**	**Late**
Initial (10)	**Transitional (5)**	**Period (7)**	**Period (6)**
(alphabetical)	(alphabetical)	(chronological)	(chronological)
Apology	Euthydemus	Cratylus	Timaeus
Charmides	Hippias Major	Phaedo	Critias
Crito	Lysis	Symposium	Sophist
Euthyphro	Menexenus	Republic 2–10	Statesman
Gorgias	Meno	Phaedrus	Philebus
Hippias Minor		Parmenides	Laws
Ion		Theaetetus	
Laches			
Protagoras			
Republic 1			

Notes:

1. The total indicated in the title of the table, giving the actual number of dialogues under consideration, does not match the sum of the totals for the groups, because the *Republic* is listed twice.
2. Offered by Rowe to illustrate a "fairly standard modern ordering," this representative classification turns out to be identical with the composition order envisaged by Gregory Vlastos (1991, pp. 46–47).
3. Rowe actually presents the first two columns in a single box containing two separate alphabetical lists strung together and separated only by a semicolon. He does not name the first list, simply following it with the second, tentatively named "transitional." The title "initial" is added above merely as a presentational convenience. The term Vlastos (1991, p. 46) uses here is "elenctic."

Source: Christopher J. Rowe: "Plato": *The Cambridge Companion to Greek and Roman Philosophy* (2003a): p. 103.

This turns out to be representative not so much in the sense of reflecting a statistical mean, mode, or median, as in the sense of adopting the position of arguably the most prominent scholar in the field, that of Vlastos (1991, pp. 46–47).

As for his illustration of the typical stylometric approach, Rowe's choice recalls the position of Ritter (1910, p. 273; 1933, pp. 27–28), while also broadly confirming the conclusions of Kahn (1996, pp. 47–48). His review of the common ground in stylometric studies can be summarized as follows:

Generic Profile of Stylometric Classification
Christopher J. Rowe
27 Dialogues (Alphabetical Order)

Group 1		**Group 2**	**Group 3**
Earlier (17)		*Transitional* (4)	*Later* (6)
Apology	Ion	Phaedrus	Critias
Charmides	Laches	Parmenides	Laws
Cratylus	Lysis	Republic	Philebus
Crito	Menexenus	Theaetetus	Sophist
Euthydemus	Meno		Statesman
Euthyphro	Phaedo		Timaeus
Gorgias	Protagoras		
Hippias Major	Symposium		
Hippias Minor			

Notes:

1. Offered by Rowe to illustrate the findings of the "nineteenth-century studies of Plato's style," this representative classification seems to be fashioned closely after the stylometric perspective of Constantin Ritter (1910, p. 273; 1933, pp. 27–28). The only significant difference is the inclusion of *Ion*, omitted by Ritter. It also matches, in broad divisions, the arrangement espoused by Charles H. Kahn (1996, pp. 47–48), who differs only in subdividing the first group into six stages and ignoring the *Hippias Major* altogether.
2. Rowe's third group is not in the exact sequence given above, as he interrupts the alphabetical order to list the *Laws* last and to append the *Critias* to the *Timaeus* with an em dash in between.
3. The temporal designations here ("earlier," "transitional," "later") are incidental rather than essential, being organizational devices adopted after and independently of the execution of the primary task of division according to stylistic variation.

Source: Christopher J. Rowe: "Plato": *The Cambridge Companion to Greek and Roman Philosophy* (2003a): p. 104.

The three groups in the stylometric classification are presumed to reflect different time periods, but this is not an essential feature of the division. As discussed earlier (§ 3.3.4.1), the stylometric project is inherently indifferent to chronological order even if the stylistic groups do in fact constitute discrete temporal clusters. The classification is based on the identification of stylistic characteristics common and peculiar to each group, the successful differentiation of which suggests that one comes first, another second, and another third, but not necessarily that one rather than another is first, second, or third. To be entirely accurate, no temporal indication of any sort, and not just a particular chronological arrangement, can be deduced from the stylometric conclusion. Any temporal inference whatsoever will be underdetermined by the stylometric evidence. What is not warranted, thereby, is not one order instead of another, but any order at all. Yet this does not undermine the viability of temporal investigations of stylometric conclusions. It is outright silly to imagine that Plato composed all of his work simultaneously, beginning and ending everything at roughly the same time, and rather counterintuitive, albeit perhaps not as silly, to assume that he shifted back and forth between the three distinctive styles with such regularity that the stylistic groups do not actually precede or follow one another while individual dialogues in fact do.

This is where anchors external to the statistical process come into play, providing bearings for the order. The conventional starting point is the assignment of last place to the group containing the *Laws*, given the testimonial tradition regarding the relative position of that dialogue (Aristotle: *Politics* 1264b26–27; Diogenes: *Lives* 3.37; Olympiodorus: *Anonymous Prolegomena* 24.13–19). The real problem is whether there is only one other group, or two as above. Given agreement both on the number of groups and on their contents, the question of their proper order would be unlikely to threaten what might otherwise constitute a rare consensus among Plato scholars. That said, common practice is to refer to stylometric groups by group number ("group 1," "group 2," and so on) rather than by any descriptive name signifying temporality ("earlier," "later," and the like). In this context, it is especially important to note that the reference for the "transitional" dialogues is entirely different in the developmental and stylometric models sketched above: The developmental reference marks a transition from the early to the middle period, while the stylometric reference indicates a transition between the first (presumed earlier) and third (presumed later) stylistic groups.

The most telling outcome of the comparison is a perfect correlation between the late period of the standard account and the final stylistic phase of the classical stylometric classification. Similarly, the early period finds substantial corroboration in the first stylistic group, as everything in the early period according to the standard account turns out to have stylistic characteristics bonding and defining enough to constitute a distinctive group. Specifically, all fourteen dialogues of the early period, leaving out the first book of the *Republic*, otherwise commonly included in that period separately from the greater body placed in the middle period, are represented in the first stylistic group. Yet this stylistic group includes more than the dialogues of the early period. It includes, in addition, three dialogues from the middle period: *Cratylus*, *Phaedo*, and *Symposium*. The main cause for disappointment is not what is added but where it comes from. These, of course, are two different ways of looking at the same problem: The standard account might not be so sensitive to the inclusion of a few more dialogues in the first stylistic group than is normally acknowledged in the early period were it not for the extraction of those dialogues from the sparsely populated middle period. Although a substantial correlation in the early period, coupled with a perfect correlation in the late period, may seem to go far toward a scientific confirmation of the standard account, the disparity in the middle is at least discouraging and possibly devastating. This is not merely because the middle period contains relatively few dialogues, wherein taking out three would make a big difference, but also because the philosophical content to be displaced thereby is of a defining nature for the middle period. Moving the *Cratylus*, *Phaedo*, and *Symposium* from the middle to the early period would completely destroy the distinction, which rests fundamentally, albeit not entirely, on the emergence of the forms in the middle period.

On the other hand, this is not exactly what is at stake. In fact, the compatibility between stylometry and developmentalism is not necessarily in question here. The inclusion of three particular dialogues in the first rather than the second stylistic group is not the same as their placement in the early rather than the middle period of the standard account. The stylometric finding does not require transferring the three defining dialogues from the middle to the early period. This is because stylistic evolution need not be aligned perfectly with philosophical development. Given that stylometric studies typically do not pursue chronology beyond the group level, the three dialogues in question may well fall at the tail end of the first stylistic group, where they would not constitute such a decisive counterexample to the standard account of developmentalism. Such an assumption would not only remove the conflict between stylometry and the standard account, but also reestablish a positive evidentiary relationship, with stylistic groups still broadly aligned with standard developmental periods. Plato's style and his philosophy need not be perfectly synchronized in terms of their turning points throughout the corpus to posit a significant correspondence between the two.

More generally, differences in Plato's style and differences in his philosophy need not converge at all, let alone being strongly or perfectly correlated, and even where they do coincide, this would neither confirm linear progress nor rule out revisionary development. Given that stylometric evaluation can be used both in validation and in refutation of the standard account, the safest conclusion that can be drawn is that the evidentiary relationship is not as straightforward as may be desired, and that the result of any appeal is inconclusive in either direction.

Nevertheless, the evidentiary gulf between stylometry and the standard developmental view grows with the level of detail offered and confirmation sought from either perspective. Nearly perfect consensus regarding a late group, corroborating its distinctness from everything else in the corpus, thereby essentially embracing a total of two groups, becomes somewhat looser when anything transitional is proposed between the late group and an initial state, and breaks down altogether around the question of the sequential order of individual dialogues. Yet stylometrists are not all so modest as to stop at the level of the group. Neither are scholars investigating chronology through other means. Quite respectable proposals, stylometric or otherwise, are on record with regard to the precise sequence of dialogues from end to end. The work of Ledger and Thesleff stand out in particular: Ledger's (1989) contribution represents the pinnacle of stylometric achievement, while the work of Thesleff (1982, 1989, 2009) is a testament to what can be accomplished independently of stylometry. Studies perfecting the micromanagement of temporal clues merit serious consideration, if not through these particular scholars, then at least through efforts in the same direction or spirit. At this point, an overview of Ledger's conclusions, based as they are on stylometry, will be more relevant to the specific survey in progress, with a brief look at Thesleff subsequently concluding the broader assessment of Platonic chronology.

3.3.4.3. Modern Stylometry: Gerard R. Ledger

Ledger's work (1989) constitutes a milestone in the development of stylometry. Breaking new ground with a timely combination of technological advancement and methodological innovation, his contribution represents a significant boost to the claim of stylometry to scientific objectivity. His initiative to track textual patterns at the level of individual letters, as opposed to studying meaningful combinations of them in words, stands as an inspiring demonstration of the possibility of insight into unconscious stylistic development. The value of such a strategy lies as much in its confirmation of the possibility of tapping into unconscious trends as it does in the particular trends it identifies and the conclusions it draws from them. The singular advantage of the approach is that exclusive focus on unconscious stylistic patterns translates into freedom from distortions associated with data contamination by deliberate manipulations of style, which, if indeed deliberate, can never be counted as part of a natural process of stylistic maturation.

The chronological order Ledger arrives at can be summarized as follows:

Extending the Frontiers of Stylometric Classification
Gerard R. Ledger
35 Dialogues (Chronological Order)

Lysis	387: Academy founded	367–366: Sicilian visit 2
399: Socrates executed	Gorgias	Letter 13
Euthyphro	Menexenus	Phaedrus
Minos*	Meno	361–360: Sicilian visit 3
Hippias Minor	Charmides	Philebus
Ion	Apology	Clitophon*
Hippias Major	Phaedo	354: Dion murdered
Alcibiades 1*	Laches	Letters 7, 3, 8
Theages*	Hipparchus*	Sophist
Crito	Rival Lovers*	Statesman
389: Sicilian visit 1	Protagoras	Laws
	Euthydemus	Epinomis*
	Symposium	Timaeus
	Cratylus	Critias
	Republic	348–347: Plato dead
	Parmenides	
	Theaetetus	

Notes:

1. All dates are B.C.
2. Ledger's own presentation incorporates numerous other dates omitted here to keep the timeline relatively free from clutter.
3. Items marked with an asterisk signify works that are not typically considered authentic. While these are not among the spuria recognized since antiquity, four are commonly rejected (*Clitophon*, *Minos*, *Rival Lovers*, *Theages*) and three are frequently questioned (*Alcibiades* 1, *Epinomis*, *Hipparchus*). The list may arguably be expanded, but other works attracting opposition (*Ion*, *Hippias Major*, *Menexenus*) attract support as well.

Source: Gerard R. Ledger: *Re-counting Plato* (1989): pp. 224–225.

The most salient difference between Ledger and stylometrists flourishing earlier is confidence and specificity, attributes that are natural allies in any exploratory project. Not only does Ledger maximize analytic specificity, namely, by focusing on the problem at the level of orthographic data instead of words, but he also digs deep to draw conclusions at the level of dialogues instead of groups of dialogues. In fact, he goes even further, assigning absolute dates to entries, already given firm relative positions in an uninterrupted sequence covering thirty-four dialogues and four letters. He does, however, express greater confidence in the relative dates than in the absolute dates. The total coverage represents everything Ledger considers authentic and nothing he does not. The inclusion of more than the typical number of dialogues reflects the fact that the method is serviceable in ascertaining authenticity as well as in determining chronology in works already considered authentic.

The specificity so impressive in unraveling the original production sequence of the entire corpus, dialogue by dialogue, also constitutes the most controversial aspect of the approach. The undertaking by Ledger demonstrates that milking stylometry for a greater yield in specificity weakens prospects for a meeting of the minds, otherwise converging at a general level since the inception of the approach. This is not to say that no two stylometrists ever disagreed before Ledger but that those satisfied with grouping dialogues rather than sequencing them have had less cause for disagreement. Does this mean that the reliability of the stylometric method, and, therefore, the plausibility of its conclusions, is inversely proportional to the strength of the claims it makes? To some extent, this, or something like this, is true of any scientific study. Errors are magnified by specificity. The pertinent question, then, might seem to be, not whether Ledger's approach is overly specific, or, his aims, too ambitious, but whether his model is prone to error. Yet this would be a step in the wrong direction, if any difficulty is assumed to be peculiar to Ledger. Indeed, Ledger can claim no more credibility for his conclusions than for his arguments, or for his findings than for his experiments, but the absence of problems in this regard does not vindicate the enterprise of stylometry as a whole.

The fallibility of stylometric chronology is not restricted to Ledger. More important, the solution to any problem with the greater specificity involved in sequencing rather than grouping dialogues cannot simply be entrusted to progress. Corresponding obstacles are not certain to be overcome through technical improvements, whether in the form of better statistical models or advancements in computer technology. This is because the underlying difficulty is not so much technical as it is conceptual. Organizational principles plausible enough in the division of the corpus into a few groups may not be as convincing in the determination of the precise position of each and every one of several dozen dialogues in an exhaustive chronology. The apparently quantitative difference between comparing groups of dialogues and comparing the dialogues themselves turns into a qualitative difference as the extension of the underlying organizational principles from one project to the other requires a leap of faith.

The growing commitment required is especially conspicuous in comparison with the more modest project, that of grouping like with like, as opposed to investigating how they might all be unlike. The provision of a full chronology implies that Plato's style was in constant transformation, with changes substantial enough to distinguish conclusively between any two works. As against this, the division of the corpus into three stylistics groups implies that Plato's style underwent a grand transformation twice, and only twice, in his life. Strictly speaking, it has no temporal implication at all, implying instead that the Platonic corpus shows two, and only two, substantial breaks in stylistic coherence, but it can safely be given a temporal extension, if not because temporal differentiation need not be implied for temporal analysis to be warranted, as submitted above, then at least because the point here is merely to test the number of breaks in question, whether or not they are temporal breaks.

Either way, the numerical claim here is not hard to believe. Two changes do not represent an extreme in either direction. Indeed, there is no set figure, or even a typical figure, for how many times the style of a writer, philosopher or not, might change significantly enough for detection. But "two" can hardly be considered outlandishly low or incredibly high. This is the extent of the doxastic commitment required by a stylometric study proposing three stylistic groups, which almost always translates into three time periods.

In contrast, any such study claiming to lay out the sequential production order of the entire collection, dialogue by dialogue, requires much more. It requires, in terms of the same criteria, accepting the far more lively scenario that Plato's style changed significantly, not just twice, but dozens of times. Specifically, it requires believing that Plato's style underwent a statistically significant transformation in every single dialogue. This, in turn, is not as easy to believe as the relatively uneventful stylistic development process implied by division into three groups.

A strong reply on behalf of Ledger is that he focuses exclusively on the unconscious elements of style. This is sufficient to confirm that Ledger was tracking the right data, or, more specifically, that he was not driving a temporal wedge between roughly concurrent projects that were deliberately processed with otherwise incongruous styles, or that he was not mistaking one dialogue as preceding another based on evidence of earlier stylistic features whereas the apparently earlier dialogue was actually composed later using the earlier style, presumably in pursuit of the best fit between argument, expression, and subject matter, though the reason does not matter.

On the other hand, confirmation that Ledger could not possibly have been deceived by Plato does not make the procedure any more responsive to stylistic changes, unconscious though they may be. The problem is not in detecting changes that are there but in detecting changes that are not. Filtering out conscious elements does not spread out the aggregate stylistic change in the corpus any more uniformly across the dialogues. It does not ensure a stylistic transformation, even a strictly unconscious one, from each dialogue to the next. Fine stylistic distinctions, after all, are no less precarious when they are unconscious than when they are conscious.

3.3.4.4. General Assessment of Stylometry

Stylometric projects are not actually all that fragile, even where they are pushed to accommodate exhaustive chronological arrangements at the level of individual dialogues. Such ambitions need not reflect badly, or at all, on stylometry, since they often combine basic stylometric findings with a plethora of other considerations, instead of letting everything hang on stylistic differences.

However, weeding out deliberate stylistic changes is not a panacea for potential problems; nor is it a license to force the method beyond its limits. Although focusing exclusively on the unconscious elements of style circumvents any problems with deliberate and therefore deceptive changes, the possibility of a false positive is not the only risk involved.

After all is said and done, stylometry fails where revision enters into the picture, and, even where this can be ruled out, it falters if production times are allowed to vary across dialogues, even on the assumption of strict succession with no overlap. Stylometric groups are less susceptible to difficulties regarding revision and variable production rates than are full stylometric chronologies, first because a revised dialogue can belong to the same group both before and after the revision, and second because a group has at least some room for overlapping production whereas a sequence has none, but the question whether the focus is on conscious or unconscious elements is an entirely different concern that makes no difference here.

Hence, division into broad groups of stylistic affinities remains a major accomplishment, despite the inherent methodological fallibility of stylometry, particularly through revision and variable production. This is not to say that a breakdown at the level of dialogues is not also a major accomplishment. It would be an even greater accomplishment save for its structural tendency to exacerbate standing threats against the basic model.

As it is, stylometric division is feasible even with the ever-present possibility of the disruption of a linear production schedule, for example, as in the scenario of producing ten dialogues in succession only to go back and revise one or two or even all for style, or as in the scenario of producing ten dialogues in succession while all along working on an eleventh far longer than any of those started and completed in order, with the longer project conceived before and finalized after the production of the others.

What keeps the widely recognized limitation from constituting a decisive objection is the very uncertainty sustaining it. The indeterminacy leaves plenty of room for mitigating factors. Chief among them is independent confirmation through evidence outside stylometry. The broad divisions identified through stylometric studies are consistent with clues in other considerations, particularly in the form of internal references linking certain dialogues to one another in short temporal chains, not to mention external anchors linking certain dialogues to familiar grounds in the world outside the text, and thereby providing additional coordinates for the arrangement of the corpus.

Such opportunities for confirmation are more likely to attach themselves to groups than to successions. For example, stylometric sequencing may fail by jumbling dialogues otherwise known on independent evidence to have been produced in a certain order, whereas all that is expected of stylometric grouping is to place them all in the same group in no particular order. Repeatability is also a factor in favor of stylometry, representing the essence of its claim to being scientific, but this, too, is more promising at the most general level of division, as demonstrated early on by independent research projects converging around comparable clusters, even before Ritter (e.g., Campbell, 1867; Dittenberger, 1881; and Lutoslawski, 1897).

3.3.4.5. Prospects for Stylometry and Standard Developmentalism

Stylometry has been invoked both to support and to oppose the standard developmental model of three productive periods defining the intellectual output of Plato. At least partial justification is available in the match between the last stylistic group and the late philosophical period. And substantial incongruity awaits in the middle, where hard core advocates of the standard account do their best spin work. If the standard developmental account is the hypothesis, and, stylometry, the test, attempts at corroboration have certainly frustrated developmentalists of that particular bent. However, given that not all developmentalists espouse the standard account, that is, the same three periods of intellectual growth, a contradiction by stylometry is not a blow to them all, especially not to those embracing developmentalism in the generic sense of the opposite of unitarianism, hence, independently of the particular course of development followed. In that case, of course, development will be defined by stylometry rather than being tested by it, since the test for a predefined course of development has not been favorable. In fact, any successful stylometric project is proof of development, and thereby of developmentalism, just not always along the same path.

The test and the hypothesis may not be jointly definitive, or even revelatory, but what can we say of stylometry and the standard account severally? Both praise and censure will have a different basis. One cannot simply agree with stylometry, or disagree with it, in the same sense that one may agree or disagree with the standard account. Stylometry cannot sensibly be doubted on the basis of its intuitive appeal, whereas that is pretty much all we have to go by in the case of the standard account, which, once the facts are laid out, is adjudicated, by and large, in terms of whether it feels right, or, to adopt a more concrete description, in terms of whether it captures, structures, and enriches the understanding one already has of Plato.

Stylometry can reasonably be faulted for vulnerability to distortions grounded in the possibility that the dialogues underwent revision and in the certainty that some took longer than others to compose in the first place, but it cannot sensibly be rejected as just another likely story lacking objective confirmation. For example, the view that the first book of the *Republic* was composed earlier than the rest of it, and released as a standalone piece known as *Thrasymachus*, or, *On Justice*, can be expected, at least on the face of it, to undermine any stylometric conclusion reached on the basis of a uniform screening of the entirety, whereupon the result would be an average that fits neither the earlier work nor the later. The scenario may be complicated even further by the possible existence of a proto-*Republic*, alternatively called the *Ideal State*, comprising most of books two through five of what we now have as the whole, and circulating far in advance of the finished product. (See, for example: Nails, 1995, pp. 116–122; 2002, pp. 324–326; Ryle, 1966, p. 61; Thesleff, 1982, pp. 102–110; 1997, pp. 149–174.) Testing such parts separately may seem to be a quick and decisive fix, but that would be to embrace figures from separate works that no longer exist, which is hardly an improvement over adopting statistical averages for the single work almost certainly put together from parts severally alien to the central tendencies in the whole. Throwing out the *Republic* altogether and testing the remainder of the corpus would clearly be an effective solution, whereby an appropriate place in the resulting chronology could be sought for the *Republic* on the basis of other considerations. This would indeed be the end of the story were the *Republic* the only snag in an otherwise smooth process, but it is instead a representative case for a general problem.

To return to the general point regarding the proper evaluation of stylometry, any opposition must be directed at the methodology rather than the conclusion since the approach is decidedly scientific. This is especially relevant to contemporary formulations, all dedicated to uncovering stylistic trends and patterns in unconscious habits of composition, with the relevant text presumably not contaminated with *ad hoc* and otherwise incongruous variations of the sort the author might have introduced deliberately. It is not, however, unique to contemporary formulations. It holds across the board, reflecting the spirit of even the earliest efforts, where the aim has always been to achieve scientific credibility, making the reliability of the method a prior concern over the accuracy of the outcome, which may, after all, even in pure guesswork, fortuitously turn out to match the historical facts.

As for developmentalism in general and the standard account in particular, scientific credibility is at the heart of the controversy. The central debate, to wit, the ongoing opposition around the tenability of the view positing three distinct productive periods, revolves around the issue of evidence. The developmental hypothesis, whether specifically in its instantiation as the standard account or in any other formulation, and whether it is supported or contradicted by stylometry, has been increasingly coming under attack. The opposition, in turn, consists largely in emphasizing the lack of hard evidence rather than in adducing counterevidence, which remains equally scarce and infirm, thereby suggesting not that developmentalism must be abandoned but that it need not be adopted. Lacking a compelling case against it, the standard developmental hypothesis is certainly not an academic abomination, and may sensibly be retained as a familiar frame of reference, useful, if for nothing else, then at least for designating a particular collection of dialogues *en bloc*. It does not merit the sacrosanct treatment it enjoyed in the twentieth century, especially as that status was founded on the inculcation of a likely story that had little to recommend it beyond explanatory power, specifically, in regard to the resolution of apparent inconsistencies in philosophical outlook between certain dialogues, chalking everything up to revisionist output, but it also does not deserve uncritical denigration just because the explanation is no longer required or welcome.

3.3.5. The Maverick's Perspective: Holger Thesleff

No discussion of Platonic chronology can be complete without taking account of the vigilant monitoring of the entire enterprise by Holger Thesleff. More aptly classified as a maverick than as an affiliate of any school of thought, Thesleff is a source well worth consulting before stringing together any number of dialogues in succession, and even before loosely placing them together in the same time period. This is not necessarily because his chronology is better than anyone else's, but because he has something to say, something relevant and incisive, about everyone else's (Thesleff, 1982, 1989, 2009). Having taken the time to formulate critical opinions on just about every proposal in the area of Platonic chronology, his firmest conviction is that the greatest obstacle is the nature of the corpus itself, not the quantity or quality of evidence or the effectiveness of investigative methods. Put simply, the corpus is a collaborative product with layer after layer of revision by multiple sources, and charting a linear chronology unfolding from a single point of origin is not even a sensible goal, let alone a manageable technical problem.

That said, Thesleff's point of view is not limited to isolated opinions on individual dialogues. He does have a conception of the whole, fluid though it may be. Thesleff himself considers his contribution "tentative, pronouncedly critical, hypothetical, and often destructive rather than constructive" (personal letter to Alican: 29 December 2009). But his own outlook is not without order. Given enough caveats, it may fairly be systematized as follows, with the notes at least as important as the body of the presentation.

Structural Scrutiny without Methodological Allegiance
Holger Thesleff
39 (26+13) Dialogues (Chronological Order)

Fully Authentic Dialogues (39)			Academy
Solo Production (21)		**Assisted (5)**	**Accretion (13)**
Apology	Laches	Timaeus	Clitophon
Gorgias	Hippias Minor	Critias	Alcibiades 1
Meno	Ion	Sophist	Theages
Phaedo	Euthyphro	Statesman	Rival Lovers
Symposium	Hippias Major	Philebus	Eryxias
Euthydemus	Cratylus		Hipparchus
Protagoras	Phaedrus		Sisyphus
Menexenus	Theaetetus		Minos
Lysis	Parmenides		Demodocus
Charmides	Republic		On Virtue
Crito			On Justice
			Laws
			Epinomis

Notes:

1. The table is chronological from the beginning of the first column to the end of the third, therein covering the fully authentic dialogues, including those produced with secretarial assistance, and it is chronological again within the last column, corresponding to works that are inspired and possibly authorized and even supervised but not written or dictated by Plato.
2. The chronology is indexed to the final edition of each dialogue, whereas Thesleff actually makes room in his timeline for the full production history of every dialogue, accounting separately for each draft released and circulated. For example, the bulk of the *Republic* comes before the *Parmenides*, but the *Parmenides* was finished before the *Republic*.
3. Among the assisted work, Thesleff takes the *Philebus* to be the closest to Plato.
4. Thesleff ascribes only one of the thirteen letters directly to Plato. He considers the *Seventh Letter* (354 BC) to have been written by Plato, between the *Philebus* and the *Laws*, though with secretarial intermediation. He considers half of the remaining dozen (*Letters* 2, 3, 4, 6, 8, 13) to have been semi-authentic accretions, all drafted between the *Hippias Major* and the *Hipparchus*, but he rejects the other half altogether (1982, pp. 233–235).
5. Excluded: *Alcibiades* 2, written in Plato's lifetime but not by Plato; *Axiochus* and *Halcyon*, both written after Plato's death (1982, pp. 231–232; personal letter to Alican: 29 December 2009).

Sources: Holger Thesleff: *Studies in Platonic Chronology* (1982); "Platonic Chronology": *Phronesis* 34 (1989): pp. 1–26; "Early Academic Editing: Plato's *Laws*" (2003: with Debra Nails): pp. 14–29; *Platonic Patterns* (2009); personal letters to Alican (7 December 2009; 29 December 2009).

In place of the familiar divisions of the standard developmental account, Thesleff gives us a primary distinction between fully authentic and semi-authentic dialogues. Fully authentic dialogues are exactly what the name might suggest, work ultimately attributable to Plato, whether in personally carrying out every aspect of the production process or in working with an assistant responsible for routine tasks unrelated to the creative effort. Semi-authentic dialogues are Academy accretions that can neither be attributed directly to Plato nor wholly divorced from him: Representing "pseudoepigraphical 'school accumulation'" (Thesleff, 1982, p. 95), these are Academic, and even Platonic, but not authentic in the strictest sense. They are likely to have been approved by Plato, but not to have been written by him, at least none in its entirety. Specifically, they represent work either begun by Plato and finished by someone else, begun by someone else and finished by Plato, or composed by someone else from a draft by Plato, or from oral suggestions by him. Even with a multitude of provisions, Thesleff claims no sharp lines between fully authentic and semi-authentic Platonic texts in circulation (1982, p. 204), admitting in fact that we may not even be able to tell the difference (1982, p. 95).

Nevertheless, he at least recognizes the distinction, and adds another, the secondary one within the realm of fully authentic dialogues, dividing them according to whether they were produced with or without secretarial assistance. Solo effort by Plato accounts for roughly half of all the dialogues in the canonical corpus, and constitutes the bulk of what Thesleff considers fully authentic work. He finds evidence of assistance in only five dialogues, all traditionally placed in the late period of the standard account, or, from the other leading perspective, all regularly showing up in the final group of stylometric classification: *Timaeus*; *Critias*; *Sophist*; *Statesman*; *Philebus*. In fact, complete convergence with the late period is precluded only by the absence of the *Laws*, which Thesleff had originally placed in the same group (1982, pp. 236–238), later declaring it a semi-authentic accumulation of the Academy (2003, pp. 14–29: with Nails).

The coincidence, however, is no indication of agreement with the standard account, which he rejects with particular urgency. The twenty-one dialogues listed under the heading of "solo production" in the Thesleff table may coincide with the sum of everything in the traditional "early" and "middle" periods, but this is where the coincidence ends, as it leaves no room for the developmental story of the standard account. We find, for example, that the *Phaedo* and the *Symposium*, otherwise standard fixtures in the middle period, are nearly ten steps ahead of the *Euthyphro*, a regular item in the early period, according to most accounts. Perhaps even more telling is the assignment of fairly late positions to Socratic dialogues such as the *Hippias Major* and, to name a semi-authentic one, the *Sisyphus*.

Yet in rejecting the standard account, Thesleff does not push an alternative paradigm. More accurately, he does not destroy systems to promote his own. To be sure, his own considerations hang together as a coherent whole, but this is not the same as starting with a hypothesis and seeking evidentiary corroboration, much less recalibrating the predictions of the model as evidence for it. He works in the opposite direction, starting with the evidence and following it to its natural conclusion. This does not necessarily make his conclusions right, but it does make them empirical as opposed to speculative. He is far more willing to give up the resulting model than to neglect, reject, or spin the available evidence, or to favor any part of it that may prove advantageous. This is not just a predisposition but a track record, as he has been known to change his mind on a magnitude that might be considered a paradigm shift if he were in fact dealing in paradigms. To cite just one example, the *Crito*, *Laches*, *Ion*, *Euthyphro*, and *Hippias Major* have gone from being semi-authentic accretions of the Academy (Thesleff, 1982, pp. 236–238) to fully authentic works of Plato (Thesleff, 2009), in fact, each ending up as a solo work, unassisted in any way, compared to an initial consignment to the fringes of authenticity.

Thesleff's perspective, at any point in time, is indeed built on an identifiable chronological sequence. But he is never as attached to the resulting layout of the whole as he is to the historical, literary, and philological evidence attendant on each part. Thesleff is insistent, before anything and above everything, that what Plato says, and what he leaves unsaid, is far more important than when he may have said it.

3.4. Pedagogical Order

A popular alternative to chronological order is pedagogical order, that is, the sequence most conducive to understanding and appreciating the philosophical content of the work. This may or may not be the order in which Plato himself intended the dialogues to be studied, which, in turn, is no easier to determine than the order in which he composed them. While difficult to prove, substantial correlation can be expected between Plato's intended order of study and his actual order of composition, given how counterintuitive it would be to line up production without regard to intended distribution. There would be little reason to produce, release, or deliver the products on a schedule that frustrates predetermined educational goals. This does not mean that the order of writing must have been identical with the intended order of reading, but if the pedagogical order was indeed established at the outset, it is reasonable to suppose that actual composition followed the predetermined program of study. On the other hand, if Plato had any preferences at all, he may well have formulated them at some time after he began writing, perhaps midway through the corpus, or possibly even toward the end. It is also conceivable that his preferences pertained only to groups of dialogues, with one group to be taken up separately from another, whether before or after, but without necessarily ordering the dialogues within each group, and without, at any rate, establishing an unbroken chain of individual dialogues from beginning to end.

The most successful approaches in this direction are likely to be those proposing an ideal reading order rather than those pursuing or reconstructing the intended reading order. Kahn (1996, pp. 42–48) has much to offer in this regard. The following table summarizes his view on the proper arrangement of the dialogues.

Pedagogical Arrangement of the Platonic Corpus
Charles H. Kahn
26 Dialogues

Group 1 (16)
Stage 1: Apology; Crito
Stage 2: Ion; Hippias Minor
Stage 3: Gorgias; Menexenus
Stage 4: Laches; Charmides; Euthyphro; Protagoras
Stage 5: Meno; Lysis; Euthydemus
Stage 6: Symposium; Phaedo; Cratylus

Group 2 (4)
Republic; Phaedrus; Parmenides; Theaetetus

Group 3 (6)
Sophist; Statesman; Philebus; Timaeus; Critias; Laws

Notes:
1. Kahn considers the first group the earliest, and, the last, the latest, while neither insisting nor denying that the stages in the first group, or the dialogues themselves, whether at the level of stages or at the level of groups, are in chronological order, though confessing that he once believed that they are.
2. Kahn actually joins the *Sophist* with the *Statesman*, and the *Timaeus* with the *Critias*, in each case with an em dash in between.

Source: Charles H. Kahn: *Plato and the Socratic Dialogue* (1996): pp. 47–48.

Kahn's contribution is original in two respects. On a collective level, dealing with the corpus as a whole, he espouses a purely pedagogical approach to organizational structure, providing a specific model based on his own insights for implementation, thereby providing an alternative to chronological order, or at least to the one in the standard developmental account. On a distributive level, dealing with the relationships between dialogues, he puts his own stamp particularly on the sixteen dialogues he brings together in the first group, adding little, if anything, to prevailing conceptions regarding the arrangement of the remainder of the corpus. This does not mean that he stands alone on both counts, collective and distributive, but that the combination makes his position profitably original.

Although Kahn's schema covers the corpus at large, his analysis focuses primarily on the first group. Indeed, the remaining dialogues, especially the six belonging to the third group, neither require nor admit radical repositioning or redistribution, as they are organized in conformity with established patterns endorsed by camps otherwise in dispute regarding the proper classification of the corpus. The second group may differ in size from what may be expected in the mainstream literature, but not so much in contents, as other accounts tend to embrace the same dialogues while perhaps adding a few from Kahn's first group. The third group, on the other hand, is particularly well-established and requires or admits little, if any, modification.

Kahn does not offer this arrangement as a deductive conclusion grounded in hard evidence. He does, of course, offer evidence. What he does not do is to suggest that the available evidence incontestably validates his interpretation, leaving no alternative. His approach is best understood in narrative rather than discursive terms. The structure he advocates is a reflection of the fact that, like the standard developmental account, Kahn has a story to tell (1996, pp. 48–59). Unlike the standard account, which tells of a disciple gradually coming into his own, Kahn tells of a master with his own agenda. This is the story of a mature philosopher sharing his views in accordance with a plan. Anything resembling development in that process is actually the episodic presentation of a fully developed system.

This is the key to Kahn's arrangement: progressive revelation rather than gradual realization. He has a twofold explanation for its motivational basis (1995, pp. 26–35; 1996, pp. 59–70): First, Plato presumably aims to harness the shock value of aporia in the service of a pedagogical structure for the whole, using episodic jolts and awakenings to confirm ignorance and arouse curiosity in the reader. In fact, Kahn considers this to be one of Plato's distinctive contributions to the genre of the *Sōkratikos logos*, blending in an aporetic flavor in a group of seven dialogues (*Laches*, *Charmides*, *Euthyphro*, *Protagoras*, *Meno*, *Lysis*, *Euthydemus*) serving as philosophical cliffhangers stimulating the audience (1996, pp. 40–42, 57–59, 95–100, 178–180). Second, and more important, Plato's views, according to Kahn, are too radical for the Athens of the time, entirely unprepared for such an otherworldly perspective. The prevailing intellectual climate thus determines the apposite mode of philosophical engagement at a public level. In spite of the fact that his views are revolutionary, or rather, precisely because of this fact, Plato, so Kahn contends, prefers to effect an evolutionary rather than revolutionary transformation.

Kahn's originality is matched only by his modesty. He fully acknowledges his debt to stylometry, retaining perhaps even less credit than he deserves. Characterizing his position as a variation on a relatively uncontroversial view that has already been sufficiently justified, his concern is more with sharing the arrangement than with validating it through anything like a rigorous proof. Actually, he does not come right out and describe his arrangement as stylistic. Nor does he unequivocally repudiate its correspondence with production order, whatever that may have been. The context does make it perfectly clear, however, that he is building on the inspiration he draws from stylometric studies dividing the corpus into three stylistic groups. Hence, insofar as he takes himself to be working with a common view long in the public domain rather than promoting an entirely new formula, between the two leading approaches, Kahn's arrangement is essentially stylistic, and only coincidentally, if at all, chronological in any sense explicating temporality.

Yet, more than anything, Kahn considers his arrangement a "proposal for an ideal reading order" (1996, p. 48). This, in the end, is what makes his perspective pedagogical. Although he might appear initially to waver between taking this to be the essence of the entire classification and identifying it exclusively with the six stages of the first group, hesitating, in other words, between a pedagogical perspective of the entire corpus and a pedagogical framework for a major chunk of it, this is consistent with the fact that everything else is typically already arranged to his liking. The emphasis on the first group is a reflection of his special concern to place everything before the *Republic* in a single group rather than allowing so-called middle period dialogues such as the *Symposium*, *Phaedo*, and *Cratylus* in the same group as the *Republic*.

Careful to avoid, to the fullest extent possible, talk of chronological order, and particularly of development, Kahn replaces the typical temporal metaphor with a spatial one, through which he proposes to monitor relative distance from the center, which, in turn, is where he places the *Republic* (1996, p. 48). Having selected a pivotal reference point to establish the bearings for the entire corpus, he lays out the dialogues in the first group in levels of systematic orientation toward the *Republic*. This, then, is the organizational principle underlying the division of the first group into stages and the ordering of both the stages among themselves and the dialogues within each stage. Accordingly, he considers the dialogues preceding the *Republic* "proleptic," that is, specifically in relation to that work, or, alternatively, "ingressive," from the same perspective. This means that the arrangement is in an order accommodating the tendency of the dialogues to anticipate one another, which, roughly speaking, is what is meant by their being proleptic, and it means further that the arrangement facilitates access to the whole, mapping out the surest path through the corpus for an adequate understanding of the whole, which is, more or less, the sense in which the order of the dialogues is said to be ingressive. This, evidently, is what makes the arrangement both stylistic and pedagogical.

The reason that Kahn is careful to avoid commitment to chronological implications or possibilities is not that he finds no correlation between his own arrangement and the order in which Plato may have actually written the dialogues, but that he finds chronological projects misguided on the whole. He is especially wary of the standard developmental account, but also, more generally, of any interpretation saddling Plato with stochastic shocks in his philosophy, or in his style, for that matter. This is not a denial of apparent development in the corpus but a rejection of the interpretation that such development is inspired rather than planned.

To be sure, Kahn is not blind to what everyone else sees: a body of writing with obvious tension and periodic redirection. He is willing to acknowledge even abrupt breaks in what is said, but never with revisionary forces as the cause or trigger. The gist of Kahn's pedagogical perspective is that differences and discrepancies between dialogues are the result of a planned progressive revelation (partly because Plato wanted to employ the pedagogical advantages of aporia but primarily because his otherworldly philosophy was too radical for its time and place) rather than indicators of an inspired development in view (1995, pp. 26–35; 1996, pp. 59–70). Hence, the anxiety regarding chronology is well-placed, as it reflects nothing more than a repudiation of the standard account.

What may not be so clear, from a methodological perspective, is the relationship between stylistic and pedagogical considerations. To put it briefly, why is the pedagogical arrangement championed by Kahn so consistent with the order suggested by stylometric studies (Ritter, 1910, p. 273; 1933, pp. 27–28; Rowe, 2003a, p. 104)? Does the arrangement most conducive to pedagogical order, or heuristic orientation, simply turn out to coincide with stylistic patterns in the whole, or is it the other way around? Is there even a difference? Indeed, there is a difference, but the answer is that two processes are operating at once. What Kahn has done is to adopt uncontroversial stylistic groups, with a view to organizing the dialogues within each group in a way promoting understanding and appreciation of the whole. This is why his intellectual biography of Plato (1996, pp. 48–59), speculative by Kahn's own admission, supports a reading order so closely aligned with stylometric evidence. His story not only matches the evidence but explains it as well. Whether the explanation is accepted is a different matter, but the match is indubitable. Nor is it a coincidence. Kahn does not simply stumble upon the best fit for the evidence; he sets out to find that fit.

All the same, it is just as important to point out that even if this were a coincidence it would not be a remarkable one. Philosophical and stylistic development are mutually independent phenomena. Accepting or rejecting one implies nothing about what is to be done with the other. Thus, it is no less consistent to think of Kahn's speculative biography of Plato as actually capturing reality, which, in turn, naturally has to be aligned perfectly with the way Plato's style in fact developed over the course of his writing career. The only question here is the accuracy of that biography, not the motivation for it. So long as it coincides with reality, it will also coincide with the prevailing facts regarding style, given that those, too, happen to be veridical.

This is by no means the only pedagogical arrangement espoused in the secondary literature. Nor is it necessarily the best or most sensible proposal. However, any judgment on the best will be largely, if not purely, subjective. And Kahn's proposal stands out as a good example of what an expert on Plato considers to be the best approach to the study of Plato.

3.5. Dramatic Order

Another option is to arrange the dialogues in the order of their dramatic dates. The central drama in the dialogues usually has some connection to external reality, and the links therein can lead to identifiable points in history, sometimes precisely, sometimes approximately. At the very least, even where absolute dates cannot be assigned to the drama, references in one dialogue to the dramatic context of another fix the position of one relative to the other. This immediately yields several definite sequences, which can then be spliced together according to external references. Even so, this is nothing like an exact science. Experts are no less likely to disagree on relative order than they are on absolute dates. Agreement tends to be limited to certain stretches of the corpus, not quite extending to the whole. Comparing the judgments of interested scholars, say, Nails (2002) and Press (2007), may help visualize the extent of expert agreement while identifying problem areas.

In her indispensable prosopography of "Plato and other Socratics," as she calls them, Nails (2002, pp. 307–330, 357–367) provides a guide to the dramatic dates of Plato's works. She does this through two separate appendixes, one offering a discussion of the dramatic date of each dialogue (appendix 1: pp. 307–330), and the other placing them all in their intended time and place, marked out with familiar historical milestones to add a sense of context (appendix 4: pp. 357–367). She reviews the entire Thrasyllan corpus except the definitions and epigrams, ending up with twenty-nine dialogues with a datable dramatic setting. Her dates for these dramas, thus excluding the letters, may be tabulated as follows:

Dramatic Dates of the Dialogues: Debra Nails
(All dates are B.C.)

Parmenides	August 450	Symposium	February 416
Protagoras	± 433/432	Eryxias	≤ 415
Alcibiades 1	Early 432	Ion	413
Alcibiades 2	Early 432 or mid-429	Lysis	Early Spring ± 409
Republic*	431–404	Euthydemus	≥ 407
Gorgias*	431–404	Meno	402
Charmides	May 429	Menexenus	Winter 401/400
Timaeus*	August 429	Theaetetus	Spring 399
Critias*	August 429	Euthyphro	Spring 399, same day
Laches	Winter 424	Sophist	Spring 399, next day
Cratylus	≤ 422	Statesman	Spring 399, same day
Clitophon	421–416	Apology	May–June 399
Hippias Major	421–416	Crito	June–July 399
Hippias Minor	421–416	Phaedo	June–July 399
Phaedrus	418–416		

Notes:

1. Dates listed are for the main action. Six dialogues also provide a framing event for the central drama: *Parmenides* (± 382); *Protagoras* (later same day); *Symposium* (± 400); *Euthydemus* (next day); *Theaetetus* (Spring 391); *Phaedo* (few weeks or months after execution).
2. The specification of a range does not signify that the event took that long but that it took place sometime during that period.
3. Dialogues marked with an asterisk are those that Nails classifies separately as problematic. She claims that no date throughout the Peloponnesian War (431–404 BC) can be ruled out for the *Republic* and the *Gorgias*, while her best estimate for the *Timaeus* and the *Critias* is August 429 BC. With regard to the *Republic*, the problem is not merely uncertainty in regard to the finished product but complexities in its production history (2002, pp. 324–326). Her earlier essay (1998) dedicated exclusively to the dramatic date of the *Republic* affords additional insight into the difficulties.
4. Nails denies discernible dramatic dates to the following thirteen dialogues: *Axiochus*; *Demodocus*; *Epinomis*; *Halcyon*; *Hipparchus*; *Laws*; *Minos*; *On Justice*; *On Virtue*; *Philebus*; *Rival Lovers*; *Sisyphus*; *Theages*.

Source: Debra Nails: *The People of Plato* (2002): pp. 307–330, 357–367.

Press (2007, pp. 72–73) meets the same basic need with greater brevity in a tabular presentation noting the dramatic dates alongside information concerning principal themes, narrative depth, dramatic setting, and interlocutor choice. His two-page presentation covers twenty-four dialogues, starting with the *Parmenides* and ending with the *Phaedo*, and omitting all that he considers spurious.

Dramatic Dates of the Dialogues: Gerald Alan Press
(All dates are B.C.)

Parmenides	450	Phaedrus	411–401
Protagoras	433–432	Euthydemus	407–405
Charmides	432–429	Gorgias	405
Philebus	< 427	Cratylus	405
Laches	424–418	Meno	403
Lysis	unknown	Theaetetus	400–399
Hippias Major	421–416	Euthyphro	400–399
Symposium	416	Sophist	400–399
Ion	> 412	Statesman	400–399
Republic	411	Apology	399
Timaeus	411	Crito	399
Critias	August 411	Phaedo	399

Notes:

1. Dates listed are for the main action, even for dialogues providing a separate framing event for the central drama.
2. The specification of a range does not signify that the event took that long but that it took place sometime during that period.

Source: Gerald Alan Press: *Plato: A Guide for the Perplexed* (2007): pp. 72–73.

Press is more selective than Nails, as he covers only the dialogues he considers authentic, rather than accounting for the entire corpus, whereas Nails dates everything she considers datable, regardless of authenticity. Among these, he considers only one indeterminate, the *Lysis*, the dramatic context of which Nails dates to the early spring of 409 BC, while Press goes only so far as assigning it a relative position. Among the thirteen dialogues Nails deems indeterminate, Press disregards twelve as spurious, but identifies the *Philebus* as having been composed sometime after 427 BC. He also excludes as spurious six dialogues Nails dates with certainty: *Alcibiades* 1; *Alcibiades* 2; *Clitophon*; *Eryxias*; *Hippias Minor*; *Menexenus*. As for the bundle of dialogues in common, in other words, those that are neither deemed indeterminate by Nails or Press nor disregarded as spurious by Press, agreement is spotty at best. In addition to the works already mentioned, specific problem areas include, but are not limited to, the following dialogues: *Cratylus*; *Critias*; *Gorgias*; *Phaedrus*; *Republic*; *Timaeus*.

No doubt, two studies do not warrant a sweeping conclusion, but prospects for a standard dramatic account are not encouraging, at least not for an undisputed one. The results of the comparison on hand are better than what might be expected of a random distribution but worse than what would be expected of a scholarly consensus. To be sure, a scientific survey might yield different results, possibly revealing a greater consensus.

In fact, expanding the sample size by just one observation, say, by adding the dramatic order worked out by Zuckert (2009), readily introduces, or uncovers, greater harmony. The addition of Zuckert shows a reasonably sharp focus around a common denominator, at least between Nails and Zuckert, if not also between all three. Her contribution on dramatic order can be encapsulated as follows:

Dramatic Dates of the Dialogues: Catherine H. Zuckert
(All dates are B.C.)

Group 1	
Laws	460–450
Epinomis	460–450
Parmenides	450

Group 2	
Protagoras	433–432
Alcibiades 1	432
Alcibiades 2	432
Charmides	429
Laches	423
Hippias Major	421–420
Hippias Minor	421–420

Group 3	
Symposium	416
Phaedrus	415
Ion	413
Clitophon	411
Republic	411
Philebus	unknown
Timaeus	409–408
Critias	409–408

Group 4	
Theages	409
Euthydemus	407
Lysis	406
Gorgias	405
Meno	402–401

Group 5	
Theaetetus	399
Euthyphro	399
Cratylus	399
Sophist	399
Statesman	399
Apology	399
Crito	399
Phaedo	399
Menexenus	387–386

Notes:

1. Dates listed are for the main action, even for dialogues providing a separate framing event for the central drama.
2. The specification of a range does not signify that the event took that long but that it took place sometime during that period.
3. Zuckert does not actually name or number the groups, but she does at least recognize them as such, separating them with horizontal lines cutting across a vertical list.

Source: Catherine H. Zuckert: *Plato's Philosophers* (2009): pp. 8–9.

Zuckert's own presentation already includes a summary in tabular form (2009, pp. 8–9). The table above merely rearranges that information to maintain parallel construction with the preceding diagrams of the other two positions, or at least not to stray far from the pattern established therein. The most conspicuous difference, both visually and logically, is that Zuckert organizes the dialogues in groups rather than leaving them in one long dramatic sequence. This is because she finds the dramatic differentiation indicative of stages, or, put differently, because she is convinced that the corpus unfolds in dramatic stages. Specifically, she contends that the groups represent distinct stages in the philosophical development of Plato's Socrates, though not of Plato himself, nor of Socrates himself. This does not mean that she ignores other leading protagonists, such as Parmenides, the Eleatic Stranger, and the Athenian Stranger. On the contrary, she finds the surest route to Plato's philosophy to be through "Plato's philosophers," paying close attention to each and every one of them, especially as they outshine or altogether replace Socrates in the lead of a particular dialogue, but she claims that the big picture is best viewed from the perspective of the dramatic Socrates.

The immediate result of the expanded sample size, now including Nails, Press, and Zuckert, is the emergence of a pattern, perhaps not with sharp borders, but in sufficient detail to make an outright denial unreasonable. On the other hand, this may be largely because Zuckert has been influenced by the work of previous scholars, as she graciously acknowledges, particularly with respect to Nails, who is the only one mentioned by name in direct connection with Zuckert's introductory material concerning dramatic order (2009, p. 9, n. 19). Moreover, the agreement is not perfect, even between Zuckert and Nails: Zuckert herself mentions disagreement regarding the *Euthydemus* and the *Lysis*. To this, we may add, just to name the glaring differences, (1) Zuckert's willingness to date the *Laws*, the *Epinomis*, and the *Theages*, none of which Nails finds sufficiently informative to include in a chronological sequence of dramatic settings, (2) Zuckert's confidence in assigning the *Gorgias* and the *Republic* each a specific year in contrast to the more conservative approach of Nails in leaving both adrift in the Peloponnesian War (431–404 BC), and (3) Zuckert's moving the *Timaeus* and the *Critias* forward by roughly two decades, and, the *Clitophon*, by at least five years.

What is novel about Zuckert is that she brings the matter, namely, the subject of dramatic order, to the forefront, and keeps it there, instead of consigning it to an introduction, digression, or appendix. She uses dramatic chronology as an overarching guide to interpreting the dialogues rather than interjecting a summary of it as incidental information.

Nevertheless, the dramatic timeline of the corpus has traditionally attracted far less attention than the order of composition. The mindset responsible for this has been shaped by a conviction that even absolute certitude in regard to dramatic dates would not leave us with a frame of reference as useful as the composition dates, nor even as useful as the composition order alone, that is, temporal precedence without fixed dates. This is not necessarily a manifestation of insensitivity to the dialogue as drama but a rejection of the corpus as drama. More accurately, it is grounded in a denial that the corpus itself is a dramatic unit, an organic whole to be mined for a unifying theme, message, or storyline, even if each dialogue is drama at its best. Fully acknowledging that the dramatic date of a single dialogue may be entirely relevant to that dialogue, perhaps even essential for a full appreciation of it, one may consistently deny that ranking the entire corpus on this basis is useful, or even meaningful, let alone that it is as important as determining the order of composition. After all, in terms of dramatic dates, the collection would have had some order or other, regardless of whether the entire sequence was planned in advance, and regardless of which dialogue was written when. Nothing else, so the argument goes, can be deduced from this information. Presumably, this is not so with the order of composition, insight into which is often expected at least to help formulate reasonable hypotheses on currently unresolved issues like possible development in Plato's thought or the intended order of study.

Yet this does not mean that the dramatic order of the dialogues is no more meaningful than, say, the alphabetical order. More and more scholars are beginning to concentrate on dramatic order, especially as the success of efforts to uncover the order of composition seems to have reached a plateau. And much of the burgeoning interest in dramatic chronology is far beyond an intellectual exercise without purpose. Zuckert, for one, insists that the dialogues tell a story when read in dramatic order (2009, p. 11). Philosophers trying to piece that story together benefit not only from the work of one another, but just as much from the findings of scholars exploring the dramatic timeline with no concern for its philosophical implications, in other words, purely as a historical or literary problem. Either way, the effort to understand Plato grows richer.

3.6. References to Plato: The Stephanus Edition

A discussion of the works of Plato, especially from a general perspective with a structural focus, as pursued here, is a good place for relevant technical and historical details on the common pagination convention. The basics are laid out as part of the separate "Note on Documentation" in the front matter introducing this book, but a more elaborate explanation, purely for the interested reader, might be in order here.

Reputable editions of Plato's work, no matter the language, display numbers and letters running down the length of the outside margin of each page. These are reference markers intended to standardize discussions of Plato through anchors to a source document serving as a navigational map. The text used for this purpose is a collection published in Geneva in 1578 by Henri Estienne (Henricus Stephanus). Commonly known as the "Stephanus edition," this is a three-volume compilation juxtaposing the Greek text with a parallel Latin translation by Jean de Serres. Each page is divided into two columns, with the left-hand side devoted to the Latin translation and the right-hand side allocated for the original. The pages are also divided conceptually, though not physically, thus, without actual breaks or gaps, into five horizontal sections marked out visually with the letters "a" through "e" printed between the two columns of text. The compartmentalization of each page in this way enables a narrower focus in reference, and constitutes the standard basis of citation in discussions of Plato.

The method of reference by "Stephanus numbers" consists in providing the title of the work (the name of the dialogue) followed, first, by the page number in the Stephanus edition, and, next, by the letter indicating the specific position on the relevant page. For example, "*Symposium* 194e" refers to the beginning of Agathon's speech in the *Symposium*.

Most discussions of Plato concern passages that are longer than the space corresponding to one letter in the Stephanus edition. If such a passage is fully contained within the space of a single page in the Stephanus edition, the reference should indicate the page number, followed by positional letters for the beginning and end of the passage, with an en dash separating the letters to indicate inclusive content. If it is longer than one page, page numbers and positional letters must be given for the beginning of the passage as well as the end, again, with inclusive reference so noted through a central en dash. For example, "*Symposium* 194e–197e" refers to Agathon's entire speech in that work.

The title of the work may be omitted from references in discussions devoted to a single dialogue with no mention of others. And where others are mentioned, they would each require the appropriate title on every mention, but the main dialogue, the one to which the discussion is devoted, may still be referenced without a title. Otherwise, the form of the reference should conform to the example given in the preceding paragraph. Thus, the title is separated by a single space from the page number, always in Arabic numerals, and the positional letter, usually in lowercase, immediately follows the page number with no space in between. Passages in dialogues divided into books, namely, the *Republic* and the *Laws*, may be cited with additional information directing readers to the relevant book. Although this is optional rather than necessary, and the level of detail superfluous, the traditional procedure, if one wishes to be particularly informative, is to give the book number in Roman numerals inserted in uppercase type, and with a blank space on either side, between the title of the work and the page number. For example, "*Republic* X 608c–611a" corresponds to the proof given in the tenth book of the *Republic* for the immortality of the soul. The Roman numeral might alternatively have been in lowercase. A growing practice in citation and documentation, not just in Plato, but in classical studies in general, is to use Arabic instead of Roman numerals in all parts of a textual reference. Thus, the same passage can be listed as "*Republic* 10.608c–611a." This is the procedure followed in this book.

The Stephanus reference scheme is sufficient to accommodate most needs. A line number can be added to narrow down the reference in linguistic or other technical discussions where the issue on hand turns on a specific word or phrase, but such pinpoint accuracy is otherwise unnecessary. Line numbers are given in concordance with the Oxford Classical Texts edition, not the Stephanus edition.

Going in the opposite direction, that is, from the most specific to the most general level of identification, any reference to the specific volume where a particular dialogue may be located in the Stephanus edition is both unorthodox and redundant. First, nobody actually consults the Stephanus edition in its original form. This is an outdated source adopted merely to unify the mode of reference in modern editions and commentaries. Therefore, directing readers to the exact volume would be pedantry, especially since the typical reader will not be following Plato through the actual edition published by Henri Estienne. Furthermore, the effort is not essential for precise identification in the original: Although each of the three volumes starts at page one, as opposed to continuing the pagination of a preceding volume, this does not necessitate reference to volume numbers, because each dialogue ends in the volume in which it starts.

The three volumes of the Stephanus edition collectively cover forty-one dialogues, all thirteen letters, and the spurious book of definitions. Coverage of the dialogues includes the two dozen that are universally recognized as authentic, the six that are contested, and eleven of the twelve that are considered spurious. This amounts to nearly everything ever attributed to Plato. The epigrams, still widely rejected by most experts, are ignored here as well. The only other item missing from the historically exhaustive list of works ascribed to Plato and still in existence is the *Halcyon*, a dialogue long known to be spurious and often attributed to Lucian of Samosata (c. 120–180), but also to others (see Diogenes: *Lives* 3.62, but compare with Taylor, 1960, p. 552, especially n. 3). This dialogue often fails to make its way into collected works editions, even into those purporting to be complete. In fact, along with the other four surviving works (*Axiochus*, *Demodocus*, *Eryxias*, and *Sisyphus*) already rejected by the time of Diogenes (*Lives* 3.62), though included in the Stephanus edition, it tends to be ignored even in a bare listing of the spurious works.

The following table is a map to the location of each dialogue in the Stephanus edition:

Stephanus Edition of Plato's Works

Title	Start	End	Length	Authenticity
Volume 1				
Euthyphro	2a	16a	14	√
Apology	17a	42a	25	√
Crito	43a	54e	22	√
Phaedo	57a	118a	61	√
Theages	121a	131a	10	spurious
Rival Lovers	132a	139a	7	spurious
Theaetetus	142a	210d	68	√
Sophist	216a	268b	52	√
Euthydemus	271a	307c	36	√
Protagoras	309a	362a	53	√
Hippias Minor (Lesser)	363a	376c	13	√
Cratylus	383a	440e	58	√
Gorgias	447a	527e	81	√
Ion	530a	542b	12	dubious
Volume 2				
Philebus	11a	67b	56	√
Meno	70a	100b	30	√
Alcibiades 1	103a	135e	33	dubious
Alcibiades 2	138a	151c	13	spurious
Charmides	153a	176d	23	√
Laches	178a	201c	23	√
Lysis	203a	223b	20	√
Hipparchus	225a	232c	7	dubious
Menexenus	234a	249e	16	dubious
Statesman	257a	311c	54	√
Minos	313a	321d	8	spurious
Republic	327a	621d	294	√
Republic 1	327a	354c	27	√
Republic 2	357a	383c	26	√
Republic 3	386a	417b	31	√
Republic 4	419a	445e	27	√
Republic 5	449a	480a	31	√
Republic 6	484a	511e	28	√
Republic 7	514a	541b	27	√
Republic 8	543a	569c	26	√
Republic 9	571a	592b	21	√
Republic 10	595a	621d	26	√
Laws	624a	969d	345	√
Laws 1	624a	650b	26	√
Laws 2	652a	674c	22	√
Laws 3	676a	702e	27	√

Stephanus Edition of Plato's Works

Title	Start	End	Length	Authenticity
Laws 4	704a	724b	20	√
Laws 5	726a	747e	22	√
Laws 6	751a	785b	34	√
Laws 7	788a	824a	36	√
Laws 8	828a	850c	22	√
Laws 9	853a	882c	29	√
Laws 10	884a	910d	26	√
Laws 11	913a	938c	25	√
Laws 12	941a	969d	28	√
Epinomis	973a	992e	20	dubious
Volume 3				
Timaeus	17a	92c	75	√
Critias	106a	121c	15	√
Parmenides	126a	166c	40	√
Symposium	172a	223d	51	√
Phaedrus	227a	279c	52	√
Hippias Major (Greater)	281a	304e	24	dubious
Letters	309a	363e	55	dubious
Letter 1	309a	310b	1	dubious
Letter 2	310b	315a	5	dubious
Letter 3	315a	319e	5	dubious
Letter 4	320a	321c	1	dubious
Letter 5	321c	322c	1	dubious
Letter 6	322c	323d	1	dubious
Letter 7	323d	352a	29	dubious
Letter 8	352b	357d	5	dubious
Letter 9	357d	358b	1	dubious
Letter 10	358b	358c	1	dubious
Letter 11	358d	359c	1	dubious
Letter 12	359c	359e	1	dubious
Letter 13	360a	363e	4	dubious
Axiochus	364a	372a	8	spurious
On Justice	372a	375d	3	spurious
On Virtue	376a	379d	3	spurious
Demodocus	380a	386b	6	spurious
Sisyphus	387b	391d	4	spurious
Eryxias	392a	406a	14	spurious
Clitophon	406a	410e	4	spurious
Definitions	411a	416a	5	spurious

3.7. Platonic Access Channels

Plato's collected works are accessible through several scholarly channels. Although the Stephanus edition marks the origin of the standard citation scheme, the current critical edition in Greek is the arrangement in the Oxford Classical Texts series. As for translations, possibilities in English originally lagged behind those in German or French, but caught up in the twentieth century with the proliferation of translations of individual dialogues and the appearance of several editions of the collected works. An extensive translation project covering twenty-nine dialogues and executed single-handedly by Benjamin Jowett became the primary source in English in the nineteenth century, remaining popular through at least the first half of the twentieth century, and is still in wide circulation owing to the expiration of its copyright, but it is no longer considered authoritative. Three collections compete for the lead among collections of English translations: The Loeb Classical Library edition is the oldest, the Bollingen edition emerged nearly half a century later, and the Hackett edition became available after another three decades. English translations by Reginald E. Allen, the first person since Jowett to tackle the corpus alone, also enjoy critical acclaim, though falling short in coverage, spanning only thirteen works. The Hackett edition seemed to be leaving the others behind in the early twenty-first century as the standard edition in English, but independent translations, both old favorites and fresh demonstrations of excellence in scholarship, are always respectable alternatives to those in collections. The definitive version in French is the omnibus appearing in the Budé collection, a classical series offering original texts in Greek or Latin, together with their translations in French, all accompanied by scholarly introductions and critical notes.

Full citation details on these collections, together with skeletal outlines of their contents, are available in the bibliographic appendix at the end of the book. The highlights may be summarized as follows:

- Oxford Classical Texts Edition (1900–1907): *Platonis Opera*. Five volumes. Edited by John Burnet with introduction and notes. Oxford, England: Oxford University Press, 1900–1907. Reprinted 1967–1968. Greek text of forty-one dialogues (ignoring only the *Halcyon*), all thirteen letters, and the spurious book of definitions. An entirely new edition has been under way to retire the old. The first volume appeared in 1995, followed by *Platonis Respublica* in 2003.

- Loeb Classical Library Edition (1914–1935): *Plato: Collected Works*. Twelve volumes. Cambridge, Massachusetts: Harvard University Press, 1914–1935. Reprinted 1961–1984. Greek text with running English translations by various hands. Includes thirty-five dialogues and all thirteen letters. All works in a single volume are translated by the same person.

- Jowett Edition (1871–1953): *The Dialogues of Plato*. Four volumes. Translated into English, with analyses and introductions, by Benjamin Jowett (1817–1893). Oxford, England: Clarendon Press, 1871. Three more editions: 1875 (five volumes); 1892 (five volumes); 1953 (four volumes). Numerous reprints, especially after entering into the public domain. Individual dialogues, twenty-nine in all, also issued severally and in clusters in various other collections. Freely available in electronic form.

- Bollingen Edition (1961): *The Collected Dialogues of Plato: Including the Letters*. Edited by Edith Hamilton and Huntington Cairns, with an introduction and prefatory notes. Bollingen Series 71. Princeton, New Jersey: Princeton University Press, 1961. English translations by various hands. Covers twenty-eight dialogues and all thirteen letters. Singularly popular in the second half of the twentieth century.

- Hackett Edition (1997): *Plato: Complete Works*. Edited, with an introduction and notes, by John Madison Cooper. Indianapolis, Indiana: Hackett Publishing Company, 1997. English translations, by various hands, of everything ever attributed to Plato, including all the works known to have been written by him as well as the spurious material. Covers forty-two dialogues, all thirteen letters, the spurious book of definitions, and the spurious collection of epigrams.

- Allen Edition (1984–2006): *The Dialogues of Plato*. Four volumes: Released individually in 1984, 1991, 1996, and 1997. English translations, with introductory, exegetical, and critical comments and analyses, by Reginald E. Allen. New Haven, Connecticut: Yale University Press, 1984–1997. The collection includes twelve dialogues, complemented by a separate translation of the *Republic*, issued by the same publisher in 2006.

- Budé Edition (1920–1956): *Platon: Oeuvres Complètes*. Fourteen volumes. Collection des Universités de France (="Collection Budé") Série Grecque. Publiée sous le patronage de l'Association Guillaume Budé. Paris, France: Société d'Édition Les Belles Lettres, 1920–1956. Greek text with running French translations by various hands. Includes forty-one dialogues (ignoring only the *Halcyon*), all thirteen letters, the epigrams, and the spurious book of definitions.

Leading English Editions of Plato's Collected Works			
Title of Work (Alphabetical)	**Publisher & Translator (Revision in Parentheses)**		
	Loeb	**Bollingen**	**Hackett**
Alcibiades 1	W.R.M. Lamb	n.a.	D.S. Hutchinson
Alcibiades 2	W.R.M. Lamb	n.a.	Anthony Kenny
Apology	H.N. Fowler	Hugh Tredennick	G.M.A. Grube
Axiochus	n.a.	n.a.	Jackson P. Hershbell
Charmides	W.R.M. Lamb	Benjamin Jowett	R.K. Sprague
Clitophon	R.G. Bury	n.a.	F.J. Gonzalez
Cratylus	W.R.M. Lamb	Benjamin Jowett	C.D.C. Reeve
Critias	R.G. Bury	A.E. Taylor	Diskin Clay
Crito	H.N. Fowler	Hugh Tredennick	G.M.A. Grube
Demodocus	n.a.	n.a.	Jonathan Barnes
Epinomis	W.R.M. Lamb	A.E. Taylor	R.D. McKirahan, Jr.
Eryxias	n.a.	n.a.	Mark Joyal
Euthydemus	W.R.M. Lamb	W.H.D. Rouse	R.K. Sprague
Euthyphro	H.N. Fowler	Lane Cooper	G.M.A. Grube
Gorgias	W.R.M. Lamb	W.D. Woodhead	Donald J. Zeyl
Halcyon	n.a.	n.a.	Brad Inwood
Hipparchus	W.R.M. Lamb	n.a.	Nicholas D. Smith
Hippias Major	W.R.M. Lamb	Benjamin Jowett	Paul Woodruff
Hippias Minor	W.R.M. Lamb	Benjamin Jowett	Nicholas D. Smith
Ion	n.a.	Lane Cooper	Paul Woodruff
Laches	W.R.M. Lamb	Benjamin Jowett	R.K. Sprague
Laws	R.G. Bury	A.E. Taylor	Trevor J. Saunders
Lysis	W.R.M. Lamb	Josiah Wright	Stanley Lombardo
Menexenus	R.G. Bury	Benjamin Jowett	Paul Ryan
Meno	W.R.M. Lamb	W.K.C. Guthrie	G.M.A. Grube
Minos	W.R.M. Lamb	n.a.	Malcolm Schofield
On Justice	n.a.	n.a.	Andrew S. Becker
On Virtue	n.a.	n.a.	Mark Reuter
Parmenides	W.R.M. Lamb	F.M. Cornford	M.L. Gill & P. Ryan
Phaedo	H.N. Fowler	Hugh Tredennick	G.M.A. Grube
Phaedrus	H.N. Fowler	Reginald Hackforth	A. Nehamas & P. Woodruff
Philebus	H.N. Fowler	Reginald Hackforth	Dorothea Frede
Protagoras	W.R.M. Lamb	W.K.C. Guthrie	S. Lombardo & K. Bell
Republic	Paul Shorey	Paul Shorey	G.M.A. Grube (C.D.C. Reeve)
Rival Lovers	W.R.M. Lamb	n.a.	Jeffrey Mitscherling
Sisyphus	n.a.	n.a.	David Gallop
Sophist	H.N. Fowler	F.M. Cornford	Nicholas P. White
Statesman	H.N. Fowler	J.B. Skemp	C.J. Rowe
Symposium	W.R.M. Lamb	Michael Joyce	A. Nehamas & P. Woodruff
Theaetetus	H.N. Fowler	F.M. Cornford	M.J. Levett (M.F. Burnyeat)
Theages	W.R.M. Lamb	n.a.	Nicholas D. Smith
Timaeus	R.G. Bury	Benjamin Jowett	Donald J. Zeyl
Letters	R.G. Bury	L.A. Post	Glenn R. Morrow
Definitions	n.a.	n.a.	D.S. Hutchinson
Epigrams	n.a.	n.a.	J.M. Edmonds (J.M. Cooper)

Part Two

DIALOGIC COMPANION

Euthyphro: Broad Outline

- Prologue and dramatic orientation (2a–5d)
  - Socrates as defendant in legal proceedings initiated by Meletus (2a–3e)
  - Euthyphro as plaintiff and prosecutor in case against his own father (3e–5a)
  - Irony: Socrates's adamant appeal for instruction by Euthyphro (5a–d)

- Ostensive approach to definition (5d–6c)
  - Definition #1: piety as the prosecution of crime as in Euthyphro's case (5d–6c)

- Guidance: the art and science of definition (6c–e)

- Extensional approach to definition (6e–11b)
  - Definition #2: piety as what is loved by (dear to) the gods (6e–7a)
  - Objection: the gods are divided in this regard (7b–8b)
  - Rejoinder: the gods are not divided about penalizing injustice (8b–9c)
  - Reorientation: Socrates redirects from the general to the universal (9c–d)
  - Definition #3: piety as what is loved by (dear to) all the gods (9d–e)

- Dilemma: "loved because holy/pious" vs. "holy/pious because loved" (10a–11b)

- Dramatic interlude: Daedalus analogy (11b–e)

- Intensional approach to definition (11e–15c)
  - Suggestion: piety as a part of justice (11e–12e)
  - Definition #4: piety as the part of justice concerning care of the gods (12e–13d)
  - Definition #5: piety as the part of justice concerning service to the gods (13d)
  - Analogy with the crafts: the end or function of service to the gods (13d–14a)
  - Definition #6: piety as the "give and take" of sacrifice and prayer (14b–15b)
  - Definition #7: piety as what is loved by the gods (15b–c)

- Epilogue (15c–16a)

Four

EUTHYPHRO

4.1. Literary Profile

Plato's *Euthyphro* is a typical aporetic dialogue, searching for a definition and concluding without one. To be precise, the discourse goes through several definitions but ends without adopting one, none having being found satisfactory. This is the basic dramatic formula in Socratic dialogues, though not without exception, as demonstrated by the deviations from the norm represented by the *Apology* and the *Crito*, neither of which is after a definition of any kind.

The concept examined in this case is piety, and, in the same fell swoop, holiness. The corresponding definition is also sought through the definienda "the pious" and "the holy," meaning, respectively, something like "that which is pious" and "that which is holy."

This plurality of terms is not due solely to ambiguities in a particularly mercurial term in the original, nor, again, solely, to scholarly preferences in translation. In the first place, the text itself provides, not just one, but two distinct sources of ambiguity, as it switches back and forth between two terms, each alone difficult enough to pin down regardless of any confusion with the other. In the second place, while translators exercising equally legitimate choices, often in competition, and sometimes in contradiction, do indeed multiply the possibilities in interpretation, the wealth of terminological choices reflects conceptual breadth present in the original and transcending language. Tracing all interpretive possibilities and taking stock of each judgment by each translator might be useful in itself, perhaps as a separate exercise, but this is not the place for it.

Nevertheless, the difference between piety and holiness is so obvious, or, rather, it is so obvious that piety and holiness are different things, even if the difference itself is not obvious, that no reader will be comfortable with the opening sentence of the second paragraph, as it bundles the two concepts together almost as if they were the same thing. Actually, this will only bother the average reader. The expert, whether a classicist or a philosopher, really, any sort of specialist in Plato, will just sigh and read on. The average reader will be restless because equating piety and holiness is counterintuitive at least as lexical synonyms. Whatever may be required to capture all the shades of meaning, at the most fundamental level, that of basic common sense, the essence of piety is a response to holiness, thus indicating a complementary relationship. Put simply, we demonstrate piety when we encounter holiness. Or maybe we do not, but, whether we actually do or not, we certainly ought to. That is what makes us pious, and it is also what identifies the object of our piety as holy.

But what do the experts know that makes them immune to the rather equivocal characterization offered through the introductory remarks of this chapter? They know that the terminology of the original is forgiving enough to frolic with impunity in translation or exegesis. Or perhaps it is so unforgiving that nothing surprises them anymore. For one thing, the discussion concerns two related but distinct terms, either one of which can reasonably be interpreted as piety or as holiness: One is *eusebeia* (εὐσέβεια), the other, *hosiótēs* (ὁσιότης). Moreover, much of the dialogue is carried out, not so much with these nouns, as with the substantive reformulation of their adjectival forms, prefacing the adjective with the definite article (*to* or τὸ), wherein "piety" is used interchangeably with "the pious," or in close correspondence with it, and, "holiness," in turn, with "the holy." The substantive use of the adjectives tends to come in pairs of opposites, at least being introduced in that way, if not also being fairly regularly invoked in that manner, as we are asked repeatedly, through Euthyphro, to reflect upon what it is that makes things pious or impious, and, as the case may be, holy or unholy. The push to identify the fundamental differences between the pious and the impious, and between the holy and the unholy, helps advance the exploration of the essential characteristics of piety and holiness. In connection with *eusebeia*, the contrast is between *to eusebēs* (τὸ εὐσεβές) and *to asebēs* (τὸ ἀσεβες). In connection with *hosiótēs*, the contrast is between *to hósion* (τὸ ὅσιον) and *to anósion* (τὸ ἀνόσιον).

The juxtaposition of *eusebeia* and *hosiótēs*, together with all the corresponding lexical categories in use, plus any inflection undertaken in the process, starts early on in the dialogue, still prevailing at the end. Euthyphro himself speaks of *to hósion* and *to anósion* (4e) as he narrates the details of his case. Socrates initially embraces these terms (4e), but he brings up *to eusebēs* and *to asebēs* (5c) in asking Euthyphro to teach him about such matters. Yet the apparently definitive question he puts to Euthyphro immediately afterwards is about *to hósion* and *to anósion* (5d). While this finally seems to establish the precise focus of the inquiry, both sets of terms remain in play through the end of the dialogue. In fact, *eusebeia* and *hosiótēs* not only seem interchangeable, with frequent switches back and forth, but they also tend to appear side by side in the same sentence (12e, 13b).

Again, the source of any ambiguity in this regard is not the alternation between two different terms picking out two altogether distinct concepts, one corresponding unequivocally to piety, and, the other, without a doubt, to holiness. What we have instead are two different terms, or, to be precise, two sets of terms, each of which can be equated or associated reasonably well with piety as well as with holiness. This is not to deny that scholars, despite substantial disagreements, have definite preferences in distinguishing between the terms in question. But even unanimous agreement would only reduce the ambiguity to the simpler scenario of two terms and two concepts, hence, still leaving us wavering between piety and holiness. Moreover, the greatest consensus among experts is not in separating piety from holiness in the original but in recognizing that the original distinction comes with additional nuances that are not exhausted by the contrast between piety and holiness. The inescapable conclusion is that the dialogue is best read in Greek.

Of course, this is not a particularly helpful assessment, as all classics are better read in their original language. Nor is steering readers away from translations the best way to hold their attention in a commentary in English. Quite the opposite, the most popular alternative to reading the original is to work with translations that stick meticulously close to the original. These, however, usually read like the Greek itself, and may not represent much of an alternative. Moreover, a translation is not the place to sort out terminological or conceptual ambiguities in the original. For that, we turn to secondary literature. Thankfully, we have had enough time over the millennia to develop a rich tradition in commentary. One piece that stands out as eminently readable in this language, while bringing out the intricacies of the original, is Burger's expository overview in "Making New Gods" (1999, pp. 39–59).

Examples can be multiplied, but the case on hand seems to call more for supplementary resources of a general nature than for direct commentaries on the dialogue itself. Insight into piety and holiness, or into their closest analogues, as they might be gleaned from generalist sources on ancient Greek culture, including moral as well as religious traditions, may be more relevant here, or at least just as much so, in comparison to one or another of the various analyses of the *Euthyphro* in its entirety. Dover's classic study, *Greek Popular Morality in the Time of Plato and Aristotle* (1994), can be consulted profitably in this regard, especially in its coverage of piety (pp. 247–268). An even better option might be to go through Mikalson's rich survey, *Greek Popular Religion in Greek Philosophy* (2010), which brings out themes especially relevant to the *Euthyphro*, dedicating a significant portion of the introductory chapter to a general discussion of religious terminology (pp. 6–15), and reserving the fourth chapter specifically for the distinction between *eusebeia* and *hosiótēs* (pp. 140–186).

Among any number of options, including that of going back to the original text, a plain discussion in English is certainly not the worst prospect. On the contrary, it can be a rewarding intellectual experience. This is because we are never really confused about whether the topic is piety or holiness. It is obviously both. Whether we are talking about piety or about holiness, we are really talking about religious duty. What is its ultimate sanction? What is its binding force? Piety and holiness, after all, are counterparts of the same concept from mortal and heavenly perspectives: Piety honors what holiness inspires, and observes what it requires.

We cannot be too far off track in approaching the *Euthyphro* with this naive yet solid distinction. That said, making the *Euthyphro* out to be entirely about religion would be to miss out on a great deal of insight into its relevance to the moral sphere. Although the subject under consideration might best be understood as "religious duty," the central import of the dedicated analysis is just as relevant to "moral duty," or, from a purely philosophical perspective, to "ethical obligation," or even to ethics in general, including both axiology and deontology.

Indeed, the work is about piety, but it is indispensable for critical reflection on righteousness or moral rectitude. No one today need consult the *Euthyphro* for guidance on religious duty, but no one can afford to ignore it for insight into the origins of the philosophical treatment of moral value and obligation. In fact, its seminal contribution, not to mention its ongoing appeal and relevance, is defined by its status as one of the earliest examples in print of moral justification and as a perennial demonstration of ethical reasoning.

Its particular relevance in this regard derives from an apparently incidental critique of divine command theory, rejected through a celebrated argument against one of the several definitions considered for piety (10a–11b). The refutation in question proceeds by reducing the perspective represented by divine command theory to the rationally less palatable end of a dilemma, amounting essentially to a challenge to any moral position based on stipulation without justification.

This feature of the dialogue is so important as to merit mention in even the briefest summary. Taking this into account, the *Euthyphro* might usefully be characterized as Plato's attack on divine command theory, dramatically laid out in the form of a quest to uncover the true meaning of piety through an ultimately inconclusive search for the proper definition of the concept. While this may not be the tidiest description possible, it is far more informative than the standard account of the work as a dialogue on piety, especially since the author is at pains to establish the independence of morality from religion.

4.1.1. Dramatic Orientation

The *Euthyphro* is a dialogue of the simplest possible form. The entire discussion takes place between two, and only two, people: Socrates and Euthyphro. Socrates is the protagonist, Euthyphro, the antagonist. They are not only the sole interlocutors but the entire *dramatis personae*. The only other mortal identified by name, albeit in passing references, is Meletus (2b, 5a–c, 12e, 15e), who figures in the *Apology* as one of Socrates's accusers in the trial ushering in the death of the master, but he does not count even as a silent character in the *Euthyphro*, where he is merely mentioned rather than present.

This Euthyphro may or may not be identical with the character of the same name in the *Cratylus*. Both are priests, the one in the *Euthyphro*, older, as evidenced by his being in a position to address the Athenian Assembly, having done so more than once and possibly on a regular basis for quite some time (3c). Other than implicit age, the two characters reveal no discernible difference, at least none that is significant. They also bear no apparent resemblance beyond name and vocation. In fact, neither is explicitly identified as a priest by profession, but the allusions in this regard are compelling, as the context in both dialogues indicates religious expertise. The character in the *Euthyphro* is introduced unequivocally as an authority on religion, so much so as to make his knowledge essential to his function or usefulness, indicating that his involvement in the field is professional (4e–5a). He is also a soothsayer, as attested to by his own admission of public divination (3b–c), as well as by the confirmation of Socrates (3e). Strictly speaking, the designation as "priest" is underdetermined by the evidence, perhaps even more so in the absence of any church to speak of, but the exegetical integrity of the text is not compromised by using the appellation as shorthand for "self-proclaimed religious expert with the gift of prophecy and an affinity for theogony." The *Cratylus* is consistent with this characterization, holding nothing to contradict it and enough to corroborate it, especially where Socrates cites Euthyphro as his source of information and inspiration regarding the genealogy of the gods (*Cratylus* 396a–e), an area of discussion where Euthyphro is demonstrably at home in the dialogue bearing his name (5e–6c).

However, the possibility of a shared character does not necessarily coincide with a dramatic intersection between the two dialogues. In other words, the reference in the *Cratylus* to Euthyphro the character does not seem to be, and certainly does not need to be, a reference to *Euthyphro* the dialogue, even if it is a reference to the same character. The *Cratylus* (396d) refers back to a discussion taking place between Socrates and Euthyphro on the morning of the dramatic date of that dialogue, specifically, putting them together at dawn on that day. But this cannot be the drama of the *Euthyphro*, which opens at an hour suitable for pursuing legal matters at a public office, accordingly, a good bit past dawn, and contains little to inspire the etymological discourse of the *Cratylus*. Moreover, the meeting of the *Euthyphro* takes place between the events of the *Theaetetus* (210d) and the *Sophist* (216a), thereby following one lengthy engagement and preceding another within twenty-four hours, both placing Socrates in the company of an entirely different set of characters from the *Euthyphro* as well as from the *Cratylus*. No room would be left to squeeze in the *Euthyphro* where its dramatic setting firmly places it in contextual relation to other works, namely, between the *Theaetetus* and the *Sophist*, if we were to interpret the dawn meeting mentioned in the *Cratylus* (396d) as a reference to the *Euthyphro*, which, to complicate matters further, would then drag the *Cratylus* along with itself into an already cramped dramatic stretch in the Platonic corpus.

Hence, the drama of the *Euthyphro* cannot safely be interpreted as blending into or leading up to that of the *Cratylus*. Such a reading would jeopardize the dramatic coherence of the greater body. To be sure, the risk of introducing a dramatic discrepancy within the collective should not be the decisive factor against a certain reading for a single dialogue, but it is not a hollow concern where the reading, to begin with, has little to recommend it other than its tenability in isolation. The mere reappearance of the character, however, carries no such risk in this case. Given the absence of any apparent reason to create a second character of the same name, profession, and general orientation, the two Euthyphros are probably one and the same. Either way, we have no external evidence of a historically significant Euthyphro flourishing in Athens around 399 BC.

No matter the degree of correspondence with reality, the dramatic setting places both Socrates and Euthyphro just outside the courthouse in the Athenian Agora. Socrates is there for arraignment in connection with multiple charges centering on impiety, the charges initiating the fateful legal process ending in his conviction and execution, while Euthyphro is engaged in a sensational project, the prosecution of his own father in a questionable murder case.

Specifically, they run into each other at the porch of the office of the *archon basileus*, a title combining the Greek words for "ruler" and "king," and often anglicized in reverse order as "king-archon." Despite the etymology, the *archon basileus* was not a king but the chief magistrate in charge of religious affairs. This was one of the nine archonships collectively inheriting the powers of the king in the political evolution of Athens over centuries, a process beginning in 1068 BC with the death of Codrus, the last of the legendary kings. The king-archon's office was the *stoa basileus* (literally "royal portico"), constructed in the fifth century before Christ in the northwest corner of the Agora. This was also the seat of the Areopagus, deriving from *Areios Pagos* (literally "Hill of Ares"), a hill hosting the council of elders during preclassical times and the chief homicide tribunal in the classical period, with the name eventually coming to denote the judicial court as well as the venue of its activities.

Headed by the *archon basileus*, the Areopagus was responsible for overseeing religious affairs and adjudicating all cases of religious offense, including murder, which, in ancient Athens, was a crime against the gods, representing a "religious pollution" sure to invoke their wrath unless handled properly, meaning rectification through formal compensatory measures as well as purification through ritual. In sum, the state's interest in homicide was not the manifestation of a general regard for the public good, or for civil order, but the result of a specific concern with religious purity (Burnet, 1924, p. 83). Hence, we find Socrates and Euthyphro at the colonnade of the courthouse, one as defendant, the other, plaintiff, in separate cases of impiety.

4.1.2. Historical Context

The dramatic setting is apposite to the philosophical discussion. The obvious connection is that the discussion on the nature of piety takes place between characters involved in legal proceedings concerning piety. The question, then, is whether this is historically accurate, that is, whether the entire setting is based in fact. The evidence is partial, clearly substantiating the Socratic case, but silent on Euthyphro.

Socrates faces charges of impiety in the indictment for having honored gods of his own invention and forsaken the ones recognized by the state (3b). He is actually accused of more than impiety, through the practice of which he allegedly leads the youth of Athens astray (2c–3a). Indeed, we find out elsewhere, in our dramatic access to the actual trial, that the formal charges against him comprise impiety, specifically in the form of heresy, combined with corrupting the youth, presumably by inspiring youngsters to adopt comparable heretical outlooks (*Apology* 24b–c).

As for Euthyphro, the legal proceedings he initiates against his father, though involving homicide, are essentially about a religious offense rather than a transgression of merely civil or criminal codes of conduct in reference to the prevailing statutory context. A twist here is that Euthyphro himself might reasonably be accused of impiety in prosecuting his own father for impiety, perhaps not so readily today, but certainly in his own day, given the filial devotion common and expected in antiquity, not merely in Athens or the Greek world but throughout the Mediterranean and deep into the heart of Asia.

Corroborating an interpretive twist as such, Euthyphro openly expresses insecurity in anticipation of an unfavorable reception of his case by the general public (4a), and reports being already under heavy criticism by his family in this regard (4d–e). He repudiates any and all wrongdoing, particularly impiety, on the grounds that his initiative is consistent with what goes on in heaven, as even the gods are known to revolt against their own fathers in the name of justice (5e–6a). This immediately sets up a contrast between the requirements of filial allegiance and those of religious reverence.

The dramatic backdrop of Euthyphro prosecuting his father for murder may or may not be based in fact. Taylor (1960, p. 146) finds the setting "too *bizarre* to be a natural fiction." In the same spirit, Allen (1984, p. 29) finds it "too good not to be true." Yet Tredennick (1969, p. 184, n. 8) sees it as a dramatic tool to illustrate a clash of pieties (between Euthyphro and Socrates) and to set the stage for Euthyphro's appeal to the doings of the gods in the traditional mythology. What is certain is that the setting is perfect for the multiple references (4e, 5e–6c, 7b, 8b) to the prevailing theogonies, particularly to the dethronement, first, of Uranus by Cronus, and next, of Cronus by Zeus, and to the great wars, namely, the Titanomachy, the war corresponding to the latter heavenly coup and taking place between the Titans and the Olympians, and the Gigantomachy, a later engagement between the Olympians and the Gigantes.

The symbolism of pitting the philosopher against the priest in a discussion of piety is vastly appropriate, especially where the overriding aim is to separate morality from religion through the aid of reason. Yet the layers of the metaphor run deeper still. Plato's characterization also brings into play opposition between the old and the young and between defending and prosecuting. In a sense, the elderly Socrates personifies the father whom the sanctimonious priest is prosecuting, while the younger Euthyphro possibly embodies the accusers and prosecutors of the martyr of philosophy. Or perhaps Euthyphro instead represents the purported victims of Socrates, those allegedly corrupted by his example and through his instruction.

At any rate, the setup is the dramatic counterpart of the public plea in the *Apology*. What the *Apology* accomplishes through argument by way of direct defense, the *Euthyphro* attempts through drama by way of demonstration. The *Apology* gives readers an opportunity to evaluate Socrates's arguments, while the

Euthyphro gives them an opportunity to evaluate his actions. Seeing him in action, particularly in connection with an issue as relevant as piety, places us in a better position later to evaluate the testimony of Socrates as he defends himself against charges of impiety.

Are Socrates's actions in the *Euthyphro* consistent with his defense in the *Apology*? Specifically, does he do or say anything that may be evidence of a heretical bent or of a corrupting influence? The two dialogues appear mutually consistent in this regard, but not necessarily in favor of innocence more than guilt. The evidence could go either way, with enough to absolve the man and plenty to convict him, whether in the *Euthyphro* or in the *Apology*, or even in any other cotemporaneous report. Regarding the charge of impiety, or heresy, the Socrates of the *Euthyphro* cannot, through the attitude he demonstrates there, reasonably be exonerated from the corresponding accusation in the *Apology*. In fact, the opposite seems nearer reason, as he openly rejects the gods, for example, in explicitly spurning the mythical accounts of the gods recognized by the state (6a–b). He also attacks the prevailing version of divine command theory, as he thwarts the priest's attempt to locate the source of holiness and piety in the gods themselves, instead, moving the determinant of such value and obligation from the heavens to the earth, and emasculating the gods while empowering mortals (6e–11b, especially 10a–11b).

As for a corrupting influence, his interaction with Euthyphro shows no intention to corrupt, if that is understood as effecting a transformation from better to worse, but a deliberate attempt to influence the priest is hard to miss or deny. After all, Socrates himself recognizes that it is not so much his opinions, but his efforts to inculcate and popularize them, that vexes Athenians (3c–d). In this connection, the symbolism in the choice of characters reveals yet another layer, emphasizing the reciprocity between teaching and learning, though the association there signals irony as well as metaphor, with Socrates asking to be enlightened by Euthyphro but instead guiding him through the logic of their discussion, and Euthyphro being eager to teach but having little to offer.

4.1.3. Tension between Philosophy and Religion

Despite the richness of the symbolism exposing layers of dramatic and philosophical tension between the two characters, a caveat is in order regarding the dangers of a facile treatment of the metaphor of philosopher and priest. Spotting and understanding a metaphor is both important and rewarding, especially with a literary genius like Plato, but missing one is probably not as infelicitous as finding one where it does not exist. Somewhere in between lies the risk of misinterpreting one intended in a slightly or perhaps even entirely different way. A tempting potential for error in this case is reading the symbolism of the opposition between philosopher and priest as a clash between philosophy and orthodoxy. To be sure, Socrates is searching for an answer based solely on reason, while Euthyphro pursues one grounded exclusively in religion, but Socrates does not symbolize opposition to the mainstream religious beliefs and practices of the typical Athenian any more than Euthyphro represents the Everyman of Athens. While the opposition between philosopher and priest is symbolic of a generic contrast between philosophy and religion, this is not a clash around the orthodox religious stance, the essence of the Greek sociocultural experience, and, in short, the ordinary way of life in Athens. Socrates is not so far from the central position implied therein, and Euthyphro is not so close.

Those approaching the *Euthyphro* as literature, particularly those initiated in critical theory but new to Plato, tend to read the religious polarity in the strongest possible sense, taking the characters to be diametrically opposed, much in the manner of good versus evil. Those reading it as philosophy, especially those trained in the analytic tradition, usually do not care one way or the other, focusing primarily and often exclusively on the definitions, with a particular interest in the emphasis on definition as a prerequisite to discussion rather than on the definitions themselves. A dramatic hint for the intended reading, which turns out to warrant a softer interpretation of the opposition around religion, is the eagerness of Euthyphro to side with Socrates on the charges against the philosopher (3b–c), not to mention Socrates's plea, ironic or not, to be tutored by Euthyphro (5a–d).

The perspective of a gentler opposition around religion has been gaining popularity, though not fully controverting claims to dramatic tension through character polarization. Its early proponents include Burnet (1924, pp. 85–87, n. 2a1; anticipated in 1914, pp. 182–184) and Taylor (1960, p. 147, especially n. 1), who, in fact, propose a reading that may be construed as opposite that of opposition: They maintain that the purpose of the *Euthyphro* is to show that Socrates is not the heretic he is made out to be, with the dialogue standing as Plato's testament to posterity that the master was accused unjustly and convicted wrongly. The crux of this interpretation is that Socrates's open opposition to the gods is not an affront to religion as practiced by his fellow citizens, who were no more impressed by the exploits of Uranus or Cronus or Zeus than was Socrates. This is supported by the complementary view that Euthyphro does not represent the Athenian orthodoxy, defined broadly as those convicting Socrates, with the priest's gift of divination (3b–c, 3e) and predilection for celestial tales (5e–6a, 6b, 6c) making his religious orientation anything but conventional, as mirrored already by his standing status as a social misfit or outcast (3c), turning into a veritable *persona non grata* upon unveiling plans to prosecute his father (4d–e, 5e–6a).

Brickhouse and Smith (2004, pp. 18–20) add that Euthyphro proves himself not to be a religious traditionalist even as he appeals to the examples set by the gods (5e–6a), in fact, especially as he does so. They find this appeal so outlandish as to call it "shocking," expressly in reference to the typical Greek estrangement from reprehensible behavior patterns reserved for the gods and shunned by mortals. This alone, they contend, is sufficient to establish that Euthyphro does not represent the prevailing praxis in religious affairs. Quite the contrary, on this interpretation, Euthyphro stands opposed to the Greek way, at least in terms of the traditional approach to religion, while it is Socrates who keeps challenging him on behalf of the conventional view that antagonism toward one's father is *prima facie* unconscionable, requiring a compelling defense (4e, 9a–b, 15d). In a sense, Socrates is prosecuting Euthyphro for impiety, as he himself is about to face charges regarding his own alleged impiety. No doubt, Brickhouse and Smith are right to find Euthyphro's position unorthodox, both in the case he pursues against his father and in the appeal he makes to the gods, whose personal and collective conflicts are meant to be a lesson on what to avoid rather than an inspiration for what to do. Cronus, after all, meets the same fate he brings to his father in dethroning him, as he himself is subsequently dethroned by his own son.

On the other hand, it might sensibly be objected, particularly against Brickhouse and Smith (2004, pp. 18–20), that Euthyphro's appeal to the exploits of the gods is not so strange since he is challenged on a point of religious propriety. Euthyphro's evaluative framework in this regard concerns what is and is not acceptable to the gods. What better guide to what is and is not acceptable to the gods than the very behavior of the kings among them?

This approach might indeed be on tenuous ground in relation to the function of myth in antiquity, and, even more generally, in regard to the standard motivation throughout history for telling stories. To be sure, some legends call for action, others warn against it, and the difference is usually perfectly clear. If it is not, the story itself is unsuccessful. In Euthyphro's case, the story of Cronus leaves no room for ambiguity. The context shows Euthyphro pursuing a course of action that is not acceptable, with rationale that is not defensible.

However, what this uncovers regarding his appeal to the gods is a mistake, not an unorthodox choice. The case he pursues is anomalous enough as it is, but it is not clear that turning to the gods for justification adds to the aberration. If the problem is that Euthyphro misinterprets the legendary struggles among the gods, deriving inspiration where he should have found deterrence, then it follows that he was right to consider the divine framework, wrong only in interpreting it, which weakens the grounds for finding him deviant in the effort. The alternative is to condemn the effort altogether, regardless of any mistake or confusion, thereby maintaining that Greeks in antiquity simply were not in the habit of justifying their actions in reference to precedents in legend. This position is difficult to separate from an outright repudiation of the social and cultural significance of mythology. Of course, if it is correct, then so much the worse for mythology, but does this really make Euthyphro any more of an oddball than he already is in prosecuting his own father? Or is it because he is prosecuting his own father that everything else about him seems amenable to classification as quirky behavior?

Overall, the arguments moderating the symbolic opposition between Socrates and Euthyphro are compelling, but not to the point of vitiating all dramatic tension between the two characters. The collaborative spirit is unmistakable (3b–c, 5a–d), and might be crucial to an accurate interpretation of the drama, but accuracy also requires recognizing that no such collaboration ever actually materializes, remaining on the level of goodwill rather than action.

Moreover, even the positive intentions turn out to be hollow, based on little more than a misunderstanding, a misguided sense of solidarity. The reciprocal signs of cooperative tendency are grounded in an ill-conceived perception of a shared interest in piety, an ideal which the two characters have entirely different ways of conceptualizing. Euthyphro, for his own part, seems eager to rush to the aid of Socrates against charges of impiety, but his eagerness is motivated by the belief that Socrates is being persecuted for being blessed with a divine sign, which Euthyphro, himself a diviner, can appreciate (3b–c). Socrates, in his turn, seems just as eager to accept the assistance of Euthyphro, begging the priest to teach him about piety, but this is the formulaic Socratic ploy to expose contradictions or other inadequacies in the opposite view by bringing it out into the open, which, in this case, makes it dramatically certain that Socrates has already identified and rejected the priest's notion of piety (5a–d). The alliance is there, but it is nothing like that between Socrates and the Thebans in the *Phaedo*. It is also far from the animosity between Socrates and Thrasymachus in the *Republic*. It lies somewhere in between, engendering cooperation without eliminating competition.

The arguments against an opposition grounded in the sociocultural fabric of the day raise important points, providing historical as well as philosophical insight, but they do not preclude tension in the juxtaposition of the philosopher and the priest as characters, though the latter may be considered as much a religious fanatic as a religious representative, certainly not one ordained by a central authority, but obviously at least some sort of sectary. Even the best reasons for rejecting a metaphorical opposition between Socrates and Athenian convictions and actions, religious or otherwise, do not overturn the symbolism in opposing a priest or religious expert with someone who openly spurns the gods immortalized by Homer and Hesiod, deified by the state, and worshipped by the people, not only through public practice but also through mystery religions, including the Dionysian, Eleusinian, and Orphic Mysteries.

The caveat remaining, on the safest general interpretation that fits the evidence, is about (1) misinterpreting Socrates as a challenge to Greek orthodoxy just because his character symbolizes reason against myth and advocates rationality in ethics against divine command theory, and about (2) mistaking Euthyphro to be representative of Athens and of Athenians at large simply because he symbolizes religious as opposed to critical thinking. Accordingly, the warning does not conflict with a symbolic reading. There is plenty of room for the basic opposition between philosopher and priest, even where the philosopher does not threaten the prevailing culture while rejecting myth and questioning authority. In fact, the warning confirms the complementary relationship between Plato's two primary objectives or achievements in the dialogue, one being the separation of morality from religion through a challenge to divine command theory, and the other being a demonstration that Socrates, charged with impiety, understands the concept better than a priest accusing a third party of the same, apparently an allegorical way of suggesting that Socrates understood piety better than even the experts, yet was still tried, sentenced, and executed for impiety.

4.2. The *Daimonion* of Socrates

The dramatic complexity of the relationship between Socrates and Euthyphro is nowhere as prominent, and philosophically extravagant, unless grounded in fact, as in their ostensibly casual bonding through the *daimonion*, that is, the divine sign that keeps the philosopher out of trouble, literally and figuratively. On the one hand, the reference to the sign (3b–c) is a clear indication of the unorthodox profile of Socrates in regard to divinity, or in relation to anything divine. On the other hand, it brings him closer with Euthyphro, who expresses approval and appreciation of the sign, with an enthusiasm approaching outright envy. Either way, the topic, or at least the concept, merits further thought, if only because it comes up again and again in the Platonic corpus, with a particularly prominent role in the *Apology*.

The reference to the sign is transliterated as often as it is translated. In fact, transliteration may well be the standard mode of reference if only because not everyone uses the same translation. In other words, the advantage of transliteration is the consistency of working with a single term in contrast to the multitude available in translation. The typical choices are: "divine guide," "divine sign," "divine signal," "divine voice," and each of these with the term "supernatural" replacing the term "divine." The word "companion" creeps in as well, usually modifying "divine," but also possibly modifying "supernatural," thus yielding "divine companion" or "supernatural companion." Sometimes the entire sequence is preceded by an acknowledgement of familiarity, making the full reference something like "familiar divine sign," which seems to be Plato's way of letting his audience know that Athenians were aware of the situation. Without further multiplying examples, even this brief survey is sufficient to demonstrate the advantage of consistently using "daimonion" to stabilize the reference.

The etymology of the term is telling but not certain. The reference in the text is to "the daimonion" (τὸ δαιμόνιον), a cognate of the more familiar "daimôn" (δαίμων), both likely having roots in the verb "daiō" (δαίω), denoting an allotment of destinies. Derivative though it may be, the diminutive, "daimonion," seems to be the preferred choice, as Plato never uses "daimôn" to refer to the sign of Socrates. He provides nothing like a definitive introduction with a comprehensive exposition, or even clear insight no matter how far from complete, but he brings the subject up frequently enough, with coverage spanning roughly one-fifth of the dialogic corpus, specifically including the following works: *Alcibiades* 1; *Apology*; *Euthydemus*; *Euthyphro*; *Phaedrus*; *Republic*; *Theaetetus*; *Theages*.

The *Apology* is the closest we get to a central account. This is not because it actually contains anything like a proper orientation, but because everything else is even more patchy, with the result that much of the information available elsewhere in Plato is already included in the *Apology*.

The superficial treatment in Plato, combined with a contradictory and equally superficial portrayal by Xenophon (*Apology* 4–5, 8, 12–13; *Memorabilia* 1.1.2–1.1.5, 4.8.1; *Symposium* 8.5), and the absence of a better alternative elsewhere, leaves a good deal of room for speculation and controversy. Even when the scope of consideration is limited to Plato, the subject affords room for disagreement. The questions reach as far as they run deep, ranging from matters of ontology to those of epistemology, and covering issues cutting across the realm of morality and religion, or the philosophy thereof.

At the most fundamental level, the ontological question crops up: What is the *daimonion*? That is to say, what sort of thing is it? What is its nature? Everyone agrees, of course, that it is a divine sign, since that much is expressly stated in the text. Where they fail to come together is on exactly what this means.

Among the various discussions surrounding the *daimonion*, arguably the most heated is its status as a source of knowledge. We know that the *daimonion* manifests itself as a supernatural voice warning Socrates when he is about to do something best not done, while remaining silent otherwise. Thus, it never provides positive counsel, engaging only in critical intervention. But where does the epistemic authority rest? How does Socrates know the *daimonion* to be reliable? The warnings of the *daimonion* are evidently epistemically serviceable, but are they infallible as well? Do they constitute a necessary condition of knowledge, or a sufficient one, or both? How exactly do they satisfy the epistemic requirements of a philosopher constantly in pursuit of the truth?

The answers revolve around a cluster of competing positions established in the late twentieth century. For example, Reeve (1989, pp. 68–73; 2000, pp. 24–39) and Vlastos (1991, pp. 157–178, 280–287) take Socrates to subordinate the guidance of the *daimonion* to the dictates of reason, thus assigning epistemic primacy to ratiocination over divination, whereas Brickhouse and Smith (1989, pp. 237–257; 1994, pp. 189–195) find him committed to heeding the warning of the *daimonion*, hence choosing divine guidance over reasoned conclusions in the event of a direct conflict. The difference is not so much that Reeve and Vlastos defend the opposite, namely, that Socrates would instead choose the rational over the divine in the event of a direct conflict, but that they do not take the possibility of conflict as seriously as do Brickhouse and Smith.

Reeve (1989, pp. 68–73) takes Socrates to be following the guidance of the *daimonion* without requiring episodic confirmation through reason, but only because of a general presumption in favor of the sensibility of divine guidance, residing, as it does, in the supreme wisdom and goodness of the gods. (Strictly speaking, the supremacy of their wisdom should be sufficient, whereupon the supremacy of their goodness would be superfluous, especially as a separate assumption, which does, however, help rule out the possibility of deliberate deception.) He thus interprets any choice favoring divine guidance over mortal reason not as an abandonment of reason but as a deference to a higher form of it (Reeve, 2000, pp. 24–39), thereby removing the conflict between piety and reason by expanding the relevant conception of rationality.

Vlastos, on the other hand, finds no conflict at all between what can be concluded through the elenchus and what is indicated by the *daimonion*, contending that divine guidance cannot be understood except through reason (1991, p. 171), and that any divine command appearing to contradict reason can be nothing but a misinterpretation (1991, p. 286). To compare, Vlastos rejects Reeve's solution of elevating divine reason above mortal reason, instead making both humans and gods subject to the universal authority of reason, undifferentiated in quality, or in any other material way, thereby guaranteeing rational harmony except in the event of error, which, if and when it occurs, would have to be on the mortal side, but without consequently indicating any conflict between ratiocination and divination.

Other controversies abound. A broad sample of these is available, for example, in a collection of essays bringing together previously published and newly commissioned material: *Reason and Religion in Socratic Philosophy* (Smith and Woodruff, 2000). The concluding chapter is particularly relevant, as it provides access to a nexus of correspondence between the foremost scholars on the epistemology of the *daimonion*, releasing an edited version of originally private discussions between Vlastos, McPherran, Brickhouse, and Smith, the last two corresponding initially as a team but later and mostly as individuals (Smith and Woodruff, 2000, pp. 176–204). Another indispensable source originates in papers from a conference in 2003 dedicated exclusively to the *daimonion*, with the contributions edited and released together as a book a couple of years later: *Socrates' Divine Sign* (Destrée and Smith, 2005).

Notwithstanding the multiplicity of the controversies surrounding it, and without prejudice to the importance of the corresponding issues, the basic concept behind the *daimonion* can accurately be explicated as divine *apotreptic* guidance. The fact that it is divine separates it from ordinary conscience. The fact that it is *apotreptic*, as opposed to *protreptic*, both standard designations in the literature, means that it is designed to dissuade rather than persuade. This underscores the negative nature of the sign, establishing it as a force of intervention rather than direction. Anything else remains open to discussion, but the basics should prove sufficient for an intelligent reception of occurrences throughout the Platonic corpus.

This is not a license to rest easy, especially if we are to take the advice of Vlastos, who identifies the problem of the *daimonion* as "the gravest of the difficulties we all have to face in our effort to make sense of Socrates" (1989, p. 1393 [=1995, p. 28]). But the vigilance required need not paralyze us in our effort to work through the references.

4.3. The Pursuit of Definition

The pursuit of definition is a common theme in Socratic dialogues: The *Euthyphro* sets out to uncover the meaning of piety; the *Laches* is after a proper account of courage; the *Lysis* explores friendship; the *Charmides* inquires into temperance; the *Hippias Major* investigates beauty; the *Meno* focuses on virtue; and the *Republic* is the monumental study on justice. While the *Republic* is not a Socratic dialogue, and might seem out of place grouped with those that are, the first of its ten books is often treated as if it were a separate work of the early period.

The purported aim in such dialogues is to find the best definition, or rather, without commitment to the possibility of degrees of accuracy in definitions, which may instead be taken simply to fail where they do not succeed, the aim may be said to be to define the object of discussion exactly as it should be defined. The goal is not to define the word in question but to uncover the true nature of the corresponding concept or phenomenon, or, put differently, to capture the conceptual essence of the corresponding object, whether concrete or abstract. Hence, Socrates is not looking for a lexical definition, though one might do, but for an accurate understanding of the subject matter.

The Socratic interest in definition, at least insofar as it is portrayed in the dialogues of Plato, is typically manifested as a logical prerequisite for fruitful and meaningful discussion. The basic reasoning here is that we must first understand what something is before we make or evaluate judgments about it.

This is sometimes construed in a stronger sense, making Socrates seem somewhat unreasonable, or more so than he usually is. The methodological concern the master exhibits here, that is, the epistemic preoccupation with definition, is sometimes called the "Socratic fallacy," a term coined by Peter Thomas Geach (1966, pp. 369–382) in a famous critique of the manifestation of such concerns in the *Euthyphro*. Geach basically saddles Socrates with the conviction that one does not know what one cannot define. Conversely, this is the notion that defining something properly is not only conclusive evidence of knowledge (of that thing) but the only acceptable evidence for it. Geach claims that Socrates holds this position, and he claims further that it is a mistake to do so. His own presentation of the fallacy is far more elegant, including all the notational apparatus befitting a philosopher laying out a position (Geach, 1966, p. 371), but it would not be too gross a distortion to describe his alleged fallacy as the mistake of thinking that understanding a term requires being able to define it, which is to say that being able to define a term is a necessary condition of knowing what its referent is.

Although scholars tend to agree that this kind of thinking is something to be avoided, if not in fact a logical fallacy, they are still divided over whether Socrates actually makes such a mistake. Resounding commentary includes work by Benson (1990, pp. 19–65), Beversluis (1987, pp. 211–223), Prior (1998, pp. 97–113), Santas (1972, pp. 127–141), Vlastos (1985, pp. 1–31, reprinted in 1994, pp.

39–66; 1990, pp. 1–16, reprinted in 1994, pp. 67–86), and Wolfsdorf (2003a, pp. 271–312; 2003b, pp. 175–188; 2004a, pp. 35–67; 2004b, pp. 75–142). While these all come out in support of Socrates, though to varying degrees and in various ways, it seems hardly necessary to cite sources supporting Geach on a point already obviously well made, so much so as to spawn a wealth of discussion over decades, fast approaching half a century.

Any one of these studies will go far toward exposing the full problem and proposing a solution. Yet the broader scope of this chapter makes it sufficient just to establish the place of definition in Socratic dialogues.

For example, we may, as in the *Meno*, want to know exactly what virtue is before we consider whether it can be taught. However, the quest for meaning is not always secondary to the main discussion. Sometimes the quest is the main event, even where it is introduced as an ancillary effort to lay the groundwork for further consideration. The search in either case is invariably inconclusive despite being unabashedly pedantic. It unfolds as a series of unsuccessful definitions usually offered by people who are purportedly experts in the relevant field, with each encounter illustrating Socrates's unwelcome habit of questioning people in his failed mission to find someone wiser than himself, as recounted in the *Apology* (20e–23d). Examples abound. Memorable ones include the following:

- Laches defines courage as fighting instead of running away in the face of the enemy (*Laches* 190e).

- Charmides takes temperance to be a kind of quietness as might be exemplified by keeping quiet and doing everything quietly (*Charmides* 159b).

- Hippias, responding to a request to define beauty, offers his estimation that a beautiful maiden is a beauty (*Hippias Major* 287e), later replacing the maiden with gold, which he believes must be the essential factor since its addition can make anything beautiful (*Hippias Major* 289e).

- Meno, initially lost in a plurality of specific virtues (*Meno* 72a), subsequently defines virtue as the capacity to govern men (*Meno* 73c–d), later revising it as the desire and ability to acquire fine things (*Meno* 77b).

- Cephalus takes justice to consist in telling the truth and paying back debts (*Republic* 1.331c–d).

- Polemarchus defines justice as rendering to each his due (*Republic* 1.331d–332a), fleshing this out as doing good to friends and evil to enemies (*Republic* 1.332a–c).

- Thrasymachus contends that justice is the advantage of the stronger (*Republic* 1.338c), though adding a couple of revisions upon further questioning (*Republic* 1.338d–339a, 1.340a–347e).

The apparent failure of a Socratic project to define something is not necessarily a negative outcome. The proper interpretation in such cases is not that Plato does not understand the meaning of justice, virtue, beauty, and so on. Nor is it that he is trying to expose Socrates as not understanding these things. The quest itself is important. Seeking answers is the essence of philosophy, ranking right up there with asking questions, both representing the ultimate use of the intellect, regardless of whether any answers are found, or found to be satisfactory. This is just as great a motivation for the quest as is the logical need to understand something before discussing it, or the dramatic need to illustrate that understanding. In the *Euthyphro*, the quest, while important in itself, is also instrumental in providing a logical and dramatic context for challenging divine command theory, and thereby showing the possibility of morality independently of religion.

Socrates and Euthyphro go through several definitions of piety, with the number of iterations ranging anywhere from two to seven, depending on which episodes count as distinct attempts at definition, as opposed to amendments to a formulation in progress. The entire process can be broken down into seven definitions in three groups:

- Ostensive
  Piety as the prosecution of crime, particularly, religious offense, as exemplified by Euthyphro's case (5d–6c full passage; 5d–e definition)
- Extensional
  Piety as pleasing the gods
  - what is loved by (dear to) the gods (6e–7a)
  - what is loved by (dear to) *all* the gods (9d–e)
- Intensional
  Piety as the part of justice concerned with religion
  - part of justice concerned with the care of the gods (12e–13d)
  - part of justice concerned with service to the gods (13d)
  - "give and take" of sacrifice and prayer in exchange for earthly blessings from heaven (14b–15b)
  - what is loved by (dear to) the gods (15b–c)

The total number can sensibly be slashed from seven to five, as with commentators who consider the first a misunderstanding rather than a definition, and, the last, an implication rather than an attempt in itself. The remaining five definitions in two groups can just as well, or nearly so, be construed as two definitions with variations. At the other extreme, the text does not contradict a linear tally of seven separate attempts, though the last (15b–c) is identical with the second (6e–7a), and need not be counted as a seventh definition just because it is the seventh attempt. Any of these approaches is reasonable, none compelling. The final count depends on the perspective for designation as a definition versus a variation. This, in turn, concerns classification rather than recognition. Scholarly disagreements arise in organizing the definitions, not in identifying the attempts.

The first definition is ostensive. This type of definition attempts to express meaning through exemplification. Euthyphro simply submits his own case as demonstrating piety. He contends that piety is what he is doing, prosecuting the guilty, specifically, for a religious crime, failure to do so being impious (5d–e). This introduces us to the standard mistake Socratic interlocutors start with in the pursuit of definition: focusing on tokens as against types, typically resulting in the delineation of contingent characteristics rather than the universal nature of the thing in question, in other words, in the identification of accidental circumstances rather than essential attributes. The definition on hand, namely, of piety as the prosecution of the guilty, reveals just this sort of confusion. Whether or not prosecuting the guilty is in fact pious, it can at most be a demonstration of piety and not an explanation of it.

This is a false start to be corrected. Indeed, Socrates quickly reproaches Euthyphro for offering an example of piety instead of a definition of it (6d–e). He reminds Euthyphro that the original query (5c–d) concerned the concept by virtue of which holy things are holy, or in reference to which they are considered so, not an enumeration of instances of holy things, acts, or phenomena. Hence, the definition is rejected, not because it is inaccurate, but because it is not even a definition, at least not in the sense stipulated in the beginning. It simply violates the criteria laid out for the joint exploration. This amounts to technical disqualification, with no need for and no recourse to refutation. On these grounds, whether we count the first definition in the grand total is a matter of preference, as it may or may not be considered a proper definition, though it is clearly an attempt in earnest. This misunderstanding helps emphasize the importance of precision in definition, not merely under the circumstances but in general.

The second definition is extensional. This type of definition covers the entire range of a term by specifying its extension, that is, the objects designated by the concept. It may be thought of as an ostensive definition that is exhaustive, embracing all possible examples. As such, it reveals the reference without clarifying the meaning. This is still not what Socrates is looking for, but it is better than the first attempt. Convinced that he has understood Socrates's instructions on procedure, Euthyphro defines piety in terms of what pleases and offends the gods (6e–7a). On this definition, depending on the translation, piety is what is loved by, dear to, or pleasing to the gods. This is not to suggest that the translation is in dispute, but that essentially the same quality can be predicated of the subject in different ways. Modern editions, at least those in English, tend to render the second definition with different terms that have the same general meaning. Piety might thus be characterized variously, even in a single translation, in terms of what is lovable, endearing, and pleasant to the gods, the pivotal point in each case being the celestial frame of reference. The definitive element is the heavenly perspective, anchoring piety directly and exclusively to the gods themselves. This makes the concept both esoteric and popular at once, esoteric because only a privileged few might have insight into what the gods truly think, and popular because little if anything in antiquity was so widely discussed as the legendary adventures of the gods, leaving hardly anyone uninformed regarding what seems to move them. Nevertheless, the definition succeeds in an important sense, as it fulfills the requirement for a universal account rising above the limitations of a demonstrative instantiation. The criterion of dearness to the gods as the foundation of piety at least purports to subsume all examples of piety under this ostensibly exhaustive formula.

Socrates appears satisfied with the general methodology, but not with the particular definition. He objects that the gods may not all love or hate the same things, in fact, that one and the same thing may be pleasing to some of the gods but not pleasing and even offensive to others, thus leaving us in the dark regarding what is and is not holy, and, therefore, pious. The remedy, also presented by Socrates, is to focus on what is dear to all of the gods without exception. This is a simple objection with a simple solution, but its presentation takes up far more room (7b–9c) than might have been necessary to communicate the logic alone. The extra room is devoted to an exploration of the nature of disagreement, particularly to its epistemic significance. This marks Plato's attempt to distinguish genuine as opposed to merely verbal or apparent disputes as those where the disagreement persists even after all the facts are sorted out to the satisfaction of all parties. These invariably prove to be about whether this or that particular does in fact instantiate a given universal, with disputes arising, for example, in discussions of whether something is beautiful, good, just, and so on. The paradigmatic contrast is between disagreements regarding which of two things is larger, or heavier, easily resolved through measuring and weighing, and disagreements about which of two courses of action is right, often sustaining opposition even with full agreement on the facts (7b–e).

The logical import of extended emphasis on the possibility of disagreement among the gods is not merely to harp on a defect in the second definition, only to usher in the third as a simple revision, but to pave the way for the subsequent treatment of piety as a part of justice. Yet the passage also holds dramatic significance in rejecting the authority of the gods, and, by implication, repudiating the moral jurisdiction and even expertise of the priests, as it portrays the gods to be no better arbiters of value than are we. Scrutinizing the theme of disagreement among the gods enables Plato to stress the futility of deference to divine judgment on issues we might be able to adjudicate just as well by ourselves, faring no better or worse than the gods, nor, therefore, than those interpreting morality strictly through the gods. Plato is at pains to show that gods and men argue about the same sorts of thing (7d, 8d), thus making it at least superfluous and almost certainly vacuous to turn to the heavens in matters that are no different on earth. The fabled and often scandalous conflicts among the gods of the Greek pantheon provide an excellent vehicle to drive this point home. The primary and recurring reference, sometimes explicit (5e–6a, 8b), sometimes implicit (4e, 6a–c, 7b), but always familiar to the classical audience, is that of the revolutionary line of succession from Uranus to Cronus to Zeus, replete with alliances and hostilities between generations, not to mention rivalries within any ruling house at any time.

(The table at the end of this chapter should be a sufficiently informative starting point for anyone interested in exploring the mythological context in greater detail.)

The emendation transforming the second definition into the third refines the prevailing conception of piety by upgrading the corresponding epistemic requirement from a heavenly consensus of unspecified strength into a unanimous agreement among the gods. Shifting the reference from the general to the universal recasts piety as what is pleasing to all of the gods, and, impiety, as what is offensive to them all, consigning ambivalent cases to a neutral category (9d–e). Under the second definition, cases of indeterminate status were limited to things that are neither loved nor hated by the gods. The third definition expands this category with the inclusion of split decisions, thereby adding anything that might be loved by some of the gods while hated by others.

This is more of a revision than a new definition. Either way, it does not stand up. The revised version is not susceptible to failure through discord among the gods, but modifying the original definition into working order finally exposes the real problem in defining piety in reference to what the gods love: The proposed definition does not really tell us what piety is; instead, it specifies a common trait shared by everything in that category, the trait of being loved by or dear to the gods. This being so, it is not truly a definition of piety but a rule of thumb for determining what things are holy and what are not. Moreover, it is not entirely effective in that capacity either, because the trait identified as common to piety is not unique to piety: Even if the gods love all that is holy and hate all that is unholy, they may love things besides the holy and hate things besides the unholy.

Socrates exposes the failure of the definition through a timeless dilemma advancing reason as a wedge between morality and religion (10a–11b). The hammer driving the wedge is a distinction between the appreciation of value for itself and the creation of value through appreciation. This axiological distinction is so seminal, especially in the development of ethics as a rational outlook, that it deserves independent consideration. Its lasting significance is in replacing stipulation with explanation: A simple declaration no longer confers value, moral or otherwise, unless supported by reason, and mere preferences or attitudes do not count as reasons, not even if they are the likes and dislikes of the gods themselves. Plato's formative treatment of this issue can be examined separately, as done here under the heading of "origination dilemma" in the next section (§ 4.4), because it is not as indispensable to modern readers as it might have been to the original audience in facilitating recognition of the shortcomings of the third definition, which fails simply because it tackles reference without conveying meaning.

The fourth definition is intensional, bringing out the internal content of the relevant concept instead of specifying the objects in its extension. This is exactly the kind of definition Socrates wants, and the kind we typically seek in consulting a dictionary. It sets up a general formula under which an indefinite number of instantiations can be subsumed, presumably covering everything that is pertinent and nothing that is not. In fact, not only does Socrates ask for this kind of definition, but he produces it himself, forcing it upon Euthyphro as he practically puts the words into the perplexed priest's mouth. Socrates identifies piety as a type of religious justice, leaving it up to Euthyphro to work out the details (12e).

The intervention of Socrates ushers in a series of three definitions approaching piety as a subset of justice, or, for all practical purposes, as the religious aspect of morality:

- Euthyphro's immediate inclination, and thus the fourth definition, counting each attempt separately from the beginning, makes piety the part of justice concerned with the care of the gods (12e–13d). The next two definitions, following in quick succession, are basically elaborations on the meaning of this one.
- The fifth definition clarifies what is meant by the "care of the gods" and reformulates it as a type of "service to the gods," given that the gods do not need to be refined or improved through our care as might domestic animals and other things we "care for," "tend to," or "look after" (13d).
- This leads to the question of what end may be achieved by such service to the gods (13d–14a). The answer, that the aim is to secure our blessings, shapes the sixth definition, accordingly turning piety into a type of "trader's art" as manifested in the "give and take" of sacrifice and prayer in exchange for earthly insurance from heaven (14b–15b).

The move from the fifth to the sixth definition may be construed as a shift from taking piety as a part of justice to taking it as an area of expertise, one characterized by skill and know-how in trade. However, this is more of an extension of interpretive possibilities, each compatible with the other, than a rejection of one for the other. In fact, the sixth definition expands the fifth, as well as the fourth, if only because the fifth expands the fourth, with the sixth finally laying out the reciprocity that demonstrates precisely what makes piety a part or kind of justice. Thus, the connection between piety and justice is not only preserved but brought out all the more clearly in the balance of the "give and take" ultimately attributed to the concept.

The final step is to demonstrate how this definition degenerates into the unacceptable one anchored to the love of the gods. As Socrates probes into the reciprocal benefits of the "give and take" involved in piety, he leads Euthyphro to the conclusion that what we get for our part is whatever it is we are praying for, and making sacrifices for, while what the gods get through our worship is what is pleasing or dear to them, thereby turning piety back into a matter of what is loved by the gods. Although Euthyphro specifically lists respect and honor among the gains of the gods, he mentions them in the context of what pleases the gods, so that the total gain is ultimately reducible to divine pleasure, the pleasure of being worshipped (15a).

In this way, the exploration of piety as a concept reverts full circle to the beginning, through a series of arguments ostensibly making headway toward an authoritative definition but actually serving as an extended illustration of the ignorance of the interlocutor, while achieving the underlying aim of debunking popular misconceptions and differentiating between morality and piety. The aim is not so much to clarify the meaning of piety as it is to free morality from its conceptual hegemony.

The decisive role of Socrates in the move from the third to the fourth definition, initiating a transition between the two main groups of definitions serving the joint effort, may make the eventual failure suspect. Given that he is the one responsible for the abrupt switch from a persistently unsuccessful attempt to define piety in terms of the love of the gods to a series of ultimately unsuccessful definitions taking piety as a part of justice, Socrates may be thought to have engineered the rather embarrassing position Euthyphro finds himself in. This is partly true. Socrates deliberately makes Euthyphro look like a dolt. On the other hand, this is not unique to a single point in the dialogue, or even to several, but expressive of the general mode of the entire exchange. The fourth definition is not the only place Socrates puts words into the mouth of the confused interlocutor. The entire dialogue after the second definition, and arguably even after the first, is an exercise in intellectual spoon-feeding, eventually to the point of acute cognitive indigestion.

Despite all this, Socrates is not to blame for the breakdown at the end, which comes about as a result of the specific ways in which Euthyphro processes the general form of the definition approaching piety as a part of justice, not as a result of that general approach itself. Socrates indeed supplies the general form, thus reorienting the discussion with a mandatory template for definition, but it is Euthyphro who contaminates it with ill-conceived details, successively working toward completing the vicious circle in the end.

While the construal of piety as a part of justice may seem to be an abrupt turn, and even a crafty one devised by Socrates to mislead Euthyphro, the connection actually goes back to the first definition, possibly the only one formulated entirely and freely by Euthyphro, that is, with no guidance from Socrates. Piety readily starts out as a type of justice, with Euthyphro immediately declaring it to be the prosecution of the guilty, particularly those guilty of a religious crime, as exemplified by his own initiative to prosecute his father for murder (5d–e). Justice, in turn, quickly rises to the top of the list of subjects about which both gods and mortals disagree (8b–9b). Accordingly, by formally nominating this perspective as a model for the fourth definition, Socrates is actually helping rather than misleading Euthyphro. The intervention reveals the basic formula through which Euthyphro might in the beginning have properly declared his specific action to be an instance of piety, thus circumventing the subsequent exploration of an understanding through heavenly preferences, but instead of taking advantage of the emerging second chance, Euthyphro misuses the formula to revert step-by-step to an approach just shown to be unworkable.

The dramatic function of repeatedly making Euthyphro look bad is not merely to indicate that the priest does not match up to the philosopher but to emphasize that religion does not determine morality. The philosophical counterpart of this is that piety, on its best definition (the sixth), before completing a full circle to a previously rejected one (the second), turns out to be little more than the religious reflection of a rational construct, with piety as justice transferring morality from the domain of religious dogma to the realm of ethical reasoning. This is a paradigm shift in the prevailing decision procedure for ethics, though it still need not be read as a threat to the Greek way of life, instead opening up the possibility of rational justification for it.

4.4. The Origination Dilemma

Roughly halfway through the dialogue, Socrates poses a question, now at the heart of value theory, then possibly inaugurating the field: Is the holy loved by (dear to) the gods because it is holy, or is it holy because it is loved by (dear to) the gods (10a)?

Euthyphro has just presented the holy as that which is loved by the gods; Socrates has raised the possibility of disagreement among the gods; and Euthyphro has responded by fortifying his position with an exhaustive reference to all gods. Socrates's question comes at the point where being loved by all of the gods becomes the operative definition of the holy, and, thereby, of piety. Presumably, what they all love is the holy, and the proper mortal response to it, whatever that may be, is piety. What Socrates wants to establish at this juncture is the inadequacy of the evidentiary link between the holy and the love of the gods. Hence, the question: Which explains the other?

This is commonly known as the "Euthyphro dilemma," sometimes with the first word italicized to anchor the reference to the dialogue instead of the character, but "origination dilemma" may be a better name altogether since the issue concerns the evidentiary or causal precedence between holiness and the love of the gods as attributes or phenomena competing as mutually exclusive explanations of each other. Accordingly, the question, placed in context, is whether holiness inspires the love of the gods, or the love of the gods confers holiness, with the epistemic fate of piety also hanging in the balance. Therefore, the "Euthyphro dilemma" is, in essence, an origination dilemma, an inquiry into which of two facts originates in the other.

The point of the question is to establish the direction of the evidentiary, explanatory, or causal relationship between holiness and the love of the gods, understood to include all of the gods. This is the turning point of the dialogue, and one of the earliest known appearances of the most fundamental question in value inquiry, arguably even representing the very inception of axiology as a critical discipline as opposed to a dogmatic system. However, a more basic issue is at work in the background: Socrates is still dissatisfied on technical grounds with the general position of Euthyphro reflected in the prevailing definition. He finds that characterizing the holy as whatever is loved by all of the gods amounts to citing a property of it, the property of being loved by all gods, and that this does not constitute a proper definition. He holds that the provisional definition gives information about holiness without clarifying or even specifying what it is. In this respect, it is no better than the initial misunderstanding which prompts Euthyphro to submit his own case as a demonstrative account of piety, or the subsequent attempt citing the love of the gods without expressly including all of the gods. The new definition is nothing but a consistent way of making the same mistake as the second definition. This is because the love of the gods does not determine holiness or piety no matter how many gods we are talking about. The real problem is not in getting them all to agree but in consulting them in the first place.

This assessment turns out to be the decisive blow against the position of the priest, as Socrates and Euthyphro proceed to a dramatic interlude in evaluation of the general course of the discussion up to that point. The smooth progression of the drama through the dilemma leaves a possible challenge untapped to its full potential. Socrates's reasoning in regard to his own question is that a thing's being holy can be an explanation of why that thing is loved by the gods, whereas a thing's being loved by the gods does not establish its holiness or piety. On this reasoning, if that which is holy is loved by the gods because it is holy, then we do not need to invoke the preferences of the gods for a definition of holiness or an understanding of piety. In fact, doing so would beg the question. Yet even though the gods become functionally redundant upon clarification of the causal confusion and evidentiary ambiguity in the definition, this is not emphasized in the dialogue. The discussion continues as if a colorless operational difficulty had been resolved, with no special attention devoted to the attendant subversion of the gods. Their removal from the moral sphere is not discussed beyond the bare minimum of words required to deny that they determine piety. Neither the logic nor the drama suffers because of this, but it is worth noting nonetheless.

The fact that Socrates couches his objection to the prevailing definition specifically in the form of the origination dilemma tends to obscure the continuity in the underlying problem, often read as a new difficulty emerging with the new definition and eliciting a new objection. On the contrary, Socrates would have been in the right to express his dissatisfaction simply by repeating the same objection to each of the first three definitions: evidentiary breakdown due to causal and explanatory irrelevance. His complaint against the entire process up to that point, not merely against this or that particular definition, is that it is geared toward producing examples or citing properties of piety instead of defining or explaining piety (11a–b). As discussed earlier (§ 4.3), this is a familiar appeal. It is the standard Socratic complaint in elenctic encounters in pursuit of meaning. In contrast, the conceptual brilliance of the dilemma, particularly the clarity of insight it affords into a general axiological problem transcending the context of the *Euthyphro*, may conceal the fact that the specific problem it addresses in the dialogue is the same difficulty persisting since the beginning of the extended effort to uncover the nature of the holy and the meaning of piety. The dilemma is so riveting, perhaps especially fascinating for us in hindsight, that we tend to lose sight of the simple and ongoing objection underlying it. This is not a mistake to be corrected, but recognizing it might help in appreciating the cohesiveness of the dialogue.

From a purely logical perspective, Socrates's objection need not be put in the form of a dilemma. Introducing the objection in the form of a question with two mutually exclusive and jointly exhaustive options enables Socrates to engage Euthyphro in a session of dialectic culminating in the failure of the prevailing definition. However, the definition does not fail because of the dilemma; it fails simply because it lays out a property of what is being defined instead of actually defining it. This reduces the logical relevance of the dilemma. This is not to say that it is employed merely as a dramatic tool to enrich the interpersonal exchange, but that it is not essential for a successful challenge to the perspective adopted by the priest. This interpretation is reinforced by the way that the second horn of the dilemma, the alternative that the holy is holy because it is loved by the gods, is dismissed far too easily, as if it were not worth serious consideration. The possibility of the love of the gods conferring piety is rejected without incident or argument. In fact, it is rejected in harmony, as Euthyphro joins Socrates the instant he understands the question posed in the dilemma (10d–e). Yet a dilemma can hardly be significant where one of the alternatives is so readily dismissible. Probing the very foundations of value theory seems to be logical overkill in the context of a debate where pointing out the present error would have been possible without the extra effort.

An indisputable dramatic feature of the dilemma is its positioning in the dialogue. It could have been introduced in immediate response to the definition of piety as what is loved by the gods, instead of waiting for the refined version accommodating the requirement for unanimous agreement among the gods. Logically, the dilemma, that is, the question and the underlying objection, belongs to the original definition invoking the love of the gods (second definition), whereas, dramatically, it enlivens the discussion of the subsequent definition (third definition). The reason for the delayed introduction is the need or desire to make room for reflection on conflict among the gods. This theme, in turn, is important at least because it lessens the severity of Socrates's alleged shortcomings in honoring the officially recognized gods of the state, if not also because it illustrates the religious dimension of the moral quagmire underlying Euthyphro's case. If the gods cannot regularly come together on questions of value, really, just the one question of what is dear to them, then Socrates can hardly be censured for failure to act in accordance with what pleases the gods. Obviously, satisfying them all at once is next to impossible, especially in anything that matters (7c–e). This result of the given conflict in heaven cannot be pushed very far, say, to establish that worshipping the gods is logistically impossible because they do not always value or want the same thing. This would be too strong a claim, at least because the gods in favor with the state are in fact worshiped, thus precluding the impossibility of that prospect. But the objection goes far toward suggesting that any shortcomings in this regard might reasonably well be sought in the gods themselves, and, this being so, it naturally undermines the efficacy of worship, whether by Socrates or by anyone else.

Although the dilemma is superfluous in controverting the third definition, which could have been handled along the lines of the same basic objection (of irrelevance) without resorting to the overzealous logical construction, it is supremely relevant to the broad initiative. Its late introduction is intended to emphasize that relevance, while allowing room for the interjection of other points, better made than not made, but not strong enough to refute Euthyphro's position, and, therefore, also not suitable to be appended merely as an afterthought following a proper refutation.

Hence, the dilemma is reserved as the *coup de grâce*, delivered after the internal contradictions surfacing in divine command theory in a polytheistic context are fleshed out through other means simultaneously serving dramatic purposes. Its resolution turns out to be as analytically overwrought as its development. The otherwise facile rejection of the horn predetermined as undesirable, or, better put, unacceptable, is accompanied by a complex yet concise chain of reasoning, presumably developed to lay out the precise logical basis for the rejection of one horn for the other, thereby demonstrating that the choice is logical rather than intuitive or arbitrary, and certainly not dogmatic. This comes in a brief passage (10e–11a) finally laying the third definition to rest while formally bringing the unfolding resolution of the dilemma to its fruition. It is distinct enough to tolerate separate consideration, and significant enough to reward the effort. This is the impetus for the following section.

4.4.1. Reductio via the Origination Dilemma

The aim of the origination dilemma is to establish the proper direction of the inferential flow under consideration. The answer Socrates is pushing for, the answer Euthyphro assents to (10d), and the one that has the greatest intuitive appeal is that the holy is loved by the gods because it is holy, with the corollary that the causal explanation fails in the other direction, in fact, explicitly repudiating the alternative that the love of the gods confers holiness or determines piety.

Having secured Euthyphro's commitment to one of the two opposing causal explanations, Socrates puts together a *reductio ad absurdum* to refute the standing definition invoking what is dear to the gods, whether in its original version open to the possibility of divine disagreement (6e–7a) or in the revised version anchored to what is dear to all the gods (9e). His contention is that what is dear to the gods, even where they are of one mind on this issue, is not the same as the holy. The reductio he sets up, beginning with the assumption to be refuted, namely, that what is dear to the gods and what is holy are the same thing (10e), can be mapped out as follows (10e–11a):

Socrates's Reductio (10e–11a) of Euthyphro's Appeal to the Gods

(P1) Dear to the gods = Holy (10e)
Position to be refuted

(P2) Holy → Loved by the gods (10d–e)
(Loved by the gods because holy)
Originally agreed causal explanation

(P3) Dear to the gods → Loved by the gods (11a)
Part of mutually implicative relationship establishing equivalence of being dear to and loved by the gods

(P4) Loved by the gods → Dear to the gods (11a)
Part of mutually implicative relationship establishing equivalence of being dear to and loved by the gods

(C) Loved by the gods → Holy (10d–e)
(Holy because loved by the gods)
Originally rejected causal explanation

Reasoning: P1 → (P2 & P3 & P4 → C)

The goal is to involve the standing definition, that is, the conception of holiness as dearness to the gods, in a logical contradiction, specifically, by demonstrating how it transforms an acceptable position into an unacceptable one. On the assumption that what is dear to the gods and what is holy are the same thing, the originally agreed (10d–e) causal explanation that the holy is loved by the gods because it is holy turns into, and, in fact, implies, the originally rejected (10d–e) causal explanation that the holy is holy because it is loved by the gods.

Socrates offers a precise if pedantic account (10e–11a) of the transformation, which is essentially a simple substitution of terms. At least in enthymematic form, the initial equivalence assumed for being dear to the gods and being holy might be considered sufficient to execute the targeted reduction to absurdity simply by switching the terms of the originally accepted (10d–e) causal explanation to arrive directly at the originally rejected (10d–e) causal explanation. This is warranted by the tacit understanding that being dear to the gods is, for all intents and purposes, the same as being loved by the gods, as suggested by common sense and evidenced by interchangeable usage throughout the dialogue. In other words, the reductio premise that what is dear to the gods and what is holy are the same thing, combined with the implicit equivalence of being dear to the gods and being loved by them, is sufficient to convert the originally accepted (10d–e) inference from the holy to the love of the gods (i.e., loved because holy) into the originally rejected (10d–e) inference from the love of the gods to the holy (i.e., holy because loved), thus producing a reduction to absurdity from Euthyphro's definition.

However, Socrates includes an extra step as he expands the implicit understanding into an explicit one, laying out a conjunction of implications in both directions between what is dear to the gods and what is loved by the gods (11a). This mutually implicative relationship, essentially a biconditional, establishes the material equivalence of being dear to the gods and being loved by them. The extra step formally validates the move from the property of being dear to the gods, as invoked in the initial equivalence assumed for refutation, to the property of being loved by the gods, as referenced in converting the originally accepted causal explanation into the originally rejected causal explanation, or, put differently, in the process of deriving the one rejected from the one accepted, and thus showing the absurdity of the initial equivalence between what is dear to the gods and what is holy.

A question that comes to mind is whether Euthyphro might convincingly have been able to respond that he never claimed what is dear to the gods and what is holy to be identical, so as to hold dearness to the gods to be exactly the same thing as the holy, having instead committed himself only to the position that the first is implied by the second, regardless of whatever else may be the case. He might indeed have taken this route with some success, especially as his considered opinion, actually, his mined response (10d–e), concerning the origination dilemma was clearly to choose the alternative that what is holy is loved by the gods because it is holy over its polar counterpart that what is holy is holy because it is loved by the gods, thus affirming that holiness implies dearness to the gods, and rejecting the alternative that dearness to the gods implies holiness. However, he would then have had to give up his persistent attempt to define holiness and explain piety in terms of dearness to the gods, which, in keeping with Euthyphro's choice in the dilemma, is not exclusive to piety, with the love of the gods including the holy, even all that is holy, but not just the holy, taking on other objects as well. Nevertheless, it seems a bit unfair to treat him as if he claimed dearness to the gods and piety to be the referents of terms that are interchangeable *salva veritate*.

4.4.2. Significance of the Origination Dilemma

Independently of whether the reductio is cleverly forced upon Euthyphro or logically apposite to the context, the origination dilemma is crucial to the discussion, and merits further consideration.

- *Holy → loved by the gods*
  (*Loved by the gods because holy*)

  If the holy is loved by the gods because it is holy, then the love of the gods is neither necessary nor sufficient for holiness or piety, but merely indicative of it. That which is indicative, on the other hand, is not conclusive, and often not even reliable, as a guide to what is holy or pious. What is loved by the gods may perchance turn out to be holy, since everything that is holy is loved by the gods, but it just as well may not, since the holy is not necessarily the only thing that is or can be loved by the gods. The guide is infallible only in a negative sense whereby anything known not to be loved by the gods can safely be ignored without further consideration of its possible holiness.

  Moreover, if what is holy is already holy independently of the love of the gods, then why can we not *ipso facto* recognize it as such, hold it dear, and love it, without inquiring into the opinions, feelings, or mental states of the gods? The definition of the holy, or rather, the ability to define the term, does not seem to require a reference to the love of the gods. In fact, if the causal direction is indeed from holiness to the love of the gods, then a definition of holiness in terms of the love of the gods would be unacceptable because it would risk including too much, namely, anything that is not holy but nevertheless loved by the gods.

- *Loved by the gods → holy*
  (*Holy because loved by the gods*)

  This alternative makes piety a heavenly opinion poll. If what is loved by the gods is holy simply because it is loved by the gods, then what makes anything holy is arbitrary, and the requirement to honor it tyrannical. This is an outright rejection of the authority and even viability of an objective value system grounded in reason, thus repudiating teleological ethics except insofar as it may be anchored specifically to core values in heaven. But it also makes any secular deontological system redundant in that any conflict with the requirements of religious duty would have to be resolved in favor of the prevailing theological standard. The only option for moral guidance is to turn to the heavens.

  Despite being severely restrictive, this is workable in principle, but the accessibility of moral guidance presents a practical problem. Under this scenario, we must have insight into the opinions and attitudes of the gods in order to be able to act in accordance with the requirements of piety, because we cannot even recognize the holy, our point of reference for piety, without bridging the epistemic distance between heaven and earth.

> Barring divine revelation on a cosmic scale, one providing general rather than preferential enlightenment, information access points are limited to mythology and the testimony of those claiming privileged insight into what is otherwise unknown. Something very much like this, even today, captures the human condition where reason is replaced by dogma.

The overall effect of the dilemma is the utter destruction of Euthyphro's position, that the holy is what all the gods love, not merely because of the reductio appended, but independently of that trick, and due to the nature of the choices available. The first horn of the dilemma (holy → loved by the gods), the one embraced by Euthyphro (10d–e), outright contradicts the definition in progress, as it makes the opinion or preference of the gods irrelevant to whatever the case may be in itself, while the second horn of the dilemma (loved by the gods → holy), being the one rejected by Euthyphro (10d–e), is what condemns us, by virtue of that rejection, to the otiose prospect represented by the first horn.

4.4.3. Analogic Development of the Origination Dilemma

Plato develops the origination dilemma with the aid of a series of parallel examples (10a–c) intended to illustrate a curiously elementary distinction in what amounts to the difference between initiating and undergoing a process, or, in the same vein, between committing an action and being affected by it. Specifically, he uses three sets of examples: carrying and being carried; leading and being led; and seeing and being seen. In each case, he carefully compares and contrasts the two correlative elements, making sure, before moving on, that Euthyphro understands the difference as well as the relationship between one and the other.

For all the fuss, this seems to establish little more than what we already know and automatically process as the basic difference between the active and passive voices (e.g., loving vs. being loved), including the obligatory coordination of that difference with matching adjustments in other grammatical elements as needed to preserve the integrity of the corresponding sentence, typically at least requiring the proper choice between the nominative and accusative cases of nouns and pronouns relevant to the context (e.g., lover vs. beloved).

The purpose appears to be simply to emphasize the right way of thinking about these fundamental conceptual relationships. Burnet (1924, pp. 127–128, n. 10a5, 10a9, 10a10, 10c1, 10c2), among others, notes that this is precisely what is going on. The apparently inordinate attention to such an elementary matter turns out to be due largely to the absence of grammatical terminology, prompting Plato's painstaking explication to make up for the inadequacies of the nascent grammatical substructure. The entire episode reflects limitations common to ancient languages rather than unique to classical Greek, but it tends to leave modern readers wondering if they are missing something making the corresponding passage more difficult than they realize. They are not. Burnet (1924, pp. 127–128, n. 10a5) warns earnestly against mistaking the effort for something more than what it is: a clarification now understood without intensive remediation thanks to a more accommodating grammatical system.

Not all commentators are content to let this stage of the discussion go with just a passing observation that it reflects a struggle to rise above the deficiencies of the existing grammatical platform. Cohen (1971, pp. 1–13) provides an extensive analysis of the distinctions, evaluating them in the greater context of the central argument (10a–11b), instead of just repeating the well-documented diagnosis that the language itself held certain limitations. Hall (1968, pp. 1–11) even provides his own translation of the passage (10a1–11a10) to compensate for the ambiguities arising in the process of making "distinctions between Greek grammatical forms that are not exactly paralleled in English" (1968, p. 1). Wolfsdorf (2005, pp. 1–71), concentrating on basically the same portion of the dialogue as the others (10a2–11b1), identifies nine separate points of controversy in the secondary literature, and proceeds to resolve each one in an ambitious effort illuminating close to half a century of Platonic metaphysics and its reception. Analytic, expository, and constructive approaches are balanced by plenty that are critical, including, for example, an assessment by Brown (1964, pp. 1–14) and an examination by Geach (1966, pp. 369–382), the latter in the same paper mentioned earlier in connection with the alleged "Socratic fallacy" (§ 4.3).

Notwithstanding the obvious scholarly interest in mulling over the examples Plato offers, a reasonably safe assessment can be offered without much analysis or argumentation, at least without having to break out the pretty fonts to symbolize the entire exchange in the notation of the predicate calculus. And that assessment, or perhaps one among many, is that the underlying intention is to illuminate the relationship between piety and the love of the gods, or, what is the same, the relationship between the holy and dearness to gods, through presumably more intuitive cases (10a–c). For example, just as the visible is seen because it is visible, rather than being visible because it is seen, so, too, is the holy loved by the gods because it is holy, rather than being holy because it is loved by the gods (10b). The same formulation can be repeated with the other two examples, namely, carrying vs. being carried, and leading vs. being led, to the same effect. Plato himself leaves nothing unsaid in this regard, as he spells out the remaining instantiations for good measure. In fact, to be perfectly accurate, he is so meticulous about this as to go through the same exercise twice for each concept: carrying, leading, and seeing (10b).

Given that piety, or the holy, is charged with value in a way that visibility and the other purely descriptive or physical cases are not, perhaps a similarly charged concept, such as desirability, would make a more fitting analogy for piety. After all, the holy is not dear to the gods merely as a matter of fact, but worthy of the love of the gods as a source of value, much in the way that the desirable is not just desired, or even necessarily so, but worthy of desire, to wit, desirable even if not in fact desired. We might, then, reformulate Plato's analogy thus: Just as the desirable is desired because it is desirable, rather than being desirable because it is desired, so, too, is the holy loved by the gods because it is holy, rather than being holy because it is loved by the gods. In either case, the strictly factual element is evidence of its value-laden counterpart, though not constituting conclusive evidence or even a necessary condition in that regard: Desire is indicative of desirability, and, the love of the gods, indicative of holiness, without the indication automatically counting as confirmation.

That said, the absence of certitude in the indicative nature of the evidence shows the fallibility, not the utter and total failure, of the evidentiary relationship. With respect to desirability, the evidentiary relationship is especially strong in the case of universal or widespread desire for something as an end in itself, and comparably weak in the case of sporadic desire for something as a means to something else, much like how unanimity among the gods in what they hold dear evinces holiness whereas discord reflects ambivalence in heaven and promotes ambiguity on earth.

More than two millennia later, another prominent philosopher, John Stuart Mill, would be accused of committing a gross fallacy in casually drawing the same connections Plato so carefully maps out here. Mill has traditionally been charged with misconstruing desirability as the condition or property of being able to be desired, in contrast to its proper construal as the condition or property of being worthy of desire, thereby allegedly equivocating between the two interpretations in the course of finding evidence for desirability in actual desires. (See, for example: Mackenzie, 1893, pp. 98–99; Moore, 1903, pp. 64–68; Sorley, 1885, pp. 60–61.) This controversy goes to the heart of Mill's notorious proof of the principle of utility in the fourth chapter of his *Utilitarianism*. Ironically, Mill was not only a renowned logician but also a child prodigy reading Plato in the original by the age children today typically finish elementary school. His misfortune seems to have been in taking shortcuts, justified though they may be, with a train of thought laid out with plodding diligence by Plato.

4.4.4. Aftermath of the Origination Dilemma

Socrates does not leave Euthyphro much to work with in the aftermath of the origination dilemma. They conclude that the love of the gods does not make anything holy, while acknowledging that all holy things attract the love of the gods. Based on this understanding, Euthyphro is expected to abandon the attempt to define holiness, or to account for piety, in reference to the love of the gods, as would, so we are led to believe, any sensible person following the argument up to that point. The causal or evidentiary link explored fails in the direction from the love of the gods to the holy, which, in turn, retains its explanatory power for the love of the gods. We can go in one direction but not the other.

Why does this undermine the logical grounds for the definitional appeal to the love of the gods? Why must the definition accommodate causality as if one thing could not be the definition of another unless it were also the cause of it, or at least the reason for it?

This is to question why the definition must stand or fall with the causal or evidentiary account attached to it by Socrates. Indeed, the relationship between the definiendum and the definiens is not necessarily a causal one, neither in general, nor here in particular. However, the consideration of a causal connection in either direction, or, with terminology possibly more fitting for abstract phenomena, the test of explanatory efficacy in either direction, as explored in both directions by Socrates, is not irrelevant to the tenability of the underlying definition here. The definition fails because it includes too much, and it includes too much because the love of the gods is not limited to the holy: All that is holy, and every instance of piety, may attract the love of the gods, thus falling in the general category sustained by the proposed definition, but things besides the holy may also attract the love of the gods, thereby cluttering the category with concepts other than holiness and piety. The love of the gods can serve at most as a rough roadmap to piety, leading us in the right general direction, but always with the possibility of error. Used as the definiens, it never fails to capture the definiendum, but it goes further than desired, exhausting the extension claimed by the holy, or by piety, as well as covering an indefinite albeit presumably not inexhaustible number of other concepts.

The origination dilemma is best understood, not merely, or even primarily, as an analysis or refutation of a definition of piety, but essentially as a reasoned rejection of divine command theory. This does not mean that the individual definitions, and possibly thereby the entire definition process, are nothing more than dramatic tools to create an occasion for philosophical rebellion against divine command theory. If they were, the definition process would not need to be continued after the introduction of the origination dilemma, successfully overturning the definition anchored to the love of the gods. The definitions are necessary, both dramatically and philosophically, independently of the position taken on divine command theory. The flip side of this regarding the origination dilemma is that it, in its own turn, carries dramatic and philosophical value beyond challenging the definitions. Its purpose is not only to undermine a specific definition but also, and more importantly, to encourage a better way of thinking about the subject matter.

4.5. Logical and Dramatic Conclusion

The *Euthyphro* ends in the typical fashion of the aporetic dialogues, leaving the main interlocutor in a state of bewilderment, confused about the one issue otherwise giving him supreme confidence and a correlative claim to fame.

The logical end of the dialogue is the failure of the final definition, specifically, its reduction to a previously rejected one (the second). Perhaps more accurately, and depending on the proper perspective on the count, the logical end is the failure of the penultimate definition as it degenerates into the final definition, which turns out to be identical to the previously rejected definition (the second) grounding holiness and piety in heavenly preferences, the dialogue's rendition of divine command theory. In a sense, the dialogue may even be said to end without a conclusion. However, although it clearly ends without having achieved its explicit aim of illuminating the nature of the holy and uncovering the true meaning of piety, it does so having reached its overarching albeit implicit goal of demonstrating the independence of morality from religion. In fact, the failure of the definition process is a vehicle for that demonstration.

The dramatic end of the dialogue complements the reasoned separation of morality and religion with perfect symbolism as it physically separates the philosopher and the priest. Without prejudice to the strength and aptness of the symbolism, this ending also stirs up significant controversy among commentators interpreting Euthyphro's exit (15e) in the final scene. The debate is over whether Euthyphro departs having already tended to the case in question or having been steered off that course by Socrates. This is assuming that the final scene depicts Euthyphro as leaving the general area. If, on the other hand, his exit from the scene marks entry into the building instead of departure from the premises, this feeds the cause for disagreement, as it creates an alternative scenario showing Euthyphro about to pursue his business inside, as opposed to having already done so or having decided not to do so.

The scenario of leaving the scene to enter the building does not attract as much support as the two sides to the central debate, partly because the frustrated interlocutor's exit from the scene of the dialogue is conspicuously hasty, and, his excuse, transparently contrived, and partly because conversational details in the beginning of the dialogue suggest that the legal process is already under way. Indeed, these considerations weaken the scenario of leaving the porch to go inside the building instead of away from the premises, but they do not rule it out. First, Euthyphro's appeal to an upcoming appointment to excuse his departure does not preclude an inward exit from the scene, because the matter alluded to in the excuse may be the very one that brought him to the portico of the king-archon's office, where he was detained in conversation until the approaching rendezvous required his immediate presence inside. This is no less believable than the scenario that the excuse pertains to business elsewhere or the scenario that it is just a pretext to get away from an insufferable encounter. Second, ongoing progress in legal action does not mean that the process requires no further management: Euthyphro could have had reason to tend to bureaucratic details following his encounter with Socrates, even if the case had already moved along sufficiently to allow meaningful discussion during the encounter and, thereby, prior to whatever needed to be done for the day. Nevertheless, the standard construction, for example, as found in Burnet (1924, p. 82) and in Brickhouse and Smith (2004, pp. 14–18), places Euthyphro on a course away from the area altogether.

The rejection of the unpopular alternative goes only so far toward explaining Euthyphro's attitude regarding his own case, that is, in regard to whether he changed his mind after speaking with Socrates. Sending him off the premises at the end still leaves us with the original interpretive question of whether he had already taken care of business before running into Socrates. To complicate matters, independently of the widely ignored alternative ending, the central debate over the closing scene is connected with a parallel ambiguity in the opening scene, where Euthyphro may be read either as having just arrived at the porch from outside the premises or as having just stepped out onto it from inside the building, the first reading portraying him about to tend to the legal matter that brought him there, and, the second, depicting him as having concluded his business for the day.

In combination, the opening (2a) and closing (15e–16a) scenes support two plausible alternatives for filling out the details of the dramatic setting left undeveloped by Plato:

- Euthyphro arrives at the king-archon's court to proceed with legal action against his father, when he runs into Socrates, has a discussion about the nature of piety and morality, and departs without carrying on with the case, presumably having changed his mind for good, or at least having abandoned the cause for the day.
- Euthyphro exits the king-archon's court, just having tended to litigation against his father, either having freshly initiated the case or having concluded a step in an ongoing process, when he runs into Socrates, has a discussion about the nature of piety and morality, and departs on a bogus excuse just to get away from the tiresome inquisitor, or on a genuine one to honor a prior commitment.

To exhaust the possibilities, the opening and closing scenes might be joined in two more ways, for a total of four combinations, given the uncertainty in the direction of both the arrival and the departure of Euthyphro. However, the two summarized above are the main interpretations dividing scholars.

Textual details are consistent with both scenarios. The fact that Euthyphro has the first line in the dialogue is sometimes taken as an indication that he is the first one at the scene, welcoming an approaching Socrates, and, in the role of a host of sorts, very likely having finished his business inside. But the same opening is also consistent with the possibility that Euthyphro is just then arriving at the scene and hailing a stationary Socrates already positioned on the porch. More important, the alternative of an earlier presence for Euthyphro does not clarify whether he would have taken any action on the case prior to speaking with Socrates, because the priest could have momentarily delayed entry into the building for any reason, including a prayer, or even a simple pause to catch his breath, despite arriving at the porch before Socrates.

In the final analysis, the answer regarding a possible shift in Euthyphro's outlook is not in the text, neither in the information transmitted through the exchange of words, nor in the imagery created thereby. The symbolism of separating the philosopher and the priest at the end is already powerful. The interpretive scenario that Euthyphro changes his mind after his encounter with Socrates enhances the drama even further, but it neither requires nor contradicts any particular scenario about where the priest goes upon departure. To be sure, the strongest ending conceivable, short of contradicting what is actually in the text, is that the philosopher corrects the misconceptions of the priest regarding piety, convincing him finally to do the right thing, which, in this case, happens to be at the intersection of ordinary morality and ethical reasoning, satisfying the requirements of both. A change of heart by Euthyphro is what every reader wants to imagine, but it would have to be classified under fan fiction rather than canon.

A telling dramatic strand running against the grain of interpretation in the stronger reading is the tone of Euthyphro, who seems more confused than convinced at each turn, and more annoyed than enlightened at the end. Be that as it may, Plato's silence, or ambiguity, regarding this scenario leaves it open, and, at any rate, does not in any way undermine the existing symbolism, particularly that of the concluding divergence of the paths of the philosopher and the priest.

In one of the earliest extant interpretations in print, Diogenes Laërtius (*Lives* 2.29) describes Socrates as having diverted Euthyphro from his purpose of prosecuting his father. While the text in Diogenes is equivocal between interpreting the dialogue and reporting an actual event, it is clear that he understands the matter, whether historical or fictional, to have been concluded with the priest being swayed by the philosopher. Brickhouse and Smith (2004, pp. 16, 18) side with Diogenes, primarily because reading Socrates as having succeeded in his engagement with Euthyphro adds to the dramatic effect of the dialogue. Others, for example, Burnet (1924, p. 82), have Euthyphro concluding his legal business for the day before running into Socrates, thus precluding the possibility of diversion, at least as far as that day is concerned.

Regardless of which reading Plato intended, if he even had a preference, the dramatic distance he puts between the two characters in the closing scene remains a perfect metaphor for the logical distance he seeks to establish between morality and religion throughout the dialogue. The right thing to do is to be decided through reason, but the promotion of this end does not turn into a rejection of ordinary morality. On the contrary, it is not the protagonist but the antagonist who is at odds with the requirements of ordinary morality, as the priest fears the negative publicity, or possibly even public backlash, likely to be attendant on his decision to prosecute his father (4a), and he is already chastised in this regard by the members of his family (4d–e). Both Socrates and Plato may have been eager in general to replace ordinary morality with philosophical ethics, but one would not know it to read the *Euthyphro*, unless, of course, one equates ordinary morality with religious reverence. We have nothing here on the order of the *Crito*'s urgent criticism of the "opinion of the many." Moreover, even where Plato, or Socrates, explicitly opposes ordinary morality, the challenge is about method, not judgment. The point is always that conclusions should be drawn through reasoning rather than adopted through inculcation, not that the result will necessarily be different. In the end, the dialogue may not have a conclusion, especially not as a formal inference from supporting premises, but it does have a message: If reason be sufficient to determine morality, religion cannot be necessary for it.

4.6. Symbolic Conclusion

Beyond the explicit conclusion of the argumentative part of the dialogue, and beyond even the general drama of the unfolding storyline, the work ends in symbolism worth considering on its own. The threads of metaphor weaving through the drama leave us with two colorful cloaks in the end, one, of Daedalus (11b–d, 15b), the other, of Proteus (15d):

- Daedalus, a legendary craftsman, was famous for his sculptures, which were so lifelike that they would get up and move about. This is one of Plato's favorite metaphors, figuring in several other dialogues, including *Alcibiades* 1 (121a), *Hippias Major* (282a), *Ion* (533a), and *Meno* (97d), and usually invoked to dramatize the point that the definitions proposed or arguments advanced are running away from their creators, or that they are running around in circles. Daedalus is a descendant of Hephaestus, the Olympian god. He is also the father of Icarus and inventor of the wax wings leading to his son's death as Icarus flies too close to the sun during their escape from the fabled Labyrinth.

- Proteus is an aquatic deity able but reluctant to foretell the future, changing his shape at will in order to avoid having to do so, though providing a reading for anyone able to capture him. Answering to Poseidon, and, in fact, himself a son of Poseidon, according to some accounts (Apollodorus: *Bibliotheca* 2.5.9), Proteus looms large in the Trojan War, both in Homeric and in other traditions. Responsible for herding Poseidon's flock of seals, he relies on his skills as a shapeshifter to steer clear of trouble with seafarers attempting to take advantage of his gift of prescience.

The cloak of Daedalus seems to be common property, as Socrates and Euthyphro each find that it suits the other. Socrates is the first to mention Daedalus (11c), but it is Euthyphro who brings up the theme calling up the reference (11b). Specifically, Euthyphro uses plain language to accuse Socrates of verbal wizardry (11b), and Socrates responds with the metaphor of Daedalus to reverse the charges (11b–d), complaining that Euthyphro's definitions do not stay put. Euthyphro is quick to adopt the analogy, throwing it right back at Socrates (11c–d). Socrates picks it up again upon the final failure of the extended definition process, blaming Euthyphro for the breakdown, but himself eager to start over (15b).

Indeed, both wear the cloak of Daedalus well, as Socrates deliberately leads Euthyphro full circle to the unacceptable position emerging with the second definition, and Euthyphro is not astute enough to recognize the path until they have traversed it in its entirety, supplying all the definitions circling around and running away at the end. Nevertheless, the cloak belongs to Socrates, at least dramatically, not only because he considers himself a descendant of Daedalus (11b–c), but also because the entire matter comes up for no other reason than that his debating style ends up frustrating Euthyphro (11b), with Socrates remaining entirely on the defensive or in a retaliatory mode on this matter through the end of the dialogue (15b).

The cloak of Proteus, on the other hand, appears to be tailor-made for Euthyphro, who eludes Socrates without giving him what he wants. Another similarity is that Euthyphro attempts to herd people, as Proteus herds seals, both in the service of the gods, Euthyphro, through his public addresses in the Athenian Assembly (3c), Proteus, through his role as Poseidon's herdsman. However, the aptness of the symbolism is best reflected in the fact that Euthyphro is a soothsayer, boasting an ability to tell the future, much like Proteus, though with the difference that Euthyphro seems to relish public divination, while Proteus, to the best of his abilities, avoids any occasion for prophesy. The similarity is stronger than the difference, at least in the sense that the sheer existence of the gift of divination is more pertinent to the basic storyline than is the question of whether it is shared with enthusiasm or drawn out by force. This is because the gift evinces insight into the opinions of the gods, whether it is used willingly or reluctantly. Moreover, the difference disappears altogether when the analogy is placed in the context of its origin in the drama, where Socrates declares Euthyphro as reluctant as Proteus in divulging information, and as elusive as the shapeshifter in evading the pursuer (15d).

In the end, responsibility for reasoning that will not stay put seems to rest with Socrates, not because his own arguments are circular, but because he forces the cloak of Daedalus upon Euthyphro, leading him to offer definitions that are severally infirm and collectively circular. And the responsibility for the termination of the effort rests with Euthyphro, who seeks an exit in the manner of Proteus when facing unpleasant business. In other words, Plato gives us a philosopher failing to pin down his opponent's arguments, on the contrary, grooming the opponent to produce arguments running around in confusion, pitted against a priest refusing to share the word from above. Another way to look at this might be as the combination of a priest whose arguments run away from him and a philosopher whose opponent runs away from him.

It is difficult to say exactly what Plato intended for us to make of the symbolism. He surely did not intend anything so serious as to determine the proper interpretation of the dialogue. There would be no point in portraying characters engaged in philosophical discussion if everything philosophical were to be expressed through metaphor and nothing through the actual arguments. Any imagery might be useful in testing an interpretation already formulated on the basis of information communicated in ordinary language, either confirming that understanding or challenging it, but no implicit guidepost in the drama can be the sole determinant of the principal philosophical message. This is not to deny the possibility of conveying deep philosophical messages through purely dramatic works. It is to deny that Plato's dialogues are purely dramatic works, and, more important, to assert positively that conveying deep philosophical messages, which may be found stamped even in greeting cards, is not the same as doing serious philosophy.

Then again, Plato is a brilliant dramatist, and it is often rewarding, at least in entertainment value, but usually also in critical insight, to pay attention to the details he provides in the dramatic backdrop, especially with respect to mythological references and allusions. For example, specific references to gods in a work reflecting on what might please the gods would seem to be a candidate for a high return on investment in time, that is, for fruitful independent scrutiny beyond what is intimated in the text.

To facilitate a start in that direction, and as promised earlier (§ 4.3), not in relation to the minor legends bringing the dialogue to a close, but in reference to the major gods inspiring Euthyphro throughout the discussion, the following table offers a springboard for exploring the mythological context, particularly the prevailing genealogy of the gods. There is no substitute for reading the original sources, most notably, Homer and Hesiod, preferably supported by early mythographical work, ideally, the monumental compendium ascribed to Apollodorus (or "pseudo-Apollodorus"), but the table should provide an adequate conceptual grounding in the theogony invoked in the *Euthyphro*. The table is based primarily on Hesiod, supplemented by relevant references to Apollodorus, but without any mention of Homer. While no serious student of mythology, or of the liberal arts in general, can afford to ignore Homer, the requirement for uniformity of focus in a concise introductory account, especially one that is tabular rather than narrative, precludes accounting for, much less settling, the divergence between Homer and Hesiod. Where both cannot or will not be studied, Hesiod is to be preferred for a thorough introduction to the ruling houses of the Greek pantheon, if only because he offers a complete theogony by design, whereas Homer provides bit and pieces in the pursuit of other ends, though making for infinitely more delightful reading.

The Ruling Houses of the Greek Pantheon

Seminal divine coupling: Uranus & Gaea

♂	Uranus (Caelus):	Mate and parthenogenic son of Gaea
♀	Gaea (Tellus):	Either primeval or daughter of Chaos
	Offspring:	Hecatoncheires, Cyclopes, Titans

The Twelve Titans — Line of Uranus & Gaea

Titanes — Sons of Uranus & Gaea

	Greek	*Roman*
♂	Oceanus	Oceanus
♂	Coeus	Coeus
♂	Crius	Crius
♂	Hyperion	Hyperion
♂	Iapetus	Iapetus
♂	Cronus	Saturn

Titanides — Daughters of Uranus & Gaea

	Greek	*Roman*
♀	Theia	Thea
♀	Rhea	Ops
♀	Themis	Themis
♀	Mnemosyne	Moneta
♀	Phoebe	Phoebe
♀	Tethys	Tethys

Addition

	Greek	*Roman*
♀	Dione	Dione

The Twelve Olympians — Line of Cronus & Rhea

First Generation — Children of Cronus & Rhea

	Greek	*Roman*
♀	Hestia	Vesta
♀	Demeter	Ceres
♀	Hera	Juno
♂	Poseidon	Neptune
♂	Zeus	Jupiter

Second Generation — Children of Zeus

	Greek	*Roman*
♀	Aphrodite	Venus
♀	Artemis	Diana
♀	Athena	Minerva
♂	Apollo	Apollo
♂	Ares	Mars
♂	Hephaestus	Vulcan
♂	Hermes	Mercury

Alternates

	Greek	*Roman*
♂	Hades	Pluto
♂	Dionysus	Liber

Notes:

1. Dione: Hesiod identifies her as a second-generation Titan, a daughter of Oceanus and Tethys, while Apollodorus moves her into the first generation as a goddess born of Uranus and Gaea.
2. Hades, a first-generation Olympian dwelling in the underworld instead of Olympus, is usually left out of the list of the twelve Olympians, with Demeter taking his place, but some, e.g., Hamilton (1942, p. 25), include Hades and leave out Demeter.
3. Dionysus (a.k.a. Bacchus), a second-generation Olympian, in later tradition displaces Hestia, a first-generation Olympian without a grand presence.

Sources:
Hesiod: *Theogony* 116–138, 453–491, 886–942.
Apollodorus: *Bibliotheca* 1.1.1–1.1.7, 1.3.1–1.3.6, 1.4.1, 3.4.3.

Apology: Broad Outline

- Prologue: opening words (17a–18a)
- Distinction: old (informal) vs. new (formal) accusations (18a–19a)

- Formal refutation (19a–28a)
  - Old accusations (standing prejudice): meddlesome public nuisance (19a–24b)
    - Overview of the accusations (19a–c)
    - Negative response: pedagogic contrast with the Sophists (19c–20c)
    - Positive account: origins of public perception of Socrates (20c–24b)
      - Assessment of the oracle of Apollo at Delphi (20e–21a)
      - Lifetime of intrusive inquisition and intervention (21b–22e)
      - Emergence and growth of hostility and prejudice (22e–23d)
  - New accusations (formal indictment): corruption & heresy (24b–28b)
    - Charges: corrupting the youth & resisting religious conformity (24b–c)
    - Response #1 to corruption charge: horse-training analogy (24c–25c)
    - Response #2 to corruption charge: neighbor analogy (25c–26a)
    - Response to heresy charge: activity implies actor (26b–28a)

- Real defense: general account and validation of conduct (28b–34b)
  - Avoiding wickedness is more important than avoiding death (28b–e)
  - Heavenly appointment as the effective source of Socrates's conduct (28e–30c)
  - Athenians would be harming themselves in executing Socrates (30c–d)
  - Socrates as God's gift to Athens (30d–e)
  - Gadfly analogy: Socrates stinging people into thought and action (30e–31c)
  - Socrates's *daimonion* steers him clear of politics (31c–32e)
  - Charges of corruptive influence contradict general satisfaction (33c–34b)

- Refusal to beg for mercy (34b–35d)
- Vote #1: 280 to 220 guilty (35e–36a)

- Intervening speech: counterproposal to the death penalty (36b–38b)
  - Alternative #1: free meals at the public expense (36b–37a)
  - Alternative #2: imprisonment, fine, or exile (37a–38b)
- Vote #2: death penalty (38b)

- Epilogue: parting speech (38c–42a)
  - Addressing opposers (38c–39d): those voting for execution
    - Analysis: reason for losing the case (38d–39b)
    - Prophecy: retribution guaranteed as others take his place as gadfly (39c–d)
  - Addressing supporters (39e–42a): those voting for acquittal
    - Confirmation: Socrates's *daimonion* acquiescent throughout the day (40a–c)
    - Death: termination of consciousness vs. safe transfer elsewhere (40c–41c)
    - Final request: asks for his sons to be nagged into righteousness (41e–42a)

Five

APOLOGY

5.1. Literary Profile

5.1.1. Dramatic Orientation

Plato's *Apology* chronicles the defense of Socrates on trial for his life. Newcomers are bound to benefit from a basic dramatic orientation, but too much guidance prior to reading the original for the first time can sterilize the experience. Preparatory directions *need not* include the broader historical context, which can be studied just as effectively after reading the dialogue, and it *should not* include the political undertones, which hold far greater interest after witnessing the trial as an impartial observer, to the extent possible, without any preconceptions regarding the outcome. What is required at the outset is not instruction but introduction, not indoctrination but information. The details most pertinent to an initial encounter are the mechanics of the legal process.

At the head of the list of relevant details comes the basic setting. The text presents, or represents, a speech by Socrates defending himself on trial for a capital offense. The indictment comprises the charges of heresy, ostensibly a specific type of impiety, and corrupting the youth. The case is prosecuted by the plaintiffs, defended by the accused, and decided by the *dikasts*, the last of these combining the functions of judge and jury. Neither the prosecution nor the defense has recourse to legal representation. Meletus, Anytus, and Lycon, having jointly initiated the legal proceedings, are responsible for carrying out the prosecution, though our dramatic access to the trial, limited as it is to the presentation by the defense, acquaints us with only one of the plaintiffs, Meletus, as he is cross-examined by the defendant. Socrates, having been duly indicted, and having heard the case by the prosecution, is responsible for his own defense, which he conducts in the form of a general address interrupted only once by dialogue, the formal exchange with Meletus. The case is adjudicated by a panel of 500 (or possibly 501) *dikasts*, but the audience also includes observers that are not connected with the trial in an official capacity.

The trial is set to be finalized within the same day, in line with standard Athenian practice in capital cases, with the verdict and the sentence determined separately. A simple majority is both necessary and sufficient for a victory by the prosecution, which, for its own part, however, faces sanctions against frivolous lawsuits, specifically in the event of failure to obtain at least one-fifth of the votes. The defendant is acquitted if the prosecution fails to obtain a simple majority. A ruling against the defendant ushers in deliberations on the appropriate punishment, with the *dikasts* choosing between the penalty originally demanded by the prosecution and an alternative proposed by the defendant upon a verdict of guilty. Socrates is found guilty as charged, and sentenced to death as demanded.

We are privy in this process to the entire presentation of the defense, entering the scene at the very beginning of the speech and leaving it upon the conclusion of the farewell address, as we witness the transformation of Socrates from a defendant into a convicted criminal, all the while proving himself to be God's gift to Athens, or, to be specific, Apollo's gift to Athens.

All this comes out perfectly well on its own, after having read the text at least once, and perhaps having discussed it with others who have done the same, but this much of a preview can make the initial experience more familiar, or at least less alien, if not more enjoyable. Anything more would impose an alien structure on that experience instead of allowing it to take shape naturally. The remainder of the chapter, however, is essential to developing a critical understanding of the dialogue following a personal encounter. This is not because the analysis here is exceptional but because it is dispassionate, detached from any interpretive platform. It brings out the important themes, questions, and debates, without framing them in a pet theory regarding the whole. The goal is not to lecture readers through an agenda of preconceived notions, but to inform and challenge them, thus engaging them in dialogue, the way Plato intended.

5.1.2. Historical Context

Plato's *Apology* is one of the only two extant records of the trial of Socrates. The other, also titled *Apology*, but often appearing as the *Defense of Socrates*, was written by Xenophon. Many other portrayals of the infamous event are known to have been produced, but all are lost, except compositions drafted as rhetorical exercises, even centuries after the event, and therefore lacking historical value. In addition to the two surviving accounts, and the multitude of comparable works that are lost, we have various independent references to the historical event. Thus, we can rest assured that such a trial actually took place. In general, we can be more confident that such a trial took place than that it took place exactly as described by Plato or by Xenophon. That said, we are better off having both accounts than just one, or none at all, and outright privileged to have either one.

The two works, purportedly recounting the exact same incident, are not as consistent as might be desired, let alone being identical, but they agree more than they disagree. As the preeminent Socrates scholar of the twentieth century, Gregory Vlastos (1991, pp. 81–106, 280–297; 1994, pp. 87–108) is one of the first sources to be consulted in regard to the historicity of the *Apology*, offering additional insight into the broader question of the general accessibility of the historical figure through the dramatic character. No approach to Socrates, and certainly none to the *Apology*, can be complete without due consideration for the various joint projects of Thomas C. Brickhouse and Nicholas D. Smith (1989, pp. 1–47, especially pp. 1–13; 1994, pp. 137–175; 2004, pp. 69–192, especially pp. 69–83). On the side of Xenophon, further enlightenment may be sought in Robin Waterfield's (1990, pp. 5–26, 29–40, 53–67) commentaries on the Socratic works, including a particularly handy catalog of the key points of convergence between Xenophon and Plato in regard to the trial (pp. 30–31).

Happily, a comparison reveals differences rather than contradictions, and leaves room for a common core, though this is not a definitive scholarly consensus, precluded, among others, by Louis-André Dorion (2006, pp. 93–109), who lays out an even longer list of key points of divergence, not just in regard to the event, but, more generally, in regard to the hero, with the conviction that the two protagonists are irreconcilable, thereby making the search for the real Socrates a futile effort. Indeed, the historicity question, running far deeper than a clash between Plato and Xenophon on the trial, merits full and separate consideration. The next section (§ 5.1.3) elaborates on the broader issue, though still observing the limits of relevance to the present undertaking, and thus aiming for explanation and documentation rather than solution, and at best providing directions for further study.

As for the trial coverage by Plato and Xenophon, the differences are not so much in the form of mutually exclusive and jointly exhaustive claims as they are in the fashion of elements in one that are missing in the other. This is not to say that direct opposition is never an issue, but that it is nowhere serious enough to require the wholesale rejection of one work for the other.

Where they clash, the one by Plato is considered authoritative, if only because Plato was present at the trial, whereas Xenophon was not. Any importance attached to this is amplified by the fact that the *Apology* is the only dialogue where Plato places himself in the audience, as trumpeted by two explicit references marking his presence (33e–34a, 38b). Xenophon, on the other hand, absent not only from the trial, but also from the city, and, in fact, from Attica altogether, can at best offer a second-hand account, appealing as he does to the testimony of Hermogenes of Alopece, who may be familiar to Plato's readers as an interlocutor in the *Cratylus* and a silent auditor in the *Phaedo* (59b).

This difference, namely, the *prima facie* evidentiary disparity between a direct and a testimonial link to the event in question, though convincing, need not be conclusive, given that the proximity of the author does not guarantee the accuracy of the report. The distance to the truth, after all, is neither spatial nor temporal. Then again, prolonged absence from the locus of evidence cannot be an advantage.

At any rate, the operative difference here is not in this or any other particular advantage that may be adduced in Plato's favor to settle a disagreement with Xenophon, but, more generally, in the overall mismatch between their intellectual legacies. Even specific reasons to favor Plato tend to be manifestations of a general prejudice in disguise. Many an apparently dispassionately reasoned consideration brought up in this regard is usually invoked as a respectable substitute for siding with Plato merely because he left an incomparably greater mark in the history of Western civilization. Yet this, to be fair, is a natural tendency shaped not so much by blind deference to the legend, but by the appeal of a safe bet in minimizing the probability of error in attempting to settle an otherwise open question.

Nevertheless, the choice is not just a matter of who the better philosopher is, or who the better writer is, but who was around, both to accompany Socrates in his last years and to contribute directly to the outflow of Socratic literature immediately afterwards. Xenophon left Athens in 401 BC, a couple of years before the death of Socrates, returning in 394 BC, following a seven-year absence, only to be exiled shortly thereafter, with an eventual repeal some twenty or so years later but no evidence that he ever returned. He simply was not around enough to establish himself as an original contributor to the rising tide of Socratic literature, to wit, the genre of the *Sōkratikos logos* (touched upon in the introductory paragraphs of chapter three). His work is widely acknowledged to be derivative, not merely on Plato, but also on other Socratics, most notably, Antisthenes of Athens and Aeschines of Sphettus (a.k.a. Aeschines Socraticus). At the very least, we can be certain that Xenophon was indebted to Plato rather than the other way around. A concise and informative overview of Xenophon's dependence on Plato can be found in Charles H. Kahn's study of the genre in *Plato and the Socratic Dialogue*, specifically in an appendix dedicated to this very comparison (1996, pp. 393–401). The same work also locates Xenophon's philosophical and literary position, in more general terms, among the disciples of Socrates (Kahn, 1996, pp. 29–35, 75–79).

Fortunately, especially for Xenophon, but also for us, a choice between Plato and Xenophon is not required except on specific issues. Yet it is an often exercised option, given that any difference at all invites comparison, and an abundance of them validates the question of which offers the more accurate depiction of the event under consideration, or the more enlightened account of the issue under discussion. In the case of the *Apology*, the conflict that crops up is notable, but not insurmountable.

The most salient disagreement in the two apologies is grounded in the same theme as the most striking point of agreement: a forsaken opportunity to circumvent conviction. Both agree that Socrates could have secured acquittal had he done everything possible toward that end. Plato attributes the deficiency of effort to Socrates's refusal to compromise his principles for the sake of acquittal, which would have come at the cost of replacing truth and reason with demagogy and flattery, whereas Xenophon, far from explaining failure to achieve acquittal, has Socrates embrace conviction as an opportunity to avoid the burden of old age. Strictly speaking, Plato, purporting to transcribe the words of Socrates, offers no commentary at all, instead boldly giving us a champion placing far greater value on justice than on acquittal, as demonstrated by a resolve to avoid wickedness before avoiding death. The divergence here, perhaps more than anywhere else, places the two accounts in competition, the Platonic, representing a philosophical outlook, and, the Xenophontic, a pragmatic one, perspectives which might not even appear at odds save for the extreme forms in which they are manifested in available. Assuming 300 business days per year, grounded in a six-day workweek and setting aside a few days for holidays, just for the sake of a provisional illustration, the final counterpenalty is equivalent to 10 years' pay, not a trifling sum by any measure.

This approach is not as universally applicable as once imagined, though the case of Socrates seems relatively safe in the face of emerging evidence against the homogeneity of price structures and labor costs in a loosely defined and conveniently expansive past that may be called nothing more scientific than "days of yore." Recent studies, for example, groundbreaking work by William T. Loomis (1998), question assumptions once taken for granted in regard to the economic and financial setting prevailing in antiquity. Chief among these is the tendency to treat the Golden Age of Greece, or even the entire classical period ranging from the fall of the last tyrant of Athens in 510 BC to the death of Alexander in 323 BC, as an immutable market governed by a static economic model and a uniform financial system. Loomis (1998, pp. 255–258) challenges several economic and financial dogmas regarding ancient markets, his foremost contribution being to debunk the myth that the Greek financial system enjoyed a singularly long and firm stretch of price stability throughout antiquity, thereby also limiting the temporal validity of one drachma as one day's pay.

Fortunately, the familiar estimate still provides a good point of reference for 399 BC. Loomis (1998, p. 257) notes that one drachma per diem was indeed the standard wage between 409 BC and 407 BC for workers engaged in the final phase of the construction of the Erechtheum (or "Erechtheion" in transliteration without Latinization), a temple dedicated to Athena Polias and Poseidon Erechtheus on the north side of the Acropolis. A rigid wage structure prevailing so close to the time of Socrates's trial, together with scattered evidence of comparable remuneration in preceding and following decades, promises ample reliability for the corresponding calculations regarding the counterpenalty.

The rate of compensation for manual labor is as reliable a benchmark as one might hope to find in comparing purchasing power over such a long period. Yet many other yardsticks are available. Brickhouse and Smith (1989, pp. 226–227) illustrate a host of these, all indicating that the counterpenalty amounted to a tidy sum: They assert, for instance, that the preliminary figure of 100 drachmas amounted to fair exchange for two oxen or 30 gallons of olive oil, while the formal counterproposal of 3,000 drachmas was enough to buy six Syrian slaves (Frost, 1971, p. 58), or, as Aristotle implies (*Nicomachean Ethics* 1134b22), to ransom 30 prisoners of war, or, as Plato indicates (*Thirteenth Letter* 361e), to provide for the dowry of a bride from all but the richest of families.

References to monetary value may continue to prove illuminating even when the scope of consideration is limited to the Platonic corpus. The *Apology* alone has five such references:

- Evenus charges 500 drachmas (five minas) to teach virtue, or, what is the same, human excellence (20b);
- The price of a book by Anaxagoras is one drachma (26d–e);
- The fine for frivolous lawsuits is 1,000 drachmas (36b);
- Socrates's provisional tender, envisaged more to highlight his ability to pay than to please the court, is 100 drachmas (38b);
- Socrates's final offer of a counterpenalty, to be financed by his friends, is 3,000 drachmas (38b).

The breakdown shows that the proposed counterpenalty of 3,000 drachmas is an amount sufficient to finance the education of six students by Evenus, to build a library of 3,000 books, or to file three lawsuits failing miserably in a court of law.

Even after the satisfaction of all concerns regarding the amount of the fine, a philosophical problem that still lingers is the reconciliation of the categorical denial of guilt with the adoption of a counterpenalty, any counterpenalty at all. The inconsistency is so glaring as to lend credence to the alternative scenario represented by Xenophon depicting Socrates as steering clear of a counterproposal in order to avoid incriminating himself (*Apology* 23). The ultimate explanation of the apparent contradiction between maintaining his innocence and proposing a counterpenalty is that Socrates does not believe that he will be harmed by parting with his money. This is why he can propose a fine as the counterpenalty without being compelled, by the inherent logic, to admitting guilt. Since he is indifferent to changes in his net worth, by proposing a fine, he is satiating the jury without inviting a true penalty and, therefore, without admitting guilt. Any other alternative, be it imprisonment or exile or anything else, would be as good as a signed confession to harm done. Moreover, the counterpenalty was to be paid by friends, not by Socrates, who, had he been fined in accordance with the final counterproposal, would not have been penalized at all. He would, by definition, still have been convicted, but this is not the same as admitting his own guilt, which the very advancement of a counterpenalty, as a first approximation, may otherwise seem to require by implication, shown here to fail because (1) Socrates never considers a monetary penalty to be personally harmful, even as he contemplates bearing the burden himself within the limits of his own ability to pay, and (2) his friends take on the financial obligation, which is the only sanction under consideration by the defense.

5.9. Sentence

Following a second voting session, this time for sentencing, the assembly decides on the death penalty (38b). Diogenes Laërtius (*Lives* 2.42) reports that the verdict for execution came with a wider margin than the initial vote to establish guilt, with an ambiguous reference to 80 more votes, pointing either to a net increase of 80 votes in the balance against Socrates or to an addition of 80 fresh votes against him, in the first case, expanding the margin from 60 to 140 votes, with a final count of 320 to 180 in favor of having him put to death, and, in the second case, expanding the margin from 60 to 220 votes, with an execution tally of 360 to 140. Either way, having fumbled the first count, the one dedicated exclusively to the establishment of guilt, Diogenes is difficult to trust on the second one, especially as he is the only source for a widening gap in moving from the verdict to sentencing.

In addition to his bad track record here, he offers an unreliable estimate in a different matter immediately after reporting the alleged addition of 80 votes: He declares that Socrates was executed a few days after the trial, whereas we know from the *Phaedo* (58a–c) that the philosopher remained on death row substantially longer than a few days, as Phaedo, the eponymous narrator of the dialogue, twice characterizes the period between the trial and the execution as a "long time," a month according to Burnet (1914, p. 192) and Taylor (1960, pp. 167–168), both probably drawing on Xenophon's report (*Memorabilia* 4.8.2) to that effect. Yet Diogenes (*Lives* 2.42) describes the same period as a "few days," despite bringing up the *Phaedo* in the same breath, and despite having access (evinced in *Lives* 2.57) to the Xenophontic record (*Memorabilia* 4.8.2) of exactly how many days Socrates happened to live after the trial.

As mentioned, a compelling reason to approach Diogenes with caution, if not to reject him altogether, is that his is the only reference on record to quantifiable growth in the opposition to Socrates between the verdict and the sentence. While a single report is all it takes to communicate the truth, the claim, if indeed true, is important enough to have made its way into many other sources, not all of which can reasonably be assumed to have perished. The silence of Plato and Xenophon is especially telling in this regard. A related difficulty is that Diogenes, never secretive about his sources, in fact, quite forthcoming in his biography of Socrates, fails to mention where he got this rather specific piece of information, becoming particularly conspicuous in that he was so meticulous as to cite two sources in the paragraph immediately preceding the one reporting the growing opposition and yet another source in the paragraph immediately following it, all in regard to points of reference having nothing to do with the number of people purported to have changed their minds regarding the defendant's innocence.

Possibly the best reason to dismiss Diogenes is the incredible psychological transformation required for anyone demanding acquittal in the initial vote to advocate execution in the final poll. This is not only psychologically counterintuitive, but also epistemically unwarranted because the second session is dedicated exclusively to the assessment of the penalty, having nothing further to do with the establishment of guilt, and thus could not possibly have revealed any evidence either to strengthen or weaken the defendant's case. The alleged shift from supporting acquittal to recommending death might even be plausibly said, on the same grounds, to be morally wrong and juridically unsound, but a possible objection here is that, the first session having established guilt, the second was intended to determine the most fitting penalty, with said determination not to be made in accordance with personal opinions regarding the guilt of the defendant but in observation of the formal verdict that the defendant is guilty as charged. All the same, any juror voting to acquit Socrates must have been tempted, at least psychologically, if not also morally, to choose the lesser of the two penalties in question.

In all fairness to Diogenes, from his frame of reference, the scenario in question is not as incredible as a motivational transformation from wanting to free Socrates to wanting to kill him. First of all, no one, not even those who voted for both conviction and execution, and especially not any of the three plaintiffs, would have wanted to create a martyr out of such an iconic maverick, only to immortalize the legend and inspire others to embrace his intellectual legacy and emulate his distinctive style. The motivation all along for seeking the death penalty was not actually to have Socrates killed but to secure the greatest possible leverage to force him to embrace exile as an alternative, or, better yet, to make a coward and a criminal out of him by placing him in a position of having to break out of prison to avoid execution. Second, and more important, the death sentence in Diogenes does not come in repudiation of an acceptable alternative but in the absence of one. The final choice in the court of Diogenes (*Lives* 2.41–42) is not between execution and a fine but between capital punishment and royal treatment (§ 5.8). Obliged to choose between two penalties, but presented instead with a choice between a penalty and a reward, the jurors may even be said to have had no choice in the matter, at least not a proper one. Hence, even if Diogenes was wrong about the counterpenalty finally adopted by Socrates, or perhaps precisely because he was wrong about it, his position on an expanding vote differential is not as far-fetched as it might have been otherwise. In other words, the widely acknowledged possibility of an erroneous starting point for Diogenes dilutes, and arguably removes, the implausibility of the psychological leap a juror would have to make in moving from supporting Socrates in the first vote to opposing him in the second.

Nevertheless, this absolves Diogenes of holding a preposterous position, not of holding a mistaken one. As it is, we can grant that Diogenes believed free meals at the Prytaneum to be the formal counterproposal, but not that this was in fact the case. What we are left with, in evaluating the alleged erosion of support for Socrates, is still the awkward combination of a presumably respectable counterproposal, or at least a marginally tolerable one, and a statistically significant shift of opinion.

Ignoring Diogenes on this particular issue, as is now the standard approach among Plato scholars, though not without important historical exceptions, as in Burnet (1914, p. 182), who uncritically adopts the tenuous account, still leaves a burning question: Why was Socrates put to death? To be more explicit, why did the jury choose the death penalty over the alternative of a fine of 3,000 drachmas? If this was not a mockingly low sum, as Brickhouse and Smith demonstrate conclusively, then money could not have been the issue (§ 5.8). If money was not the issue, why was he put to death in the face of a viable alternative?

Could the answer be that the money was not enough after all, that is, that it was too little without being insultingly inadequate? This, too, is an issue taken up by Brickhouse and Smith (1989, pp. 227–228), who readily acknowledge the possibility that the counterpenalty might not have been on par with the standard prevailing at the time, despite constituting a substantial offer worthy of serious consideration rather than indignation. They list several court decisions with fines dwarfing the penalty proposed by Socrates, though they ultimately deny that money was the decisive factor. One example that stands out is the verdict against Anaxagoras, who was banished in addition to being fined ten times the amount in question with Socrates (Diogenes: *Lives* 2.12). Apparently, the outcome for Anaxagoras was not an exception, as evidenced by the existence of other cases combining banishment with an overwhelming financial burden, specifically, the full confiscation of property (Brickhouse and Smith, 1989, p. 228).

Although the evidence available suggests that the counterpenalty proposed was at best at the low end of an acceptable range, possibly even slightly short of expectations, this does not show that Socrates was put to death for a few drachmas, or a lack thereof. He probably was never even in any serious danger of being put to death merely for a dearth of funds. The amount in question obviously paled in comparison to fines in comparable trials, but it was also demonstrably not so low as to preclude the possibility of being taken seriously. The grey area in between is surely not so confusing as to call for killing a man just to be on the safe side of proper protocol in accordance with legal precedent.

One reason that the decision to put Socrates to death cannot sensibly be attributed to an inability to match what might be considered a standard fine is that the Athenian jury appears utterly despicable under this scenario, indeed, even more so than in the popular one where the death of the philosopher is the result of a clash of ideals and conflict of interests. Another is that Socrates was a poor man whose friends had to intervene to supplement and subsidize his counterproposal, any deficiency in which would have *ipso facto* undermined the effort. As a joint effort undertaken by wealthy Athenians to ensure the adequacy of the fine to be proposed as an alternative to the death penalty, the counterpenalty is not likely to have fallen short of expectations or to have frustrated the jurors.

Admittedly, the wealth of the intervening friends, Plato, Crito, Critobulus, and Apollodorus (38b), is a qualitative assessment, largely an extrapolation from plot elements in Plato, only partially supported by historical evidence, notably in the case of Crito. Taylor (1960, pp. 166–167) interprets their support as a strenuous effort during an economically difficult period for Athens, pointing out that these were not wealthy people, except for Crito, who would have probably had to shoulder the bulk of the burden at an inconvenient time. Yet this is not the only place friends rush to the side of the philosopher, with a declaration, not only of willingness, but especially of ability, in fact, most assuredly, without insufferable hardship, to contribute funds to serve his needs. Overlapping in membership, another group, led by Crito, and including Simmias and Cebes, among "many" unidentified others, ignores consequences in an enthusiastic effort to orchestrate

Socrates's escape from prison (*Crito* 45b). Friends willing to spare no expense to break Socrates out of prison after the trial (*Crito* 44b–45c) would surely not have stopped a step short of acceptability in augmenting the sum that might have saved his life during the trial. The actual amount needed for the prison break does not turn out to be a grand burden (*Crito* 45a), which suggests that breaking out of jail was cheaper than avoiding it in the first place, but what is indicative here is that the friends are prepared to spend and risk all they have (*Crito* 44e–45a, 45b), which implies that they would have had the same attitude in supplementing the counterpenalty at the trial.

Perhaps the problem is not with the final amount offered but with the initial amount considered. This is the possibility that jurors were vexed by the preliminary consideration of a fine of 100 drachmas as a substitute for the death penalty. Although never formally proposed, the amount, even when voiced merely as a possibility, may have been disconcerting in its striking inconsistency with any range that might be considered the norm for fines in comparable cases. This possibility is closer to the root of the problem than is any concern regarding the adequacy of the official counterpenalty, but it is still not a defining juncture in the progression of the trial. The initial sum contemplated by Socrates may have been absurdly incommensurate in absolute terms, but not so much in relative terms, taking into account his finances. His poverty comes out in several dialogues, also mentioned during the trial as Socrates takes care to emphasize his humble means (38b), which Xenophon quantifies in terms of a net worth of 500 drachmas, a figure covering all assets, including the family abode (*Oeconomicus* 2.3). On this evidence, 100 drachmas turns out to be equivalent to one-fifth of the philosopher's total assets, representing a serious tender as it is, and constituting a far more substantial offer if the house is kept out of the equation on the assumption that no penalty aimed at a single person should be so harsh as to ruin his entire family. Members of the assembly were, no doubt, familiar with Socrates's basic financial profile, at least as an approximation, and it is difficult to imagine a congregation of democrats killing a man essentially for no other reason than resentment of his indigence.

Taking another step back from the formal counterpenalty, we arrive at the locus of unmitigated disaster, the declaration of public maintenance as the only fitting return for the allegations just discussed and confirmed. Although this announcement precedes any mention of a fine, it is not a provisional counterproposal later upgraded to an actual monetary penalty. Instead, it is merely Socrates's way of reiterating his innocence as a segue into his deliberations on a proper penalty. Nevertheless, it is truly scandalous. The brazen stance might have even been perceived as a mockery, though the intention was not to mock the proceedings but to emphasize the denial of guilt. The problem here is the potential estrangement of the jury by such a defiant introduction to a consideration of penalty alternatives. The reference to a reward not only sounds ridiculous in exercise of a right to specify a penalty, but also constitutes an open challenge to a court which had already reached an unfavorable decision on the issue of guilt.

Even though the entertainment of the idea of free meals at the public expense as a substitute for the death penalty was not formally registered as a counterproposal, it is a memorable expression of Socrates's considered opinion on the matter, and it must have left an indelible impression in the minds of jurors dumbfounded by the strength of conviction required to antagonize an authoritative body that might just as easily have been appeased. To be sure, the manner of delivery of the counterproposal could not sensibly have been the sole factor in eliciting a death sentence from an otherwise sympathetic jury, but it might well have been the proverbial last straw for a jury that was not very sympathetic to begin with.

5.10. Parting Speech

The remainder of the work is a farewell address with no legal bearing on the case (38c–42a). It consists of two distinct parts, the first (38c–39d), dedicated to those who voted for the death penalty, the second (39e–42a), to those who voted for acquittal. The nature of the distinction, or rather, the aim of the juxtaposition, is not immediately clear. At first glance, the apparent classification seems to mix rival camps from two different voting sessions, one, the opposition in the session determining the penalty, the other, supporters in the session establishing guilt. The death penalty was in question only in the second session, acquittal, only in the first. Thus, technically, the distinction Socrates makes in his address is not a simple one between those who consistently supported him and those who consistently opposed him throughout the whole ordeal. Yet the particular choice does not appear to have a special meaning or an overarching purpose. In other words, it does not seem to reflect an intention to categorize the jurors in a way that is mathematically or conceptually different from a generic division between those supporting and those opposing Socrates.

This is borne out by the fact that although Socrates defines the first group in explicit reference to support for the death penalty (38c–d), he also identifies it in a nonspecific sense of opposition, without mention of death or execution (39c). Assuming that those voting for the death penalty are the same as those voting for conviction, which means further, without requiring a separate assumption (other than everything else remaining the same), that those supporting the counterpenalty against the death penalty are the same as those advocating acquittal, the division is between those opposing and those supporting Socrates throughout the proceedings. On this interpretation, the choice in addressing those voting for execution rather than those voting for conviction, if not entirely random, can sensibly be attributed to a simple intention to stress the gravity of the decision. Likewise, the reason for addressing those voting for acquittal rather than those voting for the counterpenalty can safely be equated with an intention to emphasize the absence of guilt as the real essence of the support, diverted from acquittal to counterpenalty only to remain relevant to the mechanical process in the course of the trial.

Another distinction attracting attention in the farewell address concerns the attitude of Socrates regarding the authority of the court, with his recognition of legal capacity becoming explicit on a selective rather than general basis. He appears to respect his supporters, but not his opposers, as judges and jurors. Indeed, the first time Socrates uses the proper honorific title "dikast" throughout the trial is in addressing those who voted for his acquittal as distinct from those voting in opposition (40a). This comes after the pronouncement of the death sentence, prior to which he uses various forms of address such as "Athenians," "men of Athens," and "gentlemen," all devoid of formal recognition of legal status. Socrates also makes sure to attract attention to the fact that the reference as judge or juror gains propriety only at the end when all is said and done and he can address those voting for acquittal separately from those voting for conviction and capital punishment. This seems indicative of a conviction that people assigned to the case in an official capacity deserve the designation of judge or juror only if they are aligned in support of acquittal and not if they are against it.

However, it is never advisable to make too much out of dramatic subtleties, which are not always hidden troves of suppressed judgments. A competing interpretation, less plausible but possible nonetheless, could be that the term "dikast" becomes appropriate only at the end, and not before, simply because the persons in question had not yet discharged their functions as judges and jurors prior to the end of the trial, and, in fact, that it is precisely their performance of their functions as judges and jurors that brings the trial to its conclusion. True, Socrates uses the term only in reference to supporters, but this is not proof that he denies its applicability to others. Addressing people as "gentlemen" or the like is not to deny that they are also jurors. Perhaps most important, the distinction could not possibly have had any bearing on the outcome since it emerges after the pronouncement of the sentence. The neutral form of address before that is always directed at everyone without discrimination, and it is hardly of a nature to antagonize anyone except the rare eccentric inclined to take offense at being called a "gentleman" or the stickler for propriety resenting not being called a "dikast."

5.10.1. Addressing Opposers

Socrates has three messages for those voting against him: first, a quick pragmatic appraisal of their decision (38c–d); second, a reaffirmation of the prudence of his own course (38d–39b); third, a prophecy (39c–d).

Following a bald statement of the folly in martyring someone so advanced in years as to be likely to die soon enough without intervention (38c–d), he moves on to a vindication of his defensive strategy with an assessment of the effective reason for his failure to achieve acquittal (38d–39b). He claims to have lost the case because he refused to embrace the kind of speech that would have secured acquittal, not because he was unable to appease the assembly with rhetoric effective to that end. He maintains that his choice in the matter was motivated by a desire to avoid wickedness as opposed to the more common desire to avoid death.

Carrying the contrast further, he describes himself as being overtaken by death while his accusers are overtaken by wickedness.

The analysis of the outcome of the trial is followed by a prophecy (39c–d). The thrust of the message here is that retribution will be swift and strong. Socrates predicts that others will promptly take his place, and, thereby, that his originally unique position as the gadfly of Athens will become a common post permanently maintained by successive generations of enthusiastic youngsters. He warns that weeding out such people is no way to escape the moral and intellectual probe in search of a life worth living, and recommends becoming good as the best way to avoid examinations of the sort that intimidated his earlier accusers, who, in turn, bred and inspired his present accusers.

5.10.2. Addressing Supporters

The portion of the farewell address directed at supporters is roughly twice as long as the portion dedicated to those voting in opposition. With ongoing emphasis on the supreme importance of avoiding wickedness, the distinctive aim of this part of the epilogue is to console and reassure friends regarding the outcome. The reassurance offered has a spiritual (40a–c) and a metaphysical (40c–41c) component, the first, invoking the endorsement of the *daimonion* of Socrates, and, the second, disputing the sensibility of the fear of death.

Socrates takes his *daimonion* to provide external verification, constituting an additional source of confidence in the prudence and propriety of the way he conducted himself during the trial. He interprets the prolonged acquiescence of the *daimonion*, an otherwise relentless critic of bad choices, as confirmation that the way he handled the defense was neither morally nor strategically objectionable. With the *daimonion* manifested as an inner voice of supernatural origin, as opposed to the mundane phenomenology of a conscience, or comparable mental content, the appeal has a specifically religious dimension beyond the obviously spiritual one. Given further an explicit appeal to the sign's divinity (40a–b), we are left with the irony of a convicted heretic embracing religious justification.

This consideration blends into a hopeful discussion of death as a phenomenon (40c–41c). This is a brief but serious analysis proceeding on the premise that death is either the absence of consciousness, and nothing more, or a spiritual journey into another realm. Socrates is hoping for the second alternative. He wants death to turn out to be a transition to another dimension of reality, and, the afterlife, conscious existence in that setting. This is not because he is particularly troubled by the first alternative, that is, by an unequivocal end to his personal existence, but that he is excited about the prospect of continuing his mission as a gadfly. He looks forward to meeting the departed so that he can examine them much in the way that expedited his own departure. This shows just how sincere he is in discounting the exile alternative as a possible punishment in his case.

The speech by Socrates and the work by Plato end with a final request, one that is a perfect complement to Socrates's eagerness to continue the quest for knowledge and the promotion of moral integrity in the hereafter. Socrates asks that his sons be nagged in the same way that he had been nagging others, especially if the sons turn out to care more for becoming rich than for becoming good (41e–42a). This reiterates the importance of avoiding wickedness, the theme ushering in the defense proper in the transition from specific rebuttals to the general account, roughly a third of the way into the work (28b–e). The emphasis at the end becomes particularly forceful as it depicts Socrates facing certain death but preoccupied with righteousness.

5.11. Was Socrates Courting Conviction?

Next to the debate on the historicity of records, the single most engaging problem regarding the trial of Socrates is whether the outcome was his own doing. The problem is grounded in suspicions that Socrates could have secured acquittal if he wanted to, but chose not to, in fact, working in the opposite direction to force the issue and ensure a conviction. Historicity is an issue in this case as well, that is, if the problem is to determine whether the historical Socrates, as opposed to the character, chose not to defend himself to the best of his abilities. But the question can also be taken up in terms of whether Socrates as a character in the *Apology*, or, more broadly, as the main protagonist of Plato's early dialogues, or even as the central hero in the entire Platonic corpus, took a dive in the trial for his life. A similar approach could also be taken with Xenophon's Socrates, though his work is usually invoked to corroborate or question specific points in Plato's account, and to assist in the formation of a general historical portrait, as opposed to piecing together a dramatic character for literary or philosophical consideration. At any rate, the question, whether taken historically or dramatically, is compelling: Did Socrates pursue acquittal or did he pursue conviction? Or did he perhaps do neither, choosing instead to speak his mind with no regard for the outcome but the highest for truth and justice?

The Xenophontic position, touched upon earlier, is that Socrates welcomed the prospect of execution so that he might avoid the inconvenience of old age (Xenophon: *Apology* 6–9, 22–23). Taken at face value, this sounds much like suicide, at least in being an unreasonably early move toward euthanasia. Not only does it undermine the Western idealization and idolization of Socrates, grounded largely in the efforts of Plato, but it also contradicts the strong stance he is shown to take in the *Phaedo* (61c–62c) against suicide. However, this assessment is unfair to Xenophon. First, the approach of Socrates as related by Xenophon cannot be considered suicide, given that any other type of defense turns out to have been opposed by the *daimonion* (Xenophon: *Apology* 4), whose interference Socrates interprets as a heavenly indication that the gods are against prolonging his life and are thereby directing him not to put up a real fight so that he may find death without misery (Xenophon: *Apology* 5, 7–9). Second, on the issue of contradicting the *Phaedo*, the heavenly dispensation readily creates an exception removing the contradiction, but a prior consideration is that Xenophon is not obligated to be consistent with Plato.

That said, independently of whether we thus restore the *prima facie* credibility of Xenophon's story, this perspective is not in currency, and probably never was. As Xenophon himself readily admits, or rather boasts, in identifying what is unique in his contribution to the literature, he stands alone in exposing the underlying motivation driving Socrates in pursuit of conviction at the trial (Xenophon: *Apology* 1).

Xenophon's assessment of the defensive strategy followed is the extreme version of a general portrait of Socrates as not doing his best to avoid conviction. No other sympathetic account has been as unflattering, and not many in opposition create a more wretched character. What is most interesting about this is that Xenophon was at pains to honor the memory of Socrates, not to besmirch it, nor even to record and transmit a dispassionate chronicle for posterity. Be that as it may, more palatable variations tend to attract a greater following. The standard form of the suspicion that Socrates deliberately failed to avoid conviction draws on the possibility that he martyred himself, choosing death in an attempt to glorify philosophy, while defeating his accusers and opponents from beyond the grave and for all time. This makes failure in one direction success in the other, as his failure to acquit himself brings his success in vindicating philosophy, or, from the opposite perspective, his determination to vindicate philosophy turns out to require a personal sacrifice, one too great for anyone but a martyr.

In a sense, this, too, might be classified as suicide, as it is a matter of avoidable death, again, constituting an inconsistency with what Socrates says in the *Phaedo* regarding taking one's own life. Yet mitigating circumstances beg for consideration here as well. For example, Socrates reports that his *daimonion*, that unerring guardian against misdirection, has not opposed his defense (40a–c). Plato's Socrates has as much a right to take the silence of the *daimonion* during the course of the trial as encouragement, and as validation of his approach, as has Xenophon's Socrates to take the opposition of the *daimonion* to alternative strategies prior to the trial as endorsement of the defense actually presented. If so, the heavenly mandate invoked for the Xenophontic scenario is just as applicable in this case, thereby making martyrdom not only acceptable but required, or at least recommended.

As for the risk of contradicting the stance taken in the *Phaedo* against suicide, the endorsement of the gods is sufficient to remove the apparent contradiction, especially since the *Phaedo*'s main objection to suicide is its prohibition by the gods. Even if this were not the case, a contradiction here would not be as problematic as it might be under normal circumstances, because the Socrates of the *Apology* and the Socrates of the *Phaedo* need not be entirely consistent, and might not even be considered the same character, in view of the fact that the first belongs to Plato's early period, and, the second, to his middle period. In fact, as Vlastos (1991, pp. 45–80, 81–106, especially pp. 45–46) demonstrates, the problem in that regard is not in proving the dramatic division, but in associating one period with the historical Socrates, and, the other, or others, with Plato himself. Thus, the apparent contradiction is defensible on two counts, first, in shifting the responsibility where it belongs, in the court of the gods endorsing a course of action in violation of their own prohibitions, second, in appealing to the natural dramatic division between the two manifestations of the same character.

Those holding Socrates at least partially responsible for the outcome, though none so emphatically as Xenophon, include some of the most influential commentators in the history of Platonic studies: Grote (1850, pp. 399–496); Burnet (1914, pp. 180–192); Taylor (1960, pp. 156–167); Cornford (1927, pp. 302–309); Allen (1984, pp. 61–78).

Grote finds Socrates's speech in court so far from constituting a proper defense as to require announcement up front as a subheading in the table of contents to the eighth volume of his monumental work, *A History of Greece*: "Sokratês defended himself like one who did not care to be acquitted" (Grote, 1850, p. xiv). Sharing Quintilian's (*Institutio Oratoria* 2.15.30, 11.1.10) conviction that Socrates lost his life in an effort to maintain his dignity, he adds that the philosopher practically forced the court to return a verdict of guilty:

> Quintilian, indeed, expresses his satisfaction that Sokratês maintained that towering dignity which brought out the rarest and most exalted of his attributes, but which at the same time renounced all chance of acquittal. Few persons will dissent from this criticism: but when we look at the sentence, as we ought in fairness to do, from the point of view of the dikasts, justice will compel us to admit that Sokratês deliberately brought it upon himself. [Grote, 1850, p. 483; author's footnote reference marker omitted]

Grote claims Socrates to be even more at fault for receiving the death penalty than for being found guilty in the first place: "If the verdict of guilty was thus brought upon Sokratês by his own consent and cooperation, much more may the same remark be made respecting the capital sentence which followed it" (Grote, 1850, p. 483). His chief reason for blaming Socrates for failing to avoid the death penalty after conviction is the famous prefatory remarks regarding meals at the public expense as an alternative to execution:

> Subsistence in the prytaneum at the public expense, was one of the greatest honorary distinctions which the citizens of Athens ever conferred; an emphatic token of public gratitude. That Sokratês, therefore, should proclaim himself worthy of such an honor, and talk of assessing it upon himself in lieu of a punishment, before the very dikasts who had just passed against him a verdict of guilty, would be received by them as nothing less than a deliberate insult; a defiance of judicial authority, which it was their duty to prove, to an opinionated and haughty citizen, that he could not commit with impunity. [Grote, 1850, p. 485]

Grote maintains that Socrates could have saved his own life, with a sacrifice merely in arrogance rather than dignity, if he had just stated the counterproposal without the provocative introduction preceding it: "Had he proposed, with little or no preface, the substitute-fine of thirty minae with which this part of his speech concluded, there is every reason for believing that the majority of dikasts would have voted for it" (Grote, 1850, p. 485).

Burnet is likewise inclined to shift responsibility for the outcome to Socrates, so much so as to shrink from calling the speech a "defense":

> It is perfectly true, no doubt, that the *Apology* is not a defence at all, but that makes it all the more characteristic of the man. Sokrates treats the accusation with contempt, and even goes out of his way to import things into the case that were hardly of a nature to conciliate the judges. [Burnet, 1914, pp. 180–181]

Regarding the direct response to the specific allegations in the formal indictment, his reading is that "Sokrates did not stoop to defend himself against either the one charge or the other" (Burnet, 1914, p. 181). Yet he finds it self-evident that, even with this attitude, acquittal was not too far to reach: "There can be no doubt that if Sokrates had proposed exile or imprisonment till he had paid a reasonable fine, everyone would have been satisfied, but he refused to do anything of the sort" (Burnet, 1914, pp. 181–182). He maintains, with the evidentiary support of references to the *Meno* (94e) and the *Gorgias* (521c), that the driving force behind the litigation was purely political, that everyone at the trial, including Socrates, was well aware of this, and that Socrates chose to continue to inflame the underlying political sensibilities come what may:

> From this point of view one of the most important things in the *Apology* is the statement of Sokrates (39d) that his countrymen will not be able to rid themselves of criticism even if they put him to death. There are many who will take up the task of exposing them, and they will be more merciless inasmuch as they are younger. That is, to all intents and purposes, a plea of guilty to what the hints of Kallikles and Anytos suggest was the real ground of the accusation, namely, that Sokrates had fostered in young men that antidemocratic spirit which had led to the oligarchical revolutions. [Burnet, 1914, p. 187]

Burnet thus holds Socrates at least partly responsible for dying as an enemy of the state, though his assignment of blame is strictly factual rather than moral, from which standpoint he does his best to conceal undertones of approbation, sporadically surfacing in the greater context of the passage quoted.

The next generation of commentators, most notably, Taylor (1960, pp. 156–167, originally 1926) and Cornford (1927, pp. 302–309), both only slightly younger contemporaries of Burnet, but slower to come out with their principal contributions, are in general agreement regarding the role of Socrates in the way things turned out at the momentous trial. Taylor (1960, p. 166) takes issue particularly with the transition to the counterproposal, contending that Socrates put forth his initial consideration of 100 drachmas as a counterpenalty knowing full well that such an offer would be rejected. His considered opinion on the overall situation is that, immediately after sentencing, the portion of the farewell speech dedicated to an overview of reasons for losing the case (38d–39b) shows clearly "that Socrates has forced the issue, and that he could have secured his acquittal by simply 'asking for quarter'" (Taylor, 1960, p. 167). Cornford (1927, pp. 302–309) subscribes to the same general assessment, though he does not revel in the theme as thoroughly as the others, carefully sifting through the text for evidence while savoring every nuance:

> Plainly Socrates had not tried to make an effective defence: he would not slur over anything in his past that would tell against him. The misrepresentation of his character and work by the comic poets is repudiated in terms that would have been futile, as well as disingenuous, if the picture in the *Clouds* had been even a caricature of the real man. [Cornford, 1927, pp. 303–304]

Writing well over half-a-century later, Allen (1984, pp. 61–78) still assigns Socrates a prominent role in his own death, but breaks with the established critical pattern by rejecting the portrayal of the philosopher as pursuing conviction. Instead, he presents the outcome as the natural result of elevating the truth above all else: "Socrates' aim was neither acquittal nor conviction, but to tell the truth in accordance with justice, let the chips fall where they may" (Allen, 1984, p. 71). Actually, this pithy appraisal, quite the opposite of contradicting those before it, captures the exegetical essence of the perspective common to the other four scholars. The difference is not so much in the substance as it is in the emphasis. Allen brings to the foreground a distinction which goes undeclared but implicit in the others. He considers conviction to be the unguided consequence of placing a far greater value on establishing the truth than on achieving acquittal, especially as the two turn out to be mutually incompatible. Not one of the other four commentators would deny this to propose in its stead that Socrates sought conviction as an end in itself, or as an end to something other than establishing the truth in accordance with the requirements of justice. Attesting to the general convergence of his opinion with the prevailing view, Allen joins Burnet in refusing to call the Platonic text a "defense": "An apologia is a defense. But the *Apology* is something other than a defense, at least as the term is commonly understood" (Allen, 1984, p. 61).

The mainstream portrayal of Socrates as forcing the issue where he might otherwise have talked his way out of trouble is more appealing than the Xenophontic version if only because martyrdom is *prima facie* honorable whereas killing oneself to avoid growing older is not. Indeed, this is the Socrates we know.

The legendary profile handed down through the ages, and shaping our common impression, not only in the Western world but throughout the globe, is that of a man so devoted to the truth, and to what is right, as to refuse to budge in his pursuit of wisdom and devotion to righteousness even in the face of death. What is supposed to be impressive here is not the apparent philosophical indifference to death that seems to be responsible for such a disconcerted defense as we have on record. After all, an unmitigated indifference to death is one step away from an apathetic outlook on life, and neither captures what heroes are made of, today or throughout history. What is impressive, in the end, is the moral conviction that motivates a mortal opposition to unjustified coercion and unwarranted harassment, despite a passion for life, which, ironically, is demonstrated by the very lifestyle responsible for the death of Socrates. This, then, is the proper sense of interpreting the setting in terms of martyrdom, which is never an end unto itself, nor a means to a trivial or selfish end, but the advancement of a worthy cause.

Insofar as the concept of purpose, invariably an exalted one, is readily contained in that of martyrdom, no variant of the traditional view that Socrates martyred himself implies a vacuous or otiose engagement. The point is not that life is expendable, but that some things, a precious few, are more valuable. After all, the greater the value attached to life, the greater the sacrifice in giving it up, and the greater the value attached to what is achieved in consequence. What is achieved in this case is the greatest conceivable exemplar of the examined life, ending with an immortal exhortation to virtue, once more underscoring the haunting theme of the *Apology* that the meaning of life is not a merely sentient existence but a moral one (28b–d, 38d–39b). This is the sense in which Socrates, accepting death as a consequence of right action, likens himself to Achilles avenging Patroclus (28b–d). Hence, according to the image Plato sees fit to leave us with, Socrates was no more motivated by the prospect of death than was Achilles, both having risked their lives for a specific cause, and neither having pursued their respective causes merely as a self-serving opportunity to die honorably, with personal advantage of any kind, if sought at all, always subordinated to moral responsibility.

Against all this, against, that is, any sort of interpretation attributing intentional failure to Socrates, a more positive perspective depicting him as having tried his best to avoid conviction is gaining popularity. The most fervent advocates of this view are Brickhouse and Smith (1989, 2002, 2004). Rejecting any reading that may be classified under the generic notion that Socrates pursued conviction or deliberately failed to achieve acquittal, they contend that the philosopher was after acquittal all along.

Given that the natural presumption for any defendant in any trial is to work toward acquittal, the burden of proof in the debate surrounding the approach of Socrates is on those who deny that he did his best to escape conviction. On this basis, the skeptic is obligated to present, not merely random bits of evidence against the natural presumption, but a coherent interpretation of the entire trial preferably in the greater context in which it takes place, that is consistent with deliberate failure. However, the scholarly history of the event, or rather, of its records, has entertained the possibility of deliberate failure for so long that what may ordinarily be expected and accepted as a matter of course now seems to require proof.

Possibly the greatest evidence of the sincerity of the effort by Socrates is his expression of frustration with the length of time available to try a capital case (37a–b). Confident that he could have convinced the jury of his innocence had he simply had more time to defend himself, Socrates seems as far from courting conviction as conceivable. This attitude alone should suffice to keep the burden of proof on the side of the skeptic. Yet the text affords opportunities for the skeptic to build a case as well, sometimes with points specific and significant enough to shift the burden of proof or at least to demand a serious response. What Brickhouse and Smith have brought to this balance is nothing short of an exhaustive reassessment of the historical, logical, and dramatic evidence, introducing fresh perspectives on familiar considerations, and bringing to light many that were overlooked or forgotten. They have opened up the most extensive and fruitful platform dedicated to the discussion of this topic in the history of philosophy, including not only the development of arguments and the refutation of opposing viewpoints, but the compilation of an annotated repository of ancient sources underlying and sustaining the debate (Brickhouse and Smith, 2002).

Their contribution is best understood in evolutionary rather than revolutionary terms. The perspective they champion is not a revolution in the history of scholarship on the subject but the highest point of evolution in the development of an outlook taking Socrates to be partly responsible for his own death though wholly blameless in connection with it. This is the outlook that Socrates is mechanically responsible for his own death, to wit, as a catalytic agent in the causal process culminating in his execution, but free of blame as a moral agent bound by the truth and loyal to the dictates of justice. Could he have done more to achieve acquittal? Yes, no holds barred, he could have easily avoided conviction. Did he do everything possible without violating universal moral principles? Again, the answer is affirmative, perhaps requiring argument, but commonly recognized even by critics, especially those bemoaning the moral choices determining the outcome of the trial. The intersection of the two answers may safely be considered the standard view, the outgrowth of an approach under scholarly development in a dialectical process extending at least between Grote (1850) and Allen (1984) and finding its best expression in Brickhouse and Smith (1989, 2002, 2004). To be entirely accurate, this is not necessarily the standard view overall but the definitive route to a positive reading of the trial performance of Socrates. In other words, the sense in declaring this the standard view is not to prejudge the general issue in the best possible light for Socrates, but to mark out the common ground among interpretations already favorable to Socrates, whether or not the opposite perspective finds or deserves greater support.

Brickhouse and Smith did not invent this approach, but they may well be credited with having perfected it. In its most basic formulation, this is the promotion of a Socrates pursuing acquittal rather than conviction, and doing his best rather than taking a dive, but stopping short of compromising his moral integrity. This is, at least in its essentials, the budding view that Brickhouse and Smith inherited from previous generations, aptly represented by Allen's (1984, p. 71) characterization of Socrates as pursuing the truth as opposed to either acquittal or conviction. To be sure, Allen's nominal denial of a pursuit of acquittal, along with that of conviction, flatly contradicts the defining position of Brickhouse and Smith, setting up acquittal as the clear target. However, the denial in question is not an absolute rejection but a subordination of the pursuit of acquittal to the pursuit of truth in accordance with the requirements of justice. Allen's position is not that Socrates does not desire acquittal at all, or that he does not rate it any higher than conviction, but that he does not pursue it over and above everything else. The denial is not that of acquittal as an end, but that of acquittal as the ultimate end, a position reserved for the truth. Nevertheless, even if only in the course of an unhappy turn of phrase, Allen throws the baby out with the bath water, whereas Brickhouse and Smith never let go, grooming the neonatal progeny of previous generations well into maturity.

The philosophical distance between Allen, as a representative of a developing paradigm, and Brickhouse and Smith, as contributing beneficiaries, is dwarfed by the common ground between them. Mutual coexistence, possibly with some refinement and even correction on either side, is a more profitable prospect than wholesale rejection, not specifically for one approach or the other, but for progress in the right direction. The unifying pattern, then, may be characterized as a perception of Socrates in sincere commitment to a proper defense, namely, one geared toward acquittal, within the bounds of reason and morality. The shared motivational template is a drive to avoid conviction by any means except those that might require the distortion of the truth or otherwise place the agent in transgression of the principles of justice or in violation of other ethical standards. From this frame of reference, denying intentional failure, as do Brickhouse and Smith, and recognizing restrictions on a serious attempt, as do their predecessors, need not be at odds with each other.

The primary difference that sets Brickhouse and Smith apart from previous contributors to the project in progress is in the interpretation of the limitations imposed on the defense by reason and morality. Brickhouse and Smith do not count compliance with rational and moral constraints as an instance of Socrates not doing his best to achieve acquittal. Their conception of Socrates doing his best internalizes all such restrictions, so that any move, or the absence of such, to avoid violating the requirements of truth and justice is still a part of an earnest effort in full force. Their predecessors, or, perhaps more accurately, the account above of the general position represented by their predecessors, maintain a separate focus on the drive toward acquittal, on the one hand, and any rational and moral restrictions on that drive, on the other, so that a conscious effort to keep the defense on the path of truth and morality constitutes a type of restriction on the pursuit of acquittal. Thus, the restriction that is part of the central conception under one interpretation is external to it in the other, both otherwise acknowledging the same effort within the same limits. Indeed, Brickhouse and Smith (1989, pp. 41–47, 210) themselves recognize this as a point of convergence rather than divergence.

The broader debate unites Brickhouse and Smith with their predecessors, together representing a more inspiring coalition against critics accusing Socrates of intentional failure with a selfish motive, as in Xenophon's reading of premature euthanasia, or of antagonistic choices for ignoble reasons, say, haughtiness out of excessive pride, or of an ill-conceived martyrdom undertaken exclusively in the promotion of ideals, for example, the glorification of philosophy, which, if a worthy vocation in the first place, should not require gimmicks for appreciation.

That debate produces a plethora of disagreement, but the specific points of contention are reducible to a single theme: an antagonistically unconventional defense by a pompous maverick with a penchant for irony. Perhaps this characterization is conceptually too busy to constitute an indivisible whole, but it still captures the spirit of critical frustration present in any negative reception of the defense.

Among the particular issues, the most popular are those related to the counterproposal. Like Grote (1850, p. 483), critics tend to find the death sentence even more avoidable than the verdict of guilt preceding it. Already discussed at length, the inflammatory role assigned to Socrates in this regard comprises three layers of provocation:

- the allegedly offensive prefatory affirmation of reward rather than punishment as the most fitting return for the deeds laid out in the indictment;
- the purportedly insulting inadequacy of the fine of 100 drachmas initially put forth as a counterpenalty Socrates could afford on his own;
- the supposed insufficiency of the final offer of a counterpenalty of 3,000 drachmas to be financed by friends.

While all three layers receive ample attention from the critics, one feature of their collective presence often goes unnoticed, at least by the critics focused exclusively on their distributive implications. Indeed, each of these layers, as a distinct episode of antagonism, is at least superficially consistent with the semblance of a desire for conviction, but all of them together are in such genuine contradiction, with one another and with the pursuit of conviction, that they collapse under their own weight, that is, as evidence of a conscious attempt to secure conviction. The reason for the collective failure is that each episode seems far more apposite to an intention to offend than the one coming after it in the linear progression of the text. In other words, having taken the first step, Socrates would be adding nothing to the ostensible insult, in fact, working in the opposite direction, by relaxing his position from a demand for a reward to the acceptance of a light penalty, and moving even further in the wrong direction by subsequently embracing a thirtyfold increase in the amount of the fine. Each step waters down the putative insult, indistinguishable at the end from a genuine penalty. A strategy of provoking the jury into returning a guilty verdict would have been better served by stopping after the first step, or, failing that, at least after the second. The continuation to the end would seem to impede rather than facilitate the attainment of such a goal, at least through this strategy.

The three layers in fact represent two complaints, one concerning the way the offer is handled, the other, the amount proposed. The section (§ 5.8) of this chapter dedicated exclusively to the counterproposal is a fairly comprehensive dissection of the merits of the case in this regard. Nothing may fruitfully be added to the discussion there of the financial aspect of the counterpenalty except that any appeal to a quantitative deficiency now requires a direct refutation of Brickhouse and Smith (1989, pp. 225–230; 2004, pp. 166–169). Admittedly, on the issue of presentation, it is still difficult not to side with Grote (1850, p. 485), who claims that the counterpenalty would have been accepted had Socrates just offered it without the spirited speech preceding it. This is essentially the flip side of the foregoing analysis of the self-defeating nature of progressively weaker insults in the episodic development of the counterproposal from reward to penalty. The critic would be no less justified in asking, from the opposite perspective, whether the aim of acquittal would not have been better served by skipping the first two steps, to start and end with a satisfactory counterpenalty, or, failing that, at least skipping the first step, to start with an affordable one.

This, however, is the type of consideration that straddles a slippery slope between requiring Socrates to do his best to achieve acquittal and requiring him to do absolutely anything toward that end. His best, being bound by his sense of right and wrong, need not always converge with the path of least resistance toward acquittal. We cannot rightfully censure Socrates for maintaining the same high ideals for which we applaud him. Offering the counterpenalty in silence might possibly have met with a happy reception, but such a silence might also have been in conflict with his heavenly duty (28e–30c) as a moral, social, and political gadfly (30e–31c) forcing Athenians to think carefully about what they are doing. Admitting of no proof, at least none as convincing as an interview with Socrates, this scenario is not necessarily an unassailable interpretation of the way he handled the counterproposal, but the possibility alone is sufficient to vitiate the claim that he was out to offend the jury for no good reason. The constraints on a gadfly with a heavenly mandate must be kept in mind as an overarching frame of interpretation in evaluating any assumption or objection that this or that move could have been handled differently to please or appease the crowd. This is the thrust of the portrayal of Socrates as a doctor being prosecuted by a pastry chef before a jury of children (*Gorgias* 521d–e).

Stripped of the support of passages related to the counterproposal, and ignoring, for the sake of brevity, a few other references with comparably fragile relevance, the evidence against a sincere effort toward acquittal boils down to a general attitude. What remains at most is nothing but an amorphous dissatisfaction with method and style. Without a doubt, the approach is more confrontational than might be recommended for an unbridled quest for acquittal. For example, it is clearly antagonistic enough to elicit on several occasions specific reactions in protest from the audience (20e, 21a, 27b, 30c). But an accurate assessment of what goes wrong requires separating form from content.

We already know from independent records on the prevailing standards of forensic oratory that the speech was appropriate in form (§ 5.1.5). We know, therefore, not to take Socrates at his word in his opening claim to incompetence in public speaking and to ignorance of juridical rhetorical techniques (17a–18a). While disclaimers to excellence, or even to adequacy, and confessions of inadequacy are familiar instantiations of Socratic irony, this particular example finds a broader origin as the standard opening address employed by defendants appearing in court. (See, for example, Guthrie, 1975, pp. 74–80; Allen, 1984, pp. 61–78.) Dissociating oneself from the relevant skills and knowledge seems to have been common rhetorical practice, not reducible in this case to Socratic irony, which may, of course, not be denied, with any certainty, to be present simply because it is overshadowed under the prevailing circumstances. Hence, in addition to independent confirmation through literary evidence that the text of the *Apology* conforms to the standards of forensic oratory current at the time, we have two separate explanations, both satisfactory, for the opening remarks to the contrary. If the speech is structurally acceptable, then the deficiency, that is, the possible locus of impropriety, must be sought in its contents.

Conformity with the prevailing standards of forensic oratory is consistent with a dedication to acquittal, but the mechanical fit alone is not conclusive evidence against an intention to fail. For one thing, credit for the fit cannot be assigned to Socrates with any greater certainty than it can be to Plato. Moreover, even if Socrates were singularly commendable for the formulaic performance, he could not with any degree of certainty be absolved, on this basis alone, of deliberate failure, which is possible even when playing by the rules. Finally, an appeal to the technical features of the defense, namely, the formal observation of convention, as evidence of a genuine effort to avoid conviction contradicts a history of interpretation blending admiration and admonishment in regard to the blatant antagonism toward everyone involved with the case. This is the standard view, represented, for example, by Taylor (1960, pp. 156–167), who finds the words and demeanor of Socrates on trial incongruous with what may rightly be expected of a defendant seeking acquittal, noting that the defense, demonstrating a confrontational and condescending style, has been perceived "from the time of Xenophon onward to be something very much like an avowal of guilt" (Taylor, 1960, p. 157).

Indeed, the critique of Socrates as validating the allegations through the very defense expected to refute them, at least insofar as he there proves himself a pugnacious troublemaker, finds prominent historical support. For example, Epictetus attests to his being too ornery for his own good, with a belligerence inimical to exoneration:

> Why, do you think that if Socrates had concerned himself about externals, he would have said, when he appeared at his trial, "Anytus and Melitus may indeed kill me, but hurt me they cannot"? Was he so foolish as not to see that this way did not lead to safety, but the contrary? What, then, is the reason that he not only disregarded, but defied, his judges? [Epictetus: *Discourses* 2.2.13–15; Higginson translation]

He considers the truculence of Socrates to be especially conspicuous in his open refusal to beg (34b–35d):

> Be content not to entreat; yet do not proclaim that you will not entreat; unless it be a proper time to provoke the judges designedly, as in the case of Socrates. [Epictetus: *Discourses* 2.2.18; Higginson translation]

The Socratic refusal to beg actually engenders scholarly debate at deeper levels than that recognized in the abbreviated reference of Epictetus. The apparent problem is that Socrates refuses to follow the common procedure of begging for forgiveness. However, this is complicated by the fact that the refusal to follow suit in this practice seems to have been nearly as common as the convention thereby rejected. In fact, the refusal to beg for forgiveness was so strategic a device in forensic oratory as to constitute a textbook exercise of rhetorical and sophistic argument, as in the *Palamedes* of Gorgias (Guthrie, 1975, p. 74). Hence, while begging was common in the trials of the time, a refusal to beg was, done right, not a put-off but a clever rhetorical ploy, but apparently not in the haughty manner Socrates handles it. Epictetus seems to have missed the implications of a deeper layer in the debate, though his assessment could conceivably have been anchored precisely to this deeper layer, accusing Socrates, not merely of an open refusal to beg, but of an improper one.

Either way, the Socratic refusal to beg is not a pointless display of pride. It is not merely a recalcitrant refusal to participate in a tradition of slavish subservience to authority. It is, on the contrary, a demonstration (35b–c) of another kind of slavishness, a slavish obedience to the rules, partly to those of logic, making appeals to emotion irrelevant, and partly to those of ethics, making supplication wrong, both in its initiation and in its acceptance. Indeed, Socrates's refusal to beg is commonly acknowledged, for example, by Taylor (1960, p. 166) and by Allen (1984, p. 71), as having been motivated purely by a desire to avoid undermining the function of the court. Even so, the point could have been made more tactfully, or, better yet, not at all, than one that is open to misinterpretation as a defiant stance by a proven social misfit and suspected enemy of the state.

Quintilian, an older contemporary of Epictetus, forcefully brings out the importance of the interplay between form and content:

> It cannot be too earnestly inculcated that no one can speak with aptitude and propriety unless he considers not only what is to the purpose, but also what is becoming. Nor am I ignorant that these two qualities of speaking are mostly united, for what is becoming is generally to the purpose. Nor are the minds of judges conciliated by anything more than by the observance of decorum, or alienated by anything more than by violations of it. 9. The two, however, are sometimes at variance, and, when they are so, that which is becoming will be allowed the preference over that which is merely serviceable, for who does not know that nothing would have been of greater service in procuring an acquittal for Socrates than the adoption of the ordinary mode of defense on trials, the conciliation of the favor of the judges by a submissive address to them, and the careful refutation of the charges brought against him? [Quintilian: *Institutio Oratoria* 11.1.8–9; Watson translation]

Quintilian's focus is on the relationship between effectiveness and propriety in serving a given oratorical aim. This also speaks to the mismatch between form and content in the *Apology*, possibly revealing problems beyond antagonism. Put simply, by Quintilian's standards, the defense may have been not merely irreverent but also irrelevant. This is the possibility that Socrates fails not only to disprove but, more fundamentally, even to confront the formal charges as stated in the indictment, evidently in a rush instead to address old accusers and tackle perennial accusations. Strictly speaking, the theme of a deficiency in relevance is only implicit in Quintilian, who requires it without specifically declaring it absent in the Socratic case. Yet the emphasis on the importance of relevance comes in the same sentence pointing out the shortcomings of the defense, thus sanctioning a connection, if not exposing one already implicit there.

Allen (1984, pp. 61–78) picks up the theme of relevance in his own discussion of a general discrepancy between form and content. The problem is a basic functional contradiction of the kind that may exist in using iambic pentameter to carry out natural deduction in a formal system, or the notation of symbolic logic to express "emotion recollected in tranquility" à la Wordsworth. Restated in terms of the defense, then, the problem is in employing the proper rhetorical method while failing to supply it with the proper rhetoric:

> Far from attempting to prove the charges in the indictment false, it [Socrates's speech] does not even deny them. There is, then, gross incongruity between the form of the speech and its function: whereas in diction and structure it is a superb example of forensic rhetoric, in method and aim, at least in the ordinary sense, it is not rhetorical at all. [Allen, 1984, p. 64]

The tension between form and content is so strong as to undermine the entire defense, with Allen (1984, p. 66) contending that Socrates would have fared much better if he had just stuck to his promise of delivering an ordinary speech in plain language. The point is not merely that Socrates could have done better by toning down the open antagonism, but that he could have likewise improved his chances by adjusting the format. As it is, Allen (1984, p. 67) classifies the speech as rhetoric that is not rhetorical, by which he means speech that is not persuasive.

The complaint here is not that Socrates fails to win arguments, but that he fails to win the jury over. One of the greatest regrets of commentators, especially earlier ones, is Socrates's reported refusal to accept outside help to improve his prospects in court. Thus, a point of contention unrelated to the text but pertinent to the context is whether Socrates declined the *pro bono* services of Lysias, a professional speechwriter specializing in forensic oratory. As the story goes, Lysias is supposed to have prepared a speech for Socrates, especially for his use at the trial, with the philosopher refusing to adopt it for his defense on the grounds that it was, despite being a good speech in itself, not suitable for him, presumably because it was more rhetorical than philosophical. This is not mentioned by Plato or Xenophon, but it is reported by Cicero (*De Oratore* 1.54, 1.231), Quintilian (*Institutio Oratoria* 2.15.30, 11.1.9), and Diogenes Laërtius (*Lives* 2.40–41). In modern times, Grote, among others, laments Socrates's refusal to use Lysias's speech:

> The rhetor Lysias is said to have sent to him a composed speech for his defense, which he declined to use, not thinking it suitable to his dignity. But such a man as Lysias would hardly compose what would lower the dignity even of the loftiest client, though he would look to the result also; nor is there any doubt that if Sokratês had pronounced it,—or even a much less able speech, if inoffensive,—he would have been acquitted. [Grote, 1850, p. 483]

The issue is difficult to judge. On the one hand, the anecdote is likely apocryphal, especially since Plato allocates considerable room in the *Phaedrus* to a recital (230e–234c) and critique (234c–237b) of another speech by Lysias, whether authentic or imagined. This suggests that Plato, having taken the trouble to examine a relatively trivial speech of Lysias, would have at least mentioned the existence of a speech of his in connection with such an important matter as the trial for the master's life, had Lysias really written and submitted such a speech for the occasion. On the other hand, Lysias's speech taken up in the *Phaedrus* receives such a scathing review from the dramatic Socrates as to give the historical Socrates ample reason to turn down an actual speech prepared by the same rhetorician on his behalf. The Socrates of the *Phaedrus* would not trust the words of Lysias to talk the village wino into having some more wine, let alone relying upon them to defend himself in a trial for his life. In fact, the choice in the *Phaedrus* of a critical focus on the oratorical skills of Lysias, where taking up the work of any other rhetorician would have served the dialogue just as well, may well be the dramatic justification of an actual rejection. This still leaves room for puzzlement as to why such a speech is not mentioned in the *Apology*, but its omission there does not preclude its existence, as Socrates or Plato or both may simply have seen no advantage in bringing it up, Socrates in his speech, and Plato in his account of it.

Whatever the answer, the speech is now lost, and has long been so. Given that Plato and Xenophon do not mention it in their respective versions of the defense, or anywhere else, and given further that Cicero, Quintilian, and Diogenes separately confirm its existence, the effort may have followed as opposed to preceding the historical trial, having resulted from inspiration by its outcome rather than motivated by a desire to preclude that outcome. In other words, the speech may possibly have emerged as a rhetorical exercise or a demonstration of oratorical prowess instead of an actual defense intended for use by Socrates in court. It might even have been conceived as a polemical undertaking to answer the charges in the *Accusation of Socrates* by Polycrates. A later scholiast, especially one sifting through references in the absence of the original, may quite conceivably have mistaken such a speech as one prepared in advance of the trial but declined by Socrates. Both scenarios are consistent with what we know of the relationship between Socrates and Lysias, men who were evidently bound in friendship extending to the entire family, as Plato takes care to illustrate by staging his masterpiece, the *Republic*, at the house of Polemarchus, the elder brother of Lysias, and in the presence of their father Cephalus and their brother Euthydemus. Hence, the leading hypotheses are both underdetermined by the evidence, making the speech just as likely to have been a timely forensic tool as a testimonial epideictic showcase.

The crucial factor here is not Socrates's refusal to use a speech prepared by Lysias, as, no doubt, he could have done well enough on his own, but his refusal to demean himself, debase the truth, and undermine justice with words, whether put together by him or by anyone else, that could have secured his acquittal. As Socrates himself notes, he was not convicted for a lack of arguments which would have persuaded the jury, but for a lack of effrontery and shamelessness (38d). He did not think it right to secure his life and freedom at any cost.

In the end, we are left with a choice rather than a proof in the matter of the fabled speech of Lysias. This is the same choice we face in the more general matter of assessing the effectiveness of Socrates's own defense and ascertaining the aim and motivation driving that defense. One option is to embrace a Socrates defending himself to the best of his ability within the bounds of reason and morality. Where this Socrates holds back, he does so either to maintain his integrity or to preserve that of the city, oblivious in the body of the jury to the moral quagmire represented by the legal proceedings. The other option, the only competing alternative, is to interpret the same instances of defensive restraint to be indicative of a deliberate aim to facilitate conviction, whether in the pursuit of martyrdom or for any other reason. Both the available evidence and the emerging storyline favor the first option. The second cannot conclusively be proven false, but it can sensibly be rejected in advocacy of the account making a better man and a better philosopher out of Socrates.

With regard to the outcome, this interpretation properly relocates the responsibility, both causal and moral, where it belongs, at the doorstep of the state. The effort to shift some of that responsibility to Socrates, though possibly inspired spontaneously by isolated passages with a potential for misunderstanding, is motivated at least partly by the frustration of efforts to put together a causally satisfactory explanation through the charges laid out in the indictment. The formal charges are simply not defined clearly enough to constitute in the mind of an impartial observer a sufficient reason to put someone to death. This naturally motivates a search for additional considerations to complete the picture. The choices made by Socrates may indeed have forced the issue, but this is more of a distraction than a discovery in the search for the critical factor missing in the recorded history of the trial. That factor is that the trial was a reaction to a political threat, not a response to a religious offense or a civil transgression.

The best expression of this remains the incisive account of Burnet (1914, pp. 180–192), reading between the lines of extant texts, and drawing on the known facts of the historical context, to bring out the full political urgency of the need to silence Socrates. Dating back at least as far as Xenophon, this is not a novel approach, but it finds its most compelling instantiation in Burnet. Nor is it an indulgently creative undertaking bounded only by the imagination but an analytic reconstruction faithful to the facts of the case, taking care to expose rather than ignore the prosecution's perspective. Burnet devotes meticulous attention to both of the formal allegations constituting the official indictment, in each case tracing the pretext to a genuine explanation pertaining to the same general phenomenon, in this way, explaining the charge of impiety, within the bounds of religion, and, the charge of corrupting the young, within the context of interaction with the young. On each count, he finds the indictment to be an outlet for veiled frustrations, otherwise held in check by the amnesty precluding the prosecution of transgressions committed prior to 403 BC:

- Religious: The religious component of the indictment is a cover for lingering suspicions against Socrates in connection with the implication of his most intimate associates, including Critias and Alcibiades, in investigations into the religious scandals of 415 BC, witnessing an outbreak of sacrilegious activity manifested separately as the profanation of the Eleusinian Mysteries and the mutilation of the statues of Hermes.

- Pedagogic: The pedagogic component, while intimately connected with the religious, at least in terms of a resentment of the influence of Socrates on the associates involved in the religious offenses, primarily concerns the development of youngsters in his inner circle into rabid oligarchs as opposed to adherents of democracy, or at least docile followers of it.

Thus, Socrates was guilty by association. The prime culprits were Critias, Charmides, and Alcibiades, the first two, his friends, at least in the sense of interactive acquaintance, and Plato's relatives, and, the last, his lover. Critias and Charmides were both members of the most reprehensible enemy of democracy, the Thirty Tyrants, Critias being one of its two leaders. Critias had, in addition, been investigated albeit eventually exonerated in connection with the events of 415 BC, as well as allegedly participating in the oligarchic revolution of 411 BC, setting up the short-lived government of the Four Hundred. Alcibiades was a convicted offender in the sacrilegious activities of 415 BC, a confirmed traitor defecting to Sparta in the same year to avoid prosecution, and an open supporter of any antidemocratic movement, including the revolution of 411 BC.

All three were dead by the time of the indictment against Socrates. Despite each having met a violent death, they can also be said to have escaped justice, in the sense that none of them ever stood trial for the allegations on record. Socrates, of course, was not being prosecuted in their place, but he was clearly being persecuted as providing the chief or seminal inspiration for them and for all things antidemocratic. His trial in 399 BC coincided with the completion of a grand undertaking in legislative reform, including the exhaustive revision and codification of the laws in conformity with the amnesty of 403 BC. Whether or not he taught tyranny and treachery, the most notable of tyrants and traitors emerged from his inner circle. The corresponding evidence may not have been actionable, and, the actionable evidence, not sufficient, but his antidemocratic credentials were impressive enough for successful prosecution on trumped-up charges bypassing the amnesty.

The two parts of the formal indictment were in fact generic accusations, the religious component representing stock charges against philosophers (23d), as in the prosecution of Anaxagoras (26d), and the pedagogic component adding only the exhortation of others to behave in the same way (26b). The challenge on religious grounds was reserved for philosophers, and, the one on pedagogic grounds, for Sophists, with Socrates being held accountable in both roles for good measure. Ostensibly attempting to defend its religion and protect its children, Athens was in fact doing no more or no less than silencing dissent.

The effort must have drawn strength from the perverted reflection of his thoughts in the comic imagery of Aristophanes. Despite basically sound attempts to discount the influence of the travesty in Aristophanes, and to clear the intentions of the poet, placing him on good terms with Socrates, repeated exposure is sure to have had a cumulative effect on public opinion. To cite just one example, the caricature must have been too close for comfort in the image of a Socrates dethroning Zeus to make room for Vortex (Aristophanes: *Clouds* 365–385), a prime example, if there ever was one, of rejecting the gods recognized by the state in favor of new ones. Whatever the intention, no better support can be conceived for the prosecution's efforts to present Socrates as an icon of what went wrong with Athens. Already judged an enemy of the state, he thus takes the stand as the target of misdirected retaliation against the painful disintegration of the Golden

Age in a protracted state of war transforming the city from the dominant force in the region into an economic and social disaster zone under the dominion of its greatest nemesis.

None of this is verbalized in the trial, neither by the prosecution nor by the defense. The prosecution is bound by the amnesty, the defense, by the reticence of the prosecution, with the resultant absence of specificity keeping Socrates from responding to charges that are not on the table, except in the form of a general response to "old accusers." The silence of Socrates may arguably also be interpreted in terms of personal ethical standards preventing him from going into details suppressed in observation of the amnesty, with the implication that invoking such details would be tantamount to dragging the proceedings into a prohibited realm of debate and thereby forcing the court to violate the amnesty. The political overtones of the *Apology* may not be sufficiently revealing, but this is merely the reflection of scholarly scruples regarding the introduction of elements that were not already in the trial. The overt and covert operations against Socrates are so divergent as to preclude the possibility of effective treatment within the same work, thus ruling out the possibility of exposing the actual case underlying the bogus charges from within a purportedly faithful reproduction of the speech at the historical trial. Plato reveals the political connection elsewhere, primarily through allusions in the *Meno* (90a–95a, especially 94e–95a, 99e–100c) and the *Gorgias* (485e–486d, 521a–522e), as openly as must have been possible at the time, especially for a disciple of Socrates. This still may not suffice as proof that Socrates was tried unjustly, but it goes a long way toward showing that Plato believed so.

5.12. General Evaluation

Clearly, Socrates was causally effective, at least as a catalyst, in the outcome of the trial. Yet his role, whether in action or inaction, was determined by a deference to reason and morality. As if to prove his reputation as the master of irony, the man even died in tension between thought and action. Forever denying that virtue could be taught, he was condemned and executed for teaching the opposite.

Perhaps the greatest irony, possibly due at least as much to Plato as to Socrates, is a religious reference at the end of all four of the dialogues connected with the trial and execution of Socrates, as if to deny the allegation of impiety symbolically as well as rationally, hence, fully and vigorously. Some of these endings may at the same time be interpreted as a rejection of the pedagogical charge as well, at least in the sense of showing a predisposition to learn rather than teach, and to follow rather than lead.

- The *Euthyphro* (15e–16a) ends with Socrates begging Euthyphro to teach him about piety and impiety, thus providing the symbolism to reject the pedagogical as well as the religious charge, by placing Socrates in the position of a student as opposed to a teacher, and by giving him the will to understand rather than violate the requirements of piety.

- The *Apology* (42a) ends with express deference to the wisdom of God (with the context pointing to Apollo), effectively distancing Socrates from both pedagogical credentials and heretical tendencies. It also opens with a confession of ignorance ("I don't know"), though anchored to a specific context, in the very first sentence (17a). This means that the dialogue opens with Socrates admitting that he does not know and ends with Socrates affirming that only God knows, ironic enough for someone just convicted of heresy and sentenced to death for it, not to say anything of the implicit absurdity of teaching without knowing.

- The *Crito* (54e) also ends in deference to the judgment of God, this time in demonstration of the convergence of the decision of Socrates with the will of God. The context here is justification for staying put in prison. At least as the dramatic conclusion of the dialogue, the ultimate reason offered for the decision not to injure the laws and the city by escaping from prison turns out to be, after all is said and done, simply that God is leading in that direction.

- The *Phaedo* (118a) ends with a reference to a specific god, Asclepius, as Socrates names this divinity in asking Crito not to neglect their debt of sacrifice to him upon the death of Socrates. Asclepius is the god of medicine and healing and a son of Apollo. The fact that the dying thoughts of Socrates run to a god, one recognized by the state, seems telling enough in regard to where he stands on religion.

These are powerful endings, immersed in symbolism. The allegorical denial of the pedagogical component of the indictment may not come out as clearly as the contradiction of the religious component, but this is not important since the case stands or falls with the latter (*Euthyphro* 3a–b, *Apology* 26b). Strictly speaking, the allegations need not be undermined severally for both to fall because, by the admission of the prosecution (*Apology* 26b), the charge of heresy constitutes the grounds for the charge of corrupting the youth. One who is not a heretic is unlikely to make heretics out of others. Complementing this conclusion, one who claims no knowledge promises nothing to be learned, not even corruption.

Crito: Broad Outline

- Prologue (43a–44b)
  - Time and attitude: Crito bribes or finesses his way in before dawn (43a)
  - Contrast: Crito miserable vs. Socrates peaceful (43b)
  - Reason for early arrival: bring bad news (43c)
  - Delos mission: execution awaiting boat's return from Delos (43c–d)
  - Dream: death in three days (44a–b)

- Crito: escape perspective (44b–46a)
  - Proposal for a prison break (44b–d)
  - Arguments in favor of escape (44e–46a)
    - Consequentialist arguments (44e–45c)
    - Deontological arguments (45c–d)
    - Summation (45e–46a)

- Socrates: analytic assessment (46b–49e)
  - Introduction: importance of rational justification (46b–c)
  - Principle #1: superiority of expert over public opinion (46c–48b)
  - Principle #2: supremacy of morality: good-right-just (48b)
  - Methodological design: deontological focus on justice (48b–49a)
  - Guiding dictum (corollary of principles): avoid injustice at all costs (49a–e)
    - Core dictum: never deliberately act unjustly (49a)
    - Clarification: no exceptions, not even retaliation (49b)
    - Amendment: neither act unjustly nor injure anyone (49c–e)
  - Application of guiding dictum to proposal for a prison break (49e–54d)
    - Reformulation of the problem in terms of a social contract (49e–50a)
    - Personification of the Laws of Athens for greater clarity (50a–54d)

- Laws of Athens: extended application (50a–54d)
  - Introduction: relevance of the social contract (50a–e)
  - Speech #1: persuade or obey (50e–51c)
  - Speech #2: love it or leave it (51c–52d)
    - Speech #2a: staying in a city implies consent to its laws (51c–52a)
    - Speech #2b: Socrates in particular demonstrates such consent (52a–d)
  - Speech #3: overview of adversities attached to escape (52d–54d)

- Epilogue (54d–e)
  - Allegorical summation (54d)
  - Deference to the leadership of God (54e)

Six

CRITO

6.1. Dramatis Personae

Plato's *Crito* is a dialogue between Socrates and Crito. The Laws of Athens, personified by Socrates with a substantial speaking part, may be considered a third character, though this is a matter of interpretation, and one that is not of paramount importance, especially since the lines are there even if the identity or ontological status of the speaker is in dispute. The eponymous character is one of Socrates's best friends. He is a wealthy Athenian from the deme of Alopece, the hometown of Socrates. The two men are about the same age and have known each other all their lives (*Apology* 33d–e, *Crito* 43b). Being natives of the same deme, they also belong to the same tribe, Antiochis (*Apology* 32b), named after Antiochus, son of Heracles by Meda. In addition to his role in the dialogue named after himself, Crito has speaking parts in the *Phaedo* and the *Euthydemus*, and he is mentioned twice in the *Apology* (33d–e, 38b) in acknowledgement of his presence at the trial.

We know that Crito owes his wealth to farming and livestock, particularly sheep, but we do not know much about the man personally (*Euthydemus* 291e, 304c; Xenophon: *Memorabilia* 2.9.1–4). He comes across as something of a scholar in the treatment of Diogenes Laërtius (*Lives* 2.121), who claims Crito to be the author of seventeen dialogues. Although Diogenes even names each of these dialogues, all reportedly available to him in a single volume, Crito's academic achievements cannot be confirmed elsewhere, as all such references are parasitic on and reducible to this solitary record in Diogenes. No support is to be found in Plato or Xenophon, who are decidedly silent on the intellectual prowess of Crito.

In fact, both Plato and Xenophon portray him as a friend of Socrates as opposed to a fellow philosopher. This could possibly be interpreted as a choice in emphasis that merely ignores or excludes rather than denies or contradicts his other attributes in the same way that introducing John Stuart Mill as the son of the philosopher James Mill leaves open the possibility that the son is also a philosopher. Accordingly, it could conceivably be argued that Crito's Platonic roles happen to reflect the nature and strength of his friendship with Socrates, remaining silent on rather than opposed to whatever else may be said of the man. Yet independent confirmation is what makes the difference in the case of the Mills. Just as John Stuart Mill's identity as a philosopher is no secret, we might reasonably expect the author of seventeen dialogues to be acknowledged by more than one source in nearly two-and-a-half millennia.

Plato should have been among the first and most eager to note the erudition of the master's best friend. On the contrary, especially in Plato, Crito's most notable parts are episodes demonstrating the extent of his friendship with Socrates as opposed to the extent of his wit and wisdom. He is a friend of distinction, claiming and offering the utmost intimacy grounded in a closely shared history with mutual satisfaction. He is like a member of the family as he intervenes to augment and finance the counterpenalty at the trial (*Apology* 33d–e), and even more so as he closes the mouth and eyes of the philosopher's dead body after the execution (*Phaedo* 118a).

This is not to say that Crito's being a good friend to Socrates rules out the possibility of his being a scholar at the same time. Actually, quite the opposite might be expected, namely, that a good friend of Socrates would be a philosopher as well. Yet the Platonic and even the Xenophontic image we have of Crito is that of a good friend who is never seen philosophizing with Socrates. He stands out as a rare example of a recurring character engaging Socrates in extended conversation outside philosophy. This comes out most emphatically in the *Phaedo*, where his participation is exclusively in an administrative role, as he assumes a position of authority and leadership regarding the management of the schedule for the day while steering clear of intellectual discourse with anyone in the gathering. What makes the contrast particularly conspicuous is that he avoids philosophy despite the emergence and development of a gripping discussion on the immortality of the soul, which he repeatedly interrupts for routine matters but not once for a material contribution (*Phaedo* 60a–b, 63d–e, 115b–117a, 118a). He is like the master of ceremonies, organizing the event and directing the star performer, but otherwise not participating himself. Even in the *Crito*, he is more of a confidant than a debate partner.

Crito is also the father of Critobulus, a young follower of Socrates. While the relationship between Critobulus and Socrates is not entirely clear, the possibility of some sort of discipleship is suggested by the fact that Socrates names him among the young admirers whose testimonies would be pertinent to the charge of corrupting the youth (*Apology* 33d–e). However that may be, like his father, Critobulus is present both at the trial and at the prison on the last day of Socrates, whether to honor a teacher, a friend of the family, or both at once. All told, Critobulus is mentioned twice in the *Apology* (33d–e, 38b), once in the *Phaedo* (59b), and twice in the *Euthydemus* (271b, 306d), never with a speaking part.

6.2. Dramatic Setting

The entire dialogue takes place in the cell of Socrates at the Athenian prison where the condemned philosopher awaits execution. Technically, the setting is a jail as opposed to a prison, since, having been sentenced to death rather than imprisonment, Socrates is merely being held in custody there until the sentence can be carried out. Confinement is not part of his punishment but a means of assuring that he will be available for that punishment. With the difference thus understood, any reference here to prison should be interpreted as a variation serving a stream of consciousness rather than challenging the distinction.

At any rate, the distinction is not as crucial to ancient Athens as it is to penal systems prevalent in the world today. If the ancient and modern settings were comparable in all the relevant details, having been charged with capital offenses, Socrates should have been arrested and placed in jail prior to his court appearance, not just between sentencing and execution. As it is, he was not escorted from a holding cell in jail to the courthouse where the trial was held. He presumably simply walked there from his house. Thus, with neither jail nor bail preceding the trial, fine distinctions between jail and prison after the trial may be a bit pedantic. Even so, just to respect the conceptual distinction, all references here to prison are intended merely to designate the place where Socrates was confined between the trial and the execution, and not to imply anything about the legal and regulatory intricacies.

The building is no longer standing; nor is the exact location known with certainty. However, archaeological studies on the evidence of recent excavations suggest that it was situated just outside the Agora, about 100 meters southwest of the Heliaia, the law court where the trial is believed to have taken place (Vanderpool, 1980; Camp, 1992, pp. 107–108, 113–116; Freely, 2004, pp. 142–145).

Having been sentenced to death, as described in the *Apology*, Socrates is portrayed here on death row as he lives out the remainder of his days before the execution. The trial has coincided with a traditional naval mission from Athens to the island of Delos in honor of an ancient votive offering to Apollo for delivery from disaster, specifically, Cretan oppression symbolized by the Minotaur in the Labyrinth of Daedalus. Custom forbids bloodshed throughout the duration of the mission, also featured in the *Phaedo* (58a–c), and thus prevents the execution from being carried out before the return of the boat.

Meanwhile, Socrates is allowed visitors during the day. Crito is on one of his numerous visits. Arriving before the break of dawn, he has bribed his way in, anxious for the sagely convict to wake up, but careful not to disturb his sleep. His anxiety regarding the fate of Socrates is at a peak, with the imminent return of the boat from Delos signaling that time is almost up.

A caveat is in order regarding a particular subtlety dividing scholars in the characterization thus far. Although the prison guard lets Crito in prior to the start of regular visitation, and although this is mentioned in the same breath as the guard's being in Crito's debt in some unspecified manner, the combination of these facts does not necessarily point to outright bribery, which, going strictly by the text (43a), remains a possibility but not a certainty. Burnet (1924, p. 255, n. 43a8), for one, expresses confidence that the warder is in Crito's debt in connection with a prior incident having nothing to do with Crito's visit on the dramatic date of the dialogue, and he warns, on this basis, that the said obligation cannot sensibly be construed as a tip or bribe.

To be sure, the bare text neither confirms nor contradicts bribery. However, reading Crito as bribing his way in enriches the dialogue artistically as it sets up a propensity for breaking rules, minor though they may be. This, in turn, serves as the first dramatic step in a process of character development juxtaposing Socrates with an associate who does not shrink from breaking the law. Surely, the irregularity of Crito's early admission must be granted even if the corresponding passage does not bear out an instance of bribery proper, for it is the guard's prior debt, after all, that secures Crito an audience with Socrates outside regular visiting hours.

This means that the rules were broken for no other reason than a relationship of mutual interest between Crito and the guard, played out as favoritism grounded in a standing obligation. Put simply, the guard owed Crito a favor, which may or may not have been retired in full through the granting of illicit entry into the building, but was indubitably responsible for it. Perhaps Crito cannot be said, with textual certainty, to have bribed his way in, but it is clear that he finessed or finagled his way in.

Indeed, quite consistently with the character formation in progress, Crito and a few other friends have together made arrangements to bust Socrates out of prison and to see him safely out of the city. The people mentioned in this regard include, among an unnamed multitude, Simmias and Cebes, Theban friends who have arrived with a view to financing the operation. Neither is present at the scene, but both are close at hand.

Simmias is also mentioned in the *Phaedrus* (242b), but his most memorable appearance is in the *Phaedo*, where he is one of the two central interlocutors engaging Socrates in a discussion on the immortality of the soul. He is responsible for the attunement analogy (*Phaedo* 85e–86d), likening the presence of the soul in the body to that of the attunement in a lyre, both perishing immediately upon the destruction of its physical counterpart.

Cebes is the other main interlocutor in the *Phaedo*, where his mark of distinction is the weaver analogy (*Phaedo* 87a–88b), submitting the weaver of cloaks as the paradigm for the reincarnating soul, using up and going through many bodies in succession but perishing before the final one, just as the weaver weaves many cloaks but expires before his last.

Diogenes Laërtius attributes twenty-three dialogues to Simmias (*Lives* 2.124) and three to Cebes (*Lives* 2.125). All are lost except one, which turns out to have been erroneously attributed to Cebes. Nevertheless, unlike the case with Crito, these are credible claims, consistent with the portrayal of these characters by Plato, and not contradicting the occasional reference by Xenophon. All three people named in connection with the escape plans are confirmed by Xenophon (*Memorabilia* 1.2.48) to be intimate friends of Socrates.

Everything is in place for the jailbreak: Connections have been made, and funding has been guaranteed, possibly even oversubscribed, by loyal friends. All that is required is the assent of Socrates.

Crito acts as spokesperson for the inner circle, attempting to persuade Socrates to flee while he can. His role in a leadership position is fitting, given the history of his relationship with the philosopher, but it seems to contradict his earlier pledge that Socrates would not flee Athens between the trial and the execution. An often ignored passage in the *Phaedo* (115d–e) indicates that, immediately upon the conclusion of the trial, Crito had given his assurance that Socrates does not constitute a flight risk. This appears to be an attempt to spare the philosopher the inconvenience of incarceration before his execution.

An alternative interpretation, for example, by Archer-Hind (1894, p. 141, n. 115d18), is that the passage in question is a simple reminder of Crito's role in the trial as one of the four people increasing the amount of the counterpenalty and pledging to stand surety for it, or, in other words, that the passage in the *Phaedo* (115d–e) recalls one in the *Apology* (38b) rather than introducing an independent dramatic element not mentioned elsewhere.

Yet reading the passage as introducing a new fact makes better sense of it, if only because the reference fully ignores the counterpenalty as well as the other three people involved in the pledge. Burnet (1911, p. 143, n. 115d7; 1924, p. 252), Hackforth (1955, p. 187, n. 3), and Rowe (1993, p. 292, n. 115d7–8) take the passage as expanding our dramatic horizons with fresh information.

Either way, the conflict with the *Crito* is only apparent because the earlier pledge, regardless of the interpretation chosen, refers to an offer that was rejected, as evidenced by the fact that the augmented monetary fine was not the penalty imposed in the end, which voids any offers made or implied by the defense in connection with the counterproposal, and further by the fact that Socrates was not spared a stay in prison, which voids any promises Crito may have made outside the context of the counterproposal. Neither version of the pledge can sensibly be understood in unilateral terms, both versions clearly constituting contractual offers considered null and void unless accepted, and mutually binding if accepted, wherein acceptance legally binds the proposing party and creates reciprocal obligations for the responding party. Hence, on either reading, an offer was made and rejected, in which case it could no longer be binding.

Following a brief exchange of niceties, Crito presents his proposition to break Socrates out of jail and lead him out of the city, with considerable emphasis on the urgency of the matter. He is convinced that the boat will arrive on the day of the dramatic setting, and thereby that the execution will be carried out on the very next day. In contrast, Socrates claims, on the basis of the pervious night's dream foretelling his death in three days (44a–b), that the event will take place exactly one day later than anticipated by Crito. The dream with Homeric undertones is a segue into Crito's proposal, including a series of quick arguments, perhaps better described as presentations or considerations, in favor of flight to safety. The rest of the dialogue shows Socrates laying the foundations of social and political philosophy as he conducts a dispassionate analysis of the moral issues involved in the proposal, concluding ultimately that staying put would be the only morally acceptable course of action under the circumstances.

6.3. Significance of the Work

The *Crito* is one of Plato's shortest works, the absolute shortest, leaving out the dubia and spuria. It is also one of the most widely read. The dialogue is almost always bundled together with a few others in anthologies designed to introduce students to the works of Plato, or, depending on the audience, to the life and thought of Socrates. It is popular enough to find its way into even the shortest of such collections. Its invariable inclusion in volumes of this sort is a felicitous convention because the work represents one of the earliest and most cogent arguments in the social contract tradition, predating the *Leviathan* of Thomas Hobbes by a couple of millennia.

6.3.1. Place in Political Theory

David Hume, in an essay titled "Of the Original Contract," specifically acknowledges the *Crito* as a forerunner of social contract theory (*Essays* 2.12.47). Yet Plato's social contract is different from the specimens constituting the pinnacle of the social contract tradition, particularly from those envisaged by Hobbes, Locke, and Rousseau. The difference is immediately noticeable in the mechanics of the hypothetical contract serving as the core construct in each approach. The agreement in the *Crito* is between the individual and the state, or, more specifically, between each citizen and the laws governing the state, primarily the constitution, though including assent by proxy to all other legal codes as well. In contrast, the covenants in the other three examples are between people coming together for the express purpose of striking an agreement to create the state. Both kinds of contract establish the necessity of obedience to the laws of the land, whereas the latter kind, in addition, justifies the state itself.

This is not the only difference, but it is the essential one, all others being derivative of and reducible to it. One such additional difference, or, what is the same, a different perspective on the essential difference, is that Plato's contract, at least as laid out in the *Crito*, is considered severally for each citizen, who has a separate albeit standard agreement with the state, whereas mainstream examples of the social contract cover all cases with a single contract and a momentous act of covenanting.

The difference is not merely mechanical but also temporal, or, more accurately, the same difference can be considered in temporal as well as mechanical terms. Plato works with citizens contracting in a city-state, while the modern pioneers of the social contract tradition work with people contracting in the state of nature with a view to establishing a civil state. Actually, Plato considers citizens to be contracting specifically with the body of Athenian law, and not with Athens itself, but this is still, at least indirectly, a contract with the state. Hence, the state, through its legal system, is a party to the agreement in Plato's case, whereas the social contract creates and thereby predates the state in the standard case.

This difference, that is, the distinction between contracting in an established state and contracting to establish a state, is the most important point in the contrast between Plato and later social contract theorists. The direct participation of Plato's anthropomorphic legal system as a signatory also cries out for a critical comparison with the less outlandish contractors in all other social contract theories, but this aspect of the contract, though conspicuous, is a philosophically inconsequential dramatic tool. Indeed, the parties to the contract in Plato's approach reflect an unusual choice, taking artistic and philosophical liberties with the concept of personhood, here including the laws as an entity capable of entering into agreements. Yet the agreement depicted between Athenians and Athenian law is nothing more than a hypostatization representing an agreement between citizens to obey Athenian law. Anticipating later tradition, the contract here is merely hypothetical, symbolizing each individual's implicit agreement to abide by the law, but, contradicting later tradition, Plato's version preserves the prevailing order in the society into which people are born.

Plato's conception of the social contract stands out from its modern successors in its exclusive focus on the necessity of civil obedience without comment on the creation or even existence of the state, neither explaining it, nor defending its necessity, though he devotes ample attention to such issues in other works, most notably, the *Republic* and the *Laws*. Plato's concern in the *Crito* is to show why one must abide by the law. For this, he does not have to demonstrate that the state exists, which is obvious, nor to lay out why it exists, which is irrelevant, nor even to argue that it ought to exist, which is not in dispute. The version of the social contract he employs is different, and even strange, but entirely effective.

Although the particular contract Plato uses does not account for the origin of the state in the manner of the familiar template used by the moderns, it does indirectly justify the existence of the state in the course of laying out the need for restricting individual liberties for the common good and the necessity of upholding the law, with overall coverage comparable to all the rest, perhaps not through a point-by-point exposition, but certainly in being amenable to philosophical inspection on all counts. As in most other social contract theories, so, too, in Plato's theory, the individual's implicit consent resides in the absence of an attempt to change the laws or leave the country. These are the options encapsulated as "persuade or obey" in the literature focusing on the first choice, and as "love it or leave it" in the militant slogans of popular culture focusing on the second.

6.3.2. Place in Socratic Studies

Independently of its seminal position in the history of social and political philosophy, the *Crito*'s ongoing appeal is linked to the biographical insight it offers into the life, beliefs, and character of the historical Socrates, or, for those rejecting that possibility on principle, the appeal might be said to be in dramatic insight into the backstory and character development regarding Plato's Socrates.

The fact that Plato is the primary source of information on the historical Socrates makes the dialogue especially important in this regard because it stands as a unique report on certain developments in the final stretch of Socrates's life. However, its documentary value is undermined by the general uncertainty regarding the division between fact and fiction in the dramatic backdrop in Plato's works, not to mention the general exemption from historicity in the Socratic dialogue as a genre, that is, regardless of the author.

Plato's practice of using the Socrates character as a protagonist, arguably at least sometimes as a mouthpiece for his own views, makes the dramatic setting difficult to interpret, especially with no internal indication and little external confirmation of whether any particular plot or subplot is attributable to an actual event or only to a literary need. Even those denying that Plato ever uses Socrates as a mouthpiece have to contend with the possibility that not everything Plato makes the character Socrates say or do has to correspond to something actually said and done by the historical Socrates. Considerations in this regard are almost always carried into the realm of things that the historical Socrates might have said and done, which means what we may reasonably expect the historical Socrates to have said and done, which, in turn, is a judgment for which we are dependent largely on the works of Plato, thus completing the circle.

Nevertheless, the attempt is not hopeless. Scholars, time and again, turn to a select few dialogues to piece together a Platonic portrait of Socrates. The works most often consulted in such efforts include: the *Euthyphro*, following Socrates on his way to be arraigned; the *Apology*, placing him on trial for his life; the *Crito*, capturing him in prison on death row; the *Phaedo*, recounting his last day on earth as he awaits execution. Although the dramatic setting in these dialogues focuses exclusively on the final weeks of Socrates's life, the philosophical range is not limited in any way. The first dialogue on the list is a discussion of piety, ironically, led by someone about to be indicted for impiety. The second is a dramatization of the legal defense in court. The third is a contribution to the philosophy of law, fittingly enough, coming from a death-row inmate refusing to take advantage of a prison break arranged for him by his friends. The fourth is a discussion on the immortality of the soul, again, with considerable irony, led by someone scheduled to face the truth personally by the end of the day.

The *Crito* enjoys a good dramatic fit with the series of dialogues portraying Socrates near the end of his life. Yet the harmony comes with questions regarding the authenticity of the account. Socrates may have indeed taught posterity a lesson in civic responsibility by refusing to break out of prison despite the advance preparation of his friends and persistent pressure from the same, and his arguments may have been exactly as reported by Plato, presumably with the benefit of an interview with Crito, or with someone who had been briefed by Crito. On the other hand, he may have done no such thing, while the prison plot provided a convenient setting for Plato to create a dramatic work laying out foundational concepts in social and political theory. A happy medium is also believable: Perhaps Socrates's prison stay was roughly as described by Plato, who then took it upon himself to fill in the blanks through a dialogue with some degree of personal contribution in terms of both drama and philosophy.

The *Crito* is not even the only story on record regarding friendly pressure on Socrates to escape. According to Diogenes Laërtius (*Lives* 2.60, 3.36), who cites Idomeneus of Lampsacus as his source, the pressure came from Aeschines of Sphettus (a.k.a. Aeschines Socraticus), not Crito. The reason that Plato's version transfers the role of leadership to Crito, so reports Diogenes, is simply that Plato resented the devotion of Aeschines to Aristippus. What are we to make of this? The fact that Plato was closer to the scene in question than was Idomeneus (c. 325–270 BC), who lived in an altogether different world, at least temporally, does not help adjudicate the matter, because the claim is not that Plato confused the facts but that he distorted them. We may never know the truth, but the role, whether factual or imaginary, is entirely suitable for Crito, whose adoration of Socrates is well-documented elsewhere in the Platonic corpus, with his tender attention in the *Phaedo* constituting the stuff of legend and enhancing the poetic beauty of that dialogue. Even if the original honor really belongs to Aeschines, Plato's reassignment works well.

Regardless of the truth of the matter, the fact remains that both the meeting in prison and the corresponding discussion are realistic. Even if the conversation never took place as described, or at all, we can easily imagine an actual prison break being arranged by friends and turned down by Socrates. The opportunity was there. Many trials embraced harsh penalties as part of an intimidation strategy. Prosecutors who would have been content with a nonviolent alternative often demanded the death penalty just to pressure the accused into leaving the city. Exile was a favorite outcome, typically in combination with a monetary penalty, and the combination was usually the result of a counterproposal by the defendant, eager to avoid capital punishment. Illegal departure, essentially exile without the mandate, was not exactly a disappointment for the prosecution, with some of the accused fleeing before the trial, and some, shortly thereafter, both in dreadful disgrace, far worse than proper exile.

Against this background, the execution of Socrates is more like a threat gone awry. Though formally demanded by the prosecution, his death was probably not sought as an end in itself, not, that is, as the most fitting resolution, but as the surest means to secure his submission. His refusal to submit in any way must have taken most everyone by surprise, while his escape from prison would have been a relief for the prosecution and for a good many of those approving his execution. His accusers, both old and new, would have preferred to have him live out his remaining years in a shameful state of existence abroad than to have him put to death legally only to be left with the legend of a martyr of truth and justice. His escape, confirming and expanding his criminal record, would have afforded his enemies a far greater victory than his death. In sum, the historical setting was favorable to a prison break, which would not have required much force or cunning or expense, just the will.

6.4. Organizational Structure

Between a prologue (43a–44b) that establishes the basic setting and an epilogue (54d–e) that brings a swift conclusion, the dialogue can be examined in three parts, the first, presenting Crito's counsel to flee (44b–46a), the second, laying out Socrates's analysis of that advice from a moral perspective (46b–49e), and, the third, animating the Laws of Athens to introduce contractarian analysis as part of the ethical evaluation in progress (50a–54d).

Alternatively, the second and third parts might be considered a whole (46b–54d) insofar as they jointly make up the response to Crito's proposal, but this begs the question of agreement between Socrates and the Laws. Therefore, such a combination is not automatically warranted by the organizational structure of the work, instead requiring specific argumentation demonstrating cohesion. At the risk of prejudging the matter, such cohesion will have to be based on an organic fit rather than uniformity, because one part is decidedly philosophical, the other distinctly rhetorical. That said, the entire response to Crito, including the philosophical approach of Socrates as well as the rhetorical presentation of the Laws, is a disinterested critical analysis of the moral issues involved in the proposal. It is one of the earliest demonstrations of reasoning in ethics, an attempt at a resolution of moral considerations without an appeal to myth, religion, tradition, or, in general, public opinion.

The turning point (50a) in the response is the personification of the Laws of Athens as a new character, which then marks a transition from the establishment of a universal decision procedure to the execution of a specific case study. What starts out in the form of a groundwork for normative ethical assessment, arguably even a metaethical superstructure, turns into a contractarian analysis of an entirely practical matter, which Socrates examines through an imaginary dialogue with the laws, city, and state of Athens. Immediately upon expanding the character list with an anthropomorphic proxy to speak for Athenian interests (50a–d), Socrates is especially careful to give equal voice to each of the fictional representatives involved, namely, the laws, the city, and the state, and later, even the country (51a–c), in order to illustrate as fully as possible his conception of the Athenian side in the debate he stages as a one-man show. Once satisfied with the clarity of his intention, he relaxes the mode of meticulous reference to each of the fictional representatives severally, switching to heavy usage of the laws as a proxy for all.

Modern secondary literature shows a preference for denoting Socrates's debate partner as the "Laws of Athens," with the first letter of the first word capitalized. A shorter version referring to this unique character simply as the "Laws," again capitalizing the first letter, is also acceptable, provided that italicization is avoided for obvious reasons, especially when the reference is preceded by the definite article.

6.5. Crito: Escape Perspective

Crito's goal is to break Socrates out of jail and to get him out of the city before it is too late. His discussion of the prospect proceeds in two steps: He starts out with a basic proposal, which he lays out in the course of communicating his frustration concerning Socrates's predicament (44b–d), and he then moves on to a series of arguments or points favoring the proposal (44e–46a).

His anxiety regarding Socrates is twofold (44b–c): He is deeply troubled by the prospect of losing a friend, but he also dreads the disgrace attached to failure to save that friend from an avoidable death. The second part of the total disaster anticipated by Crito introduces tension between "the many" and "the few," marking a dominant theme in the dialogue and weaving in a Socratic thread running through much of Plato's early work and still operative in his middle period. Contrasting the "opinion of the many," or, to use a more colloquial expression, "public opinion," with the "opinion of the few," referring to "expert opinion," or to "technical expertise," is a distinctively Socratic approach that finds application in various contexts. The inherent idea is that expert opinion always trumps public opinion. In other words, no matter the question, the answer, if it is to be had at all, is best sought through the opinion of experts as opposed to the opinion of the masses.

Socrates immediately reproaches Crito for undue concern with public opinion (44c). He tries to shift the focus of attention from what "most people" think to what the "best people" think. Yet Crito insists that "the many" must be taken seriously, if for no other reason, then at least because of the power they wield over individuals, as evidenced tragically in the case of Socrates, which Crito takes to be a prime example of injury through public opinion anchored to false impression, or, to put it crudely, gossip fueled by disinformation (44d). Socrates denies this altogether, responding that the many can neither benefit nor harm us, since they can make us neither wise nor foolish (44d). His denial forces a special meaning on good and evil, or, what is the same, on benefit and harm, especially from the perspective of anyone who does not share the Socratic notion of the equivalence of knowledge and the good.

6.5.1. Epistemic Dimension of Morality

The prompt resistance of Socrates, interrupting Crito before any arguments at all are on the table, is an early indication of the importance of methodology. The condemnation of the opinion of the many is a Socratic trademark, here finding its most famous application as a paradigm for moral epistemology. Socrates repudiates common morality on the grounds that the public conception of what is good is not based on knowledge. He finds an irreparable epistemic deficiency in public opinion, which, he therefore contends, cannot satisfy the knowledge requirement in and of morality. The many simply do not know what is good. As in all matters, we have to turn to the few, the experts.

The difference lies in the equivalence of knowledge and the good. This means something more than that knowledge is good, or that knowing is better than not knowing, but it does not mean that "knowledge" and "good" are synonymous terms uniquely sharing the same referent. The equivalence in question is grounded in a controversial subscription to the "unity of virtue" (or the "unity of the virtues"), the principle that particular virtues are united in a single conception of virtue as wisdom, or, more accurately, that wisdom, itself a particular virtue, is also the unifying principle accounting for the unity of all particular virtues. Hence, the association is not directly between knowledge and goodness but between wisdom and virtue, but the same link holds in the former relationship as well, unless one is willing to argue that wisdom can be had without knowledge, and, virtue, without goodness. Notwithstanding scholarly disagreement, the relevant position essentially takes knowledge to be the only thing that is good as an end in itself.

Scholarly disagreement does, however, begin at this very point. Specifically, it begins with the question whether the focus on knowledge concerns the only thing that is good as an end in itself, or the only thing that is good, period, that is, the only good. The first interpretation has much to recommend it if only because it allows for the existence of other goods besides knowledge. The alternative approach, avoiding qualification of the goodness in question as an end in itself, would be required to account for the apparent existence of goods other than knowledge, or to reject it with justification, or at least to be able to deny it without contradicting our rational intuitions in this regard. The qualification "as an end in itself" avoids needless complication, is not in direct contradiction with canon, and, in fact, seems warranted, at least implicitly, by Socrates's own words in his summation of a position for the benefit of Clinias in the *Euthydemus* (281d). Perhaps most important, depicting knowledge as the only unconditional good, as opposed to the only good, has the advantage of acknowledging a multiplicity of virtues while insisting on the unity of virtue, thus admitting that other things can be good while still claiming a privileged status for knowledge.

The Socratic doctrine of the equivalence of knowledge and the good, regardless of the proper explication of the goodness in question, is the basis for the famous dictum that "to know the good is to do the good," and its corollary, that "no one does evil knowingly," both familiar themes in various dialogues (*Apology* 25d–26a; *Protagoras* 357d–358d; *Meno* 77c–78b). The clearest exposition of the underlying equivalence is the discussion in the *Protagoras* (349b) of the unity of the virtues, focusing specifically on wisdom, temperance, courage, justice, and piety, the first four of which were later designated "cardinal virtues" and adopted by the Church Fathers. The equivalence of knowledge and the good is established here through the principle of the unity of the virtues, with wisdom serving as the common denominator. Wisdom is a virtue, one of many, yet it is also a necessary ingredient in all the other virtues. The others may even be considered applications of wisdom (*sophia* or σοφία), defined as the knowledge of good and evil:

already a telling sign, and the rejection by the Laws can also be thought meaningful, insofar as the actual laws are grounded in ordinary morality, and, to a large extent, meant to preserve it. Even without any symbolism, retaliation bears the trademark of ordinary morality, not just in Athens, but throughout what was then known as the civilized world, and perhaps even more so in communities not fitting that description. Yet what makes the symbolism even stronger is the argument used against retaliation, which is ultimately rejected through the paternity analogy. Thus, Socrates uses one pillar of ordinary morality against another, making sure to distance himself from both, as he places one in the mouth of an icon of ordinary morality, while creating an entirely imaginary spokesperson for the other. This is difficult to ignore.

Moreover, Socrates's rejection of retaliation is not as significant a weapon as made out by critics finding a logical inconsistency either with another position held in the same dialogue or with other passages in other dialogues. Anything it can accomplish to this end can be accomplished just as effectively by the commitment of Socrates to the principle that we must never deliberately do injustice or injury, which already implies the corollary that we must not do them in return for the same. The burning question to settle all controversy is whether a violation of the original, overarching principle can ever be justified. Yet this is not the question asked in the *Crito*. The question asked there is whether Socrates's escape from prison and flight from Athens can be justified. His own answer is that it cannot be justified under the given circumstances. The decision procedure Socrates uses to arrive at that conclusion is the historical inception of social contract theory, which is neither controverted by the possibility of retaliation nor strengthened by its rejection.

What must be conceded at once is that Socrates might have, probably would have, and logically should have decided to stay put even if he thought that the social contract had been unilaterally violated or invalidated by the other party, and even if he found the analogic objection to retaliation irrelevant or otherwise unimpressive. After all, he is committed, by his own words, that is, without distancing himself through the Laws as a dramatic mouthpiece, twice removed from Plato, to the principle that we must never deliberately commit an injustice or injury. To return to the hypothetical scenario suggesting that he would not have been stopped by the paternalistic prohibition of retaliation had he believed that the social contract had somehow been rendered null and void by the other party, this means, of course, that he would not have been stopped by it if he had a good reason to proceed in the opposite direction. The first question that comes to mind in this context is whether he would have been stopped by anything at all. Would nothing have stopped him? At least one thing: his supreme duty never to commit an injustice or to inflict an injury, qualified in either case only by the recognition that the scope of consideration is deliberate actions. Faced with an invalid social contract and an irrelevant opposition to retaliation, he would still have been obligated to honor the first-order principle prohibiting the deliberate perpetration of injustice and of injury.

When all is said and done, is this an absolute principle? Indeed, it is, as confirmed by the repeated emphasis that its violation is *never* permissible. No spin can be put on this to make it look like Socrates is not committed to refrain, no matter the cost, from deliberately committing an injustice or injury. The only thing that might still be debated is whether escape would count as the deliberate commission of an injustice or injury, but such a debate would not free him from the unqualified rejection marking his position as an example of absolutism.

That said, the ethical absolutism in this case is decidedly different from the legal and political absolutism alleged to be a source of contradiction in the positions held by Socrates, and thereby reported or espoused by Plato. The kind of absolutism to which Socrates is committed makes him neither an advocate nor an opponent of authoritarianism. Nor does it saddle him with any particular position on obedience or disobedience to formal authority, except, of course, through the patently valid inference that he must reject obedience, or disobedience, as the case may be, in the event of a conflict with the first-order obligation to avoid the deliberate commission of injustice or injury. Nor, finally, does this refusal to harm anyone create a contradiction within the *Crito* or within the Platonic corpus. What we have is absolutism in the sense of an unqualified commitment to doing no harm deliberately. This may be too rigid a position in theory, and even an unworkable one in practice, but such respect for the moral law is a far cry from slavish obedience to political authority.

In the end, Socrates does not stay put merely to refrain from injuring the state by undermining its laws as a disobedient citizen. He remains in his cell to the end because he believes he has a contractual obligation that was neither violated nor invalidated by anything done to him by the state, and ultimately because he believes justice requires honoring that obligation. He is protecting himself, not the state. He simply does not want to be the one to give rise to an injustice or injury. In the terminology of another Socratic dictum, it is, after all, better to suffer injustice than to do injustice (*Gorgias* 474b–476a).

Phaedo: Broad Outline

- Prologue (57a–61c)

- Discussion of death and dying (61c–70b)
  Socrates's apparent eagerness to die makes the rest of the dialogue a second *Apology* for the philosopher, thus challenged to defend his "death wish"

- Proof #1: Cyclical Transformation Argument (70c–72e)
  - Logical core: cyclical generation of opposites from opposites (70c–72e)
  - Procedure: "special theory of causation" with a "doctrine of reincarnation"
  - Effect: apparently accepted and completely ignored by everyone involved

- Proof #2: Recollection Argument (72e–78b)
  - Logical core: "recollection doctrine" via paradigm of "equal sticks" (72e–77a)
  - Objection: prenatal existence is only half of the proof of immortality (77b–c)
  - Short reply: combine the first two arguments toward a complete proof (77c–e)
  - Long reply: extended response produces a third argument (78b–84b)

- Proof #3: Analogic (Affinity) Argument (78b–84b)
  - Logical core: kinship of the soul with the forms and the gods (78b–80b)
  - Speculative elaboration: fate of soul upon separation from body (80c–84b)

- Objections and Misology (84b–95a)
  - Simmias's objection: soul analogous to attunement in a lyre (85e–86d)
  - Cebes's objection: soul analogous to weaver of cloaks (87a–88b)
  - Dramatic interlude (88c–89b)
  - Warning: Socrates's warning against misology (89b–91c)
  - Reply to Simmias: contradictions in attunement analogy (91e–95a)
  - Reply to Cebes: most of what follows is a reply to Cebes (95a–107a)

- Proof #4: Causal Argument (96a–107a)
  - Natural science: empirical inquiry into particulars (96a–99d)
    - Physical causes: the initial perspective in youth (96a–97b)
    - Anaxagoras: intelligence as cause (97b–99d)
  - Rational reflection: logical inquiry into propositions (99d–107a)
    - Safest yet naive answer: forms as causes (100c–101e)
    - Safe and sophisticated answer: particulars as causes (102a–105b)
  - Logical core: "Final" or "Causal" Argument (105b–107a)
    - Part 1: soul as the cause of life (105b–e)
    - Part 2: soul as imperishable (106a–107a)

- Myth of the afterlife (107d–114e)
- Death scene of Socrates (115a–118a)

Seven

PHAEDO

7.1. Literary Profile

7.1.1. Subject and Form

The *Phaedo* is a dialogue on the immortality of the soul, taking place in the Athenian prison where Socrates awaits execution at the end of the day. Strictly speaking, this is a description of the substantive core, while the work as a whole is a dialogue about this dialogue, with the aim of communicating it.

That said, the treatment of immortality represents one of the most systematic approaches to the subject in the history of philosophy; the delivery is widely acknowledged to be a masterly display of the tools of the trade in storytelling; and the backdrop is arguably the most dramatic event in the annals of Western thought.

All this makes the work a rich source at the intersection of several fields of study. Its multidisciplinary appeal extends to philosophy, literature, and history. For the analytic philosopher, the piece offers a series of arguments on the immortality of the soul. For the literary critic, it represents one of the earliest and finest instantiations of the original template for dramatic construction. For the classical historian, it provides an authoritative account of the last day of Socrates.

This is a dialogue where the plot draws on fact rather than projecting pure fancy. The setting is an event known to have taken place. This anchor to reality, or, from a current temporal orientation, to history, enlivens the interplay between philosophy and literature. Specifically, the usual tension between argument and drama in the interpretation of Plato's dialogues is here strained further, as journalistic realism tugs against competing claims by philosophy and literature in the reading of any particular passage. A statement thought deliberately composed to support a philosophical argument, or to pursue a literary goal, might instead, or in addition, reflect a matter of fact. The inherent ambiguity makes it difficult to distinguish between plot elements representing a strict reconstruction of reality and those coming from the imagination alone.

Overinterpretation is a temptation to be avoided through conscious effort, but habituation in the opposite direction breeds a propensity to rush through the drama, ignore the symbolism, and overlook important clues and nuances. Although reading too much into the text is just as bad as not getting enough out of it, at least in the sense that both are signs of a missed target, a happy medium can be too far to reach or too hazy to recognize. It is better to err on the side of the explicit statement, missing out on a hidden meaning rather than misconstruing the one in plain sight. An incomplete appreciation of the work is more serviceable than a full appreciation of a distorted interpretation of it.

Philosophers, especially those trained in the analytic tradition, would do well to devote the bulk of their attention to the arguments, both severally and collectively. That is probably good and possibly even redundant advice for anyone reading the work, since it is, above all, a philosophical study. However, exclusive concern with the soundness of the proofs is a sure way to miss the elegance of the dialogue. A fruitful experience precludes immersion in the logic in isolation from the drama. Some of the drama will be filler, words delivering ideas in a setting staging a discussion, but not all of it can sensibly or profitably be discarded as such, even in a drive to dissect the disquisition to get at the meat of the argument. Had all his drama been filler, Plato could have just written treatises instead. The precise balance is always difficult to sort out, but particularly so in this case because the setting runs parallel to reality, so much so as to be declared a faithful report of it (58d). This exacerbates the inherent ambivalence between information and interpretation as the proper approach to the text.

Candidates for exegetical scrutiny abound. For example, readers find out at the end of the prologue that Socrates adjusts his posture, lowers his legs to the ground, and remains in this position through the rest of the discussion (61d). Is this essential information? No real insight into the philosophical position of Plato could conceivably hang on the physical position of Socrates during the final gathering. Yet if this had been entirely insignificant, Plato would not have mentioned it. If shuffling the protagonist in his seat is good symbolism for a transition from one stage to another in the development of the plot, possibly with the move into an upright position serving as an indication that the casual conversation is about to turn into a formal discussion, then Plato might be justified in portraying Socrates as shifting about even if Socrates never moved a hair. Not every detail in the drama will be so significant, and it is best not to pursue, and crucial not to find, significance where it does not exist, but the alternative should not be wholesale repudiation of the dramatic setting.

A good rule of thumb is that apparently trivial details are not necessarily trivial. That which seems negligible could have just as well been left out had it been truly pointless. Since Plato is not obligated to report everything, for example, whether Socrates was gesturing with his hands while talking, or crossing his arms while listening, what he does report can be presumed noteworthy, should at least be tested for relevance, and ought not to be set aside without due consideration.

7.1.2. Dramatic Structure and Chief Characters

The *Phaedo* offers a first-hand account of the last day of Socrates's life. Whether the work *is* such an account is open to debate, but the fact that it *contains* one is clear. The narrating character is presented as having personally been in attendance on that day, which means that the dramatic audience at the level of the narrator hears an eyewitness report, which further implies that the reader is also privy to the same account, whereas a reference to Plato's absence from the gathering, if taken at face value, complicates this construal, primarily because it places the fictional narrator closer than the author to the dramatic setting (59b). On the other hand, the author's removal from the central scene set up through his own words evinces symbolism designed to make a dramatic statement, perhaps indicating philosophical disagreement with the master, or representing a break in the corpus between reporting and doing philosophy, and need not be taken to undermine the otherwise established structure of the dialogue.

The story is narrated by Phaedo, who was with Socrates on the day he died, to Echecrates, who was not. The dramatic audience at this outermost layer is not limited to a single person: Echecrates seems to be the spokesperson of a present congregation, as evidenced by his repeated recourse to speaking in the first person plural in his interaction with Phaedo. Yet the dialogue at the level of narration is exclusively between these two characters, with the rest of the implied audience remaining silent. Both are philosophers originating outside Athens. Phaedo is from Elis, a Greek city bordering the Ionian Sea on the westernmost part of the Peloponnesus peninsula, and corresponding geographically to a prefecture of the same name in modern Greece. Echecrates is from Phlius, a city in the eastern part of the Peloponnese, specifically in Argolis, another prefecture in modern Greece. Both cities were allies of Sparta. It is interesting, if deliberate, that the story is thus removed from Athens in its narration. That is to say, anchoring the narration of the death of the greatest son of Athens to an interchange between two people who are not from Athens is pregnant with symbolism, made all the more dramatic by the fact that these people are from cities allied with or controlled by the greatest adversary of Athens.

The basic narrative structure connecting Plato with the reader houses an inner layer of dialogue where all the action takes place. At this level, the main interlocutors engaged in philosophical discourse with Socrates are Simmias and Cebes. They are both from Thebes, a Greek city north of the Cithaeron mountain range separating Boeotia from Attica. Here, too, Plato's choice is intriguing, unless it is simply a matter of fact, as the setting leaves Socrates with no Athenians as dramatic partners in debate. In fact, the imagery is strong in the opposite direction, given that Thebes, like Sparta, represented a serious threat to the dominion of Athens, famously demonstrated in its collaboration with Xerxes during the Persian invasion of 480 BC.

Simmias and Cebes are philosophers in their own right (§ 6.2). Simmias helps advance the main themes in this dialogue and attracts incidental praise in another for his unmatched enthusiasm for discourse (*Phaedrus* 242b), while the intellectual presence of Cebes is limited to this work, though he is also mentioned elsewhere in a purely dramatic context (*Crito* 45b). They are disciples of both Socrates and Philolaus, a Pythagorean philosopher somewhat senior to Socrates but his contemporary. Their interaction throughout the dialogue is logically and dramatically cohesive, with the points they raise often contributing complementary components to a particular strand of reasoning or a specific development in the plot, which is indicative of a relationship as lovers. These two characters are not typical of the Platonic interlocutors accompanying Socrates in other dialogues: They are positioned as positive participants in the philosophical process, opposing Socrates in constructive rather than destructive or obstructive ways. This fits in well with a separate record of their having pledged substantial funds to facilitate a prison break for Socrates after the trial and before the execution (*Crito* 45b).

The general pattern underlying the distribution of hometowns across characters points to a multi-layered dramatic alignment opposite Athens. The literary implication, if any, is probably not merely the isolation of Socrates as the only Athenian with a significant role in the dialogue, thereby assigning especial dramatic emphasis to his philosophical position, but also, or, perhaps, instead, a condemnation of Athens itself as the cause and place of his death. Nearly all of the dialogue takes place between Socrates and his two foreign disciples, and certainly all that is philosophical in it is fully contained in the exchange between these three people. The foreign dominion at this inner layer of drama also includes Phaedo, who not only narrates the story from the outside but actually participates in the central dialogue, albeit briefly, where Socrates turns to him for interlocution in an interlude dedicated to warding off misology (89b–90d). The philosophical exchange throughout the work can be broken down as follows according to the main interlocutors engaging Socrates in conversation:

Socrates's Partners in the Major Divisions of the *Phaedo*

"Second *Apology*"	62c–63b	Simmias
Proof #1 (Cyclical)	70c–72e	Cebes
Proof #2 (Recollection)	72e–77a	Simmias
Proof #3 (Analogic)	78b–84b	Cebes
Objection #1 (Attunement)	85e–86d	Simmias
Objection #2 (Weaver)	87a–88b	Cebes
Misology	89b–91c	Phaedo
Reply to attunement analogy	91e–95a	Simmias
Reply to weaver analogy	95a–107a	Cebes
Mythology	107d–114c	Simmias

The only other person with a notable speaking part is Crito. Appearing solely in a supporting role in the present work, Crito is a close friend of Socrates as well as the titular interlocutor of the dialogue portraying Socrates in prison after the notorious trial. Crito is the only Athenian with a speaking part besides Socrates, not counting obligatory comments by the guard and by the executioner and a brief outburst by Xanthippe in reaction to her husband's impending death. He is in attendance with his son, Critobulus, much in the way of their joint presence at the trial (*Apology* 33d–e, 38b). Although he has little to say in the *Phaedo*, he is clearly positioned as an authority figure, supervising the assembly and dictating the course of the dialogue, especially through the introduction of turns and developments opposing the natural flow of the central conversation. His lines are connected with the mechanics of the main event and not at all related to the discussion on hand. The full detachment of the character from the philosophical discussion reinforces the dramatic rejection of Athens.

Another emblematic choice in the dramatic setting, unless it is intended as no more than a factual representation, is Plato's absence from the gathering on the last day of Socrates. He is reported, somewhat tentatively, to have been ill on that day (59b). Even if the illness is an authentic report, the hesitation is pure drama, for who better to say than Plato, and, by extension, his dramatic mouthpiece, whether he was actually ill. If Plato had really been so sick as to be unable to join the master on the day of the execution, he personally would have had no encounter with doubt about the matter in recounting it in his own work. Yet he puts the illness excuse in Phaedo's mouth with an element of uncertainty, which suggests that the mention of his name serves at least some dramatic purpose even if he was in fact absent and indeed ill. The corpus contains no other reference to Plato save for an incidental confirmation of his presence at the trial of Socrates (*Apology* 34a, 38b). This canonical scarcity of self-reference makes it noteworthy that Plato explicitly confirms his presence at the trial and absence from the philosophical funeral, though the fact that both are momentous historical events, the importance of which must have been obvious even at the time of their occurrence, also supports the less exciting alternative that he was merely taking roll and reporting it.

Again, the dramatic perspective seems to suggest some sort of stand against the state. Another possibility is to read Plato's absence as his rejection of Socrates's arguments in the dialogue, but this would be a bit of a stretch. What we know of Plato and of Socrates the philosopher confirms that not all the arguments here can reasonably be stripped from Plato and transferred instead to the historical Socrates. Even if the first argument is uniquely Socratic, the rest are quite Platonic. Plato's absence can still be taken as some sort of opposition to the intellectual legacy of Socrates, but this would have to be in more general terms, perhaps signifying a critical break in the corpus between dialogues that are Socratic and those that are not, and thereby positioning the *Phaedo* as the first genuinely or entirely Platonic work. On the other hand, this is not a compelling interpretation, since such a break, if it exists at all and can be identified accurately, might just as well be placed slightly before the *Phaedo*. If Plato's absence truly has room for a metaphorical reading, the most plausible interpretation is a simple resentment of Athens. This is not only because it is simple but also because it complements the rest of the symbolism in the prologue, where political protest emerges as the central theme and any attempt to squeeze in a cloaked message, including that of philosophical disagreement, runs the risk of being lost or, worse, distractive.

Aristippus and Cleombrotus are the only other absentees exposed by name (59c). One difference here, whether significant or not, is that Phaedo volunteers the information regarding Plato's absence but discusses these two in response to a direct inquiry by Echecrates as to their whereabouts. Aristippus is from Cyrene, an ancient city just inland from the Mediterranean coast of North Africa, in a region corresponding to northeastern Libya in contemporary political geography, but originally established as a colony by Dorian Greeks fleeing a drought in Thera (modern Santorini) and later opposing Athens in the Peloponnesian War. Cleombrotus is from Ambracia, a prominent city in the Epirus region and another active force against Athens in the Peloponnesian War. Aristippus is the founder of the Cyrenaic school of philosophy, though founding credit is sometimes extended instead to his grandson of the same name because of a greater contribution to the defining position. Cleombrotus has a less impressive but more sensational reputation immortalized in anecdotes depicting an overeager philosopher committing suicide to ascend immediately to the incorporeal existence described in the *Phaedo*, with the account originating in an epigram by Callimachus of Cyrene but taken up by various other literary figures ranging from Cicero to Milton. On the day of the execution, both are reportedly in Aegina, an island situated roughly twenty-five kilometers from Athens in the Saronic Gulf, and standing as yet another rival to the illustrious center of civilization. While this peripheral probe of the two characters affords no new insight into the setting of the dialogue, it constitutes further evidence of a deliberate dramatic bias against Athens. Their joint mention could, as is always feasible in classical plots, be interpreted as an indication that they were lovers, but this is not particularly enlightening, whether fact or fiction.

If Aegina is the true birthplace of Plato, as is sometimes supposed (see § 1.2), then his placement of Aristippus and Cleombrotus there on the day of Socrates's execution may be telling in a dramatic way. But no matter how receptive we may be to symbolism, two considerations weigh in heavily against this one: first, the birthplace of Plato is more commonly acknowledged to be Athens, not Aegina; second, for all we know, Aristippus and Cleombrotus might really have been in Aegina on that day.

The most straightforward interpretation of the attendance record provided is to assume that Plato, Aristippus, and Cleombrotus were all absent as a matter of fact. A more elaborate rendition, adding some explanatory power without complicating the basic assumption, might take Plato to be drawing a contrast between his own case, tied to the legitimate excuse of illness, and the other two, whose absence he perhaps found more avoidable and less excusable. This could be why he draws attention to their absence by having Echecrates make a point of asking about them despite the fact that their absence on that day would have been indicated by their omission from Phaedo's list of attendees (59b–c), which does not seem to leave out anyone worth mentioning, given that less important figures are consigned to a generic category of anonymous auditors, who, oddly enough, all happen to be Athenians (59b).

Whatever the truth of the matter, neither reading does justice to Plato's talents as a dramatist, as both remain too tedious to demonstrate an awareness of literary effort, let alone an appreciation of artistic brilliance. At the other extreme, it is entirely possible to be too imaginative, receiving messages that were never sent, or even conceived, and reading between the lines where there is no text, literally or figuratively. Striking a balance can be difficult. If the list is meant to be interpreted, and not merely acknowledged, every name on it, even the apparently insignificant ones, merits consideration, whether mentioned to confirm attendance or to announce absence.

Together with the eponymous narrator, a total of fifteen people are identified by name in the group accompanying Socrates on his last day, excluding Xanthippe, who is in incidental contact, and ignoring others, who are both unnamed and extraneous to the central scene. Nine are Athenians and six are foreigners. One Athenian and two foreigners, all three of whom might have been expected to be there, are specifically reported absent. Echecrates, another foreigner, was also obviously absent, as he is the one asking Phaedo to recount the story. The full list includes the following people:

Last Day of Socrates
People Mentioned by Name in the Central Drama

Athenians (59b)	**Foreigners (59c)**
Present	*Present*
Apollodorus of Phaleron	Phaedo of Elis (57a)
Crito of Alopece	Simmias of Thebes
Critobulus of Alopece	Cebes of Thebes
Hermogenes of Alopece	Phaedondas of Thebes
Epigenes of Cephisia	Euclides of Megara
Aeschines of Sphettus	Terpsion of Megara
Antisthenes of Athens	*Absent*
Ctesippus of Paeania	Aristippus of Cyrene
Menexenus of Athens	Cleombrotus of Ambracia
Absent	
Plato of Collytus	

A final name worth singling out in this list is Apollodorus, not merely because he weeps the loudest (59b, 117d), but also because he is the first-level narrator of another dialogue (*Symposium* 172a–174a), and particularly because he is one of the four people (also including Plato, Crito, and Critobulus) listed as pledging a donation effecting a substantial increase, specifically to thirty times the original amount, in the fine proposed by Socrates upon the pronouncement of the verdict at the nefarious trial (*Apology* 38b).

The foregoing discussion brings out some of the implications of the most conspicuous features of the preceding list along a single common thread, an apparent repudiation of Athens. No doubt, further consideration and deeper analysis may be required to capture the true intention in the choice of characters, supposing the roster to reflect more than a journalistic report of attendees. A full understanding may require accounting for allusions that might now be obscure, such as unstated albeit then public information regarding any of the particular characters. Even the silent auditors in the audience may hold clues to the proper construal of possible hidden messages. Or the entire list of names may simply be a faithful historical record, with nothing added or omitted. The truth probably lies somewhere in between. Or, to be more precise, it is probably a mixture of fact and drama, with special emphasis on those facts serving the story or promoting the overall effect sought by the dramatist.

7.1.3. Plot Development toward Argumentation

The portion of the prologue preceding the entrance by Socrates sets up the stage for the drama and the platform of delivery for the philosophy. This brief section (57a–60a) orients the reader as to who the narrator is, what the event is, who was in attendance, and the relevant details of the circumstances.

7.1.3.1. Mission to Delos

One of the first points of reference coming out in the peripheral dialogue between the narrator and his dramatic audience concerns an unintentional yet unavoidable delay between the prosecution and execution of Socrates. As it turns out, the trial, lasting only one day, as stipulated by Athenian law (*Apology* 37a), coincided with the second day of an annual religious festival prohibiting bloodshed throughout its indefinite albeit relatively long duration (58a–c). The liturgical centerpiece of the festival is a naval mission honoring Apollo with a round-trip voyage between Athens and Delos.

Also mentioned in the preceding chapter (§ 6.2), Delos is a small island covering an area of roughly five square kilometers, slightly larger than Central Park in New York, or just under four times the size of Hyde Park in London, situated close to 150 kilometers southeast of Athens, and hallowed as the birthplace of Apollo. The religious ban on executions is said to have thus extended the time spent on death row by Socrates.

A sensible and convenient interpretation of the passage (58a–c) is that the mission to Delos was mentioned simply to record the delay and report the reason. The reference could thereby have been intended strictly as historical documentation. This is consistent, for example, with Xenophon's report (*Memorabilia* 4.8.2) that the Delian feast kept Socrates alive for thirty days after his condemnation. A literary interpretation, on the other hand, not necessarily less sensible or less convenient, might explore the symbolism, pursue dramatic clues, and mine for hidden messages. The fact that the same mission is discussed elsewhere by Plato (*Crito* 43c–44a), not to mention that the authenticity of the event is confirmed externally as a matter of historical fact, as in Xenophon, suggests that any dramatic purpose is parasitic on its reality rather than constitutive of it.

7.1.3.2. Enter Socrates

The dramatic introduction to the dialogue proper begins when Socrates joins his visitors (60a). The physical relief he reports feeling as he is released from his fetters to move freely among the company serves as a springboard for dramatic development as well as philosophical argumentation.

His appeal to Aesop (60c) to decorate apparently unstudied remarks on the connection between pleasure and pain, specifically as exemplified in his experience with the shackles, becomes a segue into a discussion of his recent experimentation with musical composition, when he is told that several people, most notably, the poet Evenus (60d), mentioned as a Sophist during the trial (*Apology* 20a–c), had been asking why he started dabbling in verse.

The contrast between pleasure and pain, both in connection with the Aesop imagery and as mentioned in passing earlier in Phaedo's narration drawing on another contrast, one between laughing and crying (59a), anticipates the first argument for the immortality of the soul, that is, the proof grounded in opposition relations.

Be that as it may, what advances the storyline in this context is the reference to poetry, revealing curiosity regarding this newfound interest of Socrates. The subsequent explanation ends with advice to the inquiring poet to make haste in following Socrates into death. The peculiarity of the advice blends into the argumentative part of the dialogue, as the counsel is first qualified by a provision against suicide and subsequently examined in its philosophical implications.

7.1.3.3. Socratic Poetry

The primary importance of the reference to Socratic poetry (60c–61c), whether grounded in fact or fiction, rests in its role as creating a dramatic opportunity for Socrates to issue a radical piece of advice stirring up an immediate and strong reaction and dictating the course of the remainder of the dialogue up to the death scene (115a–118a).

The mention of Aesop reminds Cebes that Evenus had been asking why Socrates had lately become interested in art, primarily manifested in the rendering of popular lore into verse. Socrates explains that he had taken up poetry during his imprisonment, purely in an effort to abide by the imperative in a recurring dream urging him to make art. He recounts having initially interpreted the dream as a sign to continue practicing philosophy as the finest form of art, soon afterwards taking it more literally in order to be absolved in advance of any possible noncompliance due to misunderstanding, and thus producing pieces based on the Invocation to Apollo and the fables of Aesop.

Following this brief explanatory account, meant to satisfy the curiosity of Evenus through Cebes, Socrates advises Evenus, again, through Cebes, to follow him into the afterlife as soon as possible (61b). This unorthodox recommendation is quickly amended by a reasoned prohibition of suicide, thus shifting the emphasis from urgency to enlightened enthusiasm in the advice to embrace death, but either form of the counsel is provocative enough to pique intellectual curiosity and attract rational disagreement. Indeed, all that is philosophical in the dialogue can be traced back to this unique point in the drama.

7.1.3.4. Prohibition against Suicide

Suicide is quickly agreed to be wrong, apparently not so much in deference to the cogency of the argument against it (61c–62c), but possibly due at least partly to conformity with the survival instinct, underscoring the natural aversion therein to the prospect of death, whether by one's own doing or through external factors. The quick consensus is obviously also motivated on an intellectual level by an eagerness to move on to a more general examination of death and the afterlife.

The prohibition of suicide is grounded in the belief that people are the possessions of the gods, and, therefore, that they are not authorized to interfere with the property rights of the gods in this regard, for example, by disrupting or altogether precluding the possibility of further earthly serviceability. Socrates offers this explanation as hearsay with which he agrees, and he expresses surprise that Simmias and Cebes are not already familiar with the account through their mentor Philolaus.

The cursory treatment attracts no challenge, question, or disagreement, as the audience is far more interested in hearing why death is so desirable than in discussing why one ought not to kill oneself. Since most people are not interested in killing themselves, and since those who are tend not to be swayed otherwise by reason, that issue holds little practical significance.

The prohibition invoked is a religious one, making out death to be a decision reserved exclusively for the gods. Whether or not this holds water, the larger issue is why death is desirable. The answer, stated briefly, is that death places people even closer to the gods while enabling clear and virtually unlimited access to knowledge and thereby to wisdom (62c–69e). The credibility of this view comes with an immediate prerequisite, or, from a different perspective, a direct corollary: the immortality of the soul. The rest of the dialogue is devoted to an examination of this thesis.

7.1.3.5. Second Apology

Seemingly casual advice issued for the benefit of Evenus turns into, or, more accurately, necessitates, an extended formal defense, a kind of second *Apology*. The turning point is the recommendation itself, guidance tantamount to praise for death, the purported desirability of which strikes the audience as counterintuitive and in need of proof (62c–63b). What makes the remainder of the dialogue a second *Apology*, with Socrates on trial again, this time, challenged by friends, is not merely intellectual curiosity or academic disagreement about death as a concept but disappointment in a choice embracing death as a real prospect, one looming large in the temporal context of the dramatic setting.

Despite qualifying his praise of death with a provision against suicide, Socrates himself is in the last stretch of a chosen path that may be equated, at least by analogy, with suicide. A bit of hypocrisy during the original trial might have secured acquittal (as made clear in the *Apology* at 34b–35d and 38d–39b), and mere cooperation with sympathizers would have set in motion a prison break arranged in advance and ready to be executed (as laid out in the central plot of the *Crito*). Thus, Socrates faces death after having twice refused to evade it.

This cavalier attitude toward life, particularly the absence of an effort to prolong it, is already open to question, objection, and disagreement, while the positive thesis advanced explicitly in support of the desirability of death underpins the inherent need for some sort of justification.

An apparent contradiction between the encomium to death, in the guise of advice to Evenus, and the theological approach to the impermissibility of suicide invites a full-blown discussion of the immortality of the soul. Cebes (62c–e), promptly joined by Simmias (63a), objects that, if human beings are the possessions of the gods, as declared in the argument against suicide, then people, especially philosophers, should be reluctant rather than eager to die. The objection is based on the assumption that death severs any and all ties one may have with the gods.

A direct rebuttal (63b–69e) advancing two separate points against the objection ultimately ends up further exposing the larger issue at stake, the immortality of the soul. The first point, merely rejecting rather than refuting the objection instigating it, is that death does not entail a separation from the gods, because there are both good men and good gods at the other side to accompany a soul leaving this life for the next (63b–c). The discussion is interrupted briefly by an interchange between Socrates and Crito, who is at pains to deliver the executioner's (the person responsible for administering the poison) message that talking too much tends to interfere with the efficacy of the poison, but Socrates quickly dismisses the issue (63d–e). The second point, designed to establish the desirability of death independently of any consideration regarding the gods, is that death is basically the separation of the soul from the body, a prospect especially desirable for the philosopher, whose lifelong pursuit of wisdom and knowledge is forever challenged by the limitations, distractions, and demands of the body (63e–69e). Though far richer and more respectable than the first, the second point is nevertheless argumentative rather than conclusive, thus uncovering but not settling the burning question: What happens after death?

The dual response to Cebes is more important for ushering in the proofs than for being one itself. At the center of this preparatory work is the emerging definition of death. The second point in the rebuttal defines death as the separation of the soul from the body (64c). This is reaffirmed later as "release or separation" of the soul from the body (67d). In both places, the definition of death, or that of dying, is said to coincide with the definition of philosophy, which, from this perspective, is the separation of the mental from the physical, pointing the way toward rationalism in epistemology and idealism in metaphysics. The philosopher, on this interpretation, resents the body during life, and, therefore, has no reason to fear or regret its loss in death.

Another highlight of the response is the shifting of the discussion into the realm of the forms, which are discussed rather than explained, as the audience seems to be familiar with at least the basics of the theory. (See § 2.5 for the forms and § 2.6 for their theoreticity.) Although this would not make a comprehensive orientation session for the novice, it provides useful insight into the theoretical framework of Plato's signature doctrine (65d–66a). Invoking the theory of forms, which are said to be understandable only through reason, especially when free of the influence of the senses, provides another opportunity for Socrates to defend his death wish. The theory is taken up more fully (starting from 100b) as a prelude to the final argument, where it turns out to be the single most important tool in demonstrating the immortality of the soul. As such, the philosophical portion of the dialogue can be said to begin and end with the theory of forms.

The immortality of the soul takes center stage as the topic of the day when the persistent promotion of death is challenged in regard to truth in advertising. The challenge is issued by Cebes, who refuses to consider the benefits of death without evidence of the survival of the putative beneficiary (69e–70b). He makes proof of life after death a prerequisite for the credibility of any account glorifying death. In pressing Socrates to demonstrate the soul's existence without the body, Cebes limits the kind of existence under consideration to personal rather than general or collective immortality, thus ruling out the subsistence of life at large as proof of immortality and rejecting any all-inclusive metaphysical force, entity, or state, say, something like universal energy, that is, the inherent perpetual motion in and of the universe, from satisfying the type of incorporeal existence in question.

Although the definition of death as the separation of the soul from the body begs the question of the existence of the soul, this is neither a trick nor an oversight but a mere reflection of the consensus of the time and place. The question embraced by the audience is not whether the soul exists at all but whether it continues to exist upon the destruction of the body. The apparently less demanding nature of this outlook by contemporary standards is an illusion reflecting a historical shift in perspective gradually subsuming a sense of immortality in the intension of the changing conception of the soul, parallel, in fact, to the evolving concept of soul. Hence, while the soul, in its modern conceptions, comes with an integrated sense of immortality, its origin in antiquity, the *psuchē* (ψυχή), literally "breath" or "life" or "spirit," is actually only an animating force whose immortality is a separate issue. Now invariably translated as "soul," the original "*psuchē*," or to be precise, its referent, the animating principle of life, is common and unique to all living things, so that its existence is never in question in regard to any life form. It is thus understandable that the *Phaedo* focuses on the immortality rather than the existence of the soul, whereas modern readers might require proof of its existence while granting its immortality as part of its essence. Yet the difference is not decisive in this context because any argument sufficient to establish the immortality of the *psuchē* in the classical sense would also suffice to establish the existence of an immortal soul in the modern sense.

7.2. Proof #1: Cyclical Transformation Argument

7.2.1. Logical Core

The first proof makes use of existing doctrine backed by original reasoning. It is essentially an appeal to reincarnation (or transmigration or metempsychosis) supported by an argument on causation in opposition, in other words, an argument on causal relations or directions between opposite things or states. The treatment of reincarnation is cursory, but this is because the standard formula is apparently familiar and readily agreeable among the members of the audience, who are in greater need of a justificatory exchange or revelation than an orientation session or a sales pitch.

The notion is inherently Pythagorean, as far as the Western philosophical tradition is concerned, with comparably strong representation in the mystery cults of Orpheus and Dionysus, though possibly owing its Greek presence to Indian influence rather than to spontaneous development. No matter the precise reason, the young philosophers gathered around Socrates on his last day are perfectly comfortable with the concept, regarding which the Pythagorean interlocutors might even be expected to boast some expertise, notwithstanding a surprising denial by Cebes of indoctrination in the afterlife (61d). To be entirely accurate, what Cebes denies, speaking both for himself and for Simmias, is *certain* or *definite* knowledge of such matters, not working knowledge, as evidently expected to have been transmitted through Philolaus. Accordingly, the task undertaken by Socrates is not to explain, promote, or preach reincarnation, but to produce a cogent argument in its favor.

The proof, in a nutshell, is that life and death, as a pair of opposites, come from one another, as do all pairs of opposites, and that this is a cyclical and reciprocal process demonstrating life after death.

The argument validating reincarnation makes use of a special theory of causation, special in the sense of having limited rather than general applicability. Socrates employs a causal theory governing opposition relations in order to establish death as an integral part of the reincarnation cycle he refers to as an "ancient tale." The crux of the theory is a cyclical and reciprocal process of generation between opposites, such that anything that comes to take on an attribute that has an opposite must have previously been in a state best characterized by that opposite attribute. Thus, things becoming larger must have first been smaller, those becoming smaller must have been larger, and so on for any pair of opposites. Following a few instantiations to demonstrate the way it works, the basic equation is applied to the "ancient tale" of reincarnation, toward such proof as it is susceptible of.

Socrates lays out the argument in four steps, first going through iterations of opposition to demonstrate the phenomenon in question, next establishing the generation process as reciprocal, that is, as equally relevant to and productive of both ends of an opposition, subsequently proposing life and death as a pair of opposites that fits the bill, and finally showing that the reciprocal process is cyclical, so as to preclude a terminus, not merely in life and death but in the opposition platform in general.

The first step (70e–71a) is a conceptual illustration providing an ostensibly comprehensive overview of opposition, be it in things, states, events, or attributes. Here, Socrates lists seven pairs of opposites in the following order: beautiful/ugly; just/unjust; larger/smaller; weaker/stronger; swifter/slower; worse/better; more just/more unjust. The first two pairs of opposites concern absolute phenomena, while the remaining five are relative properties stated in comparative terms, yet they all have a singular anchor, each pair denoting opposite states of one thing, and thus tracing change from one end of a continuum to the other.

The second step (71a–d) examines the relationship between any pair of opposites from the perspective of causation, or, in more definite and less controversial terms, change, becoming, or origination. The lesson here is that every pair of opposites bears two processes of generation, one, from the first to the second, and, another, from the second to the first. Socrates offers four examples of this reciprocal causal process: increasing/decreasing (as exemplified by the process of transformation from a smaller thing to a larger thing and vice versa); separating/combining; cooling/heating; falling asleep/waking up (identified as the process of transformation between being asleep and being awake). He also squeezes in among these examples a contrast between being alive and being dead, further illustrating opposite states for which reciprocal processes might be considered, but this becomes a separate step constituting the heart of the proof.

The third step (71d–72a) is the final instantiation of the general schema. Just as being asleep and being awake are opposite states brought about by the reciprocal processes of falling asleep and waking up, so, too, Socrates submits, being dead and being alive are opposite states governed by the reciprocal processes of dying and coming back to life. This is a bold stance reflecting strong commitment to the basic opposition formula in the choice of "coming back to life" or "coming to life again" as the opposite process for dying, where a deliberately noncommittal position could have been forged instead by embracing a vague alternative such as "birth" or "being born" (71e). As it is, this is a lopsided choice that distorts the parallel construction, which would seem to require the other element of the established reciprocity to be qualified by a comparable reference to repetition, reciprocity, and cyclicality, such as "dying again," or, less gracefully but also to the point, "going back to death" or "going to death again." Perhaps the cyclicality indicators ("back to *x*"; "*x* again") could have fruitfully been left out at both ends of the continuum here, since the process is guaranteed in the fourth step.

The fourth step (72a–e) is the concluding touch perpetuating the generation process in an everlasting cycle of change. This step is designed to circumvent the exhaustibility of the supply to be processed. Socrates grounds the necessity of this step in the insufficiency of finite processes to explain the ongoing and cotemporaneous existence of life and death as opposite states. The motivating concern is the inevitability of all things ending up in one state of opposition or the other, unless the reciprocal process is cyclical *ad infinitum*. Socrates illustrates this with the example that, if going to sleep were not balanced by waking up, eventually, no one awake would be left. His solution is to merge the two reciprocal processes he had already established into one never-ending cycle precluding exhaustion, expiration, or termination in either direction. This entire step could be considered superfluous from a different perspective: The perpetuity may be said to be readily implied in the sheer reciprocity of the processes it perpetuates. On this interpretation, if it is granted that the living come from the dead, and, the dead, from the living, the assent leaves no room for an objection that this cannot happen more than once, or twice, or even a countless many times, as the initial concession comes with a presumption in favor of unlimited iteration. Be that as it may, redundancy alone will hardly damage an otherwise acceptable argument.

7.2.2. Problems

7.2.2.1. Conceptual Cacophony

Life and death are not analyzed as rigorously as might be expected from an initiative to promote an immortal soul as the common thread running through their cyclical continuity. The concepts are not explored further than necessary to link them in causal connection, temporal succession, or popular conviction. This being so, the argument advances with less clarity than might be desired, or useful, or even required.

The stream of reasoning meanders through various modes of a fundamental contrast between life and death. This is not to say that the course is not clear. The basic strategy is to connect a pair of states with a pair of processes: being dead and being alive are opposite states coming about through the reciprocal processes of dying and coming back to life (71d–72a). Yet the rest of the same passage is conceptually and terminologically quite busy. The relevant range Socrates makes explicit includes the following pairs: life/death; being alive/being dead; what is living/what is dead; the living/the dead. The transformation process he posits for these opposites does not come with such variation, instead simply juxtaposing dying and coming back to life.

Exacerbating the thematic cacophony, the concept of death does not receive uniform treatment throughout the dialogue: Central usage is based on the separation of the soul and the body (64c, 67d), but the final argument draws on an implicit definition as the destruction of the soul. Actually, an understanding of death as the destruction of the soul is operative in Cebes's original challenge

(70a–b) to Socrates's death wish; it is reasserted three arguments later in Cebes's objection (86e–88b, especially 88b) to the third argument and to most of what has been said up to that point; and it is acknowledged in Socrates's recapitulation (95c–e) of that objection. But Socrates goes through three proofs arguing for the immortality of the soul in reference to death as the separation of the soul and the body before honoring the original and repeated challenge to present a proof based on death as the destruction of the soul.

Presumably, these should be the same, or at least sufficiently analogous, since the object is to establish the soul's indestructibility with particular emphasis on its separation from the body, but the separation angle can be deceptively vague. If the conception of death driving the final argument represents the definitive understanding of the subject, then the first argument is stripped of its force: If the first argument were to be reformulated to take the soul's destruction as one of the two poles in the relevant opposition, then life, or coming back to life, would have to be redefined as the creation or recreation of the soul, as opposed to the reincarnation of a soul already in existence, having been separated from a previous body but not destroyed, with the substitution undermining the meaningfulness of a reciprocal process and precluding the possibility of an eternal cycle.

The treatment of life and death is shaky enough in the first argument alone, without judging its consistency throughout the dialogue. Life is a union between the soul and the body, and, death, the dissolution of that union. This certainly draws a contrast between life and death, but it does not necessarily make opposites out of the living and the dead. Nor does reciprocal generation present itself as a necessary or even viable connection in this context. Given that life is the union of the soul and the body, living things are compound entities consisting of a soul and a body, or, in short, they are corporeal souls, or ensouled bodies. Given that death is the dissolution of that union, dead things are of two kinds, souls without bodies and bodies without souls, or, rearranging the construction, disembodied souls and inanimate bodies. On this account, what has been proven, that the dead come from the living, and, the living, from the dead, establishes merely that the soul and the body come together to form a single entity, which eventually dissolves into its constituents.

Despite the fact that the cycle established involves nothing more than separation and combination, Socrates speaks of the prospect of meeting good men and good gods upon separation, as if the soul were certain to go on living much like it does in its joint existence with the body. In fact, the afterlife is better, so much so as to make earthly existence seem like an insufferable yet mandatory chore in comparison. One wonders why the soul ever even needs a body. The momentous event from the perspective of the body is its union with the soul, but the cause for celebration for the soul is its separation from the body. Yet the separation specific to the argument does not promise such a smooth transition, familiar setting, or agreeable experience. It does not even guarantee life in the same sense. If, as Socrates contends, life is a union of soul and body, and, conversely, death is a separation of the same, and, thus, living things are, by definition, composite beings, then the soul itself is not and cannot ever be alive, just as the body on its own is denied the same possibility. The soul without a body, the incorporeal soul, is no more a life form, or living thing, than is the body without a soul, that is, the unensouled body. As the two unite and disband, ostensibly in a repeating sequence through eternity, the only time either one is in the coveted state is when they are together. This trivializes what it means for the dead to come from the living, and, the living, from the dead, even in a complete and eternal circle, because the argument tautologically attributes life only to living organisms, repudiating it as a possible property of disembodied souls. It also muddles how life and death might be understood in opposition, a relationship murky enough on its own, independently of any ambiguities in the elements nominated as examples.

A possible response is that the soul, as the quintessential animating principle of life, has a privileged status in the union, and that, being already alive, it is neither benefited by joining the body, nor harmed by leaving it behind. If so, it certainly would not be killed by separation from the body, which it does not need in the first place. Something like this must be close to how Plato would respond, and it might even be gleaned from the text without his further assistance. However, it still leaves us with the question of why we need the body at all, not merely in a general metaphysical sense, but also with respect to the cyclically reciprocal process described. The body cannot be both necessary and irrelevant to that process, and thereby to life and death.

7.2.2.2. Vague Opposition

The concept of opposition is not clear in itself. Nor is Socrates clear in his own conception of it. This creates problems for the central contrast between life and death, not to mention their various modes and derivatives. Nothing can be both living and dead at once, but things can be neither living nor dead. A rock is not a living thing, but it cannot properly be called dead. The opposition best capturing the essential distinction relevant to the context may well be between life forms and inorganic matter instead of between living things and dead things. Borrowing the terminology of formal logic, does opposition require contradiction or is contrariety sufficient? Although contradiction and contrariety are relations in the domain of propositional and predicate calculus, meaning, basically, that they apply to propositions, quantifiers, and predicates, and not to things and their names, the logical terminology affords a useful way to discuss the examples on hand, which could, if needed, be expressed in propositions or recast as predicates, before being contrasted, entirely with the same practical results.

A question to the same effect can be posed without borrowing terminology whose relevance requires demonstration and whose application needs qualification: Must opposites be jointly exhaustive as well as mutually exclusive? Perhaps the appropriate contrast is not between living things and dead things, nor between life forms and inorganic matter, but, more generally, between things that are alive and things that are not alive, the latter including things that were once alive (dead life forms) as well as those that never were (e.g., inorganic matter, incoherent energy, and, arguably, universals).

Depending on how the question is posed, contrariety, or mutual exclusivity, does not provide sufficient insight into opposition. The problem with accepting contrariety as opposition is that any two physical objects can be considered opposites in this sense, because nothing is something else instead, nor, of course, in addition, so long as we take "is" in the sense of identity. In the immortal words of Bishop Butler (1729, preface: ¶ 39), "everything is what it is, and not another thing." For example, a ball and a mall become opposites under this allowance, since nothing can be both a ball and a mall, at least not at the same time. Hence, contrariety is not restrictive enough to explicate opposition in the conventional denotation of the term. It captures all instances of opposition coincident with common sense, but it includes too much, as it fails to filter out cases we would not normally classify under opposition.

This inadequacy of contrariety to illuminate the concept of opposition pertains only to substances, not to properties or existential conditions, wherein a thing can be both hot and small, opaque and beautiful, soft and slow, and so on, or even all these things at once. Nevertheless, a categorical account of opposition requires contradiction and cannot be satisfied through mere contrariety. Indeed, opposites must be mutually exclusive, but this is not enough, as they must also be jointly exhaustive.

The ambiguity in the specific opposition on hand is skewed heavily in one direction. With reference to the dead coming from the living, which is the same as the living turning into the dead, the conceptual connection in the text is clearly between a person and a corpse, or, by extension in general terms, between the living and lifeless bodies of any organism at different times. It cannot be between the incarnate and disincarnate souls of a person because making that distinction as a premise would be to assume too much of what has to be demonstrated through argument, the disincarnate viability of the soul. It would also run against the grain of the classical notion of soul, which does not have immortality built into it. This makes it reasonable to take the transition from life to death as one from a living being to a dead one. However, the link is not so clear in the other direction, as babies do not come from corpses. On the contrary, they come from other living beings, either copulating or making other arrangements, but demonstrating rather effectively that the living come from the living, not, as Socrates claims, from the dead. If the causal flow laid out by Socrates is to be followed, where exactly do the living come from in the assertion that they come from the dead? Nowhere obvious, to be sure.

It might be objected that the contrast with dead bodies distorts the original intention, wherein the opposition relation is not anchored exclusively to the body but to the soul as well. Yet Socrates himself claims that the process of generation is evident in one direction, namely, from life to death (71e). This is an allusion to how the natural experience of death, that is, the opportunity to witness it in others, affords first-hand knowledge of the way the living end up dead. Regardless of whether the opposition relation is anchored to the body, to the soul, or to both at once, the only physical evidence available and relevant is the transition from person to corpse. The counterpart of the process, purportedly from death to life, does not proceed from corpse to body, and thus leaves a gap that cannot be filled automatically by souls in Hades.

The problem is not unique to this particular pair of putative opposites. Similar cases are legion. The opposite of hot is not necessarily cold, for not everything that is not hot is cold; some are neither hot nor cold. Is the opposite of beautiful, ugly, or is it something in between, something that can safely be predicated of what is not beautiful as well as what is not ugly? What is the opposite of jovial; is it serene or is it wretched? Even cats and dogs are contrasted in ways suggesting opposition, and, curiously, so are cats and mice, and, on occasion, cats and birds, though it is just as appropriate, or inappropriate, logically, to consider cats against maggots, magnolias, or magnesia toward the same end. But the general problem is best illustrated by examples where the extreme ends of a continuum are mutually exclusive with each other as well as with some point or region in the middle.

The potential for confusion rests in the fact that things that are both mutually exclusive and jointly exhaustive may safely be considered opposites, whereas mutually exclusive things that are not jointly exhaustive have opposition options besides each other.

People sometimes speak of an exact opposite, but the superlative is superfluous when applied to contraries or contradictories. Two things either are or are not contraries, not more or less so, and the same holds for contradictories. Exactitude adds nothing.

The examples in the text, particularly those that matter, do not illustrate the current understanding of logical opposition. Although Socrates, or Plato, cannot reasonably, and without anachronism, be criticized for failing to conform to contemporary standards, the main problem is, nevertheless, that neither these opposites nor any others, whether merely contrary or properly contradictory, actually come from each other, except in the trivial sense in which something can, over time, become relatively more demonstrative or less demonstrative of a certain property, quality, or attribute, or, in a similar vein, more apt or less apt to be described as being in a certain state or condition. Otherwise, the connection simply does not exist, as can be demonstrated through any of numerous counterexamples, such as the fact that a true proposition need neither have ever been false, nor be destined to end up false. To place life and death in the category of the larger and the smaller is to beg the question of the immortality of the soul, or at least of the continuity of personal identity between life and death.

7.2.2.3. Noncausal Opposition and Discrete Opposites

Opposition is not sufficient evidence of a causal relationship, or of any relationship whatsoever other than the bare opposition. Two things can be opposites without causing, generating, turning into, or in any way affecting each other. The attribution of a causal process to opposition works for relative (comparative) opposites in a self-referential context, but it becomes vacuous in external comparisons, and is entirely irrelevant with respect to absolute opposites. Not every pair of opposites consists of elements that must, or even can, come from or originate in each other. For example, the larger and the smaller might come from each other in the right frame of reference, but not so with the large and the small: Admittedly, that which is larger than it used to be must have been smaller than it is. But that which is larger than something else, larger, that is, at least at the present time, need not have been smaller than that thing at any other time, and, in fact, need not have ever been any different in size. Moreover, that which is said simply to be large, without explicit comparison, is almost always considered large as a member of a class of things, having never been small as a member of that same class, much in the way that a large car does not have its origins in a small car.

This case of the large and the small, troublesome even in the convenient reformulation as a contrast between the larger and the smaller, is not an aberration in an otherwise unproblematic metaphysical theory. Examples abound: good/bad; right/wrong; moral/immoral; just/unjust; love/hate; pleasure/pain; cheerful/miserable; certain/doubtful; possible/impossible; necessary/unnecessary; sufficient/insufficient; clean/dirty; clear/vague; transparent/opaque; light/dark; tall/short; hot/cold; high/low; soft/hard; loud/quiet; fast/slow. None suggests reciprocal origination.

The possibility of causal discreteness or disjunction in opposition casts doubt upon the organic relationship woven into the opposition between life and death. If not all opposites come from each other, then opposition cannot be the sole or decisive reason that life and death come from each other; further argumentation is required to establish that conclusion. The conclusion that the living come from the dead, and, the dead, from the living, is based on nothing other than the inductive argument for the cyclically reciprocal origination of opposites in each other. A single counterexample to the induction offered suffices to overturn the generalization and any instantiation grounded in it. Just as something beautiful need not have ever been ugly, so, too, something alive need not have ever been dead. The possibility is open in either case, but necessity accompanies neither. What is required, however, is not an argument showing that the soul might be immortal, particularly since that possibility, like any other, can safely be adopted even without argument. What is required, rather, is an argument confirming that the soul is immortal.

7.2.2.4. Reincarnation

A final problem is with the conclusion. This is not to rehash the logic of the argument, but to consider the conclusion as a proposition of its own, independently of how well it is supported by the given premises. Regardless of whether the argument is successful, the conclusion is in apparent conflict with the setting attendant on the scenario of reincarnation.

Specifically, reincarnation appears to be inconsistent with global population growth, at least in the absence of relevant assumptions. A remedial adjustment might be to assume that souls are produced as needed to animate new bodies. This implies that not all souls are the same age, which is not problematic in itself, but the simultaneous production of souls and bodies could be interpreted as undermining the argument from recollection presented as the second proof, though not necessarily overturning it. Furthermore, a corollary to maintaining production facilities to meet earthly demand during population growth is to furnish a waiting room at the other side for souls sitting out an earthly episode in accordance with rotating ensoulment duty during periods of population decline. None of this is absurd, but reincarnation appears to be more complicated than the deceptive simplicity of a cyclical transformation.

The flip side to tinkering with the soul supply is to be more creative with the target population. For example, perhaps the total population to be ensouled includes other rational beings in other worlds so that a fixed number of souls suffices to animate the separate stocks, some of which may be growing, while others are in decline, together amounting to a fixed total. An alternative, still affirming a constant number of souls, but, this time, without recourse to other worlds, is to avoid a deficit simply by assuming the number of readily available souls, those not currently trapped in bodies, to be large enough to accommodate earthly population growth all the way through the carrying capacity of the planet. Any of these solutions, or any other sensible way out, would do, since the problem is not an insurmountable difficulty with the scenario but a vagueness in the presentation.

An approach commanding caution, however, is the tempting scenario, a variant response to the population problem, that souls animating bodies are cut out as needed from an impersonal and inexhaustible cluster of soul-stuff constituting the singular source of all souls. The difficulty here is that the setup introduces a discrepancy between a distinctly impersonal source and an entirely personal product. It is not impossible to conceive of a personal product originating in an impersonal source, as personalization can be imagined to be a byproduct of the process, but this would be both less elegant and less clear than the assumption of precise interdimensional continuity between incarnate and disincarnate souls. What is needed is not just an *ad hoc* solution to problems peculiar to reincarnation but a sustainable ontological position that does not multiply assumptions beyond the requirements of a coherent general theory on the soul.

A real complication arises when Socrates enlarges the animation pool beyond the human species. This occurs at a later point, in a mythical account elaborating on the third argument (81e–82b). The enlargement of the cycle of reincarnation to include just about any sentient species, ranging from wolves to hawks to bees, vitiates the preservation of personal identity through the transmigration process. While Socrates never claims that reincarnation is an ongoing journey where the mind survives exactly as it is at any point in life, with all memories intact and personality the same, the kind of immortality Cebes wants demonstrated is definitely of a personal nature in the sense that what is unique to each individual is preserved through various incarnations (70a–b). What is particularly clear is a requirement to retain reasoning ability, a standard where the birds and the bees may not be able to live up to expectations, not, at any rate, to those of Cebes (70b). This, however, is not a problem with the first argument but a mismatch between the parameters of the original challenge and the extended contamination of the result supported by the argument constructed to meet that challenge.

7.2.3. Critical Assessment

The proof fails at multiple levels. The manifold breakdown can be summarized as follows:

- The approach to life and death is analytically shallow. An exigent drive to link the two concepts together supplants a more fundamental exploration of their essence. The resulting foundational setup is neither firm, nor informative, nor compelling.

- Even if the approach were analytically richer in regard to the core elements, the treatment of opposition would still be problematic. The concept itself is ambiguous between logical opposition, that is, the polarity between terms or propositions that are both mutually exclusive and jointly exhaustive, and popular opposition, which covers all other contrasts, including but not limited to mutually exclusive relations that do not exhaust the relevant range. Socrates does not state which he is considering, nor does he distinguish between these two interpretations, but he proceeds with contrary rather than contradictory pairs in his examples and arguments.

- Even if the analytic core were solid, and, the operative conception of opposition, apposite to the context, opposites would still not necessarily come from one another. A wet thing, say, a fish in water, or, better yet, the water itself, need not ever have been dry; nor is it naturally inclined, and certainly not necessarily destined, to become dry. A similar disjunction can just as sensibly be attributed to the concepts of life and death.

- Even if the argument were valid, relevant, and convincing, the conclusion would still be problematic as a judgment pertaining to the prevailing metaphysical context. Reincarnation is rather enigmatic, especially without further elaboration, and requires numerous assumptions and provisions for internal coherence, let alone general tenability.

The point here is not to destroy the argument several times over but to show that it is riddled with problems. To be sure, a single decisive defect is sufficient to overturn the proof. Bringing out all that is wrong is not necessary. However, doing so helps draw attention to an oddity begging for explanation. The fact that this is such a bad proof is at odds with the consensus that neither Socrates nor Plato is such a bad philosopher. This is not to suggest that Socrates or Plato cannot make mistakes. Yet it would be difficult for anyone, let alone a legendary philosopher, to cram so many serious blunders into a single argument.

Why does Socrates, or Plato, depending on the view of authorship, begin with such an atrocious argument? More interesting, why is this proof included in the text, given that it is superseded by others? The mere fact that the dialogue continues in pursuit of a proof of the conclusion supposedly just established is evidence that neither the author nor the protagonist is satisfied with this attempt. Why, then, even mention it?

The answer might best be sought in the drama, particularly in plot elements, diegetic strands, and mimetic features unique to the time and place but lost to readers today. A conclusive answer might require the development of a separate thesis, or several in combination, but a working hypothesis is sufficient for a plausible scenario: Perhaps the purpose of the proof is to honor or emphasize the Pythagorean context. With the central interlocutors well-versed in Pythagorean doctrine, an argument supporting reincarnation might constitute a natural fit. Or, reversing the hypothetical motive, the lame attempt at proof might be a way of debunking Pythagorean dogma without even arguing against it. This would also be more consistent with the fact that the Pythagorean interlocutors intimate an element of inadequacy in their grasp of reincarnation (61d).

Nearly as striking as the vacuity of the proof is its reception. It attracts neither praise nor censure. The absence of objection is especially conspicuous in the face of the glaring problems. Other than the final argument, apparently intended to be definitive, this is the only argument that does not draw an objection from the audience. In fact, it attracts no attention, positive or negative, instead seamlessly blending into the next proof. Why? Possibly because Plato finds it to deserve mention as an account already in circulation, but does not believe it to merit serious consideration. This would also seem to support the supposition regarding indirect homage to Pythagoreanism, or, depending on the perspective, indirect critique of Pythagoreanism, perhaps not in connection with the entire philosophy but just the notion of reincarnation, or, maybe even more narrowly, with only the particular argument considered here.

7.3. Proof #2: Recollection Argument

7.3.1. Logical Core

The second proof is introduced almost immediately upon the conclusion of the first. The only dramatic transition is a comment by Cebes, informing the audience, or, as is the case with the most important of those in attendance, reminding them, that a proof of this sort is available (72e). The central argument is not a new one but a new way of using an evidently familiar epistemological theory. The theory in question is the doctrine that learning is recollection, which holds that the original knowledge serving as the basis for recollection, that is, the knowledge by virtue of which, or, in reference to which, learning is recollection, must have been obtained or attained prior to birth, thus constituting proof of the existence of the soul prior to birth, and, by implication, its sustainability independently of the body, though the emphasis in the text is specifically on the prenatal existence of the soul rather than generally on its disembodied or disincarnate existence.

The dramatic segue into the argument operates with Cebes mentioning the recollection doctrine as an adjunct to the first argument, while addressing Simmias, who, ironically, happens to know and accept the theory invoked, but cannot remember it. Cebes touches upon two points of justification for the doctrine, both drawing on epistemological drama in another dialogue (*Meno* 81a–86c), but Socrates pursues an altogether different route here. Specifically, Cebes reports that the doctrine is corroborated (1) by the propensity to give correct answers to questions posed in a particular way in areas where one has never received any education or training, and (2) by the significance of diagrams or visual aids as facilitating such interaction, wherein they would not be pedagogically useful without recollection (73a–b).

Socrates redirects the discussion from learning in general to learning as recollection, thus leaving room, albeit unexplored, for the possibility that some learning is not recollection, and thereby introducing an implicit distinction between learning that is and is not recollection (73c). The proof he lays out on this foundation turns on knowledge of the forms as a type of recollection for which the original source cannot be found within the realm of sense experience and must be sought outside that domain, hence, in a state of independence from the senses, which points to a time preceding birth, that is, the inception of sense experience, and, presumably, the moment of union between soul and body.

The forms, originally introduced while discussing the hindrance of the body in the pursuit of wisdom (starting at 65d), become the heart of the proof in the second argument (starting at 74a). The primary form driving the argument is equality, or, as it is also known, the equal, or the equal itself, though the reasoning is applied to several other forms as well, possibly to avoid having the argument associated exclusively with a single example, on the peculiarities of which it might be thought contingent. The gist of the illustration concerning equality is the tension between its absence in the physical realm and its presence in the mind. Given that equality itself is not an object of experience, the recognition of particular things as striving after equality but falling short of it is purported to be evidence of prenatal knowledge, making the independent existence of the soul a necessary condition of *a priori* knowledge. Complementing the defining role assigned to the form of equality, the forms mentioned to demonstrate the universality of the argument include beauty, goodness, justice, and holiness (or the beautiful, the good, the just, and the holy), and, in short, anything that fits the description "what *x* itself is" (75d).

The meat of the proof is a stretch of reasoning called the "equal sticks argument" (74a–77a) after a memorable appeal to equal sticks (also translated as "logs") to illustrate the underdetermination of knowledge by sense perception. The aim is to contrast knowledge of equality with experience of it, wherein the knowledge is not and cannot be justified by the experience, thus establishing that such knowledge must have been attained prior to being wired with sense perception. Equal sticks, and later also stones, take the stage as striving after equality but falling short, hence, never going beyond merely resembling the equal itself, but thereby reflecting an assessment requiring knowledge of the equal itself, which, given the present conditions precluding such acquaintance through earthly experience, must have been known prior to birth. This illustration often divides commentators:

- A common interpretation is that the illustration depicts nearly equal sticks falling short of perfect equality, thus contrasting the approximation possible in the physical realm with the perfection reserved for the conceptual realm. This makes the central issue precision, but this is unlikely to have been Plato's main concern here because bringing sticks into alignment can hardly bridge the gap between the sensible world and that of the forms.

- Another interpretation is that sticks may appear equal to some people but not to others, equal in reference to some things but not to others (compared with, say, other sticks, or with altogether different things, such as stones), and equal at some times but not at others, whereas the equal itself is always equal in every respect. This focuses on the relativity of the equality in physical objects, and on subjective and temporal fragilities in such equality, in contrast to the absolute stability of the equal itself.

- A better interpretation is to take the contrast in question to be between sticks of the exact same size and appearance on the one hand and the equal itself on the other. This construes the illustration as showing that the equality of sticks, even if they are precisely the same length, width, depth, weight, and volume, is merely equality in size, which does not exhaust the concept of equality, and cannot, therefore, be identified with the equal itself. For those who deny that physical objects can be exactly the same size, the basic formula works just as well with triangles, squares, circles, or other geometric figures.

- Another option is to take the illustration as distinguishing between manifest and transcendent equality, that is, demonstrating that instances of the equal in particulars is not the same as the equal itself, even where the particular instantiation of equality is not lacking in precision. This is similar to the preceding interpretation except that the focus here is not merely on failure to be equal in every conceivable way but, even more rigorously, on failure to be the equal itself.

Any of these interpretations can be forced on the text, as nothing in the original rules them out. The last two seem closer to the spirit of the philosophical position inspiring the illustration in the first place. In any event, the distinction intended is between equality of some sort, or in some way, and equality without qualification, which ostensibly demonstrates that our experience of sticks and stones is not sufficient to account for our knowledge of equality. Plato cannot be cornered on this point with the objection that our acquaintance with triangles, squares, circles, and so on would be sufficient to account for our knowledge of equality without recourse to assuming prenatal existence for the soul, for he could just as sensibly deny the possibility of earthly experience of geometric figures.

The implicit distinction between learning that is and is not recollection (73c) is lost toward the end of the argument (75a onward), but this is not important, because the success of the proof does not depend on this distinction. Perhaps Plato had a lapse in precision in maintaining the distinction, or perhaps he never meant to demonstrate or imply any concern for it to begin with, the possibility remaining open but inconsequential. At any rate, the success of the argument depends neither on recollection being the only type of learning nor on learning being possible through means other than recollection.

7.3.2. Dramatic Reception

Simmias objects, with the support of Cebes, that this is only half a proof, that is, that the argument establishes the prenatal existence of the soul but not its survival of death (77b–c). Socrates has two responses, one short, the other long. The short response is a reminder that the missing half of the thesis had already been established in the first argument, and, therefore, that the two arguments in combination leave nothing out (77c–e). The long response probes the nature of the soul and its difference from the body, thereby addressing Cebes's original concern (69e–70b) that the soul might perish upon separation from the body, while meeting the revival of that concern by Simmias in response to the second argument. In this way, the long response develops into the third argument for the immortality of the soul.

7.3.3. Critical Assessment

The dramatic objection focuses on what appears to be a glaring oversight, but the recommendation to complete the proof through reference to the first argument still leaves the second one wanting, because the suggested fix acknowledges its contingency instead of establishing its success as a standalone whole. The appeal to the first argument reiterates the dramatic success of the proof therein. The first argument, never challenged by the dramatic audience, serves as a necessary foundation for the second argument, which may have been a pedagogical tool to advance the audience's initiation into the theory of forms, or a merely dramatic one to interject the theory of learning as recollection, but it also stands as an apparently superfluous adjunct to the first, as if introduced as an afterthought.

An altogether different response to the incompleteness objection might have been to trumpet a metaphysical rather than temporal gap in the possibility of knowledge of the forms. This would be to stress *that* they are known rather than *when* they are known, shifting the emphasis from the inference that they must have been known prior to birth to the corollary that knowledge is possible without the body. The magic here is the knowability of forms despite the inadequacy of sense experience to enable or facilitate that knowledge. Once such knowledge is acknowledged, the transition to a knower is no more illicit (and no less so) than the Cartesian leap, in the *cogito*, from thought or thinking to a thinker. An alternative approach of this sort could have embraced insight into the forms as a demonstration of the sustainability of the soul independently of the body, without a particular commitment to preceding or following the animation of the body.

Dramatic emphasis on an apparently crucial oversight, which turns out to be neither an oversight nor an arresting problem, leaves a number of possibly more challenging objections untouched, almost as if deliberately diverting attention away from them. The positioning of the apparent oversight as a snag in reasoning makes further scrutiny dramatically imperative, while the transformation of the extended response into the third argument limits the critical evaluation of the second argument. This is a brilliant dramatic move to dismiss the objection to the second argument while pretending to be exploring it further, and thereby keeping the dialogue moving in a seamless manner while abandoning everything accomplished up to that point. Meanwhile, the notion of forms begs for elaboration, and, the assumptions surrounding it, for justification.

Being fair to Plato in this regard requires noting that he readily concedes the point that the second argument fails unless the forms exist (76e), and that he later makes the existence of the forms a central and unquestioned hypothesis in the final argument (specifically at 99c–101e), subsequently declaring an eventual examination of the hypothesis necessary for laying the matter to rest with confidence (107b). However, additional issues that might have been debated fruitfully in the second argument include whether the forms are known or knowable at all even if they exist, and whether knowledge of them implies anything about a soul even if they exist and can be known.

At the very least, it may reasonably be objected that the argument begs the question of fundamental cognitive processes being manifested in or guided by some sort of latent knowledge of the forms. For example, belief formation through conceptualization both depends on and is proof of the existence of the forms. A backdrop of innate knowledge is not the only explanation for the ability or tendency to recognize that no two things are perfectly equal, or that equal things, whether severally or jointly, are not the same as the equal, or that the relationship between equal things is not the same as equality itself but merely a particular instance of it. Likewise, a subliminal epistemic framework is not necessary for characterizing anything as good or just or beautiful, even if we do not directly experience the good, the just, or the beautiful. In fact, it is possible instead, and just as consistent therein, to deny the existence of the forms without giving up the claim to predication, that is, without repudiating the legitimacy of attributing properties to subjects, while still advocating the existence and immortality of the soul. As it is, insight into the soul, its existence as well as its immortality, remains embedded in the intricate and otherwise conveniently discrete problem of universals.

7.4. Proof #3: Analogic (Affinity) Argument

The third proof, originating as Socrates's second and longer response to the objection to the second proof, proceeds in two parts, the first (78b–80b), foundational and logical, the second (80c–84b), speculative and mystical. The first part can be considered the argument proper, with the second constituting more of a myth than an argument. The argument is an analogic one, glorifying the soul through association with the forms and the gods, and holding its immortality evident in these relationships, while the mythical account subsequently elaborates on the fate of the soul upon separation from the body.

7.4.1. Logical Core

As the objection inspiring this argument is based on a fear that the soul might simply disintegrate or vanish into thin air upon death, the argument is designed specifically to show that the soul is not the kind of thing that can disperse, dissolve, or dissipate as such. The aim is to establish that the soul is more like the forms and the gods than it is like particular things, that is, for all intents and purposes, physical things. This introduces an essential contrast between the body as susceptible of and to change and the soul as immutable. The general similitude is also expressed specifically in terms of claims that the soul is more similar than the body to the forms and the gods, and that the body is more similar than the soul to particular things.

Although the argument is laid out in terms of loosely defined degrees of similitude, the kinship sought between the soul and the forms and the gods, not to mention that between the body and particular things, is much too strong to leave open. In effect, the resemblance should be understood to be strong enough to preclude the soul's destruction in the manner of physical objects. Put simply, and rather conveniently, the soul is so much like the forms and the gods, that it does not admit of disintegration or any other mode of termination common to mere things.

The analogy is pursued through three evidentiary observations:

- Invisibility (79a–b): The soul is invisible, thus constant and impervious to change, whereas the body is visible and amenable to change, with change in this context including, most notably, destruction.

- Intelligibility (79c–e): The soul, when united with the body, becomes erratic, confused, and dizzy, as it is dragged into the realm of particulars, whereas, by itself, it achieves wisdom through reason, as it dwells in the realm of pure thought untainted by impressions of earthly objects.

- Divinity (79e–80a): The soul is the master and ruler, and, the body, the servant and subject, in the union between the soul and the body, thus making the soul more like the divine, and, the body, more like the mortal.

The conclusion is that the soul is most like what is divine, immortal, intelligible, uniform, indestructible, and immutable, whereas the body is most like the other extreme in each of the categories represented by these predicates (80a–b). The corollary to this conclusion is that it is thus fitting for the body to be easily destroyed while the soul remains indestructible, or "very nearly so" (80b). The specific attribute of the soul that shapes its distinction from the body and its kinship with the forms and the gods turns out to be its simplicity, in other words, the fact that it is not compound or composite, and thus not liable to be separated into constituent elements (78c).

7.4.2. Critical Assessment

This argument, like all the others, simply assumes the existence of the soul and proceeds to prove its immortality. This is not necessarily problematic since that which is immortal must also exist, but if the conclusion regarding immortality rests on the assumption of an existence analogous to immortality, then the proof itself might be said to be circular. The problem, then, is not simply that the argument rests on the existence of the soul, but that it depends on and assumes the existence of the soul with an ontological profile over and above the bare minimum that may conceivably be needed to animate a body, and, in fact, bordering on outright divinity. It depends on the existence of the soul because it has to have something answering the role of resembling the forms and the gods. It assumes the existence of the soul because it uncritically assigns the soul to that role. As for the connection with divinity, the conclusion establishing the immortality of the soul turns out to require the existence of something sufficiently similar to the forms and the gods to make it immortal, and this sufficiency is generously provided in the premises explicating the nature of the soul.

The two arguments preceding this one do not rely on the existence of the soul as a formal premise: The first argument, that based on causation in opposition, makes the soul out to be a common denominator in the continuous reciprocal transformation between life and death, while the second argument, that drawing on recollection, locates the soul at the fountain of knowledge, establishing, furthering, or simply enjoying a state of wisdom prior to birth. To be sure, the existence of the soul is not questioned anywhere in the dialogue, which revels in unadulterated metaphysical dualism, but the first two arguments do not logically depend on the existence of the soul, and, in fact, might reasonably be said to demonstrate its existence, at least by implication, at the end, whereas the third argument is firmly anchored not only to the existence of the soul but to its existence as a demigod of sorts.

The soul must exist in order to resemble the forms and the gods, a resemblance which constitutes the sole proof of its immortality, which, then, requires its existence as well as its immortality instead of demonstrating either. Here, too, as mentioned or discussed in other relevant places, assuming the existence of the soul is not unreasonable in the prevailing scientific context, where living things have a soul as a matter of fact. That said, logic is timeless, and we may reasonably ask that arguments comply with its basic principles. Manipulating the essence of the soul to guarantee its immortality makes the assumption of its existence circular, and this constitutes a transgression regardless of the context.

In addition to this general problem with the proof, the specific evidentiary observations making up the argument are open to objection:

- Invisibility (79a–b): The soul's invisibility does not necessarily establish its immutability. Just as an odor, invisible though it may be, dissipates over time, so, too, might the soul. Plato's reference to invisibility, however, could be interpreted more liberally as the quality of being undetectable by any of the senses, not just by sight, so that things that cannot be seen but can be perceived by one or more of the other senses do not constitute counterexamples. Going a step further, the interpretation can be cast in terms of freedom from material existence, thus avoiding reference to sense perception altogether, whether by humans or by any other species. Even so, invisibility understood in the broadest sense is still not proof of immutability. The most that we can sensibly claim of something that is not amenable to observation, directly or indirectly, is that we do not know whether it is susceptible of change. If souls can vary in the extent to which they are moral, just, wise, and so on, becoming more so or less so over time, then they are indeed susceptible of change. And if they can change in these ways, why might they not change in other ways?

- Intelligibility (79c–e): The premise that sense experience is, despite the obvious ways in which it facilitates human reasoning, ultimately an obstacle to pure reason does not imply the conclusion that reasoning would be better, or even at all possible, in its absence. Put differently, the fact that the body undermines the soul's pursuit of wisdom does not prove that the soul can reason clearly, or at all, independently of the body. Even with the body as a hindrance to reasoning, the destruction or absence of the body could conceivably entail the destruction or absence of a reasoner. The complaint that the body impedes reasoning might well be inspired by a defective understanding imagining two things where there is one, and an outside obstacle where there is none. The limits to our insight into the forms might simply be a reflection of the fact that we just are not very good at reasoning, indicating that this is the extent of our wisdom and intelligence, given the way we are, and given that we cannot be other than the way we are. The epistemic tension between the soul and the body, specifically, the superiority of one over the other in the acquisition of knowledge, plus the burden represented by the inferior party in this regard, leaves open the question whether anything capable of reasoning survives the destruction of the body, that is, whether any intelligence remains following the moment of death.

- Divinity (79e–80a): The relationship between the soul and the body is only loosely, and not exactly, like that between ruler and subject, and the transition from a minor resemblance in this area to an analogy contrasting the divine and the mortal is neither justified in itself nor established by argument. First, the soul's hegemony over the body is not absolute. Sometimes the body's wants or needs overwhelm the will, pushing it out of alignment with what might be expected to be the demands of reason alone. This switches the roles of the ruler and the subject as they apply to the soul and the body. Second, the distinction between ruler and subject is not sufficiently similar to the distinction between divine and mortal to conclude that two things that bear the first relation must also bear the second. Two things that stand in the relation of ruler and subject, or that exist in a sufficiently analogous position, need not also exhibit the opposing characteristics essential to the distinction between the divine and the mortal. Hence, even if the relationship between the soul and the body were exactly like that between the ruler and the subject, this would not be sufficient to conclude that the relationship is also like that between the divine and the mortal. Third, the difference in identity between the ruler and the subject, or between divine and mortal beings, does not extend as clearly to the soul and the body, which operate so much like a single entity as to maintain a standing element of doubt regarding the ascription of any relationship. The reasonableness of regarding them as two separate entities goes to the heart of what is being debated.

In the final analysis, the argument begs the question in more ways than one. Not only is the soul assumed to exist, but its existence is placed well near divinity, wherein the proof of its immortality is pursued solely through a purported resemblance to things that are commonly considered indestructible, likewise, with no question regarding their existence.

More important, the indestructible things reportedly resembled, namely, the forms and the gods, represent entirely different ontological categories, at least in the sense that the forms are presumably neither sapient nor sentient nor even alive, whereas the gods are typically considered not merely alive, sentient, and sapient, but immortal to boot. Given a choice, one might prefer to be indestructible in the manner of the gods than in the manner of the forms, if, that is, either one exists at all. After all, things that do not exist at all, or, expressed with perhaps greater precision, things that are generally considered not to exist in reality, though discussed by convention as if they did exist, as in, say, the Easter Bunny, are also indestructible, without being particularly enviable in that respect. Indeed, the Easter Bunny, were it a real rabbit, would be a perishable creature, but, as it is, it is indestructible simply because things that do not exist cannot cease to exist. This, however, is not the kind of indestructibility that would satisfy the audience, be it the one portrayed in the drama or the one addressed through it.

There is, of course, a certain level of reality that accommodates the existence of even the Easter Bunny, which is, after all, a real construct, one that is, rather than is not, the hero of a genuine experience in the lives of a good many people. But, again, one hopes for more than this kind of existence, and looks for something better in fulfillment of immortality. Making the soul indestructible by placing it outside the realm of things that can be destroyed not only begs the question but also seems to trivialize the soul, running the risk of leaving it outside the realm of things that matter, and possibly even those that exist.

7.4.3. Speculative Elaboration

The argument proper blends into a speculative account of the way death works, a story recounted in the typical fashion of a Platonic myth but without the usual reference to hearsay and lore as the source of the report. The absence of effort to distinguish Socrates as a mere reporter as opposed to the progenitor or advocate of the account is striking in contrast to other Platonic myths, which usually separate the story's narrator and origin. However, this works fine because the myth is not offered in place of an argument but in support of one.

The aim is to explore further the essential distinction already drawn between the body and the soul, while glorifying philosophy as the best way of life for the soul, and thus validating the philosopher's predisposition to welcome death as a liberation from a state inimical to philosophy. The presentation starts with a contrast between the body and the soul upon the death of a person:

- The body (80c–d): Death brings decay, dissolution, and destruction, but this is a process rather than an instantaneous shift from one state to the other. Depending on the condition of the body, decomposition can even be delayed indefinitely through various preservation techniques, such as embalming. On its natural course, the process leaves intact certain body parts, such as bones and sinews, long after other parts have rotted away.

- The soul (80d–84b): Death provides a release, as the soul goes to a place, like itself, noble, pure, and invisible (80d). But what awaits it there depends on what it accomplishes here: It may depart in a state of purity, having maintained no greater association with the body than the bare requirements of the involuntary link during life, and thus holding on to nothing of the body in death. Alternatively, it may leave in a polluted state replete with desires and pleasures, lingering byproducts of an undisciplined connection with the body and of excessive fascination with earthly things. If it is released in a state of purity, it attains eternal happiness as it joins what is invisible, divine, everlasting, and wise, thus spending eternity in the company of the gods (80e–81a). If it is released in a polluted state, it retains elements of the corporeal realm, lurking in the shadowlands until reincarnation (81b–e).

Reincarnation operates with a correlation in disposition between one life and the next. Character traits nurtured in the present life determine the type of creature one comes back as. This theme is illustrated through examples in three groups:

- Group 1: Those who are predisposed to gluttony, lust, and drunkenness are reborn as donkeys (81e).

- Group 2: Those who habitually exhibit characteristics of injustice, tyranny, and robbery return as wolves, hawks, or kites (82a).

- Group 3: Those who exercise self-control but only as the result of an inherent inclination to do so, leading that type of life as a matter of natural course rather than reasoned choice, come back in a social species, such as bees, wasps, ants, and humans (82b–c).

Breaking the cycle of rebirth is a privilege reserved for philosophers, who are released in a state of purity, thereafter dwelling in the company of the gods (82b–c).

Myth is an option Plato keeps open as a dramatic license to explore what cannot be fleshed out further through observation and reasoning. Here, it supplements the argument rather than supplanting it, perhaps thereby underscoring a certain harmony between logic and tradition. After all, the affinity of the soul to the forms and the gods is more consistent with a soul that undergoes reincarnation than with one that perishes with the body, and reincarnation seems to have been, perhaps not the predominant general view, but a tenable and familiar notion, at least as far as the dramatic audience is concerned, despite the inscrutable ignorance, or, depending on the interpretation, the lack of expertise, assigned in this regard to Simmias and Cebes (61d). Proceeding in the manner of an authoritative account on the precise fate of the soul upon separation from the body, the myth facilitates the exploration of the dualism already established through argument.

Once we grant Plato this license, his account becomes a workable blueprint for the ideal human condition. But we need to remove a potential misunderstanding. According to this account, the best thing, in fact, the only reasonable thing, to do is to become a philosopher. Yet the reduction of all of life's pursuits to a single one in philosophy precludes the possibility of civilization, as it does not allow for economic specialization and the division or labor, thereby vitiating the basis for social coexistence, and possibly also individual survival. This seems to be the case even if the reference to philosophy is reinterpreted in contemporary terms as science in general. The apparent problem here is not that the social subtext of the proof is morally, politically, or economically deficient, but that the ideal or recommendation at the personal level comes with a collective implication that undermines the ideal and contradicts the recommendation.

However, the difficulty disappears if the anchor to philosophy is taken, not as the glorification of a profession or area of interest or expertise, but as a way of life in which one prepares for death by following the path of reason instead of that of the senses. Being a philosopher in this sense is a mindset rather than an occupation, and can be cultivated by people from all walks of life, regardless of what they do for a living. Indeed, this is the precise context in which philosophy is discussed, and, the philosophical life, recommended. After all, Plato is not offering vocational counseling but extolling the virtues of tending to one's soul.

7.5. Objections and Misology

Logic and speculation give way to drama as Socrates concludes the mythical account of the afterlife supplementing the central proof in the third argument for the immortality of the soul. The story is followed immediately by objections, not specifically to the third argument, or to any other in particular, but to the entire presentation laid out as proof up to that point, whereafter the rational endeavor itself loses all credibility for the audience, whose state can best be described as one of misology. The quick transitions between being impressed by and disappointed in a series of arguments, coupled with a dazzling demonstration of counterarguments defending the opposite thesis, creates a deep disappointment in what can be established through reason, both in the particular matter on hand and, even worse, in general. As disappointment in results turns into mistrust of further effort, misology becomes the central theme, marking the center of the dialogue in terms of its length as well as representing a clear break for redirection in the drama and the argument.

Socrates himself is quick and eager to discount and disown his own presentation regarding the fate of the soul upon death. This is evident in his expression of certainty that what has just been said is open to all sorts of doubt and objection, and further in his allusion to the need for a proper examination of the subject, which might reasonably have been expected of him in the first place (84c). Despite an apparent lack of confidence in the strength of the argument up to that point, Socrates is supremely confident in the conclusion, which he has demonstrably made the motivating principle of his life, about to be concluded momentarily with a swan song (84d–85b).

The explicit repudiation of what has been said by way of argument can be interpreted as anchored specifically to the mythical account of the fate of the soul instead of more generally to the entire dialogue up to that point, but that speculative portion (80c–84b), if contestable, is best challenged in what it reflects than in isolation, as it is merely a colorful instantiation in an ongoing effort to quell objections to a thesis yet to be defended in a satisfactory manner, and to patch up the holes corresponding to the objections while still rolling out the fabric of exposition.

Indeed, the logical import of the effort up to that point is limited to and by three unsatisfactory arguments:

- The first argument (70c–72e), the one anchored to the cyclical transformation of opposites into each other, merely underscores, or at best corroborates, the continuity of life in general, thus falling short of establishing personal immortality. Even in this less impressive achievement, its contribution is limited to the confirmation of a temporal relationship, not a causal one.

- The second argument (72e–77a), the one drawing on recollection, concludes with the prenatal existence of the soul, thereby offering an incomplete proof, as recognized and protested by the interlocutors. Moreover, it requires a prior commitment to what is now called "Platonic realism," the belief that the forms (or universals, to replace an idiosyncratic conception with a crude approximation in contemporary terms) exist in and of themselves, that is, that their ontological status is that of an objective and absolute reality, not to mention an additional commitment to the view that at least some knowledge, namely, that of the forms, is innate (though the ontological commitment may be interpreted as implying the epistemological one, given that the forms are not perceived in sense experience, thus reducing the two assumptions to one).

- The third argument (78b–84b), the one contrasting the essential nature of the soul with that of the body, not only begs the question of the soul's existence, but also remains inconclusive regarding its immortality, unless affinity to that which is immortal counts as proof of immortality.

Exploring an analogy pertaining to the forms and the gods, the third argument inspires Simmias and Cebes to present analogies of their own as they voice their dissatisfaction with the flow of reasoning through the first three arguments:

- Simmias (85e–86d) likens the soul to the attunement in a lyre, wherein the soul perishes with the body, just as the attunement is gone upon the destruction of its own physical counterpart.

- Cebes (87a–88b) offers an analogy involving a weaver of cloaks, with the weaver representing the soul and the cloaks representing successive incarnations, thus making the soul mortal yet more durable than the body.

The objections of the two leading interlocutors concern the perishability of the soul specifically after its separation from the body. Both had otherwise accepted the prenatal existence of the soul as demonstrated in the second argument. In fact, Cebes explicitly prefaces his objection with a confirmation of satisfaction with the recollection argument (87a). He also expresses disagreement with Simmias's analogy and with the challenge to the thesis that the soul is stronger than and otherwise superior to the body. Immediately before Socrates's response, both Simmias and Cebes reaffirm their endorsement of the recollection argument (92a).

This is where the audience enters into what Socrates calls "misology," the hatred of argument, as narrated through a specific interchange between Phaedo and Echecrates in a dramatic interlude interrupting the flow of the dialogue (88c–91c). Both objections are at least *prima facie* successful objectively, and entirely persuasive dramatically, while the members of the audience are on the verge of losing faith in reason altogether as they find points and counterpoints replacing one another in rapid succession and with comparable appeal.

At this point, Simmias has challenged the analogic argument in its entirety, proposing in its place his own analogy with the attunement objection, thus denying the superiority of the soul over the body, whereas Cebes has accepted the superiority of the soul, while rejecting the inference that the soul is everlasting, instead, demanding conclusive evidence that this is so. Their common ground is that they both accept the recollection argument and both require proof that the soul is imperishable and not merely older or more durable than the body.

7.6. Response to Simmias

The response to Simmias (91e–95a), delivered after a recapitulation (91c–d) of both objections, consists of three separate counterarguments to the attunement analogy:

- Response #1 (91e–92e): Socrates exposes a decisive conflict in Simmias's position, as he demonstrates the inconsistency of holding both, at once, that learning is recollection and that the soul is an attunement. The recollection theory of learning and the attunement conception of the soul represent mutually exclusive claims: The recollection theory supports the prenatal existence of the soul, whereas the attunement analogy makes the soul a product of the body. Simmias is fully satisfied with this counterargument, resigned to relinquish his original objection, and perhaps even prepared to concede the entire matter, but Socrates is not ready to end the rebuttal.

- Response #2 (92e–94b): Socrates's approach in the second counterargument, immediately following the first, is to carry out a *reductio ad absurdum* in the attunement analogy. He anchors this effort to what he sees as a key difference between the soul and an attunement: essential variability. His main point in this regard is that musical instruments can be tuned more fully or less fully than one another (or in comparison with themselves at different times), making attunement a matter of degree, whereas a soul cannot be more or less of a soul, and cannot, therefore, be an attunement, or similar to an attunement in any relevant respect (93a–b). This is sufficient to overturn the attunement analogy, but Socrates further argues (93b–94b) that the analogy cannot accommodate a distinction between good souls and bad souls, or between souls that are intelligent and those that are not, because to do so, that is, to ascribe goodness or intelligence to a soul, would be to posit a secondary attunement within that soul, which is itself supposed to be an attunement, the problem being that the acknowledgment of goodness or badness would embrace the very variability just rejected. In this way, the second response becomes rather convoluted as it is extended beyond the standalone challenge that the soul cannot whereas an attunement can admit of degrees (93a–b). In fact, that contrast is lost close to the midway point of the extension (93b–94b), where both turn out not to admit of degrees (93d). This is not because Socrates has already forgotten the contrast just drawn (93a–b), but because he is, at that point, and for the sake of argument, resolving that contrast in favor of the attunement analogy, thereby giving it one more chance at sensibility, with an assumption of consistency, through the provisional result that neither the soul nor an attunement can admit of degrees, and that they are thereby analogous. His assessment here is that the analogy still fails, this time because the inability to admit of degrees affords no room for a distinction between good souls and bad souls, supposedly ending up with the absurdity that all souls are equally good. Again, Simmias accept Socrates's counterargument, while Socrates moves on to another.

- Response #3 (94b–95a): The third counterargument is yet another attempt to break down the attunement analogy, no better or worse than the first two, and possibly constituting a part or continuation of the second one. The principal claim in the response here is that the soul and an attunement are not analogous, because the soul is in charge of the body whereas the attunement is entirely dependent on the instrument: The soul can oppose the body, ignoring signals and enduring states such as hunger and thirst, but the attunement always follows the lead of the instrument. Once more, without protest or question, Simmias assents to the rebuttal.

A fair assessment of the interchange between Socrates and Simmias is that their debate on the third argument, and, in general, on the nature of the soul, is inconclusive. In appraisal of Socrates's original analogy, being merely analogous to the forms and the gods, or having a nebulous kinship with them, is not conclusive evidence of the soul's immortality, proof of which would in this context require being exactly like or identical with the forms and the gods. Given that one thing cannot be exactly like each of two other things, which, at least by virtue of their duality, are not themselves exactly alike, and given further that it cannot even be exactly like one other thing while remaining itself, the proof sought would require being similar to the forms and the gods in all the relevant respects, that is, all aspects pertinent to immortality. Whichever specification is chosen, the scenario laid out by Simmias fares no better under definite standards of verisimilitude than it does as a loose analogy. Being comparable to an attunement in this or that respect, or in some unspecified general way, does not automatically make the soul an attunement, or exactly like an attunement in every respect, or in every relevant respect. Neither case considers the strength of the affinity required to make the respective analogy work, whereas what is required in each is not just any manifestation of similarity, nor a blanket generalization, but a demonstrably relevant connection. The failure of both analogies, however, would not, if indeed they do fail, indicate a stalemate, but a defeat for Socrates, since it is incumbent on him to demonstrate the affinity of the soul to the forms and the gods, whereas it is incumbent on Simmias only to overturn that analogy, not, in addition, to establish one of his own.

Socrates's original analogy is shaky enough as it is, but his variegated response to Cebes's objection is possibly even more tenuous, and, in places, outright untenable. Simmias could, quite consistently and reasonably, invalidate the first response simply by rejecting the recollection argument, undermine the second by maintaining that both souls and attunements can be better or worse examples of what they are without thereby becoming more than or less than or somehow other than what they are in essence, and counter the third by submitting that the soul merely seems to be in charge only after regularly servicing the body toward relative tranquility through the slavish satisfaction of its strongest desires and drives, including, but not limited to, water, food, sleep, and sex (not to mention the fact that all evidence of a soul, that is, the part of a person that we think of as a soul, is gone upon the destruction of the body, just as all evidence of an attunement is gone upon the destruction of the instrument). Yet Simmias does not put up a fight, as Socrates refutes the attunement analogy with a series of counter-arguments in rapid succession, moving on to Cebes's objection, thus set up as the worthier challenge.

This being so, the dispute with Simmias remains unsettled logically, though not dramatically, as the focus shifts to Cebes without objection from the audience. The move is tantamount to leaving the issue behind, not only because the two objections are different, but particularly because Cebes contradicts both Socrates and Simmias at once. He opposes Socrates by introducing the possibility that the soul might perish in one of its incarnations even if it is strong enough to survive many, while he contradicts Simmias by conceding to Socrates the point that the soul is more durable than the body.

The undertones of Socratic, or Platonic, mockery in the treatment of the objection by Simmias in contrast to the exalted value placed on the one by Cebes might influence readers to weigh the objections accordingly. However, questioning the ability of the soul to survive the destruction of its current body is as formidable a challenge as questioning its ability to survive the chain of reincarnations awaiting it. That said, the special importance attached to Cebes is not rooted in the difference between surviving one body and surviving many but in a more fundamental difference between surviving and not surviving, or, from the opposite perspective, between perishing at some point and not perishing at all. Fortunately, the facile rejection of the perspective represented by Simmias is not problematic in the end, because the final argument by Socrates turns out to be strong enough to refute both Simmias and Cebes, particularly in addressing the common denominator in the fear that the soul is the kind of thing that can perish, making it irrelevant whether it is feared to perish with one body or with the last of many. This is not to say that the final argument works, nor that it does not, but that it is not vulnerable to the attunement and weaver analogies.

7.7. Response to Cebes

Much of the remainder of the dialogue can be considered a response to Cebes, though it actually brings together an explicit reply (95a–107a), that is, the logical response setting up and culminating in the final argument for the immortality of the soul, and an allegorical one following immediately afterwards as the myth of the afterlife (107d–114e). Even the concluding section, the death scene of Socrates (115a–118a) might, in some sense, be considered part of Socrates's response to Cebes (or perhaps even Plato's response), as it is a demonstration of how a philosopher faces death. In terms of content, the response proper consists mainly of autobiographical insight into correct reasoning and procedure in causal inquiry (96a–107a), with particular emphasis on its instantiation as a causal argument for the immortality of the soul (105b–107a), which Socrates offers as a formal reply to Cebes as well as his final word on the matter.

The thrust of Cebes's objection is that the soul might be perishable even if it outlasts the body. He contends that the soul's outlasting the body is not proof of its imperishability. His chief concern is that the reincarnating soul, even if it outlasts this or that body, might perish along with the last of the series at the end of its own time. Thus, Cebes fully agrees, or at least grants, that souls are superior to bodies and can outlive them, but he rejects this as proof of the soul's immortality, which, he claims, would require imperishability instead of mere longevity.

The reincarnation dimension of the debate between Socrates and Cebes holds interesting implications that are never taken up. Three extra possibilities, all passed over in the text, must be acknowledged in the combination of the thesis that the soul is more durable than the body and the limiting amendment, that is, Cebes's objection, that durability is not conclusive evidence of everlasting existence. An incarnate soul, having previously survived any number of bodies, might, for all we know, (1) die simultaneously with its present body, (2) die after its present body but possibly before a chance for another incarnation, or (3) die before its present body, leaving it a zombie, or conceivably ushering in the scenario underlying what we consider an untimely death.

The third possibility represents a challenge for Cebes's objection, yet Socrates never pursues this route, perhaps because it does not lead anywhere useful for his own thesis. The potential challenge is that our experience is incompatible with holding both that reincarnation is a fact and that souls are longer lasting than bodies but still perishable. Reincarnation without immortality is open to the expiration of these durable yet mortal souls at any time: before or after or at the same time as any particular body with which they happen to be linked. This suggests that, had reincarnation with limited longevity been a plausible premise, we should, according to statistical probability, have been able to witness at least some instances where a soul dies before its body.

Cebes, on the other hand, could speculate in response that this is precisely what happens when people die young, thus opening the gates to instantiations of just what is sought. This, however, would not be a strong rejoinder because whether the soul dies before or simultaneously with or after the body is not clear in the case of untimely death, where the soul's expiration prior to the body is merely one of several possibilities, not an empirical observation, let alone an authoritative causal explanation. After all, we can never ascertain that a body quit working due to the death of the soul, which precludes the possibility of confirming an instance of a soul dying before its body. Nevertheless, Cebes's objection does not depend on the tenability of reincarnation. Despite the recycling that comes with the weaver analogy, the heart of the objection is not the risk of the soul's expiration at some point in the reincarnation process but the threat of the soul's expiration at some point after its present body, whether or not it ever unites with another body, thus placing the emphasis on the sheer possibility of expiration, with or without reincarnation. The independence of Cebes's position from reincarnation is also clear in Socrates's recapitulation of the objection (95a–e). Cebes could, by any count, consistently reject reincarnation without giving up his challenge.

After summarizing Cebes's objection, Socrates reevaluates the task of proving the immortality of the soul, and concludes that this is a grand undertaking requiring a full analysis of causation, particularly as it pertains to becoming and destruction (95e–96a).

7.8. Theory of Causation

Socrates launches his reply to Cebes in the form of an autobiographical account of a search for method in scientific inquiry, with especial emphasis on causation, gradually developing it into an argument for the immortality of the soul. He turns first to the *modus operandi* of natural science, namely, empirical investigation, subsequently abandoning this approach in favor of rational reflection:

Natural science:
Empirical inquiry into particulars, specifically, physical things (96a–99d)
- Physical causes: the initial perspective in youth (96a–97b)
- Anaxagoras: intelligence as cause (97b–99d)
  - Fascination: "best way to be" as generic reason "why" (97b–98b)
  - Disenchantment: "best way to be" ignored in practice (98b–99d)

Rational reflection:
Logical inquiry into propositions (99d–107a)
- Eclipse analogy (99d–100a)
- Coherence theory (100a–b)
- Forms as methodological anchor (100b–c)
- Safest yet naive account: forms as causes (100c–101e)
- Safe and sophisticated account: particulars as causes (102a–105b)
- Causal argument for the immortality of the soul (105b–107a)

The dramatic impetus for the entire sequence is the misology interlude and the ongoing preoccupation with the finality of death, which together prompt Socrates to lay out a theory of causation enabling them all to take stock of the processes of becoming and destruction, ultimately driving a wedge between destruction and the soul.

The focus on becoming includes creation as well as change, that is, it applies both to the phenomenon of coming into being after not having existed before and to the process of transformation into something different. The earlier emphasis is on becoming in the sense of change (e.g., growing larger), with parallel applications to explanations of differences between separate things (e.g., one being larger than the other), where the analysis mirrors that used in bridging a single thing before and after change. The ultimate aim is to demonstrate, through a definitive causal account, that the soul is imperishable because destruction is not the kind of change that is applicable to the soul, or, perhaps more perspicuously, because destruction cannot logically (reasonably, sensibly, or consistently) be predicated of the soul.

The preparatory autobiographical delivery lays the groundwork as it proceeds from the experiential causal explanations Socrates formulated, favored, and sought as a neophyte in natural science, to the theoretical approach he developed later, in reaction to the inadequacies of the former. The evolution of this quest for knowledge straddles a turning point where (99d–100c) the intellectual journey shifts from an empirical inquiry into particular things through the scientific method (grounded in observation) to a rationalistic inquiry into forms through theoretical reasoning (proceeding from hypotheses). The empirical operation concerns physical phenomena, whereas the rationalistic alternative is carried out as a logical analysis of concepts and propositions.

7.8.1. Natural Science

Socrates's search for a tenable theory of causation commences with his initiation into natural science (96a–99d), where he develops a mechanistic conception of cause, supporting an empirical approach to causal explanation. Frustration sinks in as he discovers shortcomings in the explanatory power of this perspective, particularly in its employment in mathematical and logical considerations. For example, he proceeds with the explanation that the cause of biological growth is nourishment (96c–d), wherein an organism becomes larger by processing its intake of additional matter, but he encounters difficulties in extending this physical account into the conceptual realm, where parallel construction requires postulating, say, that a number becomes larger through the addition of another number. One problem here, as subsequently illustrated with an example (96e–97a), is the ambiguity of whether that which is added to, or that which is added, or the two of them in combination, and therefore neither one of them in isolation, turns into the larger thing. The physical realm is not exempt from this indeterminacy, as if the awkward situation were unique to the conceptual realm, but the autobiographical account reveals its discovery in application to numbers. Otherwise, it is metaphysically just as problematic, or unproblematic, to ascertain whether the person or the food or the combination turns into the person plus the food.

Socrates reports this intellectual tour of discovery through two sets of examples, the first (96d–e), illustrating the causal account, and, the second, demonstrating corresponding problems (96e–97b). The first set consists of four examples, two physical and two conceptual:

- tall man being taller than small man by a head;
- one horse being larger than another horse by a head;
- ten being more than eight by the addition of two;
- two-cubit measure being bigger than one-cubit measure because of exceeding it by half of its own length.

These cases tend toward ambiguity between description and explanation. Using connectives for introducing cause or reason, Socrates supplies what might otherwise pass as mere description. The approach draws on or promotes equivocation on the word "by," using it to mean "because of" or "due to" in addition to its prepositional role in facilitating a comparison or reporting a difference. Causal explanation in this context seems to be a matter of restating the change or difference in question after prefacing it with terms like "by," "because of," and "due to," all of which function as operationally equivalent connectives introducing a circular account, assessment, or justification.

This approach to causation and change is reflexive, with causal explanation limited to a descriptive reflection on and of the context in which a change takes place or a difference subsists, and, the change itself, serving as the cause as well as the effect. On this platform, the standard explanation of causation and change accounts for a thing's difference from itself at another time, or from anything else at any time, in terms of the very difference for which an explanation is sought. In other words, the difference functions both as a description of the state and as the cause of it. For instance, where one person is taller than another by a head, the head is what accounts for the height difference, thus constituting an accurate description while simultaneously representing a definitive explanation or cause.

However, this is not the source of the frustration besetting Socrates in his early attempt at causal explanation. He appeals to two further examples to illustrate the real problem:

- Union, as the purported cause of one and one adding up to two, is inadequate as a causal explanation because of an inherent ambiguity in whether it is the first number one, the second number one, or both of them together that becomes two (96e–97a).

- Division, as the purported cause of one becoming two (one thing becoming two things), is likewise inadequate because it makes out the cause of two in this case to be the opposite of what it is in the first example (97a–b).

Here, too, equivocation is in play, both in regard to the word "one," used initially to express a number, but subsequently to refer to unity, demarcating something as a single thing, and with respect to the word "two," used initially to express a sum, but subsequently to refer to the separateness of discrete elements, essentially, counting them and reporting how many there are.

The real difficulty, on the other hand, the one bothering Socrates, is the indeterminacy between cause and effect, against a backdrop of equivocation on cause, reason, and condition. The first example demonstrates the difficulty of determining which one of multiple causal elements turns into the effect, while the rest play a supporting role, a tricky enough issue competing with the alternative thesis focusing on the causal role of the elements collectively rather than severally, so that a combination of them, whether including some or all, may be said to initiate the causal process and jointly bring about or turn into the effect. Socrates also finds it counterintuitive that one and one considered collectively but prior to being united (added through a mathematical operation) do not count as two, whereas the same two things indeed count as two when they are joined as such. The second example, in turn, exposes a further difficulty in the causal account by challenging the sensibility of the results of the first example while jeopardizing the tenability of its own. The explicit problem in this regard is that the cause of two in the second example becomes the opposite of what it is in the first, so that both union and division account for the same thing, or, put differently, the same thing turns out to be explicable by opposite processes.

Socrates's experience with Anaxagoras also proves unsatisfactory. The process consists of a fascination period (97b–98b) followed by disenchantment (98b–99d). Initially, Socrates is eager to follow the causal implications of Anaxagoras's doctrine that the cause of everything is intelligence. He expects to find all causal explanations in Anaxagoras firmly anchored to this position, thus proceeding on the overriding assumption that any object or phenomenon is the way it is because that is the best way for it to be. He becomes disillusioned with Anaxagoras upon discovering that this conception of intelligence does not routinely shape causal explanation.

Socrates does not explain why he does not himself adopt the method he finds fitting for Anaxagoras, in other words, the pursuit of causal explanation in terms of the best state of affairs relevant to each context. Instead, he offers a critique and moves on to an entirely different method. His chief objection is that Anaxagoras fails to distinguish between causes and necessary conditions (98b–99d), which is roughly the same problem undermining the initial approach Socrates describes taking to causal explanation (e.g., in postulating nourishment as the cause of growth).

7.8.2. Rational Reflection

Socrates leaves the method of natural science behind with playful irony, professing utter confusion regarding causal theories inspired by the physical world, or causal laws inherent therein, and twice referring to being blinded by the empirical view of physical phenomena (96c, 99e). He recommends a type of rational reflection in place of the empirical investigation employed in natural science. He describes this as a hypothetical inquiry into propositions (or into words, concepts, or theories), an undertaking he likens to observing a solar eclipse through its reflection in water, reassuring his audience that propositions remain no further from reality than do physical objects, as both are mere images or reflections of reality (99d–100a). The approach he advocates is to take a single hypothesis, the most credible one, as the anchor for a web of belief nurtured on the basis of a coherence theory of truth (100a). The hypothesis he uses is the existence of the forms, with explicit mention of the forms for beauty, goodness, and largeness, followed by a blanket reference to "all the rest" (100b).

7.8.2.1. Safest yet Naive Causal Account

Socrates develops his theory of causation around the prime hypothesis that the forms exist. His first move is to lay out what he refers to as the "safest answer" to causation, while also acknowledging that it constitutes a "naive account," which he treats as a foundational perspective to be developed. This initial step establishes the forms as causes, or as reasons, depending on the terminology apposite to the context. The cause of anything, or the reason for it, is to be sought in its corresponding form. For example, that which is beautiful is beautiful simply because it shares in the beautiful itself. The underlying formula is that the reason for any object's possession of any property is its connection with the form which that property represents.

The causal connection here is not clear. Exactly how does beauty itself make things beautiful? Stated in general terms, how does a form make a property what it is, and what is its role in an object's exhibition of that property? Socrates speculates that the link might be a type of "presence" or "communion," but he readily admits that he does not know, ultimately leaving the connection indeterminate (100d), though nonetheless functional and effective. His hesitation is not in regard to the existence or strength of the connection but in regard to its precise nature. He goes through the following examples to illustrate the relationship (100c–101c):

- Beauty makes things beautiful: beautiful things are beautiful because of the beauty in them (100c–e).
- Largeness makes things large or larger: large things are large, and, larger things, larger, because of the largeness in them (100e–101b).
- Smallness makes things small or smaller: small things are small, and, smaller things, smaller, because of the smallness in them (100e–101b).
- Ten exceeds eight because of quantity (101b).
- A two-cubit measure is greater than a one-cubit measure because of greatness (101b).
- Duality (twoness) is the cause of two coming into being when one and one are added together (101b–c).
- Unity (oneness) is the cause of one coming into being (101b–c).

Socrates concludes the safest yet naive answer with a warning that anticipates a possible objection (100d–e): He warns against confusing the veracity of the prime hypothesis with the tenability of a belief or theory supported by it. He thus anticipates a challenge to the causal account by way of a possible denial of the existence of the forms. He contends that the two issues, namely, the hypothesis and its implications, must be discussed separately. More accurately, he stipulates that they cannot be taken up jointly.

As it is, neither he nor anyone else in the congregation discusses the plausibility of the hypothesis at all. The warning remains entirely negative, making it illegitimate to challenge the existence of the forms while considering them as causes. In the final stretches of the dialogue, during the transition from reason to myth, Socrates revisits the issue by commenting that the entire argument depends on the tenability of the prime hypothesis, the proposition that the forms exist (107b). While the reference is plural in the original, which supports translations as "hypotheses," "propositions," or "assumptions," the allusion can hardly be to anything but the existence of the forms. The plurality of the expression might be explained as reflecting the plurality of the forms, though honoring each form with a separate hypothesis seems pointless. Be that as it may, the allusion, singular or plural in reference, most certainly pertains to the existence of the forms.

7.8.2.2. Safe and Sophisticated Causal Account

Socrates refines his theory of causation as he introduces some subtleties into the causal role of forms. The goal is to escape the limitations and soften the rigidity of a causal perspective where the forms have only an immediate bearing on causation, serving as a direct cause or none at all, as laid out in what Socrates considers the safest yet naive answer to causation.

The new strategy is to define essential connections between forms and particulars, thus creating a richer causal context, one accommodating a greater diversity of causal elements and relationships than afforded by the elementary scenario of the naive account. This enables explanations where the cause and the effect are connected through an intermediary instead of interacting directly, as in, say, explaining boiling water with reference to the application of fire instead of simply through an appeal to exposure to heat.

The effort at enrichment (102b–103a) is grounded in a distinction between essential and accidental (incidental) properties (qualities, attributes, characteristics, traits, or features). For example, Simmias can be taller than Socrates and shorter than Phaedo, participating in tallness and shortness simultaneously, because being tall or short are accidental, not essential properties of Simmias (102b–d). This leads to the formulation of a general causal principle:

> Causal principle #1: Parties to an opposition relation cannot be or become their own opposites while remaining what they are; they either depart (withdraw or retreat) or perish (are destroyed) upon the approach (advance or attack) of their opposites (102e–103a).

Not all translations bring out the military metaphor in the principle paraphrased above, a metaphor thenceforth invoked repeatedly through the end of the final argument for the immortality of the soul: This is the expression of opposition relations in terms of a confrontation, with one party advancing and the other either retreating or perishing. This does not necessarily mean that the party making the first move, so to speak, always dictates the terms, with the defender losing one way or the other. Indeed, all examples are in a format portraying first-mover advantages, but this is more plausibly attributable to the convenience of maintaining a uniform mode of expression than to a conscious effort to underscore such an advantage, which would, in any event, be irrelevant to the argument. The metaphor is meant to emphasize the mutual exclusivity of opposites by making exactly one of them prevail in any jointly relevant context, thus, precluding their coexistence, but doing so without prejudice to any specific party.

Independently of the import of its allegorical dimensions, the causal principle immediately draws an objection from an unidentified member of the audience (103a–c). The anonymous, and therefore dramatically unworthy, objection is that what is being said, opposites not admitting each other, contradicts the first argument (70c–72e), which works on the principle that opposites come from opposites. Socrates responds that the first argument concerns particulars while the one on hand pertains to forms, pointing out that particular things may come into being from their opposites whereas the opposite itself cannot become its own opposite.

The response is terse, and, the delivery, dispassionate. This cool and distant dismissal finds dramatic endorsement in the fact that neither of the two main interlocutors, nor anyone else in the audience, shows the slightest indication of being confused or otherwise troubled by the issue raised through the anonymous objection. Notwithstanding the often overwhelming temptation in reading Plato to look for hidden clues where none exists, the brevity of the episode may simply be due to the fact that the explanation required and provided is by its nature short, simple, and final, leaving nothing further to say on the matter. At any rate, the vapid objection fills a dramatic rather than logical need, possibly having been included in anticipation of the same question or suspicion by readers, basically to keep the record straight from the outset.

The brief coverage of the objection is followed by a series of examples designed to introduce new dimensions and possibilities in causal relations (103c–104e):

- Heat/cold vs. fire/snow (103c–e): Heat and cold are opposite forms in which fire and snow participate by necessity. The actual reference is to "the hot" and "the cold," meaning "the hot itself" as a form and "the cold itself" as a form, but the plainer translation in the contrast between "heat" and "cold" is less cumbersome without compromising the original message. The participation involved carries necessity, in the sense that fire, though it is not the same thing as the hot (heat or hotness), would not be what it is unless it were hot, and snow, though it is not the same thing as the cold (coldness), would not be what it is unless it were cold. Socrates submits that fire is incompatible with cold, and that snow is incompatible with heat, meaning that, in each case, the dependent party cannot admit, participate in, or unite with, the form opposite the one in which it participates, nor, in any way, assume its properties.

- Odd/even vs. numbers that are odd/even: (103e–104e): Odd and even are opposite forms in which odd and even numbers participate by necessity. Three is the main representative of odd numbers, and two holds that distinction among even numbers, though five and four are also named, and all odd and even numbers are included by general declaration. The leading case in point is that three, five, and half of all numbers are necessarily odd, despite not being the same as or identical with the odd (104a–b). This is accompanied by the complementary example that two, four, and the other half of all numbers are necessarily even, despite not being the same as or identical with the even (104b). The central claim here is that three and five and all other odd numbers will never admit the even, just as two and four and all other even numbers will never admit the odd.

These examples support a second causal principle:

> Causal principle #2: Nothing can admit, accommodate, or coexist with the opposite of a form with which it is essentially connected (as opposed to an accidental or incidental relationship); such an encounter or confrontation terminates immediately in either withdrawal or destruction (104b–c, 105a).

This is the gist of two different statements of what is essentially a single principle. In other words, the second causal principle is stated twice, once (104b–c) after the first group of examples, put together to demonstrate its physical relevance, and later (105a) between the introduction and discussion of the second group of examples, designed to show its conceptual relevance. Its first statement is closer to the wording of the block reference above, while its second statement makes greater use of the military metaphor of advancing and retreating and such. A discussion of one of the examples introduced but not fully examined separates the two definitional statements of the principle. This is the case of the relationship between three and the odd. Although three is not the same as the odd, it is necessarily odd, and, thus, essentially connected with the odd. As a result of this connection, it can never become the opposite, that is, even; instead, it will either withdraw or perish at the approach of the even.

The establishment of the second causal principle ushers in yet another series of examples (105a–c), this time rolling out in rapid succession to drive the point home, and blending into the final argument for the immortality of the soul. These may be examined in two parts, the first (105a–b), demonstrating the causal principle, and, the second (105b–c), constituting a part of the final argument.

First set of examples (105a–b):
- Five will never admit the even (105a).
- Ten will never admit the odd (105a).
- Double will never admit the odd (105a).
- Fractions, specifically, one-and-a-half, and the series of halves (1/2, 3/2, 5/2, . . .), and one-third, and the series of thirds (1/3, 4/3, 7/3, . . .), will never admit the whole (105a).

Second set of examples (105b–c):
- What makes a body hot is not merely heat but, specifically, fire (105b–c).
- What makes a body ill is not merely illness but, specifically, fever (105b–c).
- What makes a number odd is not merely oddness but, specifically, unity (oneness) (105b–c).

The parallel, turning into the final argument, is that what makes a body alive (exemplifying the most useful causal explanation for the presence of life in it) is not merely life itself but, specifically, the soul (105c–d).

7.8.3. Groundwork for the Final Argument

The emerging theory of causation constitutes the groundwork for the final argument, so much so that it is often regarded as part of that argument rather than as groundwork for it. Either way, careful consideration of the theory is required for an adequate understanding of the argument.

The safest yet naive answer emphasizes the forms as causes, while the safe and sophisticated answer focuses on particulars as causes. More accurately, the safest yet naive answer emphasizes the forms as direct or immediate causes, while the safe and sophisticated answer focuses on the forms as indirect or remote causes, with particulars serving as their causal agent. The reference to degrees of safety (safest vs. safe) and simplicity (naive vs. sophisticated) is directly from the text, where the first kind of answer is identified as being the safest albeit naive, also called "simple" and "unsophisticated" (100d–e), and the second kind of answer is celebrated as affording "safety of another kind" while adding sophistication (105b–c).

The problem with the first answer, motivating the move to the second, is not that it is logically, methodologically, or factually erroneous, but that it is simply unhelpful. Indeed, a beautiful thing may be so because of beauty itself, but a circular or tautological explanation of this sort does not lend itself to a deeper analysis exploring causal connections and evaluating interaction possibilities that go beyond a thing and its defining form. Overall, the search for a proper theory evolves from exclusive emphasis on particulars as ultimate causes (the method of natural science), through emphasis on forms as direct causes with no room in causation for particulars (the safest yet naive answer), finally to emphasis on particulars as direct causes and forms as indirect causes (the safe and sophisticated answer). Hence, in the end, Socrates reconciles forms and particulars in accounting for causation.

This analysis of the transition between the two accounts of causation, and the underlying interpretation of the difference therein, does not reflect a consensus among scholars. The suggestion that the emphasis is exclusively on the forms in the safest yet naive answer, and at least partly on particulars in the safe and sophisticated answer, is a matter of interpretation and ongoing debate. Hardly anyone would object seriously to the claim that the naive answer nominates the forms as causes, but many would reject the proposition that the sophisticated answer makes room for a causal role for particulars, proposing instead that it remains focused on the forms.

The source of the controversy is that the original text corresponding to the second causal principle, including its descriptive declaration as well as its elucidation through examples, does not explicitly identify the affected party in opposition relations as particulars. The absence of a textual commitment either way makes it possible to anchor the principle exclusively to the forms and to interpret clarifying examples as forms, including not only obvious instances of reference to the forms, such as the hot, the cold, the odd, and the even, but also those that might otherwise be considered physical substances, such as fire and snow, and those that are not so easy to classify either way, such as three and two.

An interpretation denying any and all reference to particulars would restrict the domain of the principle to the forms, thereby defining the sphere of application as interaction possibilities or compatibility issues between any form and the opposite of another form with which the first is essentially connected. For example, this would depict the form of fire in its aversion to that of cold, which, in turn, stands in opposition to the form of heat, with which fire has an essential connection. This interpretation should not be taken as construing fire and snow, and similarly numbers, strictly as forms, while denying the possibility of their manifestation as particulars, but as regarding the respective examples in the text to refer to the forms of fire and snow and numbers, whether or not any particulars happen to correspond to these forms.

Notwithstanding the absence of textual corroboration, at least one consideration, one grounded in philosophical aim and strategy, favors a reading embracing particulars, or, more precisely, a reading against writing them out of the causal model in development: This is the fact that ignoring particulars would defeat the purpose of searching for an explanation of why things are the way they are. Indeed, half of the satisfactory portion of that search, the naive account (100c–101e), covers the relationship between forms and particulars. The subsequent attempt in the other half, the sophisticated account (102a–105b), to refine the theoretical work in progress would hardly make sense as excluding particulars from the theory being formulated. This is not to say that the causal theory emerging through the sophisticated account is definitely reserved for relationships between forms and particulars, being inapplicable to those just between forms, but that a bend in the other direction to exclude particulars from the equation is just as erroneous. The most sensible interpretation of the sophisticated account is to take it as indifferent to the distinction between forms and particulars, applying equally well to both. Perhaps this is what Plato had in mind in laying out the theory without making an explicit commitment either way.

Plato is also silent on whether the causal agent that ushers in a form to act on a particular is itself a form or a particular. This can be taken as an endorsement of any attempt to copy his neutrality and refer to the agent simply as a "causal intermediary," without commitment to its ontological status, that is, without further effort to designate it specifically a form or a particular. Doing so should not be a requirement, especially where the aim is to ascertain whether a given causal intermediary is a form or a particular, but it should be a perfectly acceptable mode of reference in general. A comparable terminological adjustment can be considered for the thing at the receiving end of all the causal activity, if its ontological status is also found debatable: Specifically, the affected party can be called the "causal recipient" or "causal consequence" or some such designation indifferent to the distinction between forms and particulars, instead of explicitly being assumed to be a particular. However, the ambiguity between form and particular seems much stronger and more prevalent in the causal intermediary than in the causal consequence. In either case, the option of generic designation should be used as a convenience in reference, not as a veil for philosophical difficulties.

The answer might simply be that a causal intermediary can be a form or a particular, that some are forms, some particulars, and, in general, that any form or particular could conceivably be a causal agent in some relationship or other. In other words, the absence of an explicit commitment in the text might be because such intermediation works both ways, being unique to neither forms nor particulars. On the other hand, comparably plausible answers revolve around the supposition that causal intermediaries are in a class by themselves, straddling an ontological position between forms and particulars. This supposition proceeds without direct contradiction by Plato, but it finds especial credence in Aristotle's testimony, already discussed in chapter two (§ 2.5.6), that Plato in fact made room for such a category in his ontology, wherein at least the objects of mathematics, that is, numbers and geometric figures, occupy an intermediate position between forms and particulars (*Metaphysics* 987b14–17, 1059b5–14).

Indeterminacy with respect to the ontological status of numbers is particularly striking in the passage (103e–104e) where they take center stage as examples molding the template for the proof concluding the argumentative portion of the entire dialogue: An explicit reference to the "form of three" (104d) seems to favor interpreting numbers as forms, as does a subsequent reference to "threeness" (104e) and prior references (101c) to "oneness" (unity) and "twoness" (duality). None of this shows conclusively that numbers *are* forms, though establishing at least that they *have* forms, and possibly further that the reference here is to those forms. If numbers *have* forms, then they might themselves well be particulars. On the other hand, if forms of numbers are numbers, then clearly, numbers can be forms. The fact that both numbers and forms are abstract entities seems to be an additional source of confusion, as it is difficult to see the difference except specifically in reference to a number of things, whether abstract (e.g., three dreams) or concrete (e.g., three chairs). The existence of forms of numbers does not resolve the ontological status of numbers. The strongest conclusion afforded by textual references to forms of numbers is not that numbers *are* forms, though they might be, but that they *have* forms.

No confusion would arise if the ontology of numbers were captured fully by the bifurcation into forms of numbers existing purely by themselves and particular numbers invariably attached to particular things (e.g., three dreams or three chairs). Any confusion is grounded largely in the possible existence of numbers that neither dwell in the heavens as forms nor accompany particulars as particulars. This is the possibility that the number three is something altogether different from the form of three as well as from three items of any sort, similar to the way that beauty might be said to be different both from the form of beauty and from beautiful things. The exploration of every possible nuance in this respect is necessary for distinguishing what we understand in ordinary language by the number three.

The potential for ambiguity rests with the possibility, unlikely though it may be, that our ordinary intuitive conception of the number three corresponds to what is meant by the form of three, so that the number three and its form are identical. This is to endorse neither the first correspondence nor the second but to emphasize the absurdity that cannot be ruled out in the absence of further information on the rules of the game. No doubt, a form cannot be identical with that of which it is a form, at least because one is a form and the other is not. This much, Plato tells us. We know that forms are different from what they formalize, and we know the difference. But our training is in the relationship between forms and particulars. We do not know the relationship, or even the difference, between forms and numbers.

The problem is that we have a limited imagination. Numbers are already abstract enough for us. Once we leave the realm of particulars, as in, say, three chairs, we are already far enough out in la-la land with unattached numbers to pretend that yet another level of transcendence to the forms of these numbers is viable. Our abstraction capacity does not run that deep. Forms of numbers are no less troubling than forms of forms of numbers, especially since, at either point, we tend to be stuck back at numbers. This does not mean that we cannot even hope to understand Plato. We can. But we need instructions. Guesswork is not the way to go, because it risks either suffocating Plato with a rigid ontological scheme, or, less likely, burdening him with a fancier ontology than he might like. Hence, we turn to Aristotle.

The immediate difficulty, however, is not so much that Plato does not spell out his theory of numbers, or, what would be less demanding, his conception of them, but that he is not clear on precisely what he is doing with them in the *Phaedo*. Indeed, an understanding of his theory or conception of numbers might help sort out some of the confusion in the *Phaedo*, but it would do more toward clarifying the problem than toward solving it.

Regarding the benefits of deference to Aristotle, we may expect general enlightenment but not full satisfaction. As covered in greater detail in the second chapter (§ 2.5.6), being told about the distinction between formal and mathematical numbers (*Metaphysics* 1080a15–30), with the former corresponding to forms and the latter constituting a separate ontological category between forms and particulars (*Metaphysics* 987b14–17, 1059b5–14), would not settle the issue for us at this juncture. We might have even guessed as much, so tidy is the story we get through Aristotle. And the information is fallible either way, no less as a report of Aristotle than as pure speculation. What we really need by way of assistance, from Aristotle or any other trustworthy source, is not a general overview but a line-by-line commentary. We should be able to tolerate the absence of a general theory or conception quite well if we could determine, with certainty and from the text alone, what is going on in the numerical examples in the run-up to the final argument of the *Phaedo*. Instead, we have a general account grounded in testimony.

As it is, the only certainty here is that we are dealing with a type of causal explanation that proceeds with intermediation. The opacity of Plato's thought regarding numbers obscures their ontology, which our best bet is to work out through Aristotle's report that they have an intermediate status, a possibility consistent with indications that causal intermediaries also boast such a status. But how far will this get us?

Numbers and shapes seem rather strange as candidates for causation, or causal explanation, let alone as the only candidates therein. A causal account limited to the intermediation of mathematical objects looks prohibitively sterile, to say the least. Yet the novelty of the approach is not in the specific things nominated as causal intermediaries but in the separate ontological division created, or recognized, for such intermediaries. Establishing the basic category is a far thornier issue than negotiating what might or should be in it. Once causal intermediation is acknowledged as a metaphysical process, with corresponding intermediaries claiming a unique ontological category, finding candidates for membership in that category is not nearly as formidable a task. For example, the soul is often considered a causal intermediary of the sort represented by Aristotle's interpretation of Plato's conception of mathematical objects. The question here is not whether Plato finds the soul, and numbers and shapes, for that matter, to be causal intermediaries, but whether he finds them to be causal intermediaries of an intermediate ontological status, the alternative being classification either as forms or as particulars.

The debate on how to interpret this specific point in the sophisticated account of causation, while internally important at least for the sake of accuracy in capturing the original intention, becomes all the more interesting in its implications for the ontological status of the soul. The outcome has a direct bearing on whether the soul is a particular or a form or something in between. Long dividing commentators, the possibility of something in between, in addition to the strength it draws from Aristotle's testimony, rests on a nebulous distinction between forms as they are in themselves and forms as they are in their instantiations in particulars (mainly 102d–e, but also 102b–d, though less emphatically). The contrast springs up where Socrates distinguishes between forms and their manifestations in humans, specifically in discussing the "largeness in us" (102d–e) and the "smallness in us" (102e). This has the appearance of a contrast drawn in passing, that is, an otherwise unimportant turn of phrase subservient to a main point, but it could just as plausibly be interpreted as a fundamental dichotomy, with the "forms by themselves" and the "forms in us" representing two distinct ontological categories. Scholars finding the distinction deliberate and important enough to saddle Plato with a separate ontological identity for particular manifestations of forms tend to refer to these as "immanent" or "intermediate" forms to distinguish them from forms proper.

An alternative reading, one suggested by Gallop (1993, p. 99, n. 102d), is that the reference to "forms in us" is a precursor to the final argument for the immortality of the soul, where the aim is to prove the immortality of the "soul in us" as opposed to some sort of collective soul. In this way, the dialogue presumably keeps focused on satisfying the repeated and standing request, and fulfilling the corresponding promise, for proof of personal immortality.

At any rate, the main aim of taking up the forms and their instantiations separately, and thus the function of the passage regarding the presence of forms in humans, is to distinguish between essential and accidental properties, or, in the language of the forms, between a necessary connection with a form and an incidental relationship with it. Nothing in this underlying purpose and overarching development is contingent on a specific interpretation of the "forms in us," though the attempt to support one over the other might be a worthwhile effort on its own merits.

Avoiding, ignoring, or repudiating the fuzzy area between forms and particulars still leaves two possibilities for the ontological status of the soul: It could sensibly be interpreted both as a form and as a particular. Any interpretation making the soul out to be a form, whether as immanent or without qualification, would have to contend with the analogic argument (78b–80b), where the soul is merely likened to the forms and the gods. Declaring the soul analogous to the forms and the gods would be misleading and strange if the soul were in fact a form or a god. On the other hand, any interpretation making the soul out to be a particular goes against the grain of the lowly profile the dialogue reserves for particulars in contrast to the glorified presentation of the soul, which indeed bears a resemblance to the forms at least in this respect. The scarcity of linguistic evidence in the original text, or, perhaps more accurately, the flexible nature of the wording therein, to tip the balance in favor of either interpretation places extra pressure on the proper analysis of context, construction, and purpose, which seems likewise to be inconclusive in this regard.

The challenge, however, is not unique to the soul. It is an extension of the general indeterminacy between forms and particulars in the examples illustrating the second causal principle in the sophisticated account of causation. The case of the soul is no more or less difficult to adjudicate than that of numbers, which may be forms, particulars, or things of an altogether different nature. The examples that are hard to decide one way or the other could, in fact, be both, in the sense of being manifest as forms as well as particulars. For example, the case of three might plausibly be interpreted as a number fashioned after the form. Even if we fully trust Aristotle on what this might mean, what we have is a distinction between mathematical and formal numbers, and not, in addition, a map of the breakdown in the relevant passages. In the same vein, the soul could be considered a particular fashioned after the form of soul, without necessarily clarifying the corresponding arguments, in this case, with the added complication of a special ambiguity between (1) taking each soul as a particular fashioned after a generic form of soul and (2) taking each soul as a particular fashioned after the form of that specific soul. The cases of number and soul are not perfectly analogous, but the point is that the indeterminate illustrations need not be shoved into one category or the other, as they make sense both as particulars and as forms.

The problem might then be taken as one of reference instead of ontology, though combining the two possibilities instead of choosing one promises a more fruitful approach. In other words, any reading would benefit both from insight into Plato's actual words and from enlightened reasoning about the concepts introduced through those words. Unfortunately, Plato himself is not sufficiently forthcoming in this regard, as none of his writings, nor any noteworthy reports of the unwritten doctrine, clarifies the ontological status of the soul, or of numbers, and all of his works put together still fall short of communicating everything about his conception of forms and the associated theory.

Indeed, he discusses the soul in other dialogues, most notably, the *Republic*, the *Phaedrus*, and the *Timaeus*, but these, at least on face value, tend to undermine rather than confirm or clarify the account in the *Phaedo*. While such conflicts can always be attributed to the difference between Socrates and Plato, or otherwise explained as the adaptation of themes to suit specific purposes, the resolution of apparent inconsistencies at the collective level, that of the corpus as a whole, does not speak to specific problems encountered at the level of the dialogue. Again, Plato discusses the forms in numerous other works, but these do not hang together in harmony to offer a unified theory, especially given the prominence of the *Parmenides*, where he criticizes the theory, and the *Sophist*, where he reconsiders his original approach, thus leaving readers without a full positive account or a final word on the matter and with burgeoning uncertainty in their stead.

Nevertheless, the final argument for the immortality of the soul works all the same, or fails just as surely, whether the soul is taken as a particular, a form, or something in between, such as an immanent or intermediate form. The same holds for the utility of all the examples which could be interpreted as forms or particulars, or something altogether different, owing either to an unintended ambiguity or to a deliberate absence of commitment in the text.

7.9. Proof #4: Causal Argument

7.9.1. Logical Core

The final proof for the immortality of the soul is basically an instantiation of the second causal principle in the sophisticated account. In this regard, it is a terminologically fresh formulation, that is, a restatement using a different set of terms, of the analogy establishing an opposition between fire and snow on the model of a primary opposition between the hot and the cold, thus bringing out diagonal opposition relations between fire and cold and between snow and heat.

The soul is taken to be essentially connected with life, in the fashion of the essential connections between fire and heat and between snow and cold, and it is purported not to admit death, this being the opposite of life, just as fire does not admit cold, as the opposite of heat, and snow does not admit heat, as the opposite of cold.

The difference here, and thus what establishes the immortality of the soul, is that the soul's essential connection happens to be with a form whose very nature precludes death and embraces immortality, whereas the options to withdraw or perish are equally open in the other examples, such as fire faced with cold, snow faced with heat, three faced with even, and so on. We can safely rule out the outcome of perishing in the case of the soul faced with death, simply because the soul is essentially connected with the opposite of death.

7.9.2. Critical Assessment

The argument we are left with as the definitive proof of the immortality of the soul straddles an unsustainable position between equivocation and begging the question. At one end, it seems to equivocate on what constitutes the opposite of death, thereby legitimizing an otherwise illicit transition from an essential connection with life to one with immortality. At the other end, it seems to beg the question of the immortality of the soul by inferring that conclusion from an essential connection with life in the sense of a necessary rejection of death. It cannot sensibly be said to be doing both at once, but it does appear to be doing one or the other.

The argument has two distinct parts: The first part (105b–e) establishes that the soul does not and cannot admit death, and the second part (105e–107a) demonstrates that the soul, at the approach of death, safely withdraws instead of perishing. The transition seems somewhat suspicious, as the first part clearly turns on the soul's essential connection with life, while the second part ends up with the much stronger attribute of immortality.

A point of clarification regarding the transition from life to immortality, one lending credence to that transition, is that Plato is not working with two different forms here; that is, the second part of the argument does not replace the form of life with one for immortality. Plato brings immortality into play as the state or condition of that which does not and cannot admit death, much in the way that he discusses the "uneven," the "un-hot," and the "un-coolable" in the same passage (105e–106a). None of these is a new form, and the same holds for immortality. Immortality, then, turns out to be the state or property of having an essential connection with life, thus legitimately lending its name to that which never dies, that which forever subsists.

This clarification absolves the argument of charges of equivocation in the form of a deceptive and illicit transition from life to immortality, but it pushes it in the direction of begging the question. Claiming immortality on the basis of not admitting death due to an essential connection with life seems circular enough to count as a textbook example of *petitio principii*. In a fundamental sense, the final argument for the immortality of the soul is comparable to the ontological argument for the existence of God in that they both turn on the definition of the terms in question, wherein the soundness of the argument is guaranteed by the nature of the subject as defined. Sticking with an analogy closer to home, the soul rejects death for the same reason and in the same way that three cannot be odd and fire cannot be cold (106b).

The only reason that the soul is immortal is that it is essentially connected with the form of life, which can never admit the form of death, nor perish at the approach of death, leaving withdrawal as the only option. Hence, life is the very embodiment of immortality, imperishability, and indestructibility. Plato's contention is not merely that life is responsible for the presence of these qualities in the soul, but that life itself boasts these qualities, and, even more boldly, that life is their point of origin. In fact, Plato explicitly declares the form of life immortal (106d).

This raises additional questions regarding the attributes of other forms. Given that the form of life is immortal and indestructible, and, to boot, necessarily so, is the form of heat, hot, the form of cold, cold, the form of odd, odd, and so on? Sensibility seems to require rejecting this implication, which, as discussed in chapter two (§ 2.5.3), makes the theory of forms awkward and unmanageable, to say the least, but the alternative, as far as the present proof is concerned, is to give up the claim that the form of life is immortal and indestructible. To be more accurate, the alternative is to give up the claim that the form of life is uniquely and necessarily immortal and indestructible. Plato could, presumably, contend instead that life is immortal and indestructible simply by virtue of being a form, that all forms are immortal and indestructible, and that they do not otherwise take on or impart the physical or conceptual properties or qualities of the things or states which they represent or determine. This, in turn, would require giving up the final argument as a demonstration of the immortality of the soul, because the form of life would no longer have a unique claim to immortality but a generic one best not flaunted lest absolutely everything be thought immortal.

A reasonable response on behalf of Plato, again, as considered in greater detail in chapter two (§ 2.5.3), is that self-predication in forms expresses an identity claim rather than a descriptive statement. According to this reading, Plato asserts that the form of life, as the essence or purest example of life, is precisely what is meant by immortality, not that the form of life is immortal in the same way that, say, Zeus or Apollo might be immortal. Although the immortality of life is not as straightforward an example of self-predication as the justness of justice or the beautifulness of beauty, the defense works just the same, or can be rejected for the same reasons. However, even if this generic defense for self-predication is granted in this instance, it is not transitive between life and the soul, where the need for a defense of some sort seems even more urgent. The immortality of the soul, the very conclusion sought throughout the dialogue, comes with its own problems.

The final argument forges a unique link between the soul and life, an essential connection whereby the soul is invariably connected with life. Yet the soul can be no more alive than fever is ill. The entire discussion, that is, the dialogue at large, is grounded in an explicit agreement on the definition of death as the separation of the soul and the body (64c, 67d), and proceeds with a conception of life as its opposite, which is the union of the soul and the body. This is confirmed further where Socrates declares specifically that we are part body and part soul (79b). Life, then, cannot properly be predicated of a soul without a body any more than it can of a body without a soul, as it is an attribute of the combined entity, soul+body, or, less awkwardly, the ensouled body, or, conversely, the corporeal, incorporate, incarnate, or embodied soul. It might be objected that, even though life is the result of a union between soul and body, the two parts cannot be assumed to make an equal contribution to the whole, and, in fact, that the soul is the animating force in the relationship. However, this objection makes the body out to be a superfluous receptacle: If the body is not necessary for life, then the union is not necessary, and the definitions of life and death are both faulty. The objection, then, denies too much. It also accomplishes too little: What is required of the soul is not merely that it be an animating force, an inert conduit for an energy charge, but that it be alive.

So, is the soul alive? Is it a life form? This problem is sometimes tangled up in the otherwise independent controversy regarding self-predication in forms. This, in turn, means treating the soul as a form. An interpretation of the soul as a form tends to go hand-in-hand with the treatment of its claim to life as a subset or a mere specimen of the more general issue of self-predication in forms. The problem is largely the same even if the soul is not thought to be a form, or thought not to be a form. One defining difference is that the problem as it applies to the soul concerns the soul as a causal intermediary, say between a form and a particular, whereas the way it pertains to a form involves a direct relationship with a particular. But this makes no difference in terms of the common question, which might be posed thus: Does the cause boast the same quality it transfers to the effect? This basic question is the same whether it concerns the form as a direct cause or as a causal intermediary acting as the agent of the ultimate cause.

The problem as it concerns the forms in general is taken up in the *Parmenides*, but it begs for additional consideration in the specific way in which it applies to the soul in the *Phaedo*, especially as the general treatment is inconclusive in the *Parmenides*, and, as it happens, throughout the Platonic corpus. If the soul is not even alive, then it certainly cannot be immortal. More specifically, if it escapes death only because it is not the kind of thing of which life and death can meaningfully be predicated, then its immortality is meaningless, for it is no more immortal than is any substance, such as fire or water, or any concept, such as justice or beauty, or, in short, anything which never lives and never dies. Resisting death is impressive only if the subject is alive to begin with.

Burger (1984), for one, has made much of this problem, going so far as to claim that Plato's aim in the *Phaedo* is to prove the opposite of what he is commonly thought to be after. She claims that Plato is out to prove that the soul cannot survive separation from the body. The final argument becomes as crucial to her thesis as it is to Plato's. She does not reject the straightforward reading of that argument as establishing the soul's exclusion of death, but she holds Plato to his original commitment to the definition of death as the separation of the soul and the body, thus claiming that the real conclusion of the argument is that the soul cannot admit separation from the body (since it cannot admit death, and death is its separation from the body). Under this interpretation, Plato deliberately advances three bad arguments for the opposite thesis that the soul can exist independently of the body, and he does so specifically to wear down this popular Pythagorean doctrine, subsequently establishing his own position that the soul cannot exist independently of the body. Despite representing Plato as concealing too much from his less imaginative readers, and Socrates as putting on a charade for his own audience, this is a novel thesis as well as a fair challenge to the ambiguities in the dialogue.

In the final analysis, challenges and difficulties concerning the final proof, as well as those concerning the dialogue at large, have more to do with conceptualization than with inference. Problems tend to expose the ambiguity of the terms rather than the weakness of their connections. The clarification of meaning should precede any attempt to evaluate the proofs. What is at stake is not merely the immortality of the soul but the meaning of the term and the nature of the referent.

What is the soul? Granting it a physical existence would be largely counterintuitive. And rightful demands for scientific confirmation would become a constant source of frustration. On the other hand, denying it a physical existence avoids a lot of difficulties, but runs the risk of trivializing it. If the soul is neither matter nor energy, then it just might not exist at all, or not in a sense that matters to us. What is sought in such debates is the existence and immortality of a discrete sentient being, hopefully, at least as intelligent as a human. This might, in contemporary terms, be interpreted as the mind, which is not usually thought of as a material thing. How, then, does Plato's conception of the soul relate to epiphenomenalism, the view that mental states are causally inert byproducts of physical events, an echo of physiological processes and of responses to external stimuli?

We might characterize the Platonic soul, certainly not as a mental state, but perhaps as the core signature or dynamic manifestation of a particular web, network, pattern, or stream of mental states, in the final analysis, a product of brain activity. Even if this is taken as an interactive product that shapes its own source, again, call it "brain activity," its potential for independent existence is still suspect as long as it is a product of something destined to perish without exception. This is the essence of Simmias's position likening the soul to the attunement of a lyre (85e–86d), though the apparent anticipation of epiphenomenalism there does not automatically show that the soul is not immortal or that it is not significant, as if contemporary epiphenomenalism were celebrated in certitude.

Modern conceptions of the mind are not yet united in an unassailable standard model effectively contradicting everything essential to Plato's rumination on the matter. But the prospect of such a development is not the real threat to the study of Plato. The real threat is in evaluating his work in the manner of a contribution at the cutting edge of neurophilosophy. Plato is best engaged in his own terms, at the level of arguments, rather than observations, predictions, and experiments.

7.10. Mythology

Argumentation leaves its place to mythology (107d–114c) as Socrates describes the fate of the soul against a backdrop of cosmological detail, laying out a far richer account than necessary for immediate purposes, whether in terms of the drama or the logic, and offering a pictorial sketch of the universe and the human condition in context.

The mythological account has two dimensions, one outlining the setting, and, the other, supplying the scene played out in that setting. The setting is nothing less than the universe itself, wherein human existence is a negligible concern in an insignificant corner. The human condition is such that we live in a peripheral layer of reality, removed as far from what matters as are the creatures of the sea from life on the surface, leaving us as ignorant about ultimate reality as they are about what goes on beyond the water.

The fate of the soul upon death comes through with even greater detail as Socrates narrates the journey through the afterlife. The basic mechanism is a network of rivers and channels cutting through the universe, thus connecting sea and land, the diversity of which constitutes a cosmic flow of energy, wherein souls journey through eternity. The route and schedule of the journey depend on the kind of life led by the soul during its union with the body, usually proceeding along the main rivers of the central network.

The most prominent element of the cosmic architecture is Tartarus, a giant chasm penetrating the earth through and through from one end to the other. The basic landscape consists of four main rivers flowing into and out of Tartarus and connecting many regions through water and land:

- Oceanus (112e) is the greatest of the four rivers, and flows in a circle around the perimeter of Tartarus.

- Acheron (112e–113a) flows in the opposite direction, going underground, and coming out into the Acherusian Lake, where most souls are delivered and collected during the cycle of rebirth.

- Pyriphlegethon (113a–b) issues from a point between Oceanus and Acheron, flowing into a vast expanse blazing with fire, and creating its own lake.

- Cocytus (113b–c) issues and runs opposite Pyriphlegethon, which it meets at the other side of the Acherusian Lake. Its course takes it through the Stygian land, where it creates its own lake, called Styx.

The eschatological depiction of the fate of the soul makes use of this entire network, with the exception of Oceanus, which is never mentioned again. Each soul's entry into and experience in the system depends on heavenly judgment on the kind of life it has led (113d–114c):

- Those who have lived a middling sort of life in terms of goodness and piety go through Acheron to the Acherusian Lake, where they are purified, receiving reward and punishment according to desert (113d–e).

- Those coming from a morally unacceptable past enter Tartarus under conditions corresponding to the gravity of their sins. Those beyond redemption, for example, those guilty of multiple murders or sacrilegious theft, are hurled into Tartarus forever (113e). Redeemable wrongdoers are also thrown into Tartarus but reemerge on an annual basis to beg forgiveness at the Acherusian Lake, where those they have wronged congregate (113e–114b): Sinners guilty of plain homicide arrive by way of Cocytus; those guilty of patricide or matricide arrive through Pyriphlegethon. As they pass the lake, they all call upon the relevant parties for forgiveness. For each corrigible sinner, the annual schedule repeats itself until absolution.

- Those who have led an honorable life distinguished in piety are excused from systemic processing, and enjoy an existence in a pure dwelling place above the ground (114b–c).

- Those who have purified themselves through philosophy qualify for an eternal existence without reincarnation (114c).

The final category is a subset of the one preceding it, as the reference to philosophers explicitly singles them out collectively as a class among the souls who have lived in accordance with goodness and piety.

7.11. Death Scene

Myth blends into reality, as Socrates concludes his presentation and begins preparations for the sentence to be carried out. The death scene, taken at face value, is Plato's narration of an eyewitness account, though not his own, of Socrates's execution. It can also be combed for dialogue and imagery that might have philosophical or literary import as a message from Plato, beyond the explicit one from Socrates. This final chance for insight into the character of the protagonist reveals, above all, an incomparable concern for the well-being of others, combined with a marked indifference to physical pleasures and worldly matters.

Altruism emerges immediately and forcefully as a dominant theme, as the run-up to the execution discloses layer upon layer of the central character's interest in the welfare of others, even as he prepares for the end of his stay with them. The death scene opens with the depiction of a man so thoughtful as to take a bath before his own execution just to save people the trouble of washing the corpse afterwards (115a). The same sensitivity to the interests of others determines his parting counsel, as Crito asks for his final instructions. Ignoring the obvious testamentary context of Crito's request for instructions, Socrates sidesteps anything like a last will and testament, responding instead with spiritual guidance: His advice is to "take care of yourselves" (115b), which he fleshes out as leading lives along the course laid out through the discussion of the day, evidently a reference to nurturing the soul through philosophy.

The other salient theme governing character development in the final scene of the dialogue is a growing detachment from the physical world. Such dissociation is nowhere more evident or emphatic than in the haunting reply to Crito's query regarding burial instructions. Asked where he would like to be buried, Socrates responds with an evocative conviction that he is not the kind of thing that can be buried: He cannot be buried because he cannot be caught once freed of the body (115c–116a). This turns out to be the pinnacle of the otherworldly orientation driving the dialogue from the outset. The metaphysical polarity between the soul and the body is further reflected in the dramatic rift between Socrates and earthly concerns, as he refuses to take advantage of a lawful opportunity, brought up as a gentle reminder by Crito, to prolong his final moments with food, drink, and sex (116e–117a). Immediately following time spent in parting conversation with the women of his household and his three children (116b), his refusal to extend his stay by clinging to earthly pleasures draws a striking contrast between spiritual and physical engagement, with the implicit identification of the former as time well spent and the latter as a waste of time.

The portrayal of Socrates in a near-ascetic orientation regarding the needs and pleasures of the body contradicts the portrait offered in dialogues pursuing character development in the opposite direction, wherein the inimitable sage of Athens exudes a superlative zest for life, including, in the *Symposium*, a hearty appetite for food and alcohol, supported by a unique ability to drink everyone else under the table. This is not so much a contradiction in fact as it is a difference in emphasis. Even an otherwise ordinary person with a high threshold for alcohol is unlikely to want to be remembered for making a public display of that capacity his final deed on earth. Facing death with an orgy just does not seem fitting for a philosopher par excellence, fictional or historical. As for growing otherworldliness in the *Phaedo*, the hero's dramatic abandonment of the physical world serves as a metaphorical reflection of Socrates's actual departure from the same.

Righteousness, with a particular emphasis on duty and an implicit concern for justice, emerges as another powerful motif at the end of the dialogue. In fact, this is the chief enabling factor underlying the dialogue itself, which would not have been possible save for Socrates's refusal on moral grounds to participate in the prison break arranged by his friends, as related in the *Crito*. This general dramatic influence becomes conspicuously evident in an ultimate episode of obedience to authority toward the end of the dialogue, where Socrates dutifully follows the instructions of the prison personnel responsible for guard duty and administering the poison. First, he has a friendly exchange with the guard, who cannot hold back his tears after notifying him that it is time for the execution (116b–d). Next, he has a less poignant but equally civil interchange with the official charged with preparing and administering the poison (117a–c). Socrates is so much at ease with his own death that he personally seeks out the poison, which is brought in at his behest (116d), and makes a toast while raising the cup of poison to a prayer that the transition from this world to the next be a happy one (117c).

Perhaps the greatest mark of dedication to what is right and just comes at the very end of the dialogue as Socrates is about to give his last breath. His final words instruct Crito to offer a cock to Asclepius, the god of medicine and healing, in the settlement of an obligation on his behalf (118a). What is meant here is not clear. Nor is it certain whether the words belong to Socrates the philosopher or to Plato the dramatist. Yet the fact that Socrates, as he lay dying, is concerned with the settlement of a debt, even if Plato invented this ending, is consistent with what we know of the historical and the dramatic Socrates as a paragon of virtue.

The passage is easy to interpret. Securing the agreement of the scholarly community is an entirely different matter. Since the reference is hopelessly vague, and the lore delightfully rich, any sensible reading would have something to recommend it. A compelling testament to the diversity of interpretations is that the collective effort has been fertile enough to enable Peterson (2003, pp. 33–52) to list twenty-one different construals in her survey of the literature before presenting her own version.

Despite the extraordinary freedom available in the interpretive task, the basic elements should help keep any scenario sober. These are: (1) that Asclepius is a god; (2) that his domain is medicine, particularly healing, and (3) that Socrates acknowledges a debt to Asclepius.

On this basis, a plausible interpretation of the corresponding passage is that the last words of Socrates constitute a votive offering, to be understood as a metaphorical reference to being cured of all the material concerns that come with being trapped in the physical world. This interpretation is challenged by those finding it incompatible with Socrates's trademark *joie de vivre*, making it out-of-character for him to treat life as an illness. But the debt of gratitude to the god could just as well be a reference specifically to liberation from forced coexistence with the body without implying any disdain for life itself. After all, Socrates's enthusiasm for life is not necessarily for the pleasures of the flesh, but more generally for the experience of sentient and sapient existence, which he is convinced will continue after death, and which, in turn, demonstrates how he might consistently enjoy life and thank the god for being released from the body. Nevertheless, this is not the only interpretation possible. A far less dramatic yet equally plausible alternative is that the parting request is for the settlement of some other obligation unrelated to the events of the day. In either case, the final words could be taken as fact or fiction, but the limelight remains fixed on the discharge of duty regardless of the interpretation chosen.

This much about the final words of Socrates can readily be concluded from the bare statement in the text, perhaps in combination with a nominal awareness of the domain of the god chosen for the dying devotion. However, details of the corresponding legend afford deeper insight into the allegorical reference. Born to a mortal princess, Coronis, as the son of Apollo, Asclepius was so gifted in the art of healing as to bring back the dead, a deed for which he was destroyed by Zeus, yet subsequently not only resurrected but also elevated to godhood through apotheosis with the intermediation of Apollo. His name is the second to be mentioned, immediately after Apollo, in the Hippocratic Oath.

Asclepius is also mentioned in the third book of the *Republic* (3.408b–c), though not with particular reverence or admiration. Citing Pindar (*Pythian Odes* 3.55–58) and unnamed tragedians (possibly Aeschylus in *Agamemnon* 1022 ff. and Euripides in *Alcestis* 3–4), external references identified in footnotes in especially informative translations, for example, in the Loeb and Hackett editions of the collective works, Socrates in the *Republic* brings up the legend of Asclepius being struck dead by a thunderbolt from Zeus for accepting a bribe of gold to heal a rich man on the verge of death. On the authority of this reference, the cock Socrates sees fit to offer in sacrifice to Asclepius, as he himself lay dying at the end of the *Phaedo*, bears interpretation, however vacuous, as a bribe for delivery from the clutches of death. This, of course, is thoroughly repugnant to the theme of the dialogue, as well as being at variance with the portrait developed of Socrates there or elsewhere.

A better interpretation would be that the *Phaedo*'s reference to Asclepius is intended to draw a parallel between the situation of Socrates and that of the god prior to his deification. Just as Asclepius is struck dead by Zeus only to be deified later, so, too, is Socrates struck dead by Athens only to be immortalized afterwards.

Regardless of barriers to determining the precise intention in the reference, what is perfectly clear here is the irony that Socrates, dying as a convicted heretic executed for rejecting the gods recognized by the state, reserved his last words for the arrangement of a sacrifice to a god recognized by the state. This is a fitting complement to his transforming the final act of drinking the poison into an occasion for a toast-cum-prayer (117c).

7.12. Historicity in Death

The final moments of Socrates invoke the familiar issue of historicity, in fact, with even greater vigor here than in any of the proofs for the immortality of the soul. This is because the closing scene is detailed enough for scrutiny of its depiction of death by poison.

Dating at least as far back as the seventeenth century, and surviving alternating periods of neglect and reinvigoration, the primary question is whether the poison, presumably hemlock, would take effect precisely in the manner described by Plato. The answer depends more on medical, pharmacological, toxicological, and physiological considerations than on dramatic or philosophical ones, though this is not to say that classicists or philosophers would find themselves out of their element in evaluating the findings. On the contrary, their involvement promises a genuine contribution with the training to draw out more from the text itself than might strike the eye of a scientist in the natural sciences. In fact, the problem is quite suitable for a joint study, and might even demand such collaboration for a definitive solution.

What is at stake is not merely the accuracy of Plato's report of the death scene but the general reliability of his dramatic portrayal of Socrates in any context, including the trial, the prison term, and the day of execution, not to mention conspicuous plot elements in any other dialogues. Uncovering deliberate and significant factual contradictions in Plato's account here would be tantamount to proof that he falsified the record, which, no matter the reason, would, in turn, cast aspersions on the *prima facie* historicity of any and all adventures played out by his leading character. Verifying the story, on the other hand, whether in broad terms or in every detail, would add little beyond a marginal increase to his credibility as a source on the historical Socrates. This is because the death scene is one of the foremost places Plato is expected to be reporting fact rather than creating fantasy. Confirming the plausibility of the hemlock case would support that expectation, but the support would be on a scale roughly commensurate with the evidentiary contribution of a corroborating observation to a scientific theory, strengthened by yet another empirical confirmation but open to collapse with a genuine contradiction.

Refuting the account, then, would be far more sensational than upholding it. Modern attempts toward refutation include studies by Gill (1973, pp. 25–28), Ober (1977, pp. 254–258), and Graves *et al.* (1991, pp. 156–168). The most rigorous effort in the defensive camp is by Bloch (2002, pp. 255–278), who reaffirms the historical reliability of Plato's depiction of the master's death, not merely through a targeted rebuttal of specific points in previous attempts to discredit it, but through a positive account drawing on a rich history of scientific studies on the subject.

7.13. Other Arguments for Immortality

The *Phaedo* is Plato's only work on the immortality of the soul. But it is not the only one offering proof of the immortality of the soul. Three others promise such a proof: the *Republic* (Book 10), the *Phaedrus*, and the *Laws* (Book 10). To these may be added various discussions of the soul that do not attempt to prove its immortality and numerous references to it that may or may not even mention its immortality. The highlights, including the *Phaedo*, can be diagramed as follows:

Map of Focus on the Soul in the Platonic Corpus

Dialogue	**Passage**	**Pages**
Phaedo	Proof: Cyclical Argument	70c–72e
	Proof: Recollection Argument	72e–77a
	Proof: Analogic (Affinity) Argument	78b–80b
	Proof: Causal (Final) Argument	102a–107a
Republic 4	Divisions of the Soul	436a–444a
Republic 10	Proof: Soul as Resistant to Its Own Evil	608c–611a
Phaedrus	Proof: Soul as Prime Mover	245c–246a2
	Myth of the Essence and Transmigration of the Soul	246a–257a
Timaeus	World Soul	34b–36d
	Creation and Nature of the Soul via Reason	41a–44d
	Creation and Nature of the Soul via Necessity	68e–72d
	Diseases of the Soul	86b–87b
	Maintenance (Soul & Body)	87c–90d
Laws 10	Soul as the Quintessence of "Existence by Nature"	891d–893a
	Proof: Soul as Prime Mover	893b–896b
	Soul as God	896b–899d

Note: The designation of a passage as a "proof" signifies that it is a proof of the immortality of the soul.

The best companion to reading the *Phaedo* would be a complete psychology of Plato. But that is a project in itself, not to be tackled in conjunction with others, and handled admirably by Robinson (1970) and covered more recently in a collection edited by Wagner (2001). Even so, a discussion of the *Phaedo* focusing primarily, or seriously even if not primarily, on the arguments for the immortality of the soul cannot afford to ignore Plato's other arguments for the same conclusion. The remainder of this section is intended to avoid such a deficiency. A good many readers are interested in the *Phaedo* for the arguments on immortality. Those satisfied may wish to consider what else Plato has to say on the matter. Those disappointed may want to see if he does better elsewhere. Either way, further investigation is both warranted and enlightening, and the result is worth the effort.

7.13.1. *Republic* 10 (608c–611a)

7.13.1.1. Logical Core

Truncating a considerable amount of detail otherwise essential to a proper understanding, the logical progression of the central argument can be mapped out as follows:

(P1) Things can be destroyed only by their own evil (*Republic* 10.609a–b).
(P2) Evils of the soul: injustice; intemperance; cowardice; ignorance (*Republic* 10.609c).
(P3) The soul is not destroyed by its own evil (*Republic* 10.609d).
(C) The soul is immortal (*Republic* 10.610e–611a).

This is not a controversial proof. It is rejected without controversy. Dissenting opinions are typically reserved for damage control rather than denial of failure. Plato's allies in this respect, chief among them, Brown (1997), tend to be concerned with responding to derision and alleviating disappointment rather than defending the proof as a flawless one. Indeed, the proof has met with wide ridicule from respectable sources. This makes it easy to dismiss, and hard to ignore.

It is not often that one gets a chance to mock Plato, that is, with good reason. The proof merits closer investigation if only in pursuit of that opportunity, seizing it personally instead of vicariously through secondary literature. Unfortunately, the central argument tends to improve with repeated reflection, arguably leaving little to mock, though still plenty to reject. No matter how the effort pans out, progress in any direction requires fleshing out the introductory outline.

7.13.1.2. Context and Strategy

The first premise (P1) sets up a universal principle maintaining that whatever is destructible at all is destructible only through its own inherent evil (vice, defect, affliction) and by nothing else, thus ruling out the possibility of destruction by anything other than the force naturally destructive of the thing whose destruction is under consideration (*Republic* 10.609a–b).

The second premise (P2) shows where the soul fits into the general equation, or, strictly speaking, how the universal principle is instantiated in the case of the soul. The essential evil of the soul, that is, the defect attaching to it merely by virtue of what it is, includes, and is exhausted by, injustice, intemperance, cowardice, and ignorance, initially listed separately for the sake of completeness, but later grouped together, for the sake of convenience, under the general category of injustice (*Republic* 10.609c), also invoked as "injustice and the other evils" (*Republic* 10.609d). These are the privations, or, from a different perspective, the opposites, of the four cardinal virtues, justice, temperance, courage, and wisdom, taken up in several places throughout the Platonic corpus, most notably, in the fourth book of the same dialogue (*Republic* 4.427e), where they are listed together in the process of developing the celebrated analogy between the city and the soul.

The third premise (P3) supplies the final bit of input needed for a coherent argument. It adds that the soul is not destroyed by its own evil, including injustice and all the other evils subsumed under that general category (*Republic* 10.609d). These may corrupt the soul, but they cannot destroy it: They are unable to destroy the soul despite posing a natural threat to it and inflicting substantial injury.

The conclusion (C), uneventfully tapping the three premises, is that the soul is indestructible and thereby eternal and therefore immortal (*Republic* 10.610e–611a).

The heart of the argument is the first premise, which claims the lion's share of Plato's attention as well as setting the tone of critical reception for the overall proof. The premise continues to undergo development once the entire argument is laid out, after which the universal principle of destruction is explicated through examples, primarily of the destructibility of the body and of bodies, that is, other physical substances, all intended to demonstrate that nothing is destroyed by anything other than its characteristic evil, with particular emphasis on the soul's invulnerability to agents capable of destroying the body (*Republic* 10.609d–610b). This blends into a denial of any correlation between death and injustice, that is, between dying and becoming more unjust (*Republic* 10.610b–d), thus shifting some of the burden of proof to the dissenter, thereby challenged to prove that the soul becomes unjust upon death (defined implicitly as the dissolution of the union of soul and body in any life form, particularly on the evidence of *Republic* 10.609d).

7.13.1.3. Critical Assessment

The validity of the argument is not contested, as the conclusion clearly follows from the premises. Its soundness, however, is another matter. The problem is not that the premises are patently false or particularly counterintuitive, though some certainly appear to be, but that they are rather unwieldy in their speculative indulgence. In fact, the third premise (P3) is hardly objectionable, given that we do not normally think of injustice and the other evils of the soul as capable of destroying the soul. This leaves the first two premises.

The first premise (P1), reducing destruction to a predetermined causal phenomenon, rigidly configured in advance with a characteristic end for anything and everything that admits of an end, seems outright false. Yet it is not as ridiculous as it may seem upon initial encounter. It is sometimes misinterpreted as ruling out the possibility of shared causes of destruction, instead assigning a unique destructive force to all destructible things of the same kind. This would mean that nothing could be destroyed by anything that can also destroy something else, or, strictly speaking, that nothing of a certain kind could be destroyed by anything that can also destroy something of another kind, with this strict sense intended to be included in every abbreviated reference from here on out. Plato himself repudiates this as he acknowledges rust to be the inherent evil in both bronze and iron (*Republic* 10.609a).

Another misunderstanding is to take the premise as requiring exactly one cause of destruction for any given thing, or for any given kind of thing. This, however, is contradicted in the assignment of four different evils to the soul (*Republic* 10.609c). The four evils are related, to be sure, and might even be reducible to a single force under the unity of the virtues, or, in this case, the unity of the privations of the virtues, but they are also discrete, as discrete as the parts of the soul, with the causal plurality thus consistent with the central analogy of the entire work.

To summarize, the first premise leaves open both the possibility of different things having the same evil and the possibility of the same thing having different evils. The principle espoused is not that each destructible thing can be destroyed only by a singular evil unique to it and foreign to everything else, but that each destructible thing can be destroyed only by a cause naturally or essentially inimical to it, that is, by a force harmful to it by virtue of what it is.

Properly understood, this principle, and the premise advancing it, is pregnant with possibilities for vindicating itself, emerging at least as a respectable claim, as opposed to a silly one, even if it is not entirely convincing in the final analysis. The apparent problem is that, even with all possible misinterpretations identified and avoided, we are still left with the perplexing position that nothing may be destroyed by an evil alien to it. This may seem easy enough to settle, as a single counterexample would suffice to refute the principle. For instance, invoking Plato's own examples, one might object that, while rust is nominated as an evil inherent in bronze and iron, both may also be destroyed by an entirely different causal agent that does not involve oxidation, say, a thermonuclear explosion. Perhaps more perspicuously, taking another of Plato's examples, one might object that, while rot is presented as an evil inherent in wood, the latter may also be destroyed by a number of different causes, including fire, termites, beavers, and people wielding axes.

A conceivable response is that these are not counterexamples but amendments to the list of causal agents that naturally destroy this or that thing. Plato does not claim bronze or iron to be destructible only by rust, or wood to be destructible only by rot; he claims them to be destructible typically, naturally, and characteristically by these things. The central point here is that bronze and iron differ in this respect from things that are not susceptible to rust, as wood differs from things that are not susceptible to rot. Presented with additional candidates for the destruction of a substance, Plato may simply expand the list of natural evils for that substance, thereby accommodating any confirmed cases or plausible possibilities. This might run the risk of watering down the original principle to such an extent as to trivialize it altogether, but this is not as embarrassing as subscribing to a principle reducible to the absurdity of refusing to acknowledge that wood might be destroyed by something other than rot.

The second premise (P2) is comparably precarious, as it amounts to speculation on the essence of an entity that is not even perceptible. The veracity of the claim here seems difficult to judge unless one has exceptional, preferably supernatural, insight into metaphysical problems. Who knows what might be destructive of the soul? Indeed, injustice and its attendant evils may be harmful to the soul, corrupting it while falling short of destroying it, but something else may succeed where these fail. Perhaps a properly calibrated lightsaber would do the trick. If not, a sustained tachyon pulse capable of reversing the polarity of its target is always an unpleasant prospect. Would the soul survive exposure to kryptonite, or bombardment by cosmic rays? Could it handle a visit to the wrong side of an event horizon? The point is not to make light of the issue, but to demonstrate that we simply are not in the know here, no matter which side we take on the issue of personal immortality.

As we are all out of our element here, though, no doubt, some not so much as others, it would be unfair to deny (and superfluous to insist) that Plato has laid out a plausible account of what may reasonably be supposed to be the natural evil of the soul. Physical destruction requires a physical subject. Given a soul that is intelligible rather than perceptible, the corresponding destruction need not be sought in the realm of physical phenomena. And where the scope of consideration is limited to the intelligible realm, injustice, intemperance, cowardice, and ignorance hang together as an impressive ensemble of evils, each quite believable as representing a natural threat to the soul.

The upshot of all this is not that the proof is compelling, but that it is not vacuous. That said, the argument is not without fault. It seems suspiciously close to begging the question of the indestructibility of the soul. Holding something to be *indestructible because it is not destroyed by its own evil*, especially where avoiding absurdity requires being flexible enough with the definition of that evil to include any other menacing candidates that may be nominated along the way, is not far from taking that thing to be *indestructible because it is not destroyed*. Not being destroyed is no small comfort, in fact, presenting a rather enviable condition, but it is also not a cause, reason, or explanation of indestructibility. This is not necessarily an overwhelming difficulty with the proof but an example of the kind of probing that awaits it under serious scrutiny.

Even if all the causes, reasons, and explanations were in perfect order, this particular proof would have to answer for more than logical respectability. The argument here could be valid, sound, persuasive, and relevant, yet still fail to be gratifying. The question is whether the proof leaves us with a conception of soul that sounds reassuring about life after death, not just the possibility of that life, but the quality of such life as we might be susceptible of as a spectral entity unable to interact with the world around it. The position adopted regarding the indestructibility of the soul comes with a downside: An entity that cannot be destroyed by, say, a supernova in its immediate presence must be impervious to such forces because it is devoid of matter and energy, not because it has a hardy constitution. And that which is devoid of both matter and energy might just not be the kind of thing that can in fact be in the immediate presence of a supernova, or of anything else. The soul, then, is dangerously close to sounding like nothing at all instead of something glorious.

These are the same problems brought up time and again regarding God Almighty, who seems to be doing fine against such adversity. Perhaps, we can allow the soul the benefit of the doubt as well. While it may be objected that the soul is not in the same league as the Almighty, one would have a hard time convincing Plato of this. The next two proofs place the soul close enough to God to give it an impressive existence, with powers that should prove adequate for the most persnickety critic of the life it might be able to lead in the hereafter.

7.13.2. *Phaedrus* (245c–246a)

7.13.2.1. Logical Core

The proof offered in the *Phaedrus* (245c–246a) is far more controversial than the one in the *Republic* (10.608c–611a). The one in the *Phaedrus* is still debated in some form or another, while the one in the *Republic* is nearly universally rejected. The most salient difference is not that the *Phaedrus* proof still finds proponents while the *Republic* proof does not, but that the logical core of the *Phaedrus* proof is still in currency, whether attracting defense or attack, whereas nothing about the other is remembered except in academic circles. Although the enduring appeal of the proof is limited to a specific component, fully serviceable as an independent argument in another context, the proof at large makes sense only in its entirety:

(P1) Whatever moves itself is immortal (and nothing else is).
(P2) The soul moves itself.
(C) The soul is immortal (and nothing else is).

This is a condensed exposition driven by a loaded first premise. The entire argument (*Phaedrus* 245c–246a) is summarized in the opening statement (*Phaedrus* 245c) of the proof, the remainder of which is devoted to the justification of the first premise. That premise, abbreviated above, is the claim that whatever moves itself, in and of and by itself, never having required a kick-start, nor any assistance along the way, is immortal, and the only thing that is immortal. In other words, all and only those things that are capable of unassisted motion, and that are in fact in motion without assistance, are immortal. This is not the same as the material implication that a thing is immortal if it moves itself, leaving open the possibility that other things might also be immortal. It represents instead a stronger position espousing the material equivalence that a thing is immortal if and only if it moves itself.

The justification offered is that the temporal beginning and causal source of all motion must ultimately be singular self-motion, since the alternative is an infinite regress, the rejection of which leaves self-motion as the only candidate for eternal existence, and as a necessary and sufficient condition for it. As the origin of reality, that which moves itself is ungenerated and indestructible, for if it were generated it would not be the first, and if it were destructible there would be no beginning, and everything else would fall apart (*Phaedrus* 245d–e).

7.13.2.2. Context and Strategy

This, as far as we know, is the first record of a formal cosmological argument tracing the universe back to a "prime mover." The seminal formulation of that argument in Plato serves an auxiliary purpose here, as it represents the logical core of a proof for the immortality of the soul rather than constituting a standalone presentation championing a cosmic creator. The task undertaken is not merely to trace everything back to a single origin, which, even if identifiable as the soul, must be shown to be everlasting as well as primeval. This element of stability is secured, in turn, through the ostensibly self-evident claim that the source of all things accounts not merely for their creation but also for their continued existence (*Phaedrus* 245d–e).

The thrust of Plato's thesis is not so much that the soul is the only thing that moves itself, but that self-motion, herein proved to exist in the form of an ungenerated and indestructible force, or, to be precise, not merely *in* such a force but *as* such a force, is common and peculiar to the soul, the very essence of which is self-movement (*Phaedrus* 245e–246a). The proof does not rest on a devious or unconscious equivocation between the soul and self-motion; it rests on an outright identification of the two with one another. The approach thus relies not on equivocation but on equivalence, which is neither concealed nor unconscious. Plato is aware that he demonstrates the metaphysical necessity of self-motion, but he boldly equates this with the soul. Self-motion, after all, implies a self, no less than Descartes's *cogito* implies a thinker.

The reference to motion is conceived broadly to include causation, with particular relevance to creation in general and thereby to the Creation of lore. The basic strategy consists in a line of reasoning better known for its manifestation as one of the classic arguments for the existence of God. Stripped from the broader context of proof of the immortality of the soul, the supplementary argument, essentially an expansion of the logically compressed first premise, given above somewhat cryptically as the claim that "whatever moves itself is immortal (and nothing else is)," might be expanded as follows:

(P1) Everything in experience can be traced back to a cause outside itself.
(P2) The sequence cannot be infinite since this would leave the causal series itself without a cause, thus contradicting the existence of the universe (or multiverse).
(C) The ultimate source of reality must itself be uncaused (and must exist if anything at all does).

This inferential process ending up with a "prime mover" or "unmoved mover" as the ultimate source of reality represents a class of arguments commonly known as the "cosmological argument" or "argument from first cause," typically invoked as proof of the existence of God. Since this is a type of argument as opposed to a token occurrence of one, the schematic formula above is at best representative, failing both to plug all the gaps and to expose all the weaknesses. Indeed, specialists will find it either too bare and inadequately protected against common objections or too cluttered and overguarded against the same to be sufficiently representative of the class. That said, it should not be too far off target in capturing the spirit of the approach.

While the methodology originates in Plato, here in the *Phaedrus* (245c–246a), to be sure, but even more perspicuously in the *Laws* (10.893b–896b), the standard classical reference is its adoption by Aristotle (*Physics* 8.4–6; *Metaphysics* 12.1–6). It flourished in the Islamic tradition, responsible for the introduction of subtleties strengthening the basic logic, particularly the step rejecting an infinite regress, and later found its most resounding Christian rendition in the work of Thomas Aquinas (*Summa Contra Gentiles* 1.13; *Summa Theologica* 1.q2.a3). Today, the absence of a standard authority on the cosmological argument is mitigated by the availability of a plethora of sources. Craig (1979, 1980, 1993), Rowe (1975, 1978), and Smith (1993, with Craig) are widely consulted in scholarly work while also accessible at a popular level, but a perusal of most any reputable reference, specialist or generalist, should prove useful.

7.13.2.3. Critical Assessment

The history of the cosmological argument, that is, the approach handed down through the centuries, is not simply one of refinement but, more markedly, one of diversification. Variations abound with fine distinctions, many of them important. Exhaustive coverage would carry the discussion far beyond Plato, but even the cursory survey above demonstrates its immediate relevance to reflection on the existence of God. In contrast, its relation to the immortality of the soul is neither immediate, nor complete. To be blunt, if the cosmological argument were flawless, we could rest assured that God exists, but we would still require further evidence of the immortality of the soul. The same strategy is conclusive in the case of God because the requirement there is to demonstrate existence, with indestructibility built into the concept, or at least assumed instead of questioned. It does not work as well, or, dispensing with undue charity, at all, in the case of the soul, where indestructibility is precisely what is in question, while existence is assumed instead of questioned. This being so, the proof drawing on the cosmological argument turns on the assumption that the prime mover must continue to exist in order to sustain the motion it started (*Phaedrus* 245d–e).

The problem is not that the assumption is incredible, but that it is unsubstantiated. Indeed, anyone on board with an argument tracing the causal chain responsible for the entire universe to a definite and unique beginning in an uncreated creative force, ultimately responsible for all of reality while itself dependent on nothing, should find no surprise in the corollary that the force in question is eternal, indestructible, and even omnipotent. However, the argument, as it is, does not establish anything but the temporal and causal primacy of the hypothetical mover, who, or which, might quite conceivably have started a process only to disappear afterwards, presumably leaving behind a self-sustaining reality.

The prime mover need not have moved anything consciously, nor stuck around to witness the result. It need not posses sentience, let alone sapience or creative power. It is entirely conceivable that a first cause, deliberately or not, sets everything in motion and later ceases to exist, at some time, any time, after the moment of the inaugural movement, hence, disappearing after providing the initial spark, regardless of whether it had always itself been in existence or emerged spontaneously to make history without taking part in it. In short, the creator need not survive or outlast its creation, or even see it progress very far. To deny this is to beg the question of the immortality of the prime mover.

The argument is useful to establish the existence of a prime mover but not its immortality, nor even its durability or longevity. All this may be bundled up in the very concept of a prime mover, but then the corresponding achievement can at most be a proof of the existence of a being assumed to be immortal, whereas what is promised is proof of the immortality of a being agreed to exist.

All in all, Plato seems to prove too much here, apparently doing so in more ways than one. For one thing, he proves not only that the soul is immortal, but that it is the only thing that is immortal. But going even further, he proves not only that the soul is the only thing that is immortal, but that it is singularly responsible for all of Creation. It is unique in both respects. It is the one and only immortal creator. This is not stated in so many words, with emphasis and commitment commensurate with the implication, but it is the inescapable conclusion. The emphasis and commitment come later in a version of the argument taken up in the tenth book of the *Laws*. As it becomes clearer in that dialogue, although Plato seems to be proving too much by equating the soul with God, the alternative is to prove too little, with God preceding and preempting the soul as the prime mover. Identifying the soul with God turns out to be the only sensible way, whether in the

Phaedrus or in the *Laws* or anywhere else, to prove the immortality of the soul with this particular argument, that is, by invoking its status as the prime mover. The approach still leaves us with problems, but a *non sequitur* due to competition from God is not one of them.

The most serious problem is the leap in reasoning from the temporal and causal primacy of the prime mover to its temporal and causal eternality, or, focusing only on the direction relevant here, to its everlastingness. The move would be warranted with the prime mover as God, whose eternality is axiomatic rather than inferential, but not with the prime mover as the soul, whose eternality is the very conclusion to be established. The fact that these two turn out to be one and the same is not a solution to the problem but a description of it.

7.13.3. *Laws* 10 (893b–896b)

7.13.3.1. Logical Core

The proof of the *Laws* (10.893b–896b), logically identical to that of the *Phaedrus* (245c–246a), may be schematized in the same way:

(P1) Whatever moves itself is immortal (and nothing else is).
(P2) The soul moves itself.
(C) The soul is immortal (and nothing else is).

The difference is not in the proof itself but in the purpose it serves in the two dialogues. In the *Phaedrus*, the aim is to establish, against the thesis of the speech of Lysias, that the lover benefits the beloved more than the nonlover benefits the beloved, and, in fact, that the lover benefits the beloved whereas the nonlover does not. In the *Laws*, the aim is to demonstrate, as a prelude to the consideration of religious laws, specifically, in regard to legislation against impiety, that the gods exist. The same proof can sensibly be invoked for such different ends because it is not the central concern of either dialogue, contributing to each in a decidedly ancillary capacity.

The immortality of the soul contributes to the *Phaedrus* as a necessary condition of interaction with the intelligible realm of forms, where its disembodied familiarity with beauty is rekindled by love on earth as it encounters a beautiful person. The mythical process requires the survival of the soul without the body, particularly, prior to the body, and that condition is aptly fulfilled by the immortality of the soul.

The demonstration of immortality is just as crucial to the tenth book of the *Laws*, where the object is to prove the existence of the gods, at least one, and that prospect turns out to go hand-in-hand with the immortality of the soul as the prime mover, the epitome of a god, and a tenable or at least familiar representation of God.

The proof has a more direct bearing on the *Phaedrus* than on the *Laws*, as the object of the former is still to establish something about the soul, while that of the latter is all about the gods, which happen to represent an ontological category admitting the soul as a member. Nonetheless, it is indispensable to both.

7.13.3.2. Context and Strategy

In the *Laws*, the key to the connection between the soul and God, or gods, is that the prime mover is alive, as is any self-mover, and that the soul is the very essence of life. This is the point of convergence between the existence of the gods and the immortality of the soul. The gods, patently immortal if they exist at all, must be proven to exist, while the soul, obviously real, in fact, as real as life itself, must be proven to be immortal. A joint solution is possible through the recognition that God is or has a soul, or conversely, that the soul is a god. This, in turn, is effected through the acknowledgment that the prime mover is alive.

The impetus, both dramatically and logically, for the entire undertaking in the tenth book of the *Laws* is the futility of legislation against impiety, particularly atheism, if the gods do not exist. The Athenian Stranger, the protagonist replacing Socrates in the dramatic lead, echoes the Socratic paradox that no one does evil willingly and knowingly, as he attributes impiety or atheism to religious ignorance grounded specifically in three erroneous beliefs: (1) that the gods do not exist; (2) that the gods do not interfere with human affairs, presumably because they do not intervene in the world, even if they do exist; (3) that the gods can be bribed, namely, through prayer and sacrifice, to overlook crimes against religion, even if they do exist and take an active interest in the affairs of human beings. Any one of these three allegedly erroneous beliefs is sufficient for the kind of misdirection constituting impiety. Accordingly, the Athenian Stranger proceeds to overturn each one. To spell it out, he argues that the gods exist (*Laws* 10.891d–899d), that they are actively concerned with human affairs (*Laws* 10.900c–905d), and that they cannot be bribed, and, more specifically, therefore, that they cannot be persuaded, be it through prayer or sacrifice, to overlook impiety (*Laws* 10.905d–907b). Curiously, he leaves far less room for a discussion of the law itself (*Laws* 10.907d–910d) than for the supposedly prefatory demonstration of the grounds for its necessity and utility, but this only adds to the perceived value of the corresponding legislation.

The pivotal part of this progression, the thesis that the gods exist, is executed through the prime mover argument, with the mover identified first and foremost as a soul, and subsequently as a god. The same end could logically have been achieved without the intermediary step of identification as a soul, directly recognizing the prime mover as a god, or as God. Given that the purpose is to prove the existence of at least one god, so as to give meaning to legislation against impiety, any mention of a soul may seem like an unnecessary complication. Today, the same basic argument, without any reference to the soul, works just as well, or just as badly, as a proof for the existence of God.

However, this does not make the reference superfluous or extraneous in context. The soul is the principle of life, whether in humans or in beasts or in gods, and the identification of the prime mover with a soul is nothing more than a designation of it as a living being. The reference to the soul may not be necessary, even by Greek standards, but it represents a semantic, or at least scientific, equivalence rather than a logical detour. The prime mover, as the first thing to move, must have moved itself, and anything that can move itself without assistance must be alive, whether by definition or in fact, and being alive is just what is meant by being ensouled.

This works for any self-mover, thus covering the contentious scenario that a thing might be a self-mover without being the prime mover, in which case the self-mover in question would have to be recognized as alive, and thereby ensouled, simply because it is capable of unassisted motion, regardless of whether other self-movers precede it in time and trump it in causal prominence. What makes the prime mover a soul, or what gives it a soul, is not the fact that it is the first but the fact that it is its own source of motion.

At any rate, talk of the prime mover as both a soul and a god at once poses no problem: If it is a soul because it is alive, then it is a god insofar as it sets creation in motion; if it is a god because of its temporal and causal primacy, then it is a soul insofar as it is alive. The actual order of discovery in the text proceeds from its being a soul to its being a god, which makes sense, since being alive is a necessary condition for being a god, whereas being a god is sufficient though not necessary for being alive.

Regardless of whether establishing the prime mover as being or having a soul is essential for proving that it is a god, and, therefore, that at least one god exists, establishing the prime mover as a god is necessary for proving that it is immortal. This is why the argument, whether in the *Phaedrus* or in the *Laws*, does not, after all, prove too much. We would not today require evidence of divinity in order to accept the immortality of the soul, but we would require proof of indestructibility, which is satisfied by the divinity attributed to the soul.

Going by the professed aim of the relevant part of the dialogue, the *Laws* does not even offer a proof of the immortality of the soul. It offers a proof of the existence of the gods, or, strictly speaking, of at least one god, which, ensouled as the prime mover, thus constitutes proof of the immortality of the soul. In terms of the chronological development of the dialogue, the aim is to demonstrate, against the atheist, that the gods exist by nature, as opposed to existing by art (*Laws* 10.890a–e), which means showing that their existence is grounded in reality rather than merely in tradition and legislation. The effort in this direction starts out as a discussion of the soul as the quintessence of existence by nature (*Laws* 10.891d–893a), and ends up with a proof of the immortality of the soul. The connection is that the prime mover is alive, as is any self-mover, and that the soul is the very essence of life.

7.13.3.3. Critical Assessment

Although the argument does not prove too much in relation to what is required to make it work, what is required to make it work may itself be too much. What is desired is evidence of the immortality of the soul. What is required for this is uncritical assent to the claim that the soul is a god, or, alternatively, at least to the assumption that it continues to exist forever simply because it comes first in a causal series. This is to say nothing of the logical problems attached to any formulation of the cosmological argument for the existence of a prime mover, unmoved mover, or uncaused cause. Hence, in addition to asking for too much by way of silent agreement, the prime mover proof of the immortality of the soul suffers from the same problems affecting the familiar schemata for God.

7.13.3.3.1. Cosmological Argument

With proofs in two separate dialogues relying on the cosmological argument, or, to be fair, marking the historic and historical introduction of that argument, the basic strategy merits further consideration. An immediate problem with the cosmological argument is the counterintuitive operation of taking causality to be evidence of a cause without a cause, an *übercause* inaugurating all of reality but itself not subject to causation.

The standard defense is to point out that the major premise ascribes a cause to some rather than all things, thereby avoiding the contradiction in concluding with a causeless cause. The tendency is to restrict the scope of application to all contingent things, or alternatively to all finite things, depending on the deviation followed from the basic template. This produces a weaker and thus more defensible claim that everything that is contingent or finite has a cause, or, put differently, that everything that is not metaphysically necessary or temporally infinite has a cause, in contrast to the stronger and thus less defensible claim that absolutely everything has a cause.

The value of the restriction is easier to visualize in concrete than in general terms, that is, through an actual instantiation of the argument rather than through references to it. The classic statement of the argument in the Thomistic version, traditionally called the "argument from contingency," may be summarized as follows:

(P1) Every contingent being has a cause or reason for its existence.
(P2) No contingent being constitutes a sufficient cause or reason for its own existence; that is, the existence of a contingent being is never self-fulfilling or self-explanatory.
(P3) Contingent beings do not alone constitute sufficient causal or explanatory grounds for the existence of other contingent beings.
(P4) A sufficient cause or reason for the existence of contingent beings, one and all, requires the existence of a necessary being.
(P5) At least one contingent being exists.
(C) A necessary being exists.

This version accommodates the scholastic uncertainty regarding the beginning of the universe, in other words, regarding whether it has one. Designed as such, it is indifferent to whether the universe has a beginning or has always existed. The distinction between contingent and necessary beings, as the names suggest, is a distinction between beings whose existence is contingent on other things and those whose existence is not contingent on other things. The modality determines not whether they exist but why they exist if they do exist. It answers nothing more than whether they, if they do in fact happen to exist, might instead possibly not have existed. A contingent being is one that can and might but need not necessarily exist: If it exists at all, this is not because it has to. A necessary being is one that must exist unless it does not exist: If it does indeed exist, this is because it has to. Given nothing supporting its existence, nothing can take it away.

However, this formulation seems to avoid internal contradiction only at the cost of begging the question, because it employs a causal principle that applies to everything except the very thing whose existence is to be proved, and whose existence depends on its exclusion from that principle. Not everyone agrees that this is as circular as it seems, or that it even seems circular. Moreover, not every formulation of the cosmological argument uses modal terminology drawing necessity out of contingency.

For example, the "kalām cosmological argument," a term coined by Craig (1979, 1980, 1993) in reviving an Islamic stamp on the general approach, starts from the premise that "everything that begins to exist has a cause" instead of the premise that "every contingent being has a cause." All that it requires in order to assign the universe a cause is the minor premise that the "universe began to exist," or, in other words, the assumption that the universe has a beginning. The broadest outline still leaving the argument recognizable as the kalām edition may be sketched as follows:

(P1) Everything that begins to exist has a cause.
(P2) The universe began to exist.
(C) The universe has a cause.

What is missing is essential detail supporting the second premise, plus, if the argument is to be used as proof of the existence of God, personalization of the cause in the conclusion, thus bringing in God rather than leaving the cause unspecified. Details fleshing out the premise abound in current scientific theories, exemplified through the end of this section, though without any claim to expertise, and solely for purposes of illustration. As for transforming the argument into an expressly theological one, the way to invoke God should be obvious: at its simplest, a matter of appending the extra conclusion that "That cause is God," and at most requiring an extra premise clarifying or supporting the connection, usually requiring little more than stipulation.

With the same caveat regarding completeness, an alternative utilizing a modal paradigm instead of a temporal one, though without reverting to the particular modality of the Thomistic model, may be developed along the following lines:

(P1) Every event has a cause.
(P2) The universe is an event.
(C) The universe has a cause.

Either formulation is supposed to avoid problems in the argument form contingency, including, presumably, the problem of premises that severally or collectively embrace a causal principle requiring the existence of the thing whose existence is to be proven. The most salient mark of distinction in these formulations is alignment with modern cosmological views suggesting that the universe has a beginning. This is what substantiates the logical overhaul removing the burden of accommodating both possibilities, as seen in the Thomistic focus on contingency.

Nevertheless, not all problems are liable to be version-specific, and, perhaps just as important, abandoning one version for another may open up an entirely different set of problems, as readily suggested by the revisionist and expansionary history of the general approach. The ongoing drive to discover the perfect formulation, or at least one better than any in currency, may be a sign that developing version after version, which amounts to dissatisfaction with version after version, is an extended state of denial regarding the ineffectiveness of the effort. This, on the other hand, may be unfair to advocates of the strategy, as it looks like criticizing progress for producing too many results, which is hardly a liability in scientific inquiry, and is, in fact, a characteristic of science itself. Furthermore, defenders of modern reformulations of the argument from contingency, as well as advocates of the kalām edition of the general formula, and of any in addition that may genuinely merit a separate category, do not see themselves as peddling a dead argument, but as promoting the best version of a viable one.

Given an apparent stalemate, plus the fact that neither camp has a monopoly on logic and insight, supporters and critics of the cosmological argument in particular, and of the existence of God in general, often turn to scientific advances and technological breakthroughs for corroboration of their own point of view. The cosmological argument, quite apart from Plato's proof of the immortality of the soul, has indeed found renewed impetus in technological advances adding an experimental dimension to the theoretical one in the study of cosmology, parts of it becoming more and more testable, and the whole thereby more apposite to scientific discourse. A favorite arbiter in this regard is the standard cosmological model, namely, the Big Bang theory, which, curiously, is invoked with comparable enthusiasm by those arguing for and those arguing against the existence of God. One thing that is clear is that the Big Bang theory provides scientific support for the time-honored argument's minor premise, which, in any formulation, asserts something like the finitude of the universe. This premise used to be submitted purely on the basis of reasoning about causality; now, it also has the support of a scientific theory consistent with observation and experimentation.

Yet the possibility of a steady-state universe never was the critic's only, or even greatest, weapon. Evidence of an initial state consisting in a singularity does not confirm the existence of a creator or cause, or even a prior state, let alone a divine intelligence that exists forever.

A decisive question in this regard is whether the universe can be said to have a beginning in the same sense that parts of the universe, that is, observable phenomena, are said to have a beginning. In the same vein, can the universe be considered an event even though each and every event must take place in the universe, which, on this condition, must take place within itself in order to qualify as an event? No, not under these circumstances. The universe cannot be conceived to accommodate itself in any sense making it an event analogous to those taking place within it. A beginning of anything requires not just a point in time at which the thing in question comes into being and, if the beginning is to be distinct from the end, a period of time during which the thing exists, but a period of time preceding its coming into being. The same can be said of spatial dimensions, at least of the three involved in our natural perception of reality.

Hence, the beginning of anything, even of the universe itself, because of the meaning of a beginning, immediately implies a prior reality, to wit, an external reality that is prior to and inclusive of the thing in question, unless what is under consideration is the only reality whatsoever, in which case positing a beginning, for it or for anything else, is meaningless in the sense that it tells us nothing about whatever else may be the case. The very notion of an initial state of ultimate reality precludes the intelligibility of a prior state. Backtracking the current distribution of matter and energy to an initial state is an impressive accomplishment, whether demonstrated purely theoretically or with the aid of experimental confirmation, but this is not the same as discovering an independent causal force responsible for that initial state. All that is confirmed is its development into the state from which it is tracked back.

Sometimes the notion of a multiverse is invoked as a means of stepping back to give our universe the room and time it needs for the proper beginning it arguably cannot have without a transcendent receptacle, or, more specifically, a transuniversal web of reality. Indeed, our universe may be related to such a multiverse, say, through a point intersection representing the birth of our universe, which, in turn, would have to be defined as an offshoot or kind of offspring of the multiverse, itself comprising a global cluster of universes converging at a common point. Alternatively, the same scenario can be reworked for a single host universe, which may be the only other realm to consider, or which may have emerged from yet another universal host, and so on without end. The two scenarios can even be combined for a linear progression of universes spawning one another in succession with the chain terminating in a multiverse serving as a cosmic fountainhead, or with the chain itself constituting the multiverse, whether in linear fashion or by looping back on itself. The multiverse might not even be the only one of its kind, just as the universe, unique by definition, is not, in this thought experiment, allowed to stay that way. Options abound. They all have at least one thing in common. They set up shop at an indefinitely extensible distance from the original problem, the problem of a realm of existence to host the creation of the realm of existence in which we ponder these questions. The problem can thus be pushed out or back *ad infinitum*.

To be sure, our universe may be a perfectly definable event within the multiverse, and may, in that connection, have a definite cause, existing, independently of our universe, in a realm either awaiting or precluding discovery. The possibility of an ontological and cosmological superstructure wherein our universe is merely one among a multitude of universes collectively constituting a multiverse merely shifts the inconceivable beginning to a new location rather than demonstrating its possibility at the original location. The beginning thereby submitted to be conceivable for the universe is no longer the beginning of all reality but merely of a portion of it. Even if an initial state consisting in a singularity marking the beginning of our universe could be said to be an event in the multiverse, the original question can be redefined in relation to the multiverse, or in relation to wherever the evasion ends. What is wanted from the cosmological argument is not a conclusion about this or that universe but one about ultimate reality, however many universes that may correspond to. To move the target elsewhere is not a solution. To keep it moving continuously is cheating.

This does not necessarily confirm the failure of the cosmological argument. Not all of its proponents appeal to the Big Bang theory, nor invoke the possibility of a multiverse to strengthen the argument. A good many find it compelling just the way it is, while those who do seek the support of science in the ways just considered tend to have plenty to say in response to the problems discussed.

Science, of course, does not support the advocate of the cosmological argument any more than it does the opponent. For example, experiments on the quantum level of reality suggest that the connection between cause and effect may not be as strong as it seems on the level of natural observation. Quantum mechanics may thus be taken as evidence against the premise that everything, or every contingent thing, or even every event, has a cause. In fact, even without breakthroughs in quantum physics, it has long been suspected, at least as far back as Hume, that causality is an interpretive paradigm we use to make the world intelligible, and need not actually be a fact about the world itself. Given that the cosmological argument is still in currency after roughly two-and-a-half millennia, it is unlikely to go away anytime soon, or ever at all, and given that it is still thought to benefit from modification, it is unlikely ever to be perfected.

7.13.3.3.2. Plato's Proof

Plato's proof of the immortality of the soul as the prime mover, both as demonstrated in the *Phaedrus* (245c–246a) and as laid out in the *Laws* (10.893b–896b), may suffer from the same problems as the cosmological argument for the existence of God, but it cannot be exonerated together with that argument. In other words, Plato's proof, as employing the cosmological argument without being reducible to it, may fail in other ways. The proof may be flawed even if the cosmological argument is not.

A grand structural problem, in the proof of the *Phaedrus* as well as in that of the *Laws*, is the transition, already mentioned in the assessment of the approach in the *Phaedrus*, from the temporal and causal primacy of the soul to its everlastingness. The plot twist making the soul a god, or, God, a soul, takes care of that problem, given that a god proven to exist needs no further proof of being everlasting. The point of equating the soul with God becomes particularly clear in the *Laws*, but it is no less relevant in the *Phaedrus*, in both cases avoiding the disastrous alternative that the soul is not the prime mover, being preceded at least by God, or by a slew of gods, or by both the demiurge and the created gods, as in the *Timaeus* (40d–43a), which, incidentally, opens up additional possibilities with an eternal designer working with eternal ingredients.

This identification with God, despite filling gaps in both proofs, turns out to be a complication in both, as what is proven to be immortal does not seem personal enough to be compelling evidence of the survival of personal identity. What exactly is proven to be the prime mover and thereby eternal and immortal? The soul, to be sure. But whose? Mine? Yours? A multiplicity of things cannot each be the prime mover. Only one. It had better be mine. But the chances are slim. If it were mine, would I not feel more special than those around me seem to feel? Alas, I do not. I do not, for instance, feel responsible for their existence. I do not have a recollection of having set reality in motion. Yet this should be one of my fondest memories, just about my earliest memory, had I been blessed with the immortal soul of the prime mover. And everyone else should be equally justified in formulating similar judgments through introspective analyses.

The mutual inconsistency suggests that Plato might have failed in these two dialogues to prove the immortality of the soul on the level of the individual. He might have proved the existence of God instead of the immortality of the soul. He might also have proved the immortality of some kind of "soul stuff" corresponding to whatever it really is that is equated with God when he equates the soul with God. But this is not enough. This is not what is expected of a proof of the immortality of the soul. Nor will it do to claim that he never set out to prove personal immortality, and can thus be considered to have accomplished his mission in proving the immortality of the soul on a general, generic, or collective level. The immortality of some kind of mercurial and nebulous "soul stuff" can hardly account for all the personal activity going on in the myth of the *Phaedrus* (246a–257a), with the lover benefiting the beloved as person to person, in life and after death, or for the highly individualized reincarnation process in the same dialogue (*Phaedrus* 248c–249d). It is not as obviously inappropriate in the *Laws*, but since the two dialogues employ the same proof, problems are shared rather than isolated.

The best candidate for such "soul stuff" seems to be life in general, given that defining the soul as "life itself" or as "the very essence of life" is what enables Plato, in both the *Phaedrus* and the *Laws*, to attribute a soul to the prime mover, and, consequently, to identify the soul with God, or a god, specifically, on the basis of the connection making the prime mover a living being.

Such a watered-down understanding of immortality crops up in the *Symposium* (207c–208b), where Diotima declares that the only possible claim mortals can have to immortality is the natural replacement and replenishment of decaying parts, as in the preservation of an organism through cellular recycling and in the perpetuation of a species through procreation. She also draws parallels to cognitive recycling, specifically to bits of information fading in and out of memory, confirming the preservation of identity through ever-changing mental content (*Symposium* 207e–208a), and finds an even more attractive approximation to immortality in the ambition of mortals to leave behind a reputation for heroism (*Symposium* 208c–e). As far as the physical perspective of genetic replication is concerned, Diotima's view finds voice in the Athenian Stranger in the fourth book of the *Laws* (4.721b–c), where the nameless protagonist interprets immortality as the reproductive maintenance of the human race.

However, these two passages cannot be taken as conclusive evidence that Plato rejects personal immortality, whether he actually does or not, because neither claim is about the soul itself. The first is about mortals, that is, incarnate souls or ensouled bodies, in short, the composite thing, emphatically and repeatedly excluding the divine, and the second is about the human race. This cannot be the sense in which the *Phaedrus* and the *Laws* approach the immortality of the soul since no proof or argument is required for such a collective account of it as lineage extension or species perpetuation through reproduction. The continuation of a family line, the preservation of a species, and the eternity of life in general, usually quite reassuring in themselves, have nothing to do with the everlasting existence of individual consciousness. Procreation alone goes far toward endowing life in the generic sense with a reasonable claim to immortality, barring mass extinction on a cosmic scale, but it promises nothing for the individual except for a brief experience of sexual pleasure, where applicable, and a typically less transient experience of family life, again, where applicable.

Indeed, the prime mover proof of the immortality of the soul does not reduce immortality to a purely biological process such as species propagation, but it does bring comparable limits to the personalization of the phenomenon. It is clear why the prime mover should be immortal, but not so clear why I should be immortal. After all, I am not the prime mover. Perhaps I am a part of the prime mover, but the connection is difficult to confirm. Then again, perhaps I am made of the same stuff while being otherwise distinct from the prime mover. That might make me immortal if the stuff we share in common is what accounts for the immortality of the prime mover. This is indeed the best explanation for how the immortality of the prime mover might establish my own immortality.

Plato himself does not take that extra step. This may be because he finds it too obvious. It could also be because he finds it unwarranted. Or it might be because he finds the extended conclusion less important than the accomplishment preceding it. Either way, the step must be taken, and it must be legitimate, if the proof is to be useful. Existence as part of a self-perpetuating whole, possibly a cluster of creative energy, is not the same as personal immortality. The continuation of the species makes me no more immortal than the cell survived by the organism of which it is a part. What I want to know is not whether a coherent bundle of energy will always exist, and certainly not whether an incoherent one will, but whether I will always exist. The problem is not so much that nothing like this can be extracted from Plato's proof, but that he does not seem particularly anxious to do so himself.

As it is, the prime mover proof, whether in the *Phaedrus* or in the *Laws*, is limited to general or collective as opposed to personal immortality. Plato may seem to reveal his paradigm for this kind of immortality in the *Timaeus*, where we encounter something like "soul stuff," given that the human soul, presumably homogenous and isotropic, is created at once to serve all members of the species, including future generations, rather than emerging in an original multiplicity corresponding to apparent individuation, or in linear fashion as needed to populate the world. This is borne out by the description of the process as the creation of a whole subsequently divided into parts equaling in number to the stars (*Timaeus* 41d). But Plato's focus, even as late as the *Timaeus*, on reincarnation with a customizable evolution program (*Timaeus* 41e–44d, 90e–91a) requires the preservation of personal identity, and therein contradicts an interpretation of immortality in terms of generic "soul stuff."

Moreover, an appeal to the *Timaeus* for a paradigm of the soul as the prime mover has the obvious disadvantage of immediate contradiction by the soul as a creation of the demiurge (*Timaeus* 41a–44d). An equally obvious response to the apparent contradiction is that the demiurge itself is or has a soul, which might then satisfy the identification with the prime mover. Yet this might seem a bit problematic because the demiurge does not create the universe *ex nihilo*, instead working with what it finds in coexistence with itself, namely, a primordial soup of raw ingredients in chaos, which it molds rather than creates.

Actually, the beginning of the universe of the *Timaeus* can be read differently depending on whether the source is the account by reason, where the raw ingredients available include fire, air, water, and earth (*Timaeus* 31b–32c), or the account by necessity, which goes beyond these elements to posit the Platonic counterpart of subatomic particles in triangles, specifically, right triangles of particular angular formations (*Timaeus* 54d–57d). Even this does not fully capture the basic cosmological structure of the *Timaeus*, as the two references pertain to the creation of the "world body," which must be supplemented at least by an account of the "world soul" (*Timaeus* 34b–36d), preceding the body and fashioned out of "same," "other," and "being" (*Timaeus* 35a–b). However that may be, without introducing details that neither help define the problem more clearly nor inspire a solution to it, the relevant point here, clear enough as it is, is that any perspective of the cosmological model of the *Timaeus* raises the question of the cause or origin of the raw materials available in the beginning, not to mention the cause or origin of the demiurge itself, and, to be perfectly exhaustive, the cause or origin of the "model" (*Timaeus* 27d–29d) after which the demiurge shapes the given ingredients in creating the universe, unless, of course, he simply models everything after himself (*Timaeus* 29d–30b).

In short, this is like asking what caused the demiurge and the coexisting primeval stuff, and, if relevant, the cosmic template for the universe. What preceded these things? The question is motivated by the simplicity and elegance of the idea of a unique unmoved mover preceding absolutely everything, and thereby qualifying unequivocally as a prime mover, with no room for misinterpretation. Although pluralism, as in a maker coexisting with all the ingredients for the finished product, presents a less tidy platform for the prime mover proof, the objection to it is no different than the corresponding challenge to modern reformulations of the argument from first cause, typically faulted for inferring the existence of an uncaused cause from the observation that everything in our experience has a cause. If the termination of the chain to avoid an infinite regress is arbitrary or unwarranted, this is not a problem unique to Plato.

The *Timaeus* is not the place to go to vindicate the cosmological argument embraced by the *Phaedrus* and the *Laws*. It is not as hostile to the prospect as it may seem at first glance, but it certainly adds nothing to the possibility. More accurately, it does not improve the tenability of the proof for the immortality of the soul as the prime mover, though it may clarify the kind of soul proven therein to be immortal. This, with or without the insight afforded by the *Timaeus*, turns out to be too impersonal to account for the everlasting preservation of individual minds.

7.14. Implications of the Nature of the Soul

A problem unique to Plato's proofs of the immortality of the soul is the joint inconsistency, at least on the surface, of his various presentations regarding the nature of the soul, leaving readers wondering whether it is unitary or tripartite. The soul of the *Phaedo* is apparently simple, a monadic entity which, being noncomposite, is *ipso facto* indissoluble. In contrast, the soul of the *Republic*, *Phaedrus*, and *Timaeus* is explicitly complex, bringing together three essentially different components in organic coexistence. The works using the trinitarian model are not identical in the way they handle the division of the soul into parts, or, more accurately, its composition of those parts, but the basic formula brings together a *rational* part accounting for reason, a *spirited* part contributing passion, and an *appetitive* part supplying desires:

- The rational part of the soul, or simply "the rational" (*to logistikon* or τὸ λογιστικόν), representing the faculty of reason, is responsible for cognition or ratiocination. It can be thought of as the mind or intellect, especially if these are construed in a narrow sense pertaining exclusively or at least primarily to reasoning and thinking, to the exclusion of other mental states or streams of consciousness, particularly those associated with emotional content. Motivating and enabling alignment with truth, knowledge, and wisdom, this is the highest part of the soul, ideally, in charge of the other two.

- The spirited part of the soul, or simply "the spirited" (*to thumoeides* or τὸ θυμοειδές), corresponds to the seat of passion. It is the excitable element, prone to anger, especially to indignation, but also sensitive to shame, and, therefore, not inclined toward arbitrary or unprovoked aggression. As the fountainhead of personal ambition, it is driven by glory, success, victory, and, above all, honor. It is the source of courage, which, however, requiring knowledge of what to fear and what not to fear, also draws on the rational faculty. Its distinction in courage is balanced at the opposite end by responsibility for cowardice.

- The appetitive part of the soul, or simply "the appetitive" (*to epithumêtikon* or τὸ ἐπιθυμητικὸν), covers desires, particularly those representing physical, or, better yet, physiological, needs and wants, such as hunger, thirst, and sex (*Republic* 4.437d, 9.580e). Accounting for basic receptivity to pleasure in general, it is also manifested in a particular fondness for money (*Republic* 4.436a), which, then as now, constitutes a nearly universal instrument for the satisfaction of desires (*Republic* 9.580e–581a). It excels as temperance, when nurtured properly, and degenerates into debauchery, if left to its own devices.

Notwithstanding the notorious fallibility of efforts to systemize Plato, especially on a subject straddling multiple dialogues, the highlights can sensibly albeit incompletely be summarized as follows:

Organic Profile of the Tripartite Soul

	Rational	**Spirited**	**Appetitive**
Essence	reason	passion	desires
Motivator	truth	honor	pleasure
Excellence	wisdom	courage	temperance
Corruption	ignorance	cowardice	debauchery

This is only an approximation, representing a substantial sacrifice in richness, if not also in meaning. Yet it affords convenient reference, providing at least a starting point for heuristic orientation, especially if taken together with the individual summaries immediately preceding the table.

Beyond the usual loss of detail in any synoptic tabulation of complex thought, the categorization is not entirely accurate, or even clear, as abbreviated above, whether in the table or in the preceding encapsulation. Specifically, the lines of division are not as solid as may be expected between discrete parts serving different functions. Perhaps some of the difficulty comes from disruption by the superstructure imposed on a fluid theory, but not all of it is extraneous to the original.

For example, at least apparent potential for confusion may be found in the fact that pleasure is the source of motivation for the appetitive part of the soul, without thereby being restricted to that part, and thus being available as a source of motivation for the other parts as well. To be sure, the satisfaction of physiological needs is driven and reinforced by attendant pleasures, or by the elimination of painful states, but one might alternatively derive pleasure from philosophical discourse or from a competitive challenge, whereas these would be associated with the other two parts of the soul.

Likewise, desires are not unique to the appetitive part insofar as one can also desire wisdom or honor. The essential difference is that the appetitive part desires instinctively and indiscriminately, with an unbridled capacity for pleasure, while the spirited part desires in accordance with established conventions of good and bad, or right and wrong, which explains the premium on honor, and finally, the rational part desires that which is good in itself, most notably, truth, knowledge, and wisdom.

Obviously, knowledge, or at least true belief, is required, and, wisdom, helpful, for attaining excellence in the operations of each part of the soul, not just in the rational element itself. The sovereignty of the rational part satisfies this requirement, even if other questions abound, many of them focusing on the nature of the partition, that is, on whether the relationship between the whole and its parts is physical or conceptual, or, given that neither the whole nor any of its parts is physical to begin with, more properly focusing on whether the relationship is structural or perspectival. To be more specific, a structural interpretation finds organizational principles inherent in the subject, while a perspectival one finds perceptual patterns contingent on perspective, both of them indifferent to the spatiotemporal profile of the subject, but the latter externalizing instead of internalizing apparent multiplicity, which may indeed expose features or characteristics actually inherent in the subject but not as parts.

Avoiding the detail and digression required for a reasoned resolution, and forgoing the authority afforded by it, a dogmatic response to the interpretive choices is that the language, not just the Greek but the underlying logic, is organizational, indicating separate parts working in unison, indeed, as a single unit, but not as different aspects or alternating manifestations of a genetically uniform entity. More to the point, namely, in regard to the apparent problem of overlapping features or functions blurring the distinctions within the soul, the significance of the concept of a tripartite soul rests not merely on partition but at least as much on integration. The parts are inherently complementary, which is what makes a well-ordered whole possible. Neither partition nor integration requires in addition that the parts have nothing in common. The parts maintain their distinctiveness even if they run into one another, say, in the fashion of the Olympic rings symbolizing the five continents.

The structure of the soul is examined through metaphor in the *Republic* and the *Phaedrus*, and placed in anatomical context in the *Timaeus*:

- The *Republic* (4.436a–444a) offers the timeless political analogy comparing the soul to a city. Specifically, the comparison is in terms of organization and operation. The rational, spirited, and appetitive parts of the soul correspond, respectively, to the ruling, military, and working classes of a city. The ideal condition of the analogous wholes is mapped out through the placement of the cardinal virtues in the corresponding components, wisdom in the rational or ruling element, courage in the spirited or military element, and temperance in the appetitive or economically productive element, with justice, in any case, whether in the soul or in the city, consisting in each part's performance of its own function without interference from the others, thus requiring the sovereignty of the rational element and its political counterpart.

- The *Phaedrus* (246a–257a) presents the image of a chariot with a charioteer in charge of two horses, a noble white one on the right and an ugly black one on the left. The white horse is naturally cooperative, the black one, naturally unruly, and it is up to the charioteer to bring out the best in both to steer the chariot effectively. The combined force, that is, the horse-drawn chariot, including the charioteer and both horses (but not the inanimate carriage thus drawn, perhaps the allegorical counterpart of the body), symbolizes the soul, with the charioteer representing reason, the white horse corresponding to passion, and the black horse embodying desires. As in the *Republic*, the emphasis is on the rational element being in charge, with one salient difference here being the intensity of a contrast between good and bad in regard to the horses, the analogues of which are more neutrally different in the *Republic*.

- The *Timaeus* (41c–d, 44d–e, 69b–72d, 89d–90d), though not furnishing a colorful metaphor for the nature of the soul, turns out to be just as graphic in its description of the creation of the soul. The anatomical model it offers places the rational part in the head, the spirited part in the thoracic cavity, and the appetitive part in the abdominal region. Despite maintaining the tripartite model, the approach here emphasizes a primary division between an immortal element created by the demiurge and a mortal element created by gods created by the demiurge (*Timaeus* 41c–d, 69c–d). The immortal element, embodying reason, resides in the head, while the mortal part, comprising two components, the spirited and the appetitive, is situated, as described, in separate compartments in the lower regions of the body.

The basic structure and essential features of the three approaches may be summarized as follows for convenient comparison and reference:

Allegorical Anatomy of the Tripartite Soul

	Rational	**Spirited**	**Appetitive**
***Republic* 4** 436a–444a	guardians (rulers)	auxiliaries (soldiers)	general populace
Phaedrus 246a–257a	charioteer	white horse on the right	black horse on the left
Timaeus 41c–d, 44d–e, 69b–72d, 89d–90d	head 44d–e, 69e–70a	chest 70a–d	abdomen 70d–72d

All three models concern the soul itself, having nothing to do with the body, and are valid whether the soul is incarnate in a body or disembodied and roaming about the heavens. Even the anatomical paradigm of the *Timaeus* is intended merely to bring out distinctions in the essence of the soul through the more familiar imagery of natural divisions in the composition of the body. The common thread in all three is structural coherence. The *Republic* advocates functional specialization toward optimal collective operation, finding synergy in guided cooperation. The *Phaedrus* likewise posits a mutual interdependence best resolved through componential collaboration, with especial emphasis on the natural discordance to be overcome toward the achievement of organic effectiveness and efficiency. The *Timaeus* is not concerned with an explicit demonstration of organizational synergy, but it, too, stresses the importance of a balanced effort to nurture each part of the soul.

Regardless of which model is considered, the trinitarian perspective stands in stark contrast to the unitarian grounding of the *Phaedo*. The apparent discrepancy between the unitary and tripartite soul is a problem in itself, one requiring and receiving serious attention, but it has a particular bearing on Plato's proofs of the immortality of the soul. The difficulty can be especially prominent where the proof in question explicitly requires the soul to be of one nature rather than another.

The third proof of the *Phaedo* is a case in point. The argument there is particularly dependent on the soul's being simple as opposed to composite, thereby making it naturally invulnerable to decay and dissolution, especially in contrast to the body, which is open to decomposition due to its complex constitution (80c–d). In fact, the entirety of the *Phaedo* is an answer to the common fear that the soul might simply disintegrate, vanishing into thin air, a concern best voiced by Simmias in presenting the image of a soul analogous to the attunement in a lyre, capable of making good use of the body, bringing various elements into harmony, but not, in the end, surviving the body (85e–86d). A tripartite soul with a noble and a wild part held together by reason sounds like just the type of thing susceptible to disintegration.

The existence of two such diametrically opposed structural templates for the soul can be problematic even where the proof does not directly depend on the soul's being one way or the other. For example, proofs invoking opposition, as in the first and last arguments of the *Phaedo*, though having nothing else in common, that is, despite illustrating different points and serving different purposes, are liable to be complicated upon the replacement of the unitarian grounding with a trinitarian one. Each of these two proofs can be rolled out with a unitarian or trinitarian understanding of the soul, but the outcome is not guaranteed to remain the same. This automatically raises the question whether the subject of opposition taken up in the *Phaedo*, in the opening or in the closing argument, might not best be considered in terms of what constitutes an opposite to each part of the soul, given that the parts are fundamentally different, and whether what benefits, harms, or in any way affects one necessarily affects any other, or the whole.

Problems, potential or actual, are not restricted to the *Phaedo*. A unitary soul can be just as hostile to proofs advanced with a trinitarian conception as a tripartite soul is to proofs put together from a unitarian perspective. An immediate question in the move from a unitarian to trinitarian conception is whether all parts of the soul survive death. The natural inclination is an affirmative answer, no matter which proof is used. The temptation to consider a negative answer instead is the possibility of reconciling the unitarian and trinitarian conceptions of the soul by making the unitary soul correspond to the highest part of the tripartite soul, and admitting the destruction of the lower parts upon separation from the body. This, however, is not the only possibility for reconciliation. An alternative is to interpret the unitary soul of the *Phaedo* as corresponding to the entirety of the tripartite soul of the later dialogues, attributing the difference to contextual requirements for detail rather than essential characteristics of the subject. In other words, this would mean that the composite nature of the soul is somehow latent in the unitary model, flourishing into the tripartite model as needed to address different problems.

Neither explanation is entirely satisfactory as stated. The acid test seems to be whether what survives death in the *Phaedo* corresponds precisely to the highest part of the tripartite soul. Failing that, it should either correspond to the whole entity or remain altogether incompatible. The typical justification for treating the immortal soul of the *Phaedo* as the rational part of the tripartite soul is the *Phaedo*'s glorification of cognitive purification, a process hindered rather than supported by anything analogous to an appetitive or spirited element. Indeed, the *Phaedo* treats desires as little more than obstacles to the achievement of such purification, with inherent albeit less obvious contempt for anything that may correspond to the passionate element. Yet this is not as indicative as it may seem.

The greatest counterevidence is from the same dialogue: Even the unitary soul of the *Phaedo* tends to exhibit something of a composite psychology, retaining contemptible or lamentable mental content, definitely including desires and arguably also covering passions, if it leaves the body behind without having already achieved purification, subsequently lingering around graveyards and such, and eventually being reincarnated, instead of ascending to the heavens to join the forms and the gods (80c–81d). This is consistent with the evidence of the *Republic* (4.443d–e), where the soul of the just man leaves nothing to be desired in terms of unity, as justice integrates the parts of the soul, creating unity out of plurality in the process, and vitiating the possibility of partial correspondence to the monadic soul of the *Phaedo*, except possibly, with questionable relevance, in the case of the unjust man. Likewise, a partial correspondence would undermine the myth of the *Phaedrus* (246a–257a), where the soul is represented not by the charioteer alone but by the combined force of the charioteer plus horses, remaining together as a unit despite and through cyclical assignments to various physical bodies. The myth is about why souls enter a body and how they can avoid this fate. Had only the rational part been postulated to survive death, the imagery of a horse-drawn chariot would have been wholly inappropriate.

Even the *Timaeus* (41c–d, 44d–e, 69b–72d, 89d–90d), where the soul comprises both mortal and immortal elements by design, is susceptible of holistic comparison to the soul of the *Phaedo*, not necessarily limited to a partial analogy, nor even accommodating one, at least not as comfortably as may be thought upon initial consideration. The mortal part of the soul of the *Timaeus* need not, simply by virtue of the fact that it is mortal, die with the body. The mortality of this part of the soul is not intended as the absence of a potential to last forever but as the denial of an ontological status on a par either with the demiurge or with the gods created by the demiurge. Yet the ontological inferiority and causal contingency of this part of the soul does not necessarily impair its longevity. The *Timaeus* (41b) makes clear that even though the created gods are not, strictly speaking, indestructible, the demiurge, as a perfectly or at least supremely good being, will never require or permit their destruction. This means that the immortality of the created gods rests in the will of the demiurge, which, if perfectly good, is a logical guarantee of the immortality of the gods, and, if supremely though less than perfectly good, detracts nothing from immortality as a reasonable conclusion. In a similar vein, the soul in its entirety, including mortal and immortal elements, may be envisaged as being maintained in this manner, especially since the indestructibility of even the immortal part would, on the same line of reasoning as applied to the gods, be realized, not as a natural function of its own essence, but through the goodwill of the demiurge. This being so, the mortal part need not be thought of as standing in the way of the immortality of the whole.

The reasoning here may seem to rest on a confusion of categories, which, properly aligned, indicates that the gods created by the demiurge are on the same ontological level as the immortal part of the soul, also created by the demiurge, but not coinciding thereby with the mortal part of the soul, which is removed a level, having been created by the created gods instead of directly by the demiurge. This would seem to suggest that what holds for the created gods may be applicable to the immortal part of the soul supplied by the demiurge, but not, in addition, to the mortal part created by the created gods. However, the target of the analogy is not the level of the creation but the goodness of the demiurge. This carries no requirement, legitimate or otherwise, for the transitivity of ontological eminence or causal proximity. Given that this particular product of the created gods is, after all, commissioned specifically by the demiurge, and given that it turns out to be good enough to combine with the personal creation of the demiurge, then it should be good enough to preserve alongside that creation.

Hence, the partial correspondence hypothesis turns out to be underdetermined, and, in places, even contradicted, by the evidence. Despite the intuitive appeal of the hypothesis, essential features of the psychological models in the relevant dialogues indicate, upon careful consideration, that the unitary soul of the *Phaedo* cannot safely be restricted to just the highest part of the tripartite soul. Maintaining the hypothesis requires giving up too much by way of what is essential to the tripartite model, or explaining away too many incongruities with that model.

This makes full correspondence a possibility worth exploring, despite the daunting polarity between unity and plurality. The apparent incongruity may be reconciled within the limits of the available evidence without invoking alien assumptions.

A clue requiring interpretation in either case, that is, regardless of whether the correspondence is in fact partial or full, is the *Phaedo*'s anticipation of the divisions in the tripartite soul. Distinctions later constituting parts of the soul are clearly manifested in the *Phaedo* (68b–c) as personality types and character traits: lovers of wisdom; lovers of honor (or reputation); lovers of gain (or money). While these categories mark off different types of people, classifying them according to personality, and bringing out the most salient characteristic, or the one that is most relevant to the context, in designating them brave, temperate, and so on, the divisions are not mutually exclusive. This allows for complex personalities, as a brave person can at the same time be temperate, with comparable possibilities in other combinations. The central import of the passage (68b–c), revealed immediately afterwards (68d–69c), is that wisdom is the "one true currency" (69a), and that no combination without it is worthwhile, effectively precluding the possibility of bringing out the virtue associated with each psychological category, and affording only the illusion of courage, temperance, and the like, or any combination thereof.

The divisions of the tripartite soul are anticipated not merely in the *Phaedo* but arguably also in works outside Plato and predating him altogether. For example, Burnet (1911, p. 40, n. 68c2) acknowledges, in the notes to his translation of the *Phaedo*, that the trinitarian conception of the soul is implied by the psychological categories recognized in the *Phaedo* (68c), but he goes a step further to locate the original source, or at least inspiration, in the Pythagorean doctrine of the "three lives." This position is also adopted by Taylor (1960, p. 281) in his commentary on the *Republic*. Grube (1980, pp. 133–134, especially p. 133, n. 1), for one, finds the Platonic contribution so innovative as to constitute a revolution rather than an adaptation with the bulk of the credit due elsewhere. His main point is that Plato partitions the soul whereas Pythagoras categorizes people. Surely Grube is justified in the importance he attaches to the internalization of the relevant categories. However, he maintains the same sharp distinction within the Platonic corpus, specifically, between the unitarian and trinitarian conceptions of the soul, as he does between the Pythagorean and Platonic approaches. This, too, is warranted, but not to the exclusion of the possibility of reconciliation. To be sure, Grube neither finds nor leaves Plato in contradiction, admitting at least the possibility of a developing view or of one revealed as if in development.

A relevant question here would be "When?" If the difference is to be attributed to a changing view or technique, the comparison might sensibly be expected to cover a slice of time sufficient to accommodate significant development, especially one as momentous as the very foundation of psychology. Is there really enough time between the composition of the *Phaedo* and the *Republic* to allow for the emergence of such philosophically significant insight? The two dialogues are typically taken to have been produced in close temporal proximity (see tabular comparisons in § 3.3.3): Allen (1984, pp. 13–15) and Copleston (1946, pp. 138–140) place the *Republic* immediately after the *Phaedo* in the chronological layout of the corpus. Cornford (1927, pp. 310–332), Kraut (1992, p. 46, n. 57), and Vlastos (1991, pp. 46–47) also indicate a tight production schedule, allowing room for only one dialogue in between, namely, the *Symposium*. Several of these commentators, specifically, Copleston, Kraut, and Vlastos, treat the first book of the *Republic* separately, as do countless other scholars, but this does not change the consensus that the *Phaedo* and the *Republic* belong to the same period in the intellectual and literary formation of Plato. This makes it unlikely for a significant piece of insight to be manifested in one without so much as a germ of it existing in the other.

No doubt, a revolutionary idea, if it exists at all, has to emerge sometime or another. In Plato, this may perchance have coincided with a well-deserved vacation between the composition of the *Phaedo* and that of the *Republic*. Furthermore, even on the alternative assumption that Plato produced the entire corpus from the perspective of a mature philosophical position, with the benefit of a fully developed set of artistic and literary skills, grand differences can be conceived to straddle two works in close proximity. Yet a possible scenario is not the same as a plausible one. Neither actual nor simulated development makes the polarity between a unitary and tripartite soul palatable as an inconsistency. Actual development does not leave enough time, sufficient perhaps logically and metaphysically but not practically, while its semblance, either feigned or spontaneously manifested, eliminates the temporal incredibility but introduces a strategic one. Different views may be presented one after the other without fear of alienating an audience, but these best not be mutually exclusive positions on a single topic. Directly contrary views, on the other hand, may be expected to raise suspicion, enough at least to ask why a grandmaster of verbal and symbolic communication would be content to leave his audience with a conspicuous conflict.

Plato becomes all the more mercurial if the emerging paradigm is read as a thoroughgoing rejection of the standing one. On the contrary, the lines between the unitary and tripartite soul are blurred both by the *Phaedo* (68b–c), where psychological categories are predicated distributively of separate individuals as well as collectively of the same person, and by a passage in the *Republic* (9.580d–581c), where the difference between distributive and collective predication comes across as little more than a matter of perspective regarding a single principle. This methodological counterpart, or confirmation, of the *Phaedo* in the *Republic*, occurs in the ninth book, specifically in the course of a discussion of pleasures associated with the psychological categories in question (*Republic* 9.580d–583a), but it is more generally discernible in the entire trinitarian approach, which, in the final analysis, holds the ideal condition of the tripartite soul to be a unitary existence (*Republic* 4.443d–e). Plato himself indicates that the tripartite division may be representative rather than exhaustive, as he expressly allows for the possibility of categories between the three that are discussed, using a musical metaphor comparing the psychological elements in question to the highest, lowest, and mean pitches in a musical scale, while embracing the entire scale with all its pitches (*Republic* 4.443d–e). Evidently, what is important is not the actual number of parts but their plurality. This, however, is not intended as a repudiation of the psychology of the *Phaedo*, as the *Republic*'s focus on plurality even better emphasizes the importance of the unity achieved therefrom.

Underneath the visible transition from a unitarian to trinitarian presentation, we have a common psychological foundation presenting the unifying principle as wisdom in the *Phaedo* (69a–c) and as justice in the *Republic* (4.443b–444a), though, even in the latter, still under the leadership of wisdom. In fact, the alignment is even closer, as justice is not actually the unifying principle itself but the consequent state of having been unified under wisdom. This, in turn, is a state easily attributable to the *Phaedo* as well. The methodological correspondence between the relevant parts of the *Phaedo* (68b–69c) and the *Republic* (4.443b–444a, 9.580d–583a) is simply too strong to maintain the exact opposite, namely, a methodological contradiction.

Moreover, the creative distance between personality types and character traits is no greater than that between parts of the soul and parts of the city, a connection drawn in one fell swoop, in the space of a single dialogue. A certain divergence cannot be denied, but it need not be read as a rejection or contradiction of what is left behind. Taylor (1960, pp. 281–282) even warns against attaching too much importance to an account presented as tentative and revisable by Plato himself, referring specifically to an explicit emphasis on fallibility in both the introductory and the concluding comments regarding the tripartite soul (*Republic* 4.435d, 10.611b ff.).

Evidence of a special, though by no means general, methodological convergence between the psychological grounding of the *Phaedo* and that of the *Republic* constitutes sufficient motivation to pursue this hint of convergence as a possible link in a chain extending through the other dialogues adopting a trinitarian position. The various psychological models, unitarian or trinitarian, need not be taken as mutually exclusive substitutes for one another. They might instead be interpreted, both sensibly and fruitfully, as episodes of one overarching metaphor unfolding through multiple works. To be specific, they might represent philosophical and literary milestones in a progressive unification of psychological elements, with the *Phaedo* separating the rational component from the passionate and the appetitive (and largely ignoring the latter two, the functions of which are, to some degree, consigned to the body as distinct from the soul, though the clearly psychological dimension of personality types blurs this distinction), the *Republic* bringing the three together, albeit in the relatively loose coexistence represented by the imagery of social stratification, the *Phaedrus* underscoring their interaction in the more tightly integrated image of a horse-drawn chariot, and, finally, the *Timaeus* uniting them in the same body. This is at least a workable hypothesis, one that has greater explanatory power than a change of view manifested as a full philosophical reversal in the midst of a single intellectual period. Not everyone is comfortable with dividing the Platonic corpus into periods, and the *Timaeus*, at any rate, is invariably acknowledged as a temporal if not also philosophical outlier among the dialogues being discussed here, but the point is that the reversal, if it exists at all, would have to be between the *Phaedo* and the *Republic*, an unlikely position for reformulation at such a grassroots level, especially without any other substantial recalibration in the themes of the middle period, even in the nearby *Phaedrus*, silently building on the apparently new paradigm, which can just as well be read as a phase in the development or presentation of one and the same psychological outlook.

Perhaps the greatest obstacle to recognizing the *Phaedo* as part of a progressive psychological metaphor, one extending through the rest of the middle period and still unfolding as late as the *Timaeus*, is its consuming preoccupation with shedding everything extraneous to reason. The dialogue's unswerving enthusiasm for spiritual purification presents an immediate bifurcation of mental content into rational thought and everything else, with the purification in question referring to filtering out and disposing of whatever falls under the latter category. However, designating certain mental content undesirable is not the same as denying that a separate mental faculty is responsible for its production. The crucial question is this: Does purification pertain merely to flushing this mental content, or does it further require the excision of mental faculties responsible for the content? The *Phaedo* patently favors the latter, thus advocating utter and complete purification. Yet nowhere does it present this as an automatic outcome of death, that is, as a direct consequence of the separation of the soul from the body. The purification in question is an ideal to be pursued actively rather than a condition to be encountered passively. It is a distinctive achievement, not a common experience.

The *Phaedo* combines the glorification of wisdom with a reciprocal disdain for earthly pleasures, derogating them with an almost overbearing counsel for purification, indeed underscoring an unmistakable predilection for the rational element. But this is not antithetical to the psychological diversity acknowledged in later dialogues. While the *Phaedo* rejects desires and passions, it also recommends the rule of reason, impossible without something to rule over, and indicative of recognition of variegated mental content and processes. This is consistent with the later emphasis on conditioning the other parts of the soul toward the achievement and maintenance of optimum conditions in regard to the objects of their respective domains. The trinitarian approaches do not, after all, welcome the pleasures so urgently rejected by the *Phaedo*. They merely appreciate the temperance resulting from the proper calibration of receptivity to the corresponding desires, and the same holds for their view of the passions, which they recommend, not indiscriminately, but through the filter of a properly conditioned faculty exalting what is honorable and rejecting what is not.

The structural difference between the unitarian and trinitarian approaches may signify a dynamic delivery model, laying out the same idea through an evolving presentation technique, or it may indicate a developing scientific model, building on an original concept and incorporating substantive revisions as opposed to merely stylistic adjustments. Or it may be something in between, perhaps a single idea revealed over time and through multiple works, which may be no more than a different way of describing the first two possibilities, themselves possibly complementary rather than contradictory. What it is not, however, is an unmitigated contradiction. The difference tends to be exaggerated by an overeager association of purification with death. Indeed, the *Phaedo* makes much of both, but it does not guarantee purification upon death. Undesirable mental content does not automatically disappear upon the termination of electrochemical activity any more than does desirable mental content. Nor is the goal of purification peculiar to the *Phaedo*. Purification is a purposive process rather than a spontaneous transition. And its completion is a mark of distinction, not correlated with the moment of death, that is, with the instant of the separation of the soul from the body. To be sure, purification cannot be realized while incarnate in a body, and its completion, therefore, presupposes disembodiment, but this does not attach any special importance to the moment of death. In fact, even for the most successful practitioner, the process can take several lifetimes, whether in the *Phaedo* (80c–84b, 113d–114c) or in the *Phaedrus* (248c–249d) or even as late as the *Timaeus* (42a–d).

Possibly the most eloquent expression of this is in Guthrie's (1971, pp. 230–243, especially pp. 236–237) examination of Plato's conception of the soul, where the most important distinction turns out to be not the moment of death but that of escape from reincarnation. The aim is always to shed the appetites and the passions, or their equivalent in the *Phaedo*, but nowhere does this happen immediately upon separation from the body. Leaving the body behind certainly helps, but it does not guarantee purification. And this shared contingency blurs the lines between the unitary and tripartite soul.

7.15. General Evaluation

What, finally, is accomplished in regard to the immortality of the soul? Is it or is it not immortal? What does that mean in either case? And does the answer depend on the proof considered? More generally, does the outcome vary from dialogue to dialogue?

The unifying answer lies in a particular misinterpretation. More accurately, it can be seen rather clearly from that vantage point. This is the mistaken notion that a joint solution to the unitarian and trinitarian approaches requires rationality to be the only thing that survives death, that is, the only part of a person that continues to exist after the destruction of the body, which, on the contrary, is accompanied to the grave and into oblivion by all streams of consciousness, rational or otherwise. The proper answer lies in pushing out that historic moment beyond the instant of disembodiment. The tempting but indefensible interpretation is that rationality, representing the highest part of the tripartite soul, but no less relevant to its conceptual analogue in a unitary soul, or to the equivalent of this in any other mode of reference, is the only part of consciousness that survives separation from the body, whereas the interpretation actually warranted by the corpus is that this is the end product of psychological or spiritual purification, whenever that may finally be achieved as the maturity stage of a multidimensional process.

So, is the soul immortal? Yes, on every interpretation. What does that mean? It means, first and foremost, that organic life is not its own animating principle, thus pointing to an unquestioned metaphysical dualism, or rejection of epiphenomenalism. More to the point, it means that the soul survives death, whether defined as separation from the body or as destruction plain and simple. And it means this in every dialogue dealing with the issue.

The only remaining question is whether the immortality of the soul includes all of its parts. This, in more modern terms, is the question whether the entire contents of consciousness survive the destruction of the body and remain intact forever. What we really want to know here is whether immortality is personal. The point is not to press Plato on the precise configuration of the common denominator between the unitary and tripartite soul, but to press him on the perpetuation of individual consciousness, sustained indefinitely after the destruction of the body, the present one, to be sure, plus any others that may be occupied in succession. We care far less for his solution to a methodological problem than for his reassurance that immortality is personal.

The lingering cause for anxiety is that pushing out the moment of final purification, due to be realized, except by an incredible coincidence, at an unspecified point long after separation from the body, still leaves us with the prospect of eventually losing desires and passions and, in general, all mental content extraneous to pure reason. These account for a substantial part of what makes up a person, which, or who, would obviously not be exactly the same in their absence. This, of course, is putting it mildly. After all, we are not likely ever to be the same at one point as in another, with or without a body. The crucial point regarding the absence of these attributes is not whether the corresponding person would be the same but whether a corresponding person would remain at all. How much can we whittle away and still have something left, preferably something viable? The only thing we can conclude with certainty from Plato is that psychological and spiritual purification continues after the separation of the soul from the body, that this implies increasingly stronger and more extensive isolation from earthly concerns, and that the successful completion of the process is a possibility. If this is a contingency destructive of individual identity, then, indeed, the Platonist may not sensibly count on personal immortality.

Grube (1980, pp. 120–149, especially p. 148) offers a particularly insightful assessment of the potentially disappointing conclusion that Plato gives up individuality in order to make immortality work. His interpretation is that this is a windfall rather than a sacrifice, since individuality, with all the attendant passions and various other obstacles to understanding, is something to shed rather than to protect. Hence, there can be no disappointment in achieving precisely what is set up as the ultimate goal from the beginning. In fact, anything short of it would be the real disappointment.

That said, happily for those who are not philosophers in the etymological sense of the word, shedding everything outside a rational core does not seem to be a requirement. Psychological and spiritual purification is everywhere presented as hard work undertaken toward the attainment of an ultimate goal. It is an enlightened endeavor, which means that it is a voluntary one. If its fulfillment is an achievement, then it cannot be imposed on those who do not do the work, any more than it is awarded to those who do not succeed in it. The essential nature of the process would have to be contradicted to turn it into the kind of thing forced upon those who do not care for it in the first place. It follows, therefore, that philosophers can revel in the purification of the spirit, gladly giving up individuality if and when necessary, while anyone else may refrain from shedding the least bit of personal pleasure that may be retained after separation from the body. Admittedly, the loss of the body is a grand change in itself, immediately purging a substantial array of sensations otherwise promising untold delights, but if anything like the tripartite soul, or the ontological equivalent of this in a unitary model, indeed survives that separation, then this just might leave enough of a person to alleviate fears of annihilation.

Greater precision ultimately requires an answer to whether a mind freed of excess baggage, the disposable psychological matter indicated in Plato's conception of purification, is still a mind. This, in turn, is a question more fruitfully explored through current scholarship in psychology, neuroscience, and the philosophy of mind. The best that can be achieved, from any temporal perspective, is limited by the body of scientific knowledge corresponding to the relevant period. Plato stands out as having not just mastered but advanced the one corresponding to his. That is perhaps why he was able to reach across millennia to anticipate and stimulate the one corresponding to ours.

CONCLUSION

So, who is the real Plato after all? Where is the answer finally revealed? On what page? Or are these not the right questions? In all fairness, the first one is right on target, though the others may be a bit wide of the mark. It is fair to ask about the real Plato, but not so much to expect the answer to be on a specific page, in the manner of how a novel might, within the space of a single paragraph, or even that of a sentence, reveal that "the butler did it."

Some readers of fiction, a decided minority, to be sure, head straight for the last page to see how it all turns out. Many of these, most, in my experience, will still buy and read the book. They are not judging. They just want to know.

How might *Rethinking Plato* have fared in this respect? For one thing, had the book been a thriller, curious readers might have rushed to the final chapter to find out who the real Plato is. Instead, they would have gotten a commentary on the *Phaedo*. At least for their sake, then, it seems best not to let that be the end of the book.

In contrast, those reading patiently and sequentially will have quickly realized that the real Plato is not to be exposed in the final chapter, instead being explored with every word from the beginning to the end. But even these readers might require some sort of closure. Needless to say, a Cartesian quest for the real Plato is about as exciting as things tend to get in the academic world. Mentioning such a quest anywhere in the title of a book is the scholarly equivalent of announcing a pirate adventure in a movie poster. Hence, a conclusion of sorts seems to be called for by all counts.

A mechanically effective ending, to quote a disarmingly artless twentieth-century philosopher, would be simply to declare: "And that's all I have to say about that!" These are the words of Forrest Gump, the eponymous hero of a 1986 novel by Winston F. Groom, Jr. This is the stock closing Gump uses on any occasion for a public address. While it adds nothing of substance to his speech, it clearly communicates that he is done. This serves him well, as his oratorical style tends to leave audiences disoriented, and thankful for any signposts regarding the progression of his speeches. Given enough time, of course, the end of any speech will be recognized for what it is, if only because the speaker will, at some point, quit speaking altogether. But Gump prefers to announce that point out loud instead of letting it go by in silence.

While his conclusions are invariably superfluous, Gump's obsession with adding that final touch is consistent with Plato's recommendations on proper rhetorical form. Plato's memorable metaphor on speeches (*Phaedrus* 264c) lays out the structural requirements of good composition, insisting that any discourse ought to demonstrate an organic unity, with a beginning, a middle, and an end, or, in the terminology of the metaphor, a head, a body, and extremities, all suitable to one another as well as to the whole. This is timeless advice, still serving schoolchildren and seasoned writers alike.

It would be a crime for a work on Plato not to take Plato's explicit advice, especially where the work is discursive, and, the advice, on discourse. And it would be hollow deference to tack on a purely perfunctory conclusion à la Forrest Gump. Yet the kind of conclusion in order here is not necessarily ratiocinative, establishing, in a final act of reasoning, a specific thesis supported with argumentation throughout the book. Something in between seems more apposite to the case on hand.

This is neither a deductive treatise where everything builds up to a final conclusion, drawn in one defining and momentous inference, nor a page-turner where the plot thickens all the way through to a climactic end. So, the final section cannot be a conclusion in the logical or dramatic sense. If the real Plato has not graced us with his presence in the hundreds of pages following the front matter, he is not going to show up at all. The closing section can be a conclusion only in the sense of presenting concluding remarks, that is, a recapitulation and overview, perhaps with a few words about how things stand now and about directions for further work. It might alternatively have been titled "afterword" or "epilogue." But "afterword" smacks of afterthought, and "epilogue" is just a fancy way of saying the same thing. Besides, it is better to explain the kind of conclusion offered than to call it something else. Hence, the choice of "conclusion" as the title for this portion of the book.

One method of appraisal for a study of this nature is to compare it with others of its kind, or, lacking that, with others in the general area. Another is to measure its contribution to the current state of scholarship. These are best left to reviewers, commentators, and other readers. Authors themselves need not be consulted here, because, having ruminated extensively on these matters at the conception stage, they will be habitually positive in their responses. A third mode of assessment, and there may be yet others, is to weigh what was promised against what was delivered, judging whether there is a gap. This, too, is fair game for readers, but, here, the author's own assessment would also be relevant, not necessarily in trumping any challenges regarding what was accomplished but in precluding any misunderstandings about what was promised.

The primary promise, as announced at the outset, and trumpeted in the title of the book, was to rethink Plato through and through, a foundational initiative to seek out the facts anew and to put them together through a methodical process of analysis and reflection. An auxiliary promise, made and elucidated in the introduction, was to separate Plato from Socrates. And these were the only promises made, one emanating from the nature of the other and fully subordinated to it.

Regarding the primary promise, the aim was not to come up with a different story about Plato but to compose one without fear of contradicting the writer's guide, that web of belief handed down from generation to generation and accompanying the corpus proper as a veritable manual. The guiding premise was that the web itself is immensely useful, indispensible even, but that our thinking has become too rigid, and, our approach, too complacent, in our eagerness to adopt it without question. The solution envisaged was to look for Plato freely, that is, independently of where he is supposed to be according to the prevailing web of belief, or rather, sections of that web, given that the web itself is neither homogeneous nor isotropic.

This shameless reevaluation of matters already settled is what makes the quest Cartesian. And the Cartesian nature of the journey lends itself to a meditative approach, which, in the final analysis, makes the process a developing relationship of sorts, a friendship. This is not an ornate metaphor for something less impressive in ordinary language. Plato has, no doubt, already made all the friends he is ever going to have in this world. But friendship with a dead philosopher, lifting the physical constraints, is no different than friendship with a living one: It is a joint search for truth, goodness, and beauty. The list may have to be modified in accordance with the concerns and pursuits of different philosophers, but it is especially fitting in the case of Plato, who valued these things above all.

The friendship approach is certainly not a requirement. It is entirely possible to dislike Plato, or to be indifferent in that regard, or even to be ambivalent, while being hailed as the foremost authority on the subject. That would not be antithetical to the requirements of good scholarship. But it would seem to get in the way of a good time. For a good time is most assuredly to be had in the presence of good company. This is not to deny the possibility of happiness in solitude. The contrast intended is merely with the drudgery that brings expertise without passion, that natural drive that can only be created and sustained by enchantment with the subject.

Being Plato's friend, like being the friend of anyone else, does not require siding with him on everything, or even on very many things. Technically, it does not require siding with him on anything at all, though it is hard to imagine friends who disagree on absolutely everything. The requirement, at any rate, is to work with him on the problem, whatever it happens to be, rather than adopting his solution. Well put by Aristotle, as noted in the introduction, Plato is a friend, and is dear to us, but the truth is dearer.

That said, whether in agreement or in disagreement, friends of Plato, or, if one prefers, students of Plato, cannot afford to do only analysis. Nor can they afford to engage in only scholarship. They will miss much either way. Both analytical thinking and scholarly research are necessary. In the same vein, friends of Plato cannot be just philosophers, or just classicists. They must be both, possibly more, blending artistic creativity and poetic sensitivity with scientific curiosity. Only then can the fledgling relationship initiated upon reading the first dialogue, whichever one is chosen, eventually develop into a friendship with Plato.

These, of course, are the bare necessities. Friendship grows with exposure. And there is no end to exposure, especially not in this case: Even though the number of dialogues is fixed, the number of readings is not. Plato's work is so rich that each reading of each dialogue is a unique event, more enlightening and more revealing than all the ones preceding it. This is to say nothing of the virtually inexhaustible wealth of external commentary we have on record. All together, this represents abundant possibilities for developing such a friendship, or, what is the same, for getting to know the real Plato.

The main point of the friendship metaphor is to emphasize the fact that Plato is first and foremost a human being, only then a philosopher. Accordingly, the goal of this book has been to get to know the man, not just the writing he left behind. This has meant learning the details of his life, his thought, and his intellectual output, and using that understanding as a foundation for studying his individual works, represented here by a selection of dialogues revolving around the last days of Socrates. The result now stands as a comprehensive pedagogical platform on Plato. This does not mean that the book leaves nothing out, covering all the dialogues and all the themes, but that it provides the full intellectual apparatus required for doing just that. The biographical and philosophical profile developed in the first part of the book is not only itself a repository of information, and thus valuable for its own sake, but it is also just the kind of interpretive framework needed to inform the expository and critical commentary in the second part. The two parts together advance the quest for the real Plato as far as it is possible to proceed in a demonstrative initiative.

Despite the claim to a comprehensive pedagogical platform in regard to the book as a whole, the second part was offered, with full disclosure from the outset, as a representative example illustrating where critical commentary might lead in a rogue yet disciplined reading proceeding without a special effort to make things come out the way they are supposed to. Do the dialogues left out make the book incomplete? Actually, they make the process incomplete, but not the book. Obviously, covering four dialogues is not the same as covering twenty-eight, or thirty-six, or forty-two, or whatever the final tally is, depending on who is doing the counting and assuming the responsibility for weeding out spuria and dubia. But the book itself is still a comprehensive pedagogical platform, one that can be used to complete the effort. The exhaustive version of the same exercise would require going through the entire corpus, one dialogue at a time, with meticulous attention to detail. While this was neither promised nor intended here, the degree to which it is facilitated through *Rethinking Plato* can fairly be considered a measure of the book's success.

As for the auxiliary promise, the separation of Plato from Socrates, that ideal was envisioned as the instantiation of a general duty incumbent upon everyone dealing with Plato, educators as well as students, and not as a unique achievement to be realized here. The reason that it was adopted as an auxiliary goal here is that it is a natural corollary to the primary goal of rethinking Plato, especially where the aim is to bring him out from behind the veil of drama. But this has been, from the start, a guiding principle to shape the fulfillment of the primary promise, not a specific problem to be sorted out for its own sake with a separate section or chapter dedicated exclusively to that task.

In other words, the intention has not been to debate whether Socrates speaks for Plato or for himself. This is not even a fair question. It implies that he does either one or the other. It leaves no room for the possibility that he might do both at different times, nor for the possibility that he might, on occasion, do neither, speaking instead as a character that simply fits the needs of the dialogue. Moreover, these are but a mere subset of options open to Plato for expressing himself. To be blunt, Plato must have had a good many ideas, and the corpus contains plenty of characters.

Who, then, speaks for Plato? Evidently, a lot of people. Arguably, no one at all. This is a thorny issue. But it is not a new or recent one. We know that the question came up at least as far back as Diogenes Laërtius (*Lives* 3.52), who did not shrink from listing the obvious candidates (§ 2.1). The question ever since, revisited periodically, and especially lately, has been, not whether anyone of import was left out, but whether anyone at all really belongs on that list. Hence, the debate now is more about whether Plato had any mouthpieces than about who they were.

This discussion has recently been attracting so much attention that a specialized scholarly enterprise, conducted mainly through journal articles and anthologies, for example, a distinguished collection by Gerald Alan Press (2000), has evolved around the mission to identify who, if anyone, speaks for Plato, and to address the derivative though engaging problem of whether Socrates does so. These are worthy endeavors. But they approach the issue as a standalone problem with a discrete solution. This leaves room for a more general effort at a grassroots level to get to know Plato, that is, the philosopher as well as the philosophy, together with the central themes and issues surrounding both. This has been the aim of *Rethinking Plato*.

While the book, as the subtitle suggests, is a quest for the real Plato, this is not the same kind of quest as the special studies debating the possibility and identity of dramatic mouthpieces for Plato. It is not concerned with identifying specifically who, if anyone, speaks for Plato in the dialogues. If anything, it is concerned, more generally, with making holistic sense of whatever is said by whoever speaks in the dialogues. Thus, the goal here has not been simply to isolate the arguments espoused by Plato himself, but to understand how the man thinks, how he operates, what makes him tick.

Can we understand how the man thinks, and so on, without isolating the arguments actually espoused by him? This is a clever objection. It sets up, what has admittedly not been done here, as a prerequisite for what is claimed to have been done instead. Such a serious challenge deserves a straight answer. The answer is no. No, we cannot understand how the man thinks, without isolating, or, to be less pedantic about it, recognizing, the arguments espoused by him.

Is this to concede defeat in the aims of this book? Again, no. No, because everyone speaks for Plato. Perhaps some do so more than others, and, some, better than others, but it is all part of a holistic communication strategy, where, in fact, the work speaks for Plato. Put differently, the sense in which everyone speaks for Plato is not distributive but collective. Getting at the real Plato is not a matter of identifying the right mouthpiece but developing a sense of how all the pieces fit together.

But why, then, if everyone speaks for Plato, should *Rethinking Plato* place any emphasis on separating Plato from Socrates? Because Socrates is a special case. He also speaks for himself. And he is the only protagonist boasting this distinction. This alone deserves special emphasis. Moreover, Socrates is a mesmerizing character. No one is liable to admire Timaeus so much as to eclipse Plato, but this can happen with Socrates. So, it is a legitimate concern to emphasize what is Platonic in a dialogue with Socrates in the lead.

Still, the response to the "clever objection" is not quite complete. By all means, let us pay attention to what Plato has to say, but this does not require agonizing over the mouthpiece count, rendering it impossible to assign the man a single thought just because he animates characters instead of speaking directly to his audience. We have two main options: We can get stuck debating that one issue to a grinding halt. Or we can do like Diogenes, making the best of what we have. And if the problem is so intricate as to inspire the creation of its own subdivision in Plato studies, it is best left to the experts, which is what was done here.

Indeed, we cannot understand how Plato thinks, without isolating the arguments espoused by him, but this does not contradict the claim, which bears repeating at such a critical juncture, that the goal here has not been simply to isolate the arguments espoused by Plato himself, but to understand how the man thinks, how he operates, what makes him tick. The claim, then, is to have done more, not less, nor nothing at all, nor something instead. This does not mean that all of Plato's arguments in the dialogues relevant to this book have been identified as such, one by one, and announced to the reader. It means that this is an elementary exercise kept, for that very reason, underneath the surface of what has in fact been shared with the reader. In the final analysis, the confession that the book has not been a hunt for dramatic mouthpieces does not contradict the claim that it has been a quest for the real Plato.

In retrospect, the defining question is this: Has *Rethinking Plato* been worthwhile? This, of course, is a trick question: Rethinking Plato, without the italics, is always worthwhile. And it is a short step from there to transfer at least some of that value to a book of the same name, or, from the opposite perspective, that of the author, to usurp it in the name of the book. Perhaps, the same question, or one in the same spirit, would not prove so tricky if anchored to the subtitle instead of the title: Has the Cartesian quest for the real Plato been successful? As already mentioned, the quest is not finished. If nothing else, studying other dialogues, preferably all of them, would be in order. But not here and now. The difference, a planned deficit, is work for the future. Rethinking Plato, as an effort, should take over where *Rethinking Plato*, as a book, leaves off. This may sound like *Rethinking Plato* comes with homework, and, in a sense, it does, but the quest laid out in this book should prove helpful in getting it done.

WORKS CITED

Aelian (Claudius Aelianus). (1997) *Varia Historia*. Greek text with facing English translation available in the Loeb Classical Library as *Aelian: Historical Miscellany*. Translated by Nigel G. Wilson. Cambridge, Massachusetts: Harvard University Press.

Aeschylus. (2009) *Agamemnon*. Greek text with facing English translation available in the Loeb Classical Library as part of *Aeschylus: Oresteia: Agamemnon. Libation-Bearers. Eumenides*. Edited and translated by Alan H. Sommerstein. Cambridge, Massachusetts: Harvard University Press.

Allen, Reginald E. (1984) *The Dialogues of Plato*. Volume 1: *Euthyphro*; *Apology*; *Crito*; *Meno*; *Gorgias*; *Menexenus*. New Haven, Connecticut: Yale University Press.

Annas, Julia Elizabeth. (1981) *An Introduction to Plato's Republic*. Oxford, England: Oxford University Press.

———. (2003) *Plato: A Very Short Introduction*. Oxford, England: Oxford University Press.

Anonymous. (1845) *Life of Plato*. Ancient biographical account available as part of *Biographoi: Vitarum Scriptores Graeci Minores*. Edited by Anton Westermann. Brunsvigae (Braunschweig), Germany: Sumptum Fecit Georgius Westermann, pp. 388–396.

Apollodorus of Athens. (1902) *Chronicle*. The standard critical edition of the fragmentary remains is *Apollodors Chronik: Eine Sammlung der Fragmente*. Philologische Untersuchungen 16. Edited by Felix Jacoby. Berlin, Germany: Weidmannsche Buchhandlung.

———. (1921) *Bibliotheca*. Greek text with facing English translation available in the Loeb Classical Library as *Apollodorus: The Library*. Two volumes. Translated by James George Frazer. Volume 1: Books 1–3.9. Volume 2: Book 3.10–end. Epitome. Cambridge, Massachusetts: Harvard University Press.

Apuleius (Lucius Apuleius Platonicus = Lucius Apuleius Madaurensis). (1822) *De Platone et Eius Dogmate* [*On Plato and His Doctrine*]. English translation available as part of *The Metamorphosis, or Golden Ass, and Philosophical Works, of Apuleius*. Edited and translated by Thomas Taylor. London, England: Robert Triphook and Thomas Rodd.

Archer-Hind, Richard Dacre, editor. (1894) *The Phaedo of Plato*. Second edition. Greek text edited with introduction, notes, and appendices. London, England: Macmillan and Company. Originally published in 1883.

Aristophanes. (1998) *Clouds*. Greek text with facing English translation available in the Loeb Classical Library as part of *Aristophanes: Clouds. Wasps. Peace*. Edited and translated by Jeffrey Henderson. Cambridge, Massachusetts: Harvard University Press.

Aristotle. (1886) *On Poets*. Lost dialogue. Originally in three books. Fragments of the Greek text available in *Aristotelis Qui Ferebantur Librorum Fragmenta*. Edited by Valentin Rose. Third edition. Leipzig, Germany: B. G. Teubner. See also: *Philodemus, On Poems, Books 3–4, with the Fragments of Aristotle, On Poets*. Edited by Richard Janko. The Aristotelian fragments are in Part 3: "Aristotle's Dialogue *On Poets*: A New Edition of the Fragments." Oxford, England: Oxford University Press, 2010.

———. (1926) *Nicomachean Ethics*. Greek text with facing English translation available in the Loeb Classical Library as *Aristotle: Nicomachean Ethics*. Translated by Harris Rackham. Cambridge, Massachusetts: Harvard University Press.
———. (1926) *Rhetoric*. Greek text with facing English translation available in the Loeb Classical Library as *Aristotle: Art of Rhetoric*. Translated by John Henry Freese. Cambridge, Massachusetts: Harvard University Press.
———. (1929–1934) *Physics*. Greek text with facing English translation available in the Loeb Classical Library in two volumes. *Aristotle (1929): Physics, Volume 1: Books 1–4. Aristotle (1934): Physics, Volume 2: Books 5–8*. Translated by Philip Henry Wicksteed and Francis Macdonald Cornford. Cambridge, Massachusetts: Harvard University Press.
———. (1932) *Politics*. Greek text with facing English translation available in the Loeb Classical Library as *Aristotle: Politics*. Translated by Harris Rackham. Cambridge, Massachusetts: Harvard University Press.
———. (1933–1935) *Metaphysics*. Greek text with facing English translation available in the Loeb Classical Library in two volumes. *Aristotle (1933): Metaphysics, Volume 1: Books 1–9*. Translated by Hugh Tredennick. *Aristotle (1935): Metaphysics, Volume 2: Books 10–14. Oeconomica. Magna Moralia*. Translated by Hugh Tredennick and G. Cyril Armstrong. Cambridge, Massachusetts: Harvard University Press.
———. (1935) *Athenaion Politeia*. Greek text with facing English translation available in the Loeb Classical Library as part of *Aristotle: Athenian Constitution. Eudemian Ethics. Virtues and Vices*. Translated by Harris Rackham. Cambridge, Massachusetts: Harvard University Press.
———. (1955) *Sophistical Refutations*. Greek text with facing English translation available in the Loeb Classical Library as part of *Aristotle: On Sophistical Refutations. On Coming-to-be and Passing Away. On the Cosmos*. Translated by Edward Seymour Forster and David J. Furley. Cambridge, Massachusetts: Harvard University Press.
———. (1957) *De Anima*. Greek text with facing English translation available in the Loeb Classical Library as part of *Aristotle: On the Soul. Parva Naturalia. On Breath*. Translated by Walter Stanley Hett. Cambridge, Massachusetts: Harvard University Press.
———. (1995) *Poetics*. Greek text with facing English translation available in the Loeb Classical Library as part of *Aristotle: Poetics. Longinus: On the Sublime. Demetrius: On Style*. Aristotle translated by Stephen Halliwell; Longinus translated by W. Hamilton Fyfe and revised by Donald A. Russell; Demetrius translated by Doreen C. Innes and W. Rhys Roberts. Cambridge, Massachusetts: Harvard University Press.
Aristoxenus of Tarentum. (1902) *Elementa Harmonica*. Greek text and English translation available in *Aristoxenou Harmonika Stoicheia: The Harmonics of Aristoxenus*. Edited and translated, with notes, introduction, and index of words, by Henry Stewart Macran. Oxford, England: Clarendon Press.
Arnim, Hans Friedrich August von. (1896) *De Platonis Dialogis Quaestiones Chronologicae*. Rostock, Germany: Typis Academicis Adlerianis.
———. (1912) "Sprachliche Forschungen zur Chronologie der Platonischen Dialoge," *Sitzungsberichte der Kaiserlichen Akademie der Wissenschaften in Wien: Philos. Hist. Klasse*, 169:1, pp. 1–210.
Athenaeus of Naucratis. (2007–2012) *Deipnosophistae*. Greek text with facing English translation available in the Loeb Classical Library as *The Learned Banqueters*. Eight volumes. Edited and translated by S. Douglas Olson. Cambridge, Massachusetts: Harvard University Press. Volume 1 (2007): Books 1–3.106e. Volume 2 (2007):

Books 3.106e–5. Volume 3 (2008): Books 6–7. Volume 4 (2008): Books 8–10.420e. Volume 5 (2009): Books 10.420e–11. Volume 6 (2010): Books 12–13.594b. Volume 7 (2011): Books 13.594b–14. Volume 8 (2012): Book 15; General Indexes.

Augustine of Hippo, Saint. (1957–1972) *De Civitate Dei*. Latin text with facing English translation available in the Loeb Classical Library as *Augustine: City of God*. Seven volumes. Cambridge, Massachusetts: Harvard University Press. Volume 1 (1957): Books 1–3; translated by George E. McCracken. Volume 2 (1963): Books 4–7; translated by William M. Green. Volume 3 (1968): Books 8–11; translated by David S. Wiesen. Volume 4 (1966): Books 12–15; translated by Philip Levine. Volume 5 (1965): Books 16–18.35; translated by Eva M. Sanford and William M. Green. Volume 6 (1960): Books 18.36–20; translated by William Chase Greene. Volume 7 (1972): Books 21–22; translated by William M. Green.

———. (1995) *De Doctrina Christiana*. Edited and translated by R. P. H. Green. Oxford Early Christian Texts. Oxford, England: Oxford University Press. Reissued in 1997 in the Oxford World's Classics series as *Saint Augustine: On Christian Teaching*.

Barigazzi, Adelmo, editor. (1966) *Favorino di Arelate: Opere*. The critical text with introduction and commentary. Florence, Italy: Felice Le Monnier.

Benson, Hugh H. (1990) "The Priority of Definition and the Socratic Elenchus," *Oxford Studies in Ancient Philosophy*, 8, pp. 19–65.

Beversluis, John. (1987) "Does Socrates Commit the Socratic Fallacy?" *American Philosophical Quarterly*, 24:3 (July), pp. 211–223.

———. (2006) "A Defense of Dogmatism in the Interpretation of Plato," *Oxford Studies in Ancient Philosophy*, 31 (Winter), pp. 85–111.

Bloch, Enid. (2002) "Hemlock Poisoning and the Death of Socrates: Did Plato Tell the Truth?" In *The Trial and Execution of Socrates: Sources and Controversies*. Edited by Thomas C. Brickhouse and Nicholas D. Smith. Oxford, England: Oxford University Press, pp. 255–278.

Boas, George. (1948) "Fact and Legend in the Biography of Plato," *The Philosophical Review*, 57:5, pp. 439–457.

Brandwood, Leonard. (1990) *The Chronology of Plato's Dialogues*. Cambridge, England: Cambridge University Press.

Brickhouse, Thomas C., and Nicholas D. Smith. (1984) "Socrates and Obedience to the Law," *Apeiron*, 18:1 (June), pp. 10–18.

———. (1989) *Socrates on Trial*. Princeton, New Jersey: Princeton University Press.

———. (1994) *Plato's Socrates*. Oxford, England: Oxford University Press.

———. (2004) *Routledge Philosophy Guidebook to Plato and the Trial of Socrates*. New York, N.Y.: Routledge.

———, editors. (2002) *The Trial and Execution of Socrates: Sources and Controversies*. Oxford, England: Oxford University Press.

Brown, Eric Alan. (1997) "A Defense of Plato's Argument for the Immortality of the Soul at *Republic* X 608c–611a," *Apeiron*, 30, pp. 211–238.

Brown, John H. (1964) "The Logic of the *Euthyphro* 10a–11b," *Philosophical Quarterly*, 14:54 (January), pp. 1–14.

Burger, Ronna. (1984) *The Phaedo: A Platonic Labyrinth*. New Haven, Connecticut: Yale University Press.

———. (1999) "Making New Gods." Chapter 2 of *Plato and Platonism*. Edited by Johannes M. Van Ophuijsen. Washington, D.C.: Catholic University of America Press, pp. 39–59.

Burnet, John. (1892) *Early Greek Philosophy*. London, England: Adam & Charles Black.

———. (1914) *Greek Philosophy: Part 1: Thales to Plato*. London, England: Macmillan and Company.
———, editor. (1911) *Plato's Phaedo*. Greek text edited with introduction and notes. Oxford, England: Oxford University Press.
———, editor. (1924) *Plato's Euthyphro, Apology of Socrates, and Crito*. Greek text edited with introduction and notes. Oxford, England: Clarendon Press.
Butler, Joseph. (1729) *Fifteen Sermons Preached at the Rolls Chapel*. Second edition. London, England: Printed by W. Botham for James and John Knapton. Originally published in 1726 without the preface (Stanhope, 16 September 1729) containing the maxim that "everything is what it is, and not another thing" (¶ 39).
Camp, John McKesson. (1992) *The Athenian Agora: Excavations in the Heart of Classical Athens*. Second ("updated") edition. New York, N.Y.: Thames and Hudson. Originally published in 1986.
Campbell, Lewis, editor. (1867) *The Sophistes and Politicus of Plato, with a Revised Text and English Notes, by the Rev. Lewis Campbell*. Oxford, England: Clarendon Press.
Cherniss, Harold Fredrik. (1945) *The Riddle of the Early Academy*. Berkeley, California: University of California Press.
———. (1957) "The Relation of the *Timaeus* to Plato's Later Dialogues," *The American Journal of Philology*, 78:3, pp. 225–266.
Chroust, Anton-Hermann. (1967) "Plato's Academy: The First Organized School of Political Science in Antiquity," *The Review of Politics*, 29:1 (January), pp. 25–40.
———. (1973) *Aristotle: New Light on His Life and on Some of His Lost Works*. Two volumes. Volume 1: *Some Novel Interpretations of the Man and His Life*. Volume 2: *Observations on Some of Aristotle's Lost Works*. London, England: Routledge & Kegan Paul.
Cicero (Marcus Tullius Cicero). (1923) *De Divinatione*. Latin text with facing English translation available in the Loeb Classical Library as part of *Cicero: On Old Age. On Friendship. On Divination*. Translated by William Armistead Falconer. Cambridge, Massachusetts: Harvard University Press.
———. (1933) *Academicae Quaestiones*. Latin text with facing English translation available in the Loeb Classical Library as part of *Cicero: On the Nature of the Gods. Academics*. Translated by Harris Rackham. Cambridge, Massachusetts: Harvard University Press.
———. (1942) *De Oratore*. Latin text with facing English translation occupies the whole of one and a part of another of two volumes in the Loeb Classical Library. *Cicero: On the Orator: Books 1–2*. Translated by Edward William Sutton and Harris Rackham. *Cicero: On the Orator: Book 3. On Fate. Stoic Paradoxes. Divisions of Oratory*. Translated by Harris Rackham. Cambridge, Massachusetts: Harvard University Press.
Clay, Diskin. (1994) "The Origins of the Socratic Dialogue." Chapter 1 of *The Socratic Movement*. Edited by Paul A. Vander Waerdt. Ithaca, New York: Cornell University Press, pp. 23–47.
Cohen, S. Marc. (1971) "Socrates on the Definition of Piety: *Euthyphro* 10a–11b," *Journal of the History of Philosophy*, 9:1 (January), pp. 1–13.
Cooper, John Madison. (1997) "Introduction." In *Plato: Complete Works*. Edited, with an introduction and notes, by John Madison Cooper. Indianapolis, Indiana: Hackett Publishing Company, pp. vii–xxvi.

Copleston, Frederick Charles. (1946) *A History of Philosophy*. Volume 1: *Greece and Rome*. Nine volumes (1946–1974). Kent, England: Search Press; Westminster, Maryland: Newman Press.

Cornford, Francis Macdonald. (1927) "The Athenian Philosophical Schools." Chapter 11 of Volume 6 of *The Cambridge Ancient History*. Twelve volumes (1923–1939). Series edited by John Bagnell Bury, Stanley Arthur Cook, Frank Ezra Adcock, Martin Percival Charlesworth, and Norman Hepburn Baynes. Volume 6 edited jointly by the first three editors, also responsible for each of the first six volumes. Cambridge, England: Cambridge University Press, pp. 302–351.

Craig, William Lane. (1979) *The Kalām Cosmological Argument*. London, England: Macmillan.

———. (1980) *The Cosmological Argument from Plato to Leibniz*. London, England: Macmillan.

———, and Quentin Smith. (1993) *Theism, Atheism, and Big Bang Cosmology*. Oxford, England: Oxford University Press.

Dacier, André, editor. (1701) *The Works of Plato Abridg'd*. Volume 1. Two volumes. Translated by various hands from the French by André Dacier. Illustrated with notes. London, England: A. Bell. Dacier's own translation, from the Greek into French, originally appeared only two years earlier as *Les Oeuvres de Platon: Traduites en Francois avec des Remarques; Et la Vie de Ce Philosophe, avec l'Exposition des Principaux Dogmes de Sa Philosophie*. Paris, France: Chez Jean Anisson, 1699.

Dancy, Russell M. (2004) *Plato's Introduction of Forms*. Cambridge, England: Cambridge University Press.

Destrée, Pierre, and Nicholas D. Smith, editors. (2005) *Socrates' Divine Sign: Religion, Practice, and Value in Socratic Philosophy*. *Apeiron*, 38:2 (June 2005). Kelowna, B.C., Canada: Academic Printing and Publishing.

Diels, Hermann Alexander, editor. (1882–1909) *Commentaria in Aristotelem Graeca* (CAG). Edita Consilio et Auctoritate Academiae Litterarum Regiae Borussicae. Twenty-three volumes. The standard edition of ancient Greek commentaries on Aristotle. Berlin, Germany: Realschulbuchhandlung and Georg Reimer.

———. (1903) *Die Fragmente der Vorsokratiker, Griechisch und Deutsch*. Berlin, Germany: Weidmannsche Buchhandlung. Available in English through two separate volumes by Kathleen Freeman: (1) *The Pre-Socratic Philosophers: A Companion to Diels, Fragmente der Vorsokratiker*. Oxford, England: Basil Blackwell, 1946. (2) *Ancilla to the Pre-Socratic Philosophers: A Complete Translation of the Fragments in Diels, Fragmente der Vorsokratiker*. Cambridge, Massachusetts: Harvard University Press, 1948.

Dillon, John M. (2003) *The Heirs of Plato: A Study of the Old Academy (347–274 BC)*. Oxford, England: Oxford University Press.

Diodorus Siculus. (1933–1967) *Bibliotheca Historica*. Greek text with facing English translation available in the Loeb Classical Library as *Diodorus Siculus: Library of History*. Twelve volumes. Volume 1 (1933): Books 1–2.34. Volume 2 (1935): Books 2.35–4.58. Volume 3 (1939): Books 4.59–8. Volume 4 (1946): Books 9–12.40. Volume 5 (1950): Books 12.41–13. Volume 6 (1954): Books 14–15.19. Volume 7 (1952): Books 15.20–16.65. Volume 8 (1963): Books 16.66–17. Volume 9 (1947): Books 18–19.65. Volume 10 (1954): Books 19.66–20. Volume 11 (1957): Books 21–32. Volume 12 (1967): Books 33–40. Volumes 1–6 are translated by Charles Henry Oldfather, volume 7, by Charles L. Sherman, volume 8, by Charles Bradford

Welles, volumes 9–10, by Russel Mortimer Geer, and, volumes 11–12, by Francis R. Walton. Cambridge, Massachusetts: Harvard University Press.

———. (1972) *Lives of Eminent Philosophers*. Greek text with facing English translation available in the Loeb Classical Library as *Diogenes Laërtius: Lives of Eminent Philosophers*. Two volumes. Translated by Robert Drew Hicks. Reprint with introduction by Herbert Strainge Long. Volume 1: Books 1–5. Volume 2: Books 6–10. Cambridge, Massachusetts: Harvard University Press. First appearance in Loeb in 1925.

Dionysius of Halicarnassus. (1985) *De Compositione Verborum*. Greek text with facing English translation available in the Loeb Classical Library as part of the second of two volumes of *Dionysius of Halicarnassus: Critical Essays*. Translated by Stephen Usher. Cambridge, Massachusetts: Harvard University Press.

Dittenberger, Wilhelm. (1881) "Sprachliche Kriterien für die Chronologie der Platonischen *Dialoge*," *Hermes*, 16, pp. 321–345.

Dorandi, Tiziano. (1999) "Chronology." Chapter 2 of *The Cambridge History of Hellenistic Philosophy*. Edited by Keimpe Algra, Jonathan Barnes, Jaap Mansfeld, and Malcolm Schofield. Cambridge, England: Cambridge University Press, pp. 31–54.

———. (1999) "Organization and Structure of the Philosophical Schools." Chapter 3 of *The Cambridge History of Hellenistic Philosophy*. Edited by Keimpe Algra, Jonathan Barnes, Jaap Mansfeld, and Malcolm Schofield. Cambridge, England: Cambridge University Press, pp. 55–62.

Döring, Klaus. (2011) "The Students of Socrates." Chapter 2 of *The Cambridge Companion to Socrates*. Edited by Donald R. Morrison. Cambridge, England: Cambridge University Press, pp. 24–47.

Dorion, Louis-André. (2006) "Xenophon's Socrates." Chapter 7 of *A Companion to Socrates*. Edited by Sara Ahbel-Rappe and Rachana Kamtekar. Oxford, England: Blackwell Publishing, pp. 93–109.

———. (2011) "The Rise and Fall of the Socratic Problem." Chapter 1 of *The Cambridge Companion to Socrates*. Edited by Donald R. Morrison. Cambridge, England: Cambridge University Press, pp. 1–23.

Dover, Kenneth James. (1994) *Greek Popular Morality in the Time of Plato and Aristotle*. Oxford, England: Basil Blackwell; Berkeley, California: University of California Press. Reprint with corrections. Originally published in Indianapolis, Indiana: Hackett Publishing Company, 1974.

Dyer, Louis, editor. (1908) *Apology of Socrates and Crito, with Extracts from the Phaedo and Symposium and from Xenophon's Memorabilia*. Edited by Louis Dyer and revised by Thomas Day Seymour. Greek text with English introduction and vocabulary. Boston, Massachusetts: Ginn & Company. Originally published in 1885 without the extracts accompanying the two main titles and without Seymour's contribution.

Elias (sometimes identified as pseudo-Elias or replaced altogether with David). (1900) *Commentary on Aristotle's Categories*. Greek text with Latin commentary available in *Commentaria in Aristotelem Graeca* (CAG) as part of volume 18, part 1: *In Porphyrii Isagogen et Aristotelis Categorias Commentaria*. Edited by Adolf Busse. Berlin, Germany: Realschulbuchhandlung and Georg Reimer.

Else, Gerald Frank. (1957) *Aristotle's Poetics: The Argument*. Cambridge, Massachusetts: Harvard University Press.

Epicrates of Ambracia. (1880–1888) *Fragments*. Greek text with Latin commentary available in *Comicorum Atticorum Fragmenta* (CAF). Three volumes. Edited by

Theodor Kock. Leipzig, Germany: B. G. Teubner. Also available, again, in the combination of Greek text and Latin commentary, in *Poetae Comici Graeci* (PCG). Eight volumes. Edited by Rudolf Kassel and Colin Austin. Berlin, Germany, New York, N.Y.: Walter de Gruyter, 1983–2001.

Epictetus. (1865) *Discourses*. English edition published as part of *The Works of Epictetus: Consisting of His Discourses, in Four Books, The Enchiridion, and Fragments*. Translated by Thomas Wentworth Higginson from the Greek based on the text of Elizabeth Carter. Boston, Massachusetts: Little, Brown, and Co.

Euripides. (1994) *Alcestis*. Greek text with facing English translation available in the Loeb Classical Library as part of *Euripides: Cyclops. Alcestis. Medea*. Edited and translated by David Kovacs. Cambridge, Massachusetts: Harvard University Press.

Favorinus of Arelate (or Arles). (1966) *Memorabilia*. Lost work. Fragments available in *Favorino di Arelate: Opere*. The critical text, edited, with introduction and commentary, by Adelmo Barigazzi. Florence, Italy: Felice Le Monnier. A worthy alternative is *Favorin von Arelate: Der erste Teil der Fragmente: "Memorabilien" und "Omnigena Historia."* Edited, with commentary, by Eckart Mensching. Berlin, Germany: Walter de Gruyter, 1963.

———. (1966) *Miscellaneous History*. Lost work. Fragments available in *Favorino di Arelate: Opere*. The critical text, edited, with introduction and commentary, by Adelmo Barigazzi. Florence, Italy: Felice Le Monnier. A worthy alternative is *Favorin von Arelate: Der erste Teil der Fragmente: "Memorabilien" und "Omnigena Historia."* Edited, with commentary, by Eckart Mensching. Berlin, Germany: Walter de Gruyter, 1963.

Field, Guy Cromwell. (1930) *Plato and His Contemporaries: A Study in Fourth-Century Life and Thought*. London, England: Methuen & Co.

Findlay, John Niemeyer. (1974) *Plato: The Written and Unwritten Doctrines*. London, England: Routledge & Kegan Paul.

Fine, Gail. (1993) *On Ideas: Aristotle's Criticism of Plato's Theory of Forms*. Oxford, England: Oxford University Press.

Fortenbaugh, William W., Pamela M. Huby, and Anthony A. Long, editors. (1985) *Theophrastus of Eresus: On His Life and Work*. New Brunswick, New Jersey: Transaction Books.

Foucart, Paul François. (1873) *Des Associations Religieuses chez les Grecs: Thiases, Éranes, Orgéons: Avec le Texte des Inscriptions Relatives à ces Associations*. Paris, France: Chez Klincksieck.

Frede, Michael. (1967) *Prädikation und Existenzaussage*. Hypomnemata: Untersuchungen zur Antike und zu Ihrem Nachleben, No. 18. Göttingen, Germany: Vandenhoeck & Ruprecht.

Freely, John. (2004) *Strolling Through Athens: Fourteen Unforgettable Walks Through Europe's Oldest City*. London, England: Penguin Books, 1991.

Friedländer, Paul. (1928–1930) *Platon*. Two volumes. Volume 1 (1928): *Platon: Eidos, Paideia, Dialogos*. Volume 2 (1930): *Platon: Die Platonischen Schriften*. Berlin and Leipzig, Germany: Walter de Gruyter.

Frost, Frank J. (1971) *Greek Society*. Lexington, Massachusetts: Heath.

Gaiser, Konrad. (1963) *Platons Ungeschriebene Lehre: Studien zur Systematischen und Geschichtlichen Begründung der Wissenschaften in der Platonischen Schule*. Stuttgart, Germany: E. Klett. A revision of the author's postdoctoral thesis of 1960 at Eberhard Karls Universität Tübingen.

———. (1980) "Plato's Enigmatic Lecture 'On the Good,'" *Phronesis*, 25:1, pp. 5–37.

———, editor. (1988) *Philodems Academica: Die Bericht über Platon und die Alte Akademie in Zwei Herkulanensischen Papyri*. Supplementum Platonicum: Die Texte der Indirekten Platon-überlieferung 1. Stuttgart and Bad Cannstatt, Germany: Frommann-Holzboog.

Gallop, David, editor. (1993) *Plato: Phaedo*. English translation with notes. Oxford, England: Oxford University Press. Reprint separated from the original by several generations of corrected releases. Originally published in 1975.

Geach, Peter Thomas. (1966) "Plato's *Euthyphro*: An Analysis and Commentary," *Monist*, 50:3, pp. 369–382.

Gerson, Lloyd P. (2002) "Plato's Development and the Development of the Theory of Forms." Chapter 2 of *Plato's Forms: Varieties of Interpretation*. Edited by William A. Welton. Lanham, Maryland: Lexington Books, pp. 85–109.

Giannantoni, Gabriele, editor. (1990) *Socratis et Socraticorum Reliquiae*. Four volumes. Naples, Italy: Bibliopolis. Collection of *Sôkratikoi logoi*, excluding Plato and Xenophon. Greek original with Latin translation and Italian commentary.

Gill, Christopher. (1973) "The Death of Socrates," *The Classical Quarterly* (New Series), 23:1, pp. 25–28.

Gómez-Lobo, Alfonso. (1994) *The Foundations of Socratic Ethics*. Indianapolis, Indiana: Hackett Publishing Company.

Gomperz, Heinrich. (1936) "Sokrates' Haltung vor Seinen Richtern" [Socrates's Attitude Before His Judges], *Wiener Studien*, 54, pp. 32–43.

Gonzales, Francisco J. (2002) "Plato's Dialectic of Forms." Chapter 1 of *Plato's Forms: Varieties of Interpretation*. Edited by William A. Welton. Lanham, Maryland: Lexington Books, pp. 31–83.

Graves, Bonita M., G. M. Graves, A. K. Tsakopoulos, and J. P. Anton. (1991) "Hemlock Poisoning: Twentieth Century Scientific Light Shed on the Death of Socrates." In *The Philosophy of Socrates*. Edited by K. J. Boudouris (Kōnstantinos Iōannou Voudourēs). Athens, Greece: International Center for Greek Philosophy and Culture, pp. 156–168.

Griswold, Charles L., Jr. (1988) "Plato's Metaphilosophy: Why Plato Wrote Dialogues." Chapter 9 of *Platonic Writings, Platonic Readings*. Edited by Charles L. Griswold, Jr. New York, N.Y.: Routledge, Chapman & Hall, pp. 143–167.

———. (1993) "Commentary on Sayre," *Proceedings of the Boston Area Colloquium in Ancient Philosophy*, 9, pp. 200–212.

Grote, George. (1850) *A History of Greece*. Volume 8. Twelve volumes (1846–1856). London, England: John Murray.

———. (1865) *Plato, and the Other Companions of Sokrates*. Volume 1. Three volumes. London, England: John Murray.

Grube, George Maximilian Anthony. (1980) *Plato's Thought*. Reprint with new introduction, bibliographic essay, and bibliography by Donald J. Zeyl. Indianapolis, Indiana: Hackett Publishing Company. Originally published in London, England: Methuen & Co., 1935.

Gutas, Dimitri. (1985) "The Starting Point of Philosophical Studies in Alexandrian and Arabic Aristotelianism." Chapter 4 of *Theophrastus of Eresus: On His Life and Work*. Edited by William W. Fortenbaugh, Pamela M. Huby, and Anthony A. Long. New Brunswick, New Jersey: Transaction Books, pp. 115–123.

Guthrie, William Keith Chambers. (1969) *A History of Greek Philosophy*. Volume 3: *The Fifth-Century Enlightenment*. Six volumes (1962–1981). Cambridge, England: Cambridge University Press.

———. (1971) *Socrates*. Originally published as the second part ("Socrates") of the third volume (*The Fifth-Century Enlightenment* [1969]) of his larger study, *A History of Greek Philosophy*. Cambridge, England: Cambridge University Press.

———. (1975) *A History of Greek Philosophy*. Volume 4: *Plato: The Man and His Dialogues: Earlier Period*. Six volumes (1962–1981). Cambridge, England: Cambridge University Press.

———. (1978) *A History of Greek Philosophy*. Volume 5: *The Later Plato and the Academy*. Six volumes (1962–1981). Cambridge, England: Cambridge University Press.

———. (1981) *A History of Greek Philosophy*. Volume 6: *Aristotle: An Encounter*. Six volumes (1962–1981). Cambridge, England: Cambridge University Press.

Hackforth, Reginald, editor. (1955) *Plato's Phaedo*. English translation with introduction and commentary. Cambridge, England: Cambridge University Press.

———. (1972) *Plato's Philebus*. Cambridge, England: Cambridge University Press. English translation with introduction and commentary. Reprint. Originally published as *Plato's Examination of Pleasure*. Cambridge, England: Cambridge University Press, 1945.

Hall, John C. (1968) "Plato: *Euthyphro* 10a1–11a10," *Philosophical Quarterly*, 18:70 (January), pp. 1–11.

Hamilton, Edith. (1942) *Mythology*. Boston, Massachusetts: Little, Brown and Company.

Hare, Richard Mervyn. (1982) *Plato*. Past Masters. Oxford, England: Oxford University Press.

Haslam, Michael W. (1972) "Plato, Sophron, and the Dramatic Dialogue," *Bulletin of the Institute of Classical Studies of the University of London*, 19, pp. 17–38.

Hermann, Karl Friedrich. (1839) *Geschichte und System der Platonischen Philosophie*. Heidelberg, Germany: Akademische Verlagshandlung von C. F. Winter.

Hesiod. (2007) *Theogony*. Greek text with facing English translation available in the Loeb Classical Library as part of *Hesiod: Theogony; Works and Days; Testimonia*. Edited, and translated into English, by Glenn W. Most. Cambridge, Massachusetts: Harvard University Press.

Hesychius Illustrius of Miletus. (1851) *Onomatologos ē Pinax tōn en Paideia Onomastōn*. Lost work. Fragments available in the fourth volume of *Fragmenta Historicorum Graecorum* (FHG). Edited by Karl Wilhelm Ludwig Müller. Paris, France: Ambroise Firmin Didot.

Hicks, Robert Drew, editor. (1925) *Diogenes Laërtius: Lives of Eminent Philosophers*. Two volumes. Greek text with parallel English translation. Loeb Classical Library. Cambridge, Massachusetts: Harvard University Press.

Homer. (1919) *Odyssey*. Greek text with facing English translation available in the Loeb Classical Library. Two volumes. Volume 1: Books 1–12. Volume 2: Books 13–24. Translated into English by Augustus Taber Murray and revised by George E. Dimock. Cambridge, Massachusetts: Harvard University Press.

Hume, David. (1748) "Of the Original Contract." Originally published as part of *Three Essays, Moral and Political: Never Before Published; Which Compleats the Former Edition; In Two Volumes; Octavo*. London, England: A. Millar, A. Kincaid. The standard reference to the essay invokes its position as part of a later collection, *Essays, Moral, Political, and Literary* (1758), where it appears as the twelfth entry of the second volume, thus abbreviated "2.12," followed by the paragraph number corresponding to the passage in question.

Hyland, Drew A. (1995) *Finitude and Transcendence in the Platonic Dialogues*. Albany, New York: State University of New York Press.

———. (2002) "Against a Platonic 'Theory' of Forms." Chapter 10 of *Plato's Forms: Varieties of Interpretation*. Edited by William A. Welton. Lanham, Maryland: Lexington Books, pp. 257–272.

———. (2004) *Questioning Platonism: Continental Interpretations of Plato*. Albany, New York: State University of New York Press.

Irwin, Terence H. (1977) *Plato's Moral Theory: The Early and Middle Dialogues*. Oxford, England: Oxford University Press.

———. (2008) "The Platonic Corpus." Chapter 3 of *The Oxford Handbook of Plato*. Edited by Gail Fine. Oxford, England: Oxford University Press, pp. 63–87.

Isocrates. (1945) *Against Callimachus* [Oration 18]. Greek text with facing English translation available in the third of three volumes dedicated to Isocrates in the Loeb Classical Library. Volume 3: *Evagoras*; *Helen*; *Busiris*; *Plataicus*; *Concerning the Team of Horses*; *Trapeziticus*; *Against Callimachus*; *Aegineticus*; *Against Lochites*; *Against Euthynus*; *Letters*. Translated by La Rue Van Hook. Cambridge, Massachusetts: Harvard University Press.

———. (1945) *Busiris* [Oration 11]. Greek text with facing English translation available in the third of three volumes dedicated to Isocrates in the Loeb Classical Library. Volume 3: *Evagoras*; *Helen*; *Busiris*; *Plataicus*; *Concerning the Team of Horses*; *Trapeziticus*; *Against Callimachus*; *Aegineticus*; *Against Lochites*; *Against Euthynus*; *Letters*. Translated by La Rue Van Hook. Cambridge, Massachusetts: Harvard University Press.

Jacoby, Felix, editor. (1902) *Apollodors Chronik: Eine Sammlung der Fragmente*. Philologische Untersuchungen 16. Berlin, Germany: Weidmannsche Buchhandlung.

Jaeger, Werner Wilhelm. (1933–1947) *Paideia: Die Formung des Griechischen Menschen*. Three volumes. Berlin, Germany: Walter de Gruyter. Available in English as *Paideia: The Ideals of Greek Culture*. Volume 1 (1939): *Archaic Greece: The Mind of Athens*. Volume 2 (1943): *In Search of the Divine Centre*. Volume 3 (1944): *The Conflict of Cultural Ideals in the Age of Plato*. Translated by Gilbert Highet. Oxford, England: Oxford University Press. Last two volumes translated from manuscripts and published before their German counterparts.

Janko, Richard. (1984) *Aristotle on Comedy: Towards a Reconstruction of Poetics II*. Berkeley, California: University of California Press.

———. (2010) *Philodemus, On Poems, Books 3–4, with the Fragments of Aristotle, On Poets*. Oxford, England: Oxford University Press.

John (Joannes) Philoponus (alternatively: John the Grammarian or John of Alexandria). (1897) *Commentary on Aristotle's De Anima*. Greek text with Latin commentary available in *Commentaria in Aristotelem Graeca* (CAG) as volume 15: *In Aristotelis de Anima Libros Commentaria*. Edited by Michael Hayduck. Berlin, Germany: Realschulbuchhandlung and Georg Reimer. Translated into English as *Philoponus: On Aristotle On the Soul* in six volumes in the *Ancient Commentators on Aristotle* (ACA), a project carried out under the auspices of King's College London and the general editorship of Richard Sorabji. London, England: Duckworth; Ithaca, New York: Cornell University Press, 1987–present.

Judeich, Walther. (1931) *Topographie von Athen: Mit 48 Abbildungen im Text und 3 Plainen in Mappe*. Handbuch der Klassischen Altertums-Wissenschaft: volume 3, issue 2, part 2. Second edition. Munich, Germany: C. H. Beck. Originally published in 1905.

Kahn, Charles H. (1993) "Proleptic Composition in the *Republic*, or Why Book 1 Was Never a Separate Dialogue," *The Classical Quarterly* (New Series), 43:1, pp. 131–142.

———. (1995) "A New Interpretation of Plato's Socratic Dialogues," *The Harvard Review of Philosophy*, 5 (Spring), pp. 26–35.

———. (1996) *Plato and the Socratic Dialogue: The Philosophical Use of a Literary Form*. Cambridge, England: Cambridge University Press.

Kamtekar, Rachana, editor. (2005) *Plato's Euthyphro, Apology, and Crito: Critical Essays*. Lanham, Maryland: Rowman & Littlefield.

Kassel, Rudolf, and Colin Austin, editors. (1983–2001) *Poetae Comici Graeci* (PCG). Eight volumes. Greek texts with Latin commentary. Berlin, Germany, New York, N.Y.: Walter de Gruyter.

Kock, Theodor, editor. (1880–1888) *Comicorum Atticorum Fragmenta* (CAF). Three volumes. Greek texts with Latin commentary. Leipzig, Germany: B. G. Teubner.

Krämer, Hans Joachim. (1959) *Arete bei Platon und Aristoteles: Zum Wesen und zur Geschichte der Platonischen Ontologie*. Heidelberg, Germany: Carl Winter Universitätsverlag. The author's doctoral dissertation. Available in English as *Plato and the Foundations of Metaphysics: A Work on the Theory of the Principles and Unwritten Doctrines of Plato with a Collection of the Fundamental Documents*. Translated by John R. Catan. Albany, New York: State University of New York Press, 1990.

Kraut, Richard. (1981) "Plato's *Apology* and *Crito*: Two Recent Studies," *Ethics*, 91:4 (July), pp. 651–664.

———. (1984) *Socrates and the State*. Princeton, New Jersey: Princeton University Press.

———. (1988) "Reply to Clifford Orwin." In *Platonic Writings, Platonic Readings*. Edited by Charles L. Griswold, Jr. New York, N.Y.: Routledge, Chapman & Hall, pp. 177–182.

———. (1992) "Introduction to the Study of Plato." In *The Cambridge Companion to Plato*. Edited by Richard Kraut. Cambridge, England: Cambridge University Press, pp. 1–50.

Lasserre, François, editor. (1987) *De Léodamas de Thasos à Philippe d'Oponte: Témoignages et Fragments*. La Scuola di Platone, No. 2. Naples, Italy: Bibliopolis. Greek text with translation and commentary in French.

Ledger, Gerard R. (1989) *Re-counting Plato: A Computer Analysis of Plato's Style*. Oxford, England: Clarendon Press.

Loomis, William T. (1998) *Wages, Welfare Costs and Inflation in Classical Athens*. Ann Arbor, Michigan: University of Michigan Press.

Lutoslawski, Wincenty. (1897) *The Origin and Growth of Plato's Logic, with an Account of Plato's Style and of the Chronology of His Writings, by Wincenty Lutoslawski*. London, England: Longmans, Green, and Co.

Lynch, John Patrick. (1972) *Aristotle's School: A Study of a Greek Educational Institution*. Berkeley and Los Angeles, California: University of California Press.

MacDowell, Douglas Maurice. (1978) *The Law in Classical Athens*. Ithaca, New York: Cornell University Press.

Mackenzie, John Stuart. (1893) *A Manual of Ethics: Designed for the Use of Students*. London, England: W. B. Clive, University Correspondence College Press.

Marrou, Henri Irénée. (1956) *A History of Education in Antiquity*. Translated by George Lamb from the third edition (1955) of the French original. New York, N.Y.: Sheed and Ward. Originally published as *Histoire de l'Education dans l'Antiquité*. Paris, France: Éditions du Seuil, 1948.

McCoy, W. James. (1975) "The Identity of Leon," *The American Journal of Philology*, 96, pp. 187–199.

Meinwald, Constance C. (1991) *Plato's Parmenides*. Oxford, England: Oxford University Press.

———. (1992) "Good-bye to the Third Man." In *The Cambridge Companion to Plato*. Edited by Richard Kraut. Cambridge, England: Cambridge University Press, pp. 365–396.

Mensching, Eckart, editor. (1963) *Favorin von Arelate: Der erste Teil der Fragmente: "Memorabilien" und "Omnigena Historia."* The critical text with commentary. Berlin, Germany: Walter de Gruyter.

Mikalson, Jon D. (2010) *Greek Popular Religion in Greek Philosophy*. Oxford, England: Oxford University Press.

Moore, George Edward. (1903) *Principia Ethica*. Cambridge, England: Cambridge University Press.

Morrow, Glenn Raymond. (1960) *Plato's Cretan City: A Historical Interpretation of the Laws*. Princeton, New Jersey: Princeton University Press.

Mosshammer, Alden A. (1976) "Geometrical Proportion and the Chronological Method of Apollodorus," *Transactions of the American Philological Association (1974–.)*, 106, pp. 291–306.

Müller, Karl Wilhelm Ludwig, editor. (1841–1870) *Fragmenta Historicorum Graecorum* (FHG). Five volumes. Paris, France: Ambroise Firmin Didot.

Nails, Debra. (1995) *Agora, Academy, and the Conduct of Philosophy*. Dordrecht, Netherlands: Boston, Massachusetts: Kluwer Academic Publishers.

———. (2000) "Mouthpiece Schmouthpiece." Chapter 1 of *Who Speaks for Plato? Studies in Platonic Anonymity*. Edited by Gerald Alan Press. Lanham, Maryland: Rowman & Littlefield, pp. 15–26.

———. (2002) *The People of Plato: A Prosopography of Plato and Other Socratics*. Indianapolis, Indiana: Hackett Publishing Company.

———. (2006a) "The Life of Plato of Athens." Chapter 1 of *A Companion to Plato*. Edited by Hugh H. Benson. Oxford, England: Blackwell Publishing, pp. 1–12.

———. (2006b) "The Trial and Death of Socrates." Chapter 1 of *A Companion to Socrates*. Edited by Sara Ahbel-Rappe and Rachana Kamtekar. Oxford, England: Blackwell Publishing, pp. 5–20.

———, and Holger Thesleff. (2003) "Early Academic Editing: Plato's *Laws*." In *Plato's Laws: From Theory into Practice: Proceedings of the VI Symposium Platonicum: Selected Papers*. Edited by Samuel Scolnicov and Luc Brisson. Sankt Augustin, Germany: Academia Verlag, pp. 14–29.

Notopoulos, James A. (1939) "The Name of Plato," *Classical Philology*, 34:2 (April), pp. 135–145.

Ober, William. (1977) "Did Socrates Die of Hemlock Poisoning?" *New York State Journal of Medicine*, 77, pp. 254–258.

Oldfather, William Abbott. (1938) "Socrates in Court," *The Classical Weekly*, (Whole Number 844), 31:21 (25 April), pp. 203–211.

Olympiodorus the Younger of Alexandria. (1902) *Prolegomena and Commentary on Aristotle's Categories*. Greek text with Latin commentary available in *Commentaria in Aristotelem Graeca* (CAG) in volume 12, part 1: *Prolegomena et in Categorias Commentarium*. Edited by Adolf Busse. Berlin, Germany: Realschulbuchhandlung and Georg Reimer.

———. (1956) *Commentary on the First Alcibiades of Plato*. Critical text and indices. Edited by Leendert Gerrit Westerink. Amsterdam, Netherlands: North-Holland Publishing Company. Second edition, a corrected reprint, published in Amsterdam, Netherlands: Adolf M. Hakkert, 1982.

———. (1962) *Anonymous Prolegomena to Platonic Philosophy*. [Traditionally albeit erroneously attributed to Olympiodorus.] Greek text with English translation. Edited and translated by Leendert Gerrit Westerink. Amsterdam, Netherlands: North-Holland Publishing Company.

Owen, Gwilym Ellis Lane. (1953) "The Place of the *Timaeus* in Plato's Dialogues," *The Classical Quarterly* (New Series), 3 (January–April), pp. 79–95.

———. (1965) "Aristotle on the Snares of Ontology." In *New Essays on Plato and Aristotle*. Edited by Renford Bambrough. London, England: Routledge & Kegan Paul, pp. 69–95.

———. (1970) "Plato on Not-Being." Chapter 12 of *Plato: A Collection of Critical Essays*. Volume 1: *Metaphysics and Epistemology*. Edited by Gregory Vlastos. Garden City, New York: Anchor Books, Doubleday, pp. 223–267.

Pelletier, Francis Jeffry. (1990) *Parmenides, Plato, and the Semantics of Not-Being*. Chicago, Illinois: University of Chicago Press.

Peterson, Sandra Lynne. (2003) "An Authentically Socratic Conclusion in Plato's *Phaedo*: Socrates' Debt to Asclepius." In *Desire, Identity, and Existence: Essays in Honor of T. M. Penner*. Kelowna, B.C., Canada: Academic Printing & Publishing, pp. 33–52.

Philip, James A. (1970) "The Platonic Corpus," *Phoenix*, 24:4, pp. 296–308.

Philodemus of Gadara. (1902) *Academicorum Philosophorum Index Herculanensis*. Fragmentary remains (Papyrus Herculanensis 164, 1021) edited by Siegfried Mekler, who is responsible for the modern title. Berlin, Germany: Weidmannsche Buchhandlung.

Photius. (1959–2003) *Bibliotheca* [=*Myriobiblon*]. The standard critical edition is a French undertaking in ten volumes: *Bibliothèque*. Greek text with running French translations, accompanied by introductory essays and critical notes. Edited and translated by René Henry. Collection des Universités de France (="Collection Budé") Série Grecque. Publiée sous le patronage de l'Association Guillaume Budé. Paris, France: Société d'Édition Les Belles Lettres.

Pindar. (1997) *Pythian Odes*. Greek text with facing English translation available in the Loeb Classical Library as part of *Pindar: Olympian Odes. Pythian Odes*. Edited and translated by William H. Race. Cambridge, Massachusetts: Harvard University Press.

Plato. (1578) *Platonis Opera Quae Extant Omnia*. Three volumes. Greek texts with running Latin translations by Jean de Serres, laid out in a two-column format. Edited by Henri Estienne (Henricus Stephanus). Geneva, Switzerland.

———. (1701) *The Works of Plato Abridg'd*. Two volumes. Translated by various hands from the French by André Dacier. Illustrated with notes. London, England: A. Bell, 1701. Dacier's own translation, from the Greek into French, was published two years earlier as *Les Oeuvres de Platon*. Paris, France: Chez Jean Anisson, 1699.

———. (1804–1828) *Platons Werke*. Three volumes. German translations, with critical commentary, by Friedrich Daniel Ernst Schleiermacher. Berlin, Germany: Realschulbuchhandlung and Georg Reimer.

———. (1804) *The Works of Plato, viz. His Fifty-Five Dialogues, and Twelve Epistles*. Five volumes. English translations by Thomas Taylor and Floyer Sydenham. London, England: Printed for Thomas Taylor by R. Wilks, Chancery-Lane, and sold by E. Jeffery and R. H. Evans, Pall-Mall.

———. (1848–1854) *The Works of Plato: A New and Literal Version, Chiefly from the Text of Stallbaum*. Six volumes. English translations by Henry Cary, Henry Davis, and George Burges. Bohn's Classical Library. London, England: Henry G. Bohn.

———. (1871–1953) *The Dialogues of Plato*. Four volumes. English translations, with analyses and introductions, by Benjamin Jowett. Oxford, England: Clarendon Press, 1871. Three more editions: 1875 (five volumes); 1892 (five volumes); 1953 (four volumes). Numerous reprints, especially after entering into the public domain.

———. (1900–1907) *Platonis Opera*. Five volumes. Critical texts with introductions and notes. Edited by John Burnet. Oxford Classical Texts. Oxford, England: Oxford University Press. Reprinted 1967–1968. A new edition has been under way since 1995.

———. (1914–1935) *Plato: Collected Works*. Twelve volumes. Greek texts with facing English translations. All works in a single volume are translated and edited by the same person. Loeb Classical Library. Cambridge, Massachusetts: Harvard University Press. Reprinted 1961–1984.

———. (1920–1956) *Platon: Oeuvres Complètes*. Fourteen volumes. Greek texts with running French translations by various hands. Collection des Universités de France (="Collection Budé") Série Grecque. Publiée sous le patronage de l'Association Guillaume Budé. Paris, France: Société d'Édition Les Belles Lettres.

———. (1961) *The Collected Dialogues of Plato: Including the Letters*. English translations by various hands. Edited by Edith Hamilton and Huntington Cairns, with an introduction and prefatory notes. Bollingen Series 71. Princeton, New Jersey: Princeton University Press.

———. (1984–2006) *The Dialogues of Plato*. Four volumes. English translations, with introductory, exegetical, and critical comments and analyses, by Reginald E. Allen. New Haven, Connecticut: Yale University Press. The collection comprising twelve dialogues in four volumes (1984–1997) is complemented by a separate translation of the Republic, issued by the same publisher in 2006.

———. (1997) *Plato: Complete Works*. English translations by various hands. Edited, with an introduction and notes, by John Madison Cooper. Indianapolis, Indiana: Hackett Publishing Company.

Plutarch (Lucius Mestrius Plutarchus). (1918) *Life of Dion*. Greek text with facing English translation available in the Loeb Classical Library as part of *Plutarch: Lives*, Volume 6. (*Dion and Brutus. Timoleon and Aemilius Paulus*.) Translated by Bernadotte Perrin. Cambridge, Massachusetts: Harvard University Press.

———. (1967) *Adversus Colotem*. [*Against Colotes*.] Greek text with facing English translation available in the Loeb Classical Library as part of *Plutarch: Moralia*, Volume 14. (*That Epicurus Actually Makes a Pleasant Life Impossible. Reply to Colotes in Defence of the Other Philosophers. Is "Live Unknown" a Wise Precept? On Music*.) Translated by Benedict Einarson and Phillip H. De Lacy. Cambridge, Massachusetts: Harvard University Press.

Polycrates of Athens. (c. 393 BC) *Accusation of Socrates*. Lost work advocating the case of Athens against Socrates. Known only through secondary accounts, such as those in Xenophon (*Memorabilia* 1.2.9–1.2.61), Isocrates (*Busiris* 11.4–6), Quintilian (*Institutio Oratoria* 2.17.4, 3.1.11), or Diogenes Laërtius (*Lives* 2.38–39).

Popper, Karl Raimund. (1945) *The Open Society and Its Enemies*. Two volumes. Volume 1: *The Spell of Plato*. Volume 2: *The High Tide of Prophecy: Hegel, Marx, and the Aftermath*. London, England: G. Routledge & Sons.

Press, Gerald Alan. (2007) *Plato: A Guide for the Perplexed*. London, England: Continuum International Publishing Group.

———, editor. (2000) *Who Speaks for Plato? Studies in Platonic Anonymity*. Lanham, Maryland: Rowman & Littlefield.

Prior, William J. (1998) "Plato and the 'Socratic Fallacy,'" *Phronesis*, 43:2 (May), pp. 97–113.

Quintilian (Marcus Fabius Quintilianus). (1856) *Institutio Oratoria*. English edition available in Bohn's Classical Library as *Institutes of Oratory*. Two volumes. Translated by John Selby Watson. London, England: Henry G. Bohn.

Reale, Giovanni. (1975–1980) *Storia della Filosofia Antica*. Five volumes. Milan, Italy: Vita e Pensiero. Reorganized in four volumes for an English edition translated by John R. Catan and published as *A History of Ancient Philosophy*. Albany, New York: State University of New York Press, 1985–1990.

———. (1984) *Per una Nuova Interpretazione di Platone: Rilettura Della Metafisica dei Grandi Dialoghi alla Luce Delle "Dottrine Non Scritte."* Milano, Italy: Vita e Pensiero. Translated and edited by John R. Catan and Richard Davies as *Toward a New Interpretation of Plato: A Rereading of the Metaphysics of the Great Dialogues in the Light of the Unwritten Doctrines*. Washington, D.C.: Catholic University of America Press, 1997.

Reeve, Charles David Chanel. (1989) *Socrates in the* Apology*: An Essay on Plato's* Apology *of Socrates*. Indianapolis, Indiana: Hackett Publishing Company.

———. (2000) "Socrates the Apollonian." Chapter 2 of *Reason and Religion in Socratic Philosophy*. Edited by Nicholas D. Smith and Paul B. Woodruff. Oxford, England: Oxford University Press, pp. 24–39.

Rickless, Samuel Charles. (1997) *Plato's Forms in Transition: A Reading of the Parmenides*. Cambridge, England: Cambridge University Press.

Riddell, James, editor. (1867) *The Apology of Plato, with a Revised Text and English Notes, and a Digest of Platonic Idioms*. Oxford, England: Clarendon Press.

Ritchie, David George. (1902) *Plato*. New York, N.Y.: Charles Scribner's Sons.

Ritter, Constantin. (1910) *Platon: Sein Leben, Seine Schriften, Seine Lehre*. Volume 1. Two volumes (1910–1923). Munich, Germany: Oskar Beck.

———. (1933) *The Essence of Plato's Philosophy*. Translated from the German original by Adam Alles. London, England: George Allen & Unwin. Originally published as *Die Kerngedanken der Platonischen Philosophie*. Munich, Germany: E. Reinhardt, 1931.

Robinson, Thomas M. (1970) *Plato's Psychology*. Toronto, Canada: University of Toronto Press.

Rose, Valentin, editor. (1886) *Aristotelis Qui Ferebantur Librorum Fragmenta*. Third edition. The standard source for fragments traditionally attributed to Aristotle. Leipzig, Germany: B. G. Teubner. The second edition appeared, with the same title, as part of the Prussian Academy's collection of Aristotle's works: *Aristotelis Opera: Edidit Academia Regia Borussica*. Berlin, Germany: Georg Reimer, 1870. Originally published as *Aristoteles Pseudepigraphus*. Leipzig, Germany: B. G. Teubner, 1863.

Rosen, Stanley. (1983) *Plato's Sophist: The Drama of Original and Image*. New Haven, Connecticut: Yale University Press.

———. (1988) *The Quarrel Between Philosophy and Poetry: Studies in Ancient Thought*. New York, N.Y.: Routledge.

———. (1991) "Is Metaphysics Possible?" *The Review of Metaphysics*, 45:2 (December), pp. 235–257.

Ross, William David. (1951) *Plato's Theory of Ideas*. Oxford, England: Clarendon Press.

Rowe, Christopher J. (2003a) "Plato." Chapter 4 of *The Cambridge Companion to Greek and Roman Philosophy*. Edited by David N. Sedley. Cambridge, England: Cambridge University Press, pp. 98–124.

———. (2003b) "Plato, Socrates, and Developmentalism." In *Desire, Identity and Existence: Essays in Honour of T. M. Penner*. Edited by Naomi Reshotko. Kelowna, B.C., Canada: Academic Printing & Publishing, pp. 17–32.

———. (2006a) "Interpreting Plato." Chapter 2 of *A Companion to Plato*. Edited by Hugh H. Benson. Oxford, England: Blackwell Publishing, pp. 13–24.

———. (2006b) "Socrates in Plato's Dialogues." Chapter 9 of *A Companion to Socrates*. Edited by Sara Ahbel-Rappe and Rachana Kamtekar. Oxford, England: Blackwell Publishing, pp. 159–170.

———. (2007) *Plato and the Art of Philosophical Writing*. Cambridge, England: Cambridge University Press.

———, editor. (1993) *Plato: Phaedo*. Greek text with introduction and commentary. Cambridge, England: Cambridge University Press.

Rowe, William Leonard. (1975) *The Cosmological Argument*. Princeton, New Jersey: Princeton University Press.

———. (1978) *Philosophy of Religion: An Introduction*. Belmont, California, Wadsworth Publishing Company.

Rusten, Jeffrey S., editor. (2011) *The Birth of Comedy: Texts, Documents, and Art from Athenian Comic Competitions, 486–280*. Translated by Jeffrey Henderson, David Konstan, Ralph Rosen, Niall W. Slater, and Jeffrey Rusten. Baltimore, Maryland: Johns Hopkins University Press.

Ryle, Gilbert. (1966) *Plato's Progress*. Cambridge, England: Cambridge University Press.

Sallis, John. (1975) *Being and Logos: The Way of Platonic Dialogue*. Pittsburgh, Pennsylvania: Duquesne University Press.

Santas, Gerasimos Xenophon. (1972) "The Socratic Fallacy," *Journal of the History of Philosophy*, 10:2 (April), pp. 127–141.

———. (1979) *Socrates: Philosophy in Plato's Early Dialogues*. London, England: Routledge & Kegan Paul.

Sayre, Kenneth M. (1983) *Plato's Late Ontology: A Riddle Resolved*. Princeton, New Jersey: Princeton University Press.

———. (1988) "Plato's Dialogues in Light of the *Seventh Letter*." Chapter 6 of *Platonic Writings, Platonic Readings*. Edited by Charles L. Griswold, Jr. New York, N.Y.: Routledge, Chapman & Hall, pp. 93–109.

———. (1993a) "Hans J. Kraemer: Plato and the Foundations of Metaphysics," *Ancient Philosophy*, 13, pp. 167–184.

———. (1993b) "Why Plato Never Had a Theory of Forms," *Proceedings of the Boston Area Colloquium in Ancient Philosophy*, 9, pp. 167–193.

———. (1995) *Plato's Literary Garden: How to Read a Platonic Dialogue*. Notre Dame, Indiana: University of Notre Dame Press.

———. (1996) *Parmenides' Lesson: Translation and Explication of Plato's Parmenides*. Notre Dame, Indiana: University of Notre Dame Press.

———. (2002) "Do Forms Have a Role in Plato's *Philebus*?" Chapter 6 of *Plato's Forms: Varieties of Interpretation*. Edited by William A. Welton. Lanham, Maryland: Lexington Books, pp. 169–191.

Schleiermacher, Friedrich Daniel Ernst, editor. (1804–1828) *Platons Werke*. Three volumes. Berlin, Germany: Realschulbuchhandlung and Georg Reimer. Held in high regard in their own right, separately from the translations themselves, the introductions are available in English in a single volume published as *Schleiermacher's Introductions to the Dialogues of Plato*. Translated by William Dobson. Cambridge, England: J. & J. J. Deighton, 1836.

Sedley, David N. (2003) *Plato's Cratylus*. Cambridge, England: Cambridge University Press.

Sextus Empiricus. (1933) *Pyrrhōneioi Hypotypōseis* (PH). Greek text with facing English translation available in the Loeb Classical Library as *Sextus Empiricus: Outlines of Pyrrhonism*. Translated by Robert Gregg Bury. Cambridge, Massachusetts: Harvard University Press.

Shorey, Paul. (1903) *The Unity of Plato's Thought*. Chicago, Illinois: University of Chicago Press.

———. (1933) *What Plato Said*. Chicago, Illinois: University of Chicago Press.

Simplicius of Cilicia. (1882–1895) *Commentary on Aristotle's Physics*. Greek text with Latin commentary available in two volumes in *Commentaria in Aristotelem Graeca* (CAG). Volume 9 (1882): *In Aristotelis Physicorum Libros Quattuor Priores Commentaria* [*Physics* 1–4]. Volume 10 (1895): *In Aristotelis Physicorum Libros Quattuor Posteriores Commentaria* [*Physics* 5–8]. Edited by Hermann Alexander Diels. Berlin, Germany: Realschulbuchhandlung and Georg Reimer. Translated into English as *Simplicius: On Aristotle On Physics* in multiple volumes (eight during 1989–2002, three still pending) in the *Ancient Commentators on Aristotle* (ACA), a project carried out under the auspices of King's College London and the general editorship of Richard Sorabji. London, England: Duckworth; Ithaca, New York: Cornell University Press, 1987–present.

Smith, Nicholas D., and Paul B. Woodruff, editors. (2000) *Reason and Religion in Socratic Philosophy*. Oxford, England: Oxford University Press.

Sorley, William Ritchie. (1885) *On the Ethics of Naturalism*. Edinburgh, Scotland: William Blackwood and Sons.

Stone, Isidor Feinstein. (1988) *The Trial of Socrates*. New York, N.Y.: Anchor Books, Doubleday.

Storey, Ian C., editor. (2011) *Fragments of Old Comedy*. Three volumes. Edited and translated by Ian C. Storey. Loeb Classical Library. Cambridge, Massachusetts: Harvard University Press. Volume 1: *Alcaeus to Diocles*. Volume 2: *Diopeithes to Pherecrates*. Volume 3: *Philonicus to Xenophon. Adespota*.

Strauss, Leo. (1946) "On a New Interpretation of Plato's Political Philosophy," *Social Research*, 13:3 (Fall), pp. 326–367.

———. (1952) *Persecution and the Art of Writing*. Glencoe, Illinois: Free Press. Reissued: Westport, Connecticut: Greenwood Press, 1973. Chicago, Illinois: University of Chicago Press, 1988.

———. (1964) *The City and Man*. Chicago, Illinois: Rand McNally.

———. (1983) *Studies in Platonic Political Philosophy*. Chicago, Illinois: University of Chicago Press.

Strycker, Emile de, and Simon Roelof Slings. (2005) "Plato's *Apology* of Socrates." Chapter 5 of *Plato's Euthyphro, Apology, and Crito: Critical Essays*. Edited by Rachana Kamtekar. Lanham, Maryland: Rowman & Littlefield, pp. 72–96. Originates in Emile de Strycker's work in progress, posthumously edited and completed by Simon Roelof Slings, and published with the same main title in Volume 137 of *Mnemosyne: A Journal of Classical Studies* (Bibliotheca Classica Batava): Supplementum 0169–8958. Leiden, Netherlands: E. J. Brill, 1994.

Swift Riginos, Alice. (1976) *Platonica: The Anecdotes Concerning the Life and Writings of Plato*. Leiden, Netherlands: E. J. Brill.
Szlezák, Thomas Alexander. (1985–2004) *Platon und die Schriftlichkeit der Philosophie*. Two volumes. Volume 1 (1985): *Interpretationen zu den Frühen und Mittleren Dialogen*. Volume 2 (2004): *Das Bild des Dialektikers in Platons Spaten Dialogen*. Berlin, Germany: Walter de Gruyter.
———. (1993) *Platon Lesen*. Stuttgart, Germany: Frommann-Holzboog. Translated into English by Graham Zanker as *Reading Plato*. London, England: Routledge, 1999.
Tarán, Leonardo. (1981) *Speusippus of Athens: A Critical Study with a Collection of the Related Texts and Commentary*. Leiden, Netherlands: E. J. Brill.
Tarrant, Harold. (1993) *Thrasyllan Platonism*. Ithaca, New York: Cornell University Press.
Taylor, Alfred Edward. (1908) *Plato*. London, England: Archibald Constable & Co.
———. (1960) *Plato: The Man and His Work*. Seventh edition. New York, N.Y.: Methuen & Co. Originally published in 1926.
Tennemann, Wilhelm Gottlieb. (1839) "Life of Plato." First appearance in English as part of *Selections from German Literature*. Translated and edited by Bela Bates Edwards and Edwards Amasa Park. Andover, Massachusetts: Gould, Newman, and Saxton, pp. 311–367. Originally published as "Leben des Plato," the biography of Plato in the first volume (1792, pp. 1–80) of the author's *System der Platonischen Philosophie*. Four volumes. Leipzig, Germany: Johann Ambrosius Barth, 1792–1794.
Thesleff, Holger. (1982) *Studies in Platonic Chronology*. Helsinki, Finland: Societas Scientiarum Fennica.
———. (1989) "Platonic Chronology," *Phronesis*, 34:1, pp. 1–26.
———. (1993) "Looking for Clues: An Interpretation of Some Literary Aspects of Plato's Two-Level Model." Chapter 2 of *Plato's Dialogues: New Studies and Interpretations*. Edited by Gerald Alan Press. Lanham, Maryland: Rowman & Littlefield, pp. 17–45.
———. (1997) "The Early Version of Plato's *Republic*," *Arctos*, 31, pp. 149–174.
———. (1999) *Studies in Plato's Two-Level Model*. Helsinki, Finland: Societas Scientiarum Fennica.
———. (2009) *Platonic Patterns: A Collection of Studies*. Las Vegas, Nevada: Parmenides Publishing. A collection of Thesleff's previously published work, including, in addition to four articles, the following books: *Studies in the Styles of Plato* (1967); *Studies in Platonic Chronology* (1982); Studies in *Plato's Two-Level Model* (1999).
Thomas Aquinas, Saint. (1924) *Summa Contra Gentiles*. Literally translated by the English Dominican Fathers from the latest Leonine edition. Five volumes. London, England: Burns, Oates & Washbourne.
———. (2006) *Summa Theologiæ*. Sixty volumes plus index. Latin text with facing English translation. Cambridge, England: Cambridge University Press. A reprint, with minor emendations, mostly of typographical errors, of the English Dominican output known as the "Blackfriars edition," the collection was originally conceived and produced under the general editorship of Father Thomas Gilby, O.P. London, England: Eyre and Spottiswoode; New York, N.Y.: McGraw–Hill, 1964–1973.
Travlos, John. (1971) *Pictorial Dictionary of Ancient Athens*. London, England: Thames and Hudson.
Tredennick, Hugh, editor. (1969) *Plato: The Last Days of Socrates: Euthyphro, The Apology, Crito, Phaedo*. Reprint with revisions. English translations of the dialogues, each with an introduction and notes. London, England: Penguin Books. Originally published in 1954.

Tzetzes, Johannes. (1826) *Chiliades*. Critical text available as *Historiarum Variarum Chiliades*. Edited by Theophilus Kiesslingius (Johann Gottlieb Kiessling). Leipzig, Germany: Friedrich Christian Wilhelm Vogel.

Ueberweg, Friedrich. (1872) *History of Philosophy: From Thales to the Present Time*. Volume 1: *History of the Ancient and Mediaeval Philosophy*. Two volumes (1872–1874). Translated, from the fourth edition of the German original, by George Sylvester Morris, with additions by Noah Porter and a preface by the editors of the Philosophical and Theological Library. Authorized translation, revised by the author. New York, N.Y.: Charles Scribner's Sons. Originally published as *Grundriss der Geschichte der Philosophie*. Three volumes. Berlin, Germany: E. S. Mittler und Sohn, 1862–1866.

Vanderpool, Eugene. (1980) "The State Prison of Ancient Athens." In *From Athens to Gordion: The Papers of a Memorial Symposium for Rodney S. Young, Held at the University Museum, the Third of May, 1975*. Edited by Keith DeVries. Philadelphia, Pennsylvania: University of Pennsylvania Press, pp. 17–31.

Vlastos, Gregory. (1954) "The Third Man Argument in the *Parmenides*," *The Philosophical Review*, 63, pp. 319–349. Reprinted, with an addendum, in *Studies in Plato's Metaphysics*. Edited by Reginald E. Allen. London, England: Routledge & Kegan Paul, 1965, pp. 231–263 (addendum: pp. 261–263). Also reprinted as chapter 12a of his *Socrates, Plato, and Their Tradition*, the second volume of his *Studies in Greek Philosophy*. Edited by Daniel W. Graham. Princeton, New Jersey: Princeton University Press, 1995, pp. 166–190. Chapter 12b of the same volume contains his "Addendum to the Third Man Argument in the *Parmenides*" (pp. 191–193). The next two chapters lay out his replies to selected criticism: Chapter 12c presents "Addenda to the Third Man Argument: A Reply to Professor Sellars" (pp. 194–203). Chapter 12d is a "Postscript to the Third Man: A Reply to Mr. Geach" (pp. 204–214).

———. (1963) "H. J. Kraemer: Arete bei Platon und Aristoteles," *Gnomon*, 35, pp. 641–655. Reprinted with an added appendix in his *Platonic Studies*. Second edition. Princeton, New Jersey: Princeton University Press, 1981, pp. 379–403.

———. (1985) "Socrates' Disavowal of Knowledge," *Philosophical Quarterly*, 35, pp. 1–31. Reprinted as chapter 2 of his *Socratic Studies*. Edited by Myles Burnyeat. Cambridge, England: Cambridge University Press, 1994, pp. 39–66.

———. (1989) "Divining the Reason: Review of Brickhouse and Smith, *Socrates on Trial*," *Times Literary Supplement*, 4:524 (15–21 December), p. 1393. Reprinted as chapter 3 of his *Socrates, Plato, and Their Tradition*, the second volume of his *Studies in Greek Philosophy*. Edited by Daniel W. Graham. Princeton, New Jersey: Princeton University Press, 1995, pp. 25–29.

———. (1990) "Is the 'Socratic Fallacy' Socratic?" *Ancient Philosophy*, 10, pp. 1–16. Reprinted as chapter 3 of his *Socratic Studies*. Edited by Myles Burnyeat. Cambridge, England: Cambridge University Press, 1994, pp. 67–86.

———. (1991) *Socrates, Ironist and Moral Philosopher*. Ithaca, New York: Cornell University Press.

———. (1994) *Socratic Studies*. Edited by Myles Burnyeat. Cambridge, England: Cambridge University Press.

———, Thomas C. Brickhouse, Mark L. McPherran, and Nicholas D. Smith. (2000) "Socrates and His *Daimonion*: Correspondence Among the Authors." Edited by Paul B. Woodruff. In *Reason and Religion in Socratic Philosophy*. Edited by Nicholas D. Smith and Paul B. Woodruff. Oxford, England: Oxford University Press, pp. 176–204.

———, editor. (1971) *The Philosophy of Socrates: A Collection of Critical Essays.* Garden City, New York: Anchor Books, Doubleday.

Wagner, Ellen, editor. (2001) *Essays on Plato's Psychology.* Lanham, Maryland: Lexington Books.

Wallach, John Robert. (2001) *The Platonic Political Art: A Study of Critical Reason and Democracy.* University Park, Pennsylvania: Pennsylvania State University Press.

Waterfield, Robin, editor. (1990) *Xenophon: Conversations of Socrates.* Translated by Hugh Tredennick and Robin Waterfield, and edited with new material by Robin Waterfield. London, England: Penguin Books.

Weiss, Roslyn. (1998) *Socrates Dissatisfied: An Analysis of Plato's Crito.* New York, N.Y.: Oxford University Press.

Welton, William A., editor. (2002) *Plato's Forms: Varieties of Interpretation.* Lanham, Maryland: Lexington Books.

Westermann, Anton, editor. (1845) *Biographoi: Vitarum Scriptores Graeci Minores.* Brunsvigae (Braunschweig), Germany: Sumptum Fecit Georgius Westermann.

White, Stephen A. (2000) "Socrates at Colonus: A Hero for the Academy." Chapter 9 of *Reason and Religion in Socratic Philosophy.* Edited by Nicholas D. Smith and Paul Woodruff. Oxford, England: Oxford University Press, pp. 151–175.

Whitehead, Alfred North. (1929) *Process and Reality: An Essay in Cosmology.* Gifford lectures delivered in the University of Edinburgh during the session 1927–28. Cambridge, England: Cambridge University Press. Subsequently published in a "corrected edition" edited by David Ray Griffin and Donald W. Sherburne. New York, N.Y.: The Free Press, 1978. The famous analogy of Western philosophy ("the European philosophical tradition") as a series of footnotes to Plato is on p. 39 of the "corrected edition."

Wieland, Wolfgang. (1982) *Platon und die Formen des Wissens.* [*Plato and the Written Word.*] Gottingen, Germany: Vandenhoeck & Ruprecht.

Wilamowitz-Moellendorff, Enno Friedrich Wichard Ulrich von. (1881) *Antigonos von Karystos.* Volume 4 of Philologische Untersuchungen. Berlin, Germany: Weidmannsche Buchhandlung.

Williams, Bernard Arthur Owen. (2006) "Plato: The Invention of Philosophy." Chapter 10 of *The Sense of the Past: Essays in the History of Philosophy.* Edited, with an introduction, by Myles Burnyeat. Princeton, New Jersey: Princeton University Press, pp. 148–186. Article originally published as a book of the same name, appearing as volume 23 of the Great Philosophers Series. London, England: Phoenix, 1998.

Wolfsdorf, David Conan. (2003a) "Socrates' Pursuit of Definitions," *Phronesis*, 48:4, pp. 271–312.

———. (2003b) "Understanding the 'What-Is-*F*?' Question," *Apeiron*, 36:3, pp. 175–188.

———. (2004a) "The Socratic Fallacy and the Epistemological Priority of Definitional Knowledge," *Apeiron*, 37:1, pp. 35–67.

———. (2004b) "Socrates' Avowals of Knowledge," *Phronesis*, 49:2, pp. 75–142.

———. (2005) "*Euthyphro* 10a2–11b1: A Study in Platonic Metaphysics and Its Reception Since 1960," *Apeiron*, 38:1, pp. 1–71.

———. (2008) *Trials of Reason: Plato and the Crafting of Philosophy.* Oxford, England: Oxford University Press.

Woodbridge, Frederick James Eugene. (1929) *The Son of Apollo: Themes of Plato.* Boston, Massachusetts: Houghton Mifflin Company.

Woozley, Anthony Douglas. (1979) *Law and Obedience: The Arguments of Plato's Crito*. Also contains an English translation of the dialogue. Chapel Hill, North Carolina: University of North Carolina Press.

Wycherley, Richard Ernest. (1962) "Peripatos: The Athenian Philosophical Scene—II," *Greece & Rome* (Second Series), 9:1 (March), pp. 2–21.

———. (1978) *The Stones of Athens*. Princeton, New Jersey: Princeton University Press.

Xenophon. (1918–1921) *Hellenica*. Greek text with facing English translation available in the Loeb Classical Library as *Xenophon: Hellenica*. Two volumes. Volume 1 (1918): Books 1–4. Volume 2 (1921): Books 5–7. Translated by Carleton L. Brownson. Cambridge, Massachusetts: Harvard University Press.

———. (1925) *Hiero*. Greek text with facing English translation available in the Loeb Classical Library as part of *Xenophon: Scripta Minora*. Translated by Edgar Cardew Marchant and Glen Warren Bowersock. Cambridge, Massachusetts: Harvard University Press.

———. (1990) *Apology* [*Socrates' Defence*]. English translation available as part of a single-volume collection of his Socratic works published as *Conversations of Socrates*. Translated by Hugh Tredennick and Robin Waterfield, and edited with new material by Robin Waterfield. London, England: Penguin Books.

———. (1990) *Memorabilia* [*Memoirs of Socrates*]. English translation available as part of a single-volume collection of his Socratic works published as *Conversations of Socrates*. Translated by Hugh Tredennick and Robin Waterfield, and edited with new material by Robin Waterfield. London, England: Penguin Books.

———. (1990) *Oeconomicus* [*The Estate-Manager*]. English translation available as part of a single-volume collection of his Socratic works published as *Conversations of Socrates*. Translated by Hugh Tredennick and Robin Waterfield, and edited with new material by Robin Waterfield. London, England: Penguin Books.

———. (1990) *Symposium* [*The Dinner-Party*]. English translation available as part of a single-volume collection of his Socratic works published as *Conversations of Socrates*. Translated by Hugh Tredennick and Robin Waterfield, and edited with new material by Robin Waterfield. London, England: Penguin Books.

Yonge, Charles Duke, editor. (1853) *Diogenes Laërtius: The Lives and Opinions of Eminent Philosophers*. Bohn's Classical Library 43. London, England: Henry G. Bohn.

Young, Charles M. (1994) "Plato and Computer Dating: A Discussion of Gerard R. Ledger, *Recounting Plato: A Computer Analysis of Plato's Style* and Leonard Brandwood, *The Chronology of Plato's Dialogues*," *Oxford Studies in Ancient Philosophy*, 12, pp. 227–250.

Zeller, Eduard. (1876) *Plato and the Older Academy*. English translation of "Plato und die ältere Akademie," a portion of the author's three-volume *Die Philosophie der Griechen*, corresponding to the second section of the second part of the second volume in its third edition (1875), the correspondence being identified as such in the preface to the translation. Translated by Sarah Frances Alleyne and Alfred Goodwin. London, England: Longmans, Green, and Co. The full set in German was originally published in Tübingen, Germany: Ludwig Friedrich Fues, 1844–1852.

Zeyl, Donald J., editor. (2000) *Timaeus*. English translation, including a substantial introduction, by Donald J. Zeyl. Indianapolis, Indiana, Hackett Publishing Company.

Zuckert, Catherine H. (2009) *Plato's Philosophers: The Coherence of the Dialogues*. Chicago, Illinois: University of Chicago Press.

Appendix

BIBLIOGRAPHIC GUIDE TO FURTHER STUDY

1. Collected Works

1.1. Greek Editions

Stephanus Edition (1578): *Platonis Opera Quae Extant Omnia*. Three volumes. Greek text with running Latin translation by Jean de Serres, laid out in a two-column format. Edited by Henri Estienne (Henricus Stephanus). Geneva, Switzerland: 1578. Includes forty-one dialogues (ignoring only the *Halcyon*), all thirteen letters, and the spurious book of definitions. Volume 1: *Euthyphro*; *Apology*; *Crito*; *Phaedo*; *Theages*; *Rival Lovers*; *Theaetetus*; *Sophist*; *Euthydemus*; *Protagoras*; *Hippias Minor*; *Cratylus*; *Gorgias*; *Ion*. Volume 2: *Philebus*; *Meno*; *Alcibiades* 1; *Alcibiades* 2; *Charmides*; *Laches*; *Lysis*; *Hipparchus*; *Menexenus*; *Statesman*; *Minos*; *Republic*; *Laws*; *Epinomis*. Volume 3: *Timaeus*; *Critias*; *Parmenides*; *Symposium*; *Phaedrus*; *Hippias Major*; *Letters*; *Axiochus*; *On Justice*; *On Virtue*; *Demodocus*; *Sisyphus*; *Eryxias*; *Clitophon*; *Definitions*.

Oxford Classical Texts Edition (1900–1907): *Platonis Opera*. Five volumes. Edited by John Burnet with introduction and notes. Oxford Classical Texts. Oxford, England: Oxford University Press, 1900–1907. Reprinted 1967–1968. Greek text of forty-one dialogues, all thirteen letters, and the spurious book of definitions. Oxford treats thirty-five dialogues as genuine, six as spurious, and ignores the *Halcyon* altogether. Volume 1 (1900): *Euthyphro*; *Apologia Socratis*; *Crito*; *Phaedo*; *Cratylus*; *Theaetetus*; *Sophista*; *Politicus* [*Statesman*]. Volume 2 (1901): *Parmenides*; *Philebus*; *Symposium*; *Phaedrus*; *Alcibiades* 1; *Alcibiades* 2; *Hipparchus*; *Amatores* [(*Rival*) *Lovers*]. Volume 3 (1903): *Theages*; *Charmides*; *Laches*; *Lysis*; *Euthydemus*; *Protagoras*; *Gorgias*; *Meno*; *Hippias Major*; *Hippias Minor*; *Io* [*Ion*]; *Menexenus*. Volume 4 (1902): *Clitopho*; *Res Publica*; *Timaeus*; *Critias*. Volume 5 (1907): *Minos*; *Leges* [*Laws*]; *Epinomis*; *Epistulae* [*Letters*]; *Definitiones*; Spuria [*De Justo*; *De Virtute*; *Demodocus*; *Sisyphus*; *Eryxias*; *Axiochus*].

Oxford Classical Texts [New] Edition (1995–present): *Platonis Opera*. Five volumes. A new edition designed to replace Burnet's 1900–1907 contribution to the same series. Oxford Classical Texts. Oxford, England: Oxford University Press, 1995–present. Volume 1 (1995): *Euthyphro*; *Apologia*; *Crito*; *Phaedo*; *Cratylus*; *Theaetetus*; *Sophista*; *Politicus* [*Statesman*]. Edited by E. A. Duke, W. F. Hicken, W. S. M. Nicoll, D. B. Robinson, and J. C. G. Strachan. *Republic*: *Platonis Respublica* (2003). Edited by Simon Roelof Slings.

Burnet [Minor] Edition. John Burnet also prepared the Greek manuscripts of selected dialogues for publication outside the *Platonis Opera*. Featuring extensive notes and commentary, these editions are all related to the trial and execution of Socrates: *Plato's Phaedo*. Oxford, England: Oxford University Press, 1911. *Plato's Euthyphro, Apology of Socrates, and Crito*. Oxford, England: Clarendon Press, 1924. Reprinted in New York, N.Y.: AMS Press, 1977.

1.2. English Editions

Dacier Edition (1701): *The Works of Plato Abridg'd.* Two volumes. Translated by various hands from the French by André Dacier. Illustrated with notes. London, England: A. Bell, 1701. Publisher's full description on title page: *The Works of Plato Abridg'd: With an Account of His Life, Philosophy, Morals, and Politicks; Together with a Translation of His Choicest Dialogues, viz., Of: Human Nature; Prayer; Wisdom; Holiness; What One Ought to Do; Immortality of the Soul; Valour; Philosophy.* Dacier's own translation, from the Greek into French, had appeared only two years earlier as *Les Oeuvres de Platon: Traduites en Francois avec des Remarques; Et la Vie de Ce Philosophe, avec l'Exposition des Principaux Dogmes de Sa Philosophie.* Paris, France: Chez Jean Anisson, 1699. The effort was the first appearance in print of a collected works edition in French, and the first again in English. Despite covering only ten dialogues, it remained the most popular edition of Plato in the eighteenth century. Volume 1: *Alcibiades* 1; *Alcibiades* 2; *Theages*; *Euthyphro*. Volume 2: *Apology*; *Crito*; *Phaedo*; *Laches*; *Protagoras*; *Rival Lovers*. Six of the works were first-ever appearances in English: *Alcibiades* 1; *Alcibiades* 2; *Theages*; *Euthyphro*; *Laches*; *Protagoras*.

Taylor and Sydenham Edition (1804): *The Works of Plato, viz. His Fifty-Five Dialogues, and Twelve Epistles.* Five volumes. Translated by Thomas Taylor and Floyer Sydenham. London, England: Printed for Thomas Taylor by R. Wilks, Chancery-Lane, and sold by E. Jeffery and R. H. Evans, Pall-Mall, 1804. Publisher's full description on title page: *The Works of Plato, viz. His Fifty-Five Dialogues, and Twelve Epistles, Translated from the Greek; Nine of the Dialogues by the Late Floyer Sydenham, and the Remainder by Thomas Taylor: With Occasional Annotations on the Nine Dialogues Translated by Sydenham, and Copious Notes by the Latter Translator; in which is Given the Substance of Nearly All the Existing Greek MS. Commentaries on the Philosophy of Plato, and a Considerable Portion of Such as Are Already Published.* Volume 1: General Introduction; Explanation of Certain Terms Peculiar to the Platonic Philosophy; Life of Plato; *Alcibiades* 1; *Republic*; Additional Notes on *Alcibiades* 1; Additional Notes on *Republic*. Volume 2: *Laws*; *Epinomis*; *Timaeus*; *Critias*; Additional Notes on *Timaeus*. Volume 3: *Parmenides*; *Sophist*; *Phaedrus*; *Hippias Major*; *Symposium*; Additional Notes on *Parmenides*; Additional Notes on *Phaedrus*. Volume 4: *Theaetetus*; *Statesman*; *Minos*; *Apology*; *Crito*; *Phaedo*; *Gorgias*; *Philebus*; *Alcibiades* 2. Volume 5: *Euthyphro*; *Meno*; *Protagoras*; *Theages*; *Laches*; *Lysis*; *Charmides*; *Hippias Minor*; *Euthydemus*; *Hipparchus*; *Rival Lovers*; *Menexenus*; *Clitophon*; *Ion*; *Cratylus*; *Letters*; Additional Notes on *Cratylus*. Actually contains thirty-five rather than fifty-five dialogues. The books of the *Republic* and those of the *Laws* are counted as individual dialogues, inflating the total by nine in the first case, eleven in the second, and twenty in all. Together with the letters taken as a whole, the collection accounts for the entirety of the traditional tetralogical scheme of thirty-six works, though it covers twelve rather than thirteen letters, omitting the thirteenth as no less apocryphal than the dialogues handed down from antiquity as known spuria within the Platonic corpus.

Bohn's Classical Library Edition (1848–1854): *The Works of Plato: A New and Literal Version, Chiefly from the Text of Stallbaum.* Six volumes. Translated by Henry Cary, Henry Davis, and George Burges. Bohn's Classical Library. London, England: Henry G. Bohn, 1848–1854. The first volume is by Cary, the second, by Davis, and, the rest, by Burges. Volume 1 (1848): *Apology*; *Crito*; *Phaedo*; *Gorgias*; *Protagoras*; *Phaedrus*; *Theaetetus*; *Euthyphro*; *Lysis*. Volume 2 (1849): *Republic*; *Timaeus*; *Critias*. Volume 3

(1850): *Meno*; *Euthydemus*; *Sophist*; *Statesman*; *Cratylus*; *Parmenides*; *Symposium*. Volume 4 (1851): *Philebus*; *Charmides*; *Laches*; *Menexenus*; *Hippias Major*; *Hippias Minor*; *Ion*; *Alcibiades* 1; *Alcibiades* 2; *Theages*; *Rival Lovers*; *Hipparchus*; *Minos*; *Clitopho*; *Letters*. Volume 5 (1852): *Laws*. Volume 6 (1854): *The Doubtful Works [Epinomis; Axiochus; Eryxias; On Virtue; On Justice; Sisyphus; Demodocus; Definitions; Timaeus Locrus]; with Lives of Plato, by Diogenes Laërtius, Hesychius, and Olympiodorus; Introductions to His Doctrines, by Alcinous and Albinus; the Notes of Thomas Gray; and a General Index to the Entire Work*. The collection amounts to forty-four works, including all thirty-six items in the traditional tetralogical scheme as well as the bulk of the spuria. It even adds *Timaeus Locrus* (a.k.a. *The Treatise of Timaeus the Locrian on the Soul of the World and Nature*), but it leaves out the *Halcyon* and the *Epigrams*.

Jowett Edition (1871–1953): *The Dialogues of Plato*. Four volumes. Translated into English, with analyses and introductions, by Benjamin Jowett (1817–1893). Oxford, England: Clarendon Press, 1871. Two more editions, both in five volumes, were issued by the same publisher during the translator's lifetime, the second, appearing in 1875, and, the third, in 1892. A fourth edition, revised by Donald James Allan and Harold Edward Dale, was released, again, by the same publisher, in four volumes in 1953. Numerous reprints have been available in various forms, especially since the work's entry into the public domain. The individual dialogues, numbering twenty-nine in all, have been and continue to be issued severally and in clusters in various collections. They are all freely available in electronic form. Structure of the third edition, the last in Jowett's lifetime: Volume 1: *Charmides*; *Lysis*; *Laches*; *Protagoras*; *Euthydemus*; *Cratylus*; *Phaedrus*; *Ion*; *Symposium*. Volume 2: *Meno*; *Euthyphro*; *Apology*; *Crito*; *Phaedo*; *Gorgias*; Appendix 1: *Hippias Minor*; *Alcibiades* 1; *Menexenus*; Appendix 2: *Alcibiades* 2; *Eryxias*. Volume 3: *Republic*; *Timaeus*; *Critias*. Volume 4: *Parmenides*; *Theaetetus*; *Sophist*; *Statesman*; *Philebus*. Volume 5: *Laws*; Index to the Writings of Plato. The *Republic* was also published separately from the collection in a third edition (so numbered as it follows the first two and precedes the third of the collection) released as *The Republic of Plato*. Oxford, England: Clarendon Press, 1888.

Loeb Classical Library Edition (1914–1935): *Plato*. Twelve volumes. Greek text with running English translations by various hands. Loeb Classical Library. Cambridge, Massachusetts: Harvard University Press, 1914–1935. Reprinted numerous times. Covers the entire range of canonical works, including thirty-five dialogues and all thirteen letters, and leaving out only items traditionally recognized as spuria. All the works in a single volume are translated by the same person, as noted in parentheses: Volume 1 (1914): *Euthyphro*; *Apology*; *Crito*; *Phaedo*; *Phaedrus* (H. N. Fowler). Volume 2 (1924): *Laches*; *Protagoras*; *Meno*; *Euthydemus* (W. R. M. Lamb). Volume 3 (1925): *Lysis*; *Symposium*; *Gorgias* (W. R. M. Lamb). Volume 4 (1926): *Cratylus*; *Parmenides*; *Hippias Major*; *Hippias Minor* (H. N. Fowler). Volume 5 (1930): *Republic* 1–5 (Paul Shorey). Volume 6 (1935): *Republic* 6–10 (Paul Shorey). Volume 7 (1921): *Theaetetus*; *Sophist* (H. N. Fowler). Volume 8 (1925): *Statesman*; *Philebus*; *Ion* (H. N. Fowler). Volume 9 (1929): *Timaeus*; *Critias*; *Clitophon*; *Menexenus*; *Letters* (R. G. Bury). Volume 10 (1926): *Laws* 1–6 (R. G. Bury). Volume 11 (1926): *Laws* 7–12 (R. G. Bury). Volume 12 (1927): *Charmides*; *Alcibiades* 1; *Alcibiades* 2; *Hipparchus*; *Rival Lovers*; *Theages*; *Minos*; *Epinomis* (W. R. M. Lamb).

Bollingen Edition (1961): *The Collected Dialogues of Plato: Including the Letters*. Edited, with an introduction and prefatory notes, by Edith Hamilton and Huntington Cairns. Bollingen Series 71. Princeton, New Jersey: Princeton University Press, 1961. English translations of twenty-eight dialogues and all thirteen letters. All dialogues are listed here in alphabetical order for convenience in reference, with the letters appended at the end, and the translator's name noted in parentheses for each item: *Apology* (Hugh Tredennick); *Charmides* (Benjamin Jowett); *Cratylus* (Benjamin Jowett); *Critias* (A. E. Taylor); *Crito* (Hugh Tredennick); *Epinomis* (A. E. Taylor); *Euthydemus* (W. H. D. Rouse); *Euthyphro* (Lane Cooper); *Gorgias* (W. D. Woodhead); *Hippias Major* (Benjamin Jowett); *Hippias Minor* (Benjamin Jowett); *Ion* (Lane Cooper); *Laches* (Benjamin Jowett); *Laws* (A. E. Taylor); *Lysis* (J. Wright); *Menexenus* (Benjamin Jowett); *Meno* (W. K. C. Guthrie); *Parmenides* (F. M. Cornford); *Phaedo* (Hugh Tredennick); *Phaedrus* (Reginald Hackforth); *Philebus* (Reginald Hackforth); *Protagoras* (W. K. C. Guthrie); *Republic* (Paul Shorey); *Sophist* (F. M. Cornford); *Statesman* (J. B. Skemp); *Symposium* (Michael Joyce); *Theaetetus* (F. M. Cornford); *Timaeus* (Benjamin Jowett); *Letters* (L. A. Post). The collection omits the entirety of the traditional spuria as well as seven canonical dialogues the editors deem spurious: *Alcibiades* 1; *Alcibiades* 2; *Clitophon*; *Hipparchus*; *Minos*; *Rival Lovers*; *Theages*. This was the standard English collection of Plato in the second half of the twentieth century until the appearance of the Hackett edition in 1997.

Allen Edition (1984–2006): *The Dialogues of Plato*. Four volumes. Translated into English, with introductory, exegetical, and critical comments and analyses, by Reginald E. Allen. New Haven, Connecticut: Yale University Press, 1984–1997. Covering only twelve dialogues, the contribution is known more for its intellectual depth, with particularly enlightening commentaries, than for its physical breadth. Yet it stands as the most extensive and successful solo effort in more than a century since Jowett. Volume 1 (1984): *Euthyphro*; *Apology*; *Crito*; *Meno*; *Gorgias*; *Menexenus*. Volume 2 (1991): *Symposium*. Volume 3 (1996): *Ion*; *Hippias Minor*; *Laches*; *Protagoras*. Volume 4 (1997): *Parmenides* (revision of his earlier translation published in 1983). The collection proper is complemented by a separate translation of the *Republic*, appearing in 2006 through the same publisher. Translations of the *Apology* and *Crito* in the first volume originate in his *Socrates and Legal Obligation*. Minneapolis, Minnesota: University of Minnesota Press, 1980.

Hackett Edition (1997): *Plato: Complete Works*. Edited, with an introduction and notes, by John Madison Cooper. Indianapolis, Indiana: Hackett Publishing Company, 1997. English translations of everything ever attributed to Plato, including all the works known to have been written by him as well as the spurious material. Covers forty-two dialogues, all thirteen letters, the spurious book of definitions, and the spurious collection of epigrams. All dialogues are listed here in alphabetical order for convenience in reference, with everything else (letters, definitions, epigrams) appended at the end, and the translator's name noted in parentheses for each item: *Alcibiades* 1 (D. S. Hutchinson); *Alcibiades* 2 (Anthony Kenny); *Apology* (G. M. A. Grube); *Axiochus* (Jackson P. Hershbell); *Charmides* (Rosamond Kent Sprague); *Clitophon* (Francisco J. Gonzalez); *Cratylus* (C. D. C. Reeve); *Critias* (Diskin Clay); *Crito* (G. M. A. Grube); *Demodocus* (Jonathan Barnes); *Epinomis* (Richard D. McKirahan, Jr.); *Eryxias* (Mark Joyal); *Euthydemus* (Rosamond Kent Sprague); *Euthyphro* (G. M. A. Grube); *Gorgias* (Donald J. Zeyl); *Halcyon* (Brad Inwood); *Hipparchus* (Nicholas D. Smith); *Hippias Major* (Paul Woodruff); *Hippias Minor* (Nicholas D. Smith); *Ion* (Paul Woodruff); *Laches* (Rosamond Kent Sprague); *Laws* (Trevor J. Saunders); *Lysis* (Stanley Lombardo); *Menexenus* (Paul Ryan); *Meno* (G. M. A. Grube);

Minos (Malcolm Schofield); *On Justice* (Andrew S. Becker); *On Virtue* (Mark Reuter); *Parmenides* (Mary Louise Gill and Paul Ryan); *Phaedo* (G. M. A. Grube); *Phaedrus* (Alexander Nehamas and Paul Woodruff); *Philebus* (Dorothea Frede); *Protagoras* (Stanley Lombardo and Karen Bell); *Republic* (G. M. A. Grube, revised by C. D. C. Reeve); *Rival Lovers* (Jeffrey Mitscherling); *Sisyphus* (David Gallop); *Sophist* (Nicholas P. White); *Statesman* (C. J. Rowe); *Symposium* (Alexander Nehamas and Paul Woodruff); *Theaetetus* (M. J. Levett, revised by Myles F. Burnyeat); *Theages* (Nicholas D. Smith); *Timaeus* (Donald J. Zeyl); *Letters* (Glenn Raymond Morrow); *Definitions* (D. S. Hutchinson); *Epigrams* (J. M. Edmonds, revised by John Madison Cooper). Quickly became the standard collection of Plato's works in English translation.

1.3. Other Editions

Schleiermacher Edition (1804–1828): *Platons Werke*. Three volumes. Translated from the Greek into German, with extensive critical commentary, by Friedrich Daniel Ernst Schleiermacher. Berlin, Germany: Realschulbuchhandlung and Georg Reimer, 1804–1828. Volume 1, part 1 (1804): *Phaedrus*; *Lysis*; *Protagoras*; *Laches*. Volume 1, part 2 (1805): *Charmides*; *Euthyphro*; *Parmenides*; *Apology*; *Crito*; *Ion*; *Hippias Minor*; *Hipparchus*; *Minos*; *Alcibiades* 2. Volume 2, part 1 (1805): *Gorgias*; *Theaetetus*; *Meno*; *Euthydemus*. Volume 2, part 2 (1807): *Cratylus*; *Sophist*; *Statesman*; *Symposium*. Volume 2, part 3 (1809): *Phaedo*; *Philebus*; *Theages*; *Erastae*; *Alcibiades* 1; *Menexenus*; *Hippias Major*; *Clitophon*. Volume 3, part 1 (1828): *Republic*. A second edition of the collection appeared in 1817, before the third volume, thus covering only and both of the first two volumes. The reason that the collection is broken down into three volumes and six parts, as opposed to the simpler structure of six volumes with no further divisions, is that the superstructure of three volumes follows Schleiermacher's division of Plato's works into three groups, while the substructure of parts reflects choices in time management in the production schedule of the translation project. The output is not limited to the genuine works of Plato, as evidenced at least by the inclusion of the *Erastae*, which Schleiermacher deemed patently spurious, but translated nonetheless. His death in 1834 precluded the completion of the effort, missing the *Timaeus*, *Critias*, *Laws*, and *Epinomis*, which would have collectively rounded out the third volume. Two centuries later, the contribution remains authoritative, still valued for the translations as well as the commentary, with the introductions to the dialogues attracting international readership. The introductions were translated into English by William Dobson as *Schleiermacher's Introductions to the Dialogues of Plato*. Cambridge, England: J. & J. J. Deighton, 1836.

Budé Edition (1920–1956): *Platon: Oeuvres Complètes*. Fourteen volumes. Greek text with running French translations, accompanied by introductory essays and critical notes. Collection des Universités de France (="Collection Budé") Série Grecque. Publiée sous le patronage de l'Association Guillaume Budé. Paris, France: Société d'Édition Les Belles Lettres, 1920–1956. Includes forty-one dialogues (ignoring only the *Halcyon*), all thirteen letters, the epigrams, and the spurious book of definitions. The editors take twenty-nine of the dialogues to be genuine and twelve of them to be spurious. The following is a list of the authentic dialogues in the order in which they appear in the Budé edition, purportedly laid out in the actual chronological order: *Hippias Minor*; *Alcibiades* 1; *Apology*; *Euthyphro*; *Crito*; *Hippias Major*; *Charmides*; *Laches*; *Lysis*; *Protagoras*; *Gorgias*; *Meno*; *Phaedo*; *Symposium*; *Phaedrus*; *Ion*; *Menexenus*; *Euthydemus*; *Cratylus*; *Republic*; *Parmenides*; *Theaetetus*; *Sophist*; *Statesman*; *Philebus*; *Timaeus*; *Critias*; *Laws*; *Epinomis*. The twelve spurious dialogues, again in sequential order, are as follows: *Alcibiades* 2; *Hipparchus*; *Minos*; *Rival Lovers*; *Theages*; *Clitophon*; *On Justice*; *On Virtue*; *Demodocus*; *Sisyphus*; *Eryxias*; *Axiochus*. New editions of individual dialogues have been known to be released on a sporadic basis, with no formal announcement of a comprehensive renewal initiative. Examples include the *Phaedo* (1983), the *Phaedrus* (1985), and the *Symposium* (1989).

2. Selected Dialogues

2.1. Euthyphro

2.1.1. Editions

Adam, James. *Platonis Euthyphro: With Introduction and Notes*. Greek text with extensive English commentary. Cambridge, England: Cambridge University Press, 1890.

Allen, Reginald E. "The Euthyphro." English translation of the dialogue, with introductory, exegetical, and critical comments and analyses, published as part of the first volume of his renditions offered collectively as *The Dialogues of Plato*. New Haven, Connecticut: Yale University Press, 1984, pp. 27–58.

Burnet, John. "Euthyphro." Greek text, edited with introduction and notes, and constituting part of a minor collection bringing together his versions of other Socratic dialogues, published together as *Plato's Euthyphro, Apology of Socrates, and Crito*. Oxford, England: Clarendon Press, 1924. The collection was reprinted in New York, N.Y.: AMS Press, 1977. Burnet's text of each of the three dialogues was originally published as part of the first volume of *Platonis Opera*, dedicated to eight dialogues: *Euthyphro, Apologia Socratis, Crito, Phaedo, Cratylus, Theaetetus, Sophista, Politicus* [*Statesman*]. Edited by John Burnet. Oxford Classical Texts. Oxford, England: Oxford University Press, 1900. The second edition of the larger work was released by the same publisher in 1922.

Church, Frederick John. "Euthyphro." English translation of the dialogue, introduced as part of his larger contribution released as *The Trial and Death of Socrates; Being the Euthyphron, Apology, Crito, and Phaedo of Plato*. London, England: Macmillan and Company, 1880. Several reprints, both as a whole and in parts, for example, with the first three dialogues bundled up with the death scene from the *Phaedo*, published in a single edition as *Plato: Euthyphro, Apology, Crito; With the Death Scene from the Phaedo*. Edited, with an introduction, by Robert D. Cummings. New York, N.Y.: Macmillan Publishing Company, 1956.

Cooper, Lane. "Euthyphro." Translated into English, with an introduction and prefatory notes, as part of his rendition of *Plato on the Trial and Death of Socrates: Euthyphro, Apology, Crito, Phaedo*. Ithaca, New York: Cornell University Press, 1941. Cooper's translation also appeared in the Bollingen edition of *The Collected Dialogues of Plato: Including the Letters*. Edited by Edith Hamilton and Huntington Cairns. Princeton, New Jersey: Princeton University Press, 1961, pp. 169–185.

Duke, E. A., W. F. Hicken, W. S. M. Nicoll, D. B. Robinson, and J. C. G. Strachan. "Euthyphro." Greek text with critical apparatus, appearing as part of the first volume of the New Edition of *Platonis Opera*, the collected works of Plato in the Oxford Classical Texts Series. The volume consists of eight dialogues: *Euthyphro, Apologia, Crito, Phaedo, Cratylus, Theaetetus, Sophista, Politicus* [*Statesman*]. Oxford, England: Oxford University Press, 1995.

Fowler, Harold North. "Euthyphro." English translation of the dialogue, with an introduction and parallel Greek text, appearing as part of the first volume of Plato's collected works in twelve volumes in the Loeb Classical Library. Cambridge, Massachusetts: Harvard University Press, 1914, pp. 1–59.

Griffith, Tom. "Euthyphro." English rendition of the dialogue, constituting part of his collection of translations published together, with a general introduction by Jane O'Grady, as *Plato: Symposium and the Death of Socrates*. Wordsworth Classics of World Literature. Hertfordshire, England: Wordsworth Editions Limited, 1997, pp. 59–82.

Grube, George Maximilian Anthony. "Euthyphro." English edition of the dialogue, originally packaged in a Socratic set incorporating some of his other translations, jointly published as a volume titled *The Trial and Death of Socrates: Euthyphro, Apology, Crito, Death Scene from Phaedo*. Indianapolis, Indiana: Hackett Publishing Company, 1975. The collection became available in a second edition, with corrections, in 1980, and in a third, incorporating revisions by John Madison Cooper, in 2000. Grube's translation of the *Euthyphro* also appeared in the same publisher's *Five Dialogues: Euthyphro, Apology, Crito, Meno, Phaedo*. Indianapolis, Indiana: Hackett Publishing Company, 1981. This slightly larger collection came out in a second edition, incorporating revisions by John Madison Cooper, in 2002. Grube's rendition of the *Euthyphro* here (together with his translations of the other four dialogues in the corresponding volumes) constitutes part of the definitive collection released by the same publisher: *Plato: Complete Works*. Edited, with an introduction and notes, by John Madison Cooper. Indianapolis, Indiana: Hackett Publishing Company, 1997, pp. 1–16.

Heidel, William Arthur. *Plato's Euthyphro: With Introduction and Notes*. Greek text with extensive English commentary. Greek Series for Colleges and Schools. New York, N.Y.: American Book Company, 1902.

Jowett, Benjamin. "Euthyphro." English translation of the dialogue, introduced as part of the second volume of his renditions offered collectively as *The Works of Plato*. Oxford, England: Clarendon Press, 1871. The second edition of the collection was published in 1875, the third in 1892, both during the translator's lifetime, while the fourth appeared posthumously in 1953. Numerous reprints have been following in various forms, especially in inexpensive editions, for example, *Plato: Six Great Dialogues: Apology, Crito, Phaedo, Phaedrus, Symposium, The Republic*. Mineola, New York: Dover Publications, 2007. All Jowett texts are freely available online.

Rowe, Christopher J. "Euthyphro." English rendition of the dialogue, constituting part of his collection of translations published together, with introductions and notes, as *Plato: The Last Days of Socrates: Euthyphro, Apology, Crito, Phaedo*. London, England: Penguin Books, 2010, pp. 6–28.

Tredennick, Hugh. "Socrates in Action: Euthyphro." English translation of the dialogue, with an introduction and notes, appearing as part of his rendition of *Plato: The Last Days of Socrates: Euthyphro, The Apology, Crito, Phaedo*. London, England: Penguin Books, 1954. New edition, with corrections, published in 1959. Reprinted, with revisions, in 1969. Later reissued in a revised translation, including new introduction and notes, all by Harold Tarrant, published in 1993.

2.1.2. Commentaries

Allen, Reginald E. *Plato's "Euthyphro" and the Earlier Theory of Forms*. London, England: Routledge & Kegan Paul, 1970.

Benson, Hugh H. "The Priority of Definition and the Socratic Elenchus," *Oxford Studies in Ancient Philosophy*, 8 (1990), pp. 19–65.

Beversluis, John. "Does Socrates Commit the Socratic Fallacy?" *American Philosophical Quarterly*, 24:3 (July 1987), pp. 211–223.

Brown, John H. "The Logic of the *Euthyphro* 10a–11b," *Philosophical Quarterly*, 14:54 (January 1964), pp. 1–14.

Burger, Ronna. "Making New Gods." Chapter 2 of *Plato and Platonism*. Edited by Johannes M. Van Ophuijsen. Volume 33 of Studies in Philosophy and the History of Philosophy. Washington, D.C.: Catholic University of America Press, 1999, pp. 39–59.

Burns, Steven A. M. "Doing Business with the Gods," *Canadian Journal of Philosophy*, 15:2 (June 1985), pp. 311–325.

Cohen, S. Marc. "Socrates on the Definition of Piety: *Euthyphro* 10a–11b," *Journal of the History of Philosophy*, 9:1 (January 1971), pp. 1–13. Reprinted as chapter 3 of *Plato's Euthyphro, Apology, and Crito: Critical Essays*. Edited by Rachana Kamtekar. Lanham, Maryland: Rowman & Littlefield, 2005, pp. 35–48.

Dimas, Panos. "Euthyphro's Thesis Revisited," *Phronesis*, 51:1 (2006), pp. 1–28.

Edwards, Mark Julian. "In Defense of Euthyphro," *The American Journal of Philology*, 121:2 (Summer 2000), pp. 213–224.

Furley, William D. "The Figure of Euthyphro in Plato's Dialogue," *Phronesis*, 30:2 (1985), pp. 201–208.

Geach, Peter Thomas. "Plato's *Euthyphro*: An Analysis and Commentary," *Monist*, 50:3 (1966), pp. 369–382. Reprinted as chapter 2 of *Plato's Euthyphro, Apology, and Crito: Critical Essays*. Edited by Rachana Kamtekar. Lanham, Maryland: Rowman & Littlefield, 2005, pp. 23–34.

Hall, John C. "Plato: *Euthyphro* 10a1–11a10," *Philosophical Quarterly*, 18:70 (January 1968), pp. 1–11.

Hoerber, Robert G. "Plato's *Euthyphro*," *Phronesis*, 3:2 (1958), pp. 95–107.

Kim, Alan. "A Chiastic Contradiction at *Euthyphro* 9e1–11b5," *Phronesis*, 49:3 (2004), pp. 219–224.

McPherran, Mark L. "Socratic Piety in the *Euthyphro*," *Journal of the History of Philosophy*, 23:3 (July 1985), pp. 283–309.

McPherran, Mark L. "The Aporetic Interlude and Fifth Elenchus of Plato's *Euthyphro*," *Oxford Studies in Ancient Philosophy*, 25 (Winter 2003), pp. 1–37.

McPherran, Mark L. "Socratic Religion." Chapter 6 of *The Cambridge Companion to Socrates*. Edited by Donald R. Morrison. Cambridge, England: Cambridge University Press, 2011, pp. 111–137.

O'Sullivan, Brendan. "The *Euthyphro* Argument (9d–11b)," *The Southern Journal of Philosophy*, 44:4 (2006), pp. 657–675.

Prior, William J. "Plato and the 'Socratic Fallacy,'" *Phronesis*, 43:2 (May 1998), pp. 97–113.

Rosen, Frederick. "Piety and Justice: Plato's *Euthyphro*," *Philosophy*, 43:164 (April 1968), pp. 105–116.

Santas, Gerasimos Xenophon. "The Socratic Fallacy," *Journal of the History of Philosophy*, 10:2 (April 1972), pp. 127–141.

Vlastos, Gregory. "Socrates' Disavowal of Knowledge," *Philosophical Quarterly*, 35 (1985), pp. 1–31. Reprinted as chapter 2 of his *Socratic Studies*. Edited by Myles Burnyeat. Cambridge, England: Cambridge University Press, 1994, pp. 39–66.

Vlastos, Gregory. "Is the 'Socratic Fallacy' Socratic?" *Ancient Philosophy*, 10 (1990), pp. 1–16. Reprinted as chapter 3 of his *Socratic Studies*. Edited by Myles Burnyeat. Cambridge, England: Cambridge University Press, 1994, pp. 67–86.

Wolfsdorf, David Conan. "Socrates' Pursuit of Definitions," *Phronesis*, 48:4 (2003), pp. 271–312.

Wolfsdorf, David Conan. "Understanding the 'What-Is-*F*?' Question," *Apeiron*, 36:3 (2003), pp. 175–188.

Wolfsdorf, David Conan. "The Socratic Fallacy and the Epistemological Priority of Definitional Knowledge," *Apeiron*, 37:1 (2004), pp. 35–67.

Wolfsdorf, David Conan. "Socrates' Avowals of Knowledge," *Phronesis*, 49:2 (2004), pp. 75–142.

Wolfsdorf, David Conan. "*Euthyphro* 10a2–11b1: A Study in Platonic Metaphysics and Its Reception Since 1960," *Apeiron*, 38:1 (2005), pp. 1–71.

2.2. Apology

2.2.1. Editions

Adam, James. *Platonis Apologia Socratis: With Introduction, Notes, and Appendices*. Greek text with extensive English commentary. Cambridge, England: Cambridge University Press, 1887.

Allen, Reginald E. "The Apology." English translation of the dialogue, with introductory, exegetical, and critical comments and analyses, published as part of the first volume of his renditions offered collectively as *The Dialogues of Plato*. New Haven, Connecticut: Yale University Press, 1984, pp. 59–104.

Burnet, John. "Apology of Socrates." Greek text, edited with introduction and notes, and constituting part of a minor collection bringing together his versions of other Socratic dialogues, published together as *Plato's Euthyphro, Apology of Socrates, and Crito*. Oxford, England: Clarendon Press, 1924. The collection was reprinted in New York, N.Y.: AMS Press, 1977. Burnet's text of each of the three dialogues was originally published as part of the first volume of *Platonis Opera*, dedicated to eight dialogues: *Euthyphro, Apologia Socratis, Crito, Phaedo, Cratylus, Theaetetus, Sophista, Politicus* [*Statesman*]. Edited by John Burnet. Oxford Classical Texts. Oxford, England: Oxford University Press, 1900. The second edition of the larger work was released by the same publisher in 1922.

Church, Frederick John. "Apology." English translation of the dialogue, introduced as part of his larger contribution released as *The Trial and Death of Socrates; Being the Euthyphron, Apology, Crito, and Phaedo of Plato*. London, England: Macmillan and Company, 1880. Several reprints, both as a whole and in parts, for example, with the first three dialogues bundled up with the death scene from the *Phaedo*, published in a single edition as *Plato: Euthyphro, Apology, Crito; With the Death Scene from the Phaedo*. Edited, with an introduction, by Robert D. Cummings. New York, N.Y.: Macmillan Publishing Company, 1956.

Cooper, Lane. "Apology." Translated into English, with an introduction and prefatory notes, as part of his rendition of *Plato on the Trial and Death of Socrates: Euthyphro, Apology, Crito, Phaedo*. Ithaca, New York: Cornell University Press, 1941.

Duke, E. A., W. F. Hicken, W. S. M. Nicoll, D. B. Robinson, and J. C. G. Strachan. "Apologia." Greek text with critical apparatus, appearing as part of the first volume of the New Edition of *Platonis Opera,* the collected works of Plato in the Oxford Classical Texts Series. The volume consists of eight dialogues: *Euthyphro*, *Apologia*, *Crito*, *Phaedo*, *Cratylus*, *Theaetetus*, *Sophista*, *Politicus* [*Statesman*]. Oxford, England: Oxford University Press, 1995.

Fowler, Harold North. "The Apology." English translation of the dialogue, with an introduction and parallel Greek text, appearing as part of the first volume of Plato's collected works in twelve volumes in the Loeb Classical Library. Cambridge, Massachusetts: Harvard University Press, 1914, pp. 61–145.

Griffith, Tom. "Apology." English rendition of the dialogue, constituting part of his collection of translations published together, with a general introduction by Jane O'Grady, as *Plato: Symposium and the Death of Socrates*. Wordsworth Classics of World Literature. Hertfordshire, England: Wordsworth Editions Limited, 1997, pp. 83–113.

Grube, George Maximilian Anthony. "Apology." English edition of the dialogue, originally packaged in a Socratic set incorporating some of his other translations, jointly published as a volume titled *The Trial and Death of Socrates: Euthyphro, Apology, Crito, Death Scene from Phaedo*. Indianapolis, Indiana: Hackett Publishing Company, 1975. The collection became available in a second edition, with corrections, in 1980, and in a third, incorporating revisions by John Madison Cooper, in 2000. Grube's translation of the *Apology* also appeared in the same publisher's *Five Dialogues: Euthyphro, Apology, Crito, Meno, Phaedo*. Indianapolis, Indiana: Hackett Publishing Company, 1981. This slightly larger collection came out in a second edition, incorporating revisions by John Madison Cooper, in 2002. Grube's rendition of the *Apology* here (together with his translations of the other four dialogues in the corresponding volumes) constitutes part of the definitive collection released by the same publisher: *Plato: Complete Works*. Edited, with an introduction and notes, by John Madison Cooper. Indianapolis, Indiana: Hackett Publishing Company, 1997, pp. 17–36.

Jowett, Benjamin. "Apology." English translation of the dialogue, introduced as part of the second volume of his renditions offered collectively as *The Works of Plato*. Oxford, England: Clarendon Press, 1871. The second edition of the collection was published in 1875, the third in 1892, both during the translator's lifetime, while the fourth appeared posthumously in 1953. Numerous reprints have been following in various forms, especially in inexpensive editions, for example, *Plato: Six Great Dialogues: Apology, Crito, Phaedo, Phaedrus, Symposium, The Republic*. Mineola, New York: Dover Publications, 2007. All Jowett texts are freely available online.

Riddell, James. *The Apology of Plato, with a Revised Text and English Notes, and a Digest of Platonic Idioms*. Greek text with extensive English commentary. Oxford, England: Clarendon Press, 1867.

Rowe, Christopher J. "The Apology of Socrates ('Socrates' Defence')." English rendition of the dialogue, constituting part of his collection of translations published together, with introductions and notes, as *Plato: The Last Days of Socrates: Euthyphro, Apology, Crito, Phaedo*. London, England: Penguin Books, 2010, pp. 32–62.

Stokes, Michael C. *Plato: Apology. With an Introduction, Translation and Commentary*. Greek and English texts on facing pages, combined with introduction and commentary in English. Warminster, England: Aris & Phillips, 1997.

Tredennick, Hugh. "Socrates on Trial: The Apology." English translation of the dialogue, with an introduction and notes, appearing as part of his rendition of *Plato: The Last Days of Socrates: Euthyphro, The Apology, Crito, Phaedo*. London, England: Penguin Books, 1954. New edition, with corrections, published in 1959. Reprinted, with revisions, in 1969, pp. 45–76. Later reissued in a revised translation, including new introduction and notes, all by Harold Tarrant, published in 1993. Tredennick's translation was also published in the Bollingen edition of *The Collected Dialogues of Plato: Including the Letters*. Edited by Edith Hamilton and Huntington Cairns. Princeton, New Jersey: Princeton University Press, 1961, pp. 3–26.

Tyler, William Seymour. *Plato's Apology and Crito; With Notes*. Greek text with extensive English commentary. New York, N.Y.: D. Appleton and Company, 1860. Revised edition, with the assistance of Henry Mather Tyler, published in 1887.

2.2.2. Commentaries

Blyth, Dougal. "Socrates' Trial and Conviction of the Jurors in Plato's *Apology*," *Philosophy & Rhetoric*, 33:1 (2000), pp. 1–22.

Brickhouse, Thomas C., and Nicholas D. Smith. *Socrates on Trial*. Princeton, New Jersey: Princeton University Press, 1989.

Brickhouse, Thomas C., and Nicholas D. Smith, editors. *The Trial and Execution of Socrates: Sources and Controversies*. Oxford, England: Oxford University Press, 2002.

Brickhouse, Thomas C., and Nicholas D. Smith. "The Origin of Socrates' Mission," *Journal of the History of Ideas*, 44:4 (October–December 1983), pp. 657–666.

Brickhouse, Thomas C., and Nicholas D. Smith. "Socrates' First Remarks to the Jury in Plato's *Apology of Socrates*," *The Classical Journal*, 81:4 (April–May 1986), pp. 289–298.

Colaiaco, James A. *Socrates Against Athens: Philosophy on Trial*. New York, N.Y., and London, England: Routledge, 2001.

Gomperz, Heinrich. "Sokrates' Haltung vor Seinen Richtern" [Socrates's Attitude Before His Judges], *Wiener Studien*, 54 (1936), pp. 32–43.

Hackforth, Reginald. *The Composition of Plato's Apology*. Cambridge, England: Cambridge University Press, 1933.

Josiah Ober. "Socrates and Democratic Athens." Chapter 7 of *The Cambridge Companion to Socrates*. Edited by Donald R. Morrison. Cambridge, England: Cambridge University Press, 2011, pp. 138–178.

Kraut, Richard. "Plato's *Apology* and *Crito*: Two Recent Studies," *Ethics*, 91:4 (July 1981), pp. 651–664.

Leibowitz, David. *The Ironic Defense of Socrates: Plato's Apology*. Cambridge, England: Cambridge University Press, 2010.

Metcalf, Robert. "The Philosophical Rhetoric of Socrates' Mission," *Philosophy & Rhetoric*, 37:2 (2004), pp. 143–166.

Miller, Paul Allen, and Charles Platter. *Plato's Apology of Socrates: A Commentary*. Greek text with introduction, notes, and commentary in English. Oklahoma Series in Classical Culture. Norman, Oklahoma: University of Oklahoma Press, 2010.

Millett, Paul. "The Trial of Socrates Revisited," *European Review of History*, 12:1 (March 2005), pp. 23–62.

Morrison, Donald R. "On the Alleged Historical Reliability of Plato's *Apology*," *Archiv für Geschichte der Philosophie*, 82:3 (2000), pp. 235–265. Reprinted as chapter 6 of *Plato's Euthyphro, Apology, and Crito: Critical Essays*. Edited by Rachana Kamtekar. Lanham, Maryland: Rowman & Littlefield, 2005, pp. 97–126.

Oldfather, William Abbott. "Socrates in Court," *The Classical Weekly*, (Whole Number 844), 31:21 (25 April 1938), pp. 203–211.

Prior, William J. "The Historicity of Plato's *Apology*," *Polis*, 18 (2001), pp. 41–57.

Reeve, Charles David Chanel. *Socrates in the* Apology*: An Essay on Plato's* Apology *of Socrates*. Indianapolis, Indiana: Hackett Publishing Company, 1989.

Roochnik, David L. "*Apology* 40c4–41e7: Is Death Really a Gain?" *The Classical Journal*, 80:3 (February–March 1985), pp. 212–220.

Strycker, Emile de, and Simon Roelof Slings. *Plato's Apology of Socrates: A Literary and Philosophical Study with a Running Commentary*. Emile de Strycker's work in progress, posthumously edited and completed by Simon Roelof Slings. Volume 137 of *Mnemosyne: A Journal of Classical Studies* (Bibliotheca Classica Batava): Supplementum 0169–8958. Leiden, Netherlands: E. J. Brill, 1994.

2.3. Crito

2.3.1. Editions

Adam, James. *Platonis Crito: With Introduction, Notes, and Appendix*. Greek text with extensive English commentary. Cambridge, England: Cambridge University Press, 1888. Second edition published in 1893.

Allen, Reginald E. "The Crito." English translation of the dialogue, with introductory, exegetical, and critical comments and analyses, published as part of the first volume of his renditions offered collectively as *The Dialogues of Plato*. New Haven, Connecticut: Yale University Press, 1984, pp. 105–129.

Burnet, John. "Crito." Greek text, edited with introduction and notes, and constituting part of a minor collection bringing together his versions of other Socratic dialogues, published together as *Plato's Euthyphro, Apology of Socrates, and Crito*. Oxford, England: Clarendon Press, 1924. The collection was reprinted in New York, N.Y.: AMS Press, 1977. Burnet's text of each of the three dialogues was originally published as part of the first volume of *Platonis Opera*, dedicated to eight dialogues: *Euthyphro, Apologia Socratis, Crito, Phaedo, Cratylus, Theaetetus, Sophista, Politicus* [*Statesman*]. Edited by John Burnet. Oxford Classical Texts. Oxford, England: Oxford University Press, 1900. The second edition of the larger work was released by the same publisher in 1922.

Church, Frederick John. "Crito." English translation of the dialogue, introduced as part of his larger contribution released as *The Trial and Death of Socrates; Being the Euthyphron, Apology, Crito, and Phaedo of Plato*. London, England: Macmillan and Company, 1880. Several reprints, both as a whole and in parts, for example, with the first three dialogues bundled up with the death scene from the *Phaedo*, published in a single edition as *Plato: Euthyphro, Apology, Crito; With the Death Scene from the Phaedo*. Edited, with an introduction, by Robert D. Cummings. New York, N.Y.: Macmillan Publishing Company, 1956.

Cooper, Lane. "Crito." Translated into English, with an introduction and prefatory notes, as part of his rendition of *Plato on the Trial and Death of Socrates: Euthyphro, Apology, Crito, Phaedo*. Ithaca, New York: Cornell University Press, 1941.

Duke, E. A., W. F. Hicken, W. S. M. Nicoll, D. B. Robinson, and J. C. G. Strachan. "Crito." Greek text with critical apparatus, appearing as part of the first volume of the New Edition of *Platonis Opera,* the collected works of Plato in the Oxford Classical Texts Series. The volume consists of eight dialogues: *Euthyphro*, *Apologia*, *Crito*, *Phaedo*, *Cratylus*, *Theaetetus*, *Sophista*, *Politicus* [*Statesman*]. Oxford, England: Oxford University Press, 1995.

Fowler, Harold North. "Crito." English translation of the dialogue, with an introduction and parallel Greek text, appearing as part of the first volume of Plato's collected works in twelve volumes in the Loeb Classical Library. Cambridge, Massachusetts: Harvard University Press, 1914, pp. 147–191.

Griffith, Tom. "Crito." English rendition of the dialogue, constituting part of his collection of translations published together, with a general introduction by Jane O'Grady, as *Plato: Symposium and the Death of Socrates*. Wordsworth Classics of World Literature. Hertfordshire, England: Wordsworth Editions Limited, 1997, pp. 115–132.

Grube, George Maximilian Anthony. "Crito." English edition of the dialogue, originally packaged in a Socratic set incorporating some of his other translations, jointly published as a volume titled *The Trial and Death of Socrates: Euthyphro, Apology, Crito, Death Scene from Phaedo*. Indianapolis, Indiana: Hackett Publishing Company, 1975. The collection became available in a second edition, with corrections, in 1980, and in a third, incorporating revisions by John Madison Cooper, in 2000. Grube's translation of the *Crito* also appeared in the same publisher's *Five Dialogues: Euthyphro, Apology, Crito, Meno, Phaedo*. Indianapolis, Indiana: Hackett Publishing Company, 1981. This slightly larger collection came out in a second edition, incorporating revisions by John Madison Cooper, in 2002. Grube's rendition of the *Crito* here (together with his translations of the other four dialogues in the corresponding volumes) constitutes part of the definitive collection released by the same publisher: *Plato: Complete Works*. Edited, with an introduction and notes, by John Madison Cooper. Indianapolis, Indiana: Hackett Publishing Company, 1997, pp. 37–48.

Jowett, Benjamin. "Crito." English translation of the dialogue, introduced as part of the second volume of his renditions offered collectively as *The Works of Plato*. Oxford, England: Clarendon Press, 1871. The second edition of the collection was published in 1875, the third in 1892, both during the translator's lifetime, while the fourth appeared posthumously in 1953. Numerous reprints have been following in various forms, especially in inexpensive editions, for example, *Plato: Six Great Dialogues: Apology, Crito, Phaedo, Phaedrus, Symposium, The Republic*. Mineola, New York: Dover Publications, 2007. All Jowett texts are freely available online.

Rowe, Christopher J. "Crito." English rendition of the dialogue, constituting part of his collection of translations published together, with introductions and notes, as *Plato: The Last Days of Socrates: Euthyphro, Apology, Crito, Phaedo*. London, England: Penguin Books, 2010, pp. 66–82.

Tredennick, Hugh. "Socrates in Prison: Crito." English translation of the dialogue, with an introduction and notes, appearing as part of his rendition of *Plato: The Last Days of Socrates: Euthyphro, The Apology, Crito, Phaedo*. London, England: Penguin Books, 1954. New edition, with corrections, published in 1959. Reprinted, with revisions, in 1969, pp. 79–96. Later reissued in a revised translation, including new introduction and notes, all by Harold Tarrant, published in 1993. Tredennick's translation was also published in the Bollingen edition of *The Collected Dialogues of Plato: Including the Letters*. Edited by Edith Hamilton and Huntington Cairns. Princeton, New Jersey: Princeton University Press, 1961, pp. 27–39.

Tyler, William Seymour. *Plato's Apology and Crito; With Notes*. Greek text with extensive English commentary. New York, N.Y.: D. Appleton and Company, 1860. Revised edition, with the assistance of Henry Mather Tyler, published in 1887.

2.3.2. Commentaries

Brickhouse, Thomas C., and Nicholas D. Smith. "Socrates and Obedience to the Law," *Apeiron*, 18:1 (June 1984), pp. 10–18. Reprinted as chapter 9 of *Plato's Euthyphro, Apology, and Crito: Critical Essays*. Edited by Rachana Kamtekar. Lanham, Maryland: Rowman & Littlefield, 2005, pp. 163–174. Originates in a paper presented at assemblies of various organizations, including the Tennessee Philosophical Association (1980), the Southern Society for Philosophy and Psychology (1981), and the Western Division of the American Philosophical Association (1981).

Brickhouse, Thomas C., and Nicholas D. Smith. "Socrates and the Laws of Athens," *Philosophy Compass*, 1:6 (2006), pp. 564–570.

Colaiaco, James A. *Socrates Against Athens: Philosophy on Trial*. New York, N.Y., and London, England: Routledge, 2001.

Colson, Darrel D. "*Crito* 51a–c: To What Does Socrates Owe Obedience?" *Phronesis*, 34:1 (1989), pp. 27–55.

Congleton, Ann. "Two Kinds of Lawlessness: Plato's *Crito*," *Political Theory*, 2:4 (November 1974), pp. 432–446.

D'Amato, Anthony. "Obligation to Obey the Law: A Study of the Death of Socrates," *Southern California Law Review*, 49 (1975–1976), pp. 1079–1108.

Euben, J. Peter. "Philosophy and Politics in Plato's *Crito*," *Political Theory*, 6:2 (May 1978), pp. 149–172.

Hall, Matthew R. "Guilty but Civilly Disobedient: Reconciling Civil Disobedience and the Rule of Law," *Cardozo Law Review*, 28:5 (2007), pp. 2083–2132.

Hanna, Nathan. "Socrates and Superiority," *The Southern Journal of Philosophy*, 45:2 (Summer 2007), pp. 251–268.

Kraut, Richard. *Socrates and the State*. Princeton, New Jersey: Princeton University Press, 1984.

Kraut, Richard. "Plato's *Apology* and *Crito*: Two Recent Studies," *Ethics*, 91:4 (July 1981), pp. 651–664.

Kraut, Richard. "Reply to Clifford Orwin." In *Platonic Writings, Platonic Readings*. Edited by Charles L. Griswold, Jr. New York, N.Y.: Routledge, Chapman & Hall, 1988, pp. 177–182.

Martin, Rex. "Socrates on Disobedience to Law," *The Review of Metaphysics*, 24:1 (September 1970), pp. 21–38.

Momeyer, Richard W. "Socrates on Obedience and Disobedience to the Law," *Philosophy Research Archives*, 8 (1982), pp. 21–53.

Orwin, Clifford. "Liberalizing the *Crito*: Richard Kraut on Socrates and the State." In *Platonic Writings, Platonic Readings*. Edited by Charles L. Griswold, Jr. New York, N.Y.: Routledge, Chapman & Hall, 1988, pp. 171–176.

Penner, Terry. "Two Notes on the *Crito*: The Impotence of the Many, and 'Persuade or Obey,'" *The Classical Quarterly*, 47:1 (1997), pp. 153–166.

Rosen, Frederick. "Obligation and Friendship in Plato's *Crito*," *Political Theory*, 1:3 (August 1973), pp. 307–316.

Steadman, Geoffrey D. "The Unity of Plato's *Crito*," *The Classical Journal*, 101:4 (April–May 2006), pp. 361–382.

Stokes, Michael C. *Dialectic in Action: An Examination of Plato's Crito.* Swansea, Wales: Classical Press of Wales, 2005.

Weinrib, Ernest J. "Obedience to the Law in Plato's *Crito*," *American Journal of Jurisprudence*, 27 (1982), pp. 85–108.

Weiss, Roslyn. *Socrates Dissatisfied: An Analysis of Plato's Crito.* New York, N.Y.: Oxford University Press, 1998.

Woozley, Anthony Douglas. *Law and Obedience: The Arguments of Plato's Crito.* Also contains an English translation of the dialogue. Chapel Hill, North Carolina: University of North Carolina Press, 1979.

Young, Gary. "Socrates and Obedience," *Phronesis*, 19:1 (1974), pp. 1–29.

2.4. Phaedo

2.4.1. Editions

Archer-Hind, Richard Dacre. *The Phaedo of Plato.* Greek text edited with introduction, notes, and appendices. London, England: Macmillan and Company, 1883. Second edition released in 1894 by the same publisher.

Bluck, Richard Stanley. *Plato's Phaedo.* Translated into English, with introduction, notes, and appendices. London, England: Routledge & Kegan Paul, 1955.

Brann, Eva, Peter Kalkavage, and Eric Salem. *Plato's Phaedo.* English translation of the dialogue, with introduction and glossary. Focus Philosophical Library. Newburyport, Massachusetts: Focus Publishing, R. Pullins Co., 1998.

Burnet, John. *Plato's Phaedo.* Greek text edited with introduction and notes. Oxford, England: Oxford University Press, 1911. Burnet's text was originally published as part of the first volume of *Platonis Opera*, dedicated to eight dialogues: *Euthyphro, Apologia Socratis, Crito, Phaedo, Cratylus, Theaetetus, Sophista, Politicus* [*Statesman*]. Edited by John Burnet. Oxford Classical Texts. Oxford, England: Oxford University Press, 1900. The second edition of the larger work was released by the same publisher in 1922.

Church, Frederick John. "Phaedo." English translation of the dialogue, introduced as part of his larger contribution released as *The Trial and Death of Socrates; Being the Euthyphron, Apology, Crito, and Phaedo of Plato.* London, England: Macmillan and Company, 1880. Several reprints, both as a whole and in parts, with the *Phaedo* available either by itself in its entirety or through the death scene bundled up in a collection with the other three dialogues. For example, the full text of the *Phaedo* was issued separately as *Plato: Phaedo.* Edited, with an introduction, by Fulton H. Anderson. New York, N.Y.: Macmillan Publishing Company, 1951. Subsequently, the original collection was reissued with the *Phaedo* stripped down to the death scene: *Plato: Euthyphro, Apology, Crito; With the Death Scene from the Phaedo.* Edited, with an introduction, by Robert D. Cummings. New York, N.Y.: Macmillan Publishing Company, 1956.

Cooper, Lane. "Phaedo." Translated into English, with an introduction and prefatory notes, as part of his rendition of *Plato on the Trial and Death of Socrates: Euthyphro, Apology, Crito, Phaedo.* Ithaca, New York: Cornell University Press, 1941.

Duke, E. A., W. F. Hicken, W. S. M. Nicoll, D. B. Robinson, and J. C. G. Strachan. "Phaedo." Greek text with critical apparatus, appearing as part of the first volume of the New Edition of *Platonis Opera,* the collected works of Plato in the Oxford Classical Texts Series. The volume consists of eight dialogues: *Euthyphro,*

Apologia, Crito, Phaedo, Cratylus, Theaetetus, Sophista, Politicus [*Statesman*]. Oxford, England: Oxford University Press, 1995.

Fowler, Harold North. "Phaedo." English translation of the dialogue, with an introduction and parallel Greek text, appearing as part of the first volume of Plato's collected works in twelve volumes in the Loeb Classical Library. Cambridge, Massachusetts: Harvard University Press, 1914, pp. 193–403.

Gallop, David. *Plato: Phaedo*. English translation with extensive notes. Clarendon Plato Series. Oxford, England: Clarendon Press, 1975. Reprinted with corrections: 1983, 1986, 1988. Gallop's text was later issued, with condensed notes, in the World's Classics Series. Oxford, England: Oxford University Press, 1993.

Griffith, Tom. "Phaedo." English rendition of the dialogue, constituting part of his collection of translations published together, with a general introduction by Jane O'Grady, as *Plato: Symposium and the Death of Socrates*. Wordsworth Classics of World Literature. Hertfordshire, England: Wordsworth Editions Limited, 1997, pp. 133–211.

Grube, George Maximilian Anthony. "Phaedo." An English rendition of the final scene of the dialogue first appeared as part of a collection of some of his other translations, published together as *The Trial and Death of Socrates: Euthyphro, Apology, Crito, Death Scene from Phaedo*. Indianapolis, Indiana: Hackett Publishing Company, 1975. The collection became available in a second edition, with corrections, in 1980, and in a third, incorporating revisions by John Madison Cooper, in 2000. Grube's first full translation of the *Phaedo* emerged as an independent volume released in 1977 as a second edition by the same publisher. His translation of the *Phaedo* also appeared in the publisher's *Five Dialogues: Euthyphro, Apology, Crito, Meno, Phaedo*. Indianapolis, Indiana: Hackett Publishing Company, 1981. This slightly larger collection was reissued in a second edition, incorporating revisions by John Madison Cooper, in 2002. Grube's rendition of the *Phaedo* here (together with his translations of the other four dialogues in the corresponding volumes) constitutes part of the definitive collection released by the same publisher: *Plato: Complete Works*. Edited, with an introduction and notes, by John Madison Cooper. Indianapolis, Indiana: Hackett Publishing Company, 1997, pp. 49–100.

Hackforth, Reginald. *Plato's Phaedo*. English translation of the dialogue, with introduction and commentary. Cambridge, England: Cambridge University Press, 1955.

Jowett, Benjamin. "Phaedo." English translation of the dialogue, introduced as part of the second volume of his renditions offered collectively as *The Works of Plato*. Oxford, England: Clarendon Press, 1871. The second edition of the collection was published in 1875, the third in 1892, both during the translator's lifetime, while the fourth appeared posthumously in 1953. Numerous reprints have been following in various forms, especially in inexpensive editions, for example, *Plato: Six Great Dialogues: Apology, Crito, Phaedo, Phaedrus, Symposium, The Republic*. Mineola, New York: Dover Publications, 2007. All Jowett texts are freely available online.

Rowe, Christopher J. *Plato: Phaedo*. Greek text edited with an introduction and commentary. Cambridge, England: Cambridge University Press, 1993.

Rowe, Christopher J. "Phaedo." English rendition of the dialogue, constituting part of his collection of translations published together, with introductions and notes, as *Plato: The Last Days of Socrates: Euthyphro, Apology, Crito, Phaedo*. London, England: Penguin Books, 2010, pp. 87–170.

Tredennick, Hugh. "The Last Conversation: Phaedo." English translation of the dialogue, with an introduction and notes, appearing as part of his rendition of *Plato: The Last Days of Socrates: Euthyphro, The Apology, Crito, Phaedo*. London, England: Penguin

Books, 1954. New edition, with corrections, published in 1959. Reprinted, with revisions, in 1969, pp. 99–183. Later reissued in a revised translation, including new introduction and notes, all by Harold Tarrant, published in 1993. Tredennick's translation was also published in the Bollingen edition of *The Collected Dialogues of Plato: Including the Letters*. Edited by Edith Hamilton and Huntington Cairns. Princeton, New Jersey: Princeton University Press, 1961, pp. 40–98.

2.4.2. Commentaries

Ahrensdorf, Peter J. *The Death of Socrates and the Life of Philosophy: An Interpretation of Plato's Phaedo*. Albany, New York: State University of New York Press, 1995.
Bedu-Addo, J. T. "The Role of the Hypothetical Method in the *Phaedo*," *Phronesis*, 24:2 (1979), pp. 111–132.
Bloch, Enid. "Hemlock Poisoning and the Death of Socrates: Did Plato Tell the Truth?" In *The Trial and Execution of Socrates: Sources and Controversies*. Edited by Thomas C. Brickhouse and Nicholas D. Smith. Oxford, England: Oxford University Press, 2002, pp. 255–278.
Bluck, Richard Stanley. "ὑποθέσεις in the *Phaedo* and Platonic Dialectic," *Phronesis*, 2:1 (1957), pp. 21–31.
Bluck, Richard Stanley. "Forms as Standards," *Phronesis*, 2:2 (1957), pp. 115–127.
Bluck, Richard Stanley. "Plato's Form of Equal," *Phronesis*, 4:1 (1959), pp. 5–11.
Bostock, David. *Plato's Phaedo*. Oxford, England: Oxford University Press, 1986.
Brentlinger, John. "Incomplete Predicates and the Two-World Theory of the *Phaedo*," *Phronesis*, 17:1 (1972), pp. 61–79.
Burge, Evan Laurie. "The Ideas as Aitiai in the *Phaedo*," *Phronesis*, 16:1 (1971), pp. 1–13.
Burger, Ronna. *The Phaedo: A Platonic Labyrinth*. New Haven, Connecticut: Yale University Press, 1984.
Calder, William Musgrave, III. "The Spherical Earth in Plato's *Phaedo*," *Phronesis*, 3:2 (1958), pp. 121–125.
Dorter, Kenneth. *Plato's Phaedo: An Interpretation*. Toronto, Canada: University of Toronto Press, 1982.
Dorter, Kenneth. "Equality, Recollection and Purification," *Phronesis*, 17:3 (1972), pp. 198–218.
Frede, Dorothea. "The Final Proof of the Immortality of the Soul in Plato's *Phaedo* 102a–107a," *Phronesis*, 23:1 (1978), pp. 27–41.
Gallop, David. "Plato's 'Cyclical Argument' Recycled," *Phronesis*, 27:3 (1982), pp. 207–222.
Gentzler, Jyl. "'Sumphônein' in Plato's *Phaedo*," *Phronesis*, 36:3 (1991), pp. 265–276.
Gilead, Amihud. *Platonic Odyssey: Philosophical-Literary Inquiry into the Phaedo*. Amsterdam, Netherlands; Atlanta, Georgia: Editions Rodopi B.V., 1994.
Gill, Christopher. "The Death of Socrates," *The Classical Quarterly* (New Series), 23:1 (1973), pp. 25–28. Reprinted in *The Trial and Execution of Socrates: Sources and Controversies*. Edited by Thomas C. Brickhouse and Nicholas D. Smith. Oxford, England: Oxford University Press, 2002, pp. 251–255.
Gosling, Justin Cyril Bertrand. "Similarity in *Phaedo* 73b Seq." *Phronesis*, 10:2 (1965), pp. 151–161.
Graves, Bonita M., G. M. Graves, A. K. Tsakopoulos, and J. P. Anton. "Hemlock Poisoning: Twentieth Century Scientific Light Shed on the Death of Socrates." In *The Philosophy of Socrates*. Edited by K. J. Boudouris (Kōnstantinos Iōannou

Voudourēs). Athens, Greece: International Center for Greek Philosophy and Culture, 1991, pp. 156–168.

Haynes, Prichard P. "The Form Equality, as a Set of Equals: *Phaedo* 74b–c," *Phronesis*, 9:1 (1964), pp. 17–26.

Huby, Pamela M. "*Phaedo* 99d–102a," *Phronesis*, 4:1 (1959), pp. 12–14.

Keyt, David. "The Fallacies in *Phaedo* 102a–107b," *Phronesis*, 8:2 (1963), pp. 167–172.

McPherran, Mark L. "Matthen on Castañeda and Plato's Treatment of Relational Statements in the *Phaedo*," *Phronesis*, 28:3 (1983), pp. 298–306.

Matthen, Mohan. "Plato's Treatment of Relational Statements in the *Phaedo*," *Phronesis*, 27:1 (1982), pp. 90–100.

Matthen, Mohan. "Relationality in Plato's Metaphysics: Reply to McPherran," *Phronesis*, 29:3 (1984), pp. 304–312.

Matthews, Gareth B., and Thomas A. Blackson. "Causes in the *Phaedo*," *Synthese*, 79:3 (June 1989), pp. 581–591.

Mills, K. W. "Plato's *Phaedo* 74b7–c6," *Phronesis*, 2:2 (1957), pp. 128–147, and *Phronesis*, 3:1 (1958), pp. 40–58.

Morgan, Michael L. "Sense-Perception and Recollection in the *Phaedo*," *Phronesis*, 29:3 (1984), pp. 237–251.

Morris, Michael. "Socrates' Last Argument," *Phronesis*, 30:3 (1985), pp. 223–248.

Morrison, J. S. "The Shape of the Earth in Plato's *Phaedo*," *Phronesis*, 4:2 (1959), pp. 101–119.

Ober, William. "Did Socrates Die of Hemlock Poisoning?" *New York State Journal of Medicine*, 77 (1977), pp. 254–258.

Peterson, Sandra Lynne. "An Authentically Socratic Conclusion in Plato's *Phaedo*: Socrates' Debt to Asclepius." In *Desire, Identity, and Existence: Essays in Honor of T. M. Penner*. Kelowna, B.C., Canada: Academic Printing & Publishing, 2003, pp. 33–52.

Plass, Paul. "Socrates' Method of Hypothesis in the *Phaedo*," *Phronesis*, 5:2 (1960), pp. 103–115.

Reeve, Michael D. "Socrates's Reply to Cebes in Plato's *Phaedo*," *Phronesis*, 20:3 (1975), pp. 199–208.

Rist, John M. "Equals and Intermediates in Plato," *Phronesis*, 9:1 (1964), pp. 27–37.

Rosenmeyer, Thomas G. "The Shape of the Earth in the *Phaedo*: A Rejoinder," *Phronesis*, 4:1 (1959), pp. 71–72.

Schiller, Jerome P. "*Phaedo* 104–105: Is the Soul a Form?" *Phronesis*, 12:1 (1967), pp. 50–58.

Shipton, Kirsty M. W. "A Good Second-Best: *Phaedo* 99b ff." *Phronesis*, 24:1 (1979), pp. 33–53.

Stough, Charlotte L. "Forms and Explanation in the *Phaedo*," *Phronesis*, 21:1 (1976), pp. 1–30.

Vlastos, Gregory. "Reasons and Causes in the *Phaedo*," *The Philosophical Review*, 78:3 (July 1969), pp. 291–325.

Wedin, Michael V. "αὐτὰ τὰ ἴσα and the Argument at *Phaedo* 74b7–c5," *Phronesis*, 22:3 (1977), pp. 191–205.

2.5. Republic

2.5.1. Editions

Adam, James. *The Republic of Plato*. Greek text, edited with critical notes, commentary, and appendices. Two volumes, the first containing the first five books, and, the second, the last five and indexes. Cambridge, England: Cambridge University Press, 1902. Not a translation, but a Greek edition accompanied by extensive English commentary, both withstanding the test of time. Preceded by a text only edition (without commentary) appearing through the same publisher in 1897. Second edition, with an introduction by D. A. Rees, issued, again, by the same publisher, in 1963.

Allen, Reginald E. *The Republic*. English translation of the dialogue, with introductory, exegetical, and critical remarks. New Haven, Connecticut: Yale University Press, 2006.

Bloom, Allan David. *The Republic of Plato*. English translation of the dialogue, with notes, an interpretive essay, and a new introduction. New York, N.Y. Basic Books, 1968. Second edition in 1991.

Cornford, Francis Macdonald. *The Republic of Plato*. English translation of the dialogue, with introduction and notes. Oxford, England: Oxford University Press, 1941.

Davies, John Llewelyn, and David James Vaughan. *Republic*. English translation of the dialogue. Hertfordshire, England: Wordsworth Editions Limited, 1997.

Griffith, Tom. *Plato: The Republic*. Edited by Giovanni (John) R. F. Ferrari. English translation of the dialogue. Cambridge Texts in the History of Political Thought. Cambridge, England: Cambridge University Press, 2000.

Grube, George Maximilian Anthony. *Plato: Republic*. English translation of the dialogue. Indianapolis, Indiana: Hackett Publishing Company, 1974. Second edition incorporates revisions by Charles David Chanel Reeve: Indianapolis, Indiana: Hackett Publishing Company, 1992. The text of the second edition, as revised by Reeve, also appears in the definitive collection released by the same publisher: *Plato: Complete Works*. Edited, with an introduction and notes, by John Madison Cooper. Indianapolis, Indiana: Hackett Publishing Company, 1997, pp. 971–1223.

Jowett, Benjamin. "The Republic." English translation of the dialogue, introduced as part of the second volume of his renditions offered collectively as *The Works of Plato*. Oxford, England: Clarendon Press, 1871. The second edition of the collection was published in 1875, the third in 1892, both during the translator's lifetime, while the fourth appeared posthumously in 1953. The *Republic* was also issued separately from the collection in a third edition (so numbered because it follows the first two and precedes the third of the collection) released as *The Republic of Plato*. Translated into English, with introduction, analysis, marginal analysis, and index. Oxford, England: Clarendon Press, 1888. Numerous reprints, both of the collection and of the *Republic*, have been following in various forms, especially in inexpensive editions, for example, *Plato: Six Great Dialogues: Apology, Crito, Phaedo, Phaedrus, Symposium, The Republic*. Mineola, New York: Dover Publications, 2007. All Jowett texts are freely available online.

Lee, Henry Desmond Pritchard. *Plato: The Republic*. English translation of the dialogue. London, England: Penguin Books, 1955. Second edition, with revisions, in 1974. Reprinted, with additional revisions, in 1987. Third edition, with an introduction by Melissa Lane, in 2007.

Lindsay, Alexander Dunlop. *The Republic of Plato*. English translation with introduction. London, England: J. M. Dent & Co., 1906. Second edition published in 1908 and reprinted, with corrections, in 1910 by J. M. Dent & Sons. Third edition released, with corrections and enlarged introduction, in 1923 by the same publisher. Issued in 1935 as the publisher's standard edition of the *Republic* in its classics series known as Everyman's Library, replacing the Spens text used in that series since its inception in 1906. Released in a new edition, still in Everyman's Library, in 1976 as *Plato: The Republic*, edited by Renford Bambrough, with an introduction and explanatory notes. Reprinted in 1992, with a new introduction by Alexander Nehamas and a bibliography and chronology.

Sachs, Joe. *Plato: Republic*. English translation of the dialogue. Focus Philosophical Library. Newburyport, Massachusetts: Focus Publishing, R. Pullins Co., 2007.

Shorey, Paul. *Plato: The Republic*. Two volumes. Greek text, with parallel English translation, constituting the sixth (1930) and seventh (1935) volumes of Plato's collected works in twelve volumes in the Loeb Classical Library. Cambridge, Massachusetts: Harvard University Press, 1930–1935. Shorey's translation also appears in the Bollingen edition of *The Collected Dialogues of Plato: Including the Letters*. Edited by Edith Hamilton and Huntington Cairns. Princeton, New Jersey: Princeton University Press, 1961, pp. 575–844.

Slings, Simon Roelof. *Platonis Respublica*. Greek text, edited with critical apparatus. Standard critical edition replacing the previous entry for the *Republic* (1902) in the Oxford Classical Texts Series. Second item to appear in the *Platonis Opera* commissioned to supersede the 1900–1907 collection edited by John Burnet. Oxford, England: Oxford University Press, 2003.

Spens, Harry. *The Republic of Plato: In Ten Books*. English translation with a preliminary discourse, by the translator, on the philosophy of the ancients. Glasgow, Scotland: Robert & Andrew Foulis, 1763. Celebrated as the first English edition of the dialogue. Included in 1906 as a flagship volume (No. 64), with an introduction by Richard Garnett, in Everyman's Library, inaugurated that year. London, England: J. M. Dent & Co., 1906. Reprinted several times in the same series, by J. M. Dent & Sons, until its replacement in 1935 by the Lindsay rendition, originally published in 1906.

Waterfield, Robin. *Plato: Republic*. English translation of the dialogue. Oxford, England: Oxford University Press, 1993.

2.5.2. Commentaries

Annas, Julia Elizabeth. *An Introduction to Plato's Republic*. Oxford, England: Oxford University Press, 1981.

Benardete, Seth. *Socrates' Second Sailing: On Plato's Republic*. Chicago, Illinois: University of Chicago Press, 1989.

Blackburn, Simon. *Plato's Republic: A Biography*. Books That Changed the World. New York, N.Y.: Grove/Atlantic, 2007.

Brown, Eric Alan. "A Defense of Plato's Argument for the Immortality of the Soul at *Republic* X 608c–611a," *Apeiron*, 30 (1997), pp. 211–238. Reprinted in *Essays on Plato's Psychology*. Edited by Ellen Wagner. Lanham, Maryland: Lexington Books, 2001, pp. 297–322.

Craig, Leon Harold. *The War Lover: A Study of Plato's Republic*. Toronto, Canada: University of Toronto Press, 1994.

Cross, Robert Craigie, and Anthony Douglas Woozley. *Plato's Republic: A Philosophical Commentary*. London, England: Macmillan; New York, N.Y.: St. Martin's Press, 1964.

Ferrari, Giovanni (John) R. F. *City and Soul in Plato's Republic*. Sankt Augustin, Germany: Academia Verlag, 2003. Reissued in Chicago, Illinois: University of Chicago Press, 2005.

Ferrari, Giovanni (John) R. F., editor. *The Cambridge Companion to Plato's Republic*. Cambridge, England: Cambridge University Press, 2007.

Howland, Jacob. *The Republic: The Odyssey of Philosophy*. Twayne's Masterwork Studies. New York, N.Y.: Twayne Publishers, 1993. Reissued in Philadelphia, Pennsylvania: Paul Dry Books, 2004.

Kahn, Charles H. "Proleptic Composition in the *Republic*, or Why Book 1 Was Never a Separate Dialogue," *The Classical Quarterly* (New Series), 43:1 (1993), pp. 131–142.

Kraut, Richard, editor. *Plato's Republic: Critical Essays*. Lanham, Maryland: Rowman & Littlefield Publishers, 1997.

Murphy, Neville Richard. *The Interpretation of Plato's Republic*. Oxford, England: Clarendon Press, 1951.

Nails, Debra. "The Dramatic Date of Plato's *Republic*," *The Classical Journal*, 93:4 (April–May 1998), pp. 383–396.

Nettleship, Richard Lewis. "The Theory of Education in Plato's *Republic*." Third essay in *Hellenica: A Collection of Essays on Greek Poetry, Philosophy, History and Religion*. Edited by Evelyn Abbott. London, England: Rivingtons, 1880, pp. 61–165. Reissued separately in book form as *The Theory of Education in the Republic of Plato*. Edited by William Bishop Owen. Chicago, Illinois: University of Chicago Press, 1906.

Nettleship, Richard Lewis. *Lectures on the Republic of Plato*. London, England: Macmillan and Company, 1901. Originally published as the second of two volumes of *Philosophical Lectures and Remains of Richard Lewis Nettleship*, appearing there with the title "Lectures on Plato's 'Republic.'" Edited, with a biographical sketch, by Andrew Cecil Bradley and Godfrey Rathbone Benson. London, England: Macmillan and Company, 1897.

Pappas, Nickolas. *Routledge Philosophy Guidebook to Plato and the Republic*. New York, N.Y.: Routledge, 1995. Second edition in 2003.

Reeve, Charles David Chanel. *Philosopher-Kings: The Argument of Plato's Republic*. Princeton, New Jersey: Princeton University Press, 1988. Reprinted in Indianapolis, Indiana: Hackett Publishing Company, 2006.

Rice, Daryl H. *A Guide to Plato's Republic*. Oxford, England: Oxford University Press, 1998.

Rosen, Stanley. *Plato's Republic: A Study*. New Haven, Connecticut: Yale University Press, 2005.

Santas, Gerasimos Xenophon, editor. *The Blackwell Guide to Plato's Republic*. Malden, Massachusetts: Blackwell Publishing, 2006.

Thesleff, Holger. "The Early Version of Plato's *Republic*," *Arctos*, 31 (1997), pp. 149–174.

White, Nicholas P. *A Companion to Plato's Republic*. Indianapolis, Indiana: Hackett Publishing Company, 1979.

2.6. Letters

Bury, Robert Gregg. "Epistles." English translation of the letters, with an introduction and parallel Greek text, appearing as part of the ninth volume of Plato's collected works in twelve volumes in the Loeb Classical Library. Cambridge, Massachusetts: Harvard University Press, 1929, pp. 383–627.

Morrow, Glenn Raymond. "Letters." English translation of the letters, issued as part of Plato's collected works edited by John Madison Cooper and known as the Hackett edition: *Plato: Complete Works*. Indianapolis, Indiana: Hackett Publishing Company, 1997, pp. 1634–1676.

Post, Levi Arnold. *Thirteen Epistles of Plato*. English translation with introduction and notes. Oxford, England: Clarendon Press, 1925. The bare translation later appears as "Letters" in the Bollingen edition of *The Collected Dialogues of Plato: Including the Letters*. Edited by Edith Hamilton and Huntington Cairns. Princeton, New Jersey: Princeton University Press, 1961, pp. 1560–1606.

3. Classical Sources

Aelian (Claudius Aelianus). *Varia Historia*. Greek text with facing English translation available in the Loeb Classical Library as *Aelian: Historical Miscellany*. Translated by Nigel G. Wilson. Cambridge, Massachusetts: Harvard University Press, 1997.

Aeschylus. *Agamemnon*. Greek text with facing English translation available in the Loeb Classical Library as part of *Aeschylus: Oresteia: Agamemnon. Libation-Bearers. Eumenides*. Edited and translated by Alan H. Sommerstein. Cambridge, Massachusetts: Harvard University Press, 2009.

Anonymous. *Life of Plato*. An ancient biographical account that still remains rather obscure, with print availability concentrated in the middle of the nineteenth century. Published as part of *Biographoi: Vitarum Scriptores Graeci Minores*. Edited by Anton Westermann. Brunsvigae (Braunschweig), Germany: Sumptum Fecit Georgius Westermann, 1845, pp. 388–396. Also available in a prestigious nineteenth-century edition of the *Lives* of Diogenes Laërtius: *Diogenis Laertii de Clarorum Philosophorum Vitis, Dogmatibus et Apophthegmatibus Libri Decem*. Edited by Carel Gabriel Cobet. Paris, France: Ambroise Firmin Didot, 1850. Considered the source of certain biographical details in St. Augustine of Hippo (*De Civitate Dei* 8.11; *De Doctrina Christiana* 2.28.43) and in Photius (*Bibliotheca* 249, a codex actually on the life of Pythagoras).

Apollodorus of Athens. *Bibliotheca*. Compendium of Greek mythology historically attributed to Apollodorus (born c. 180 BC), but long confirmed to contain references placing it well past his lifetime, and now believed to have been compiled roughly three centuries later. Citation alternatives avoiding the traditional anachronism include ascription to Pseudo-Apollodorus as well as direct reference to the work without mention of author. Translated into English as *The Library*. Greek text with parallel English translation by Sir James George Frazer. Two volumes. Volume 1: Books 1–3.9. Volume 2: Book 3.10–16 and Epitome. Loeb Classical Library. Cambridge, Massachusetts: Harvard University Press; London, England: William Heinemann, 1921. Reprinted numerous times, including: 1939; 1954; 1956; 1961; 1963; 1976; 2002.

Apollodorus of Athens. *Chronicle* (*Chronika* or Χρονικά). A lost history of the Greek world, covering more than a full millennium from the fall of Troy (no later than the twelfth century before Christ, according to tradition) to the time of the author (born c. 180 BC). Based on the work of Eratosthenes of Cyrene (c. 285–194 BC), whose *Chronographiai*, also lost, likewise goes back to the fall of Troy but ends with the death (323 BC) of Alexander the Great. Apollodorus extends the timeline a couple of centuries forward. The *Chronicle* is composed in verse, specifically, in iambic trimeter, to facilitate memorization. Widely popular in its day, and for quite some time beyond, it is now available only in fragments. Dates are given in reference to the office terms of the Athenian archons, possible to track down even today, and done so famously by Felix Jacoby in *Apollodors Chronik: Eine Sammlung der Fragmente*. Philologische Untersuchungen 16. Berlin, Germany: Weidmannsche Buchhandlung, 1902. This is still the standard critical edition of the fragmentary remains.

Apuleius (Lucius Apuleius Platonicus = Lucius Apuleius Madaurensis). *De Platone et Eius Dogmate* (*On Plato and His Doctrine*). An overview in Latin of Plato's physics (natural philosophy), ethics (moral philosophy), and logic (concerning interpretation, or the categorical syllogism), laid out in three separate "books," with a biographical account serving as the introduction to the first book. English translation available as part of *The Metamorphosis, or Golden Ass, and Philosophical Works, of Apuleius*. Edited and translated by Thomas Taylor. London, England: Robert Triphook and Thomas Rodd, 1822. French translation, with running Latin text on facing pages, available as part of *Opuscules Philosophiques [Du Dieu de Socrate; Platon et sa Doctrine; Du Monde] et Fragments*: Edited and translated by Jean Beaujeu. Collection des Universités de France (="Collection Budé") Série Latine. Publiée sous le patronage de l'Association Guillaume Budé. Paris, France: Société d'Édition Les Belles Lettres, 1973. Second edition published in 2002.

Aristophanes. *Clouds*. Greek text edited by Kenneth James Dover with an introduction and commentary in English. Oxford, England: Clarendon Press, 1968. Numerous translations, including Jeffrey Henderson's rendition, with introduction and notes, appearing in the Focus Classical Library as *Aristophanes: Clouds*. Newburyport, Massachusetts: Focus Publishing, R. Pullins Company, 1992. Later bundled with Henderson's translations of *Wasps* and *Peace*, together constituting the second of four volumes of the plays of Aristophanes appearing in the Loeb Classical Library. Greek text with parallel English translation. Cambridge, Massachusetts: Harvard University Press, 1998.

Aristotle. *Corpus Aristotelicum*. The standard critical edition is *Aristotelis Opera: Edidit Academia Regia Borussica*. Five volumes. The Greek text of the complete works of Aristotle, prepared, under the general editorship of Immanuel Bekker, by the Prussian Academy of Sciences. Berlin, Germany: Georg Reimer, 1831–1870.

Aristotle. *Fragments*. Although the fragments are, in a sense, an integral part of the *Corpus Aristotelicum*, and are, in fact, included in the Prussian Academy's collection of Aristotle's works, the version there has long been superseded by a newer edition outside that collection. The standard critical edition has always been the compilation by Valentin Rose, but that book has evolved over time, joining the Prussian Academy collection only during a part of its natural life cycle, or, perhaps more accurately, growing beyond its instantiation there. Bearing the title *Aristoteles Pseudepigraphus*, clearly indicating Rose's contention that the fragments are all spurious, the first edition immediately filled a need in scholarship. (Leipzig, Germany: B. G. Teubner, 1863.) Rose later expanded this work for inclusion in the

Prussian Academy's *Aristotelis Opera*, where it was published as part of the fifth volume. (Berlin, Germany: Georg Reimer, 1870.) He subsequently enlarged it even further, securing it a place in the Bibliotheca Scriptorum Graecorum et Romanorum Teubneriana. (Leipzig, Germany: B. G. Teubner, 1886.) Constituting the third edition, this remains the authoritative source in the citation of fragments, though it is liable to be replaced by more recent initiatives. Citations usually give the fragment number in Arabic numerals, preceded by the abbreviation "fr." plus a single space, and followed by a single space plus the name "Rose" (or, in lieu of "Rose," a capital "R" with a superscript "3" denoting the third edition).

Aristotle. *Collected Works in English*. The standard English edition of the Aristotelian corpus is *The Complete Works of Aristotle: The Revised Oxford Translation*. Two volumes. Edited by Jonathan Barnes. Princeton, New Jersey: Princeton University Press, 1984. Originally published in twelve volumes, known collectively as The Oxford Translation of Aristotle, and titled *The Works of Aristotle*. Edited by John Alexander Smith and William David Ross. Oxford, England: Clarendon Press, 1908–1952. The original edition also appeared, with the same title, as volumes 8 and 9 of the Great Books of the Western World, a series managed by the University of Chicago, under the general editorship of Robert Maynard Hutchins. Chicago, Illinois: Encyclopaedia Britannica, 1952. Another common translation is *The Basic Works of Aristotle*. Edited, with an introduction, by Richard McKeon. New York, N.Y.: Random House, 1941. Reissued with an introduction by C. D. C. Reeve. New York, N.Y.: Modern Library, 2001. As always, the Loeb Classical Library presents a respectable alternative: Greek text with parallel English translation. Twenty-three volumes. Cambridge, Massachusetts: Harvard University Press, 1926–2002. Contents, with publication dates of subsequent editions listed after a slash following that of the original: Volume 1 (1938): *Categories. On Interpretation. Prior Analytics*. Translated by Harold P. Cooke and Hugh Tredennick. Volume 2 (1930): *Posterior Analytics. Topica*. Translated by Hugh Tredennick and E. S. Forster. Volume 3 (1955): *On Sophistical Refutations. On Coming-to-Be and Passing Away. On the Cosmos*. Translated by E. S. Forster and D. J. Furley. Volume 4 (1929): *Physics*, Books 1–4. Translated by P. H. Wicksteed and F. M. Cornford. Volume 5 (1934): *Physics*, Books 5–8. Translated by P. H. Wicksteed and F. M. Cornford. Volume 6 (1939): *On the Heavens*. Translated by W. K. C. Guthrie. Volume 7 (1952): *Meteorologica*. Translated by H. D. P. Lee. Volume 8 (1936/1957): *On the Soul. Parva Naturalia. On Breath*. Translated by W. S. Hett. Volume 9 (1965): *History of Animals*, Books 1–3. Translated by A. L. Peck. Volume 10 (1957/2002): *History of Animals*, Books 4–6. Translated by A. L. Peck. Volume 11 (1970/1991): *History of Animals*, Books 7–10. Translated by D. M. Balme. Volume 12 (1937): *Parts of Animals. Movement of Animals. Progression of Animals*. Translated by A. L. Peck and E. S. Forster. Volume 13 (1942): *Generation of Animals*. Translated by A. L. Peck. Volume 14 (1936): *Minor Works. On Colours. On Things Heard. Physiognomics. On Plants. On Marvellous Things Heard. Mechanical Problems. On Indivisible Lines. The Situations and Names of Winds. On Melissus, Xenophanes, and Gorgias*. Translated by W. S. Hett. Volume 15 (1936): *Problems*, Books 1–21. Translated by W. S. Hett. Volume 16 (1937): *Problems*, Books 22–38. *Rhetorica ad Alexandrum*. Translated by W. S. Hett and Harris Rackham. Volume 17 (1933): *Metaphysics*, Books 1–9. Translated by Hugh Tredennick. Volume 18 (1935): *Metaphysics*, Books 10–14. *Oeconomica. Magna Moralia*. Translated by Hugh

Tredennick and G. Cyril Armstrong. Volume 19 (1926): *Nicomachean Ethics*. Translated by Harris Rackham. Volume 20 (1935/1981): *Athenian Constitution. Eudemian Ethics. Virtues and Vices*. Translated by Harris Rackham. Volume 21 (1932): *Politics*. Translated by Harris Rackham. Volume 22 (1926): *The Art of Rhetoric*. Translated by J. H. Freese. Volume 23 (1927/1995): *Aristotle: Poetics. Longinus: On the Sublime. Demetrius: On Style*. (Aristotle translated by Stephen Halliwell; Longinus translated by W. Hamilton Fyfe, revised by Donald A. Russell; Demetrius translated by Doreen C. Innes from an "Idea" by W. Rhys Roberts.) Second edition of volume 23, first appearing in 1995, was reprinted, with corrections, in 1999.

Aristoxenus of Tarentum. *Elementa Harmonica*. Peripatetic philosopher remembered mainly for his contributions to music theory. This is partly because he was a trained musician as well as an eminent musicologist, and partly because his only extant albeit incomplete work, *Elementa Harmonica*, is a treatise on music. Otherwise, he is noted as a prolific writer, evidently comfortable with a broad range of topics within the domain of philosophy. As a student of Aristotle, one of his greatest attractions for Plato scholars is his report of his master's estimation of Plato's famous lecture on the good (*Elementa Harmonica* 2.30–31). The Greek text and English translation of the treatise are available in *Aristoxenou Harmonika Stoicheia: The Harmonics of Aristoxenus*. Edited and translated, with notes, introduction, and index of words, by Henry Stewart Macran. Oxford, England: Clarendon Press, 1902.

Athenaeus of Naucratis. *Deipnosophistae*. Written around the end of the second century after Christ, this a succession of dialogues bringing together the fictionalized intelligentsia of imperial Rome in leisurely discussions over a wide range of issues collectively providing deep and broad insight into the sociocultural essence and nuances of the time. The dramatic backdrop is a series of banquets, where the conversation may range from literature to gastronomy to sexual mores. The work is held in especially high esteem for its discussion of and quotations from ancient works that were available to the author but not to us. Greek text with running English translation available in the Loeb Classical Library as *The Learned Banqueters*. Eight volumes. Edited and translated by S. Douglas Olson. Cambridge, Massachusetts: Harvard University Press, 2007–2012. Volume 1 (2007): Books 1–3.106e. Volume 2 (2007): Books 3.106e–5. Volume 3 (2008): Books 6–7. Volume 4 (2008): Books 8–10.420e. Volume 5 (2009): Books 10.420e–11. Volume 6 (2010): Books 12–13.594b. Volume 7 (2011): Books 13.594b–14. Volume 8 (2012): Book 15; General Indexes.

Augustine of Hippo, Saint. *De Civitate Dei*. Latin text with facing English translation available in the Loeb Classical Library as *Augustine: City of God*. Seven volumes. Cambridge, Massachusetts: Harvard University Press, 1957–1972. Volume 1 (1957): Books 1–3; translated by George E. McCracken. Volume 2 (1963): Books 4–7; translated by William M. Green. Volume 3 (1968): Books 8–11; translated by David S. Wiesen. Volume 4 (1966): Books 12–15; translated by Philip Levine. Volume 5 (1965): Books 16–18.35; translated by Eva M. Sanford and William M. Green. Volume 6 (1960): Books 18.36–20; translated by William Chase Greene. Volume 7 (1972): Books 21–22; translated by William M. Green.

Augustine of Hippo, Saint. *De Doctrina Christiana*. Edited and translated by R. P. H. Green. Oxford Early Christian Texts. Oxford, England: Oxford University Press, 1995. Reissued in 1997 in the Oxford World's Classics series as *Saint Augustine: On Christian Teaching*.

Cicero (Marcus Tullius Cicero). *Academicae Quaestiones*. Originally published in 45 BC. Released as part of one of the six volumes dedicated to Cicero's philosophical treatises in the Loeb collection organized in twenty-nine volumes collectively recognized as the standard edition of his works. Volume 19 (1933): *Philosophical Treatises: On the Nature of the Gods; Academics*. Translated by Harris Rackham. Latin text with parallel English translation. Loeb Classical Library. Cambridge, Massachusetts: Harvard University Press, 1933. Also translated into English by Charles Duke Yonge as part of *The Academic Questions, Treatise De Finibus and Tusculan Disputations, of M. T. Cicero, with a Sketch of the Greek Philosophers Mentioned by Cicero. Literally translated by C. D. Yonge, B.A.* London, England: Henry G. Bohn, 1853.

Cicero (Marcus Tullius Cicero). *De Divinatione*. Originally published in 44 BC. Appears in one of the six volumes dedicated to Cicero's philosophical treatises in the twenty-nine volume Loeb collection constituting the standard edition of his works. Volume 20 (1923): *Philosophical Treatises: On Old Age. On Friendship. On Divination*. Translated by William Armistead Falconer. Latin text with parallel English translation. Loeb Classical Library. Cambridge, Massachusetts: Harvard University Press, 1923. Also edited by Arthur Stanley Pease and published as volumes 6 (1920) and 8 (1923) of the University of Illinois Studies in Language and Literature. Urbana, Illinois: University of Illinois, 1920–1923. Reprinted in New York, N.Y.: Arno Press, 1979.

Cicero (Marcus Tullius Cicero). *De Oratore*. Originally produced in 55 BC as a monograph in three books, the work occupies the whole of one and a part of another of the five volumes dedicated to Cicero's rhetorical treatises in the Loeb collection spanning twenty-nine volumes and constituting the standard edition of his works. Volume 3 (1942): *Rhetorical Treatises: On the Orator*, Books 1–2. Translated by Edward William Sutton and Harris Rackham. Volume 4 (1942): *Rhetorical Treatises: On the Orator*, Book 3; *On Fate*; *Stoic Paradoxes*; *On the Divisions of Oratory*. Translated by Harris Rackham. Latin text with parallel English translation. Loeb Classical Library. Cambridge, Massachusetts: Harvard University Press, 1942.

Diodorus Siculus. *Bibliotheca Historica*. Universal history of Diodorus of Sicily, a Greek historian flourishing in the first century before Christ. Arranged in forty books: Books 1–5 and Books 11–20 are preserved in their entirety, the rest, in fragments. Available in various collections, for example, the one in the Loeb Classical Library: *Library of History*. Twelve volumes. Greek text with parallel English translation. Cambridge, Massachusetts: Harvard University Press, 1933–1967. Volume 1 (1933): Books 1–2.34. Translated by Charles Henry Oldfather. Volume 2 (1935): Books 2.35–4.58. Translated by Charles Henry Oldfather. Volume 3 (1939): Books 4.59–8. Translated by Charles Henry Oldfather. Volume 4 (1946): Books 9–12.40. Translated by Charles Henry Oldfather. Volume 5 (1950): Books 12.41–13. Translated by Charles Henry Oldfather. Volume 6 (1954): Books 14–15.19. Translated by Charles Henry Oldfather. Volume 7 (1952): Books 15.20–16.65. Translated by Charles L. Sherman. Volume 8 (1963): Books 16.66–17. Translated by Charles Bradford Welles. Volume 9 (1947): Books 18–19.65. Translated by Russel Mortimer Geer. Volume 10 (1954): Books 19.66–20. Translated by Russel Mortimer Geer. Volume 11 (1957): Books 21–32. Translated by Francis R. Walton. Volume 12 (1967): Books 33–40. Translated by Francis R. Walton.

Diogenes Laërtius. *Lives and Opinions of Eminent Philosophers*. An ancient (c. 200–500) biographical reference work on Greek philosophers. The conventional form of citation is by the name of the author alone (often abbreviated as "DL") because the exact title of the original is not certain, with the surviving manuscripts using various lengthy formulations showing substantial freedom of expression, and because the practice of citation by the name of the author becomes feasible in the absence of other extant works of significance by Diogenes. The title used above captures the spirit of the content and something of the common denominator in what has been handed down through the ages. Prized for its use of a great many sources no longer in existence, the initiative is just as widely and passionately repudiated for the same thing, that is, for stitching together various bits of information, ostensibly all that was available, without due critical consideration, thus often falling short of the mark in internal consistency. An edition in the mid-nineteenth century enjoyed critical acclaim through the end of the millennium: *Diogenis Laertii de Clarorum Philosophorum Vitis, Dogmatibus et Apophthegmatibus Libri Decem*. Greek original and Latin translation in adjacent columns on the same page. Edited by Carel Gabriel Cobet. Paris, France: Ambroise Firmin Didot, 1850. The standard critical edition today is *Diogenis Laertii Vitae Philosophorum*. Three volumes. First two volumes edited by Miroslav Marcovich (1999); third volume, dedicated exclusively to indexes, edited by Hans Gärtner (2002). Bibliotheca Scriptorum Graecorum et Romanorum Teubneriana. Munich and Leipzig, Germany: K. G. Saur [later Walter de Gruyter], 1999–2002. The definitive English translation is *Lives of Eminent Philosophers*. Two volumes. Greek text with parallel English translation by Robert Drew Hicks. Loeb Classical Library. Cambridge, Massachusetts: Harvard University Press, 1925. Reprinted with an introduction by Herbert Strainge Long, 1972. See also Charles Duke Yonge's rendition as *The Lives and Opinions of Eminent Philosophers*. Bohn's Classical Library 43. London, England: Henry G. Bohn, 1853.

Dionysius of Halicarnassus. *De Compositione Verborum*. Translated into English by William Rhys Roberts as *On Literary Composition, Being the Greek Text of the De Compositione Verborvm: Edited with Introduction, Translation, Notes, Glossary, and Appendices; by W. Rhys Roberts*. London, England: Macmillan and Company, 1910. Also appears in a translation by Stephen Usher, with an introduction and parallel Greek text, as the second volume of *The Critical Essays* in the Loeb Classical Library edition of the works of Dionysius of Halicarnassus. Cambridge, Massachusetts: Harvard University Press, 1974–1985.

Elias (sometimes identified as pseudo-Elias or replaced altogether with David). *Commentary on Aristotle's Categories*. Greek text with Latin commentary available in *Commentaria in Aristotelem Graeca* (CAG) as part of volume 18, part 1 (1900): *In Porphyrii Isagogen et Aristotelis Categorias Commentaria*. Edited by Adolf Busse. Berlin, Germany: Realschulbuchhandlung and Georg Reimer, 1882–1909. Neither available nor planned in the *Ancient Commentators on Aristotle* (ACA), the definitive English collection of the commentaries.

Epicrates of Ambracia. *Fragments*. Greek text with Latin commentary available in *Comicorum Atticorum Fragmenta* (CAF). Three volumes. Edited by Theodor Kock. Leipzig, Germany: B. G. Teubner, 1880–1888. Also available, again, in the combination of Greek text and Latin commentary, in *Poetae Comici Graeci* (PCG). Eight volumes. Edited by Rudolf Kassel and Colin Austin. Berlin, Germany, New York, N.Y.: Walter de Gruyter, 1983–2001.

Epictetus. *Works*. Various collections, for example, the one in the Loeb Classical Library. Two volumes. Greek text with parallel English translation by William Abbott Oldfather. Cambridge, Massachusetts: Harvard University Press, 1925–1928. Volume 1 (1925): *Discourses*, Books 1–2. Volume 2 (1928): *Discourses*, Books 3–4; *Fragments*; The *Encheiridion*. A collection in English without the original is *The Works of Epictetus: Consisting of His Discourses, in Four Books, The Enchiridion, and Fragments*. Translated by Thomas Wentworth Higginson from the Greek based on the text of Elizabeth Carter. Boston, Massachusetts: Little, Brown, and Co., 1865. Another English edition is *The Discourses of Epictetus; with the Encheiridion and Fragments*. Translated, with notes, a life of Epictetus, and a view of his philosophy, by George Long. Bohn's Classical Library. London, England: G. Bell, 1877.

Euripides. *Alcestis*. Greek text with facing English translation available in the Loeb Classical Library as part of *Euripides: Cyclops. Alcestis. Medea*. Edited and translated by David Kovacs. Cambridge, Massachusetts: Harvard University Press, 1994.

Favorinus of Arelate (or Arles). *Works and Fragments*. Flourishing during the reign of Hadrian, roughly half a millennium after the death of Socrates, Favorinus was a philosopher, a sophist, an orator, and, evidently, above all, something of a polymath. Securing, for some time, a place in the court of Hadrian, he enjoyed considerable fame in both Rome and Athens, though falling out of favor in both, before regaining his position at least in the former. No more than a few speeches survive from an otherwise substantial intellectual output. Yet fragments can be found scattered throughout derivative works, as later writers have made liberal use of his contributions. His *Memorabilia* and his *Miscellaneous History* have been especially popular in this regard, both serving as a sourcebook for encyclopedic works such as the *Suda* and for compliers such as Diogenes Laërtius and Aulus Gellius. The works of Favorinus are also valued for the references they contain to other lost works that were extant in his own time. A reputable modern edition of his works, including the extant speeches as well as all fragmentary remains, together with his references to secondary sources lost to us, is *Favorino di Arelate: Opere*. The critical text, edited, with introduction and commentary, by Adelmo Barigazzi. Florence, Italy: Felice Le Monnier, 1966. A comparable contribution from German scholarship is *Favorin von Arelate: Der erste Teil der Fragmente: "Memorabilien" und "Omnigena Historia."* Edited, with commentary, by Eckart Mensching. Berlin, Germany: Walter de Gruyter, 1963.

Hesiod. *Theogony*. Edited, and translated into English, by Glenn W. Most as part of the first volume of the coverage of Hesiod by the Loeb Classical Library. Greek text with parallel English translation in prose. Cambridge, Massachusetts: Harvard University Press, 2006–2007. Volume 1 (2006): *Theogony; Works and Days; Testimonia*. Volume 2 (2007): *The Shield; Catalogue of Women; Other Fragments*.

Hesychius Illustrius of Miletus. *Onomatologos ē Pinax tōn en Paideia Onomastōn*. A lost biographical survey of eminent writers. Dates back to the sixth century. Although the original is lost, many of its entries have either been excerpted or reproduced entirely in other works, including the *Bibliotheca* of Photius and the *Suda*. Fragments are available in the fourth volume of *Fragmenta Historicorum Graecorum* (FHG). Edited by Karl Wilhelm Ludwig Müller. Paris, France: Ambroise Firmin Didot, 1851.

Homer. *Odyssey*. Translated into English by Augustus Taber Murray and revised by George E. Dimock. Two volumes. Volume 1: Books 1–12. Volume 2: Books 13–24. Greek text with parallel English translation in prose. Loeb Classical Library. Cambridge, Massachusetts: Harvard University Press; London, England: William Heinemann, 1919. Reprinted numerous times.

Isocrates. *Works*. Various collections, including, most notably, the edition in the Loeb Classical Library. Three volumes. Greek text with parallel English translation. Cambridge, Massachusetts: Harvard University Press, 1928–1945. Volume 1 (1928): *To Demonicus*; *To Nicocles*; *Nicocles* or *The Cyprians*; *Panegyricus*; *To Philip*; *Archidamus*. Translated by George Norlin. Volume 2 (1929): *On the Peace*; *Areopagiticus*; *Panathenaicus*; *Against the Sophists*; *Antidosis*. Translated by George Norlin. Volume 3 (1945): *Evagoras*; *Helen*; *Busiris*; *Plataicus*; *Concerning the Team of Horses*; *Trapeziticus*; *Against Callimachus*; *Aegineticus*; *Against Lochites*; *Against Euthynus*; *Letters*. Translated by La Rue Van Hook.

John (Joannes) Philoponus (alternatively: John the Grammarian or John of Alexandria). *Commentary on Aristotle's De Anima*. Greek text with Latin commentary available in *Commentaria in Aristotelem Graeca* (CAG) as volume 15 (1897): *In Aristotelis de Anima Libros Commentaria*. Edited by Michael Hayduck. Berlin, Germany: Realschulbuchhandlung and Georg Reimer, 1882–1909. Translated into English as *Philoponus: On Aristotle On the Soul* in six volumes in the *Ancient Commentators on Aristotle* (ACA), a project carried out under the auspices of King's College London and the general editorship of Richard Sorabji. London, England: Duckworth; Ithaca, New York: Cornell University Press, 1987–present. The volumes in the *Ancient Commentators on Aristotle* are not numbered: *On the Soul* 1.1–1.2 (2005): translated by Philip van der Eijk. *On the Soul* 1.3–1.5 (2006): translated by Philip van der Eijk. *On the Soul* 2.1–2.6 (2005): translated by William Charlton. *On the Soul* 2.7–2.12 (2005): translated by William Charlton. *On the Soul* 3.1–3.8 (2000): translated by William Charlton. *On the Soul* 3.9–3.13 (2000): translated by William Charlton (published together with *Stephanus: On Aristotle On Interpretation*, likewise translated by William Charlton).

Olympiodorus the Younger of Alexandria. *Anonymous Prolegomena to Platonic Philosophy*. Greek text with English translation. Translated into English, with introduction and indices, by Leendert Gerrit Westerink. Amsterdam, Netherlands: North-Holland Publishing Company, 1962. Anonymous lecture notes dating from the sixth-century Neoplatonist school of Alexandria and traditionally albeit mistakenly attributed to Olympiodorus.

Olympiodorus the Younger of Alexandria. *Commentary on the First Alcibiades of Plato*. Critical text and indices. Edited by Leendert Gerrit Westerink. Amsterdam, Netherlands: North-Holland Publishing Company, 1956. Second edition, a corrected reprint, published in Amsterdam, Netherlands: Adolf M. Hakkert, 1982. Comprises notes from a series of lectures on *Alcibiades* 1, with a biographical introduction, which is often excerpted as a *Life of Plato* (*Olympiodori Vita Platonis*) in older editions of the complete works of Plato, for example, in English translation in the sixth volume of the Bohn edition: *The Works of Plato: A New and Literal Version, Chiefly from the Text of Stallbaum*. Bohn's Classical Library. London, England: Henry G. Bohn, 1854, pp. 232–240. The biographical portion also appears in *Olympiodori, Ammonii, Iamblichi, Porphyrii et aliorum Vitae Platonis, Aristotelis, Pythagorae, Platoni et Isidori*. Edited by Anton Westermann. Paris, France: Ambroise Firmin Didot, 1862, pp. 1–4.

Olympiodorus the Younger of Alexandria. *Prolegomena and Commentary on Aristotle's Categories*. Greek text with Latin commentary available in *Commentaria in Aristotelem Graeca* (CAG) in volume 12, part 1 (1902): *Prolegomena et in Categorias Commentarium*. Edited by Adolf Busse. Berlin, Germany: Realschulbuchhandlung and Georg Reimer, 1882–1909. Neither available nor planned in the *Ancient Commentators on Aristotle* (ACA), the definitive English collection of the commentaries.

Philodemus of Gadara. *Academicorum Philosophorum Index Herculanensis*. A history of Academic philosophy from Plato to Antiochus of Ascalon. Fragmentary remains (Papyrus Herculanensis 164, 1021) edited by Siegfried Mekler, who is responsible for the modern title. Berlin, Germany: Weidmannsche Buchhandlung, 1902. Partly superseded by an edition of narrower scope in Konrad Gaiser's *Philodems Academica: Die Bericht über Platon und die Alte Akademie in Zwei Herkulanensischen Papyri*. Supplementum Platonicum: Die Texte der Indirekten Platon-überlieferung 1. Stuttgart and Bad Cannstatt, Germany: Frommann-Holzboog, 1988. Gaiser's edition, originally intended as part of a larger project, never realized, covers Plato through Arcesilaus, leaving out the later Academy.

Photius. *Bibliotheca* [=*Myriobiblon*]. A literary encyclopedia by the Byzantine scholar Photius (c. 810–893), revered in his own time as the Ecumenical Patriarch of Constantinople (858–867, 877–886), and now venerated as St. Photios the Great in the Eastern Orthodox churches. Covering roughly fourteen hundred years of literature from the classical age to the time of Photius, the *Bibliotheca* is essentially a collection of 280 book reviews by the patriarch, summarizing, outlining, and commenting on works he himself had read, though not on all the works he had read, as evidenced by the absence of classical works known to have been common reading material for the learned. Valuable in its own right, the study is also prized as a source of information on works lost today but available then. Nearly half of its coverage corresponds to works no longer in existence. The emphasis is on theology and ecclesiastical history, while philosophy and poetry are decidedly absent. Nothing of the Platonic corpus is covered, but several entries are directly relevant to Plato, including the following by codex number: 151; 154; 155; 156; 247. Biographical details are generally agreed to come from the *Onomatologos* of Hesychius Illustrius of Miletus. The standard critical edition is a French undertaking in ten volumes: *Bibliothèque*. Greek text with running French translations, accompanied by introductory essays and critical notes. Edited and translated by René Henry. Collection des Universités de France (="Collection Budé") Série Grecque. Publiée sous le patronage de l'Association Guillaume Budé. Paris, France: Société d'Édition Les Belles Lettres, 1959–2003.

Pindar. *Pythian Odes*. Greek text with facing English translation available in the Loeb Classical Library as part of *Pindar: Olympian Odes. Pythian Odes*. Edited and translated by William H. Race. Cambridge, Massachusetts: Harvard University Press, 1997.

Plutarch (Lucius Mestrius Plutarchus). *Adversus Colotem*. [*Against Colotes*.] Greek text with facing English translation available in the Loeb Classical Library as part of *Plutarch: Moralia*, Volume 14. (*That Epicurus Actually Makes a Pleasant Life Impossible. Reply to Colotes in Defence of the Other Philosophers. Is "Live Unknown" a Wise Precept? On Music.*) Translated by Benedict Einarson and Phillip H. De Lacy. Cambridge, Massachusetts: Harvard University Press, 1967.

Plutarch (Lucius Mestrius Plutarchus). *Lives*. Commonly called *Parallel Lives* (*Bioi Parallèloi*), or *Plutarch's Lives*, or simply *Lives*, this is a collection of biographies pairing Greek and Roman personalities for comparative study. Published in the year 75, the work covers twenty-three pairs of lives, plus four individual accounts, for a total of fifty biographies. The standard critical edition dates back to the nineteenth century: *Vitae Parallelae*. Four volumes. Edited by Karl Heinrich Ferdinand Sintenis. Leipzig, Germany: B. G. Teubner, 1839–1846. Second edition released, by the same publisher, in five volumes in 1852–1855. A roughly cotemporaneous alternative, known as the "Bekker edition," after the editor, or as the "Tauchnitz edition," after the publisher, provides the convenience of numbered divisions for each of the chapters: *Vitae inter se Comparatae*. Five volumes. Edited by Immanuel Bekker. Leipzig, Germany: Bernhard Tauchnitz, 1855–1857. Several English translations are available. The Loeb edition constitutes the bulk of the publisher's Plutarch collection: *Lives*. Greek text with parallel English translation. Eleven volumes. Translated by Bernadotte Perrin. Loeb Classical Library. Cambridge, Massachusetts: Harvard University Press, 1914–1926. A rendition by Arthur Hugh Clough in the middle of the nineteenth century continues to be favored today: *Plutarch's Lives: The Translation Called Dryden's. Corrected From the Greek and Revised by Arthur Hugh Clough*. Boston, Massachusetts: Little, Brown, and Company, 1859. This is an overhaul of an edition prepared under the supervision of John Dryden and published in 1683. The Clough edition is still available, for example, as *The Lives of the Noble Grecians and Romans*. Two volumes. New York, N.Y.: Modern Library, 1979.

Polycrates of Athens. *Accusation of Socrates* [c. 393 BC]. Lost work advocating the case of Athens against Socrates, though not as a formal part of the infamous trial. External evidence puts the date of composition several years after the trial (Diogenes Laërtius: *Lives* 2.38–39). Possibly drafted as an oratorical exercise, the work is known to us only through external references or commentary, such as those by Xenophon (*Memorabilia* 1.2.9–1.2.61), Isocrates (*Busiris* 11.4–6), and Quintilian (*Institutio Oratoria* 2.17.4, 3.1.11), in addition to Diogenes.

Quintilian (Marcus Fabius Quintilianus). *Institutio Oratoria*. Various collections, for example, the one in the Loeb Classical Library. Latin text with parallel English translation. Seven volumes, the last two reserved for the *Declamationes Minores*, one of two sets of declamations attributed to him with some dispute. Cambridge, Massachusetts: Harvard University Press, 2002–2006. Volume 1 (2002): *The Orator's Education* 1, Books 1–2. Edited and translated by Donald A. Russell. Volume 2 (2002): *The Orator's Education* 2, Books 3–5. Edited and translated by Donald A. Russell. Volume 3 (2002): *The Orator's Education* 3, Books 6–8. Edited and translated by Donald A. Russell. Volume 4 (2002): *The Orator's Education* 4, Books 9–10. Edited and translated by Donald A. Russell. Volume 5 (2002): *The Orator's Education* 5, Books 11–12. Edited and translated by Donald A. Russell. Volume 6 (2006): *The Lesser Declamations* 1. Edited and translated by D. R. Shackleton Bailey. Volume 7 (2006): *The Lesser Declamations* 2. Edited and translated by D. R. Shackleton Bailey. Also translated into English, with notes, by John Selby Watson, as *Institutes of Oratory*. Two volumes. Bohn's Classical Library. London, England: Henry G. Bohn, 1856.

Sextus Empiricus. *Pyrrhōneioi Hypotypōseis* (PH). Various English editions are available. The Loeb Classical Library offers Robert Gregg Bury's translation as *Sextus Empiricus: Outlines of Pyrrhonism*, constituting the first of its four volumes of the collected works of Sextus Empiricus. Greek text with running English translation on facing pages. Edited by Thomas Ethelbert Page, Edward Capps, and William Henry Denham Rouse. Cambridge, Massachusetts: Harvard University Press, 1933. A newer alternative is *The Skeptic Way: Sextus Empiricus's Outlines of Pyrrhonism*. Translated, with introduction and commentary, by Benson Mates. Oxford, England: Oxford University Press, 1996. A third option is *Sextus Empiricus: Outlines of Scepticism*. Translated by Julia Elizabeth Annas and Jonathan Barnes. Cambridge, England: Cambridge University Press, 1994. Reissued six years later with a new introduction and a few minor emendations, all by Jonathan Barnes. Cambridge Texts in the History of Philosophy. Cambridge, England: Cambridge University Press, 2000.

Simplicius of Cilicia. *Commentary on Aristotle's Physics*. Greek text with Latin commentary available in two volumes in *Commentaria in Aristotelem Graeca* (CAG), the standard edition of ancient Greek commentaries on Aristotle. Volume 9 (1882): *In Aristotelis Physicorum Libros Quattuor Priores Commentaria* [*Physics* 1–4]. Volume 10 (1895): *In Aristotelis Physicorum Libros Quattuor Posteriores Commentaria* [*Physics* 5–8]. Edited by Hermann Alexander Diels. Berlin, Germany: Realschulbuchhandlung and Georg Reimer, 1882–1909. Translated into English as *Simplicius: On Aristotle On Physics* in multiple volumes in the *Ancient Commentators on Aristotle* (ACA), a project carried out under the auspices of King's College London and the general editorship of Richard Sorabji. London, England: Duckworth; Ithaca, New York: Cornell University Press, 1987–present. The volumes in the *Ancient Commentators on Aristotle* are not numbered: *Physics* 1.1–1.2 (commissioned). *Physics* 1.3–1.4 (commissioned). *Physics* 1.5–1.9 (commissioned). *Physics* 2 (1997): translated by Barrie Fleet. *Physics* 3 (2002): translated by James O. Urmson. *Physics* 4.1–4.5, 4.10–4.14 (1992): translated by James O. Urmson. *Physics* 4.6–4.9 (1994): translated by James O. Urmson (published as part of *On Aristotle On the Void*, also including the commentary of Philoponus on Aristotle's *Physics*, translated by Paul Lettinck). *Physics* 5 (1997): translated by James O. Urmson. *Physics* 6 (1989): translated by David Konstan. *Physics* 7 (1994): translated by Charles Hagen. *Physics* 8.6–10 (2001): translated by Richard McKirahan.

Suidas. *Suda* (=*Souda*). Traditionally attributed to a certain Suidas, later identified and still widely accepted to be the name of the work rather than the compiler, this is a Byzantine lexicon dating back to the tenth century. The current preference is toward calling the work "the *Suda*" as opposed to any of several variants, with most scholars classifying its authorship as anonymous, though the consensus is not unanimous. Boasting more than 30,000 entries, ranging from the briefest note to compendious coverage, this represents a gargantuan effort more in line with a modern encyclopedia than a conventional lexicon. It is cherished for its copious references to and extractions from sources now unavailable to us. Its biographical accounts, including the one on Plato, are derived from the *Onomatologos ē Pinax tōn en Paideia Onomastōn*, a lost work on eminent writers, by Hesychius Illustrius of Miletus. The standard critical edition of the *Suda* in currency today originates in the first half of the twentieth century: *Suidae Lexicon*. Five volumes. Edited by Ada Adler. Leipzig, Germany: B. G. Teubner, 1928–1938. Early on in the second decade of the twenty-first century, the only English edition, still in progress at the time, was an online initiative: The Suda On Line (www.stoa.org/sol/). Listings are codified by "Adler numbers," alphanumeric strings uniquely assigned to each headword. Searches may be conducted accordingly. The Adler number for the primary entry on Plato is "pi,1707": everything in between the quotation marks is to be entered exactly as displayed.

Thomas Aquinas, Saint. *Summa Contra Gentiles*. Available in English as *The "Summa Contra Gentiles" of St. Thomas Aquinas*. Literally translated by the English Dominican Fathers from the latest Leonine edition. Five volumes. London, England: Burns, Oates & Washbourne, 1924. Also available as *On the Truth of the Catholic Faith: Summa Contra Gentiles*. Five volumes. Translated by Anton C. Pegis, James F. Anderson, Vernon J. Bourke, and Charles J. O'Neil. Garden City, N.Y.: Doubleday, 1955–1957.

Thomas Aquinas, Saint. *Summa Theologiæ*. Available in English as *The "Summa Theologica" of St. Thomas Aquinas*. Literally translated by Fathers of the English Dominican Province. Twenty-one volumes plus index. London, England: Burns, Oates & Washbourne, 1912–1925. Second and revised edition released by the same publisher in 1920. Reissued in three volumes in New York, N.Y.: Benziger Brothers, 1947–1948. Reprinted in five volumes in Westminster, Maryland: Christian Classics, 1981. Originally credited to the aforementioned Dominican priests as a group, remaining anonymous as individuals, the translation turned out to have been the personal achievement of Father Laurence Shapcote, O.P., the extent of whose contribution was revealed in 1934 in another publication: the introduction to the third volume of *On the Power of God* (p. v), the English Dominican translation of *Quæstiones Disputatæ de Potentia Dei*. A bilingual edition of the *Summa Theologiæ*, with Latin text and facing English translation, was prepared by the Cambridge Blackfriars under the general editorship of Father Thomas Gilby, O.P. London, England: Eyre and Spottiswoode; New York, N.Y.: McGraw–Hill, 1964–1973. Sixty volumes plus index. This collection was reprinted, with the correction of typographical errors, as *St. Thomas Aquinas: Summa Theologiæ*, comprising the same number of volumes as the original. Cambridge, England: Cambridge University Press, 2006.

Thucydides. *History of the Peloponnesian War*. Available in various collections, for example, the one in the Loeb Classical Library. Four volumes. Greek text with parallel English translation. Cambridge, Massachusetts: Harvard University Press, 1919–1923. Volume 1 (1919): Books 1–2. Volume 2 (1920): Books 3–4. Volume 3 (1921): Books 5–6. Volume 4 (1923): Books 7–8 and General Index. Translated by Charles Forster Smith. The classic English translation is that of Thomas Hobbes in 1629, still available as volumes 7–9 of the collection of his major works in English published as *The English Works of Thomas Hobbes of Malmesbury: Now First Collected and Edited by Sir William Molesworth, Bart*. Eleven volumes. London, England: John Bohn, 1839–1845.

Tzetzes, Johannes. *Chiliades*. A twelfth century Byzantine scholar, Johannes Tzetzes (c. 1110–1180), is known for his commentaries on ancient works and for his own compositions in verse. His most famous work is a compilation of miscellany drafted in "political verse," a metric form thought to originate with him. Tzetzes himself called this work a *Book of Histories*, specifically, a *Book of Histories in Political Verse*, but it has come down to us as *Chiliades*, after the title chosen by the first editor of the published manuscript: *Historiarum Variarum Chiliades*. The modern critical edition displays both names on the title page, the original one, in Greek (βιβλίον ιστορικόν το δια στίχων πολιτικών), and, the official one, in Latin (*Historiarum Variarum Chiliades*). Edited by Theophilus Kiesslingius (Johann Gottlieb Kiessling). Leipzig, Germany: Friedrich Christian Wilhelm Vogel, 1826.

Xenophon. *Works*. Various compilations, for example, the one in the Loeb Classical Library. Seven volumes. Greek text with parallel English translation. Cambridge, Massachusetts: Harvard University Press, 1914–1998. Volume 1 (1918): *Hellenica*, Books 1–4. Translated by Carleton L. Brownson. Volume 2 (1921): *Hellenica*, Books 5–7. Translated by Carleton L. Brownson. Volume 3 (1998): *Anabasis*. Translated by Carleton L. Brownson; revised by John Dillery. Volume 4 (1923): *Memorabilia; Oeconomicus; Symposium; Apology*. Translated by Edgar Cardew Marchant and Otis Johnson Todd. Volume 5 (1914): *Cyropaedia*, Books 1–4. Translated by Walter Miller. Volume 6 (1914): *Cyropaedia*, Books 5–8. Translated by Walter Miller. Volume 7 (1925): *Hiero; Agesilaus; Constitution of the Lacedaemonians; Ways and Means; Cavalry Commander; Art of Horsemanship; On Hunting; Constitution of the Athenians*. Translated by Edgar Cardew Marchant and Glen Warren Bowersock. A shorter collection focusing exclusively on the Socratic writings in English translation is available through Penguin as *Conversations of Socrates*. Translated by Hugh Tredennick and Robin Waterfield, and edited with new material by Robin Waterfield. London, England: Penguin Books, 1990. The contents exhaust the Socratic works of Xenophon: *Socrates' Defence* (*Apology*); *Memoirs of Socrates* (*Memorabilia*); *The Dinner-Party* (*Symposium*); *The Estate-Manager* (*Oeconomicus*). Includes a general introduction by Waterfield, as well as separate introductions, again, by Waterfield, to each of the four works.

4. Secondary Literature

Ahbel-Rappe, Sara, and Rachana Kamtekar, editors. *A Companion to Socrates*. Oxford, England: Blackwell Publishing, 2006. Contents: Part 1: Socrates in Antiquity. Section 1: Biography and Sources. Debra Nails: "The Trial and Death of Socrates" (pp. 5–20). Christian Wildberg: "Socrates and Euripides" (pp. 21–35). Paul Woodruff: "Socrates Among the Sophists" (pp. 36–47). Richard Janko: "Socrates the Freethinker" (pp. 48–62). Anthony A. Long: "How Does Socrates' Divine Sign Communicate with Him?" (pp. 63–74). Susan Prince: "Socrates, Antisthenes, and the Cynics" (pp. 75–92). Louis-Andre Dorion: "Xenophon's Socrates" (pp. 93–109). Kenneth Lapatin: "Picturing Socrates" (pp. 110–155). Section 2: Plato. Christopher J. Rowe: "Socrates in Plato's Dialogues" (pp. 159–170). Heda Segvic: "No One Errs Willingly: The Meaning of Socratic Intellectualism" (pp. 171–185). George Rudebusch: "Socratic Love" (pp. 186–199). John Bussanich: "Socrates and Religious Experience" (pp. 200–213). Rachana Kamtekar: "The Politics of Plato's Socrates" (pp. 214–227). Richard Kraut: "The Examined Life" (pp. 228–242). Roslyn Weiss: "Socrates: Seeker or Preacher?" (pp. 243–253). Harold Tarrant: "Socratic Method and Socratic Truth" (pp. 254–272). Section 3: Hellenistic Philosophy. Eric Alan Brown: "Socrates in the Stoa" (pp. 275–284). Tad Brennan: "Socrates and Epictetus" (pp. 285–297). Richard Bett: "Socrates and Skepticism" (pp. 298–311). Part 2: Socrates After Antiquity. Section 4: From the Medieval Period to Modernity. Ilai Alon: "Socrates in Arabic Philosophy" (pp. 317–336). James Hankins: "Socrates in the Italian Renaissance" (pp. 337–352). Daniel R. McLean: "The Private Life of Socrates in Early Modern France" (pp. 353–367). Nicholas P. White: "Socrates in Hegel and Others" (pp. 368–385). Section 5: The Modern Period. Paul Muench: "Kierkegaard's Socratic Point of View" (pp. 389–405). James Porter: "Nietzsche and 'The Problem of Socrates'" (pp. 406–425). Francisco J. Gonzalez: "The Socratic Hermeneutics of Heidegger and Gadamer" (pp. 426–441). Jonathan Lear: "The Socratic Method and

Psychoanalysis" (pp. 442–462). Mark Buchan: "Lacan and Socrates" (pp. 463–475). Avi Mintz: "From Grade School to Law School: Socrates' Legacy in Education" (pp. 476–492). Hayden W. Ausland: "Socrates' Definitional Inquiries and the History of Philosophy" (pp. 493–510).

Allen, Reginald E. *Socrates and Legal Obligation*. Minneapolis, Minnesota: University of Minnesota Press, 1980. Includes his translations of the *Apology* and the *Crito*, both later appearing, bundled together with his renditions of four other dialogues (*Euthyphro*, *Meno*, *Gorgias*, *Menexenus*), in the first volume of his collection published as *The Dialogues of Plato*. New Haven, Connecticut: Yale University Press, 1984.

Allen, Reginald E., editor. *Studies in Plato's Metaphysics*. International Library of Philosophy and Scientific Method. London, England: Routledge & Kegan Paul, 1965.

Annas, Julia Elizabeth. *Platonic Ethics, Old and New*. Ithaca, New York: Cornell University Press, 1999.

Annas, Julia Elizabeth. *Plato: A Very Short Introduction*. Oxford, England: Oxford University Press, 2003.

Annas, Julia Elizabeth. "What Are Plato's Middle Dialogues in the Middle Of?" Chapter 1 of *New Perspectives on Plato: Modern and Ancient*. Edited by Julia Elizabeth Annas and Christopher J. Rowe. Cambridge, Massachusetts: Harvard University Press, 2002, pp. 1–23.

Annas, Julia Elizabeth, and Christopher J. Rowe, editors. *New Perspectives on Plato: Modern and Ancient*. Cambridge, Massachusetts: Harvard University Press, 2002. Originates in the proceedings of a colloquium held at the Center for Hellenic Studies, Washington, D.C.: Trustees for Harvard University, August 1999.

Arieti, James A. *Interpreting Plato: The Dialogues as Drama*. Savage, Maryland: Rowman & Littlefield Publishers, 1991.

Arnim, Hans Friedrich August von. *De Platonis Dialogis Quaestiones Chronologicae*. Vorlesungsverzeichnis der Universität Rostock für das Wintersemester 1896. Rostock, Germany: Typis Academicis Adlerianis, 1896.

Arnim, Hans Friedrich August von. "Sprachliche Forschungen zur Chronologie der Platonischen Dialoge," *Sitzungsberichte der Kaiserlichen Akademie der Wissenschaften in Wien: Philos. Hist. Klasse*, 169:1 (1912), pp. 1–210.

Benson, Hugh H., editor. *A Companion to Plato*. Oxford, England: Blackwell Publishing, 2006. Contents: Debra Nails: "The Life of Plato of Athens" (pp. 1–12). Christopher J. Rowe: "Interpreting Plato" (pp. 13–24). William J. Prior: "The Socratic Problem" (pp. 25–35). Part 1: Platonic Method and the Dialogue Form. Mary Margaret McCabe: "Form and the Platonic Dialogues" (pp. 39–54). Charles M. Young: "The Socratic *Elenchus*" (pp. 55–69). Russell M. Dancy: "Platonic Definitions and Forms" (pp. 70–84). Hugh H. Benson: "Plato's Method of Dialectic" (pp. 85–99). Part 2: Platonic Epistemology. Gareth B. Matthews: "Socratic Ignorance" (pp. 103–118). Charles H. Kahn: "Plato on Recollection" (pp. 119–132). Deborah K. W. Modrak: "Plato: A Theory of Perception or a Nod to Sensation?" (pp. 133–145). Michael Ferejohn: "Knowledge and the Forms in Plato" (pp. 146–161). Part 3: Platonic Metaphysics. Terry Penner: "The Forms and the Sciences in Socrates and Plato" (pp. 165–183). Mary Louise Gill: "Problems for Forms" (pp. 184–198). Cynthia Freeland: "The Role of Cosmology in Plato's Philosophy" (pp. 199–213). David N. Sedley: "Plato on Language" (pp. 214–227). Michael White: "Plato and Mathematics" (pp. 228–243). Mark L. McPherran: "Platonic Religion" (pp. 244–259). Part 4: Platonic Psychology. Thomas C. Brickhouse and Nicholas D. Smith: "The Socratic Paradoxes" (pp. 263–

277). Fred D. Miller, Jr.: "The Platonic Soul" (pp. 278–293). Charles David Chanel Reeve: "Plato on Eros and Friendship" (pp. 294–307). Gerasimos Xenophon Santas: "Plato on Pleasure as the Human Good" (pp. 308–322). Part 5: Platonic Ethics, Politics, and Aesthetics. Daniel Devereux: "The Unity of the Virtues" (pp. 325–340). David Keyt: "Plato on Justice" (pp. 341–355). Nicholas P. White: "Plato's Concept of Goodness" (pp. 356–372). Susan Sauvé Meyer: "Plato on the Law" (pp. 373–387). Christopher Janaway: "Plato and the Arts" (pp. 388–400). Part 6: Platonic Legacy. Christopher Shields: "Learning About Plato from Aristotle" (pp. 403–417). Anthony A. Long: "Plato and Hellenistic Philosophy" (pp. 418–433). Sara Ahbel-Rappe: "Plato's Influence on Jewish, Christian, and Islamic Philosophy" (pp. 434–451).

Beversluis, John. *Cross-Examining Socrates: A Defense of the Interlocutors in Plato's Early Dialogues*. Cambridge, England: Cambridge University Press, 2000.

Beversluis, John. "Socratic Definition," *American Philosophical Quarterly*, 11 (1974), pp. 331–336.

Beversluis, John. "A Defense of Dogmatism in the Interpretation of Plato," *Oxford Studies in Ancient Philosophy*, 31 (Winter 2006), pp. 85–111.

Biffle, Christopher. *A Guided Tour of Five Works by Plato: With Complete Translations of Euthyphro, Apology, Crito, Phaedo (The Death Scene), "Allegory of the Cave."* Mountain View, California: Mayfield Publishing Company, 1988. Second edition in 1995, third in 2001.

Blondell, Ruby. *The Play of Character in Plato's Dialogues*. Cambridge, England: Cambridge University Press, 2002.

Boas, George. "Fact and Legend in the Biography of Plato," *The Philosophical Review*, 57:5 (1948), pp. 439–457.

Boudouris, K. J. (Kōnstantinos Iōannou Voudourēs), editor. *The Philosophy of Socrates*. Athens, Greece: International Center for Greek Philosophy and Culture, 1991.

Bowen, Alan C. "On Interpreting Plato." Chapter 3 of *Platonic Writings, Platonic Readings*. Edited by Charles L. Griswold, Jr. New York, N.Y.: Routledge, Chapman & Hall, 1988, pp. 49–65.

Boys-Stones, George R., and Johannes H. Haubold, editors. *Plato and Hesiod*. Oxford, England: Oxford University Press, 2010.

Brandwood, Leonard. *A Word Index to Plato*. Leeds, England: Maney & Son, 1976.

Brandwood, Leonard. *The Chronology of Plato's Dialogues*. Cambridge, England: Cambridge University Press, 1990. Revision of his doctoral dissertation presented and accepted as *The Dating of Plato's Works by the Stylistic Method: A Historical and Critical Survey*. London, England: University of London Press, 1958.

Brickhouse, Thomas C., and Nicholas D. Smith. *Plato's Socrates*. Oxford, England: Oxford University Press, 1994.

Brickhouse, Thomas C., and Nicholas D. Smith. *The Philosophy of Socrates*. Boulder, Colorado: Westview Press, 2000.

Brickhouse, Thomas C., and Nicholas D. Smith. *Routledge Philosophy Guidebook to Plato and the Trial of Socrates*. New York, N.Y.: Routledge, 2004.

Brickhouse, Thomas C., and Nicholas D. Smith. "Socrates and the Unity of the Virtues," *The Journal of Ethics*, 1 (1997), pp. 311–324.

Brickhouse, Thomas C., and Nicholas D. Smith. "Socrates' *Daimonion* and Rationality." Chapter 4 of *Socrates' Divine Sign: Religion, Practice, and Value in Socratic Philosophy*. *Apeiron*, 38:2 (June 2005), pp. 43–62. Edited by Pierre Destrée and Nicholas D. Smith. Kelowna, B.C., Canada: Academic Printing and Publishing, 2005.

Brisson, Luc. "Premises, Consequences, and Legacy of an Esotericist Interpretation of Plato," *Ancient Philosophy*, 15 (1995), pp. 117–134.
Burnet, John. "The Socratic Doctrine of the Soul." Second Annual Philosophical Lecture. Henriette Hertz Trust. Lecture delivered on 26 January 1916 before the British Academy. *Proceedings of the British Academy*, 7 (1915–1916), pp. 3–27. London, England: Humphrey Milford, Oxford University Press, 1916.
Calder, William M., III, Bernhard Huss, Marc Mastrangelo, R. Scott Smith, and Stephen M. Trzaskoma, editors. *The Unknown Socrates: Translations, with Introductions and Notes, of Four Important Documents in the Late Antique Reception of Socrates the Athenian*. Presents the relevant texts in their original language (Greek or Latin) together with an English translation of each: (1) Diogenes Laërtius: *Life of Socrates*. (2) Libanius: *Apology of Socrates*. (3) Maximus of Tyre: *Whether Socrates Did the Right Thing When He Did Not Defend Himself*. (4) Apuleius: *On the God of Socrates*. Wauconda, Illinois: Bolchazy-Carducci Publishers, 2002.
Cameron, Alan. "The Last Days of the Academy at Athens," *Proceedings of the Cambridge Philological Society*, 195 (New Series 15), (1969), pp. 7–29.
Campbell, Lewis. *The Sophistes and Politicus of Plato, with a Revised Text and English Notes, by the Rev. Lewis Campbell*. Oxford, England: Clarendon Press, 1867.
Campbell, Lewis. "On the Place of the *Parmenides* in the Chronological Order of the Platonic Dialogues," *The Classical Review*, 10 (1896), pp. 129–136.
Cherniss, Harold Fredrik. *The Riddle of the Early Academy*. Berkeley, California: University of California Press, 1945.
Cherniss, Harold Fredrik. "The Relation of the *Timaeus* to Plato's Later Dialogues," *The American Journal of Philology*, 78:3 (1957), pp. 225–266. Reprinted as chapter 17 of *Studies in Plato's Metaphysics*. International Library of Philosophy and Scientific Method. Edited by Reginald E. Allen. London, England: Routledge & Kegan Paul, 1965, pp. 339–378. Also released as chapter 21 of the collection of his essays published, on the occasion of his seventieth birthday, as *Harold Cherniss: Selected Papers*. Edited by Leonardo Tarán. Leiden, Netherlands: E. J. Brill, 1977, pp. 298–339.
Chroust, Anton-Hermann. *Socrates, Man and Myth: The Two Socratic Apologies of Xenophon*. London, England: Routledge & Kegan Paul; Notre Dame, Indiana: University of Notre Dame Press, 1957.
Chroust, Anton-Hermann. "Plato's Academy: The First Organized School of Political Science in Antiquity," *The Review of Politics*, 29:1 (January 1967), pp. 25–40.
Clay, Diskin. "The Origins of the Socratic Dialogue." Chapter 1 of *The Socratic Movement*. Edited by Paul A. Vander Waerdt. Ithaca, New York: Cornell University Press, 1994, pp. 23–47.
Cornford, Francis Macdonald. "The Athenian Philosophical Schools." Chapter 11 of Volume 6 of *The Cambridge Ancient History*. Twelve volumes (1923–1939). Series edited by John Bagnell Bury, Stanley Arthur Cook, Frank Ezra Adcock, Martin Percival Charlesworth, and Norman Hepburn Baynes. Volume 6 edited jointly by the first three editors, also responsible for each of the first six volumes. Cambridge, England: Cambridge University Press, 1927, pp. 302–351. Socrates is in pp. 302–310, Plato is in pp. 310–332, and Aristotle is in pp. 332–351. Volume 6 was reprinted with corrections in 1933.
Crombie, Ian M. *An Examination of Plato's Doctrines*. Two volumes. Volume 1 (1962): *Plato on Man and Society*. Volume 2 (1963): *Plato on Knowledge and Reality*.

London, England: Routledge & Kegan Paul; New York, N.Y.: Humanities Press, 1962–1963.

Dancy, Russell M. *Plato's Introduction of Forms*. Cambridge, England: Cambridge University Press, 2004.

Desjardins, Rosemary. "Why Dialogues? Plato's Serious Play." Chapter 7 of *Platonic Writings, Platonic Readings*. Edited by Charles L. Griswold, Jr. New York, N.Y.: Routledge, Chapman & Hall, 1988, pp. 110–125.

Destrée, Pierre, and Nicholas D. Smith, editors. *Socrates' Divine Sign: Religion, Practice, and Value in Socratic Philosophy. Apeiron,* 38:2 (June 2005). Kelowna, B.C., Canada: Academic Printing and Publishing, 2005. Contents: Luc Brisson: "Socrates and the Divine Signal According to Plato's Testimony: Philosophical Practice as Rooted in Religious Tradition" (pp. 1–12). Mark L. McPherran: "Introducing a New God: Socrates and His *Daimonion*" (pp. 13–30). Gerd Van Riel: "Socrates' Daemon: Internalisation of the Divine and Knowledge of the Self" (pp. 31–42). Thomas C. Brickhouse and Nicholas D. Smith: "Socrates' *Daimonion* and Rationality" (pp. 43–62). Pierre Destrée: "The *Daimonion* and the Philosophical Mission: Should the Divine Sign Remain Unique to Socrates?" (pp. 63–79). Roslyn Weiss: "For Whom the *Daimonion* Tolls" (pp. 81–96). Mark Joyal: "*To Daimonion* and the Socratic Problem" (pp. 97–112). Michel Narcy: "Socrates Sentenced by His *Daimôn*" (pp. 113–125). Louis-André Dorion (Matthew Brown, translator): "The *Daimonion* and the *Megalêgoria* of Socrates in Xenophon's *Apology*" (pp. 127–142). Aldo Brancacci: "The Double *Daimôn* in Euclides the Socratic" (pp. 143–154).

Dillon, John M. *The Heirs of Plato: A Study of the Old Academy (347–274 BC)*. Oxford, England: Oxford University Press, 2003.

Dittenberger, Wilhelm. "Sprachliche Kriterien für die Chronologie der Platonischen *Dialoge*," *Hermes*, 16 (1881), pp. 321–345.

Döring, Klaus. "The Students of Socrates." Chapter 2 of *The Cambridge Companion to Socrates*. Edited by Donald R. Morrison. Cambridge, England: Cambridge University Press, 2011, pp. 24–47.

Dorion, Louis-André. "Xenophon's Socrates." Chapter 7 of *A Companion to Socrates*. Edited by Sara Ahbel-Rappe and Rachana Kamtekar. Oxford, England: Blackwell Publishing, 2006, pp. 93–109.

Dorion, Louis-André. "The Rise and Fall of the Socratic Problem." Chapter 1 of *The Cambridge Companion to Socrates*. Edited by Donald R. Morrison. Cambridge, England: Cambridge University Press, 2011, pp. 1–23.

Dorter, Kenneth. *Form and Good in Plato's Eleatic Dialogues: The Parmenides, Theaetetus, Sophist, and Statesman*. Berkeley, California: University of California Press, 1994.

Dyer, Louis, editor. *Apology of Socrates and Crito, with Extracts from the Phaedo and Symposium and from Xenophon's Memorabilia*. Edited by Louis Dyer and revised by Thomas Day Seymour. Greek text with English introduction and vocabulary. Boston, Massachusetts: Ginn & Company, 1908. Originally published in 1885 without the extracts accompanying the two main titles and without Seymour's contribution.

Ferrari, Giovanni (John) R. F. "Socratic Irony as Pretence," *Oxford Studies in Ancient Philosophy*, 34 (2008), pp. 1–33.

Field, Guy Cromwell. *Socrates and Plato: A Criticism of Professor A. E. Taylor's "Varia Socratica."* Oxford, England: Parker & Co.; London, England: Simpkin, Marshall & Co., 1913.

Field, Guy Cromwell. *Plato and His Contemporaries: A Study in Fourth-Century Life and Thought*. London, England: Methuen & Co., 1930. Second edition in 1948.

Findlay, John Niemeyer. *Plato: The Written and Unwritten Doctrines*. International Library of Philosophy and Scientific Method. London, England: Routledge & Kegan Paul, 1974.

Fine, Gail. *On Ideas: Aristotle's Criticism of Plato's Theory of Forms*. Oxford, England: Oxford University Press, 1993.

Fine, Gail, editor. *The Oxford Handbook of Plato*. Oxford, England: Oxford University Press, 2008.

Fowler, David H. *The Mathematics of Plato's Academy: A New Reconstruction*. Oxford, England: Clarendon Press, 1987. Second edition in 1999.

Frede, Michael. *Prädikation und Existenzaussage*. Hypomnemata: Untersuchungen zur Antike und zu Ihrem Nachleben, No. 18. Göttingen, Germany: Vandenhoeck & Ruprecht, 1967.

Friedländer, Paul. *Platon*. Two volumes. Volume 1 (1928): *Platon: Eidos, Paideia, Dialogos*. Volume 2 (1930): *Platon: Die Platonischen Schriften*. Berlin and Leipzig, Germany: Walter de Gruyter, 1928–1930. Second edition in 1954. Second edition translated into English in three volumes by Hans Meyerhoff with the general title *Plato*. Volume 1 (1958): *Plato: An Introduction*. Volume 2 (1964): *Plato: The Dialogues, First Period*. Volume 3 (1969): *Plato: The Dialogues, Second and Third Periods*. Princeton, New Jersey, Princeton University Press, 1958–1969.

Gadamer, Hans-Georg. *Wahrheit und Methode: Grundzüge einer Philosophischen Hermeneutik*. Tübingen, Germany: J. C. B. Mohr, 1960. Numerous editions, the sixth and final one appearing in 1990. The fifth (1986) and sixth (1990) editions were issued successively, with the latter replacing the former, as the first volume of Gadamer's collected works in German, released as *Gesammelte Werke*. Ten volumes. Tübingen, Germany: J. C. B. Mohr, 1985–1995. Translated into English as *Truth and Method* by Garrett Barden and John Cumming. New York, N.Y.: Seabury Press; London, England: Sheed & Ward, 1975. Second English edition, with revised translation by Joel Weinsheimer and Donald G. Marshall: New York, N.Y.: Crossroad Publishing Company, 1989. Reissued: New York, N.Y.; London, England: Continuum International Publishing Group, 2004.

Gadamer, Hans-Georg. *Die Idee des Guten zwischen Plato und Aristoteles*. Heidelberg, Germany: Universitätsverlag Winter, 1978. The English edition appeared as *The Idea of the Good in Platonic-Aristotelian Philosophy*. Translated by P. Christopher Smith. New Haven, Connecticut: Yale University Press, 1986.

Gadamer, Hans-Georg. *Dialogue and Dialectic: Eight Hermeneutical Studies on Plato*. Collection of essays previously published separately in German. Translated and edited, with an introduction and annotation, by P. Christopher Smith. New Haven, Connecticut: Yale University Press, 1980.

Gaiser, Konrad. *Platons Ungeschriebene Lehre: Studien zur Systematischen und Geschichtlichen Begründung der Wissenschaften in der Platonischen Schule*. Stuttgart, Germany: E. Klett, 1963. A revision of the author's postdoctoral thesis of 1960 at Tübingen University (Eberhard Karls Universität Tübingen). An enlarged edition was released by the same publisher in 1968. An appendix bringing together sources on the "unwritten doctrine" is of particular interest: "Testimonia Platonica. Quellentexte zur Schule und Mündlichen Lehre Platons."

Gaiser, Konrad. "Plato's Enigmatic Lecture 'On the Good,'" *Phronesis*, 25:1 (1980), pp. 5–37.

Gaye, Russell Kerr. *The Platonic Conception of Immortality and Its Connexion with the Theory of Ideas: An Essay which Obtained the Hare Prize, 1903*. London, England: C. J. Clay and Sons, 1904.

Gerson, Lloyd P. "Plato's Development and the Development of the Theory of Forms." Chapter 2 of *Plato's Forms: Varieties of Interpretation*. Edited by William A. Welton. Lanham, Maryland: Lexington Books, 2002, pp. 85–109.

Gerson, Lloyd P. "Plato on Identity, Sameness, and Difference," *The Review of Metaphysics*, 58 (2004), pp. 106–132.

Gerson, Lloyd P. "Platonism and the Invention of the Problem of Universals," *Archiv für Geschichte der Philosophie*, 87 (2004), pp. 1–26.

Gerson, Lloyd P. "Platonism in the Ethics of Aristotle," *Oxford Studies in Ancient Philosophy*, 22 (2004), pp. 217–249.

Gerson, Lloyd P. "What is Platonism?" *Journal of the History of Philosophy*, 43 (2005), pp. 253–276.

Gerson, Lloyd P. "Platonic Knowledge and the Standard Analysis," *International Journal of Philosophical Studies*, 14 (2006), pp. 455–474.

Glucker, John. *Antiochus and the Late Academy*. Issue No. 56 of *Hypomnemata: Untersuchungen zur Antike und zu ihrem Nachleben*. Göttingen, Germany: Vandenhoeck und Ruprecht, 1978.

Gómez-Lobo, Alfonso. *The Foundations of Socratic Ethics*. Indianapolis, Indiana: Hackett Publishing Company, 1994.

Gonzales, Francisco J. "Plato's Dialectic of Forms." Chapter 1 of *Plato's Forms: Varieties of Interpretation*. Edited by William A. Welton. Lanham, Maryland: Lexington Books, 2002, pp. 31–83.

Griswold, Charles L., Jr., editor. *Platonic Writings, Platonic Readings*. New York, N.Y.: Routledge, Chapman & Hall, 1988.

Griswold, Charles L., Jr. "Plato's Metaphilosophy: Why Plato Wrote Dialogues." Chapter 9 of *Platonic Writings, Platonic Readings*. Edited by Charles L. Griswold, Jr. New York, N.Y.: Routledge, Chapman & Hall, 1988, pp. 143–167.

Griswold, Charles L., Jr. "Commentary on Sayre," *Proceedings of the Boston Area Colloquium in Ancient Philosophy*, 9 (1993), pp. 200–212.

Grote, George. *Plato, and the Other Companions of Sokrates*. Three volumes. London, England: John Murray, 1865. Subsequent editions by the same publisher: 1867; 1875 (posthumous); 1885 (four volumes). Reissued several times. Still in print, for example, in the form of an unabridged facsimile of the first edition in three volumes: Boston, Massachusetts: Adamant Media Corporation, 2005.

Grube, George Maximilian Anthony. *Plato's Thought*. London, England: Methuen & Co., 1935. Reprinted, with new introduction, bibliographic essay, and bibliography by Donald J. Zeyl. Indianapolis, Indiana: Hackett Publishing Company, 1980.

Guthrie, William Keith Chambers. "Plato's Views on the Nature of the Soul." In *Entretiens sur l'Antiquité Classique*. Tome 3: *Recherche sur la Tradition Platonicienne*. Vandoeuvres-Genève, Switzerland: Fondation Hardt pour l'Étude de l'Antiquité Classique, 1957, pp. 2–19. Reprinted with minor modifications, limited to supplanting or supplementing Greek terms with English equivalents, in *Plato: A Collection of Critical Essays*. Volume 2: *Ethics, Politics, and Philosophy of Art and Religion*. Edited by Gregory Vlastos. Garden City, New York: Anchor Books, Doubleday, 1971, pp. 230–243.

Hackforth, Reginald. *Plato's Philebus*. Cambridge, England: Cambridge University Press, 1972. English translation of the dialogue, with introduction and commentary. Originally published as *Plato's Examination of Pleasure*. Cambridge, England: Cambridge University Press, 1945.

Hackforth, Reginald. *Plato's Phaedrus*. English translation of the dialogue, with introduction and commentary. Cambridge, England: Cambridge University Press, 1952.

Hare, Richard Mervyn. *Plato*. Past Masters. Oxford, England: Oxford University Press, 1982.

Harte, Verity. *Plato on Parts and Wholes: The Metaphysics of Structure*. Oxford, England: Oxford University Press, 2002.

Haslam, Michael W. "Plato, Sophron, and the Dramatic Dialogue," *Bulletin of the Institute of Classical Studies of the University of London*, 19 (1972), pp. 17–38.

Hermann, Karl Friedrich. *Geschichte und System der Platonischen Philosophie*. Heidelberg, Germany: Akademische Verlagshandlung von C. F. Winter, 1839.

Hughes, Bettany. *The Hemlock Cup: Socrates, Athens and the Search for the Good Life*. London, England: Jonathan Cape, 2010. New York, N.Y.: Alfred A. Knopf, 2011.

Hyland, Drew A. *Finitude and Transcendence in the Platonic Dialogues*. SUNY Series in Hegelian Studies. Albany, New York: State University of New York Press, 1995.

Hyland, Drew A. *Questioning Platonism: Continental Interpretations of Plato*. SUNY Series in Contemporary Continental Philosophy. Albany, New York: State University of New York Press, 2004.

Hyland, Drew A. "Against a Platonic 'Theory' of Forms." Chapter 10 of *Plato's Forms: Varieties of Interpretation*. Edited by William A. Welton. Lanham, Maryland: Lexington Books, 2002, pp. 257–272.

Irwin, Terence H. *Plato's Moral Theory: The Early and Middle Dialogues*. Oxford, England: Oxford University Press, 1977.

Irwin, Terence H. "The Platonic Corpus." Chapter 3 of *The Oxford Handbook of Plato*. Edited by Gail Fine. Oxford, England: Oxford University Press, 2008, pp. 63–87.

Jaeger, Werner Wilhelm. *Paideia: Die Formung des Griechischen Menschen*. Three volumes (1933, 1944, 1947). Berlin, Germany: Walter de Gruyter, 1933–1947. First volume reissued in a second edition in 1935. Translated into English in three volumes by Gilbert Highet with the general title *Paideia: The Ideals of Greek Culture*. Volume 1 (1939): *Archaic Greece: The Mind of Athens*. Volume 2 (1943): *In Search of the Divine Centre*. Volume 3 (1944): *The Conflict of Cultural Ideals in the Age of Plato*. Oxford, England: Oxford University Press, 1939–1944. Second and third volumes of the English collection translated from the author's manuscripts and published before their German counterparts. First volume of the English collection reissued in a second edition in 1945.

Kahn, Charles H. *Plato and the Socratic Dialogue: The Philosophical Use of a Literary Form*. Cambridge, England: Cambridge University Press, 1996.

Kahn, Charles H. "A New Interpretation of Plato's Socratic Dialogues," *The Harvard Review of Philosophy*, 5 (Spring 1995), pp. 26–35.

Kahn, Charles H. "On Platonic Chronology." Chapter 4 of *New Perspectives on Plato: Modern and Ancient*. Cambridge, Massachusetts: Harvard University Press, 2002, pp. 93–127. Edited by Julia Elizabeth Annas and Christopher J. Rowe. Originates as a contribution to a colloquium held at the Center for Hellenic Studies, Washington, D.C.: Trustees for Harvard University, August 1999.

Kamtekar, Rachana, editor. *Plato's Euthyphro, Apology, and Crito: Critical Essays*. Lanham, Maryland: Rowman & Littlefield, 2005. Contents: Mark L. McPherran: "Justice and Pollution in the *Euthyphro*" (pp. 1–22). Peter Thomas Geach: "Plato's *Euthyphro*: An Analysis and Commentary" (pp. 23–34). S. Marc Cohen: "Socrates on the Definition of Piety: *Euthyphro* 10a–11b" (pp. 35–48). Gregory Vlastos: "Socratic Piety" (pp. 49–71). Emile de Strycker and Simon Roelof Slings: "Plato's *Apology* of Socrates" (pp. 72–96). Donald R. Morrison: "On the Alleged Historical Reputability of Plato's *Apology*" (pp. 97–126). Terence H. Irwin: "Was Socrates Against Democracy?" (pp. 127–149). Myles F. Burnyeat: "The Impiety of Socrates" (pp. 150–162). Thomas C. Brickhouse and Nicholas D. Smith: "Socrates and Obedience to the Law" (pp. 163–174). Richard Kraut: "*Dokimasia*, Satisfaction, Agreement" (pp. 175–209). David Bostock: "The Interpretation of Plato's *Crito*" (pp. 210–228). Verity Harte: "Conflicting Values in Plato's *Crito*" (pp. 229–260).

Klagge, James C., and Nicholas D. Smith, editors. *Methods of Interpreting Plato and His Dialogues*. Oxford Studies in Ancient Philosophy, Supplementary Volume. Oxford, England: Clarendon Press, 1992.

Krämer, Hans Joachim. *Arete bei Platon und Aristoteles: Zum Wesen und zur Geschichte der Platonischen Ontologie*. Heidelberg, Germany: Carl Winter Universitätsverlag, 1959. (Abhandlungen der Heidelberger Akademie der Wissenschaften. Philosophisch-historische Klasse. Jahrgang 1959:6). The author's doctoral dissertation. Translated into English by John R. Catan as *Plato and the Foundations of Metaphysics: A Work on the Theory of the Principles and Unwritten Doctrines of Plato with a Collection of the Fundamental Documents*. Albany, New York: State University of New York Press, 1990.

Krämer, Hans Joachim. "Retraktationen zum Problem des Esoterischen Platon," *Museum Helveticum*, 21 (1964), pp. 137–167.

Kraut, Richard, editor. *The Cambridge Companion to Plato*. Cambridge, England: Cambridge University Press, 1992. Contents: Richard Kraut: "Introduction to the Study of Plato" (pp. 1–50). Terence H. Irwin: "Plato: The Intellectual Background" (pp. 51–89). Leonard Brandwood: "Stylometry and Chronology" (pp. 90–120). Terry Penner: "Socrates and the Early Dialogues" (pp. 121–169). Ian Mueller: "Mathematical Method and Philosophical Truth" (pp. 170–199). Gail Fine: "Inquiry in the *Meno*" (pp. 200–226). Michael L. Morgan: "Plato and Greek Religion" (pp. 227–247). Giovanni (John) R. F. Ferrari: "Platonic Love" (pp. 248–276). Nicholas P. White: "Plato's Metaphysical Epistemology" (pp. 277–310). Richard Kraut: "The Defence of Justice in Plato's *Republic*" (pp. 311–337). Elizabeth Asmis: "Plato on Poetic Creativity" (pp. 338–364). Constance C. Meinwald: "Good-bye to the Third Man" (pp. 365–396). Michael Frede: "Plato's Sophist on False Statements" (pp. 397–424). Dorothea Frede: "Disintegration and Restoration: Pleasure and Pain in Plato's *Philebus*" (pp. 425–463). Trevor J. Saunders: "Plato's Later Political Thought" (pp. 464–492).

Lamm, Julia A. "The Art of Interpreting Plato." Chapter 5 of *The Cambridge Companion to Friedrich Schleiermacher*. Edited by Jacqueline Mariña. Cambridge, England: Cambridge University Press, 2005, pp. 91–108.

Ledger, Gerard R. *Re-counting Plato: A Computer Analysis of Plato's Style*. Oxford, England: Clarendon Press, 1989.

Lutoslawski, Wincenty. *The Origin and Growth of Plato's Logic, with an Account of Plato's Style and of the Chronology of His Writings, by Wincenty Lutoslawski*. London, England: Longmans, Green, and Co., 1897.

McCabe, Mary Margaret. "Plato's Ways of Writing." Chapter 4 of *The Oxford Handbook of Plato*. Edited by Gail Fine. Oxford, England: Oxford University Press, 2008, pp. 88–113.

McPherran, Mark L. *The Religion of Socrates*. University Park, Pennsylvania: The Pennsylvania State University Press, 1996.

Malcolm, John. *Plato on the Self-Predication of Forms: Early and Middle Dialogues*. Oxford, England: Clarendon Press, 1991.

Mayhew, Robert. *Plato: Laws 10*. Oxford, England: Oxford University Press, 2008. English translation with commentary.

Meinwald, Constance C. *Plato's Parmenides*. Oxford, England: Oxford University Press, 1991.

Meinwald, Constance C. "Good-bye to the Third Man." In *The Cambridge Companion to Plato*. Edited by Richard Kraut. Cambridge, England: Cambridge University Press, 1992, pp. 365–396.

Moravcsik, Julius. *Plato and Platonism: Plato's Conception of Appearance and Reality in Ontology, Epistemology, and Ethics, and Its Modern Echoes*. Oxford, England: Blackwell Publishers, 1992.

Morrison, Donald R., editor. *The Cambridge Companion to Socrates*. Cambridge, England: Cambridge University Press, 2011. Contents: Louis-André Dorion: "The Rise and Fall of the Socratic Problem" (pp. 1–23). Klaus Döring: "The Students of Socrates" (pp. 24–47). David K. O'Connor: "Xenophon and the Enviable Life of Socrates" (pp. 48–74). David Konstan: "Socrates in Aristophanes' *Clouds*" (pp. 75–90). Paul Woodruff: "Socrates and the New Learning" (pp. 91–110). Mark L. McPherran: "Socratic Religion" (pp. 111–137). Josiah Ober: "Socrates and Democratic Athens" (pp. 138–178). Hugh H. Benson: "Socratic Method" (pp. 179–200). Christopher J. Rowe: "Self-Examination" (pp. 201–214). Richard Bett: "Socratic Ignorance" (pp. 215–236). Melissa Lane: "Reconsidering Socratic Irony" (pp. 237–259). Terry Penner: "Socratic Ethics and the Socratic Psychology of Action: A Philosophical Framework" (pp. 260–292). Christopher Bobonich: "Socrates and Eudaimonia" (pp. 293–332). Charles L. Griswold, Jr.: "Socrates' Political Philosophy" (pp. 333–354). Anthony A. Long: "Socrates in Later Greek Philosophy" (pp. 355–380).

Morrow, Glenn Raymond. *Plato's Cretan City: A Historical Interpretation of the Laws*. Princeton, New Jersey: Princeton University Press, 1960. Reissued in 1993 with a new foreword by Charles H. Kahn.

Nails, Debra. *Agora, Academy, and the Conduct of Philosophy*. Dordrecht, Netherlands: Boston, Massachusetts: Kluwer Academic Publishers, 1995.

Nails, Debra. *The People of Plato: A Prosopography of Plato and Other Socratics*. Indianapolis, Indiana: Hackett Publishing Company, 2002.

Nails, Debra. "Plato's 'Middle' Cluster," *Phoenix*, 48:1 (Spring 1994), pp. 62–67.

Nails, Debra. "Mouthpiece Schmouthpiece." Chapter 1 of *Who Speaks for Plato? Studies in Platonic Anonymity*. Edited by Gerald Alan Press. Lanham, Maryland: Rowman & Littlefield, 2000, pp. 15–26.

Nails, Debra. "The Life of Plato of Athens." Chapter 1 of *A Companion to Plato*. Edited by Hugh H. Benson. Oxford, England: Blackwell Publishing, 2006, pp. 1–12.

Nails, Debra. "The Trial and Death of Socrates." Chapter 1 of *A Companion to Socrates*. Edited by Sara Ahbel-Rappe and Rachana Kamtekar. Oxford, England: Blackwell Publishing, 2006, pp. 5–20.

Nails, Debra, and Holger Thesleff. "Early Academic Editing: Plato's *Laws*." In *Plato's Laws: From Theory into Practice: Proceedings of the VI Symposium Platonicum: Selected Papers*. Volume 15 of International Plato Studies. Edited by Samuel Scolnicov and Luc Brisson. Sankt Augustin, Germany: Academia Verlag, 2003, pp. 14–29.

Nettleship, Richard Lewis. *Philosophical Lectures and Remains of Richard Lewis Nettleship*. Two volumes. Edited, with a biographical sketch, by Andrew Cecil Bradley and Godfrey Rathbone Benson. London, England: Macmillan and Company, 1897. The two volumes were reissued separately in 1901 by the same publisher, the first appearing as *Philosophical Remains of Richard Lewis Nettleship*, and the second released as *Lectures on the Republic of Plato*.

Notopoulos, James A. "The Name of Plato," *Classical Philology*, 34:2 (April 1939), pp. 135–145.

Ophuijsen, Johannes M. Van, editor. *Plato and Platonism*. Volume 33 of Studies in Philosophy and the History of Philosophy. Washington, D.C.: Catholic University of America Press, 1999.

Owen, Gwilym Ellis Lane. *Logic, Science, and Dialectic: Collected Papers in Greek Philosophy*. Posthumously published collection of seminal papers in Greek philosophy, including the Presocratics as well as Plato and Aristotle, and focusing mainly on logic, metaphysics, and the philosophy of science. Edited by Martha Craven Nussbaum. Ithaca, New York: Cornell University Press, 1986.

Owen, Gwilym Ellis Lane. "The Place of the *Timaeus* in Plato's Dialogues," *The Classical Quarterly* (New Series), 3 (January–April 1953), pp. 79–95. Reprinted as chapter 16 of *Studies in Plato's Metaphysics*. International Library of Philosophy and Scientific Method. Edited by Reginald E. Allen. London, England: Routledge & Kegan Paul, 1965, pp. 313–338. Also included in the collection of Owen's essays published posthumously as *Logic, Science, and Dialectic: Collected Papers in Greek Philosophy*. Edited by Martha Craven Nussbaum. Ithaca, New York: Cornell University Press, 1986, pp. 65–84. Later appeared as chapter 13 of *Plato: Critical Assessments*, Volume 3. Edited by Nicholas D. Smith. Routledge Critical Assessments of Leading Philosophers. London, England: Routledge, 1998, pp. 251–272.

Owen, Gwilym Ellis Lane. "Aristotle on the Snares of Ontology." In *New Essays on Plato and Aristotle*. Edited by Renford Bambrough. London, England: Routledge & Kegan Paul, 1965, pp. 69–95. Reprinted in his *Logic, Science, and Dialectic: Collected Papers in Greek Philosophy*. Edited by Martha Craven Nussbaum. Ithaca, New York: Cornell University Press, 1986, pp. 259–278.

Owen, Gwilym Ellis Lane. "Plato on Not-Being." Chapter 12 of *Plato: A Collection of Critical Essays*. Volume 1: *Metaphysics and Epistemology*. Edited by Gregory Vlastos. Garden City, New York: Anchor Books, Doubleday, 1970, pp. 223–267.

Patterson, Richard. *Image and Reality in Plato's Metaphysics*. Indianapolis, Indiana: Hackett Publishing Company, 1985.

Pelletier, Francis Jeffry. *Parmenides, Plato, and the Semantics of Not-Being*. Chicago, Illinois: University of Chicago Press, 1990.

Philip, James A. "The Platonic Corpus," *Phoenix*, 24:4 (1970), pp. 296–308.

Popper, Karl Raimund. *The Open Society and Its Enemies*. Two volumes. Volume 1: *The Spell of Plato*. Volume 2: *The High Tide of Prophecy: Hegel, Marx, and the Aftermath*. London, England: G. Routledge & Sons, 1945.

Press, Gerald Alan. *Plato: A Guide for the Perplexed*. London, England: Continuum International Publishing Group, 2007.

Press, Gerald Alan, editor. *Plato's Dialogues: New Studies and Interpretations*. Lanham, Maryland: Rowman & Littlefield, 1993.

Press, Gerald Alan, editor. *Who Speaks for Plato? Studies in Platonic Anonymity*. Lanham, Maryland: Rowman & Littlefield, 2000.

Press, Gerald Alan. "The Logic of Attributing Characters' Views to Plato." Chapter 2 of *Who Speaks for Plato? Studies in Platonic Anonymity*. Edited by Gerald Alan Press. Lanham, Maryland: Rowman & Littlefield, 2000, pp. 27–38.

Prior, William J. "Socrates Metaphysician," *Oxford Studies in Ancient Philosophy*, 27 (2004), pp. 1–14.

Prior, William J. "The Socratic Problem." Chapter 3 of *A Companion to Plato*. Edited by Hugh H. Benson. Oxford, England: Blackwell Publishing, 2006, pp. 25–36.

Reale, Giovanni. *Storia della Filosofia Antica*. Five volumes. Milan, Italy: Vita e Pensiero, 1975–1980. Numerous editions. Reorganized in four volumes for an English edition translated by John R. Catan and published as *A History of Ancient Philosophy*. Volume 1 (1987): *From the Origins to Socrates*, translated from the fourth Italian edition. Volume 2 (1990): *Plato and Aristotle*, translated from the fifth Italian edition. Volume 3 (1985): *The Systems of the Hellenistic Age*, translated from the third Italian edition. Volume 4 (1990): *The Schools of the Imperial Age*, translated from the fifth Italian edition. Albany, New York: State University of New York Press, 1985–1990.

Reale, Giovanni. *Per una Nuova Interpretazione di Platone: Rilettura Della Metafisica dei Grandi Dialoghi alla Luce Delle "Dottrine Non Scritte."* Milano, Italy: Vita e Pensiero, 1984. Numerous editions. Translated from the tenth edition and edited by John R. Catan and Richard Davies as *Toward a New Interpretation of Plato: A Rereading of the Metaphysics of the Great Dialogues in the Light of the Unwritten Doctrines*. Washington, D.C.: Catholic University of America Press, 1997.

Reeve, Charles David Chanel. "Socrates the Apollonian." Chapter 2 of *Reason and Religion in Socratic Philosophy*. Edited by Nicholas D. Smith and Paul B. Woodruff. Oxford, England: Oxford University Press, 2000, pp. 24–39.

Richard, Marie-Dominique. *L'enseignement Oral de Platon: Une Nouvelle Interprétation du Platonisme*. Paris, France: Editions du Cerf, 1986.

Rickless, Samuel Charles. *Plato's Forms in Transition: A Reading of the Parmenides*. Cambridge, England: Cambridge University Press, 1997.

Ritchie, David George. *Plato*. New York, N.Y.: Charles Scribner's Sons, 1902.

Ritter, Constantin. *Neue Untersuchungen über Platon*. Munich, Germany: Oskar Beck, 1910.

Ritter, Constantin. *Platon: Sein Leben, Seine Schriften, Seine Lehre*. Two volumes. Munich, Germany: Oskar Beck, 1910–1923.

Ritter, Constantin. *Die Kerngedanken der Platonischen Philosophie*. Munich, Germany: E. Reinhardt, 1931. Translated into English by Adam Alles as *The Essence of Plato's Philosophy*. London, England: George Allen & Unwin, 1933.

Robinson, Thomas M. *Plato's Psychology*. Toronto, Canada: University of Toronto Press, 1970. Second edition in 1995.

Rosen, Stanley. *Plato's Sophist: The Drama of Original and Image*. New Haven, Connecticut: Yale University Press, 1983.

Rosen, Stanley. *The Quarrel Between Philosophy and Poetry: Studies in Ancient Thought*. New York, N.Y.: Routledge, 1988.

Rosen, Stanley. *Plato's Statesman: The Web of Politics*. New Haven, Connecticut: Yale University Press, 1995.

Ross, William David. *Plato's Theory of Ideas*. Oxford, England: Clarendon Press, 1951. Second edition released by the same publisher in 1953.

Ross, William David. "The Problem of Socrates," *Proceedings of the Classical Association*, 30 (1933), pp. 7–24.

Rowe, Christopher J. *Plato*. New York, N.Y.: St. Martin's Press, 1984. Second edition published in London, England: Bristol Classical Press, 2003.

Rowe, Christopher J. *Plato and the Art of Philosophical Writing*. Cambridge, England: Cambridge University Press, 2007.

Rowe, Christopher J. "Plato." Chapter 4 of *The Cambridge Companion to Greek and Roman Philosophy*. Edited by David N. Sedley. Cambridge, England: Cambridge University Press, 2003, pp. 98–124.

Rowe, Christopher J. "Plato, Socrates, and Developmentalism." In *Desire, Identity and Existence: Essays in Honour of T. M. Penner*. Edited by Naomi Reshotko. Kelowna, B.C., Canada: Academic Printing & Publishing, 2003, pp. 17–32.

Rowe, Christopher J. "Interpreting Plato." Chapter 2 of *A Companion to Plato*. Edited by Hugh H. Benson. Oxford, England: Blackwell Publishing, 2006, pp. 13–24.

Rowe, Christopher J. "Socrates in Plato's Dialogues." Chapter 9 of *A Companion to Socrates*. Edited by Sara Ahbel-Rappe and Rachana Kamtekar. Oxford, England: Blackwell Publishing, 2006, pp. 159–170.

Rutherford, Richard B. *The Art of Plato: Ten Essays in Platonic Interpretation*. Cambridge, Massachusetts: Harvard University Press, 1995.

Ryle, Gilbert. *Plato's Progress*. Cambridge, England: Cambridge University Press, 1966.

Sallis, John. *Being and Logos: The Way of Platonic Dialogue*. Pittsburgh, Pennsylvania: Duquesne University Press, 1975. Second edition published in Atlantic Highlands, New Jersey: Humanities Press International, 1986. Third edition released with a different subtitle as *Being and Logos: Reading the Platonic Dialogues*. Bloomington, Indiana: Indiana University Press, 1996.

Santas, Gerasimos Xenophon. *Socrates: Philosophy in Plato's Early Dialogues*. London, England: Routledge & Kegan Paul, 1979.

Sayre, Kenneth M. *Plato's Late Ontology: A Riddle Resolved*. Princeton, New Jersey: Princeton University Press, 1983. Reissued with a new introduction and additional essay ("Excess and Deficiency at *Statesman* 283c–285c"). Las Vegas, Nevada: Parmenides Publishing, 2005.

Sayre, Kenneth M. *Plato's Literary Garden: How to Read a Platonic Dialogue*. Notre Dame, Indiana: University of Notre Dame Press, 1995.

Sayre, Kenneth M. *Parmenides' Lesson: Translation and Explication of Plato's Parmenides*. Notre Dame, Indiana: University of Notre Dame Press, 1996.

Sayre, Kenneth M. "Plato's Dialogues in Light of the *Seventh Letter*." Chapter 6 of *Platonic Writings, Platonic Readings*. Edited by Charles L. Griswold, Jr. New York, N.Y.: Routledge, Chapman & Hall, 1988, pp. 93–109.

Sayre, Kenneth M. "Hans J. Kraemer: Plato and the Foundations of Metaphysics," *Ancient Philosophy*, 13 (1993), pp. 167–184.

Sayre, Kenneth M. "Why Plato Never Had a Theory of Forms," *Proceedings of the Boston Area Colloquium in Ancient Philosophy*, 9 (1993), pp. 167–193.

Sayre, Kenneth M. "Do Forms Have a Role in Plato's *Philebus*?" Chapter 6 of *Plato's Forms: Varieties of Interpretation*. Edited by William A. Welton. Lanham, Maryland: Lexington Books, 2002, pp. 169–191.

Schleiermacher, Friedrich Daniel Ernst. *Schleiermacher's Introductions to the Dialogues of Plato*. Translated by William Dobson. Cambridge, England: J. & J. J. Deighton, 1836. English translations of Schleiermacher's introductions to his own translations of Plato's dialogues from the Greek into German, with the collection originally appearing in three volumes as *Platons Werke*. Berlin, Germany: Realschulbuchhandlung and Georg Reimer, 1804–1828.

Schofield, Malcolm. "Plato in His Time and Place." Chapter 2 of *The Oxford Handbook of Plato*. Edited by Gail Fine. Oxford, England: Oxford University Press, 2008, pp. 36–62.

Sedley, David N. *Plato's Cratylus*. Cambridge, England: Cambridge University Press, 2003.

Sedley, David N. "The End of the Academy," *Phronesis*, 26:1 (1981), pp. 67–75. Review of John Glucker's *Antiochus and the Late Academy* (Issue No. 56 of *Hypomnemata: Untersuchungen zur Antike und zu ihrem Nachleben*. Göttingen, Germany: Vandenhoeck und Ruprecht, 1978).

Seeskin, Kenneth. *Dialogue and Discovery: A Study in Socratic Method*. Albany, New York: State University of New York Press, 1987.

Shields, Christopher. "Learning About Plato from Aristotle." Chapter 27 of *A Companion to Plato*. Edited by Hugh H. Benson. Oxford, England: Blackwell Publishing, 2006, pp. 403–417.

Shorey, Paul. *The Unity of Plato's Thought*. Chicago, Illinois: University of Chicago Press, 1903. Originates as part of the sixth volume of the Decennial Publications of the University of Chicago, 1903, pp. 129–214. Numerous reprints as a standalone book by the original publisher as well as by others.

Shorey, Paul. *What Plato Said*. Chicago, Illinois: University of Chicago Press, 1933.

Smith, Nicholas D., editor. *Plato: Critical Assessments*. Four volumes. Volume 1: *Problems of Interpretation and Method*. Volume 2: *The Early Dialogues*. Volume 3: *The Middle Dialogues*. Volume 4: *The Late Dialogues*. New York, N.Y.: Routledge, 1998.

Smith, Nicholas D., and Paul B. Woodruff, editors. *Reason and Religion in Socratic Philosophy*. Oxford, England: Oxford University Press, 2000. Contents: Richard Kraut: "Socrates, Politics and Religion" (pp. 13–23). C. D. C. Reeve: "Socrates the Apollonian?" (pp. 24–39). Robert Parker: "The Trial of Socrates: And a Religious Crisis?" (pp. 40–54). Gregory Vlastos: "Socratic Piety" (pp. 55–73). Thomas C. Brickhouse and Nicholas D. Smith: "Socrates' Gods and the *Daimonion*" (pp. 74–88). Mark L. McPherran: "Does Piety Pay?" (pp. 89–114). Asli Gocer: "A New Assessment of Socratic Philosophy of Religion" (pp. 115–129). Paul B. Woodruff: "Socrates and the Irrational" (pp. 130–150). Stephen A. White: "Socrates at Colonus" (pp. 151–175). Gregory Vlastos, Thomas C. Brickhouse, Mark L. McPherran, and Nicholas D. Smith (Paul B. Woodruff, editor). "Socrates and His *Daimonion*: Correspondence Among the Authors" (pp. 176–204).

Stalley, Richard F. *An Introduction to Plato's Laws*. Indianapolis, Indiana: Hackett Publishing Company, 1983.

Sternfeld, Robert, and Harold Zyskind. *Plato's Meno: A Philosophy of Man as Acquisitive*. Carbondale and Edwardsville, Illinois: Southern Illinois University Press, 1978.

Stocks, John Leofric. "Plato and the Tripartite Soul," *Mind* (New Series), 24:94 (April 1915), pp. 207–221.

Stokes, Michael C. *Plato's Socratic Conversations: Drama and Dialectic in Three Dialogues*. Baltimore, Maryland: Johns Hopkins University Press, 1986.

Stone, Isidor Feinstein. *The Trial of Socrates*. New York, N.Y.: Anchor Books, Doubleday, 1988.

Strauss, Leo. *Persecution and the Art of Writing*. Glencoe, Illinois: Free Press, 1952. Reissued: Westport, Connecticut: Greenwood Press, 1973. Chicago, Illinois: University of Chicago Press, 1988.

Strauss, Leo. *The City and Man*. Chicago, Illinois: Rand McNally, 1964. An enlarged version of his Page-Barbour lectures delivered at the University of Virginia in the spring of 1962.

Strauss, Leo. *Studies in Platonic Political Philosophy*. Published posthumously with an introduction by Thomas L. Pangle. Chicago, Illinois: University of Chicago Press, 1983.

Strauss, Leo. "On a New Interpretation of Plato's Political Philosophy," *Social Research*, 13:3 (Fall 1946), pp. 326–367.

Swift Riginos, Alice. *Platonica: The Anecdotes Concerning the Life and Writings of Plato*. Columbia Studies in the Classical Tradition, No. 3. Leiden, Netherlands: E. J. Brill, 1976.

Szlezák, Thomas Alexander. *Platon und die Schriftlichkeit der Philosophie*. Two volumes. Volume 1 (1985): *Interpretationen zu den Frühen und Mittleren Dialogen*. Volume 2 (2004): *Das Bild des Dialektikers in Platons Spaten Dialogen*. Berlin, Germany: Walter de Gruyter, 1985–2004.

Szlezák, Thomas Alexander. *Platon Lesen*. Stuttgart, Germany: Frommann-Holzboog, 1993. Translated into English by Graham Zanker as *Reading Plato*. London, England: Routledge, 1999.

Szlezák, Thomas Alexander. "Notes sur le Débat autour de la Philosophie Orale de Platon," *Les Études Philosophiques*, (1998/1), pp. 69–90. [Numbering of volumes discontinued starting with issues corresponding to 1968–1969.]

Tarrant, Harold. *Thrasyllan Platonism*. Ithaca, New York: Cornell University Press, 1993.

Tarrant, Harold. "Where Plato Speaks: Reflections on an Ancient Debate." Chapter 5 of *Who Speaks for Plato? Studies in Platonic Anonymity*. Edited by Gerald Alan Press. Lanham, Maryland: Rowman & Littlefield, 2000, pp. 67–82.

Taylor, Alfred Edward. *Plato*. London, England: Archibald Constable & Co., 1908.

Taylor, Alfred Edward. *Varia Socratica: First Series*. St. Andrews University Publications, No. 9. Oxford, England: James Parker & Co., 1911.

Taylor, Alfred Edward. *Plato: The Man and His Work*. London, England: Methuen & Co., 1926. Numerous editions (1926, 1927, 1929, 1937, 1948, 1949, 1960) and reprints. Seventh edition published in New York, N.Y.: Methuen & Co., 1960.

Taylor, Alfred Edward. *Socrates*. London, England: P. Davies, 1932.

Taylor, Alfred Edward. "Plato's Biography of Socrates." Address delivered on 28 March 1917 before the British Academy. *Proceedings of the British Academy*, 8 (1917–1918), pp. 93–132. London, England: Humphrey Milford, Oxford University Press, 1917.

Tejera, Victorino. *Rewriting the History of Ancient Greek Philosophy*. Volume 59 of the Contributions in Philosophy Series. Westport, Connecticut: Greenwood Publishing Group, 1997.

Tennemann, Wilhelm Gottlieb. "Life of Plato." First appearance in English as part of *Selections from German Literature*. Translated and edited by Bela Bates Edwards and Edwards Amasa Park. Andover, Massachusetts: Gould, Newman, and Saxton, 1839, pp. 311–367. Originally published as "Leben des Plato," the biography of Plato in the first volume (1792, pp. 1–80) of the author's *System der Platonischen Philosophie*. Four volumes. Leipzig, Germany: Johann Ambrosius Barth, 1792–1794. The biographical portion is critically acclaimed, so much so as to earn the unqualified recommendation of Schleiermacher (1836, p. 1), who refers his own readers to the life of Plato available through Tennemann.

Thesleff, Holger. *Studies in the Styles of Plato.* (*Acta Philosophica Fennica*, Fascicle 20.) Helsinki, Finland: Societas Philosophica Fennica, 1967.

Thesleff, Holger. *Studies in Platonic Chronology.* (*Commentationes Humanarum Litterarum*, Volume 70.) Helsinki, Finland: Societas Scientiarum Fennica, 1982.

Thesleff, Holger. *Studies in Plato's Two-Level Model.* (*Commentationes Humanarum Litterarum*, Volume 113.) Helsinki, Finland: Societas Scientiarum Fennica, 1999.

Thesleff, Holger. *Platonic Patterns: A Collection of Studies.* Las Vegas, Nevada: Parmenides Publishing, 2009. A collection of Thesleff's previously published contributions to Platonic scholarship. In addition to four articles, the collection includes the following books: *Studies in the Styles of Plato* (1967); *Studies in Platonic Chronology* (1982); Studies in *Plato's Two-Level Model* (1999).

Thesleff, Holger. "Platonic Chronology," *Phronesis*, 34:1 (1989), pp. 1–26.

Thesleff, Holger. "Looking for Clues: An Interpretation of Some Literary Aspects of Plato's Two-Level Model." Chapter 2 of *Plato's Dialogues: New Studies and Interpretations.* Edited by Gerald Alan Press. Lanham, Maryland: Rowman & Littlefield, 1993, pp. 17–45.

Thesleff, Holger. "The Philosopher Conducting Dialectic." Chapter 4 of *Who Speaks for Plato? Studies in Platonic Anonymity.* Edited by Gerald Alan Press. Lanham, Maryland: Rowman & Littlefield, 2000, pp. 53–66.

Tigerstedt, Eugène Napoléon. *Interpreting Plato.* Stockholm Studies in History of Literature, No. 17. Acta Universitatis Stockholmiensis, Stockholms Universitet. Stockholm, Sweden: Almqvist & Wiksell International, 1977.

Trapp, Michael B., editor. *Socrates from Antiquity to the Enlightenment.* Center for Hellenic Studies, King's College, London. Aldershot, England, Ashgate Publishing, 2007.

Trapp, Michael B., editor. *Socrates in the Nineteenth and Twentieth Centuries.* Center for Hellenic Studies, King's College, London. Aldershot, England, Ashgate Publishing, 2007.

Tress, Daryl McGowan. "Relations and Intermediates in Plato's *Timaeus.*" Chapter 6 of *Plato and Platonism.* Edited by Johannes M. Van Ophuijsen. Washington, D.C.: Catholic University of America Press, 1999, pp. 135–162.

Vander Waerdt, Paul A., editor. *The Socratic Movement.* Ithaca, New York: Cornell University Press, 1994.

Vlastos, Gregory. *Platonic Studies.* Princeton, New Jersey: Princeton University Press, 1973. Second edition (reprint with corrections) in 1981.

Vlastos, Gregory. *Plato's Universe.* Seattle, Washington: University of Washington Press, 1975. Reprinted with a new introduction by Luc Brisson. Las Vegas, Nevada: Parmenides Publishing, 2005.

Vlastos, Gregory. *Socrates, Ironist and Moral Philosopher.* Ithaca, New York: Cornell University Press, 1991.

Vlastos, Gregory. *Studies in Greek Philosophy.* Two volumes. Volume 1 (1993): *The Pre-Socratics.* Volume 2 (1995): *Socrates, Plato, and Their Tradition.* Edited by Daniel W. Graham. Princeton, New Jersey: Princeton University Press, 1993–1995.

Vlastos, Gregory. *Socratic Studies.* Edited by Myles Burnyeat. Cambridge, England: Cambridge University Press, 1994.

Vlastos, Gregory, editor. *Plato: A Collection of Critical Essays.* Volume 1 (1970): *Metaphysics and Epistemology.* Volume 2 (1971): *Ethics, Politics, and Philosophy of Art and Religion.* Garden City, New York: Anchor Books, Doubleday, 1970–1971.

Vlastos, Gregory, editor. *The Philosophy of Socrates: A Collection of Critical Essays.* Garden City, New York: Anchor Books, Doubleday, 1971.

Vlastos, Gregory. "The Third Man Argument in the *Parmenides*," *The Philosophical Review*, 63 (1954), pp. 319–349. Reprinted, with an addendum, in *Studies in Plato's Metaphysics*. Edited by Reginald E. Allen. London, England: Routledge & Kegan Paul, 1965, pp. 231–263 (addendum: pp. 261–263). Also reprinted as chapter 12a of his *Socrates, Plato, and Their Tradition*, the second volume of his *Studies in Greek Philosophy*. Edited by Daniel W. Graham. Princeton, New Jersey: Princeton University Press, 1995, pp. 166–190. Chapter 12b of the same volume contains his "Addendum to the Third Man Argument in the *Parmenides*" (pp. 191–193). The next two chapters lay out his replies to selected criticism: Chapter 12c presents "Addenda to the Third Man Argument: A Reply to Professor Sellars" (pp. 194–203). Chapter 12d is a "Postscript to the Third Man: A Reply to Mr. Geach" (pp. 204–214).

Vlastos, Gregory. "H. J. Kraemer: Arete bei Platon und Aristoteles," *Gnomon*, 35 (1963), pp. 641–655. Reprinted with an added appendix in his *Platonic Studies*. Second edition. Princeton, New Jersey: Princeton University Press, 1981, pp. 379–403.

Vlastos, Gregory. "Plato's 'Third Man' Argument (*Parm.* 132a1–b2): Text and Logic," *Philosophical Quarterly*, 19 (1969), pp. 289–301. Reprinted with revisions and appendixes in his *Platonic Studies*. Second edition. Princeton, New Jersey: Princeton University Press, 1981, pp. 342–365.

Vlastos, Gregory. "Self-Predication and Self-Participation in Plato's Later Period," *The Philosophical Review*, 78:1 (1969), pp. 74–78. Reprinted with corrections in his *Platonic Studies*. Second edition. Princeton, New Jersey: Princeton University Press, 1981, pp. 335–341.

Vlastos, Gregory. "A Metaphysical Paradox." In his *Platonic Studies*. Second edition. Princeton, New Jersey: Princeton University Press, 1981, pp. 43–57. Reprinted in *Plato's Republic: Critical Essays*. Edited by Richard Kraut. Lanham, Maryland: Rowman & Littlefield, 1997, pp. 181–196.

Vlastos, Gregory. "Divining the Reason: Review of Brickhouse and Smith, *Socrates on Trial*," *Times Literary Supplement*, 4:524 (15–21 December 1989), p. 1393. Reprinted as chapter 3 of his *Socrates, Plato, and Their Tradition*, the second volume of his *Studies in Greek Philosophy*. Edited by Daniel W. Graham. Princeton, New Jersey: Princeton University Press, 1995, pp. 25–29.

Vlastos, Gregory, Thomas C. Brickhouse, Mark L. McPherran, and Nicholas D. Smith. "Socrates and His *Daimonion*: Correspondence Among the Authors." Edited by Paul B. Woodruff. In *Reason and Religion in Socratic Philosophy*. Edited by Nicholas D. Smith and Paul B. Woodruff. Oxford, England: Oxford University Press, 2000, pp. 176–204.

Wagner, Ellen, editor. *Essays on Plato's Psychology*. Lanham, Maryland: Lexington Books, 2001. Contents: Ellen Wagner: "Introduction" (1–32). Part 1: The Nature of the Soul. Cass Weller: "Fallacies in the *Phaedo* Again" (pp. 35–50). Christopher Charles Whiston Taylor: "The Arguments in the *Phaedo* Concerning the Thesis that the Soul is a *Harmonia*" (pp. 51–68). Ellen Wagner: "Supervenience and the Thesis that the Soul is a *Harmonia*" (pp. 69–88). Part 2: The Tripartite Soul. John Madison Cooper: "Plato's Theory of Human Motivation" (pp. 91–114). Nicholas D. Smith: "Plato's Analogy of Soul and State" (pp. 115–136). Christopher Shields: "Simple Souls" (pp. 137–156). Bernard Arthur Owen Williams: "The Analogy of City and Soul in Plato's *Republic*" (pp. 157–168). Jonathan Lear: "Inside and Outside the *Republic*" (pp. 169–202). Christopher Bobonich: "Akrasia and Agency in Plato's *Laws* and *Republic*" (pp.

203–237). Part 3: Arguments for Immortality of the Soul. David Bostock: "The Soul and Immortality in Plato's *Phaedo*" (pp. 241–262). David Gallop: "Plato's 'Cyclical' Argument Recycled" (pp. 263–280). Dorothea Frede: "The Final Proof of the Immortality of the Soul in Plato's *Phaedo* 102a–107a" (pp. 281–296). Eric Alan Brown: "A Defense of Plato's Argument for the Immortality of the Soul at *Republic* X 608c–611a" (pp. 297–322). Thomas R. Robinson: "The Argument for Immortality in Plato's *Phaedrus*" (pp. 323–333). Richard Bett: "Immortality and the Nature of the Soul in the *Phaedrus*" (pp. 335–361).

Wallach, John Robert. *The Platonic Political Art: A Study of Critical Reason and Democracy*. University Park, Pennsylvania: Pennsylvania State University Press, 2001.

Waterfield, Robin. *Why Socrates Died: Dispelling the Myths*. London, England: Faber and Faber; New York, N.Y.: W. W. Norton & Co., 2009.

Waugh, Joanne. "Socrates and the Character of Platonic Dialogue." Chapter 3 of *Who Speaks for Plato? Studies in Platonic Anonymity*. Edited by Gerald Alan Press. Lanham, Maryland: Rowman & Littlefield, 2000, pp. 39–52.

Welton, William A., editor. *Plato's Forms: Varieties of Interpretation*. Lanham, Maryland: Lexington Books, 2002.

Welton, William A. "Introduction: Plato's Mysterious Forms." Introduction to *Plato's Forms: Varieties of Interpretation*. Edited by William A. Welton. Lanham, Maryland: Lexington Books, 2002, pp. 1–29.

White, Nicholas P. *Plato on Knowledge and Reality*. Indianapolis, Indiana: Hackett Publishing Company, 1976.

White, Stephen A. "Socrates at Colonus: A Hero for the Academy." Chapter 9 of *Reason and Religion in Socratic Philosophy*. Edited by Nicholas D. Smith and Paul Woodruff. Oxford, England: Oxford University Press, 2000, pp. 151–175.

Wieland, Wolfgang. *Platon und die Formen des Wissens*. [*Plato and the Written Word.*] Gottingen, Germany: Vandenhoeck & Ruprecht, 1982.

Williams, Bernard Arthur Owen. *Plato: The Invention of Philosophy*. Volume 23 of the Great Philosophers Series. London, England: Phoenix, 1998. Reprinted in *The Great Philosophers: From Socrates to Turing*. Edited by Ray Monk and Frederic Raphael. London, England: Weidenfeld and Nicholson, 2000, pp. 39–75. Also released as chapter 10 of *The Sense of the Past: Essays in the History of Philosophy*. Edited, with an introduction, by Myles Burnyeat. Princeton, New Jersey: Princeton University Press, 2006, pp. 148–186.

Williams, Bernard Arthur Owen. *The Sense of the Past: Essays in the History of Philosophy*. Edited, with an introduction, by Myles Burnyeat. Princeton, New Jersey: Princeton University Press, 2006. Brings together twenty-five previously published essays by Williams on the history of philosophy, each corresponding to a single chapter, seven of them on Socrates and Plato, with the collection itself appearing posthumously.

Wilson, Emily R. *The Death of Socrates: Hero, Villain, Chatterbox, Saint*. Profiles in History Series. London, England: Profile Books; Cambridge, Massachusetts: Harvard University Press, 2007.

Wolfsdorf, David Conan. *Trials of Reason: Plato and the Crafting of Philosophy*. Oxford, England: Oxford University Press, 2008.

Wolfsdorf, David Conan. "Plato and the Mouth-Piece Theory," *Ancient Philosophy*, 19 (1999), pp. 13–24.

Wolfsdorf, David Conan. "Interpreting Plato's Early Dialogues," *Oxford Studies in Ancient Philosophy*, 27 (Winter 2004), pp. 15–40.

Wood, Kelsey. *Troubling Play: Meaning and Entity in Plato's Parmenides*. Albany, New York: State University of New York Press, 2005.

Woodbridge, Frederick James Eugene. *The Son of Apollo: Themes of Plato*. Boston, Massachusetts: Houghton Mifflin Company, 1929.

Young, Charles M. "Plato and Computer Dating: A Discussion of Gerard R. Ledger, *Recounting Plato: A Computer Analysis of Plato's Style* and Leonard Brandwood, *The Chronology of Plato's Dialogues*," *Oxford Studies in Ancient Philosophy*, 12 (1994), pp. 227–250.

Zeller, Eduard. *Plato and the Older Academy*. English translation of "Plato und die ältere Akademie," a portion of the author's three-volume *Die Philosophie der Griechen*, corresponding to the second section of the second part of the second volume in its third edition (1875), the correspondence being identified as such in the preface to the translation. Translated by Sarah Frances Alleyne and Alfred Goodwin. London, England: Longmans, Green, and Co., 1876. The full set in German was originally published in Tübingen, Germany: Ludwig Friedrich Fues, 1844–1852.

Zeyl, Donald J., editor. *Timaeus*. English translation, including a substantial introduction, by Donald J. Zeyl. Indianapolis, Indiana, Hackett Publishing Company, 2000.

Zuckert, Catherine H. *Plato's Philosophers: The Coherence of the Dialogues*. Chicago, Illinois: University of Chicago Press, 2009.

5. General References

Algra, Keimpe, Jonathan Barnes, Jaap Mansfeld, and Malcolm Schofield, editors. *The Cambridge History of Hellenistic Philosophy*. Cambridge, England: Cambridge University Press, 1999.

Allen, Danielle. "Imprisonment in Classical Athens," *The Classical Quarterly* (New Series), 47:1 (1997), pp. 121–135.

Andrewes, Antony. "The Arginousai Trial," *Phoenix*, 28 (1974), pp. 112–122.

Barigazzi, Adelmo, editor. *Favorino di Arelate: Opere*. The critical text with introduction and commentary. Florence, Italy: Felice Le Monnier, 1966.

Barkan, Irving. "Imprisonment as a Penalty in Ancient Athens," *Classical Philology*, 31:4 (October 1936), pp. 338–341.

Burnet, John. *Early Greek Philosophy*. London, England: Adam & Charles Black, 1892. Second edition in 1908. Third edition in 1920. Fourth edition published posthumously in 1930. Reprinted numerous times, for example, as an unabridged facsimile of the third edition: Boston, Massachusetts: Adamant Media Corporation, 2005.

Burnet, John. *Greek Philosophy: Part 1: Thales to Plato*. London, England: Macmillan and Company, 1914. Reprinted numerous times, with the designation "Part 1" dropped from the full title sometime after the author's death, coinciding with the fourth printing in 1928.

Butler, Joseph. *Fifteen Sermons Preached at the Rolls Chapel*. London, England: Printed by W. Botham for James and John Knapton, 1726. The preface (Stanhope, 16 September 1729), the source of the memorable declaration that "everything is what it is, and not another thing" (¶ 39), was added in the second edition (1729).

Camp, John McKesson. *The Athenian Agora: Excavations in the Heart of Classical Athens*. New York, N.Y.: Thames and Hudson, 1986. Second ("updated") edition published in 1992.

Chroust, Anton-Hermann. *Aristotle: New Light on His Life and on Some of His Lost Works*. Two volumes. Volume 1: *Some Novel Interpretations of the Man and His Life*. Volume 2: *Observations on Some of Aristotle's Lost Works*. London, England: Routledge & Kegan Paul, 1973.

Copleston, Frederick Charles. *A History of Philosophy*. Nine volumes. Kent, England: Search Press; Westminster, Maryland: Newman Press, 1946–1974. Volume 1 (1946): *Greece and Rome*. Volume 2 (1950): *Augustine to Scotus*. Volume 3 (1953): *Ockham to Suárez*. Volume 4 (1960): *Descartes to Leibniz*. Volume 5 (1959): *Hobbes to Hume*. Volume 6 (1960): *Wolff to Kant*. Volume 7 (1963): *Fichte to Nietzsche*. Volume 8 (1966): *Bentham to Russell*. Volume 9 (1974): *Maine de Biran to Sartre*. Reprinted several times, including Doubleday's compressed arrangement comprising three books of three volumes each. New York, N.Y.: Doubleday, 1985. Plato is in volume 1 (1946), pp. 127–265.

Craig, William Lane. *The Kalām Cosmological Argument*. London, England: Macmillan, 1979.

Craig, William Lane. *The Cosmological Argument from Plato to Leibniz*. London, England: Macmillan, 1980.

Craig, William Lane, and Quentin Smith. *Theism, Atheism, and Big Bang Cosmology*. Oxford, England: Oxford University Press, 1993.

Davies, John Kenyon. *Athenian Propertied Families, 600–300 B.C.* Oxford, England: Clarendon Press, 1971.

Diels, Hermann Alexander, editor. *Die Fragmente der Vorsokratiker, Griechisch und Deutsch*. Berlin, Germany: Weidmannsche Buchhandlung, 1903. Numerous editions and reprints. The fourth edition, the last in the author's lifetime, appeared in 1922. Anglophone access is available through two separate volumes by Kathleen Freeman: (1) *The Pre-Socratic Philosophers: A Companion to Diels, Fragmente der Vorsokratiker*. Oxford, England: Basil Blackwell, 1946. (2) *Ancilla to the Pre-Socratic Philosophers: A Complete Translation of the Fragments in Diels, Fragmente der Vorsokratiker*. Based on the fifth edition of the original (1937). Cambridge, Massachusetts: Harvard University Press, 1948.

Diels, Hermann Alexander, editor. *Commentaria in Aristotelem Graeca* (CAG). Edita Consilio et Auctoritate Academiae Litterarum Regiae Borussicae. Twenty-three volumes. The standard edition of ancient Greek commentaries on Aristotle. Berlin, Germany: Realschulbuchhandlung and Georg Reimer, 1882–1909.

Dorandi, Tiziano. "Chronology." Chapter 2 of *The Cambridge History of Hellenistic Philosophy*. Edited by Keimpe Algra, Jonathan Barnes, Jaap Mansfeld, and Malcolm Schofield. Cambridge, England: Cambridge University Press, 1999, pp. 31–54.

Dorandi, Tiziano. "Organization and Structure of the Philosophical Schools." Chapter 3 of *The Cambridge History of Hellenistic Philosophy*. Edited by Keimpe Algra, Jonathan Barnes, Jaap Mansfeld, and Malcolm Schofield. Cambridge, England: Cambridge University Press, 1999, pp. 55–62.

Dover, Kenneth James. *Greek Popular Morality in the Time of Plato and Aristotle*. Oxford, England: Basil Blackwell; Berkeley, California: University of California Press, 1974. Reprinted, with corrections, in Indianapolis, Indiana: Hackett Publishing Company, 1994.

Else, Gerald Frank. *Aristotle's Poetics: The Argument*. Cambridge, Massachusetts: Harvard University Press, 1957.

Fortenbaugh, William W., Pamela M. Huby, and Anthony A. Long, editors. *Theophrastus of Eresus: On His Life and Work*. New Brunswick, New Jersey: Transaction Books, 1985.

Foucart, Paul François. *Des Associations Religieuses chez les Grecs: Thiases, Éranes, Orgéons: Avec le Texte des Inscriptions Relatives à ces Associations*. Paris, France: Chez Klincksieck, 1873.

Freely, John. *Strolling Through Athens: Fourteen Unforgettable Walks Through Europe's Oldest City*. London, England; New York, N.Y.: Penguin Books, 1991. Also published in London, England; New York, N.Y.: Tauris Parke Paperbacks, 2004.

Frost, Frank J. *Greek Society*. Lexington, Massachusetts: Heath, 1971. Numerous editions, the fifth published in Boston, Massachusetts: Houghton Mifflin Company, 1997.

Gaiser, Konrad, editor. *Philodems Academica: Die Bericht über Platon und die Alte Akademie in Zwei Herkulanensischen Papyri*. Supplementum Platonicum: Die Texte der Indirekten Platon-überlieferung 1. Stuttgart and Bad Cannstatt, Germany: Frommann-Holzboog, 1988. Gaiser's edition of the history of Academic philosophy in the *Academicorum Philosophorum Index Herculanensis* attributed to Philodemus of Gadara. This edition covers only a portion of the original, corresponding specifically to the succession from Plato through Arcesilaus, leaving out the later Academy.

Garland, Robert. *Introducing New Gods: The Politics of Athenian Religion*. Ithaca, New York: Cornell University Press, 1992.

Giannantoni, Gabriele. *Socratis et Socraticorum Reliquiae*. Collegit, Disposuit, Apparatibus Notisque Instruxit Gabriele Giannantoni. Four volumes. Naples, Italy: Bibliopolis, 1990. Collection of *Sōkratikoi logoi*, excluding Plato and Xenophon. Greek original with Latin translation and Italian commentary. Revised and enlarged edition of *Socraticorum Reliquiae*. Four volumes. Naples, Italy: Bibliopolis, 1983–1985.

Grote, George. *A History of Greece*. Twelve volumes. London, England: John Murray, 1846–1856. Numerous reprints, some omitting the indefinite article leading the title. Released as a "new edition," the final version during the author's lifetime introduces a subtitle: *A History of Greece: From the Earliest Period to the Close of the Generation Contemporary with Alexander the Great*. London, England: John Murray, 1869–1870. Reissued posthumously in ten volumes. The work devotes an entire chapter spanning nearly a hundred pages to Socrates: chapter 68 of volume 8 corresponding to pp. 399–496 in the original edition of 1850. Plato gets his own tome (*Plato, and the Other Companions of Sokrates*) instead of an independent chapter here, but he is discussed in this collection as well, with a particularly prominent presence in chapters 67 (pp. 317–399) and 68 (pp. 399–496) of volume 8 and in chapters 83 (pp. 1–54) and 84 (pp. 54–128) of volume 11. The chapter numbers remain the same in the "new edition" as well as in the subsequent ten-volume format, but the volume and page numbers tend to change.

Gutas, Dimitri. "The Starting Point of Philosophical Studies in Alexandrian and Arabic Aristotelianism." Chapter 4 of *Theophrastus of Eresus: On His Life and Work*. Edited by William W. Fortenbaugh, Pamela M. Huby, and Anthony A. Long. New Brunswick, New Jersey: Transaction Books, 1985, pp. 115–123.

Guthrie, William Keith Chambers. *The Greek Philosophers: From Thales to Aristotle*. London, England: Methuen & Co., 1950.

Guthrie, William Keith Chambers. *A History of Greek Philosophy*. Six volumes. Cambridge, England: Cambridge University Press, 1962–1981. Volume 1 (1962): *The Earlier Presocratics and the Pythagoreans*. Volume 2 (1965): *The Presocratic Tradition from Parmenides to Democritus*. Volume 3 (1969): *The Fifth-Century*

Enlightenment. Volume 4 (1975): *Plato: The Man and His Dialogues: Earlier Period*. Volume 5 (1978): *The Later Plato and the Academy*. Volume 6 (1981): *Aristotle: An Encounter*. The third volume was reissued in 1971 as two separate books: The first part, originally titled "The World of the Sophists" as a physical part of the third volume, was released by itself as *The Sophists*, while the second part, originally titled "Socrates," appeared in an independent edition under the same name.

Hamilton, Edith. *Mythology*. Boston, Massachusetts: Little, Brown and Company, 1942. Reprinted numerous times, including a 1998 edition by Back Bay Books, an imprint of the original publisher. Also available as *Mythology: Timeless Tales of Gods and Heroes*. New York, N.Y.: Warner Books, 1999.

Hamilton, Edith. *The Greek Way*. New York, N.Y.: W. W. Norton & Company, 1991. Originally published in 1930 with five fewer chapters. Subsequently published in its current form in 1942 as *The Great Age of Greek Literature*. Also appeared as *The Greek Way to Western Civilization* in a few editions. Title fixed since the early 1960s.

Hume, David. "Of the Original Contract." Originally published as part of *Three Essays, Moral and Political: Never Before Published; Which Compleats the Former Edition; In Two Volumes; Octavo*. London, England: A. Millar, A. Kincaid, 1748. Envisaged as a supplement to *Essays, Moral and Political* (1741–1742). Contents include "Of National Characters," "Of the Original Contract," and "Of Passive Obedience," all incorporated in the same year into the third edition of *Essays, Moral and Political* (1748), and afterwards into *Essays and Treatises on Several Subjects* (1753–1756), and finally into *Essays, Moral, Political, and Literary* (1758). The standard reference to the essay invokes its position in the latest version of the collection, *Essays, Moral, Political, and Literary* (1758), where it appears as the twelfth entry of the second volume, thus abbreviated "2.12" (optionally with Roman numerals for the volume number) followed by the relevant paragraph number of the specific citation.

Hunter, Virginia. "The Prison of Athens: A Comparative Perspective," *Phoenix*, 51:3–4 (1997), pp. 296–326.

Jacoby, Felix, editor. *Apollodors Chronik: Eine Sammlung der Fragmente*. Philologische Untersuchungen 16. Berlin, Germany: Weidmannsche Buchhandlung, 1902.

Janko, Richard. *Aristotle on Comedy: Towards a Reconstruction of Poetics II*. Berkeley, California: University of California Press, 1984.

Janko, Richard. *Philodemus, On Poems, Books 3–4, with the Fragments of Aristotle, On Poets*. Oxford, England: Oxford University Press, 2010.

Jones, Nicholas F. *The Associations of Classical Athens: The Response to Democracy*. Oxford, England: Oxford University Press, 1999.

Judeich, Walther. *Topographie von Athen: Mit 48 Abbildungen im Text und 3 Plainen in Mappe*. Handbuch der Klassischen Altertums-Wissenschaft: volume 3, issue 2, part 2. Munich, Germany: C. H. Beck, 1905. Second edition, released by the same publisher, in 1931.

Kassel, Rudolf, and Colin Austin, editors. *Poetae Comici Graeci* (PCG). Eight volumes. Greek texts with Latin commentary. Berlin, Germany, New York, N.Y.: Walter de Gruyter, 1983–2001.

Kock, Theodor, editor. *Comicorum Atticorum Fragmenta* (CAF). Three volumes. Greek texts with Latin commentary. Leipzig, Germany: B. G. Teubner, 1880–1888. Reprinted in Utrecht, Netherlands: HES, 1976.

Kuhn, Thomas Samuel. *The Structure of Scientific Revolutions*. Chicago, Illinois: University of Chicago Press, 1962. Second edition in 1970. Third edition in 1996.

Lasserre, François, editor. *De Léodamas de Thasos à Philippe d'Oponte: Témoignages et Fragments*. La Scuola di Platone, No. 2. Naples, Italy: Bibliopolis, 1987. Greek text with translation and commentary in French.

Loomis, William T. *Wages, Welfare Costs and Inflation in Classical Athens*. Ann Arbor, Michigan: University of Michigan Press, 1998.

Lynch, John Patrick. *Aristotle's School: A Study of a Greek Educational Institution*. Berkeley and Los Angeles, California: University of California Press, 1972. A revision of the author's doctoral dissertation: Yale, 1970. Concentrated discussion of Plato and the Academy in pp. 54–67.

MacDowell, Douglas Maurice. *Athenian Homicide Law in the Age of the Orators*. Manchester, England: Manchester University Press, 1963.

MacDowell, Douglas Maurice. *The Law in Classical Athens*. Ithaca, New York: Cornell University Press, 1978.

Mackenzie, John Stuart. *A Manual of Ethics: Designed for the Use of Students*. University Correspondence College Tutorial Series. London, England: W. B. Clive, University Correspondence College Press, 1893. Numerous editions, with revisions, enlargements, and rewriting.

McCoy, W. James. "The Identity of Leon," *The American Journal of Philology*, 96 (1975), pp. 187–199.

Marrou, Henri Irénée. *Histoire de l'Education dans l'Antiquité*. Paris, France: Éditions du Seuil, 1948. Available in English, based upon the third edition (1955) of the French, as *A History of Education in Antiquity*. Translated by George Lamb. New York, N.Y.: Sheed and Ward, 1956. Reissued in Madison, Wisconsin: University of Wisconsin Press, 1982.

Mensching, Eckart, editor. *Favorin von Arelate: Der erste Teil der Fragmente: "Memorabilien" und "Omnigena Historia."* The critical text with commentary. Berlin, Germany: Walter de Gruyter, 1963.

Mikalson, Jon D. *Greek Popular Religion in Greek Philosophy*. Oxford, England: Oxford University Press, 2010.

Moore, George Edward. *Principia Ethica*. Cambridge, England: Cambridge University Press, 1903. Reprinted numerous times, with alterations, if any, limited to the correction of misprints and of grammatical errors. Reissued posthumously with additional material, including: a "Preface to the Second Edition" (never realized) and two essays, "Free Will" (1912) and "The Conception of Intrinsic Value" (1922). Edited with an introduction by Thomas Baldwin. Cambridge, England: Cambridge University Press, 1993.

Mosshammer, Alden A. "Geometrical Proportion and the Chronological Method of Apollodorus," *Transactions of the American Philological Association (1974–.)*, 106 (1976), pp. 291–306.

Müller, Karl Wilhelm Ludwig, editor. *Fragmenta Historicorum Graecorum* (FHG). Five volumes (1841, 1848, 1849, 1851, 1870). Paris, France: Ambroise Firmin Didot, 1841–1870.

Parker, Robert. *Athenian Religion: A History*. Oxford, England: Oxford University Press, 1996.

Rose, Valentin, editor. *Aristoteles Pseudepigraphus*. Fragments traditionally attributed to Aristotle as representing his lost works, though the editor considers them all spurious. Leipzig, Germany: B. G. Teubner, 1863.

Rose, Valentin, editor. *Aristotelis Qui Ferebantur Librorum Fragmenta*. Enlarged version of the editor's earlier collection of fragments in *Aristoteles Pseudepigraphus*. Prepared specifically for the Bekker edition of the Corpus Aristotelicum: *Aristotelis Opera: Edidit Academia Regia Borussica*. Volume 5 (1870): 1463–1589. Berlin, Germany: Georg Reimer, 1870. Subsequently enlarged further and published separately from the Bekker edition, instead taking its place in the Bibliotheca Scriptorum Graecorum et Romanorum Teubneriana. Leipzig, Germany: B. G. Teubner, 1886. Constituting the third edition (going back to *Aristoteles Pseudepigraphus* (1863), this is the standard critical edition used in the citation of fragments. The common form is to give the fragment number in Arabic numerals, preceded by the abbreviation "fr." plus a single space, and followed by a single space plus the name "Rose" (or simply the initial "R" with a superscript "3" indicating the third edition).

Rosen, Stanley. *The Limits of Analysis*. New York, N.Y.: Basic Books, 1980.

Rosen, Stanley. "Is Metaphysics Possible?" *The Review of Metaphysics*, 45:2 (December 1991), pp. 235–257.

Rowe, William Leonard. *The Cosmological Argument*. Princeton, New Jersey: Princeton University Press, 1975.

Rowe, William Leonard. *Philosophy of Religion: An Introduction*. Belmont, California, Wadsworth Publishing Company, 1978. Numerous editions, including a fourth in 2007.

Rusten, Jeffrey S., editor. *The Birth of Comedy: Texts, Documents, and Art from Athenian Comic Competitions, 486–280*. Translated by Jeffrey Henderson, David Konstan, Ralph Rosen, Niall W. Slater, and Jeffrey Rusten. Baltimore, Maryland: Johns Hopkins University Press, 2011.

Sorabji, Richard, editor. *Ancient Commentators on Aristotle* (ACA). A project to translate the principal Greek commentaries on Aristotle into English. Still in progress as of the publication date of this book, the initiative as it stood at that time included eighty-eight volumes already published, with a further thirty or so expected to be added in due course. The volumes in the *Ancient Commentators on Aristotle* are not numbered. All work is undertaken under the auspices of King's College London and with the general editorship of Richard Sorabji. London, England: Duckworth; Ithaca, New York: Cornell University Press, 1987–present.

Sorley, William Ritchie. *On the Ethics of Naturalism*. Edinburgh, Scotland: William Blackwood and Sons, 1885. Second, "revised" edition released in 1904 by the same publisher as: *The Ethics of Naturalism: A Criticism*.

Storey, Ian C., editor. *Fragments of Old Comedy*. Three volumes. Edited and translated by Ian C. Storey. Loeb Classical Library. Cambridge, Massachusetts: Harvard University Press, 2011. Volume 1: *Alcaeus to Diocles*. Volume 2: *Diopeithes to Pherecrates*. Volume 3: *Philonicus to Xenophon. Adespota*.

Tarán, Leonardo. *Speusippus of Athens: A Critical Study with a Collection of the Related Texts and Commentary*. Leiden, Netherlands: E. J. Brill, 1981.

Travlos, John (Traulos, Iōannēs). *Pictorial Dictionary of Ancient Athens*. Prepared with the collaboration of the German Archaeological Institute. Translated from the Greek manuscript. London, England: Thames and Hudson, 1971. Originally published as *Poleodomikē Exelixis tōn Athēnōn* (Πολεοδομική Εξέλιξις των Αθηνών). Athens, Greece: [s.n.], 1960.

Ueberweg, Friedrich. *Grundriss der Geschichte der Philosophie*. Three volumes. Berlin, Germany: E. S. Mittler und Sohn, 1862–1866. English edition published as *History of Philosophy: From Thales to the Present Time*. Two volumes. Translated, from the fourth German edition, by George Sylvester Morris, with additions by Noah Porter and a preface by the editors of the Philosophical and Theological Library. Authorized translation, revised by the author. New York, N.Y.: Charles Scribner's Sons, 1872–1874. Volume 1 (1872): *History of the Ancient and Mediaeval Philosophy*. Volume 2 (1874): *History of Modern Philosophy*.

Vanderpool, Eugene. "The State Prison of Ancient Athens." In *From Athens to Gordion: The Papers of a Memorial Symposium for Rodney S. Young, Held at the University Museum, the Third of May, 1975*. Edited by Keith DeVries. University Museum Papers 1. Philadelphia, Pennsylvania: University of Pennsylvania Press, 1980, pp. 17–31.

Whitehead, Alfred North. *Process and Reality: An Essay in Cosmology*. Gifford lectures delivered in the University of Edinburgh during the session 1927–28. Cambridge, England: Cambridge University Press, 1929. Subsequently published in a "corrected edition" edited by David Ray Griffin and Donald W. Sherburne. New York, N.Y.: The Free Press, 1978. The famous analogy of Western philosophy ("the European philosophical tradition") as a series of footnotes to Plato is on p. 39 of the "corrected edition."

Wilamowitz-Moellendorff, Enno Friedrich Wichard Ulrich von. *Antigonos von Karystos*. Volume 4 of Philologische Untersuchungen. Berlin, Germany: Weidmannsche Buchhandlung, 1881.

Wilson, Emily R. *The Death of Socrates*. Cambridge, Massachusetts: Harvard University Press, 2007.

Wycherley, Richard Ernest. "Peripatos: The Athenian Philosophical Scene—I," *Greece & Rome* (Second Series), 8:2 (October 1961), pp. 152–163.

Wycherley, Richard Ernest. "Peripatos: The Athenian Philosophical Scene—II," *Greece & Rome* (Second Series), 9:1 (March 1962), pp. 2–21.

Wycherley, Richard Ernest. *The Stones of Athens*. Princeton, New Jersey: Princeton University Press, 1978.

Zeller, Eduard. *Die Philosophie der Griechen: Eine Untersuchung über Charakter, Gang und Hauptmomente ihrer Entwicklung*. Three volumes. Tübingen, Germany: Ludwig Friedrich Fues, 1844–1852. Subsequent editions bear a slightly different title: *Die Philosophie der Griechen in ihrer Geschichtlichen Entwicklung*. Evolved through numerous editions, though, strictly speaking, the growth in question was driven by individual volumes, and, in fact, by parts of volumes issued as separate books, all of which came together at a variable pace of renewal that did not correspond to definite chronological breaks between uniform editions of the set as a whole. The third volume was organized in two parts published separately from the outset. The second volume was split into two parts, each a standalone book, starting with the second edition of the volume. The first volume followed suit, starting with its own fifth edition. Some parts were issued in a greater number of editions, while others came in fewer editions, and this tended to obscure the edition number of the corresponding volumes. A rate differential also existed between volumes, thus posing the same indeterminacy for the set as a unit. Even so, it has, of course, been possible at any time to put together a definitive edition of the set from the latest edition of each part and volume. Consensus seems to have settled on the Reisland edition, sometimes called the "seventh edition," edited by Franz Lortzing, Wilhelm Nestle, and Eduard Wellmann. Leipzig, Germany: O. R. Reisland, 1919–1923. English translations were pursued piecemeal as separate projects, determined largely by the production schedule of the original: *A History of Greek Philosophy from the Earliest Period to the Time of Socrates*, translated by Sarah

Frances Alleyne (1881). *Socrates and the Socratic Schools*, translated by Oswald J. Reichel (1868, 1877, 1885). *Plato and the Older Academy*, translated by Sarah Frances Alleyne and Alfred Goodwin (1876, 1888 ["new edition"], both based on the second section of the second part of the second volume in its third edition [1875], according to the preface in the translation). *Aristotle and the Earlier Peripatetics*, translated by Benjamin Francis Conn Costelloe and John Henry Muirhead (1897). *A History of Eclecticism in Greek Philosophy*, translated by Sarah Frances Alleyne (1883).

ABOUT THE AUTHOR

Born in Jackson, Mississippi, to Turkish parents, the author started life as a stranger in a strange land, as he explored the Bible Belt of the Deep South with a name like Necip Fikri Alican. His formative years also included exposure to Turkey, where the name seemed more familiar, but, the land, even stranger.

Thus conditioned from childhood with a taste for odd combinations, he got a chance, as he entered college, to test the workable limits of eclecticism. The first step in this direction was undergraduate studies at Millsaps College, where he earned a B.B.A. in 1985 and a B.A. in 1986, graduating *magna cum laude* with a triple major in business administration, economics, and philosophy. The next step was the M.B.A. program of Vanderbilt University, where he finished up in 1988 with a concentration in finance at the Owen Graduate School of Management. The final touch was graduate work in philosophy, a field in which he received an A.M. in 1990 and a Ph.D. in 1994, both at Washington University in St. Louis, where his specialty was ethics, broadly conceived, but his work was decidedly historical, and, his approach, distinctively analytic.

His intellectual pursuits continue to include scholarly work in philosophy and economics. He is interested in several periods and figures in the history of Western philosophy, particularly in its nascency with the Greeks and in its revival with the Enlightenment.

He is the author of *Mill's Principle of Utility: A Defense of John Stuart Mill's Notorious Proof.* As intimated in the title, this is a scholarly monograph vindicating Mill's proof of the principle of utility. The motivating spark for it was not that the principle is so compelling but that the proof has been so misunderstood. Hence, it is more about the proof than the principle. To elaborate, the book examines and endorses Mill's approach to ethical theory from a strictly methodological perspective, that is, from the standpoint of the viability of the moral reasoning inherent in the ethical system advocated, independently of the strengths and weaknesses of utilitarianism itself as a school of thought.

Alican has also been pursuing less defensive and more constructive projects. Plato and Kant account for the bulk of his current research interests in philosophy, while his recent studies in economics focus separately on Turkey and the European Union as well as on relations between the two.

INDEX OF NAMES

nobiliary particles suppressed without exception,
even against any prevalent conventional form,
otherwise usually adopted in the main body

INDEX OF SUBJECTS

VIBS

The **Value Inquiry Book Series** is co-sponsored by:

Adler School of Professional Psychology
American Indian Philosophy Association
American Maritain Association
American Society for Value Inquiry
Association for Process Philosophy of Education
Canadian Society for Philosophical Practice
Center for Bioethics, University of Turku
Center for Professional and Applied Ethics, University of North Carolina at Charlotte
Central European Pragmatist Forum
Centre for Applied Ethics, Hong Kong Baptist University
Centre for Cultural Research, Aarhus University
Centre for Professional Ethics, University of Central Lancashire
Centre for the Study of Philosophy and Religion, University College of Cape Breton
Centro de Estudos em Filosofia Americana, Brazil
College of Education and Allied Professions, Bowling Green State University
College of Liberal Arts, Rochester Institute of Technology
Concerned Philosophers for Peace
Conference of Philosophical Societies
Department of Moral and Social Philosophy, University of Helsinki
Gannon University
Gilson Society
Haitian Studies Association
Ikeda University
Institute of Philosophy of the High Council of Scientific Research, Spain
International Academy of Philosophy of the Principality of Liechtenstein
International Association of Bioethics
International Center for the Arts, Humanities, and Value Inquiry
International Society for Universal Dialogue
Natural Law Society
Philosophical Society of Finland
Philosophy Born of Struggle Association
Philosophy Seminar, University of Mainz
Pragmatism Archive at The Oklahoma State University
R.S. Hartman Institute for Formal and Applied Axiology
Research Institute, Lakeridge Health Corporation
Russian Philosophical Society
Society for Existential Analysis
Society for Iberian and Latin-American Thought
Society for the Philosophic Study of Genocide and the Holocaust
Unit for Research in Cognitive Neuroscience, Autonomous University of Barcelona
Whitehead Research Project
Yves R. Simon Institute

Titles Published

Volumes 1 - 215 see www.rodopi.nl

216. James R. Watson, Editor, *Metacide: In the Pursuit of Excellence.* A volume in **Holocaust and Genocide Studies**

217. Andrew Fitz-Gibbon, Editor, *Positive Peace: Reflections on Peace Education, Nonviolence, and Social Change.* A volume in **Philosophy of Peace**

218. Christopher Berry Gray, *The Methodology of Maurice Hauriou: Legal, Sociological, Philosophical.* A volume in **Studies in Jurisprudence**

219. Mary K. Bloodsworth-Lugo and Carmen R. Lugo-Lugo, *Containing (Un)American Bodies: Race, Sexuality, and Post-9/11 Constructions of Citizenship.* A volume in **Philosophy of Peace**

220. Roland Faber, Brian G. Henning, Clinton Combs, Editors, *Beyond Metaphysics? Explorations in Alfred North Whitehead's Late Thought.* A volume in **Contemporary Whitehead Studies**

221. John G. McGraw, *Intimacy and Isolation (Intimacy and Aloneness: A Multi-Volume Study in Philosophical Psychology, Volume One)*, A volume in **Philosophy and Psychology**

222. Janice L. Schultz-Aldrich, Introduction and Edition, *"Truth" is a Divine Name, Hitherto Unpublished Papers of Edward A. Synan, 1918-1997.* A volume in **Gilson Studies**

223. Larry A. Hickman, Matthew Caleb Flamm, Krzysztof Piotr Skowroński and Jennifer A. Rea, Editors, *The Continuing Relevance of John Dewey: Reflections on Aesthetics, Morality, Science, and Society.* A volume in **Central European Value Studies**

224. Hugh P. McDonald, *Creative Actualization: A Meliorist Theory of Values.* A volume in **Studies in Pragmatism and Values**

225. Rob Gildert and Dennis Rothermel, Editors, *Remembrance and Reconciliation.* A volume in **Philosophy of Peace**

226. Leonidas Donskis, Editor, *Niccolò Machiavelli: History, Power, and Virtue.* A volume in **Philosophy, Literature, and Politics**

227. Sanya Osha, *Postethnophilosophy.* A volume in **Social Philosophy**

228. Rosa M. Calcaterra, Editor, *New Perspectives on Pragmatism and Analytic Philosophy*. A volume in **Studies in Pragmatism and Values**

229. Danielle Poe, Editor, *Communities of Peace: Confronting Injustice and Creating Justice*. A volume in **Philosophy of Peace**

230. Thorsten Botz-Bornstein, Editor, *The Philosophy of Viagra: Bioethical Responses to the Viagrification of the Modern World*. A volume in **Philosophy of Sex and Love**

231. Carolyn Swanson, *Reburial of Nonexistents: Reconsidering the Meinong-Russell Debate*. A volume in **Central European Value Studies**

232. Adrianne Leigh McEvoy, Editor, *Sex, Love, and Friendship: Studies of the Society for the Philosophy of Sex and Love: 1993–2003*. A volume in **Histories and Addresses of Philosophical Societies**

233. Amihud Gilead, *The Privacy of the Psychical*. A volume in **Philosophy and Psychology**

234. Paul Kriese and Randall E. Osborne, Editors, *Social Justice, Poverty and Race: Normative and Empirical Points of View*. A volume in **Studies in Jurisprudence**

235. Hakam H. Al-Shawi, *Reconstructing Subjects: A Philosophical Critique of Psychotherapy*. A volume in **Philosophy and Psychology**

236. Maurice Hauriou, *Tradition in Social Science*. Translation from French with an Introduction by Christopher Berry Gray. A volume in **Studies in Jurisprudence**

237. Camila Loew, *The Memory of Pain: Women's Testimonies of the Holocaust.*. A volume in **Holocaust and Genocide Studies**

238. Stefano Franchi and Francesco Bianchini, Editors, *The Search for a Theory of Cognition: Early Mechanisms and New Ideas*. A volume in **Cognitive Science**

239. Michael H. Mitias, *Friendship: A Central Moral Value*. A volume in **Ethical Theory and Practice**

240. John Ryder and Radim Šíp, Editors, *Identity and Social Transformation, Central European Pragmatist Forum, Volume Five.* A volume in **Central European Value Studies**

241. William Sweet and Hendrik Hart, *Responses to the Enlightenment: An Exchange on Foundations, Faith, and Community.* A volume in **Philosophy and Religion**

242. Leonidas Donskis and J.D. Mininger, Editors, *Politics Otherwise: Shakespeare as Social and Political Critique.* A volume in **Philosophy, Literature, and Politics**

243. Hugh P. McDonald, *Speculative Evaluations: Essays on a Pluralistic Universe.* A volume in **Studies in Pragmatism and Values.**

244. Dorota Koczanowicz and Wojciech Małecki, Editors, *Shusterman's Pragmatism: Between Literature and Somaesthetics.* A volume in **Central European Value Studies**

245. Harry Lesser, Editor, *Justice for Older People,* A volume in **Values in Bioethics**

246. John G. McGraw, *Personality Disorders and States of Aloneness (Intimacy and Aloneness: A Multi-Volume Study in Philosophical Psychology, Volume Two),* A volume in **Philosophy and Psychology**

247. André Mineau, *SS Thinking and the Holocaust.* A volume in **Holocaust and Genocide Studies**

248. Yuval Lurie, *Wittgenstein on the Human Spirit.* A volume in **Philosophy, Literature, and Politics**

249. Andrew Fitz-Gibbon, *Love as a Guide to Morals.* A volume in **Ethical Theory and Practice**

250. Ronny Miron, *Karl Jaspers: From Selfhood to Being.* A volume in **Studies in Existentialism**

251. Necip Fikri Alican, *Rethinking Plato: A Cartesian Quest for the Real Plato.* A volume in **Philosophy, Literature, and Politics**

CPSIA information can be obtained at www.ICGtesting.com
Printed in the USA
BVOW030011161012
302705BV00002B/11/P